production/operations management

McGRAW-HILL SERIES IN MANAGEMENT

KEITH DAVIS, *consulting editor*

production/ operations management:

CONTEMPORARY POLICY FOR MANAGING OPERATING SYSTEMS

RICHARD I. LEVIN
Professor of Business
University of North Carolina

CURTIS P. McLAUGHLIN
Associate Professor of Business
University of North Carolina

RUDOLF P. LAMONE
Professor of Business
University of Maryland

JOHN F. KOTTAS
Associate Professor of Business
University of North Carolina

McGraw-Hill Book Company
New York · St. Louis · San Francisco · Düsseldorf · Johannesburg
Kuala Lumpur · London · Mexico · Montreal · New Delhi · Panama
Rio de Janeiro · Singapore · Sydney · Toronto

PRODUCTION/OPERATIONS MANAGEMENT:

Contemporary Policy for Managing Operating Systems

Library of Congress Catalog Card Number 73–172259

07–037369–8

1 2 3 4 5 6 7 8 9 0 K P K P 7 9 8 7 6 5 4 3 2 1

This book was set in News Gothic by The Maple Press Company, and printed and bound by Kingsport Press, Inc. The designer was Wladislaw Finne; the drawings were done by John Cordes, J. & R. Technical Services, Inc. The editors were Richard F. Dojny, Cynthia Newby, and Claudia A. Hepburn. John A. Sabella supervised production.

contents

vii

PART FOUR
OPERATING AND CONTROLLING
THE PRODUCTION/OPERATIONS
MANAGEMENT SYSTEM

preface

Many new texts for production and operations management have been offered in the last several years. Their existence reflects a felt need for an improved structure and pedagogy for teaching in this area. This book was designed to meet that need as expressed through an extensive market survey and five years of development. Our objective has been to provide the appropriate production/operations management (POM) book for a target segment of the academic market. It has not been our intention to be all things to all users, and we have tailored our presentation to meet the comments of a large number of professors who have expressed considerable frustration with existing texts.

We anticipate that this book will be most useful for a wide range of users from the junior-senior level of undergraduate courses to the first year of many master's programs. Its objectives, format, and order of difficulty all have been designed for that level, which is characterized by a lack of business experience, an awakening mathematical fluency, and a concern for management as a whole and as a meaningful social process.

Our surveys of experienced instructors showed consistent response in four areas of concern:

1) That the textbook they use be pedagogically sound, yet still teachable to students with mathematical-statistical backgrounds limited to three or four semesters of instruction

2) That the book project production/operations management as an integrated discipline or approach and not as a collection of institutional material or mathematical models

3) That, as over three-quarters of the respondents noted, the area be approached from a policy point of view and that the implications of the techniques and approaches that are taught reflect the larger, total organizational view, as well as the POM viewpoint

4) That the approach draw upon the wealth of experience and creative activity in POM beyond the walls of industrial plants

We have tried to meet these desires. All quantitative material presented in this text can be mastered by any student who understands algebra, elementary probability theory, and elementary differential calculus. Whenever possible, we have included noncalculus derivations as well.

In response to the "lack of order" complaints, we have arranged the material into four major parts which follow the logic of POM theory and practice. Part 1 introduces the basic concepts of system, analysis, and synthesis, which are generic to the tasks of production/operations management. Part 2 further defines these concepts in the specific language and experiences of the organizations in which function and organizational subsystems interface. It then describes the external environments to which they interface individually and as a whole. Part 3 deals with the processes by which a POM system is physically and organizationally designed for efficient and effective performance. And Part 4 focuses on the problems of control and evaluation in the POM organization once it is designed and is in operation.

In response to the complaints about the way in which specific quantitative models tend to appear and then reappear in many POM texts, we have limited coverage of common models to a single presentation, and we have placed linear programming in a comprehensive appendix in the interest of continuity and balance in the basic text. Some users may not find the menu of quantitative models as broad as in some texts; hence, we suggest the use of the traditional lecture method to bring in as much additional information as desirable. Our basic criteria for inclusion have centered on approaches which currently seem to be offering operational solutions to applied problems whether sophisticated or not, specifically those problems that POM managers *must* deal with, regardless of the state of the quantitative art.

To impart a "policy" approach to the book, we have allocated considerable space in the development of each topic to the relationship between it and the broader strategic issue in the organization and to the possible areas of conflict between POM and other functional areas. It is our hope that this will help train managers who do not lose sight of the broad implications of their area decisions and thus become unwitting practitioners of organizational suboptimization. We recognize that the converse may occur, that the student will perceive that there is no such thing as a functional area solution. If we must err, we hope we have done so in favor of a general management viewpoint.

We have made an earnest attempt to draw illustrations and examples from nonmanufacturing segments of the private sector of the economy and from the many large operating systems of the public sector. The reader will find represented in this text hospital situations, the tasks of the air traffic controller, and the back room operations of a brokerage house. We are of a single mind that public systems offer a significant challenge to production/operations management and one of considerable future import to the lives and interests of the students.

As this book comes to fruition, there are many people who over the long period of preparation have made contributions and have lent support to this task. In this case they are too numerous to thank publicly, as we have done so privately. To all we now say a well-deserved "Thank you." A special vote of thanks must go to the publisher, who, as on previous ventures, has helped so much with this undertaking.

Of course, the errors (and there are undoubtedly many) are our full responsibility. Over the time we promise to clean them up as they are brought to our attention and to continue to improve this text. We hope that our contribution will be rewarded in the way we see as most important, by attracting competent and creative students to the challenges of production/operations management.

Richard I. Levin
Curtis P. McLaughlin
Rudolf P. Lamone
John F. Kottas

production/operations management

part

INTRODUCTION AND BASIC CONCEPTS

one

chapter

INTRODUCTION TO OPERATING SYSTEMS

one

In any organization made up of individuals with common *objectives,* someone has to make things happen. They have to get goods made and out the door, take care of waiting patients, build a tower of Babel, plan the fraternity party, cook the steaks, and put on a Broadway show. These people have to make a *system operate* in the best possible way to meet the group's objectives. To an inexperienced observer, the systems that produce goods and services are vast, complex, and impersonal. Yet in reality, they are composed of small *subsystems* at every level which are understandable and personally managed, and exhibit on a small scale the attributes of their larger cousins, the corporation, the governmental system, and the health care system.

THE PRODUCTION FUNCTION

The primary focus of this text is that organizational function commonly called *production.* This function usually is responsible for the management of

3

a *process* or procedure intended to *convert* (transform) a set of *inputs* into a predetermined set of *outputs* in accordance with the objectives assigned to that production system.

Traditionally, to provide for specialization, the firm has been organized into three basic functional groups: marketing, finance, and production. The marketing group generates the demand; the financial group generates the capital; and the production group generates the supply of output. All these groups can at one point or another be evaluated as operating systems, and you will encounter many "gray areas" in the material offered in your courses where one functional area or another claims intellectual jurisdiction over certain functions. Both marketing and production will study the distribution and location of warehousing and service facilities. Finance and production will both emphasize methods of resource allocation important to the design and evaluation of investments. From our point of view, it is not important to settle these jurisdictional disputes. What is important is that you view such activities as alternative ways of structuring your analysis, so that you see the underlying processes operating in each area and can make rational decisions concerning them.

The function of the production manager is that of *putting together inputs of men, capital, materials, information, and energy; and transforming them into products and services in the quantity, quality, time, and location that will best meet the organization's objectives.* In an organization with a market orientation, this may mean that the process will have to be balanced between what marketing can sell and the best profit opportunities. In a public agency, it may mean balancing client needs against the available budget. In each case, there will be a set of *tradeoffs* to be made between multiple goals and the available resources. These tradeoffs will involve the decisions that are the essence of operating system (production process) *design.* Substitution of capital equipment for men, often called *mechanization* or *automation,* and other substitutions of inputs for each other represent another type of design tradeoff. It is this infinite variety of potential tradeoffs that makes production management so dynamic. As market demands shift and advancing technology modifies the factor combinations available, decisions and modifications are constantly required in even the most successful processes.

SYSTEMS

The word "system" has many uses, all stemming from the initial recognition that a system is a complex of functionally related components designed to achieve a predetermined objective. A *closed* system is one which contains all the attributes necessary for evaluation and manipulation for a designated

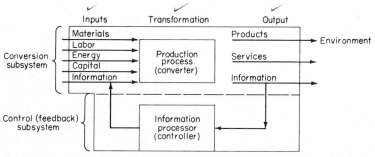

Figure 1-1 *A simple system description of operating systems*

purpose. An *open* system is one which is subject to outside influences. In real life, the complexity of relationships and influences is so great that no system involving people and society is a closed system. Yet we may deal with a system for specific purposes as if it were closed in order to analyze its components and interactions.

The simplest conception of a system is one which very closely resembles the process outlined in Figure 1-1. It contains two subsystems (sets of components and interrelationships viewed as components of an aggregated larger system). The *conversion process* is one subsystem. The second is a *control subsystem* which is a component of any managed system. It involves the feedback of information from the output of the converter to an information processor. This information processor may be all or partly human. The information processor is itself a subsystem which can be generalized as having the several component functions described in Figure 1-2. Note that the information output of the production subsystem serves as the input to the control system. This information is produced in a form which may or may not be suitable for decision making. For example, the producer of electric cable may make 50,000 feet of cable per hour and experience 320 defects in a $7\frac{1}{2}$-hour production shift, yet quality standards may be expressed in terms of the number of defects in each thousand feet of cable. The sensor component then has to monitor the appropriate output measures of units produced and defects and transmit these measures to a comparer. The comparer checks the observed standards stored in the

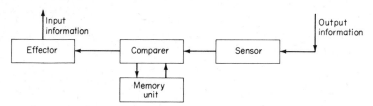

Figure 1-2 *Components of an information processor in feedback control*

memory component and sends signals to the effector unit whenever corrections should be made to adjust product quality.

These descriptions of a production system are extremely brief. They serve to introduce concepts and terms which will be used throughout this book. Chapters 2 and 3 illustrate the concepts of systems in more detail. The relationship of the production subsystem to the rest of the firm and to the environment is explained much more fully in Chapters 4 and 5.

PRODUCTION/OPERATIONS MANAGEMENT (POM) ✸

Historically, many of the concepts discussed in this text have been associated with manufacturing processes leading to the production of tangible products. But, as our society has experienced an even faster rate of growth in the production of services, in the development of information systems, and in the many large-scale, one-of-a-kind projects like the NASA space activities, the applicability of the same concepts to a much wider variety of human endeavors has become clearer.

Inputs must be converted *efficiently* and *effectively* into the desired outputs, whether the organization is profit or nonprofit, private or governmental, whether the output is tangible or intangible, a product or a service. Table 1-1 illustrates the varied nature of outputs from operating systems. All these outputs involve processing operations which must be managed and operated. Marshalling blood donors to provide a reliable supply geared to the varying needs of hospitals for five or six blood products of several types is very much like manufacturing frozen foodstuffs by gathering perishable

Table 1-1   *Types of outputs from operating systems*

	Tangible	Intangible
Profit-oriented	Cars	Advertising
	Soap	Brokerage
	Airplane rides	Accounting
	Computers	Nursing home care
	Records, LP	
Nonprofit:	Blood	Mutual life insurance
Private	Research reports	Cooperative food marketing
	Low rent housing	Hospitalization
Governmental	Electricity	Medical research
	Bridge crossings	Police protection
	Garbage collection	Education

products in the countryside and putting out several varieties and package sizes. Perhaps in another way, blood collection is like the allocation of airline seats to meet the seasonal demands of summer vacationers. One also might investigate the similarities among the behavior of a line of cars behind the tollbooths on the Golden Gate bridge, the orders awaiting processing in the computers of a Wall Street brokerage house, the family in Ann Arbor, Michigan trying to place a call to Grandma in Phoenix, Arizona on Christmas day, and the processing of orders for lilac and orange Corvettes at the Chevrolet assembly plant. This ability to identify similarities in processes and systems in a great variety of activities is one of the primary objectives behind the emphasis on systems in our approach to the overall topic of production/operations management, referred to as POM throughout this book. *Conceptually POM includes all types of productive work which are geared to the criteria of efficiency and effectiveness.*

EFFICIENCY

In engineering texts, efficiency is very carefully defined. It is the ratio of useful output to input, usually expressed in terms of energy in and out, or of material utilized. This measure is dimensionless and must take on a value between zero and one. In many production processes, this is a useful measure of the current state of the process. For the firm as a whole, however, it is a dangerous idea. The total system of the firm has to convert one set of inputs into a different set of outputs of much greater economic value so that the difference is sufficient to cover all processing costs and make a sufficient contribution toward covering overhead expenses and meeting the organization's objectives for rate of return on capital invested. Even a nonprofit corporation can be treated as one with a target rate of return; it merely happens to equal to zero. In POM literature, you will see the objective of efficiency improvement used in both senses—input conservation and enhancement of the *value added* by processing. The latter emphasis is closely related to the value added term used by economists in national income accounting, except that it may be applied to the much less aggregated operations within the firm.

EFFECTIVENESS

Many times you may have heard the old joke about the operation that was a success except that the patient died. Medical care may be delivered very efficiently, but it must still do the job. In many chapters of this book, you will find the words "efficiency" and "effectiveness" used together to serve as a reminder that the items which are quantified in dollars are not the only factors which must be evaluated in POM decisions. Starr suggests that any measure of effectiveness must take into account:

1. Costs of running the system
2. Quality of output
3. Production rate and production capacity
4. Flexibility to adjust to changing circumstances
5. Social value of the system[1]

As you will see in Chapter 3, these factors do not all move in the same direction in most alternative designs suggested for a POM system. Therefore, decision making involves many tradeoffs among very different factors until one is satisfied that the system is highly effective.

EVOLVING CONCEPTS IN POM

Man has been engaged in productive individual and group activities since prehistoric times. He has continually specialized tasks for greater efficiency and effectiveness and adopted new technologies. But the idea that these activities could be studied bit by bit (analyzed), conceptualized as abstractions (modeled), and then recombined (synthesized) into improved activities is a relatively new one. At first, societies were all concerned primarily with food, shelter, and defense, but soon individual artisans began to appear who could perform specific tasks better than others and made these their full-time function. Expanding trade and political relationships enabled whole groups to concentrate on products and services. Goods were exchanged, Greeks came (usually as slaves) to Rome to teach wealthy young Romans, mercenary units were added to the armies, and rulers traveled for days to Delphi to consult the oracle. Throughout the Middle Ages, these activities rested specifically with guilds, religious orders, and social groups, often on a hereditary basis. This form of assignment of tasks continues to exist in the caste groups of India and the tribal systems of Asia, Africa, and South America.

During and following the Renaissance, a technological and intellectual basis was established for the Industrial Revolution. Physical phenomena became a desirable subject for study; the printed word moved the information; commerce joined government, agriculture, warfare, and the religious orders as a fit vocation for educated men; and people began to concentrate more on the material rather than on the spiritual. As new techniques and materials developed which were combined with the new, more powerful, more reliable steam engine, the factory system became the preferred method

[1] M. K. Starr, *Production Management: Systems and Synthesis* (Englewood Cliffs, N.J.: Prentice-Hall, Inc., 1964), p. 32.

of organization of work. Hand labor no longer limited the size and scope of productive organizations. Improved metallurgy and machine design led to the idea of interchangeable parts, which allowed further flexibility in manufacture and assembly, and to early concepts of mass production. With these new and more complex methods of organization a need gradually arose for improved management techniques.

It is important to recognize the fact that most ideas important to POM have existed in the POM environment for a long time. What is relatively new is the systematization, abstraction, and widespread dissemination of these concepts and techniques under one title or another (e.g., management science, operations research, systems analysis, industrial engineering). The Venetians had a remarkable assembly line for outfitting war galleys by the fourteenth century. The programmed punched card of our computer era was the basis of the Jacquard loom which was invented about 1805 and was used for weaving complex patterns. Charles Babbage in England wrote about management problems in manufacture in 1832 and suggested the design of a computer by 1834.

The missing ingredients were a common language of discussion and a method of analysis for POM problems. By the turn of the century, organizations had grown huge, and yet the main responsibility for decisions remained with the worker and his foreman. Deliveries of inputs and outputs were uncoordinated and uncertain, and worker turnover was high in an era of low job security, poor employee training, and lack of management control. It remained easier to fire the worker who failed to deliver than to show him how to plan and perform effectively.

AGE OF ANALYSIS

With the increasing technology came new men with scientific and engineering training. These men were skilled in scientific methods of observation and analysis. They quite naturally applied their skills to their new duties as process developers and managers. Henry Towne, the engineer president of Yale & Towne Manufacturing Company, urged members of the American Society of Mechanical Engineers in 1886 to take a stronger interest in management problems. Captain Henry Metcalfe and many others engaged in private (contract) and public (arsenal) manufacture of arms greatly improved parts interchangeability, process flow and scheduling, and machine tool efficiency and flexibility.

Then in 1895, Frederick W. Taylor reported on a series of experiments with wage incentives which was the start of a stream of thought and work aimed at scientific work management in POM activities. He advocated the same systematic and scientific approach he had earlier used to develop a new method of tempering tool steel. Not a popular man among employers,

Taylor continued to write about his experiments and developed a set of associates which included Henry Gantt, Morris Cooke, and Harrington Emerson, who all made major contributions to scientific management. Taylor's *Principles of Scientific Management* (1911) remains a classic in this field. Jobs were studied and broken down into components. Methods were evaluated and modified, and more objective standards of performance were set for carefully trained and selected laborers. New methods of analysis were developed by these people who frequently were called "efficiency experts." Present-day descendants of these methods and their uses are described in detail in Chapters 9 and 10.

The disciples of Taylor continued to encounter resistance to their approaches from those whose efficiency and private skills were being questioned and from social observers who felt that their views of the worker were too mechanistic and that their views of the productive system were too narrow, too local, and too short-ranged.

Experiments involving workers, and other findings of the social sciences, have provided a leavening for those who wish to see a more humanistic approach to management decision making and to the design of production tasks. The systems concepts outlined in Chapter 2 provide an intellectual basis for a much broader view of the firm and of the human and organizational environment in which it operates.

AGE OF SYNTHESIS

The work of Taylor and his successors emphasized breaking tasks down into their most minute components and reassembling them into highly efficient, mass-production systems capable of economical manufacture of long runs of highly standardized products and dependent on the supervision of large numbers of men and machines doing repetitive tasks. But as Skinner[2] has suggested, the importance of such processes may be dwindling in our society. Increasing affluence has led to a desire for quality at the expense of cost, for variety and style, for service and delivery. The substitution of capital for labor has placed a higher priority on making the right decisions from the start, while technological change has shortened the useful life of products and processes. He argues that

> the job of production management in most industries is greatly different
> from what it was 15 years ago. With the mechanization of part of
> direct labor and much of management's paperwork and short-term
> scheduling decisions, managers may now spend more of their time
> on tomorrow's equipment and systems, and less on today's personnel

[2] C. Wickham Skinner, "Production Under Pressure," *Harvard Business Review,* 44 (November-December 1966), pp. 139–46.

assignments and grievances, parts shortages, and one-at-a-time machine choices. Here is an opportunity, but it comes at a price. To take advantage of it, more planning and system-designing skills are needed. There is an increasing requirement for specialists, and the production manager must be able to direct these experts and not be overwhelmed by them.

Since World War II, these new techniques and the experts who develop them have multiplied rapidly. Variously called "management science," "systems analysis," and "operations research," these disciplines have developed capabilities to abstract and manipulate (model) complex systems and to deal with their complexity, variety, and uncertainty in an improved but still imperfect manner. We shall see many of these abstractions in schematic and mathematical forms in later chapters. These experts have drawn freely on the findings of the basic disciplines of mathematics, applied psychology, and computer science to deal with large problems such as capital equipment analysis, allocation of scarce resources, determination of best product mix, product design, process design, scheduling, inventory management, and quality control. You will be introduced to the more basic aspects of these techniques in the appropriate chapters of this book.

The mathematically and scientifically oriented techniques associated with management science are not necessarily new. F. W. Harris of Westinghouse Electric began in 1913 using the simple economical ordering quantity formula that you will learn. At Bell Telephone Laboratories, the basic aspects of probability theory for system design were outlined by T. C. Fry in 1928 and those for quality control by W. Shewhart in 1931. What is new since World War II is the building of a systematic body of knowledge intended for use in any and all fields by trained specialists; new is the idea that the skills and tools of varied sciences were applicable to convoy design, tanker routing, bombing patterns, and antisubmarine warfare, and then after the war to equipment design, warehouse location, planning surgical procedures, scheduling bank computers, etc.

Starr has summarized the importance of synthesis as follows:

Great stress has always been placed on analysis in the production management field. But synthesis has not been similarly favored. The explanation is that synthesis has been relegated to intuition and judgment of executives. It shall continue to be, but not exclusively. There is a basis for objective synthesis. The desire for synthesis is not academic. Pre-designed systems of partial or full automation must be synthesized in an external and objective fashion. There is no other way.

To achieve synthesis we must be able to identify structure that will permit the simultaneous consideration of all production factors. For

example, we cannot determine the best production process for unit
x and for unit y independently and then put the two together; there
may be a different best process for units x and y when considered
together. Similarly, the decision problem concerning what materials
handling equipment to use interacts with problems running the gamut
from plant selection and product line composition to how many ashtrays
the company will keep in stock for its employees. A limited supply
of investment funds and restrictions of other resources creates a situation which requires overall treatment of factors. Separate analytic
results that indicate a number of best subsystem strategies will seldom
sum together to yield an overall best strategy.

The problem of synthesis is too complex to permit the exclusive use
of judgment. It is too large for a purely methodological treatment
also. Properly used, the combination of objective and subjective treatments can be synergistic. (The total effect of the system is greater
than the sum of the individual effects of the parts of the system
operating independently.)[3]

The relationships and the methodological treatments mentioned by
Starr are the models and systems concepts developed by operations researchers and management scientists. They are applicable to many different activities involving highly varied production technologies. Starr has suggested
that analysis and then synthesis have progressed further in production management because (1) the outputs are more easily measured, (2) the operations are primarily internal and thus are treated more effectively as closed
systems, (3) production has a history of rigorous design, and that all three
reasons are compatible with the introduction of the computer. Another related
reason would seem to be the ample supply of technically trained personnel,
usually engineers, who started out to design nonhuman systems components
but have progressed to applying their approaches to man-machine systems
as well.

The computer has not yet changed the nature of the management
decision-making process. While the computer has been used to digest and
process larger and more varied information much more quickly, the organization of the effort and the rules for selecting and evaluating the data remain
unchanged. As H. A. Simon has suggested, the computer has been taking
over from middle management the solving of many well-structured problems,[4] but the tasks of supervision and the solution of ill-structured problems
remain as the challenge of the future for human managers.

[3] Starr, *op. cit.*, p. 54.
[4] H. A. Simon, *The New Science of Management Decision* (New York: Harper and Brothers, 1960).

CHANGES TO COME

In reality, we have only started to achieve the full power of our ability to process, analyze, and synthesize data. Beer[5] has argued that this is because our conceptions of business organizations and their decision-making processes are constrained by the limitations of the human hand, eye, and brain. Only gradually can we comprehend and apply radically new approaches which are beyond our own capacities. Only gradually will we begin to see how the organization can respond to these new capabilities and how it can manage systems well beyond the present absorptive capacity of any one manager alone. Some potential for changes may come about quite rapidly as we develop computer systems which "learn" and are capable of reprogramming themselves.

Already, centralized resource allocation models used in large corporations have made possible a degree of analysis and improved design well beyond the ability of local managers to plan. What looks like an *optimal* (best possible) system of operation for the manager of an East Coast oil refinery may be *suboptimal* in the light of the worldwide availability of crude oil and the demand for products experienced by his company. For the same reasons, the domains of the functional areas—marketing, finance, and production—have become less independent as models have been developed to integrate decision making about items such as product mix and allocation of production capacity.

Man, however, will still maintain many processing advantages over machines. Simon summarized man's retained comparative advantage as "(1) the use of his brain as a flexible general-purpose, problem-solving device, (2) the flexible use of his sensory organs and hands, and (3) the use of his legs, on rough terrain as well as smooth, to make this general purpose sensing-thinking-manipulating system available wherever it is needed."[6] He sees men as necessary to small, low-volume tasks; to solve ill-structured problems; to design, maintain, and modify machines; to manage people; and to provide personal services where face-to-face human interaction is an important part of the product. This would imply a more varied, more rewarding life for those who are employed.

Since Simon's projection, the factor of consumption versus environmental pollution has gained considerable public attention. It now seems possible that the output of goods may be constrained by the availability of raw materials, the consumption of energy, and the disposal of waste

---

[5] Stafford Beer, *Management Science; The Business Use of Operations Research* (Garden City, N.Y.: Doubleday and Company, Inc., 1967).
[6] H. A. Simon, "The Corporation: Will It Be Managed by Machines?", in Anshen and Bach, eds., *Management and Corporations 1985* (New York: McGraw-Hill Book Company, 1960).

products. But a constraint on the production of physical goods need not necessarily imply a halt to economic growth. We could continue to have an expansion of the services in which the human contact is an integral part, as well as an emphasis on those activities which conserve resources and reprocess wastes. Just because our vaunted productivity has led us to social and ecological problems, there is no reason to abandon the methodologies developed to enhance these processes. The same methodologies coupled with modified objectives and social values represent the logical approach to the changes that are necessary for the next generation of improvements.

ORGANIZATION OF THIS BOOK

To educate you further in these methodologies is the objective of the authors. Systems concepts are amplified in Chapter 2, while in Chapter 3, the general methodological approaches to decision making are presented together with a few models of wide applicability. Relationships among the functions of the firm are examined in Chapter 4. The system is opened up in Chapter 5 through consideration of the relationships between the POM system and the environment.

Chapters 6 through 10 deal with the design of operating systems and with the detailed methods which have been developed to provide for efficient and effective operation. Chapter 6 presents the process by which the output products and services are designed and specified. The processes by which they are produced are the topics of Chapters 7, 8, and 9. Once the products and processes have been designed, it becomes necessary to measure the inputs and outputs to determine the effectiveness of the design and its operation. Chapter 10 focuses on the topic of measurement and its importance to the POM system. We mentioned earlier that location and availability of the output was an important attribute of the system, so facilities location is the topic of Chapter 11.

No matter how good the design process has been, the system must be operated in response to changing demands and capabilities. Chapters 12 through 16 outline the techniques available for dealing with the problems of system dynamics and control. Chapter 12 introduces these topics and emphasizes the complexities involved in determining and utilizing the output capacity of a system over time. The demand on a system is uncertain, and good forecasting is essential if management is going to be prepared to adjust to it. Chapter 13 presents the topic of forecasting for planning, while Chapter 14 covers the techniques of planning for capacity over the longer run based on these forecasts. Chapter 15 deals with the uses of inventory as a method of storing capacity and with the models available to plan and control its use in a highly rational manner. Shorter-run scheduling and production control are the subjects of Chapter 16. The remaining attribute of the system is the quality of its output which can be used to respond to market demands and to alter operating capacity. This area is outlined in Chapter 17 and completes the array of aspects of the productive system you may be expected to control as an interested and educated management decision maker.

QUESTIONS

1. What is the production function? Describe how a college library might be viewed as a production function.
2. What is the function of a production manager? Is this function different from the function of a marketing manager? Explain.
3. Assume that you have been assigned the job of designing and producing an electronic error-detection system. As always, your resources are limited. You have been asked to consider three cost categories: (1) research and development costs, (2) investment costs, i.e., those costs beyond the development phase necessary to introduce the new system, and (3) operating costs, i.e., recurring costs of operating, supporting, and maintaining the system. Discuss the tradeoff possibilities that might exist between the cost categories and the goal of producing an effective error detection system at a minimum cost.
4. The term "operations management" implies the applicability of production concepts to a much wider variety of human endeavors. Explain.
5. Explain why an engineering definition of efficiency is not applicable to economic systems.
6. Distinguish between efficiency and effectiveness.
7. From a historical viewpoint, we have progressed from an efficiency orientation to an effectiveness orientation. Explain.
8. What characteristics distinguish the age of analysis from the age of synthesis?
9. Explain why analysis and synthesis have progressed further in production management relative to other functional fields.
10. Discuss the impact of the computer in the field of production operations management.

CASE

Mr. Robert Minte has been in the field of hospital administration for 15 years. Recently, he became the chief hospital administrator of a large sub-

urban hospital. Within a short period of time in his new position, he uncovered a number of problems within the hospital, most significant of which
were critical shortages of both medical and nonmedical supplies, poor patient
feeding, and increasing costs in the laundry facility. Minte decided to hire
an assistant to help him solve these problems.

After turning down a number of applicants for the job, a young man,
Roger Hefler, walked into the administrator's office, requested, and was
granted an interview. Hefler told Minte that he had been a production manager for a local manufacturing firm and felt that he could help solve many
of the hospital's operating problems. Minte just shook his head in amazement
and said, "Is this some kind of a joke, a production manager applying
for a job to help me solve problems in a hospital! How can a production
manager, however ingenious you are Hefler, come into my hospital and
learn enough about it to help me find solutions to problems that give me
difficulty? It took me years to learn what I know about hospital administration,
and I don't know enough to solve these problems."

Assume you are Hefler, how would you answer Minte's question?

RESEARCH PROJECT

Using the following list of references, write a brief report contrasting the
scientific management movement with present-day concepts of POM.

1. Fillipetti, George, *Industrial Management in Transition* (Homewood:
   Richard D. Irwin, Inc., 1946).
2. George, Claude S., Jr., *The History of Management Thought* (Englewood Cliffs, N.J.: Prentice-Hall, Inc., 1968).
3. Mee, J. F., *Management Thought in a Dynamic Society* (New York:
   New York University Press, 1963).
4. Starr, Martin K., "Evolving Concepts in Production Management,"
   Elwood S. Buffa, ed., *Readings in Production and Operations Management* (New York: John Wiley & Sons, Inc., 1966).

chapter
THE SYSTEMS CONCEPT
two

Given the complexity of large-scale operations, it becomes almost impossible to view the many segments of the production function solely as a group of separate entities within the total organization. Effective managers have never completely ignored the interrelationships that exist among the functional components of the organization. The problem, however, confronting managers today is finding better ways and means of developing a conceptual framework which more precisely and effectively ties together all functional efforts, contributions, and knowledge.

One clearly emerging conceptual framework is the systems concept. The major impact of this deceptively simple concept has yet to be felt. According to Cleland and King, the systems concept is much more widely discussed than understood. "Probably no concept has ever had more lip service paid to it; undoubtedly few concepts have ever been more widely applied by people who did not know they were doing so, and perhaps no concept has been more widely ignored by people who should know better."[1]

---

[1] David I. Cleland and William R. King, *Systems, Organizations, Analysis, Management: A Book of Readings* (New York: McGraw-Hill Book Company, 1969), p. 47.

This chapter abstracts the essence of the systems concept and separates it from any specific functional area. The emphasis is not on what is actually being done, nor what can readily be done. The objective is the development of a conceptual framework and an operational philosophy within which the traditional management functions of planning, controlling, organizing, and directing can be integrated more effectively. The actual application of this conceptual framework to the field of production/operations management is discussed in subsequent chapters.

✓ WHAT IS A SYSTEM?

A *system* may be defined as *an interconnected complex of functionally related components designed to achieve a predetermined objective.* There are several significant points in this definition. First, there must be an established arrangement of the components, activities, or functions. In any system, there is a coherent rather than a random collection of elements. In other words, we acknowledge relatedness by examining the relationships among the elements making up the collection. Hence, we turn a collection into what might be called an "assemblage." The way in which these components interact must be defined. In setting out a pattern of interaction in a given set of relationships, we convert an assemblage into a systematically arranged assemblage. Furthermore, there must be some objective which the system is designed to achieve. A systematically arranged assemblage does not constitute a system until some unifying purpose is devised for it. We have a *system,* then, when we bring to a collection of objects coherence, pattern, and purpose. To recognize these characteristics and to determine how they affect a given system is half the battle. This point sounds trivially obvious. But, we frequently underestimate the magnitude of that task. Finally, implicit in any definition of a system is the concept of an organized or complex whole—the assembly or combination of the components into a unitary whole. Indeed, the Greek word for "organized whole," "systēma," is appropriately descriptive of the conceptual phase of the modern systems approach.

This definition is applicable to many types of systems, whether physical,

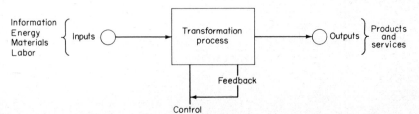

Figure 2-1 *Input-output process model of a subsystem*

biological, behavioral, or social. The generality and scope of the concept are illustrated in examples such as production system, hospital system, penal system, Copernican system, nervous system, welfare system. In fact, we are surrounded by systems and subsystems. The concept provides us with a framework for analyzing complex phenomena. If systems did not exist, we would invent them.

THE PRODUCTION/OPERATIONS FUNCTION AS A SYSTEM

The POM system may be viewed as a structure of subsystems, each of which has the following basic characteristics: inputs, a transformation process, outputs, and a feedback process. Figure 2-1 illustrates how various inputs enter into some process which transforms the set of inputs into some set of outputs. Within the POM system, we discover many configurations of the input-output process model. Figure 2-2 shows a very simple straight-line or serial configuration in which the output of one process becomes the input of another process. For example, the output of one department within the plant, say a completed subassembly, becomes the input to another department which uses the subassembly to produce a finished product. Figure 2-3 illustrates a parallel configuration in which the outputs from three subsystems, *A, B,* and *C,* are brought together as inputs into a subsystem *D.* A large national bakery, for example, may have its own flour mill, egg farm, and sugar refinery. Each of these processes represents subsystems of the total production system of the firm. The output of each of these subsystems is combined as inputs to the bakery itself.

Finally, Figure 2-4 shows a more complicated system which employs both the serial and parallel configurations and which illustrates the interrelationships that are characteristic of POM systems often encountered in practice. Notice that the information output from process *C* is fed back to process *A* for purposes of control. Similarly, process *E* is dependent upon information output from process *F.* For the same reason, process *C* is dependent upon process *F* and process *D* upon process *E.* The essential point here is that the information necessary to control subsystems *A, C, D,* and *E* is not

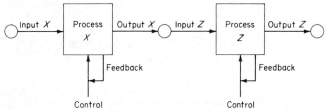

Figure 2-2   *Serial subsystem configuration*

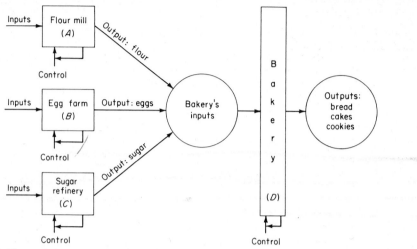

Figure 2-3 *Parallel subsystem configuration*

generated solely within those subsystems. Consequently, they are interconnected with and dependent upon other subsystems. In this sense, then, a POM system may be viewed as an interdependent grouping of subsystems, each related to its successor, each performing a different function in the chain, but each united in the achievement of the common goal.

THE POM SYSTEM AS AN OPEN SYSTEM

All living systems are open systems in that they interact with their environment. Figure 2-5 illustrates how the POM system is itself a subsystem within its environment. The POM system is influenced by, and influences, its internal and external environments. In some cases, the influence between the various interfaces is well-defined, in others, ill-defined. A more detailed study of the interfaces shown in Figure 2-5 will be presented in Chapters 4 and 5.

It is essential that a system interact with its environment if it is to grow. Thus, to isolate the system from its environment is to rob the system of its viability. In some cases, if you take pieces out of a viable system in order to study them, or if you insist on considering the behavior of parts of the system as if the rest of it did not exist, they either stop functioning or begin to behave atypically. Yet, how often in an organization do we find a manager being held responsible for getting his own bit of the organization system right, regardless of the rest; and how often do we hear that if managers succeed in this, their success represents success for the whole organization? As was pointed out in Chapter 1, this narrow concept of

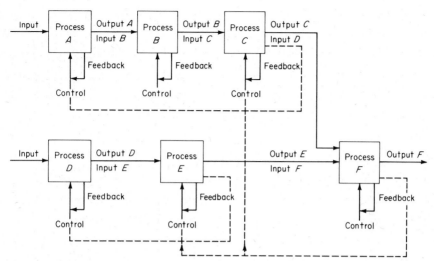

Figure 2-4 *An integrated feedback configuration*

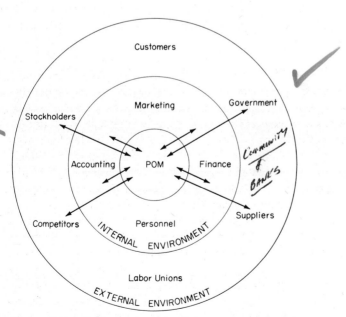

Figure 2-5 *Environmental interfaces with production/operations management system*

efficiency is a dangerous idea for the organization as a whole. The desired or optimal outcome does not necessarily result from the more narrowly conceived but carefully designed actions of subsystem managers.

THE SYSTEMS CONCEPT AND THE
PRODUCTION/OPERATIONS MANAGER

At this point, we want to examine the way in which the systems concept provides the manager with a framework for managing the complexity of "everything depends upon everything else" in an orderly way. Given that the activity of any subsystem within an organization has some effect on the activity of every other subsystem, the evaluation of any decision or action requires the identification of all *significant* interactions and their combined impact on the performance as a whole, not merely on the subsystem originally involved. According to Ackoff and Rivett:

> This orientation is quite contrary to what might be called the "natural"
> inclination of researchers or managers to cut a very complex problem
> "down to size," and isolate it from its environment. That is, we tend
> to eliminate aspects of a problem which make it difficult to solve,
> and thereby we reduce it to one that can be handled by "standard"
> techniques or by judgment based on experience. The system's orienta-
> tion, on the other hand, moves in the opposite direction; it deliberately
> expands and complicates the statements of problems until all the sig-
> nificant interacting components are contained within it.[2]

The use of the word "significant" is very important here, because not all interactions in a system are significant and measurable. This basic idea is perhaps better understood by example than by abstract and general discussion.

Consider a warehousing operation where the costs are excessive.[3] The high costs are apparently related to a great deal of overcrowding and congestion in the warehouse, with work frequently piling up at certain times in the operation, particularly during peak periods. Now, in terms of the industrial engineer, the problem might be seen as follows: "How can we modify the materials handling procedures in such a way as to reduce or eliminate the congestion, overcrowding, and piling up of work, and thus reduce our costs?" Given this statement of the problem, you don't have to be an indus-

---

[2] Russell L. Ackoff and Patrick Rivett, *A Manager's Guide to Operations Research* (New York: John Wiley & Sons, Inc., 1964), p. 10.
[3] Based on an example by Allen Harvey, "This Systems Engineering Approach to Cost Reduction and Control," *Cost Reduction at Work* (New York: American Management Association, 1958), pp. 30–32.

trial engineer to come up with a range of possible solutions. These might include, for example, adding more warehouse space, improving the layout and/or procedures, and introducing some mechanization. Any or all of these approaches may result in a reduction of the high costs. Yet, no matter how brilliant the engineering or how bad the warehousing operation, the effectiveness of cost reduction effort has been limited by the implicit assumptions that were made concerning the nature of the cost problems in the warehouse.

Now, let's take the same warehousing operation, with the same set of conditions, and broaden our assumptions to include the possibility that the flow through the warehouse actually depends largely on factors outside of the warehouse. We have, in a sense, opened the door of our warehousing subsystem and brought into play a new set of related variables. These might include, say, the size and shape of the materials that are brought into the warehouse, their sequence and rate of delivery and withdrawal. What about order-filling and shipping procedures, and in fact, the company's sales forecasting? Are these organized in such a way as to maintain the most effective flow through the warehouse?

The point here is that this new set of assumptions immediately changes our statement of the cost problem. Why? We have identified the significant interactions between the warehousing subsystem and other subsystems within the organization. In so doing, we now recognize that the causes of the high costs in the warehouse may not lie solely with the functioning of the warehouse, but may be largely rooted in factors outside it.

We may carry this example one step further. Having identified and recognized the interrelationships among the subsystems that affect the warehousing operation, we can no longer accept any statement of the problem in terms of warehousing costs alone. If, for example, the reduction in warehousing costs led to impaired customer service, decreased the efficiency of handling reorders, or in any way detracted from the total profitability of the company, what would have been accomplished? Nothing! Thus from a systems viewpoint, a more correct statement of the problem is as follows: "How can we eliminate the congestion, overcrowding, and work pile-up in the warehouse in such a way as to achieve an optimal balance among our objectives of reducing warehousing costs, maintaining specific standards of customer service, meeting certain sales requirements, and increasing the total profitability of the company?"

What originally appeared to be a simple and isolated problem in the warehouse turned out to be interrelated with a number of other operating problems in the company. By expanding the problem, the solutions to the parts could be interconnected to define performance in terms of the organization as a whole. The systems orientation goes beyond those local improvements, which may result in overall loss of effectiveness.

LESSONS TO BE ABSORBED

There are several important general conclusions that can be drawn from our example of the warehouse problem. First, *effectiveness in an organization exists only when all its subsystems are in proper relationship to one another.* We cannot escape the problem of complexity by ignoring it. This is, in fact, what we do when we attempt to break it down and deal piecemeal with the elements that make up the total strategy of the firm. In a sense, problems have really not become more complex; rather, the systems concept and the corresponding developments in systems analysis and technology have provided a capability for dealing with the complexity that always existed.

Any particular component performs a function in relation to, or in cooperation with, a large number of interrelated components, and its effects are as dependent upon those interrelationships as upon its own inherent characteristics. Thus, in addition to the variables associated with each individual subsystem, another set of variables enters the picture as soon as these components are viewed as a whole. The whole is greater than the sum of its parts taken separately. We can say, then, that the general behavior of a system is determined more by the interactions than by the things that interact.

Of course, for certain kinds of analyses, we may want to treat the subsystem as if it were a closed system and ignore or hold constant other interrelated variables. But, in the end, the results of the analysis must be integrated with the system of variables which actually exists in the organization with all its complexity. To eliminate such complexity and enforce simplicity for its own sake destroys one of the essential characteristics of the system being defined. We should be as concerned with the impracticality inherent in oversimplification as by that involved in magnitude and complexity.[4]

Another lesson to be absorbed concerns the independence or dependence of objectives. Whenever there is no conflict between objectives—that is, when the attainment of one objective is independent of others, or the interactions are mutually supportive—the manager can solve his decision problems separately. Unfortunately, this is seldom the case. *Organizational objectives are, for the most part, interdependent and involve tradeoffs.* This means that optimization of one objective can result in a lower degree of attainment for others, a condition generally referred to as *suboptimization.* We could have, for example, solved the problem of the high costs in the warehouse case in terms of the warehouse alone. But such a solution would have been suboptimal with respect to overall objectives. Instead, the problem had to be expanded to include several interdependent objectives. Achieving

⁴ E. Bakke, "Concept of the Social Organization," M. Haire, ed., *Modern Organization Theory* (New York: John Wiley & Sons, Inc., 1961), pp. 72–73.

the optimal solution means finding the *best balance* among the whole set of conflicting objectives.

This point cannot be stressed too strongly. For example, each subsystem's request for capital investment funds is generally accompanied by a watertight story justifying why the investment yield would exceed the return on investment required by top management. But in order to make the best decision among these competing requests, we would have to evaluate the behavior of the entire system assuming that each change had been made. We must do more than examine the alleged benefits of the investment in a particular subsystem because of the impact the change will make throughout the system. In the final analysis, there is "no functional profit, no functional loss, no functional investment, no functional risk, no functional product, and no functional image of the company. There is only a unified company product, risk, investment, and so on."[5] Management's ultimate concern is total company performance.

In most cases, it is impossible to enhance simultaneously the achievement of all relevant objectives. For example, we cannot simultaneously maximize the quality of a product and minimize the cost of manufacturing that product. What we can do is optimize a given objective subject to the restrictions and limitations imposed by the other objectives. For example, we can maximize the quality of a product subject to the condition that we will not spend more than a given number of dollars on materials, equipment, manpower, and other production factors; or, we can minimize the manufacturing costs of a given product subject to some specified quality level or other production restrictions.[6]

Finally, *when a problem is first observed in one area of an organization, there is a tendency to find a solution that is completely contained in that area and to use methods of solution that fit the established procedures in that area.* Problems, however, have no respect for organizational structure. The successful implementation of the systems concept is dependent largely on your ability to recognize this fact. Bringing within the scope of analysis interactions previously considered out of bounds will, in most cases, greatly enhance the power and effectiveness of the analysis.

THE TRANSFORMATION PROCESS

Up to this point, we have said little about how the transformation process converts some input into some output. A purchasing department may, for

---

[5] Peter Drucker, "Long-range Planning—Challenge to Management Science," *Management Science* (April 1959), pp. 238–249.

[6] Martin K. Starr, *Production Management Systems and Synthesis* (Englewood Cliffs, N.J.: Prentice-Hall, Inc., 1964), pp. 36–37.

example, process purchase requisitions by hand or by computer. The bakery may transform its inputs of flour, sugar, eggs, and so on into a set of outputs—bread and cakes—using hand mixers or automatic mixers, gas or electric ovens. For purposes of identifying and analyzing the interrelationships among the various subsystems and synthesizing these interrelationships into some meaningful whole, we may specify only the inputs and outputs. We observe what takes place viewing the transformation process as a black box which represents an abstraction of a complex grouping of functionally related components. Anything may be going on inside the box.

Even when we study the detail inside the transformation process, we shall have to simplify the relationships that arise. At times, POM is concerned primarily with the details of the transformation process that takes place in each of the black boxes. In some POM problems, for example, we may be given a set of input and output conditions for the specified system; the operations manager's job, then, may be to restructure the transformation process of the system to meet these specifications most effectively. In other problems, the operations manager may wish to predict the outputs from the system, given specified input conditions. To do this, he would isolate the inputs and outputs and attempt to determine which elements within the conversion process would affect his prediction.

POM is also concerned with synthesizing all the transformation processes into some meaningful whole. This concern for synthesis forces the operations manager to treat the conversion process as a black box, either because he does not wish to deal with further detail, or because he is not able to penetrate the boundary of the black box. Professor Hare provides us with an example:

> If we wished to know in complete detail why a particular dog wags
> his tail, we would need to destroy the dog to trace his nerve structure,
> to cite one form of analysis. This, however, would still not explain
> in complete detail why the dog wagged its tail. For the dog's owner,
> a black box approach is entirely satisfactory: "My dog wags his tail
> when I give him a bone." . . . In other words at some level of refine-
> ment, we say "enough!" and lump together what we do not know
> or care to discover.[7]

When viewing the system as an interconnected complex of functionally related transformation processes—each with its own set of inputs and outputs—we are assuming some stability on the part of the conversion process, be it a machine process, a human process, or some combination of both. That is, for purposes of prediction, we assume the conversion process will

---

[7] Van Court Hare, Jr., *Systems Analysis: A Diagnostic Approach* (Harcourt, Brace, & World, Inc., 1967), p. 29. See also pp. 27–51 for a more complete discussion of the transformation process.

continue to operate in the future as it has in the past. We accept information output from the computer without concern for the internal electronic structure of the computer. We are, out of necessity, forced to accept the black-box concept in many cases in our everyday decision-making process.

Furthermore, we recognize in this black-box thinking the self-organizing properties of systems. For example, if there exist alternative courses of action at any given point in the system at any given time, then a decision is required to resolve the alternatives. Sometimes this means the manager must make the choice. But sometimes the system itself effectively makes the choice. These self-organizing properties are extremely important in the decision-making process of a system. "No manager has time to make conscious, deliberated choices each time an alternative exists. Management relies more heavily than it often realizes on the system's intrinsic ability to do the right thing—and this includes sensible behavior on the part of workers who know nothing of the company's policies as such."[8] Therefore, in specifying the decision properties of a system, the decision maker must distinguish between the self-organizing ones and those that require managerial intervention.

In summary, we need not always be concerned with the details of the conversion process. Remember the behavior of a system is determined more by the interactions than by the things that interact. This approach guides us in categorizing what is relatively stable or changing in a given situation. The stability assumption, for example, may fail if the transformation process is permitted to operate outside its previously tested range; or it may fail if a major change takes place in the combination of inputs; or over a period of time, the internal structure of the process itself may be altered and hence fail to produce the predetermined output. This approach also helps us in examining the vulnerability of the system to changes in environment, the dependence or independence of various transformation processes, and the compatibility of outputs to inputs. These conclusions are inferred from the interrelationships and not from information about the details of all the transformation processes.

THE CONTROL PROCESS

The function of the control process is to make the system operate true to the objectives which the system was designed to achieve. The control function includes the measurement of output, the comparison of output with some standard, and the adjustment, if necessary, of the inputs and/or

8 Stafford Beer, *Management Science: The Business Use of Operations Research* (Garden City, N.Y.: Doubleday & Company, Inc., 1968), p. 128.

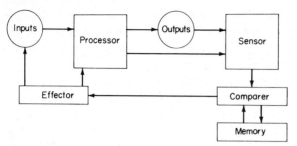

Figure 2-6 *The control process system*

the conversion process to restore the system to its predetermined plan. There are five basic elements in all control systems:

1. The *transformation process* represents the activity that is being controlled. In general, it converts inputs into outputs.
2. The *sensor* is a device which measures characteristics or conditions of the process or the output.

3. The *comparer* is a device which compares the information received from the sensor with a predetermined value or standard. It is in a sense an error-detector.
4. The *memory* is a device which holds the standard, value, or specified characteristics of the output and process.
5. The *effector* is a device which is capable of modifying the process or the mix of inputs in response to signals from the comparer and memory.[9]

Figure 2-6 illustrates the relationships among the five elements. The sensor measures the characteristics of the output and the processor. This information is then sent to the comparer which compares the measures to the predetermined standards housed in the memory unit. If there is no *significant* deviation in the compared results—the measures fall within allowable limits—the effector takes no action to change the status of the inputs or processor. If a significant deviation exists, the effector takes the corrective action necessary to bring inputs or process into conformance with the desired characteristics.

The control process need not be automated. The human operator in charge of some machine process and observing the instrument readings may detect significant deviation of the actual performance of the process from some desired standard and take corrective action by manipulating several valves or levers. In this case, the human operator serves as the sensor,

[9] Richard J. Hopeman, *Systems Analysis and Operations Management* (Columbus, Ohio: Charles E. Merrill Books, Inc., 1969), pp. 134–141.

the comparer, the memory unit, and the effector. He observes the reading, decides what is meant, what action should be taken to correct the process, and whether or not the corrective action is sufficient. This is what control is all about: measure, compare, correct, and check the result.

Of course, the limitations of the human system and the increasing complexity of modern technological systems have forced the development of automatic or self-regulating control processes. The general notion of automatic control is not a new thing. Self-regulating mechanisms are an inherent characteristic of many processes in nature, living and nonliving. Temperature control within the human system is one obvious example of a self-regulating process. The thermostat is another example of a self-regulating mechanism in physical systems. While the concepts underlying self-regulating systems are indeed old, the formulation and exploitation of the principles of automatic control are relatively new. Most books that talk about control begin their analysis with a discussion of self-regulating mechanisms, and for a very good reason. The fundamental concepts underlying these mechanisms provide fruitful clues for understanding and talking sensibly about the nature of management control in large systems.

SELF-REGULATING SYSTEMS AND FEEDBACK

A concept fundamental to all control processes is feedback. Information is the basis of control, since the adjustment of future actions is based upon information about past performance. Feedback, in general, expresses interdependence of one part of a system with another. The classical example of a thermostat demonstrates its characteristics. When the room temperature falls below some desired level, the thermostat closes a circuit to start the heating system, and the temperature rises. Conversely, as the temperature rises to the selected level, the thermostat opens the circuit to turn off the heating system. In this example, the reading of the thermometer within the thermostat represents information about the room temperature which is fed back to open or close a circuit, which in turn controls the temperature. Thus the reading on the thermometer and the temperature of the room are interdependent. This type of system is generally referred to as a *closed-loop system* as shown in Figure 2-7.

Not all automatic control processes are of the closed-loop type. For example, the thermostat might be placed outside in the open air and connected to the heating system so that the outside temperature regulates the heating system. In this open-loop system, the room temperature provides no feedback; it has no effect on the operation of the activity controlled—the heating system. Another example would be a street-lighting system controlled by a timing mechanism. At specified times in the evening and morning,

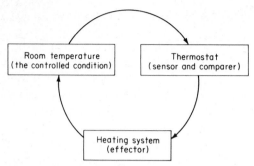

Figure 2-7   *A closed-loop system*

the lights are turned on and off. It does not measure the system being controlled—light. On a dark overcast day, lights might be needed; but, being an independent unit, the timing device would not recognize the need for light. This does not mean that open-loop systems are necessarily bad or useless; in some cases, they work very well. They do, however, have some limitations. The open-loop controller must be developed to meet each particular application. Moreover, it can handle only standard conditions.

The feedback control system avoids these limitations. It is interdependent with the controlled activity, and it is capable of dealing with a variety of conditions. In many street-lighting systems, a photoelectric cell continuously measures the local daylight level, and the lights will go on during a dark storm as well as at dusk.

Feedback control systems cannot operate without some error; it is, in fact, the error which is depended upon to bring about the correction. The objective, of course, is to make the error as small as possible.

CHARACTERISTICS OF FEEDBACK SYSTEMS

Now let us look at some of the performance characteristics of feedback systems. Essentially, we are interested in determining what happens when a system is disturbed, i.e., what happens to output when the input is changed. Change in input may mean, for example, new materials, more or fewer workers, new labor union requirements, more or less cash available, and so on. To examine the effect of a change in input, we assume first that the system is in a steady state, i.e., the input and output are constant. Any change in input at this point will cause feedback, and the output will fluctuate around the predetermined output level. The output will, in a sense, begin to search or hunt back and forth around the desired level. This fluctuating or oscillatory behavior is characteristic of all feedback systems. If the input quantity begins to oscillate in value, then the output quantity also will begin to oscillate, not simultaneously or necessarily in the same way but with the same frequency.[10] The task in management control, therefore, is to sufficiently dampen the oscillation such that the output quantity quickly reaches the desired level.

The various patterns of oscillatory behavior are more conveniently shown in graphical form. Figure 2-8a shows the output of a system in continuous but stable oscillation. To explain this pattern, we must understand that control is exercised by *negative feedback*. That is, the information fed back represents the difference between actual and desired output. Hence, the pattern of motion resulting from negative feedback is opposite to the original motion resulting from a change in input. Now in a closed-loop system without any time lag between input oscillation and output oscillation, the correct amount of negative feedback would prevent oscillatory behavior in output. Unfortunately, in most systems, when there is some change in the inputs or process, it takes some time before the output of the system adjusts to the change and settles down to the desired level. The fact that output oscillation lags behind input oscillation enormously complicates the subject of feedback systems. Figure 2-8a, then, shows a system in which the feedback

[10] Arnold Tustin, "Feedback," in *Automatic Control* by the editors of *Scientific American* (New York: Simon & Schuster, Inc., 1955), p. 16.

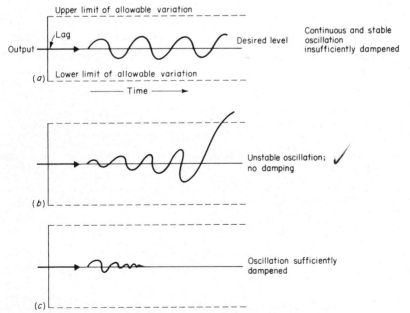

Figure 2-8   *Patterns of oscillation in feedback systems*

is opposite in direction and equal in force to the original change. Thus the oscillation maintains itself, like a dog chasing its own tail.

Figure 2-8b illustrates unstable oscillation. This may happen when we take corrective action which is greater than the error, thus amplifying the original disturbance. In other words, we may overexaggerate the error. This overcompensation may cause the oscillations to grow until the system is out of control or, worse, destroyed. Many of us have no doubt experienced the consequences of overcompensation. For example, in trying to avoid hitting an animal which suddenly darts out onto the highway, we may overcompensate, swerving the car sometimes violently right and left. Depending on the amount of overcompensation and other conditions (road surface, tires, etc.), we may bring the car back into control; or, unfortunately, in some cases, we may end up in a tree—system destroyed.

The desired pattern of response in a feedback control system is shown in Figure 2-8c. Although there is some initial oscillation, it is quickly dampened out when the feedback is less than output. Essentially, this is what we mean when we say that the system is "in control." If the system is disturbed during its steady state, the output is disturbed as well; but, if the system is in control, then oscillation is sufficiently dampened to restore the output to the desired level. The word "stability" best describes a system that is in control. If a system is unstable, a disturbance may lead to violent oscillations.

What can we learn from our discussion of feedback control systems? First, the design of a POM control system should involve a consideration of the following basic factors:

1. *The sensitivity of the system,* i.e., how sensitive is the system to the degree of variation between the desired level and the level which results before corrective action is taken. We should not have to take panic measures to achieve stability; neither should constant surveillance and intervention be necessary.

2. *The amount of feedback used.* This determines the pattern of oscillation generated as a result of some disturbance in the system's inputs or process.

3. *Time lag.* Control in some cases, for example, may involve periodic inspections to determine whether the specified variable is in control. When the inspection system shows that the variable is going out of control, a sequence of corrective steps may begin to bring the variable back in control. However, any one of these steps may go wrong and may widen the time gap between error detection and error correction. Notice that there are at least three types of time lag:

   (a) The time between the onset of the change and discovery of the induced error.

(b) The time between the discovery and notification of the error via the feedback mechanism.

(c) The time between receipt of notice and corrective action.

Time lag is perhaps the principal enemy of the operations manager, when developing a POM control system. Happiness is finding a way to reduce it. In automatic or self-regulating control devices, controllability is implicit in the device. "Variables are brought back into control *in the act of and by the act of* going out of control."[11] This is achieved through continuous and automatic comparison of actual output against the desired standard and continuous and automatic feedback of corrective action. Ideally, then, we would like to develop a control system which acts before, rather than after, the variable goes out of control, i.e., the variable going out of control should advertise the fact rather than continuing until someone identifies it. This type of control describes the concept of intrinsic control, or self-regulation as distinguished from regulation.

THE LAW OF REQUISITE VARIETY

Susceptibility to control is a function of the complexity of a system's behavior pattern and of the range of variations under which it can maintain that pattern. Complexity is not so much a function of the physical size of a system as it is a function of the variety of possible combinations of events that can occur in the system. For example, if an organization has 200 workers who work independently on identical jobs, control problems may not be significant, because the total operation can be reduced to the operation of one worker, multipled 200 times. But, consider another firm in which the production department contains 10 different processes. Assume that the products made by this second firm require various sequences through some number of these 10 processes, i.e., one product needing only 3 processes, another 6, and so on. In this small firm, the number of possible ways in which r processes may be chosen from the total n (in this example, 10) processes for converting inputs into a given product is so large (in the millions) that *complete* control is not possible. Complexity, therefore, is a function of the variety of events which the manager can encounter to achieve adequate control.

Why is it important to consider variety in the design of control processes? One of the laws of *cybernetics,* the science of control, is that the variety of conditions that can be handled by a control process must be *at least* as great as the variety of the system to be controlled—commonly

[11] Beer, *op. cit.,* p. 147.

referred to as Ashby's law of requisite variety.[12] In mass production or flow shop processing, this condition generally can be met. Oil refineries, chemicals, paper products, soap, glass, cement, and bricks are all examples of industries in which sophisticated control processes have been developed. When production, however, consists of a series of independent operations, the production possibilities increase to such an extent that it is impossible to measure objectively all possible conditions that might exist. It is this very complexity of certain systems that causes a breakdown of the principle of *management by exception.* It becomes difficult, if not impossible, in some cases to determine what really is an exception.

Although conceptually simple, the law of requisite variety has important implications for the designer of a control process.[13] First, to be effective, the control process must have at least as many matching alternatives as the defined system can exhibit. Hence, it establishes a minimum requirement on the requisite variety of actions the controller must have. In many cases, the control process will have many more alternatives so that an appropriate set is in reserve to meet a given problem, but it can never have less than the requisite number.

Next, the law indicates two principal ways of adjusting the control process to meet the requirements of the system to be controlled: (1) increase the variety of the control process, or (2) reduce the variety of the system to be controlled. Hare provides us with the following example:

> The biological organism is able to counter changes in the environment, such as moderate changes in humidity, temperature, and oxygen content of the air, but it cannot handle all possibilities. To survive, the organism must restrict the range of its environment. Thus we do not take baths in liquid nitrogen, reside in furnaces, or confer at the tail end of a jet engine.[14]

Therefore, a control process can be expected to stabilize the specified output of a system within certain limits. For the operations manager, this requires a proper understanding of the concepts of volume, capacity, and rate of flow or throughput, all of which will be discussed in subsequent chapters. It also requires an understanding of the number of alternative combinations of events which the operations manager may encounter. In too many cases, gross errors have been made in establishing control processes by accepting the system as it exists at the present time. Almost inevitably, by next week, or next month, or next year, some of the conditions will have changed, and the system will no longer be the same. Only when we

---

[12] Hare, *op. cit.,* pp. 135–154. See also W. Ross Ashby, *An Introduction to Cybernetics* (New York: John Wiley & Sons, Inc., Science Editions, 1963), pp. 202–218.

[13] Hare, *op. cit.,* pp. 143–145.

[14] *Ibid.,* p. 144.

sufficiently define the system can we begin to measure the number of possible states it can take on. If we indicate the complexity of a system by measuring its variability, a great deal will depend on how the system is defined and on who defines it. We will discuss the establishment of system boundaries in a later section of this chapter.

LARGE MANAGERIAL SYSTEMS AND SELF-CONTROL

In subsequent chapters, the concepts of control discussed thus far will be applied to areas such as production control, inventory control, and quality control. These are examples of the way in which the operations manager attempts to control situations of high variety by dividing them into subsystems and then setting up adequate subcontrollers to cope with the variety implicit in the situation. However, when we speak of control within the *whole* of the operations management function, we have a much larger and much more complicated situation. It is complicated because of the rich interaction between each of the subsystems in the total system. It is also complicated because the proliferation of variety is increased.

We must now extend our discussion of control to take into account these much larger and more complicated systems. We have already mentioned briefly the self-organizing properties of systems. Let us now examine this concept as it applies to control of large managerial systems. In studying the control of total systems, we can learn a great deal from the cybernetics of ecology, or control within living systems. Living systems are intrinsically self-controlled. Stafford Beer gets this point across in the following example:

> We know . . . that there are myriads of insects and small beasts
> all around us, and we know that these proliferate at fantastic rates.
> And yet we never stop to ask ourselves how it is that we are not
> drowned in a sea of caterpillars, squeezed to death by frogs (just
> think of all that frog spawn), or pecked to death by birds. It is not
> an easy question to answer, even though one fully appreciates the
> basic device that nature uses—the device whereby things eat each
> other. Thinking strictly in managerial terms, it is really fantastic that
> the whole system works. Indeed, on the few occasions when something
> goes slightly wrong, we are moved more to annoyance than to wonder;
> we complain that there is a plague of ants, or that some blight has
> killed off our roses. But these rare exceptions should persuade us
> of the fantastic efficacy of the control system at large.
>
> There are no managers, no controllers, no sub-controllers, no bureau-
> cracy, and no paper work, in an ecological control system. There is
> instead intrinsic control. A particular population tending to increase

is *ipso facto* short of food and its breeding rate falls . . . We have
here a vast network of interacting governors. The network is so complicated that ecologists will rarely agree to the identification of any one
on its own. They talk instead about food webs, and regard the very
complexity of the system as its main stabilizing feature. By this I
mean . . . that there is no unique feedback, no unsupported control
loop, on which the whole system depends. And just because of this,
the whole business is an excellent model of business itself.[15]

In the system described above, proliferating variety is controlled by
another population of living organisms which prey on the first. All systems,
living or artificial, must be capable of proliferating requisite variety, if they
expect to maintain control. Think for a moment about a policeman trying
unsuccessfully to straighten out a traffic jam at a busy intersection. He
is unsuccessful because he does not have requisite variety. Now the traffic
tie-up eventually clears, but only because the residual variety required has
been supplied by the drivers themselves. As another example, consider the
operations manager who, after reviewing some report, finds that twice as
much money as is really necessary is tied up in inventory. On the basis
of this report, he sends a memorandum to the relevant departments indicating that all the various types of inventory stocks must be cut by 50 percent.
Supposedly, this should solve the problem; but it does not, because the
system proliferates so much variety. Not all inventory stocks are twice as
large as they should be—the figure is just an average. Some of the inventory
stocks may be at the correct level, so when they are cut by 50 percent
they no longer are adequate. Not providing the requisite variety, the manager
does not succeed in controlling the situation. What happens at this point
is analogous to our description of control in living systems. The manager's
subordinates will come up with the necessary variety to circumvent the
manager's poor decision. In a sense, the system has implicitly arranged
its own stability but at an added dollar cost. This property is in fact a
characteristic of all large complex systems.[16]

The type of control mechanism with which we have been dealing is
known as a "homeostat," the basic control mechanism used by nature.
It promotes homeostasis which is that characteristic of an organism which
holds some critical variable steady within physiological limits (body temperature, again, is a good example).[17] Another property of the homeostat is
ultrastability: the capacity in a system to regain equilibrium after any type
of disturbance including types the designer did not have in mind. The opera-

---

[15] Beer, *op. cit.*, pp. 151–153.
[16] For more extensive study of the properties of self-regulating systems and examples of
the design of such systems see Stafford Beer, *Decision and Control* (New York: John Wiley &
Sons, 1966), pp. 253–400.
[17] *Ibid.*, p. 289.

tions manager may frequently be confronted with types of disturbances that he may not have considered when he arranged the set of management controls. Furthermore, as the system adjusts to the unexpected disturbances, we would expect the system to improve the performance on the basis of experience. In other words, we expect the system to learn, to grow, to evolve. Of course, in some cases, the self-organizing properties exhibited by some systems may be unsatisfactory; that is, they may be change-defeating and hence self-defeating. Companies may overload their internal structure in their search for growth. They may oversell and overcommit. They may become so preoccupied with their own stability that they simply die.

Our discussion of large management systems and self-control provides us with a basis for the development and analysis of complex control systems. Production control, inventory control, quality control, and other control activities to be discussed in this book are not simply a collection of separate and specialized functions. No one of these activities represents the key mechanism of management control. Successful control of the POM system as a whole depends on one's ability to both understand the process involved and coalesce these many activities around a central theme. Furthermore, an understanding of self-regulation in systems provides the operations manager with some basis for identifying what is self-regulating about the POM system. This in turn tells him what is not self-regulating about the system and points out those areas in POM where greater process understanding and more emphasis on system optimization will produce greater total benefits.

SYSTEM BOUNDARIES

It has already been argued that no system can in fact be completely isolated from its environment. Hence, in selecting the components of a given system and in defining the relationships, the operations manager will be confronted with an infinite number of possibilities unless he defines the relevant boundaries of the given system. Furthermore, given the complexity of a system as measured by the variety of possible actions or events within the system, the operations manager must establish the scope of his system in order to define, analyze, and control the system meaningfully. The objective in defining system boundaries is to establish a balance between the variety of the system to be handled by the manager and the manager's resources.

To delineate a system for a given purpose is to decide what elements and relationships must be included and what can be excluded. Some of the interactions between a given system and its environment may not be significant. They are irrelevant and could be eliminated without affecting the behavior of the system. Some of the interactions may be significant to the behavior of the system, but they are interactions over which we have no control. For example, until we can control the weather, it is a part, not of a system, but of a system's environment, no matter how critically it may affect the operation of a system. On the other hand, there are other relationships which, if ignored, will not permit a complete understanding of the behavior of a system. These relationships, of course, must be identified.

From a systems viewpoint, the nature of the decision problem determines the definition of system boundaries. Boundaries are not a question of physical reality, since there is no point at which a system ceases entirely to react to its environment. The point here is that the arbitrary, traditional boundaries found in many organizations today emphasize more the parts and segments of the structure than the interrelationships and integration of activities. While it is true that the people running organizations realize that the divisions they have created are artificial, they do not regard them as particularly dangerous. Accepting the conventional boundaries uncritically can inflict heavy penalties on the firm. Remember, decision problems have no respect for organizational structure.

If the boundaries of a system are improperly defined, a great deal of waste and confusion will result when this system interacts with other systems. Some examples, by Richard Farmer, may be helpful here:

> A. In the United States, automotive transportation is regarded as a system which is independent of other kinds of transportation systems . . . In turn, the transportation system, as a whole, has been seen as independent of social systems, such as the city. What this results in is evident. City bus companies (operating as independent systems) are faced with serious problems or even destroyed, because auto facilities are constructed without a consideration of these facilities' effect on public transit . . . The planning of parking space is made by organizations which have nothing to do with the highway department, and this causes thousands of cars to be parked in congested city streets when no space is available elsewhere . . .
>
> B. Today's water pollution problem arose because it was previously assumed that the individual users need not concern themselves with how others were making use of the same water. Thus, city A and firm B dump wastes in a river upstream. Downstream, city C uses the same water for drinking. As long as the cities are far enough apart, this is not a particular problem, but as urban population and industry grow, a time will come when the entire waterway is one long sewer. . . . [18]

[18] Richard N. Farmer, *Management in the Future* (Belmont, Calif.: Wadsworth Publishing Company, Inc., 1967), pp. 66–67.

The above examples illustrate how many problems are the result of poor analytic breakdown of systems and how greater attention to systems concepts might have avoided, or at least decreased, the negative aspects of these problems.

CONCLUSIONS

In this chapter, we have presented a conceptual framework and an operational philosophy within which the various operations management functions can more effectively be integrated. The operations manager deals with process design, facilities design, product design, and many other factors. The systems concept provides a way in which these and other aspects of operations can be synthesized into a whole.

The presentation of the systems concept has been minimal; otherwise, it would fill the entire book. We have attempted only to present the basic concepts underlying the notion of a system: the input-output process, the transformation process, the concept of the open system, the control process, complexity and the law of requisite variety, self-regulating systems and feedback, stability and ultrastability. Having now been exposed to these concepts, you might well say that all of this is entirely obvious. Of course it is obvious—with hindsight. In general, we might say that all the great natural laws are obvious, too. But this by no means diminishes their importance. Besides, if the systems concept is so obvious, why do we try to disobey it all the time? And why is it that although this disobedience results in ineffective management of operations, we still do not recognize what has gone wrong?

Given our minimum treatment of the details of the various aspects of the field of operations management to this point, the presentation of the systems concept may have been somewhat abstract. We have relied heavily on your power of imagination to assimilate the material presented. The framework will come alive as you move through the remaining chapters of the book. Failure to absorb and extend the concepts presented in this chapter will, in the end, result in your having some knowledge of the various aspects of the field of operations management but no knowledge of how it *all* works.

QUESTIONS

1. What is a system?
2. A collection of objects, i.e., processes, operations, offices, departments, does not in itself constitute a system. Explain.

3. Explain why, and in what way, the following are examples of systems. Furthermore, for each of the following give some examples of possible inputs, outputs, and transformation processes.
   (a) Hospital system
   (b) Criminal justice system
   (c) Transportation system
   (d) Production system

4. The purchasing subsystem within The Wagner Co. is partially described in the following diagram.

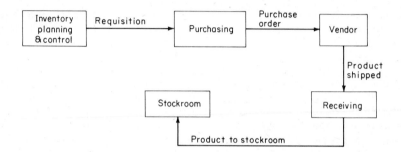

Expand the diagram such that it represents an integrated feedback system, i.e., identify and diagram the information feedback loops.

5. Why must a system interact with its environment to grow?

6. Contrast what might be called the traditional approach to problem formulation with the systems approach.

7. We cannot escape the problem of complexity by ignoring it. Explain.

8. What is suboptimization? How is it related to the systems concept?

9. Assume that a product is processed through ten different operations. If we optimized the efficiency of each operation, then the set of operations taken as a whole will be optimized. Do you agree? Explain.

10. For many types of problems, we can achieve only a constrained optimal solution. Give some examples to indicate your understanding of constrained optimal solutions.

11. In our examination of a system, at what point and for what reasons do we treat the transformation process as a black box? What major assumption is made in viewing the transformation process as a black box?

12. Why are we sometimes concerned with the details of the transformation process?

13. Discuss the elements common to all control systems.

14. Discuss the characteristics of feedback systems.

15. What do we mean when we say the system is in control?

16. The sensitivity of the system, the amount of feedback used, and the

time lag should be considered in the design of any control system. Why?

17. What is the law of requisite variety? What important implications does this law have for the designer of a control process?
18. Describe the control mechanism known as a homeostat. In what way might the operations manager benefit from his understanding of the homeostat?
19. What determines the relevant system boundaries for the analysis of problems? Are system boundaries a function of physical reality?
20. From your own experiences, give some examples of improperly defined system boundaries.

CASE

The BUGO Corporation was a relatively successful, medium-sized firm. The top executives had recently attended a 3-day seminar on the systems concept. The president called a meeting of the executive staff to examine the possibility of implementing the systems concept in the organization. The reactions of the executive staff were varied. Several of the executives felt that the concept was "a heck of a lot of hot air," "too abstract to be practical," "a lot of mumbo jumbo that I don't understand," "only suitable for large complex organizations." Others felt that the concept was a mechanistic one focusing heavily on optimizing economic objectives and recognizing very little the social and psychological needs of individuals. Still other executives believed that the concept was a sound one but at this point could not evaluate how the concept would affect their traditional functions. "What impact will this concept have on our functions of planning, organizing, and controlling; and what changes must we make in order to effectively utilize the systems concept?"

What are your reactions to the observations made by the executive staff? Describe these reactions in the form of a written report to the president. The following references may be helpful.

1. Johnson, Richard A. et al., *The Theory and Management of Systems,* 2d ed. (New York: McGraw-Hill Book Company, 1967), pp. 303–329.
2. Schoderbek, Peter P., *Management Systems, A Book of Readings* (New York: John Wiley & Sons, Inc., 1967), pp. 145–215.
3. Hare, Van Court, Jr., *Systems Analysis: A Diagnostic Approach* (New York: Harcourt, Brace & World, Inc., 1967), pp. 413–442.

chapter

DECISION MAKING FOR POM SYSTEMS

three

The manager differs from most other employees in that he takes full responsibility for making and implementing a sequence of decisions to carry out the functions for which he has full authority. He may make these decisions himself or he may delegate that responsibility and authority. What he cannot delegate, however, is the responsibility for the quality of the outcome in his area. Yet, he is not a free agent in all of his decisions by any means. He is limited by company, by procedures and customs, and by the impact of what he does upon other parts of the organization and upon his environment.

The way he reaches his decisions differentiates the professionally trained manager from his counterparts. We indicated in Chapter 2 how the manager learns to conceptualize his organization as a system and as a subsystem of larger systems. The systems view that he develops provides the intellectual structure for his operating decisions—his picture of the important factors to be evaluated and manipulated and the interrelationships to be considered in the design of a system and in the assessment of its performance. This structure is not permanent. He reevaluates and revises it to meet changing reality much as the artist does with his visual world.

THE ART OF MODELING

Systems analysis is a powerful rationalizing tool. Yet it is still a mixture of art and science. Analysis is a pervasive attribute of the good manager's approach to decision making but so is the art of structuring the situation correctly and in sufficient, but not overwhelming, detail. Morris[1] puts his finger on a tender point when he observes that

> If one grants that modeling is and, for greatest effectiveness, probably ought to be, an intuitive process for the experienced, then the interesting question becomes the pedagogical problem of how to develop this intuition. What can be done for the inexperienced person who wishes to progress as quickly as he can toward a high level of intuitive effectiveness in management science? What can be done for the experienced person whose mind "draws a blank" when seeking to model some management problem?

Certainly Morris intended that these would be rheotrical questions. He proposes a description of the modeling process which would seem generally applicable and also suggests some reasons behind the differences between the experiences of solving problems and the reports of their solutions. He notes that the articles in journals and the chapters of texts always state the abstractions (models) used in the most concise and logical terms. This is how the writer wishes to appear after the fact, not how he actually did it. What is communicated to the reader is the justification of the analysis but not its unfolding or "discovery."

MODELING PROCESS

The process of modeling a system is a sequential one. The first step is inspecting the complex of data and impressions which we perceive as reality to find analogies or associations with known systems or methodological approaches. Generally, this involves gross simplification of that reality until a simple model can be set up and put to work. Once that happens, the process of *enrichment* and *enhancement* starts. New components are added to the system concept or model to move from the simplest abstraction toward the more complex and hopefully more realistic analysis. This is essen-

[1] W. T. Morris, "On the Art of Modeling," *Management Science, 13* (August 1967), p. B-707.

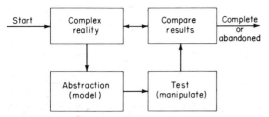

Figure 3-1 *The process of modeling*

tially the *looping* or *iterative* procedure described by Figure 3-1. The first abstraction is tested to see what resulting actions it suggests. These actions are then compared with the other information the manager has about the behavior of the real world. If they seem plausible and acceptable, the procedure is finished, and we have the basis for a decision. If not, then the process choices are (1) a revision of the model, (2) occasionally a revision of the decision-maker's view of reality, or (3) abandonment of the approach as nonproductive, i.e., the anticipated values from further analysis do not outweigh the anticipated costs. Revision of the model may involve either further simplification or enrichment and enhancement.

Morris[2] suggests as a procedure:

1. Factor the system problem into simpler problems.
2. Establish a clear set of analytical objectives.
3. Seek analogies.
4. Consider a specific numerical instance of the problem.
5. Where possible, establish some symbols representing values and relationships.
6. Write down all known relationships and assumptions.
7. Manipulate the relationships for potential solutions.
8. If a tractable model is obtained, enrich it. Otherwise, simplify it further.

Tractability, as Morris[3] uses it, means capable of a solution in theory and in application. He also has suggested as other measures of an effective modeling outcome:

1. *Relatedness* to previously tested models.
2. *Transparency* in the sense that the model is easily interpreted and confirmed intuitively.
3. *Robustness* in terms of relative insensitivity to the assumptions characterizing it.
4. *Fertility* in the variety of deductive consequences produced.
5. *Ease of enrichment.*

[2] Morris, *op. cit.*
[3] Morris, *op. cit.*

To this he might well have added economy in the value of the deductive consequences and of the cost of development and manipulation.

NORMATIVE AND DESCRIPTIVE SYSTEMS OF ANALYSIS

It is the implication of all writings on analysis and synthesis that there exists a sought-for objective of an identifiable best (optimal) solution. This implication of "one best way" is called a normative approach, one which every self-respecting decision-maker *ought* to achieve. Models exist, particularly those representing system components, whose purposes are descriptive, but these are considered second class citizens by many. Yet descriptive models are necessary predecessors of normative ones and are equally important to the process of analysis and synthesis. In many cases, descriptive models are illuminating enough to lead to new, intuitively developed changes which accomplish alone many of the improvements later attained with an optimal, mathematically derived solution.

Sometimes it may appear that POM material consists primarily of a body of tools and analytical techniques borrowed from economics, engineering, mathematics, statistics, the physical sciences, operations research, and management science. But there is a fundamental added ingredient—the commitment to make the system operate well regardless of whether or not the problem is mathematically tractable. This further implies a commitment to avoid suboptimization through acceptance of easy solutions to tractable closed-systems analysis while ignoring important but unquantifiable interrelationships. The principal objective is the best outcome in the time allowed, regardless of whether or not the method of getting there is elegant and precise.

THE PROCESS OF ANALYSIS

The first step in any analysis has to be a comprehensive description of the system, followed by an attempt to express these relationships, where possible, in a diagram, equation, or other set of symbols. Certainly, mathematical equations are the most precise and concise expressions of relationships, but others are valuable when the system cannot be quantified. It is necessary to define the inputs and outputs and the process variables which determine conversion and flow rates in the system. From this, you can expand your analysis of the design of the system based on the performance specifications for the output.

For example, one can separate the two activities of performance specification and output and process engineering. The former sets the objectives of

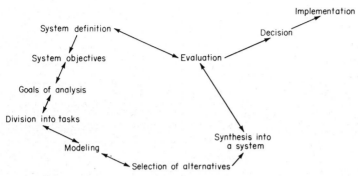

Figure 3-2 *The process of analysis*

the analysis. The latter can then be delegated to specialists who provide the information and the designs needed to develop the alternatives to be considered in the final stages of decision making. Without these alternatives, there are no choices to be made, nothing to search, and nothing to synthesize into an improved operating system. Figure 3-2 represents this fact in a diagram of the process of analysis.

The analyses of the specialists are likely to appear in the form of more detailed studies of specific subsystems like inventory or scheduling, or in the generation of design alternatives, and in the suggestion of the specific ways in which their alternatives should be implemented. But someone has to take the responsibility of deciding which model-building approach is most relevant to some aspect of a current problem, and how the results can be combined with other information to improve operations. It is this analysis (breaking down) and synthesis (putting together) that makes it necessary that the would-be manager know something about the many models available to him, and how they can be used.

AN EXAMPLE—MODELS FOR COST-VOLUME-PROFIT RELATIONSHIPS

One of the most commonly used models of an organization deals with the relationships between volume of output, costs, and profits. These relationships are critical to almost all major decisions and to the evaluation of most alternative cost-volume structures.

REVENUE RELATIONSHIPS

At a selected price, sales revenue will increase steadily as volume increases. Revenue from a product can be estimated by multiplying the number of units to be sold by the unit price. Total sales revenue is the sum of the revenues from the products being offered. In this case, total sales revenue ignores income from nonoperating sources, such as investments or sale of assets.

COST RELATIONSHIPS

The costs of a firm are multiple. Some are the materials and labor which go directly into a unit of output. Others are incurred in more generalized activities such as the marketing of goods, the salaries of maintenance men, and the fees for members of the board of directors. All of these costs are classified as either *variable* (changing directly with the volume of output), or *fixed* (unaffected in the short run by volume changes). Variable costs include those materials, labor, packaging, freight, fuel, supplies, and sales commissions chargeable directly to a unit of production and varying directly with changes in its output volume.

CONTRIBUTION

The difference between revenue per unit and variable cost per unit is called *contribution per unit*. In economists' terms, contribution is the difference between marginal revenue and marginal cost. The *total contribution* from all products of the company should be greater than the sum of all fixed costs. The amount by which the company's total contribution exceeds its total fixed costs is called *profit*. If the fixed costs exceed the total contribution, the difference is called a *loss*. Where the two (contribution and fixed costs) are equal, the firm breaks even for the accounting period. The volume at which the two are equal is called the *breakeven point*. Obviously, the businessman is interested in knowing whether or not his anticipated sales volume is above or below the breakeven point. He wishes to avoid the ignominy of a red ink position wherever possible.

GRAPHICAL APPROACH

Figure 3-3 is a typical graphic representation of these relationships. The fixed costs do not change and therefore are parallel to the *x* or volume axis. To them, the wedge representing variable costs (which do change directly with volume) is added to make up the total cost line. The intersection of the total revenue line with the total cost line represents the breakeven point. To the right of that point, the vertical distance between the two lines represents the profit at that point, while distances to the left are losses.

More complex models certainly are needed by companies where the relationships are not that simple. For example, the variable costs per unit might rise sharply above a certain volume if that volume was the maximum

capacity of the plant and only overtime operations could produce more volume. Fixed costs might also rise as volume increases. Foremen's salaries
might be fixed if a single shift is adequate to produce the needed volume,
but they may rise sharply when a second shift is added. But once the
basic model is mastered, these embellishments are relatively easy to incorporate into the model.

ALGEBRAIC APPROACH

Few of us are good enough draftsmen to get very accurate answers with
the graphic approach. Graphs are an easy way to remember what gets added
to what. But since they do not give us the numerical answers we want,
we generally rely on the algebraic representation of the same values. First,
let us hang labels on some of our symbols.

Let

TR = total revenue in dollars
p = selling price (net) per unit in dollars
x = volume sold or produced in units.

$$TR = xp \tag{3-1}$$

Let

TC = total cost (fixed plus variable)
TVC = total variable cost
TFC = total fixed cost
v = variable cost per unit in dollars

$$TVC = xv \tag{3-2}$$
$$TC = TVC + TFC = xv + TFC \tag{3-3}$$

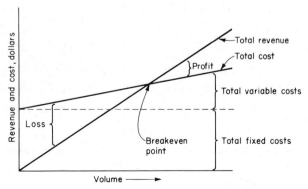

Figure 3-3   *Basic cost-volume-profit curves*

At the breakeven point

$$TR = TC$$

and

$$xp = xv + TFC \tag{3-4}$$

Therefore, we know that the breakeven point in units is

$$x = \frac{TFC}{p - v} \tag{3-5}$$

and in dollars

$$TR = xp = \frac{TFC}{1 - v/p} \tag{3-6}$$

(Note that the above equations are for a single product company only.)

RESPONSE TO CHANGES

It is possible also to represent, either graphically or algebraically, changes in profits with changes in the selling price per unit, the number of units sold, the fixed cost total, or the variable costs per unit. Figure 3-4 shows the impact of such changes. Furthermore, it is possible to have more than one of these variables change, but the algebraic model quickly adjusts for such multiple changes.

MULTIPLE PRODUCTS

The typical manufacturer has more than one line of goods and can change the price or cost of one line without necessarily changing the others. Most realistic problems, therefore, have to be solved with a multiple product approach to cost-volume-profit relationships. Here the use of the model must be more imaginative. Let us look at the example of the Henry-Don Furniture Company which makes four products (or classes of similarly priced and costed products), with the following characteristics:

Product	Last Year's Volume	Price	Variable Cost	Revenue
A1	5,000 units	$20	$15	$100,000
A2	6,000	22	16	132,000
B1	3,000	37.50	28	112,500
B2	2,000	40	30	80,000
				$424,500

Fixed costs last year were $85,000.

The contribution from $A1$ was $25,000 (5,000 $\times$ $5), from $A2$ it was $36,000, from $B1$ $28,500, and from $B2$ $20,000. The total was $109,500 which exceeded TFC by $24,500. There is a breakeven dollar volume in the multiple product case calculated as follows:

Product	Contribution per Dollar of Sales		Revenue as a Percent of Total Sales		Weighted Contribution
A1	$5/$20 = .250	$\times$	.235	=	.059
A2	$6/$22 = .272	$\times$	.312	=	.085
B1	$9.50/$37.50 = .253	$\times$	.266	=	.067
B2	$10/$40 = .250	$\times$	.187	=	.047
			1.000		.258

Since,

$$TR = \frac{TFC}{1 - v/P} \qquad (3\text{-}6)$$

$$TR = \frac{\$85,000}{.258}$$

$$= \$329,000$$

If, however, the proportion of products changes when that volume falls, then the breakeven level will have to be recalculated.

Models are useful only if they can be used to gain information about specific management decisions. Henry-Don, for example, has set up a profit target of $50,000 for next year and hopes to achieve this through the introduction of a new product C with a price of $60 per unit and a variable cost per unit of $40. At the new level of operations, the total fixed cost would be $92,000. We know that the current products give a contribution of $109,500 ($85,000 + $24,500). To reach the desired level of $142,000 ($92,000 + $50,000), would require an increase in contribution of $32,500 ($142,000 — $109,500). Since product C yields a contribution of $20 per unit ($60 — $40), then it will take sales of 1,625 units to reach the desired profit level.

On the other hand, it is possible to see how many units of new product C would be needed to get the profit level back up to its former value of $24,500. Since fixed costs were increased $7,000, $7,000/20 or 350 units would have to be sold to get back where we were.

It also is possible to see what the price would have to be to achieve the target level of profit ($50,000) if product C could sell only 1,000 units. The four old products leave Henry-Don $32,500 short of the desired contribution of $142,000. This means that the target can be reached only if the 1,000 units of C contribute $32.50 each. Since the variable costs are $40

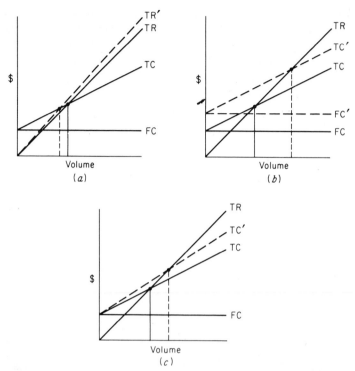

Figure 3-4 *Three separate changes in variables affecting profits. The solid lines represent the original conditions. Broken lines represent the changes. (a) Here the selling price per unit was raised. The vertical broken line shows how the BEP was lowered. (b) Here fixed costs were raised. The vertical broken line shows by how much the BEP increased. (c) Here the change was an increase in variable costs. As in (b), the vertical broken line shows that the change raised the BEP.**

per unit, this means that a selling price of $72.50 per unit would be required.

There are many other problems in which the cost-volume-profit relationships are important and where the model outlined above can be used quite effectively. Other authors have given examples related to equipment selection, make-or-purchase decisions, advertising programs, choice of channels of distribution, and plant additions.

PROBABILISTIC MODELS

Among the many questions that one might have about the Henry-Don case is whether or not the sales volume of the four old products would stay

*From Levin and Kirkpatrick, *Quantitative Approaches to Management,* 2d ed. (New York: McGraw-Hill Book Company), p. 25.

constant. No one knows for sure. This is the type of risk that is so funda-mental to all business decisions. The businessman must develop his best estimates of the value that a variable such as sales or costs can take on and must consider the likelihood that each possible value will occur.

Suppose, for example, that a manufacturer of shoes wishes to order a shipment of shoe laces. He has ordered shoe laces in the past, and his rec-ords show the following deliveries in recent periods.

Delivery Time	Number of Occurrences
5 days	20
6	5
7	10
10	4
11	2
12	6
15	3
28	1

When placing his next order, the manufacturer can use these values to reach his decision about how much time to allow for delivery. If he recalls that the 28-day delivery was the result of a strike and that no such strike is now likely, he would eliminate that observation from his consideration, because it was due to atypical conditions. Thus 50 occurrences remain to be considered.

The number of days taken to receive the order is a *random variable.* For any given order, the delivery is unknown, but it appears that there are 20 chances in 50 that it will be 5 days, 5 chances out of 50 that it will be 6 days, etc. These ratios, expressed as decimal fractions, are called "probabilities" or in some cases are called "percent chances." These are the type of data that the weather bureau gives. When the weatherman says there is a "10 percent chance of rain," he means that when he has seen weather information like today's, it has rained 10 times out of 100 on the average and has not rained 90 times out of 100. Note that the probabilities would be 0.10 and 0.90 respectively, and that the probabilities for all mutually exclusive events must add up to 1.00.

What should our shoe manufacturer expect his delivery to be? If he is interested in a single average figure, he should use the *expected value* (weighted average) of the delivery time. Table 3-1 shows the calculation of the expected value for the shoe manufacture. This does not imply that any one shipment will take 7.58 (the expected value) days. It means that if there are decisions to be based on the length of the delivery period, it will be best to use 7.58 as the average value rather than any other.

The usual factor for decision making, however, is not average days

Table 3-1 *Calculation of expected value for the delivery period*

Orders Received In	Probability of This Value	Weighting
5 days	20/50 = 0.40	5 × 0.40 = 2.00
6	5/50 = 0.10	6 × 0.10 = 0.60
7	10/50 = 0.20	7 × 0.20 = 1.40
10	4/50 = 0.08	10 × 0.08 = 0.80
11	2/50 = 0.04	11 × 0.04 = 0.44
12	6/50 = 0.12	12 × 0.12 = 1.44
15	3/50 = 0.06	15 × 0.06 = 0.90
	Total probability = 1.00	Expected value = 7.58

to achieve delivery, but rather how early to reorder, and this is a question of expected costs. This type of model will be discussed in Chapter 15. It involves expected costs rather than just expected delivery times. If costs are high in terms of delayed production when there are no shoe laces, the manager might well choose to order 7, 10, 11, 12, or even 15 days before he needs them, providing that the offsetting costs of having the early arriving materials on hand are not too high. As you will learn, there are real costs to having goods sitting around ahead of time too.

CONTINUOUS PROBABILITY MODELS

The expected delivery time of 7.58 days was based on probabilities for a set of specific values of the random variable. This approach involves *discrete* probability. But these delivery times might have taken on any value in whole or partial units. Therefore, a *continuous variable* might have been used and a quite different set of calculations called for.

Consider, for example, a case in which past daily sales of a product for a representative 30-day period are as listed in Table 3-2. These thirty values can be plotted on a graph as in Figure 3-5. The mean sales per day is 14 (420/30).

When, in Figure 3-5, we draw a line through the points, we find that it takes the *approximate* shape of the often-cited normal curve. If we are

Table 3-2 *Daily demand*

Quantity Sold per Day:	3	5	7	9	10	13	17	18	19	20	22	26	33
Days:	1	2	2	3	4	5	4	3	2	1	1	1	1

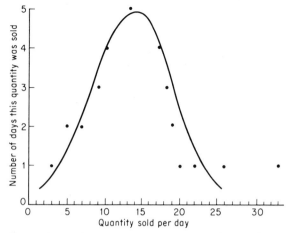

Figure 3-5   *Continuous distribution of past daily sales*

satisfied that this curve is an adequate representation of the process behind the observed demand, then we can act as if the demand is a normally distributed random variable with a mean of 14 units per day. We can take advantage of the known properties of the normal curve as part of our model of decision making.

Other curves would be used where the values are more widely dispersed from their mean and still others where the values are even more tightly grouped around their mean. These two situations are illustrated in Figure 3-6.

STANDARD DEVIATION

One statistical measure of the tendency of data to group or disperse around their own mean is called the "standard deviation." To make important man-

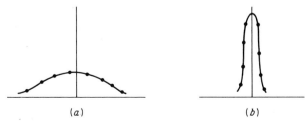

Figure 3-6   *Two variant curves. (a) The values are widely dispersed away from their mean. (b) The values are tightly grouped about their mean.*

agement inferences from these data, we must have both the correct mean and the correct standard deviation. The latter is computed as follows:

Step 1: Subtract the mean from each of the observed values.
Step 2: Square each difference computed in step 1.
Step 3: Add together the products of the squared differences for each observed point times that point's frequency of occurrence.
Step 4: Divide the total in step 3 by the number of points to determine average squared difference.
Step 5: Determine the square root of the average squared difference computed in step 4. This is the standard deviation.

The standard deviation for the data shown in Table 3-2 is calculated in Table 3-3.

USING THE STANDARD DEVIATION

Now that we know that the representative 30-day sales data can be represented by a normal distribution with a mean of 14 units and a standard deviation of 6.49—so what? Well, as you will learn in a later chapter, it is possible for the manager to determine the specific probability of selling an item that is required for the stocking of that item to be profitable before he decides whether or not to stock it. Assume that this probability is 0.44, and that he orders only a day's supply once daily. This means that he will order up to the amount that will sell in at least 44 percent of the days and then stop. It is widely known that about 68 percent of sales will fall between 14 plus 6.49 units and 14 minus 6.49 (between 20.49 and 7.51 units). About 95 percent of all sales will fall between $14\pm$ (2×6.49) units (between 26.98 and 1). There are standard statistical tables readily available which show the proportion of all values in a distribution which is contained

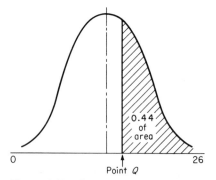

Figure 3-7 *Continuous probability distribution; 0.44 of the area under the curve is shaded*

within any given number of standard deviations from the mean. The whole area under the curve in Figure 3-7 represents a probability of 1.00. The area under the curve to the right of a vertical line representing any given sales quantity shows the probability of having demand equal to or greater than that quantity.

Figure 3-7 illustrates the 0.44 probability which we assumed must exist before it would pay to order another unit each day. If a manager stocks a larger quantity, the right-hand shaded area will fall below 0.44, and he expects to loose on that marginal additional unit. Looking up the results in standard statistical tables, we find that the point Q is .15 standard deviations to the right of the mean (14 units). A standard deviation is 6.49 units; thus point Q is $14 + (0.15 \times 6.49) = 14.9735$ units to the right of the mean. This suggests that 15 units should be ordered daily.

Table 3-3 *Calculating the standard deviation*

Step 1	Step 2	Step 3
		Add the Products of the Squared Differences Times
Subtract the Mean from Each Value	*Square Each of the Differences*	*the Frequency of Occurrence*
$3 - 14 = -11$	$(-11)^2 = 121$	$1 \times 121 = 121$
$5 - 14 = -9$	$(-9)^2 = 81$	$2 \times 81 = 162$
$7 - 14 = -7$	$(-7)^2 = 49$	$2 \times 49 = 98$
$9 - 14 = -5$	$(-5)^2 = 25$	$3 \times 25 = 75$
$10 - 14 = -4$	$(-4)^2 = 16$	$4 \times 16 = 64$
$13 - 14 = -1$	$(-1)^2 = 1$	$5 \times 1 = 5$
$17 - 14 = 3$	$(3)^2 = 9$	$4 \times 9 = 36$
$18 - 14 = 4$	$(4)^2 = 16$	$3 \times 16 = 48$
$19 - 14 = 5$	$(5)^2 = 25$	$2 \times 25 = 50$
$20 - 14 = 6$	$(6)^2 = 36$	$1 \times 36 = 36$
$22 - 14 = 8$	$(8)^2 = 64$	$1 \times 64 = 64$
$26 - 14 = 12$	$(12)^2 = 144$	$1 \times 144 = 144$
$33 - 14 = 19$	$(19)^2 = 361$	$1 \times 361 = 361$
		$\overline{1{,}264}$

Step 4 Determine the average squared difference $1{,}264/30 = 42.13$
Step 5 Determine the square root of the average squared difference

$$\sqrt{42.13} = 6.49$$

The standard deviation is 6.49.

Probabilistic models are among the most useful tools available to the POM team.

CONSTRAINED DECISION MAKING

The POM organization also operates in an environment where there are limits or *constraints* on what can be done. Many choices must be made in allocating scarce resources among projects, manpower among tasks, capacity among product lines, and capital among competing requests. Therefore, some of our most important models deal with ways of determining what would be the best way of assigning these resources to achieve specific goals.

Take as an example the Henry-Don Furniture Company situation outlined earlier in this chapter. Table 3-4 gives the information about the five products planned for next year, together with information concerning the labor hours consumed in the manufacture of each. This labor factor has been added because the management realizes that a shortage of skilled labor in the vicinity of their plant will limit their capacity to 81,850 labor hours for the year.

You will recall that this volume of sales will meet the company's new profit target of $50,000. But obviously, it cannot be achieved. It requires 2,400 (84,250 − 81,850) more labor hours than are available. The task then is to find a model which allows Henry-Don to reach its profit goal under these constrained conditions. Our objective is to *improve the contribution per unit of scarce resources.* Here it would mean improving the contribution per labor hour, since we wish to raise contribution and cannot raise the available hours. Table 3-5 lists the contribution per labor hour for each of the five products.

Since the greatest contribution per unit is achieved with product *C* and the least with product *B2*, it would appear that the expansion of sales

Table 3-4 *Data for determining Henry-Don output with constrained labor input*

Product	Anticipated Volume	Contribution/ Unit	Labor Hours/Unit	Total Labor Hours	Contribution
A1	5,000	$ 5	3	15,000	$ 25,000
A2	6,000	6	3.5	21,000	36,000
B1	3,000	9.50	6	18,000	28,500
B2	2,000	10	7	14,000	20,000
C	1,625	20	10	16,250	32,500
	17,625			84,250	$142,000

Table 3-5 *Contribution per labor hour from Henry-Don products*

Product	Contribution/ Unit	Labor Hours/Unit	Contribution/ Labor Hour
A1	$ 5	3	$1.667
A2	6	3.5	1.714
B1	9.50	6	1.583
B2	10	7	1.429
C	20	10	2.000

of product C at the expense of product $B2$ would be the best alternative, assuming the market would take the added demand for product C at no additional marketing expense.

We are short 2,400 man-hours. Since Henry-Don has as its objective a $142,000 contribution, we will have to substitute higher contribution labor for lower. Every dollar contribution from product C consumes 0.5 hours (10 hrs/$20) and from product $B2$ it consumed 0.7 (7 hrs/$10). Thus each dollar contribution substituted when product C replaces $B2$ requires 0.2 hours less labor. Henry-Don is short 2,400 hours and still wants $142,000 contribution. This means that $12,000 of contribution [2,400/(0.7 − 0.5)] will have to be moved from $B2$ to C, if they are to meet their objective with only 81,850 hours. This would imply adding 600 units of C ($12,000/$20 per unit) and dropping 1,200 units of $B2$ ($12,000/$10 per unit). Table 3-6 verifies that this is the desired solution in terms of both total contribution and total labor hour needs.

There are many other substitutions which are feasible. Which one is best will depend on the demands of the marketplace and whether or not there are any other constraints. The typical firm has many constraints and many situations where these substitutions can be made. The technique called

Table 3-6 *Solution to the constrained Henry-Don problem*

Product	Quantity	Contribution	Total Labor Hours
A1	5,000	$ 25,000	15,000
A2	6,000	36,000	21,000
B1	3,000	28,500	18,000
B2	2,000 − 1,200 = 800	8,000	5,600
C	1,625 + 600 = 2,225	44,500	22,250
		$142,000	81,850

"linear programming" can be used to analyze many such situations. It is described in detail in an appendix and utilized in several later chapters. You should become familiar with it at some point in your education. Where the linear programming model's specific conditions do not apply, a number of alternative techniques are available, but they are well beyond the scope of this text.

CONCLUSION

In this chapter, we have discussed the art of modeling and several basic models which we hope will get you used to the idea of seeing POM situations in quantitative terms. They are an important, early step in understanding and structuring a situation explicitly before you seek a solution.

The four types of models introduced here are among the most important in POM. The overall relationship between cost-volume-profit is fundamental to the objectives and the survival of the firm. The discrete and continuous probability cases are important analytically and philosophically. Once you see that most events have a number of available outcomes, each with its own probability, you will respond very differently to uncertainty and to risk. Unfortunately, we could only scratch the surface of this area of probability and statistics. We would strongly urge you to study this area in more detail. The model of the substitution of one resource for another is an important one for both business and economics. It is the same type of marginal analysis that you have seen in your economics courses. This is as it should be. Business administration, including POM, is an economic activity. Other models and more intensive uses of all four models will appear in later chapters where they will be applied to common POM decision environments.

QUESTIONS

1. "Modeling is a process of abstraction." Explain what is meant by this statement. Discuss the usefulness of a model that has a very low degree of abstraction versus a model with a very high degree of abstraction.
2. What is the ultimate test of a model?
3. Describe the modeling process.
4. What are the purposes of a model? Give some examples of mathematical and nonmathematical models.
5. How would you simplify a mathematical model?
6. What do we mean by a normative approach to model building?
7. Discuss the relationship between normative and descriptive models.
8. What is the process of analysis? How is it related to the model building process?

9. What are the assumptions underlying the cost-volume-profit model? In what ways do these assumptions limit the use of this model as a decision-making tool?

10. Assume firm A has high-fixed costs and low-variable costs and firm B has high-variable costs and low-fixed costs. In terms of the cost-volume-profit model, explain the positions of the two firms in an extended period of economic recession.

11. Is the cost-volume-profit model a short-range or long-range decision-making aid? Explain.

12. How does the cost-volume-profit model represent system structure, i.e., inputs, outputs, the transformation process, interactive components, and so on?

13. How can the breakeven point be lowered?

14. Define expected value.

15. "The expected value of demand next month is 2,000 units." How would you interpret this statement?

16. Distinguish between discrete and continuous probability models.

17. What does the standard deviation tell us?

18. Define constrained optimization.

PROBLEMS

1. The Serelee Corporation produces chairs. An analysis of their accounting data shows the following:

Fixed cost	$50,000 per year
Variable cost	$2 per chair
Capacity	30,000 chairs
Selling price	$7 per chair

(a) Compute the breakeven point in number of chairs.

(b) How many chairs must the company sell to show a profit of $30,000?

(c) What is the fixed cost per chair at 75 percent capacity?

(d) The addition of a new process will double fixed costs but cut variable costs in half. What is the new breakeven point?

(e) What is the profit if the sales prediction is 20,000 chairs?

(f) Suppose the sales prediction is given in terms of a discrete probability distribution as shown below. What is the expected value of the profit?

Sales prediction	10,000	15,000	20,000	25,000	30,000
Probability	.10	.20	.40	.20	.10

2. The Butts Corporation produces feed for horses, hogs, cattle, and dogs. From available records, we are given the following:

Feed for	Selling Price Per Ton	Variable Cost Per Ton	Expected Sales
Horses	$30	$15	$40,000
Hogs	40	16	20,000
Cattle	36	16	25,000
Dogs	32	12	15,000

Annual fixed costs $80,000

   (a) Find the total contribution per overall sales dollar with the present product mix.
   (b) Find the breakeven point in dollars.

3. The Aarsands Co. is considering the installation of one of two types of machines. A long-run sales forecast indicates that sales will not fall below 8,200 units per year for the next 5 years, the expected life of each machine. Machine A will increase fixed costs by $20,000 per year but will reduce variable costs by $6 per unit. Machine B will increase fixed costs by $4,000 per year but will reduce variable costs by $4 per unit. Variable costs are now $20 per unit. At what point are you indifferent as to which machine to purchase? Which machine should be purchased?

4. The Midi Corporation currently buys exhaust valves for its motors at $2.50 each. An estimate of the cost to the company to manufacture these valves reveals that the fixed costs will be $4,800 per year, and the variable costs per valve will be $1.25. Each motor requires one exhaust valve, and Midi's annual capacity is 6,000 motors per year. Does it pay the company to manufacture its own valves?

5. Here is a discrete distribution of past sales:

Quantities Buyers Bought	Number of Days Occurred	Probability of Occurrence
20 units	10	.10
25 units	30	.30
40 units	50	.50
60 units	10	.10

Selling price is $10 per unit, and the cost is $6 per unit. Assume the product has no salvage value. If 25 units are stocked every day, what will be the expected profit per day over the long run?

6. Using the information given in problem 5, what will be the number of units to stock daily to maximize profit?

7. The Alexander Company has average daily sales of 60 units with a standard deviation of 10 units. Units sell for $10 each and cost $5. There is no salvage value. The manager must be .30 sure of selling at least an additional unit before it would pay him to stock that unit. What is the optimum level of stock which it should carry?

8. Assume that Henry-Don Furniture (Tables 3-4 and 3-5 in the text material) had experienced a brief strike reducing its available labor hours per year to 81,350; assume also that the maximum market for product C is 2,200 units. Provide a revision of the solution in Table 3-6 which takes into account these new events.

part

INTERNAL AND EXTERNAL INTERFACES

two

chapter

THE INTERNAL ENVIRONMENT

four

This chapter defines the significance of the interfaces between the production/operations management (POM) system and the larger internal systems
and subsystems of the organization.

The presentation centers around a conceptual
diagram of the POM system with supporting diagrams and narrative explanation keyed to it. The
central diagram (Figure 4-1) shows POM, marketing,
finance and accounting, management, and the information system as systems within the framework
of the organizational system. The major interfaces
between POM and the rest of the organization are
represented by appropriate flows of orders, material, cash, and information.

The organization is bounded by an environment made up of all the political-legal, economic,
and sociological factors which affect it. The flows
between the environment and the marketing, POM,
finance and accounting, and management systems
also take the form of orders, materials, cash, and
information. At the center is the information system
which serves to connect all the systems via the informational flows that provide control, information,
and feedback.

We shall examine first the interfaces between marketing and POM, including the role of information, both historical and forecast. Second, we shall discuss the POM system and the two major modes of production as they relate to and are affected by the rest of the organization. Third, the POM system will be related to the finance and accounting system both in terms of operating and capital investment cash flows. Fourth, we shall show how the general management system relates to the production system by providing its philosophy, policy, objectives, and organization. And finally, we will demonstrate how the information system interrelates and integrates all systems within the organization.

THE MARKETING SYSTEM

All business activity must start with a customer need. An organization exists because there is a market for its product or service. The objectives of any organization, therefore, must be the production of goods and services needed or desired by the consumer. In this context, the marketing system discovers and transmits the needs of consumers to the total organization, including the POM system which supplies these needs.

In Figure 4-1, the marketing system is shown together with the other systems to which it relates via the information flows. Orders and other information in the form of marketing and product research are collected from the external environment by the marketing system while advertising, promotion, and sales activity flow out to influence that environment. Marketing sets up its relationships with the other systems based on control information furnished by POM, and finance and accounting. The marketing system provides feedback in the form of sales forecasts, product development information, marketing strategies, and marketing programs.

The specific functions and activities assigned to the marketing system fall into three broad categories: planning, sales, and service. Operating within these three areas, the marketing system must supply management and the other systems in the organization with responsible and reliable forecasts of what response will be required to satisfy the market. A properly prepared forecast will show management what to expect in the way of sales volume and profits, and it will give the other systems information with which to schedule their operations.

In its relationship to POM, marketing interprets the demand for future periods and translates this demand into units of production and desired delivery schedules. Marketing in turn expects POM to:

1. Provide production facilities—plants, equipment, and personnel
2. Provide adequate quality control
3. Sustain technological growth and improvement and economic viability

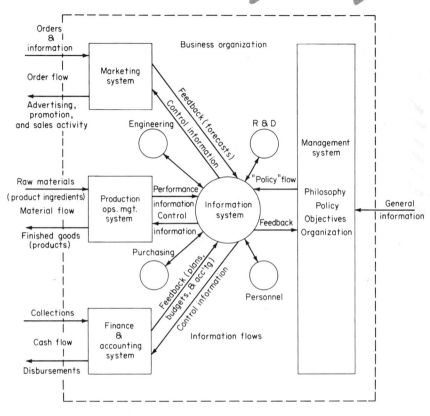

Figure 4-1 *General diagram of the relationship between the POM system and the rest of the organization*

The production process comes only after a product has been *approved* for production. Prior to approval, a potential product goes through a great deal of planning and reviewing. And long before a product or service is put into production, marketing must work with POM to resolve jointly important issues such as:

1. Product design
2. Equipment needed for production
3. Facilities available: kind, location, amount, manpower
4. Quality control
5. Raw-material storage, handling, and use
6. Inventory needs, including finished-product inventory
7. Possible production and delivery schedules
8. Costs: of tooling, of production
9. ENGINEERING

Sales Forecast → Production

9. Possible use of substitute materials
10. Pilot tests and controls
11. Product service[1]

Because it interfaces with the market, marketing should be prepared to furnish POM data such as:

1. Size of potential market
2. Volume of production needed to meet anticipated market needs
3. Desired finished goods inventories
4. Anticipated changes in production of other products
5. Anticipated delivery schedules: amounts, location, timing
6. Packaging needs
7. Special characteristics to be stressed in the marketing program[2]

This exchange of information cuts across many lines and involves many activities within the organization. Before marketing can commit itself to POM, it must develop complete market studies, accurate forecasts, alternate marketing programs, and information on dealer and customer needs.

CONFLICTING OBJECTIVES

At the point where the marketing system and the POM system interface, there is always the possibility of organizational conflict arising because of different preferences in these two systems. For example, the manager of a POM system might want long design lead times, simple design, few models with standard components, long and inflexible order lead times, strict production schedules, long production runs, infrequent design or model changes, standard size orders, ease of fabrication, and less strict quality standards.

On the other hand, the manager of the marketing system might want short design lead times, special product features, many models with custom components, short and flexible order lead times, scheduling to meet emergency orders, short runs with many models, frequent model changes, custom orders, and tight quality control.

This latent and often very real conflict of system goals has been captured in anecdotal form in a joke about two lion hunters, one a marketing manager and the other a POM manager. After a long trek into lion country, they had pitched their tent and retired for the night. The marketing manager arose earlier than his companion and desirous of proving his mettle as a hunter went out to look for lions. As the story goes, he was shortly surprised by a very large lion which chased him in the direction of the tent. By very adroit maneuvering, the marketing manager was able to get to

---

[1] Harper W. Boyd, and Steuart Henderson Britt, *Marketing and Administrative Action* (New York: McGraw-Hill Book Company, 1963), p. 679.
[2] *Ibid.*

the tent with the lion in hot pursuit. As he dashed through the tent, he awakened a very startled POM manager and exclaimed, "O.K., I've captured one; you take care of him while I find us another."

The organizational moral of this story is a simple one: the marketing manager is portrayed as creating a fairly intractable problem for his companion. In a more ordinary organizational setting, the "capturing" of the lion might be likened to selling an order by promising immediate delivery with full knowledge that the POM facilities are already far overloaded. In still another sense, the lion anecdote could describe a situation where a sale was made by promising a certain modification of a standard item without prior evaluation by the POM staff, only to find later that it could not be made with present tools and equipment. A final example of this type of behavior would be the case where an order for far fewer units than the minimum economic production run was accepted by marketing in order to effect the sale. In all three of these examples, the action taken by marketing was taken in light of their perceived preference, i.e., increasing sales. One cannot easily argue with this seemingly parochial point of view especially in the face of dollar sales quotas. The cost of lost sales is often seen by marketing to be infinite regardless of its true magnitude.

From the POM point of view, the three examples above all represent additional headaches. POM would rather not modify standard products; they would rather not manufacture items in less than economic batches; and they surely would not like to break into an established production schedule to satisfy a customer who was promised an unrealistic delivery date. From a motivational point of view, POM perceives that it is probably evaluated on the basis of production cost and not on the extent to which it accommodates the marketing function with favors. In such a situation, given the fact that each of the three examples will probably increase cost, POM is not overly happy at the thought of having to accommodate what it sees as a series of poor marketing decisions.

REDUCING SYSTEM CONFLICT

A vital requirement for top management then is to maximize the extent to which it promotes complete cooperation between these two functions, i.e., insuring that they act as a system of two smaller systems and not as two separate systems. This is the stage that organizations should be approaching today, an integration of marketing and POM such that they complement each other. In the case of the order which was promised too early, for example, many companies publish realistic delivery schedules which sales representatives can quote and which POM is responsible for meeting. Failure to meet a realistic schedule is clearly assessable against POM in these cases. If, in this situation, a sales representative wishes to promise delivery in a shorter interval than the schedule indicates, marketing is required to indicate specifically which previously scheduled order must be delayed. In this sense, the marketing system controls customer satisfaction and is simultaneously responsible for the tradeoffs that are required to do so. Since it is assumed the POM facility is fully utilized in this example, it seems only logical that marketing both control and take responsibility for such changes in the schedule.

In the case of production lots smaller than those considered to be economical, this situation can often be handled quite easily. In many organizations, the manufacture of such size lots is authorized when requested by marketing. The additional cost per unit of producing in smaller batches is either charged as a selling expense or allowed as a legitimate production cost by means of a flexible production budget, making POM more willing to accommodate marketing because the evaluation system will not treat this action unfavorably.

In each of these examples, management decisions can encourage organizational flexibility, i.e., the mechanism for accommodating customers has been allowed to function, and thus marketing has been allowed to respond quickly to what it perceives to be *marketing problems.* On the other hand, the economic costs of these responses have not accrued to POM and what POM perceives as a *production problem,* i.e., increased costs, has not been allowed to preclude a proper reaction.

To provide for an organizational resolution of such intrasystem conflicts as these just mentioned, it is necessary to maintain a climate which:

1. States explicitly the decision rules under which the system is normally expected to operate.
2. Sets the conditions under which exceptions to these rules are allowable and the extent of exceptions permitted.
3. Provides a mechanism which determines if the tradeoff involved in each of these decisions is worthwhile from the organizational point of view.
4. Insures that no system component which is a party to a worthwhile tradeoff is economically or organizationally penalized for being involved with that action.

Unless all four of these conditions are met, it is difficult to create an organizational environment which encourages cooperation between system components. One particular difficulty today is the absence of accounting procedures which illuminate all dimensions of a proposed tradeoff. For example, it is one thing to measure the increased cost per unit occasioned by smaller production runs; it is clearly another to attempt to measure the probable lost future sales from a customer who is antagonized by late deliveries.

THE PRODUCTION/OPERATIONS MANAGEMENT SYSTEM

Once the consumer's needs are assessed, the POM system plans the products, processes, and operations methods required. Planning information flows into operations where needs are translated into physical goods and services. Once the consumer purchases the goods or services, his needs are satisfied but the system continues to operate. To obtain maximum effectiveness, the POM system must be apprised of changes in consumer needs. Thus the system becomes a dynamic entity, reacting to changes in market demand by altering its products, size of output, and manufacturing and distribution techniques.

The POM system, like any other system within the organization, contains those elements or variables over which it has direct control, whereas the environment surrounding the system contains the variables which affect or are affected by the system but over which there is little control. In Figure 4-1, the POM system's internal environment is the area within its own box. The area between the POM box and the dotted organizational boundary represents an area in which cooperative action between POM and other systems can take place. The area outside of the dotted lines represents the organization's environment.

Any POM system consists of eight basic elements:

1. Forecasting facility requirements
2. Designing the total production facility
3. Planning output levels
4. Planning inventory levels
5. Controlling work input
6. Controlling work output
7. Feedback
8. Replanning

The POM system converts a set of inputs into a specified set of outputs. The inputs include such elements as labor, raw materials, machines and equipment, and financial resources. The inputs are processed, or themselves process in turn certain other inputs to produce the marketed good or service. The concept of production/operations management, as defined above, is broad enough to apply to any transformation process which fits the input—output construct. Examples of the inputs, processes, and outputs for different kinds of POM systems are shown in Table 4-1.

THREE DIFFERENT POM SYSTEMS

POM systems are characterized by the flow of materials, information, or people. In Figure 4-1, the POM system was related to the environment

Table 4-1   *Inputs, processes, and outputs for different kinds of production/operations management systems*

Facility	Input	Conversion Process	Output
Bank			
Teller window	Customers	Cash checks, make deposits	Serviced customers
Accounting office	Canceled checks, deposit slips, etc.	Adjust balances of accounts	Status of accounts, reports
Supermarket			
Store and display shelves	Merchandise	Receive, unpack, and store on shelves	Merchandise ready for sale
Checkout counters	Customer with purchases	Checkout, add up bill, receive payment, and make change; package	Customer with purchases, less cash
Factory			
Manufacturing facility	Raw material, parts and supplies	Change shape or form by fabrication and assembly; package	Completed parts and products
Hospital			
Patient's rooms, operating rooms, laboratories, etc.	Patients	Examinations, shots, tests, operations, etc.	Discharged patients

through the flow of materials: raw materials in and finished goods out. Material flow may encompass raw materials, pieces of equipment, people, paper forms, or products. The flow of materials can occur through either a network of machines and/or personnel. POM processes typically are classified as either *flow shop, job shop,* or *project* depending on their flow and network characteristics. All three types fit within the framework of the POM system as it relates to the organization. Figures 4-2 and 4-3 illustrate respectively the flow shop and job shop configurations.

A "flow shop" involves a continuous, uninterrupted flow of objects through various operations or a continuous flow of operations to some object which remains stationary. Figure 4-2 is an illustration of a very simple flow shop system with the material flow and the information flow illustrated.

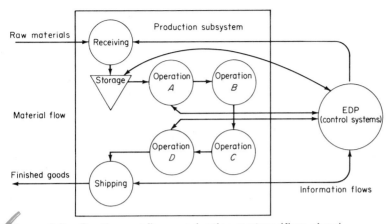

Figure 4-2 *Continuous flow production system (flow shop)*

The flow shop is best represented by the mass-production-type plant used to manufacture consumer goods where there is a limited variety in the output and each unit of output goes through the same sequence of operations. Output is not designated to a particular customer and machines are very often designed as special purpose for the production of a single product or group of products. Flow may or may not be continuous. Automobiles, appliances, and soft drinks are examples of flow shop products.

An intermittent POM system (a "job shop"), as shown in Figure 4-3, is the direct opposite of the flow system. Production is in batches, often

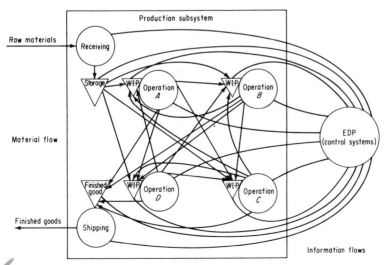

Figure 4-3 *Intermittent flow production system (job shop)*

for individual orders for specific customers or for finished goods inventory with an extensive product line. The job shop is characterized by a variable routine of the flow. Jobs flow through the system via different routes depending on the tasks required. The facilities and machines are almost always general purpose, meaning that they can be adjusted for a variety of outputs. Examples of job shops are specialty metal fabricating plants, automobile service centers, and hospitals.

A "project" is a production system designed to produce only one product or a limited number of large jobs. It is essentially a job shop differing only in the size or scope of the job it can handle. The job is usually stationary, with the production resources being brought to it. The fabrication of space vehicles, the erection of a bridge, and the repairing of large machinery are examples of projects.

Each of these POM systems has different methods and techniques of design, planning, and control, although there are general concepts which apply to all three. For example, both flow and job shops can have finished goods inventories. However, the job shop usually has the greater inventory, i.e., work-in-progress, raw materials, and finished goods and therefore requires the greater information flow and control. In some job shop cases, however, the system operates off an order backlog and thus has no finished goods inventory.

OTHER INTERFACES

Interfaces between POM and other organizational units, including research and development, engineering, purchasing, and personnel, are represented in Figure 4-1 by the smaller circles. Research and development and engineering work with information flows between marketing, POM, management, and the information system to effect product development and production planning and control, as well as quality control. Purchasing uses information flows on purchases, inventory control, traffic, receiving and warehousing, and quality control, while personnel is responsible for flows concerning manpower planning, wages and salaries, labor relations, employee services, and personnel records. These departments produce their own information flows connecting with POM, finance and accounting, management, the information system, and the environment.

THE MARKETING–POM INTERFACE

A more detailed schematic view of the interrelationships and interdependencies between the marketing and POM systems is given in Figure 4-4. In this portrayal, product and market research and sales forecasting provide

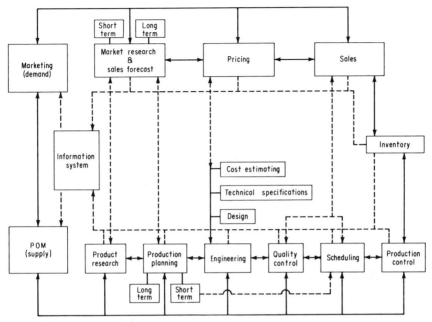

Figure 4-4 *Interfaces between the POM and marketing systems*

the primary data and thus the primary goals to which total system operations are directed. The product and market research function interacts more with the long-term market conditions than the short term. In a highly competitive industry, a keen awareness of future market conditions plays a major role in the economic survival of the firm. If the firm is to survive and grow, it must have new products and services to meet the changing needs of its customers. Existing products and services must be updated continually, and market research and sales forecasting should outline future opportunities for product research.

Long-run market research and sales forecasting also must be coordinated carefully with long-run production planning. Only through such efforts can plans for expansion of plant and equipment be carried out economically. As expansion or new product introduction seem warranted by future growth possibilities, engineering becomes involved with product research and production planning.

Cost must be considered together with technical specifications and expressed in product design and process design. This is also the time to determine equipment specifications and the need for additional personnel, since a new product, new process, or new service may require additional more highly trained men and more sophisticated machines.

Market research and sales forecasting must also interface with production planning in the short run. The product output mix may be modified to meet existing demands. Proper scheduling methods must be established and maintained to meet the daily sales requirements. Short-term production planning also requires communications between sales and production control to establish the proper inventory levels. This is necessary to meet fluctuations in customer demands and provide for good customer relations.

Short-term forecasts also are needed to establish proper raw materials and goods-in-process inventories. Various mathematical models have been built which help determine economic order quantities, optimum reorder points, and economic production lot sizes. Short-term sales forecasting is a basic input to all of these models. Also related to inventory control and sales forecasting is storage and warehouse capacity. These capacities are a function of both long-term and short-term sales forecasts.

The pricing function in the marketing system requires an input from the engineering function. Market research and production planning also play vital roles in the pricing decision. When a particular new product is being contemplated by marketing, the engineering department estimates the labor and material required for production. The choice of a production method in cases like this depends heavily upon initial forecasts of sales volume made by marketing. For example, if a product can be manufactured by hand, by semi-automatic machinery, or by a fully automated process, the choice among these alternatives is not solely a technical decision but is based firmly upon the economics of the situation. Take the example illustrated in Table 4-2 and Figure 4-5. If sales projections are high, the lowest unit cost will result from use of fully automated production methods. With a more moderate sales level, it will be economically sounder to use a less automated method so that the average fixed cost per unit of the machinery is not excessive. Finally, if sales of this new product are anticipated to be quite low, it may be much wiser to produce the output by hand and avoid all capital costs.

Table 4-2 *Cost-volume—method relationships*

Production Method	Hand Work	Semi-automatic	Fully Automatic
Direct Labor	$3.20	$ 1.40	$ .25
Direct Material	.60	$ .60	$ .60
Capital Cost Over Product Life for Machinery	$ .00	$400,000	$900,000

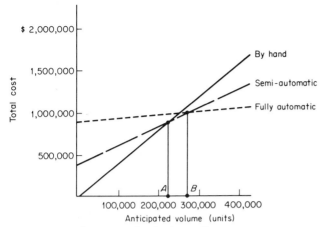

Figure 4-5 *Cost graph of alternatives*

The same information is shown graphically in Figure 4-5. Here we have illustrated the total cost of producing by the three alternative methods. For anticipated sales below point *A,* the hand method yields the lowest total cost; for production budgets between points *A* and *B,* the semi-automatic method is least costly; and for anticipated volumes above point *B,* production by the fully automatic method yields the lowest total production cost over the projected life of the product. This hypothetical example points up still another vital interdependence between the POM and marketing systems. Is the pricing decision exclusively a marketing decision in this case? Could one approach a pricing decision intelligently without the cost figures of Table 4-2 and Figure 4-5? Of course not, because in this case and most others we might cite, price is both determined by and helps determine (through its effect on sales volume), the production method to be utilized. This interface may become more important if, for example, higher volume forces a change in production method from semi-automatic to fully automatic causing us to lose the $400,000 investment we made in the semi-automatic process. Once again, the ability to forecast remains of vital importance not only to the marketing system but also to the POM system as it seeks to operate most effectively.

Finally, for this system to be fully effective, it must be linked by a communications system that will provide all areas with the information they need. There must be not only direct communication between each of the various functions under marketing and POM but also a system that will gather, store, calculate, and transmit vital data required by each of these functions.

THE FINANCIAL AND ACCOUNTING SYSTEM

THE FINANCIAL SYSTEM

As can be seen from Figure 4-1, all cash flows between the organization and the external environment revolve around the finance and accounting system. All other monetary data within the formal organization are in the form of information flows.

While we know that money itself does not flow between the various systems, we must recognize it as one of the dimensions of the inputs to the POM system. Figure 4-6 indicates the point at which the money dimension enters into the POM cycle and shall thus be used as a framework for discussing some of the interfaces between finance, accounting, and the POM system.

Figure 4-6 illustrates schematically the relationship between the POM system and the finance and accounting system. The section of the money accounts block labeled "physical plant" represents the long-term investment of money and is therefore usually referred to as fixed capital. Although the physical plant is not directly consumed in making a product, it eventually loses value due to wear and/or obsolescence. Therefore, this loss in value must be allocated to the cost of the products in the form of depreciation expense. Hence we have a small "stream" of physical plant shown entering the production process as equipment is being used up, and we have part of the money obtained from sales shown as flowing back into the "physical plant" block. Changes in the scale of plant would come in response to

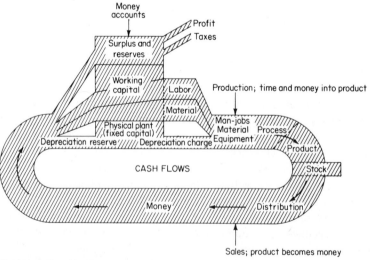

Figure 4-6   *Money, time, and the POM system*

changing production requirements resulting from actual or forecasted changes in demand.

Even though all capital expenditures are made with the hope of increasing profits, the ways in which profits are affected will vary. Some of the categories into which capital investment may be classified are:[3]

1. To replace worn-out plant and equipment so as to be able to maintain current production levels.
2. To secure plant and equipment necessary to expand production of existing products.
3. To replace obsolete equipment with more efficient processes, either to reduce costs or increase output or both.
4. To add capacity so as to produce or handle new product lines.
5. To expand distribution facilities.
6. To integrate operations toward sources of raw material.
7. To improve product quality.
8. To improve general plant efficiency, working conditions, or employee morale.
9. To improve efficiency of employees or management.

An interaction between the POM and financial system takes place each time there is a capital request for one or more of the items contained in the above list. For example, if the POM system requests a new piece of machinery to speed up or simplify the manufacture of a given product, the POM supervisor may be asked to estimate the production output rate, labor input, expected scrap loss, and raw material usage appropriate to the new equipment. Finance will take this information and calculate the cost of this method versus the method currently being used. The value of any assets which will be discarded or sold is also considered, as well as. present versus proposed depreciation differentials. Tax savings or expenditures are estimated to arrive at the total amount of out-of-pocket cost related to the new product. Any volume changes or product mix alterations are considered in evaluating the total impact of the project upon existing plant profitability. The total profit is compared to the total related investment to determine the return on investment, the criterion generally used to accept or reject the project.

The final section of the money accounts block, "working capital," is much more volatile. Cash flows from this account reimburse labor and material and meet operating expenses; collections from sales flow back in to replenish this account. Because working capital is the difference between current assets and current liabilities, it follows that the shorter the time lag between (1) payment for raw materials and labor needed to produce a product, and (2) collections from the sale of that product, the greater

[3] Ernest W. Walker, *Financial Planning and Policy* (New York: Harper & Brothers, 1961), p. 130.

the volume of output which can be supported by a given amount of working capital.

To complete our analysis of the money flow in Figure 4-6, let us follow the flow clockwise from the money accounts block. The money flowing from this block satisfies the obligations for labor, materials, and taxes and provides a return to the stockholders in the form of dividends. Labor and material then enter the production process and are converted over time into output. This output is either held in inventory until it is sold and distributed or produced and sold without going through a finished goods inventory (as in the case of a job shop operating off an order backlog). In either case—upon sale—the output becomes money (or a money surrogate—accounts receivable), which flows back into the money accounts block from which we started. Through its control of inventories and process flows, POM can influence these accounts markedly.

Before concluding our discussion of money flow, let us look at one further point. Although we have discussed money flow in general terms, it is important that we recognize the various levels of control implicit in this system. Three distinct levels of control can be defined as follows:

1. Actual cash collections and disbursements
2. Cost accounting and other control work for operating decisions
3. Long-range financial planning or budgeting

THE ACCOUNTING SYSTEM

The accounting system contributes to the total system by performing the following functions:

1. Internal control
2. Cash control
3. Budgeting
4. Asset valuation
5. Internal audit and review
6. External reports
7. Assigns costs to appropriate functions
8. Measures of effectiveness

The POM system and the accounting system interface from the inception of the idea for a product through its developmental stages until it is sold and taxes are paid on the profits. The following are some of the specific functions of the accounting system of particular assistance to the POM system:

1. Accumulation of operating data to form a starting point for standards.
2. Accumulation of costs of a job, a time period, or a process.

3. Assignment of general costs to profit centers.
4. Determination of profits or losses of profit centers.
5. Determining the financial value of the work-in-process.
6. Determining the financial value of raw material and finished goods inventories.
7. Providing cost status of jobs or work-in-process.

Data stored or previously reported in the accounting records are input data for feasibility studies and analyses that estimate the profitability of a proposed project. Consider, for example, the interaction which develops between the POM system and the accounting subsystem when an organization receives a request to evaluate the potential of a completely new product. POM typically is given the data regarding demand, specifications, materials, etc. From this, they estimate the speed of the equipment, the probable man-hours required in processing, the projected scrap rate, and any suggested modifications to the given material formulation. These estimates are given to accounting for translation into plant standard cost including the allocation of departmental overhead in accordance with predetermined criteria. Accounting also determines the amount of investment to be associated with the new product's production. This might include, in addition to actual fixed asset expenses, working capital to support the accounts receivable generated by selling the new product and the inventories needed to maintain an adequate supply of the new product.

Accounting might then project useful data based on the following format:

1. Forecast units of annual demand
2. Investment in fixed assets, inventory, and accounts receivable
3. Investment per unit
4. Gross selling price per unit
5. Freight, returns, and allowances
6. Net selling price
7. Standard cost of manufacture
8. Manufacturing variances
9. Plant profit
10. Corporate overhead (selling, general, and administrative estimated as a percent of net selling price)
11. Corporate profit from this product
12. Return on investment

In any system, accounting methods are based on work measurement. Initially, standards for performing each operation are established by industrial engineers. They are useful for establishing a bid price for jobs and products, for payment of employees, for product costing, for measuring effectiveness, and as standards of product quality. Work performance of employees is measured by comparing actual hours worked with output produced. Data to effect these comparisons are available from the accounting system.

Since the greatest majority of POM systems accomplish their objectives by the combination of labor and materials, cost accounting begins at the time materials are ordered. When the raw materials are received, they are entered on records. As they are used, they are identified with a particular job or process. Their cost, like the individual labor hours, becomes part of the cost of the finished product, and they lose physical identity at the point when they are withdrawn from stock and enter the manufacturing process. Each job or process must be identified with the amount of raw materials consumed.

An important function of accounting during the manufacturing process is that of monitoring progress. Data fed into the accounting system form the basis of reports and information feedback which can enhance the overall performance of the firm. Properly designed systems can distinguish between productive time and time not spent directly upon production. Consolidation of the time cards from specific work groups will show the performance of those groups when measured against previously established standards. Standards can be utilized to monitor learning rates of new employees. Accounting information on the distribution and productivity of labor can indicate if areas are understaffed or overmanned.

THE INFORMATION SYSTEM

In Figure 4-1, the information system was shown at the center of the entire organization. The information system incorporates both policy flow *from* management and information flow *to* management. Proper development and implementation of an information system will help management to determine when and how the work should be done, the necessary work components, and the contribution of each such component. An information system accommodates information both from the external environment and from the various other systems within the organization.

Information system design begins with a refining of the initial problem definition. Systems analysts and designers lay out the "general logic" of the system, identify and specify the interface between components of the system, and define the necessary data inputs, the appropriate processing of data, and the system's desired end results. The system thus designed is often put into operation via computer programs designed to accept the raw data, to help effect decisions wherever possible, and to output required summary information.

POM APPLICATIONS OF INFORMATION SYSTEMS

The number of ways in which the power of information systems can be applied to the POM system is limited more by the initiative and imagination of management than by any other constraint except cost. Below is a list of information system applications in POM; it is by no means exhaustive but does serve to indicate the broad scope of possible applications. Immediately following the list, we shall discuss in some detail several of the more prominent applications. Some of the terms may be unfamiliar to you, but they will be outlined in the appropriate sections of this book.

1. Inventory control
2. Cost control
3. Reporting the status of orders
4. Production scheduling
5. Establishing and maintaining standards
6. Forecasting and scheduling materials requirements
7. Control of work-in-process
8. Issuing work orders
9. Quality control
10. Machine load records
11. Routing jobs through a process
12. Maintenance planning, scheduling, and control
13. Numerical control of machines
14. Preventive maintenance planning
15. Make-or-buy decisions
16. Manpower utilization
17. Labor efficiency records
18. Engineering changes
19. Air traffic control
20. Control of traffic flows in major cities
21. Scheduling of hospital operations (For example: scheduling of patients' treatments in a clinic with limited facilities)
22. Improving stock exchange information flow
23. Integrating hotel-chain operations (For example: reservation and registration systems)
24. Aiding clerical routines in banks

APPLICATION EXAMPLES

The original POM systems applications tended to be more static than dynamic in relating the effect of current decisions to future decision-making flexibility and vice versa. The principal advance that has taken place is in combining new, more dynamic tools with previously static tools. The new methods that result sometimes enable simultaneous evaluation of hundreds of factors to arrive at better POM decisions. An example of what can result is the fact that a division of the Honeywell Corporation was able to reduce the number of its warehouses from 85 to 1 over a 2-year period. The method: an information analysis covering such factors as historical buying patterns, lead times, demands on each warehouse, most common orders, and order frequency for each product. The study convinced management that it could service all orders from one warehouse at no loss in speed and efficiency.

A growing POM application of information systems today is in the area of inventory control. This includes control of purchased parts ordered from outside vendors, parts in transit, and parts banks at specific working locations. The computerized inventory control system at Ryerson Inc., a Chicago steel supplier, uses programmed decision rules to decide when and how much to buy. Programmed into this system are the rates of demand for all items, how that demand has varied historically, steel mill delivery lead times, frequency of availability, a computation which takes into account the relative costs of stockouts versus those of carrying extra inventory, and finally, an economically determined best-order quantity and reorder point. The company has been able to reduce significantly the amount of inventory that must be held.

But computer-based inventory systems can do even more than what has been described above. If a company has factories, offices, and warehouses scattered throughout the country, it is possible to design a multiple monitoring system at a central control point. To illustrate: Westinghouse Electric Corporation has facilities (plants, warehouses, etc.), located in different parts of the United States; in total, these amount to almost 400 "information points." All these are connected electronically to a control center in Pittsburgh. Whenever an order is received, it is flashed to a computer in Pittsburgh, and within seconds a chain reaction of responses takes place automatically in the POM system. Here are just a few:

1. The order is sent to the appropriate warehouse. If the item should be out of stock, the order is transferred to the nearest warehouse.
2. Invoices and other necessary bookkeeping operations are carried out in the central office, and salesmen's commissions and other regular costs are computed.
3. Warehouse records are brought up to date, and as inventory levels reach predetermined reorder points, orders are sent out to factories for replenishment.

An example of a completely integrated information system, i.e., one that performs functions across several systems within the organization, is one in use at the Vendo Company. The company produces dispensers for hot, cold, and frozen foods. Although it theoretically produces only seven versions of these dispensers, the complexity in the POM system is somewhat complicated by the company's policy of designing machines to customer specifications.

In essence, the company's system encompasses and implements the POM system from planning and procurement of parts, through each step of production scheduling, requisitioning, manufacturing, material movement, and inventory control. The complexities of this system are handled within the computer.

The starting point of the system is an annual sales forecast to support the production schedule. The computer expands this schedule into parts requirements, level by level, taking all lead times into consideration. Thus, the required stock level of every component is developed in relation to completion dates. Scheduling changes are made which cover both purchased and fabricated parts and assemblies. All bill-of-materials (list of parts) data are stored in the computer. By feeding in a finished product number, the company can "build a machine," that is, get a complete bill-of-materials for it, in a few minutes.

The Vendo system monitors all POM activities. As required, it produces a master operating record for each part which shows, by week for up to 20 weeks, the projected status on hand, on order, and when the part is due in relation to when it is needed. The computer also produces a weekly composite report of the entire production schedule and a daily report of all production scheduled on the final assembly line.

POM systems have benefited enormously from simulation techniques used in conjunction with information systems. Briefly, the goal of simulation is to describe systems and develop workable solutions on the basis of structured trial-and-error methods. POM inventory policies, for example, can be simulated. More nearly optimum inventory policies, including purchase quantity and warehousing, can be determined. Where there is a probability distribution for differing demands, out-of-stock conditions and inventory investment for various policies can be examined. In the public sector, traffic flows can be simulated. Under the guidance of those conducting traffic simulations, vehicles can be moved in various directions. Different timings of signal lights and multiple one-way and other street arrangements can be compared to determine the best arrangement. Aircraft flight under assumptions as to failure of various parts and systems can also be simulated. The optimum location of spare parts inventory as well as the most advantageous location of repair crews and facilities can thus be determined.

REMOTE DATA COLLECTION SYSTEMS

While computers provide the information necessary to prevent, for example, costly errors and missed production schedules, these data often do not get into proper hands in time to be effective. Remote data collection (RDC) systems enable the POM manager to know the instant a machine breaks down, the moment a critical inventory item runs low, or the second a quality inspector spots a serious defect. Moreover, RDC systems prepare running accounts of the number of people working on a job, the tools and materials they use, and the location and status of all work-in-process. Figure 4-7 illustrates schematically a remote data collection system.

Remote data collection starts at the input stations (1) placed at key locations throughout the process. Into these instruments, machine operators, quality control inspectors, and foremen feed production information as it happens. These data are instantly flashed to an information collector (2) which automatically checks and combines it with data from other stations. The collector either produces punched cards or punched paper tape (3) for further processing by office machines or electronically feeds data directly to a computer (4) where it is stored. As the computer gathers information, it compares it with predetermined schedules and other criteria in its memory and, when necessary, flashes instructions directly to foremen or other POM supervisors through the printer on the production floor (5). On a regular schedule—several times each day, for example—the computer prepares reports for POM (6) that help reduce production errors and adjust improper work flow. At any time, executives may query the system for up-to-the-minute data on all work-in-process. Besides monitoring production, the RDC system usually keeps track of attendance, provides the basic data for complex incentive-type payrolls, and enables POM personnel to keep a constant check on job costs and obtain maximum utilization of both men

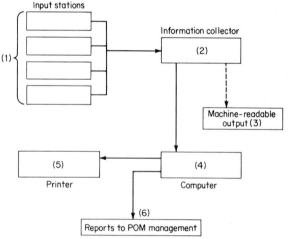

Figure 4-7   *Remote data collection (RDC) system*

and machines. Parts (2), (3), and (4) of the system are often integrated into one single unit—a large computer.

The impact of RDC on POM systems can be illustrated by an example. Lockheed Aircraft Corporation has installed an elaborate RDC system in its California division; it has 206 remote input units. In all, about 10,000 messages are fed into the system each working day; some are simple, others quite complex. This division is organized like a gigantic job shop. About 65,000 different job orders are being worked on at once. To track down and check any one of these *manually* would be a tedious job. Through the RDC system, this can be attained by inserting a card with the job number into a remote input unit. This information is then sent to a large computer. The computer searches its memory and sends back a report that is printed at the remote station. It tells where the job is currently located, the number of parts involved, and exactly what work has been done so far. Furthermore, it estimates when the job will be completed. The whole process takes only a few seconds.

POSSIBLE ORGANIZATIONAL ROLES FOR POM

Production/operations management is considered a system within the organization as a whole. It continually interacts with other major systems of the firm. This interaction has increased over time to the point where the boundaries of POM often overlap with the boundaries of other areas. POM personnel no longer limit their interests or efforts solely to matters of technology, equipment handling, and engineering. As we have indicated, attention is now given to such considerations as marketing forecasts, and financial and accounting data. Individual departments are becoming increasingly aware of the need to appraise factors that fall outside their normal boundaries. Organizations now realize, for example, that decisions in marketing and finance have a significant impact on POM decisions and that the reverse is also quite true.

HISTORICAL POM ROLES

Historically, POM has sometimes been characterized by a strict cost orientation, whereas marketing has been directed more toward the ultimate consumer. Clearly these objectives can be at variance with one another. Modern organizational texts point out that firms are becoming increasingly aware of the need to take the overall organizational viewpoint in decision making, rather than limit decision making to the objectives of one or more particular systems. Though this trend toward a "global" point of view continues to develop, in many firms the particular systems never achieve a rapport with each other or with the major organizational goals themselves. This lack of role congruity may have disastrous effects.

The role of POM changes over time. Cost efficiencies are becoming less and less the dominant consideration in strategic POM planning, due to the fact that the profit leverage of production efficiencies has declined. With higher universal levels of technology, competition often is able to arrive at equivalent cost efficiencies. Production costs often are no longer the overwhelming component of selling price.

SUPPORTIVE VERSUS DOMINANT ROLES

At a particular point in the development of the organization, top management may feel strongly that the best interests of growth lie with a strong marketing approach. Efforts to increase sales may result temporarily in a supportive role for POM. This "production at any cost" philosophy may require the POM system to sacrifice cost and quality objectives in order to achieve maximum outputs; but as POM becomes more dedicated to a single objective, the amount of coordination with other systems may diminish. In situations like this, strong lines of communication are generally lacking. If POM is geared only to satisfying marketing criteria, it frequently loses its own objective measurements. There may be little dialogue between POM and accounting control and review. The physical size of the operation will not necessarily diminish, but its organizational importance will. From an organizational point of view, POM will not assume a positive role again until a point is reached where POM can no longer support the demands of marketing as a viable system.

The opposite extreme, with top management emphasis on POM at the expense of other segments of the organization is also rare. Organizations committed to a singular "production" philosophy generally find in the longer run that failure to assess and plan for marketing viability becomes a limiting constraint on operations. Management more typically attempts to achieve balance between the POM system and the rest of the organization, rather than placing complete emphasis on POM or subordinating it. Realistic managements are aware of the need for a POM system which fits the organization, supports its roles, but does not dominate it.

POM ROLE IN SERVICE ORGANIZATIONS

The role of the POM system would be much different in service organizations than it would be in organizations involved in the manufacture of products. Operations in service-oriented businesses frequently consist primarily of record maintaining activities and data computations. An example of this type or arrangement is in a banking firm or retail establishment, where the POM procedure is devoted largely to handling financial transactions or servicing the incoming and outgoing flows of customers. The collected data are transformed into customer statements and decision-supporting analysis. The POM system may not require extensive informational flows or communications with the other systems in the organization. Processes will usually be repetitive in nature, facilitating uniform inputs. Consequently, the POM system may temporarily assume a lesser role in total organizational strategy. However, several securities dealers recently found themselves in serious trouble with the Securities and Exchange Commission for not being able to process the flow of work through their "back offices." Failure to make their POM system a viable part of their total strategy had led to the point where an active marketing strategy was severely constrained by POM inadequacies. Several firms were forced to curtail marketing activities for considerable periods of time; in several cases, this even led to the closing of sales offices at various locations across the country, and the closing of the stock exchanges one day a week.

ROLE DETERMINANTS

One often encounters difficulty in assuming that as an ironclad rule, the POM role will ultimately be determined by the nature of the POM process. In some service organizations, POM may play a subordinate role; however, in other service environments, POM may become critical to the functioning of the entire organization and assume a major role. In distribution warehousing, for example, close attention must be given to inventory control. This requires close coordination between POM and both purchasing and finance to ensure that the organization avoids having excessive working capital involved in nonrevenue producing assets. Such an arrangement often creates a major role for the POM system.

Some organizations produce a high volume of standardized products. The POM system in this environment can adjust to stable demand over time without necessarily requiring close relations or continuous communication with other departments. Inputs are likely to be similar and predictable, possibly resulting in separated working situations. However, when the firm is producing highly diversified products, the need for reciprocity in communications and clarification of objectives and tactics is much stronger. The POM system, in these cases, must coordinate very closely with marketing forecasts to develop adequate inventory control and scheduling policies. Close attention must be paid to the issue of inventory levels and minimization of stockout conditions. Labor skills are likely to be diverse so that POM must effectively coordinate with personnel management. In this type of environment, POM will develop and play a major role in total organizational activities.

Often, the significant factors in determining the role of POM within the organization are the nature of the technological processes and the characteristics of the inputs to the POM system. Generally, the more intricate the transformation processes are, the more significant a role POM will play. Typically, more technology involves more numerous inputs. To control these inputs properly, the POM role must be able to receive informational inputs from all systems and to provide required decision flows in return. In certain cases, the technology can be very involved and the physical inputs relatively simple. The processing of wood pulp is an example of this situation. Here, the POM system plays a dominant role.

There is simply no categorical answer to questions regarding the best organizational role for the POM system. Each organization decides this question based on its current objectives and within the constraints imposed by its own personnel and facilities. These types of strategic decisions are made typically by first designing a total organizational strategy, then defining the most appropriate supporting roles for each system in the organization.

QUESTIONS

1. How do external environmental factors affect an organization? Give specific examples of four such factors.
2. Can an organization influence its external environmental factors? Give two specific examples of how this can happen.
3. In what ways does the finance and accounting system relate to the POM system?
4. How does the marketing system relate to the POM system? What specific kinds of information passes between these two systems?
5. Define flow shop, job shop, and project. Which characteristics are common to all three of these forms? Which are different?
6. What kind of information is basic to any POM decision? What are the minimum informational needs of any POM decision?
7. Why is an information system necessary to any organization? What would you state as the symptoms of an ineffective information system?
8. Are cost and efficiency considerations of equal relevance in all POM decisions? Why? Where are they most relevant?
9. What role would POM play in Sears, Roebuck Company? What would be the typical kinds of POM activities in that organization?
10. Which system do you feel is most important to the Xerox Company: marketing, POM, or finance and accounting? Why?
11. What is the POM system in a data processing organization? Is this a job shop, a flow shop, or a project?

12. What is the POM system in a hospital? What are the major activities it engages in? Is such a system a flow shop, a job shop, or a project?

13. Discuss the implications of designing a POM system which is totally responsive to a marketing policy of being able to supply every possible sale.

14. Suppose that General Motor's Pontiac Division went to considerable expense to develop a highly successful automobile bumper which subsequently caused that division's profits to increase by 10 percent. Now the Buick Division wants to copy the bumper, thus avoiding the research and development cost. The head of the Pontiac Division objects to this request. If you were the president of the corporation, what would you say? Justify your answer.

15. Why might a corporate executive be dissatisfied even though a system analyst had designed a model which would optimize the performance of the POM system?

16. POM in a manufacturing firm may be briefly described in terms of these two basic functions: (1) acquiring inputs and (2) converting those inputs into outputs, in a form and at a time and place appropriate to the needs of the next operation and, finally, the ultimate consumer. This description is also appropriate to the POM system in nonmanufacturing organizations. Give the major inputs, describe the conversion process, and list the major outputs for each of the following activities:

    (a) A legal office
    (b) A retailer
    (c) An investment firm
    (d) A physician's office
    (e) A bank
    (f) A computer
    (g) A university

CASE: ORANGE PRODUCTS MANUFACTURING COMPANY

Frank Field, the production manager of Orange Products Manufacturing Company, was sitting in his office, reflecting upon what he viewed as an impossible backlog of unfilled orders in the plant. Shortly, he received a phone call from Sam Wrigley, the company sales manager.

"Frank, I just wanted to know when we can ship that special order for Dearborn Wholesalers?"

"Darn it, Sam, that order was due out last week; I was told that we would make the schedule on that one; do you mean to tell me that it hasn't been shipped?"

Sam went on to review a similarly late status on four or five other orders expected to be shipped during the past week or so.

"Sam, I tell you what, let me check with Jim Wilde, my expediter, and I'll call you back tomorrow, O.K.?"

"O.K., thanks, Frank. Oh, by the way, our salesman in Chicago called a couple of hours ago and reported that he had landed that Acme Special order we've been working on for 2 months. Remember you will have to begin shipment on that next week."

"Darn it, Sam, I told you we could begin shipment on the Acme order 8 weeks from the time we got the order; now you tell me, 7 weeks later, that we got the order, and you expect our boys in the shop to lay everything aside to get it out."

"Don't worry, Frank. I know your guys out there can do it; besides, you know that unless we can promise something special on delivery dates, we have a hard time with our competition. I'll call back tomorrow to see about those other late orders. Oh, by the way, Frank, there are one or two engineering modifications on those late orders which have been called in by customers this week; I'll get our boys to rush them right down to the shop; hope they don't hold you up too much."

Frank reflected a while, after his call from Sam, on the problems of operating a large job shop. Five minutes later, his phone rang again.

"Mr. Field, this is Sally Dart, the president's secretary; would you hold on just a minute for Mr. Teel?"

"Frank, Myron Teel here; I've just seen the February figures on shop cost and work-in-process inventory, and quite frankly, I'm afraid we're getting into serious trouble on both counts. Frank, we simply cannot run a first-class sales operation and then back it up with production inefficiencies like these. I'd like to see you in my office tomorrow morning at 9:00 to discuss this situation."

As Frank hung up the phone, he remembered that he was supposed to call Jim Wilde, the expediter, to find out the status on things down in the shop.

CASE: CHATAM OPERATING ASSOCIATES

Steve Cramer, the founder of Chatam Operating Associates, was presiding over a meeting of the three principal stockholders. Chatam had been formed just a month ago as an organization which would perform contract janitorial services for large office buildings.

"Gentlemen, I asked you to meet here this morning to help me set up the organizational structure of our company. I am a firm believer in organization, and I know that with our planned work force of over 150 employees, early attention to the details of organization will pay off in the future. You all know that beginning in March, we must start performance on contracts in 11 buildings in this city. I would like us, this morning, to address ourselves to these questions: (1) What should our organization look like? (2) What are the major responsibilities of each department within our organization? (3) How should these departments fit together in the sense of coordination among them, and (4) What kinds of systems will we need to ensure that our goals are being reached. Who would like to begin this morning?"

chapter

PRODUCTION/OPERATIONS MANAGEMENT AND

THE EXTERNAL ENVIRONMENT

five

The production/operations management system is an internal entity of the organization. In much the same manner as the total organization is affected by its external environment, the POM system is also affected by its environment. In fact, outside forces, as we shall observe, have a very significant effect upon decisions made within the POM system. These environmental forces cannot be treated lightly nor can intensive study of the POM system take place in a black-box type of atmosphere. True, the POM manager may have varying degrees of control on the environment and thus varying degrees of control over the constraints the environment places on his decisions; but whatever the degree of control he can exercise, the external environment must be considered in every decision affecting the POM system. The purpose of this chapter is (1) to define the external environment, (2) to indicate the ways it affects decisions within the POM system, (3) to indicate ways in which management can ascertain the nature of their environment and forecast changes in its character, and (4) to show ways in which POM system managers can cope effectively with the environment.

THE EXTERNAL ENVIRONMENT DEFINED

The external environment can be defined as those factors that exist outside and beyond the control of the organization. This environment can be separated into three classifications: political-legal, economic, and sociological. The POM system is directly influenced by each of these environmental factors, and if they can be specifically identified, the production organization will adapt to its environment more efficiently and function at a higher level of effectiveness.

POLITICAL-LEGAL

A given law, or political event, can cause an organization to vary its POM processes, thus affecting its performance. Included in the relevant legal structure are such codes as business law, general law, and labor law.

Business law includes rules governing trademarks, patents, etc. These factors have direct implications for planning within the POM system. For example, patents cannot be infringed directly by competitors. As a result, major investments in patented machines and specialized production methods can be made with little fear of competition. Patent production will allow the operating managers to reap the benefits of process innovation.

A second category of business law is the antitrust laws. If the purpose of antitrust legislation is to increase competition within a given industry, prices will likely diminish. As a result, pressure for increasing efficiency and lower costs is inevitable. This demand on the part of top management will force the POM system to adapt its present production methods to meet competition.

General law includes laws governing the health, welfare, and safety of employees. These regulations often lead the POM system to change its methods and policies. For example, recent mining disasters in the United States, which claimed the lives of a number of miners, have raised the level of public concern toward mining safety. There is already legislation which promotes the safety of mine workers, and additional public pressure will probably demand more restrictive measures. Any required, additional safety measures could alter the present methods of mining, and thus cause a change in the POM system in general. Obviously, pollution control legislation will also have far reaching effects on POM systems.

Perhaps the most profound of the legal considerations affecting the POM system is labor law. Among the various labor considerations are hours and conditions of work, bargaining powers, tenure and job security, and unemployment compensation plans. These social policies have forced the POM system to adapt to a totally new environment. For example, laws that govern hours and conditions of work force the POM system to focus more attention on meeting output quotas within a specified time. Provisions must be made within the system to cope with this external force. Another example is the minimum wage law. The typical result of such legislation is for operating managers to shift their input factors by using less labor and more capital.

Political practices of government often influence POM decisions. An example is the effect of monetary and fiscal policy on the structure of output. If the government decides to increase the money supply or to reduce taxes, more income is available to the consumer. As a result, demand curves for certain products or services may shift to the right. With increased demand facing the individual companies, POM systems may tend to shift their orientation to maximizing output by altering their factor inputs or product mix. Another political factor to be considered is defense policy. Since billions of dollars are spent each year in this area, many firms plan their POM system around the actions of the Department of Defense. *Restrains companies from freezing union Activities.*

ECONOMIC FACTORS

Economic factors are perhaps the most obvious and influential constraints affecting the POM system. They include changes in technology, changes in the level of demand, changes in consumer tastes, and general economic factors, i.e., the state of the economy. *Has stimulated POM system*

AMERICAN ECONOMIC LIFE

The security and affluence of economic life for most Americans have fostered significant trends in both consumption and investment behavior. Individuals have become increasingly aware of the social and political forces now being exerted to stabilize economic fluctuations (in contrast to policies in effect prior to John Maynard Keynes). The consumer has adjusted his consumption behavior from one that accepted the standardized offerings from industry (such as the Model T Ford), to one which demands and expects style and innovation. Although the range of choices available in the early 1900s was often limited because of the rigidity associated with mass production, the fact remains that the consumer accepted this situation. This attitude prevailed because he was temporarily content to have mere access to these products at reasonable prices, and because his economic power had been limited and unstable in the basically agrarian economy prior to World War I.

The pattern of consumer demand has been altered partly as a result of a widespread and basic reappraisal of one's economic stability and growth in light of recent experience and future expectations. This perceptual framework has been treated in two recent economic theories. One idea, advanced by Dusenberry and Modigliani, postulates that an individual's present consumption is a function of his past previous peak in income.[1] Alternately, Milton Friedman asserts that present consumption is greatly determined by one's perception of his "permanent" income (income over the next 11 to 15 years).[2] It would logically appear that both are correct to a degree and are credible when taken together as a composite explanation of behavior in the marketplace. In accepting this position for his experience since the 1930s, the consumer has come to regard fluctuations in his income as short-term occurrences while gauging his behavior to coincide with long-run perceptions.

An equally powerful trend has evolved during this period of economic growth and rising confidence in the durability of the American economic system. Under these conditions, industry has become increasingly eager to invest vast amounts of capital and time in the process of technological innovation. Prior to the twentieth century, most (if not all) of the technological breakthroughs were the result of personal motivation. As the country grew larger and more economically sophisticated, business more fully realized the profit potentials inherent in the concept of innovation (and style). Consequently, firms began to pursue change actively in hopes of capitalizing upon untapped consumer markets or productivity-stimulating inventions. Thus, technological change became an integral part and/or concern for the POM system. The magnitude of this change is illustrated when we observe that about $\frac{1}{3}$ of our products in 1960 were unknown 10 years earlier, and that 58 percent of our 1970 products were not in existence in 1960.

MAXIMUM PRODUCTIVE VARIETY

Martin Starr relates the POM system to the consumers' desire for *maximum productive variety* (or maximum changes).[3] Basically, he states that a firm begins with an orientation focused primarily on production. However, with the advent of technology and technological progress, improvements in production bring about a change described as the consumers' demand for *maximum productive variety*. The force for this change comes from the marketplace, but the means for change resides within the POM system. Therefore new methodologies must be developed within the POM organization to meet the consumers' demand for variety. Seasonal patterns within this demand also affect the POM system. When the sales forecasting method-

---

[1] J. S. Dusenberry, *Income, Savings, and the Theory of Consumer Behavior* (Cambridge: Harvard University Press, 1959).

[2] Milton Friedman, *A Theory of the Consumption Function* (Princeton: Princeton University Press, 1957).

[3] Martin Starr, "Modular Concept—A New Concept," *Harvard Business Review, 43* (November 1965), pp. 131–142.

ology does not adequately track these patterns and the demand for the company's products changes radically, the POM system is forced to adopt radical, internal adjustments. These may include shifting between long production runs and smaller batches or making major changes in employment levels.

MAXIMUM PRODUCTIVE VARIETY AND THE POM SYSTEM

The effect of the consumers' desires for maximum productive variety on the POM system is significant. In dealing with this consumer trait, one quickly perceives its effect upon product design for one example. Product design activity is so severely constrained by the desires of consumers that product design is less engineering in origin or nature and more correctly a set of decisions derived largely from the marketplace. As the final design emerges, one may be sure that in large measure its color, form, variety, etc., were all determined by an environment external to the POM system.

Consumer demands in the automobile industry, for example, force manufacturers to assemble many different models and types. Just how much of an effect this desire for variety has had on the industry can be seen from this quotation.

> With the current body styles, interior and exterior colors and optional built in equipment, (it has been said) that one manufacturer could build a car a minute for 90 years without duplication.[4]

The result of the demand for variety on the POM system is to increase greatly the complexity of the planning and scheduling function and to decrease significantly the length of production runs. However, in order to maintain some semblance of production-line technology, the POM system must produce only a limited number of basic models. From these basic styles, it must satisfy the consumer's seemingly insatiable desire for variety by adding equipment options to the customer's order and thereby "customizing" the product. Unfortunately, such a system creates scheduling nightmares as far as maintaining adequate stocks of parts. Flexibility in production scheduling, astute inventory control, and effective material analysis are essential for survival.

MAXIMUM PRODUCTIVE VARIETY AND FACILITIES DESIGN

The consumer demand for maximum productive variety has an equally powerful effect upon POM decisions in the area of physical facilities including the choice of an appropriate production mode. In fact, one can say that

---

[4] T. H. Manlin, "Linking Supplier to Customer by Computer Network," *Iron Age, 199* (February 23, 1967), p. 52.

the facilities design decision is one derived largely from the marketplace. Manufacturers involved in style-oriented businesses (fashion dresses, for example) would hardly set up permanent production lines for each of their separate styles. The manufacturing life expectancy of a particular dress style may be only 5 weeks. This fact makes automated production-line technologies almost useless in this situation. On the other hand, a manufacturer of wooden pencils, assured of a fairly stable product technology, would likely invest considerable capital in creating a high technology flow shop manufacturing facility. What is important in these two examples is the fact that even though production-line technology *could* have been applied in both cases, it was the marketing dimension of the product which directed the final choice of a facilities design and not the technical characteristics of the product.

MAXIMUM PRODUCTION VARIETY, AN INDUSTRY EXAMPLE

The powerful effect of consumer desires for maximum productive variety upon the POM system is demonstrated dramatically in the fashion garment industry. At the beginning of each season, the fashion goods producer must plan the manufacturing process to be used in meeting sales requirements. Part of his product line may consist of simple garments with a few operations; the other part may consist of complex garments with many operations requiring considerably more direct labor. This is in contrast to the work clothing manufacturer who may each year make a dungaree with 38 operations and a fixed direct labor content. It is obvious that the same POM techniques cannot apply in each case. While the work clothing producer can maintain his POM process intact from year to year, the fashion goods producer must replan his process for each season. In a fashion plant, it is essential that this procedure be efficient and accurate if the current product line is ever to be profitable.

The enormous disparity in inventories required to support a fashion garment factory versus one producing staple items (men's slacks, for example) is shown in a survey by the American Apparel Manufacturer's Association. The survey indicates that the throughput time (the time garments are actually *in* the production process) for style factories was found to range from 11 to 45 days. This compares to throughput time of less than a week for factories producing staple items. This problem of handling throughput effectively is proportional to the number of styles. Finally, the balancing of work so that each operator receives a steady flow of garments is greatly complicated by the fact that style garments do not require identical labor operations.

Another study by the American Apparel Manufacturers Association showed considerable differences in excess costs as the style factor increased.

	Staple Factory	Semistyle Factory	Style Factory
Make-up Pay	2.3%	3.5%	6.0%
Transfer Pay	3.5	5.7	8.7
Unmeasured Work	—	0.2	0.5
Machine Delay	0.1	0.1	0.1
Waiting Time	0.1	0.2	0.4
Repairs	0.5	0.6	0.8
Overtime Premium	0.5	0.7	1.0
Totals	7.0%	11.0%	17.5%

The categories of excess cost are defined as follows: (1) make-up pay—dollars paid to bring total wage up to plant minimum guarantee in the event incentive earnings are not equal to this value, (2) transfer pay—wages paid to supplement operator's pay when transferred to a new operation or style, (3) unmeasured work—wages paid for operations for which no production standard has been established.

THE NEED FOR FLEXIBILITY

Although changes in the environment have been profitable for organizations with POM systems flexible enough to adapt to altered conditions, the increased need for innovativeness and flexibility in POM systems is more critical and more difficult to achieve than ever before. This stems from the basic nature of most long-term capital investments and the tendency of product life cycles to become shorter and shorter. New equipment, sometimes entire plants, becomes obsolete too quickly for healthy paybacks. Production planning and control systems scarcely get operating effectively before new ones are needed. Worker training is so time-consuming and expensive that many plants have had to reduce the work requirements to small, more easily mastered parts. These factors now make it necessary for POM to take a serious interest in the people who buy these products and services and how the items are used. It can be a matter of organizational survival. Better long-run forecasts obviously lead to greater long-run effectiveness.

It must be stressed that the need for flexibility is not confined to manufacturers. Service organizations such as banks and hospitals are more concerned than ever with the problem of matching their operating systems to the changing social and economic needs of the public. Hospitals in particular have suffered from an inability to adapt their POM system, much less explore the possibilities offered in radical alterations in the very concept of what a hospital does. The recent flurry of nursing home and out-patient centers has been a response to this inflexibility and should provide the hospitals with some relief so that they might have greater incentive to attack their more vital POM problems. Government is another area which has developed such rigid POM facilities and methods that it is becoming more and more ineffective in dealing with the myriad of problems it faces. Debate rages almost daily over the structure and operation of programs such as those involved with eliminating poverty and administering welfare. Until proper POM systems are conceived for these and similar programs, rigidity and ineffectiveness may continue to be characteristic of many efforts in this direction.

SOCIOLOGICAL FACTORS

Perhaps the most difficult of the external environmental variables affecting the POM system are the sociological constraints. These factors can be defined, in this context, as the attitudes and values that act to influence the motivation, behavior, and performance of individuals. Here the individuals are employees working in formal organizations.

Each individual brings with him to the organization a basic set of needs. His productivity in the organization rests on the extent to which his position and duties satisfy his needs. For example, in addition to other needs, a employee has a need for recognition, for accomplishment, for participation, for affiliation, and for achievement. In order that this employee continue to find his work environment satisfying, that environment must in some way help fulfill all these stated needs. Since the productivity of individuals and of their work groups depends in large measure upon the extent to which POM systems managers design and maintain a "need-fulfilling" environment, the studies of the leading researchers in the area of work sociology are of significant importance.

The traditional view of management direction and control has come to be known as "Theory X." This theory holds that the average worker has an inherent dislike of work and will avoid work if he can. Because of this dislike, the worker must be coerced, controlled, directed, and even threatened with punishment to get him to put forth adequate effort. This theory maintains that the average worker prefers to be directed and has relatively little ambition.

A theory developed by Douglas McGregor, "Theory Y," assumes, on the other hand, that the average human being does not inherently dislike work. Depending upon controllable conditions, work may be a source of satisfaction. It also assumes that under the conditions of modern industrial life, the intellectual potentialities of the average worker are only partially utilized.[5] Theory Y places the responsibility for worker satisfaction and efficiency directly on management.

[5] Douglas McGregor, *The Human Side of Enterprise* (New York: McGraw-Hill Book Company, 1960).

UNFILLED NEEDS ARE MOTIVATORS
SATISFACTION THEN SELF ACTUATION / ① SOCIAL CONTACT / RECOGNITION
② ... / ③ SELF ACTUATION

PRODUCTION/OPERATIONS MANAGEMENT AND THE EXTERNAL ENVIRONMENT   **105**

A. H. Maslow proposes that man is a wanting animal, and that as soon as one of his needs is satisfied, another appears in its place. These needs are organized in a series of levels—a hierarchy of importance—and progress from physiological needs, through love and esteem, to self-actualization.

As a need is satisfied, it is no longer a motivator of behavior (a fact unrecognized in Theory X). People deprived of opportunities to satisfy their important needs at work, behave on the job with indolence, passivity, unwillingness to accept responsibility, resistance to change, willingness to follow the demagogue, and unreasonable demands for economic benefits.[6]

In attempting to fulfill the individual needs of employees, the POM system may encounter difficulty. For example, after researching the needs for participation and accomplishment, Frederick Herzberg has outlined in his work an approach called "job enrichment."[7] This goes far beyond the older ideas of job enlargement (which recommended letting the employee perform two or more tasks to reduce the effects of monotony). Herzberg's job enrichment program involves employee participation in decisions affecting his job, even to the point of letting employees determine most suitable, individual work methods. One can appreciate the problems involved in letting each employee determine his own work methods particularly if the practice in the past has been to insist upon rigid standardization of method. By the same token, the modern organization is fully aware of the effect and value of increased motivation and interest upon efficiency. More and more POM managers are experimenting with Professor Herzberg's ideas.

Another important area of research involving the motivation of employees has been investigated by David McClelland, a social-psychologist. McClelland has directed his research at the need of the individual employee to achieve, a need which he says is paramount in determining the ultimate performance of that employee. The employee's need to achieve is significantly increased when several factors are present in the work environment.[8] Perhaps the most important is that the work environment must allow the employee to take calculated (moderate) risks in performing his job; that is, the job must be designed so that it provides a moderate risk taking opportunity for the employee. According to McClelland, the drive to achieve (and thus produce), is highly dependent upon the presence of this opportunity. From the POM point of view, increasing the need for employees to achieve would then involve the design of an environment where work was not reduced, specialized, or routinized to the point where the risk-taking element was eliminated. Of course, it is not an easy task to design such

[6] A. H. Maslow, *Motivation and Personality* (New York: Harper & Row, 1954).

[7] F. Herzberg, B. Mausner, and B. Snyderman, *The Motivation to Work*, 2d ed. (New York: John Wiley & Sons, 1959).

[8] David McClelland, *The Achieving Society* (Princeton: D. Van Nostrand Co., 1961).

a work environment, but enlightened POM system managers are also experimenting with the results of this kind of research.

The research of Rensis Lickert indicates that individual motivation and productivity of employees are highly dependent upon the leadership styles of those who manage the work environment. Lickert contends that in work environments where work is completely standardized and where excessively demanding work standards and output controls are used as the primary means of motivation, the interest and productivity of the work force ultimately declines. Conversely, Lickert's work indicates that when management focuses on maintaining morale and interest, productivity and profits increase.[9] The message for POM system managers is a strong one; Lickert is suggesting that an environment where involvement in one's job is more important than controls will produce higher levels of output and efficiency. Progressive managers today examine with interest Lickert's work although they also see the difficulties involved in implementing this type of leadership system particularly in high-volume, standardized POM facilities.

A person's attitudes toward his work are a significant determinant of his productivity. If the work environment causes these attitudes to be hostile, or if one's job does not provide satisfaction, this inbalance will have important repercussions on the POM system. The normative message seems to be that POM decisions affecting the work environment must always examine human values as a relevant input factor.

DETERMINING THE NATURE AND DIRECTION
OF THE EXTERNAL ENVIRONMENT: FORECASTING

Forecasting enables POM systems to cope with changing environments by projecting the past and the present into the future. Predictions take the form of estimates known as demand forecasts. This prognosis may be based on past experience as revealed by records, on appraisal of consumer demand, and on the economic value of products and services to be sold in comparison with the value and appeal of those offered by competitors. Broad company policies as well as sales and advertising programs are considered in formulating forecasts.

The demand forecast is the link between the evaluation of external factors and the management of the organization's internal affairs. A forecast of demand of some type exists, at least implicitly, whenever management makes a decision in anticipation of future demand, whether this decision is to expand facilities or to manufacture another run of a particular item to

---

[9] Rensis Likert, *New Patterns in Management* (New York: McGraw-Hill Book Company, 1961).

restore inventory balances. The question of whether demand forecasts are useful is no longer argued. The real issue is how to forecast demand more reliably in order to enable the organization and its POM system to react more effectively.

More and more organizations have come to recognize the need for formal forecasts of some type and have set up formal methods for obtaining them. These formal procedures in many cases, however, are restricted to rather broad, i.e., organization-wide forecasts covering periods from a quarter to a year. Many times management fails to recognize, however, that implicit forecasts are made at a great many levels in the organization. For example, one often finds forecasting decisions which have an important influence on production-planning operations being made by storekeepers or stockroom clerks with little or no procedural or policy guidance. Determination of types of forecasts required and establishment of procedures governing these forecasts are fundamental steps in the organization of a well-conceived POM system. Chapter 13 will treat in detail the various forecasting methods available to management.

FORECASTING AND THE POM SYSTEM

The importance of forecasting to the POM system varies in different types of organizations. Companies that develop new products and whose immediate sales problem is the creation of new markets often have little interest in general business conditions. Such companies, however, are prone to underestimate the usefulness of general business forecasting and may not see the potential dangers that threaten their markets. An annual sales forecast is still needed by companies that are selling in rapidly expanding markets in order to establish a uniform weekly or monthly production rate and to gain the other advantages of stabilized production.

Organized forecasting is more necessary in companies where seasonal and cyclical fluctuations are violent. For example, consumer demand for staple foods and clothing fluctuate least over the period of the larger industry cycles. Companies in these industries need to give the state of general business only secondary consideration. On the other hand, companies in the durable goods industries, such as steel, automobiles, and similar lines, find general business forecasting not only more necessary but also more difficult.

Forecasting annual sales is desirable even in the smallest manufacturing firms if there is a large seasonal factor in sales. Production and employment can be stabilized during the year by transferring the fluctuations in sales from production to finished goods inventory, but this requires careful planning of funds flows and storage facilities.

Forecasting the course of general business and the sales of individual products becomes more important as the length of the POM process increases. The risk of doing business increases with the length of time from the procurement of raw materials to the sale of the product to the user. Tire and soap manufacturing companies, for example, are greatly concerned about the future prices of their imported raw materials because of the long time between purchase of materials and their use in production. Forecasting is relatively less important for companies which have constant stable demands and relatively short POM processes.

Forecasting is also needed because of the combination of uncertainty in resupply time and the uncertainty in demand. The following kinds of POM decisions require forecasting to overcome these uncertainties:

1. Physical facility capacity
2. Raw material purchases
3. POM system planning and control
4. Human resource planning

PHYSICAL FACILITY CAPACITY

When customer orders are received, it is a costly mistake to have too much or too little capacity. When too much capacity has been created by optimistic long-range demand forecasts, operations must proceed at uneconomically low rates. If capacity has been limited by pessimistic long-range forecasts, some orders cannot be filled. Either a very high or very low rate of operation increases the per-unit cost. Of course, no manager can expect to attain a level of orders which is equal to his capacity at all times. What he *can* hope for, however, is a capacity which will not generate prohibitively high costs in less prosperous periods. To achieve these conditions, he must know something about the long-term demand for his products and services and knowledge of the lead time necessary to add more capacity. Satisfactory knowledge of long-term demand would lead him to design his capacity at reasonable levels.

RAW MATERIAL PURCHASES

In some industries, raw materials required for the production process have long purchase lead times. This might be due to long transportation or production times, import difficulties, or seasonal availability. For example, some food companies need to forecast their markets 2 years in advance because they contract for crops still to be planted. Forecast errors in these environments can and do cause serious problems in the POM system.

POM SYSTEM PLANNING AND CONTROL

Production planning translates demand forecasts into production schedules. It determines material, personnel, and equipment requirements and prepares detailed area or department schedules. It also attempts to maintain raw materials and finished goods inventories at proper levels. Production planning has been extensively used in many companies to stabilize seasonal production schedules in order to allow long, efficient production runs.

A major purpose of forecasting is to enable the company to maintain more economical stock levels by anticipating demand more closely. Forecasting errors cause inventory mistakes, that is, carrying too little or too much. If too little is carried, the company loses the profit from sales lost through stockout. If too much is carried, the company bears an unnecessary cost through tying up its capital and risking obsolescence or perishability.

HUMAN RESOURCE PLANNING

Good forecasts can help management stabilize production and employment by removing or at least dampening the impact of seasonal variations in sales. Stabilized employment can mean better labor relations, lower employee turnover, and reduced labor costs.

Better forecasting will be needed by managements to deal constructively with the increasing demands of labor and the general public for employment security. Guaranteed annual wages, employment seniority, transferable pension rights, and severance pay all make the cost of poor human resource planning significant, and each emphasizes further the value of good forecasting.

PROVIDING POM SYSTEM FLEXIBILITY IN A DYNAMIC ENVIRONMENT

As long as consumer tastes and income increase, it seems probable that they will continue to place great emphasis upon style and new want satisfaction. Industry has little reason to believe that it can or should alter this outlook. A significant goal of any POM system must be the simultaneous achievement of some degree of production-line technology *and* the maintenance of POM system flexibility within the constraints imposed by a fickle external environment.

Flexibility to meet customer demand and future uncertainties is a joint overall responsibility within the firm and cannot be attained through parochial philosophies and timetables. It will be useful to examine briefly some individual areas within the POM system with specific attention to policies designed to provide flexibility in adapting to change in the external environment. At this point, we are more interested in the general issue of providing flexibility as opposed to a detailed examination of certain policies. Later chapters will treat responses to the need for flexibility in greater detail.

FLEXIBILITY IN FACILITIES DESIGN

Production facilities should be designed to accommodate potential fluctuations in the level of demand. Besides demand, other factors contributing to a need for flexibility include: (1) new products, (2) obsolescence of processes or machines, (3) human resource problems, and (4) the need for cost reductions. Since all facilities can be changed at some cost, a truly flexible facility is one that can be changed at minimum cost.

As between the flow shop and the job shop layout, the more flexible of the two is the job shop. It makes possible the production of a wide variety of products, facilitates the allocation of machines to jobs, and reduces vulnerability to breakdown. Other specific benefits attributed to this plan are that it allows the efficient production of a wide variety of small quantity items and minimizes disruption of equipment and personnel when phasing out old products or phasing in new ones. Minimization of costly obsolescence due to product change and easy replacement or rearrangement of one process area without affecting other areas is also possible.

The principal deficiency of job shops has been that they do not always permit the lowest product cost. If, however, there is a strong consumer's preference for maximum productive variety, these extra costs can probably be passed on to the consumer with little difficulty. Under certain conditions where the costs must be absorbed by the company, the long-run benefits of maintaining market position by retaining production flexibility may still justify the job shop mode of production.

On the other hand, a flow shop arrangement is optimal for higher volumes and operates at a lower cost per unit output. Its primary disadvantage is that it is considerably less flexible than its job shop counterpart and thus quite vulnerable to changes in consumer taste and product design.

FLEXIBILITY IN MATERIAL HANDLING

To build flexibility into material handling designs, the POM manager seeks the total system which will best meet his needs instead of looking for specific equipment. For example, he may decide to move machines or men to the material instead of moving the material through fixed processes.

Most material handling equipment is in either one of two classes: fixed-path or variable-path movement. In the fixed-path class are conveyors, cranes, and pipelines. On the other hand, trucks, powered or manual, are the most common members of the variable-path class. Variable-path equipment offers more flexibility where a number of different jobs are being performed in different places on a variety of different machines. Conversely, fixed-path equipment is the most economical for flow shop operations.

In an environment in which products and technology are constantly changing, care must be taken to avoid large investments which might impede future adaptive system changes. Developing technology has provided some interesting innovations in material handling flexibility. A trend is developing to unite automation and flexibility. Examples are remotely controlled cranes, belt conveyors capable of moving materials around corners, movements of equipment and parts directed by computers, and lift trucks with a variety of attachments to boost their flexibility.

FLEXIBILITY IN ASSEMBLY

Assembly is another area in which flexibility must be maintained. Industries are bearing greater and greater costs in order to maintain a nonrigid assembly process. Assembly tends to be labor-intensive and since wages have risen steadily, assembly wages have become a greater part of manufacturing costs. Recent surveys indicate that industries such as machinery and transportation equipment average about 54 percent of their direct labor cost in assembly. Furthermore, assembly appears to have created a technological constraint in regard to automation. Faced with these rising costs, companies have renewed their efforts to update assembly techniques while maintaining or even increasing flexibility.

One method of increasing flexibility is through modular construction. Subassemblies are prebuilt then combined later according to individual customer requirements. This procedure allows: lower inventory of work-in-process and finished goods, maintenance of complex shipping schedules, and matching productivity with demand. There is less worry about changes in demand, no heavy investment in finished goods not in demand, and no complete unit is built until the customer's order is received. This concept has been put into practice at Westinghouse's General Control Division in Buffalo. In this case, the division offers a virtually infinite variety of control cabinets. They are constructed from 200 basic sheet metal parts and can be assembled quickly with fasteners. The parts are mass produced then assembled to fit individual specifications.

FLEXIBILITY IN PROCESSES

Implementing some of the new POM processes while simultaneously maintaining production flexibility is quite a challenge. Because the wider range of products being offered by firms today has led to shorter lead times and shorter production runs, automatic processing systems are at a disadvantage in providing economies in the process. To begin with, an automated system is designed to operate economically at a particular output rate—usually a high one. This places a heavy responsibility on the marketing function because it must sell the output of the automated system and try to overcome the fluctuations in demand. Secondly, the design of the product affects the design of the system, and characteristically, the designing and building of special purpose automated systems is very costly. For this reason, once a system is constructed for a particular product, it is liable to be obsolete as soon as the product is. Indeed, rapid payback is an absolute requirement in view of the risks being born by the company in committing itself to a rigid production system. Finally, an automated system is often inflexible in regard to the inputs or materials that it can handle.

POM systems are often forced to cope with many variations or styles while being expected to maintain flexibility and some semblance of a production line process. One feasible and practical solution is to manufacture four or five basic models of a product and vary them according to color, style, options, etc. In this way, a certain degree of production-line technology is maintained at the same time that the consumers' desire for increased variety is satisfied. For example, in the automobile industry, manufacturers assemble several basic models or types of cars and solve the issue of variety by varying each model according to color, options, etc.

Specific solutions to the problem of process flexibility have been adopted by Chrysler Corporation. In 1967, Chrysler Corporation installed a computer network which linked the company's 7 United States car assembly plants, Chrysler's own 26 parts manufacturing plants, and 97 independent suppliers. Chrysler Corporation is apparently using the system to gain the flexibility it needs to react swiftly to dealer orders and still maintain reasonable inventory levels. The improved reaction ability comes from shortening of communication times rather than production or shipment times.

Earlier in this chapter, we reviewed the necessity for garment manufacturers to produce many styles within the same physical facility. The need for flexibility is of course most severe in the "style factories," that is, where most of the product line is materially changed each selling season. POM systems in these environments cope with the complexity which results and its effect upon scheduling and control by a fairly well-organized procedure.

An essential first step in the procedure is a knowledge of the styles to be produced and the approximate quantities of each. Given this information, the POM system must make a detailed analysis of the entire product line. The object of this analysis is to find similarities among the styles thereby assigning them to a product "group." The net result is that of reducing a complex product line of many styles to a smaller number of product groups. The similarities should reflect similarity of operations, sequence, work content, etc. Once the product line has been reduced to these groupings, the actual production can be planned.

The approach is to set up a common parts section for all styles. This means that the sewing machine operator can stay on the same operation even though the style may change. As an example, the operator assigned to the "make collar" operation might switch from a round to a square collar. This is much easier than to switch from "make collar" to "sideseam." Systems are thus set up by operation rather than by style. This simple innovation has resulted in productivity increases as high as 50 percent in some style shops.

FLEXIBILITY IN HUMAN RESOURCE UTILIZATION

Today much thought and effort goes into devising nonrigid POM systems aimed at increasing human satisfaction within the work environment. Some of this work involves a recognition of the deficiencies of automated lines and a movement toward a revival of the "craftsman" concept of manufacturing. Organizations attempt to provide increased job satisfaction by making the workers' tasks more interesting and by increasing their responsibility, i.e., letting them handle additional assembly steps and even some of the inspection. Results indicate decreased rejects and scrappage, and increased morale. In one Worthington Corporation installation, for example, nine short lines have replaced two long ones. Various heating products are assembled by two-man teams. Each team is responsible for assembly and testing. The names of team members are placed inside the packages. Quality is higher, and the short assembly line allows greater flexibility in scheduling.

Useful insights into how workers view their jobs and how POM systems can properly respond were gained from a study of an automobile plant by Charles R. Walker and Robert H. Guest.[10] From the standpoint of the worker, the automobile factory has certain characteristics which are typical of mass production:

1. Most jobs are mechanically paced.
2. The jobs are clearly repetitive.
3. There is a low skill requirement.
4. Social interaction is severely limited.

Typical comments of the workers were that there was not enough time to do the job right if any trouble was encountered. They disliked the fact that if you ever got behind, it was very difficult to catch up. One worker's comment aptly summed up his sentiment: "The work isn't hard; it's the never ending pace . . . The guys yell "Hurrah' whenever the line breaks down . . . You can hear it all over the plant."

There was a widespread belief among employees that the machine

[10] Walker and Guest, "The Man on the Assembly Line," *Organizations and Human Behavior* (Englewood Cliffs, N.J.: Prentice-Hall, Inc., 1967).

had completely taken over and on mass-production lines the worker had no influence on quality. Also the management felt that the worker no longer cared or got satisfaction from doing a good job (as in Theory X). On the contrary, half the workers interviewed in the auto plant were discouraged because they felt they were unable to do the quality job expected of them.

In situations such as this, management must be interested in modifying on-the-job conditions of work to increase efficiency and worker satisfaction. By improved methods of recruiting and selection, the organization can increase the hiring of workers who prefer or are indifferent to mechanical pacing and thus improve total worker efficiency.

The major clue to improvement however is found in providing features in a job which appeal to the worker's needs:

1. Social interaction to break the monotony.
2. Enough operations on a particular job to give variety.
3. Opportunity to work back up the line or build up a backlog and get a "breather."
4. Opportunity to alternate between jobs of substantially different character.[11]

Present technology in mass production often renders impractical the implementation of many of these suggestions. One striking finding of the auto plant study, however, was the psychological importance even minute changes had on worker motivation. There are many opportunities today for worker satisfaction and efficiency through minor POM process designs which appeal to the worker's psychological needs.

CONCLUSION

In this chapter, we have shown how both the design and operation of POM systems are affected by the characteristics of their environment. Implicit in this discussion has been the hypothesis that continued economic viability of any operating system demands that the system possess the ability to forecast environmental changes and the flexibility to react to these changes. Specific examples of operating systems which have been successful in adopting this posture were offered. The next several chapters will treat in detail the methodology by which this sytem posture can be attained.

QUESTIONS

1. State the ways in which the major factors in the nation's economy affect POM systems.

[11] *Ibid.*

2. Do you think that such economic factors will have a greater or lesser effect on most POM systems in the next decade? Justify your answer.

3. Why are accurate forecasts of demand necessary for the effective operation of POM systems? What would you suggest are the symptoms of a POM system that suffers from inadequate demand forecasts?

4. What issues would have to be faced in deciding how large to build a plant to manufacture lasers? What kinds of informational needs are there in a decision of this type?

5. When sales forecasts have been too optimistic, what effects are felt by the POM system? What happens when sales forecasts have been too low?

6. Can a firm maintain flexibility as it increases its use of automation? How is this possible?

7. It has been offered as a hypothesis that in mass-production lines, workers have little or no influence on the quality of the finished product. Do you agree? Explain your position.

8. What kinds of things can be done to make the job more interesting for a production worker who must drill several hundred identical holes each day?

9. How should the financial implications of reducing boredom be treated? What are the significant costs of avoiding boredom on the part of workers? What are the relevant benefits an organization can expect?

10. Suppose it were accepted that industrial robots would replace 40 percent of production workers over the next 10 years. What are the implications of this for POM managers? What plans should be made now?

11. Is the cost of providing POM system flexibility very visible to top management? Is it as visible as say an excessive scrap cost? How would top management know whether too much flexibility or too little flexibility was being maintained?

12. What are the three most significant social developments during the last decade in terms of their effect upon POM systems? What in your opinion, has been the most significant legal development in terms of its effect on POM systems during the same period?

13. Which one of the following reasons is the most likely reason why it is necessary for some POM systems to produce-to-order instead of maintaining an inventory: (a) low expected demand, (b) uncertainty of product specifications, (c) the uncertainty of demand, (d) the type of manufacturing facility. Why?

14. Do you agree or disagree with this statement: The use of a product basis for specializing the POM facility rather than a functional basis makes coordination and control much simpler. What are your reasons?

15. Would there be distinguishable differences in the POM system of a small firm as opposed to a very large firm? What would be the nature of any such differences?

16. What kinds of constraints to action in POM systems are created by the political process in the environment? Give five examples of such phenomena.

CASE: THE WENDEL COMPANY

The Wendel Company manufactures children's dresses; its annual sales volume is about $4 million. Children's dresses enjoy two heavy selling seasons: "back-to-school" (dresses for this period have to be available in the retail establishments by July 15 each year) and "Easter" (dresses for Easter season must be available to the retailer by February 1 each year). There are two other much smaller seasons: summer and Christmas. The two largest selling seasons account for 70 percent of the total sales volume; the back-to-school season alone accounts for 45 percent of the total annual sales volume of the Wendel Company.

The marketing–POM strategy that has been followed by the Wendel Company is as follows: A sample line of dresses (approximately 100 different styles) is prepared for the back-to-school season. This is shown to retailers by the company sales force sometime in February; orders are taken at that time. When sufficient orders warranting the manufacture of one style have been received, the company then orders the necessary material and puts that style into production. Although this marketing–POM strategy avoids the manufacture of dresses which would not be attractive to retailers and thus minimizes end of year dumping of unsold styles, it creates other problems for the Wendel Company. Since 45 percent of the annual volume is done in such a short time, the plant cannot keep up with orders once they start coming in, with the result that in the past back-to-school season, the company was unable to produce $400,000 worth of orders it had accepted; at the same time, retail stores returned approximately $175,000 worth of back-to-school dresses which had arrived at the stores after September 15 (too late for the back-to-school season). The same problem exists with respect to other selling seasons, but, of course, the dollar magnitude is somewhat less.

The sales manager of the Wendel Company is quite concerned over the poor performance of the company with respect to timely shipment of orders. The POM manager is also quite concerned over the fact that having to wait for an accumulation of orders before beginning production causes him to have to hire and train large numbers of employees for short production seasons, only to discharge them at the end of that season. The sales manager maintains that this is simply the nature of the dress business and cannot be helped; he has suggested that the POM manager hire employees at the beginning of each season at a faster rate. The POM manager, on the other hand, has suggested several times that the sales manager should forecast sales and authorize the production of certain items far in advance of the actual season. The sales manager rejected this idea as being impossible, given the nature of the children's dress industry.

You are the president of the Wendel Company and have called a meeting of the sales manager and POM manager to discuss possible solutions to this problem.

CASE: KNIGHTDALE PRODUCERS

Knightdale Producers is a commercial producer of chickens; in their operation, they incubate eggs, hatch them, and then feed the chickens until they reach approximately 3 pounds. At that time, they are sold to a commercial processor.

Knightdale Producers has used local farm labor in their operation. None of the jobs is very skilled, and they have been able in the past to secure enough labor in the local area at a very low wage rate. Labor accounts for approximately 40 percent of their total cost of production. Knightdale earns a return of 11 percent on invested capital.

Knightdale Producers has just been notified that their operation is covered under new state legislation proposed for enactment during the next 6 months. If this legislation is passed, Knightdale Producers will be required to double their present wage rates. What specific action do you propose the company take now in light of this information? Indicate each step you feel is necessary, and state what the step is designed to accomplish.

part

DESIGNING THE PRODUCTION/OPERATIONS MANAGEMENT SYSTEM

three

chapter

OUTPUT DESIGN

six

The development of an actual product design involves the consideration of many relevant factors.
In this chapter, we shall concentrate on four. First
among those discussed is *materials and processing
considerations:* marketability, durability, cost, and
demand-meeting ability. Crucial to the product's
performance, reliability, and production cost are
the *specifications and tolerances* which need to
be established for each of its components. The
use of *standardization and interchangeability* of
parts and products whenever possible helps consumers and reduces production, inventory and
marketing costs. The last product design factor
discussed here is *human engineering*, which
examines those aspects of product design which
consider the potential interface between the
finished product and its projected users.

MATERIALS AND PROCESSING CONSIDERATIONS

OVERALL COST OF RAW MATERIAL is most imp.

POSSIBLE CHOICES

One of the most critical decisions in the design
process is the choice of raw materials. Some of the

121

components of a product may be selected on the basis that the present state of technology or common usage dictates only one economic alternative (e.g., 2 by 4s in basic construction of private homes or tungsten filament in incandescent light bulbs). In most instances, however, there does exist a range of choices in the selection of raw materials. A bridge could be made of reinforced concrete or structural steel; an egg carton could be made of fiberboard, pressed paper, or molded plastic foam. When a choice is to be made, the designer will want to select the material which offers the most desirable physical characteristics at the least possible cost. Thus he will analyze each alternative raw material from the standpoint of *desirability* of the product to the customer and of *cost* of both raw material and processing to the firm.

When analyzing the appeal of the finished product to the potential buyer, many factors play important roles. The product is often expected to be durable; consider the appeal of lightweight durability needed in a tennis racket. Sometimes attractiveness is paramount; consider, for example, the value of eye-catching packaging for a breakfast cereal. Another critical decision involves the market segment in which this product is designed to compete. In some cases, status or novelty value may be critical while in others low price may supersede all other factors. The option of luxurious leather upholstery may have real appeal to Mercedes Benz buyers but may be totally meaningless to potential VW owners.

Important for POM purposes, however, once marketing has narrowed the group of alternatives to those acceptable to the consumer, are the costs of inputs and of raw material processing. The cost of the input can be a routine matter of finding would-be suppliers (if, indeed, they have not already made contact on their own initiative), and of collecting price estimates. However, determining the processing cost is considerably more complex. Of real importance is the cost of tooling and setting up machines to handle a particular raw material. Another consideration pertains to the amount of labor that is required for processing and handling. Some materials may need a high level of quality control, and others may vary in the amount of labor that is required for processing and handling. When considered jointly, all of these considerations of cost and appeal in selection of raw materials and processing can easily become complicated.

AN EXAMPLE OF CHOICE

To illustrate the choice process, let us consider the example of a medium-sized manufacturer of color television sets. The firm must decide on a material for the cabinet of a new, 117 square inch, portable, color television that it is going to add to its product line. The marketing staff indicates that this set will be bought as a first or replacement set by apartment dwellers and by those of limited means desiring a color television. It will also be an ideal set for those wanting a second or third television set. It is anticipated that the firm will sell 100,000 units a year.

Consumer acceptance. A vice president of the firm has asked the design group to prepare studies on each of three possible materials for the cabinet (wood, plastic, and sheet metal), and to make recommendations as to the advisability of each. The design group reports that with respect to consumer appeal, each of the materials under consideration has its own inherent advantages and disadvantages. Most of the sampled, potential buyers like the look and feel of wood. A well-finished wood cabinet creates an image of a high quality, expensive, and handcrafted product. Yet because it is relatively heavy in weight, it is subject to scratches and gouges, has little moisture resistance, and as a housing for a portable-television has questionable value.

With a plastic material, the design group indicates a much lighter cabinet could be achieved. By utilizing the new, more durable and crack resistant plastics, the cabinet would have greater scratch and dent resistance than either wood or metal. Further, it is the most moisture resistant of the three. On the negative side is the poor image one segment of the consumer sample (those over 35 years old) has of plastics. This group commonly associates all plastics with those early products of the 1940s and 1950s which readily cracked upon impact or with weather changes and which were then associated with an inferior quality product. On the other hand, the younger market segment positively associates attractive plastic with a desirable, modern appearance.

The design group reports that by using sheet metal a somewhat lighter cabinet could be achieved. It would also have high crack resistance. Unfortunately, metal is the most easily dented of the three materials, and it needs to have some kind of protective finish to protect the surface against corrosion. Although there exists the possibility of using a thicker and necessarily heavier sheet metal (virtually eliminating the denting problem), the resulting cabinet would weigh about the same as a comparable plastic one and would also be difficult to form into a cabinet. While a sheet metal cabinet conjures up images of mass production, most people have neither a strong bias for nor against a properly and attractively finished one.

Raw material considerations. Results of investigating the cost of materials necessary to build an attractive, durable, crack and dent resistant cabinet are the following. Good quality plastics are as expensive to produce as all but the most costly hardwoods. When considering all costs, the least expensive to produce from the raw materials and manufacturing standpoint is the sheet metal one. A wood grained vinyl covering may be added at minimal expense to enhance the cabinet's appearance and appeal. Indeed, with an additional expenditure, both the plastic and metal case can take advantage over the appeal of wood (through a simulated wood-grain finish), without having to become involved with its shortcomings.

Processing considerations. The three materials also differ in processing considerations. The firm already has an excellent woodworking shop which makes the wood cabinets for the firm's console television line. Although the cabinet shop is presently operating at capacity, it is readily expandable. For a small investment (when compared to the purchase cost of plastic molding and sheet metal working equipment), the additional saws, sanders, planers, and spray guns could be quickly obtained. The firm currently does not have a plastic molder of sufficient capacity to make the cabinets. Such a machine would cost at least $80,000. In addition, this machine would require special expensive dies to shape the cabinet. As for stamping and forming presses for producing sheet metal cabinets, the firm already has these. Further, the existing presses have enough idle capacity to supply the needed production. However, if sheet metal cabinets are chosen and if business keeps increasing as it has in the past few years, an additional press would be needed to meet the increased total demand. Cabinet stamping and forming tooling would have to be made immediately. Again the expense would run into many thousands of dollars and would take several months to prepare.

Labor considerations. Whichever cabinet type is selected, additional labor will be needed. Several additional cabinetmakers and finishers would have to be hired if wood were selected. Being members of a declining trade in the firm's area, such workers would be difficult to hire. Both other material alternatives do not require such intensive and specialized labor. Each would necessitate only one additional worker who would be semiskilled and easily hired. If plastic were used, this worker would operate the semi-automatic molding equipment. Were metal cabinets chosen, the additional employee would be needed to finish the cabinets. Thus, both the plastic and metal options involve less labor cost and pose smaller potential problems in finding qualified employees.

None of the case alternatives appears to present significant quality control problems. Most defects in wood cabinets are easily reworkable. Plastic molding technology is such that no problems should arise if the dies are kept clean and the temperature setting is carefully adjusted. Similarly, stamping and forming of sheet metal cases can be expected to involve no undue difficulties, as long as the dies are maintained. It is expected, however, that it will take some weeks before the sheet metal finisher has satisfactorily mastered his job.

Making the choice. The firm's vice president approached the choice of the best cabinet alternative based on the facts presented to him by this design study. He quickly eliminated wood because of cost and performance considerations. The cost to produce 100,000 wood cabinets a year would be much greater than either of the other alternatives. Further reinforcing his opinion was the fact that this new product had to be not only durable without special handling but also portable. On both counts, wood failed.

Making the choice between plastic and metal was a more difficult one. The favorable wood image could be transferred to both plastic and metal through the use of a simulated wood grain finish. At 100,000 units a year, the material-plus-labor costs were comparable as were the costs of tooling. Counterbalancing each other was the dentability of the metal cabinet with both the consumer misconception of the durability of the plastic and its heavier weight. The vice president concluded that the decision rested upon the choice between a definite investment in a plastic molder or the possibility of having to buy additional metal presses. Although both had the same present value to the firm, he justified his choice of the metal cabinet covered with a wood-grained vinyl in the following manner. If the new portable set wasn't a success, the firm would not be stuck with a major investment of the plastic molder for which few alternative uses could be found. On the other hand, if new set sales increased above their expected 100,000 unit level, the chances are good that the whole product lines' sales would also increase and that the new presses would be needed anyway.

DESIGN SPECIFICATIONS AND TOLERANCES

Another important aspect of product design is the problem of determining design specifications. A design specification is composed of a statement of an ideal value or characteristic of a product and the allowable deviation from this ideal. This acceptable deviation is known as a *tolerance*. A designer might, for example, specify the thickness of a piece of sheet steel used in making a part be 0.1 inches $\pm$0.001 inches, the percent composition by weight of rocket fuel to be 5 percent $\pm$0.25 percent of a particular chemical compound, a surface to be flat within $\pm$0.0001 inches; or all angles of a gear to be within $\pm$0.1 degrees of the stated values.

While the need for the ideal part of the specification is clear, one might, however, question in today's world of mass production of seemingly identical products why we should worry about deviations from an ideal; after all, one would think that all the output was the same. This is not true if you measure very closely. Consider a press which stamps out hundreds of sheet steel parts an hour. The dies forming the cutting surfaces will obviously wear with time. The sheet steel will vary in thickness and, thus, in the force required to cut it. The steel corporation's processing is not perfect either. The press operator may not always get the sheet perfectly positioned on the die. The press itself has a certain degree of slippage between its parts. Vibrations and variations in the sheets and their positioning will cause the press to perform slightly different each time a part is stamped out.

As a result of such variations, it is necessary for the designer to define not only the desired value but also the permissible variation from it in order that parts can be assembled into a product which will function properly. Workers involved in one small part of a process have no way of knowing what accuracy is required unless they are so informed by the tolerance limits.

How does the designer know which degree of accuracy will be an appropriate tolerance for a particular product? Obviously a certain tolerance will be necessary if the product is to be standardized, functional, and interchangeable. Unnecessary precision, however, as we shall see, often leads to increased production cost because of its effect on raw materials, labor, tooling, and quality control.

To understand the process of selecting specifications, it is first necessary to distinguish between overall specifications and those individual part specifications necessary to ensure that overall specifications will be achieved. If you examine the literature which is packed with a stereo set, you often find such technical specifications as the set's maximum harmonic distortion, music power, and channel separation. By no means are these listed specifications the complete product specifications; they are merely summary statistics. In order to ensure that these qualities will be present in all products, the manufacturer uses many other specifications on the subassemblies, parts, and materials going into the stereo. Without the latter, he could not be even reasonably sure that the product would be similar to what he claims.

Initially, the overall specifications take the form of goals for the design process and may be based on any number of diverse criteria such as salability, reliability, profitability, or the firm's capability for achieving these characteristics. Using the selected overall goals, a search is begun for a product design which will achieve these specifications. Material and part specifications must be developed such that, when the materials are transformed into the parts and assembled, the finished product meets its overall specifications. This goal setting process can, as in the case of a jet transport, take years, because of the complexities, possibilities, and tradeoffs involved. Occasionally, it may be necessary or desirable to change some of the overall specifications when it becomes clear that the existing ones cannot be met at an economically reasonable cost in the available time.

PROCEDURE FOR CHOOSING SPECIFICATIONS

A critical phase of this overall process is developing the part specifications. The choosing of part specifications can be described as a three-step procedure.

1. *The most desired or basic value of the specification should be selected* in light of the part's function and its relationship to the other

aspects of the part design. Thus, an automotive engineer who is trying to determine the diameter for the pistons of an automobile engine must base his selection on the prespecified horsepower (overall specification), and on the tradeoffs between combinations of length of piston movement and piston diameter each of which can be used to achieve the desired horsepower. While the procedure sounds relatively simple, it actually involves a number of complex engineering calculations.

2. *The loosest tolerance about the desired value that still will produce the product's overall specifications should be determined.* Often there exists a maximum amount of part variation which allows the part to be assembled and function properly. Since different products have different functions, the degree of tightness of this critical variation of tolerance can vary significantly. For an example of this concept compare air rifle shot which typically have a roundness variation observable with the naked eye to precision ball bearings used in a research instrument. The latter may be within a few millionths of an inch of being perfectly spherical. To operate a railroad train safely at a maximum speed of 60 miles per hour requires a track road bed whose maximum lateral deviation per 100 feet is no more than $\frac{1}{2}$ inch. However, to safely operate one of the high speed trains on the Boston-Washington corridor whose maximum speed will approach 150 miles per hour requires that there be no more than $\frac{1}{16}$ of an inch of variation. Sometimes even a critical tolerance is beyond technological capability. A well-known example involves the transistor. Even though the principle of the transistor had been known for many years, it wasn't until the 1950s that molecule-to-molecule bonding techniques were developed which made this replacement for the vacuum tube possible. In many other cases, only the most extreme conditions of dust-free handling and super precision tooling can produce a limited quantity of goods meeting exacting tolerances.

3. Finally, *the most economical tolerance satisfying the critical tolerance should be chosen.* Since the critical tolerance is the loosest acceptable one, the chosen tolerance will always be as tight or tighter than the former.

In many cases, the most economical tolerance for a part is its critical tolerance. Tighter tolerances mean higher quality raw material, more highly skilled labor, more precise equipment, and higher costs to produce the part. When the critical tolerance is not the most economical one, other cost factors have obviously come into consideration. Sometimes by tightening selected part tolerances, the cost to assemble the part can be significantly reduced. Thus, a product design should seek that tolerance level which not only satisfies the crucial level but which also minimizes the manufacturing cost of all the parts *plus*

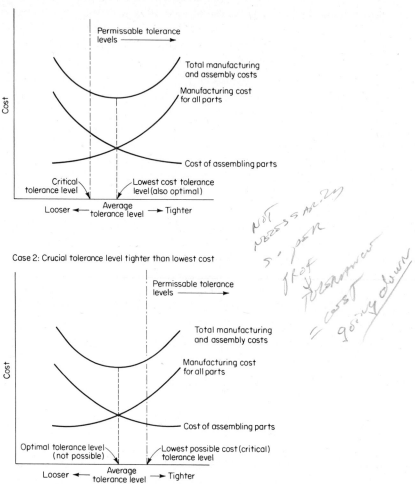

Figure 6-1 *Selecting the most economical part tolerances*

the cost of assembling them. Figure 6-1 depicts the selection of the most economical tolerance. In case (1), the tolerance level that was finally selected is *tighter* than the critical tolerance level because that selection minimizes total cost in case (2). The optimal tolerance level from a total cost point of view is not physically feasible hence the critical tolerance level is selected.

The selection of a most economical part tolerance is clearly predicated on the assumption that the most economic processing methods will be used in achieving each of the feasible part tolerances. For the production of any part, there usually exists a variety of processes

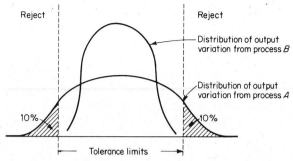

Figure 6-2 *Two processes with different tolerance-meeting capabilities*

which will produce the same product. Figure 6-2 shows two processing alternatives, *A* and *B*, and their tolerance meeting capabilities; each of these capabilities is described by its distribution of output variation for the characteristic in question. Such variation for a particular process arises from the raw material variations, from variations in the manner in which the workers produce each part, and from the inherent variations in the processing equipment. No machine functions exactly the same each time. While part of a machine's variation is due to wear, another part stems from the machine's clearance (the fact that its own parts do not fit perfectly). From Figure 6-2 we can see that process *B* is more capable than *A* since almost all of *B*'s output can meet the tolerance while at least 20 percent of process *A*'s output will be

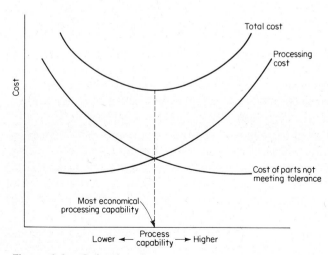

Figure 6-3 *Selecting the most economical process for a particular tolerance*

rejected. This does not mean that process *B* is necessarily the more economical alternative of the two. The final choice will depend on the total cost including *both* the part manufacturing cost and the cost of the rejects. It could easily happen that the extra cost of process *B* would be *more* than the cost of the rejects produced by process *A*. Such would very likely be the case in a situation where raw material costs were negligible compared to the total cost of production.

In general, the more capable, and hence, the more expensive the process, the lower the amount of money lost in the rejects. Figure 6-3 shows the typical nature of these two costs as a function of process capability. The process choice is optimum where the sum of the two costs is minimum.

STANDARDIZATION AND INTERCHANGEABILITY

Another important facet of product design is the industry-wide standardization of parts and products. The dimensions of items such as lightbulbs, screws, nuts and bolts, tin cans, brick, concrete block, and sheet steel have long been standardized so that the products of all manufacturers producing them may be used interchangeably.

This arrangement is beneficial to producers and consumers. The producer can be assured of a potentially large market, making it possible to take advantage of the economics of high-volume production. The purchaser will incur less expense by being able to buy ready-made goods of a consistent dimension at lower cost. Secure in the knowledge that exact replacements will always be available, he need not build up large inventories or be unduly concerned with the future cost of these replacements or of their availability in a particular section of the country. And he need not be bothered with having to design and manufacture special parts of equivalent function to those standard parts already available. Imagine the greatly increased expense and bother to the consumer if all manufacturers of lamps and lighting fixtures produced their own size bulbs and if none of these could be interchanged. Imagine, too, the fantastic inventories of replacement parts for automobiles if each model of each brand of car required entirely different components down to the smallest screw. Consider also the difficulty to the manufacturer who would have to produce such an endless variety of parts. The American National Standards Institute, Inc., the Society of Automotive Engineers, and the American Society for Testing Metals are organizations which have developed standards and which have promoted industry-wide cooperation in adhering to them.

Although most industry-wide standardization is initiated by the desire for convenience and economy, some standardization practices are instituted to comply with government regulation and control. Pasteurization of milk leads to a uniformly germ-free product, and quality grading or sizing of such food items as meat, eggs, and fresh fruit has produced useful guidelines for the purchaser. The safety specifications for automobiles and the ICC regulation of the public carriers, airlines, trains, and buses are other examples.

Standardization of certain products within a particular firm is advantageous both from the standpoint of design and cost. If an existing part can be incorporated into a new design, no new tooling or labor training may be necessary, and the increased volume will typically lower costs. On the other hand, excessive standardization within one firm can reduce the firm's competitive capability by narrowing the range of choice the firm offers to its consumers.

Always press for standardization

HUMAN ENGINEERING

A product should be designed so that it may be easily used. If a hand tool is to be employed effectively, it should conform to the shape of the hand and not require any unusual or undue position or force in its operations. Knobs and dials should be within comfortable reach and any markings on them should be readily recognized. Any tool or machine should be safe to use. In each of these cases, human engineering is the term applied to the design function which is concerned with the interface of the machine with its user or operator.

Although the basic ideas of human engineering had been incorporated into the design of products for many years, the design of clothing, cockpits, and oxygen masks for the Air Corps during World War II gave the field a tremendous impetus. Today a whole discipline has evolved from using and developing measurements of the human body; serious study of its capabilities and limitations is necessary in order to design clothing, equipment, workplaces, and signals. Examples of the extent of these studies can be seen from the figures and tables in this section which form a part of our examination of the human engineering procedure.

The procedure for the human engineering of a product has four steps:

1. *Identify what human characteristics or physical senses are needed to interact with the product in order for it to fulfill its function.* A ballpoint pen or knife must fit comfortably into a hand. A desk lamp must provide shadowless illumination with a minimum of visual glare. In some cases, more than one factor comes into play; for example,

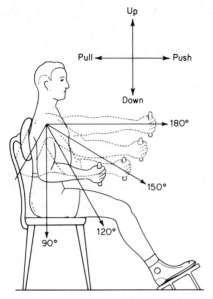

Up

Pull ← → Push

Down

Side view of subject in study on arm strength, showing various angular positions of upper arm. For each position, maximum strength was determined for pull, push, up, and down movements as well as for in and out movements as shown below.

180°

150°

120°

90°

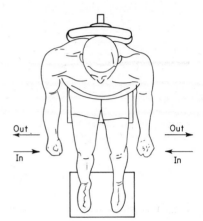

Out

In

Out

In

Top view of subject shown in above. The in and out movements were made at each of the arm positions shown above.

Arm Strength, in Pounds, of Movements in Various Directions for Different Angular Positions of Upper Arm

(For 5th percentiles and means)

Angle of arm, degrees	5th percentile		Mean		5th percentile		Mean	
	Left	Right	Left	Right	Left	Right	Left	Right
	Pull				Push			
180	50	52	116	120	42	50	126	138
150	42	56	112	122	30	42	111	123
120	34	42	94	104	26	36	99	103
90	32	37	80	88	22	36	83	86
60	26	24	64	63	22	34	80	92
	Up				Down			
180	9	14	41	43	13	17	35	41
150	15	18	52	56	18	20	41	47
120	17	24	54	60	21	26	51	58
90	17	20	52	56	21	26	49	53
60	15	20	44	49	18	20	46	51
	In				Out			
180	13	20	43	50	8	14	30	34
150	15	20	47	54	8	15	29	33
120	20	22	45	53	10	15	30	34
90	16	18	48	50	10	16	33	37
60	17	20	50	52	12	17	32	42

Figure 6-4. *Man's ability to exert selected forces [From E. J. McCormick, Human Factors Engineering, 2d ed. (New York: McGraw-Hill Book Company, 1964), Figs. 8-13, 8-14, and Table 8-2, pp. 232–233.]*

automotive seating should conform to the contours of the body in a manner which minimizes fatigue as well as maximizes the degree of unrestricted vision.

2. *Identify the users.* Define the physical or sensory characteristics of the users. Since women are the primary users of kitchens, kitchen appliances should be designed for their use, taking into account their smaller stature and lesser ability to exert force. Studies have shown that truck drivers are typically physically larger than the average man; consequently, truck cabs should be designed with more than normal room and space in them. Writing instruments for preschool and primary age children should be larger in diameter that those designed for older ones because their manual dexterity and hand-eye coordination is not as fully developed.

3. *Analyze the nature of user characteristics.* If a product requires force to operate, then that force which the user can comfortably exert should be identified. Figure 6-4 illustrates the results of one of the several studies made in this area. The designer of chairs and sofas must examine the lower leg heights, seat to back of knee distances, hip widths, etc., of Figures 6-5 and 6-6. Comparable anthropological data are also available for children. Indeed there probably exists a chart for any anthropological measure in which the designer might have an interest.

Some products involve the production of sound, either as a primary function as in the case of a warning buzzer or as a noisy by-product of an essential operation, such as a typewriter, vacuum cleaner, or electric turbine. In the former case, the designer must address himself to the production of effective or pleasing sound. The buzzer should be audible to the majority of the population without causing undue discomfort to those with very acute hearing (see Figure 6-7). Noise that goes above the level of comfortable speech, as in the case of certain high-speed machines, can cause hearing loss or damage.

Vision plays an important part in the use of some products. Knowledge of line of sight when sitting is helpful in designing the tilt of theater or auditorium seating. Fields of vision influence the arrangement of auto, airplane, and machinery instrument panels. Numerous studies have been conducted on instrument layout and design. Figures 6-8 and 6-9 give the result of two of these. Note the significant improvements which can be made through proper design.

4. The final step in the human engineering of a product, is to *identify the critical portion of the user's distribution.* Having made this identification, one determines an appropriate design parameter.

	Dimensional Element	Dimension (in inches except where noted)	
		5th Percentile	95th Percentile
	Weight	132 lb	201 lb
A	1 Vertical reach	77.0	89.0
	2 Stature	65.0	73.0
	3 Eye to floor	61.0	69.0
	4 Side arm reach from CL of body	29.0	34.0
	5 Crotch to floor	30.0	36.0
B	1 Forward arm reach	28.0	33.0
	2 Chest circumference	35.0	43.0
	3 Waist circumference	28.0	38.0
	4 Hip circumference	34.0	42.0
	5 Thigh circumference	20.0	25.0
	6 Calf circumference	13.0	16.0
	7 Ankle circumference	8.0	10.0
	8 Foot length	9.8	11.3
	9 Elbow to floor	41.0	46.0
C	1 Head width	5.7	6.4
	2 Interpupillary distance	2.27	2.74
	3 Head length	7.3	8.2
	4 Head height	—	10.2
	5 Chin to eye	—	5.0
	6 Head circumference	21.5	23.5
D	1 Hand length	6.9	8.0
	2 Hand width	3.7	4.4
	3 Hand thickness	1.05	1.28
	4 Fist circumference	10.7	12.4
	5 Wrist circumference	6.3	7.5
E	1 Arm swing, aft	40 degrees	40 degrees
	2 Foot width	3.5	4.0
F	1 Shoulder width	17.0	19.0
	2 Sitting height to floor (std chair)	52.0	56.0
	3 Eye to floor (std chair)	47.4	51.5
	4 Standard chair	18.0	18.0
	5 Hip breadth	13.0	15.0
	6 Width between elbows	15.0	20.0
G	0 Arm reach (finger grasp)	30.0	35.0
	1 Vertical reach	45.0	53.0
	2 Head to seat	33.8	38.0
	3 Eye to seat	29.4	33.5
	4 Shoulder to seat	21.0	25.0
	5 Elbow rest	7.0	11.0
	6 Thigh clearance	4.8	6.5
	7 Forearm length	13.6	16.2
	8 Knee clearance to floor	20.0	23.0
	9 Lower leg height	15.7	18.2
	10 Seat length	14.8	21.5
	11 Buttock-knee length	21.9	36.7
	12 Buttock-toe clearance	32.0	37.0
	13 Buttock-foot length	39.0	46.0

Note: All except critical dimensions have been rounded off to the nearest inch.

Figure 6-5 *Selected dimensions of the male human body, ages 18 to 45 [From W. E. Woodson and D. W. Conover,* Human Engineering Guide for Equipment Designers, *2d ed. (Berkeley: University of California Press, 1966).]*

	Dimensional Element	Dimension (in inches except where noted)	
		5th Percentile	95th Percentile
	Weight	102 lb	150 lb
A	1 Vertical reach	69.0	81.0
	2 Stature	60.0	69.0
	3 Eye to floor	56.0	64.0
	4 Side arm reach from CL of body	27.0	38.0
	5 Crotch to floor	24.0	30.0
B	1 Forward arm reach	24.0	35.0
	2 Chest circumference (bust)	30.0	37.0
	3 Waist circumference	23.6	28.7
	4 Hip circumference	33.0	40.0
	5 Thigh circumference	19.0	24.0
	6 Calf circumference	11.7	15.0
	7 Ankle circumference	7.8	9.3
	8 Foot length	8.7	10.2
	9 Elbow to floor	34.0	46.0
C	1 Head width	5.4	6.1
	2 Interpupillary distance	1.91	2.94
	3 Head length	6.4	7.3
	4 Head height	—	9.0
	5 Chin to eye	—	4.25
	6 Head circumference	20.4	22.7
D	1 Hand length	6.2	7.3
	2 Hand width	3.2	4.0
	3 Hand thickness	0.84	1.14
	4 Fist circumference	9.1	10.7
	5 Wrist circumference	5.5	6.9
E	1 Arm swing, aft	40 degrees	40 degrees
	2 Foot length	3.2	3.9
F	1 Shoulder width	13.0	19.0
	2 Sitting height to floor (std chair)	45.0	55.0
	3 Eye to floor (std chair)	41.0	51.0
	4 Standard chair	18.0	18.0
	5 Hip breadth	12.5	15.4
	6 Width between elbows	11.0	23.0
G	0 Arm reach (finger grasp)	22.0	33.0
	1 Vertical reach	39.0	50.0
	2 Head to seat	27.0	38.0
	3 Eye to seat	25.0	32.0
	4 Shoulder to seat	18.0	25.0
	5 Elbow rest	4.0	12.0
	6 Thigh clearance	3.5	6.0
	7 Forearm length	14.0	18.0
	8 Knee clearance to floor	17.0	22.0
	9 Lower leg height	13.5	18.8
	10 Seat length	13.0	23.0
	11 Buttock-knee length	18.0	27.0
	12 Buttock-toe clearance	27.0	37.0
	13 Buttock-foot length	34.0	49.0

Note: All except critical dimensions have been rounded off to the nearest inch.

Figure 6-6 *Selected dimensions of the female human body, ages 18 to 45 [From W. E. Woodson and D. W. Conover,* Human Engineering Guide for Equipment Designers, *2d ed. (Berkeley: University of California Press, 1966), pp. 5-18, 5-19.]*

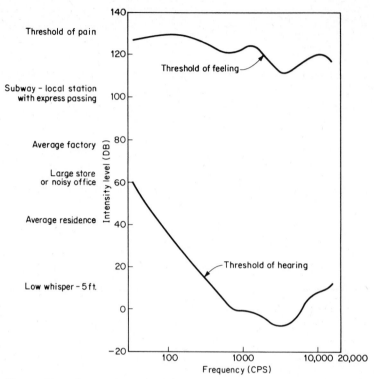

Figure 6-7 *Some characteristics of hearing and sound [From W. E. Woodson and D. W. Conover,* Human Engineering Guide for Equipment Designers, *2d ed. (Berkeley: University of California Press, 1966), Fig. 6-7, p. 4-10.]*

APPLYING HUMAN ENGINEERING

To illustrate the four-step process of human engineering, let us consider a very common example. One element in designing airline seats is determining their width, an especially critical problem where space is at such a high premium. Clearly, the critical users are those passengers who are of the widest girth. Referring to Figures 6-5 and 6-6, we see that width between elbows (dimension F-6), is the critical dimension and, that more women fall into this category at its extremes than do men. One possible approach might be to design to accommodate the widest passenger—the proverbial circus fat lady. As is usually the case, however, this is impractical from a cost standpoint. The vast majority of passengers do not need seats that wide and would be unwilling to pay the increased fare which would result from fewer seats per plane. Consequently, designers decide on an arbitrary *maximum* percentage of users that will be inconvenienced by a particular design. If 2.5 percent had been selected, for example, the seat width would be placed at about 23 inches which is the 95th percentile for women. A seat 23 inches wide inconveniences almost no males. As a consequence, the maximum percentage of passengers inconvenienced by this dimension is 0 percent for men and at most 5 percent for women, yielding an approximate percentage of 2.5 for total passengers inconvenienced assuming the passengers are one-half female. There is nothing sacred about the 2.5 percent figure except that most designers feel that it is often representative of a good balance between inconvenience and cost. For this reason, many of the studies of human characteristics summarize their findings by giving the 5th and the 95th percentile. As we have seen, this was the case with Figures 6-5 and 6-6.

Although the conscious development of a design which disregards the needs of certain users may seem unfair, it is also unfair to make the majority of the users bear the disproportionate cost or inconvenience of extending the design to these relatively few users. We should not lose sight of the fact that users who find themselves at a characteristic extreme have learned almost subconsciously to adapt to the inconveniences. Seven-foot men gain

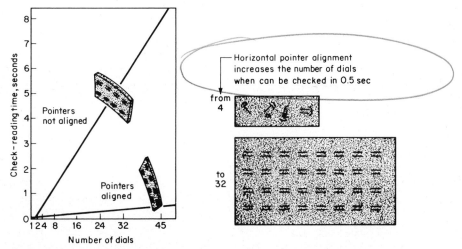

Figure 6-8 *Illustration of two patterns of dial pointers for indicating a "normal" condition. For the four dials, the white area indicates the normal condition; in the larger group, the 9 o'clock alignment indicates normal. The left part indicates the relative times required for check-reading various numbers of dials for the two patterns. [From E. J. McCormick,* Human Factors Engineering, *2d ed. (New York: McGraw-Hill Book Company, 1964), Fig. 6-14, p. 145.]*

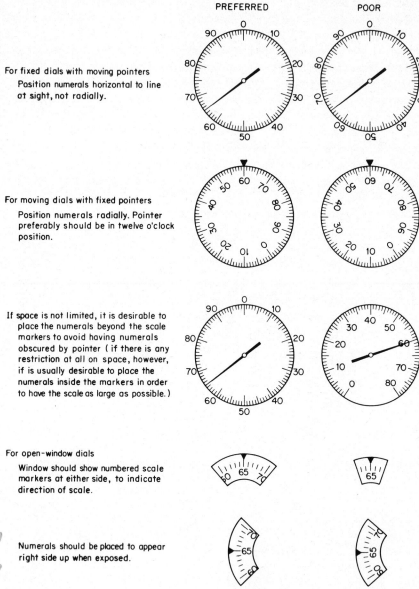

Figure 6-9. *Preferred practices in the printing of numerals on visual instruments [From E. J. McCormick,* Human Factors Engineering, *2d ed. (New York: McGraw-Hill Book Company, 1964), Fig. 6-8, p. 139.]*

FREDRich TAYLOR - Efficiency Studies.

a sixth sense about ducking while hard-of-hearing people get hearing aids, and large ladies learn to turn sideways in tight situations.

Nevertheless, extreme caution should be exercised in employing any inconvenience factor. Indeed, the word *inconvenience* must be just that: it is a term used only when inconvenience is involved, not when there is definite danger involved to everyone. Problems involving weight carrying are especially representative here. Consider the absurdity of an elevator cable designed for 95 percent of the maximum load, i.e., one that would send people crashing down the shaft one out of every twenty lifts. Here is the situation where engineers design for a maximum load then increase the design by a safety factor of 3 or 4 to protect against unforeseen circumstances and the effects of general wear and tear on the vehicle.

THE MATHEMATICS OF INCONVENIENCE FACTORS

There are also situations where a designer would like to use an inconvenience factor that does not appear directly in Figures 6-5 or 6-6. It is possible to transform the data available in these tables to whatever information he desires. Suppose for example, the airline seat designer wanted to reduce the inconvenience factor to 0.5 percent for the first-class seats. Again he would begin by observing the width between elbows of the critical user—the women. The dimension he needs is the one for the 99th percentile since they make up somewhere near half of the passengers. (Accommodating 99 percent of the women automatically ensures that almost no men are inconvenienced; thus the average percent of men and women accommodated is about 99.5.) Finding the inconvenience factor presents no problem because the distribution of variation associated with human characteristics can usually be closely approximated by a normal distribution, a fact which allows one to easily compute the value of any desired percentile. To determine the percentile, e.g., the 99th, it is necessary to utilize the properties of the normal distribution described in Appendix 1. The procedure can be summarized as follows.

1. Find the mean of the distribution of the user characteristic.
2. Find the standard deviation of that characteristic.
3. Determine how many standard deviations from the mean the desired accommodation percentile is.
4. Convert the answer in step 3 to the unit of measure being utilized.

   Using these four steps, let's compute the first class airline seat width which will accommodate 99 percent of women passengers (99.5 percent of all passengers).

1. From Figure 6-6, we find the 5th and 95th percentile values of the width between elbow measurement to be 11 and 23 inches respectively.

Since the normal distribution is symmetrical around its mean, any two values equidistant from the mean can be averaged to yield the mean; thus the mean is $(11 + 23)/2 = 17$ inches.

2. Next, from the body of the normal distribution table in Appendix 1, we can see that the 95th percentile is 1.65 standard deviations from its mean; in other words, 23 inches is 1.65 standard deviations from 17 inches, or one standard deviation is $(23 - 17)/1.65 = 3.63$ inches.

3. Since we want to accommodate 99 percent of the women, we need to determine how many standard deviations the 99th percentile value is from the mean; in the body of the normal distribution table, we find that answer to be 2.33.

4. Finally, since we already know that one standard deviation is 3.63 inches, 2.33 standard deviations must be $(3.63 \times 2.33) = 8.5$ inches. Thus we would design our seat width to be $(17 + 8.5)$ inches or 25.5 inches.

OTHER CONSIDERATIONS IN HUMAN ENGINEERING

The design implications of these calculations should be clear. If for example, you want to inconvenience no more than 5 percent of the users, you must design to meet the needs of 95 percent of the users. If the critical users are the ones with the largest characteristic values (as would be the case when you are designing clearances), the design value is the 95th percentile. If, however, the critical users are the ones with the smallest characteristic values (as would be the case when designing products requiring reach or force to operate), the design value would be the 5th percentile. With aspects of products like chair-seat height and stove height, the critical users are those with the largest *or* smallest characteristic value. To minimize the impact on these people then, the design value should be the 50th percentile.

Before he goes through the above procedures, any designer should consider the possibility that the product can be designed to make it unnecessary (or at least less necessary) to inconvenience *any* users. Adjustable ironing boards, adjustable automobile seats and steering wheels, and volume controls on telephones illustrate this thought. In some cases, such accommodation may be too costly.

To close this introduction to the area of human engineering, we consider one further example. For many years, hand irons were made with the cord coming out of the side away from the right-hand users body. Although there are approximately four right-handers for every left-handed user, such an arrangement was extremely awkward to the left-handed person who found himself constantly being struck by the cord. By simply designing the cord so that it would come out of the back of the handle, inconvenience to all users, whether right- or left-handed, was averted at minimal cost to the manufacturers.

QUESTIONS

1. The introduction of the Mustang into the Ford line was a marketing triumph. What previously unsatisfied segment of the market did it appeal to? How was the Mustang designed to attract this market segment?

2. Explain how product design affects production cost in (a) the clothing industry? (b) the small appliance industry? (c) the construction industry?

3. Upon overhearing the following statement by one of his furniture designers, the owner of a small furniture company fired the man: "As a furniture designer, my objective is to design the highest quality furniture on the market." In what type of firm might this action be justified and why?

4. Discuss the implications of the Postal Service standardizing the design of Post Office buildings. Why could or could not the same basic design be scaled up or down to meet the volume needs of the area it is to serve?

5. Holiday Inns, Inc. claims one of the reasons for its success is standardization. To what operational areas are they referring? What advantages and disadvantages do you see in their standardization?

6. Give examples and explanations of situations where one might not design for part interchangeability.

7. What are the basic objectives in establishing product tolerances?

8. Characterize a hypothetical situation where the tightening of selected part tolerances from their crucial level can result in cost reductions?

9. How would you go about selecting a manufacturing process whose output had to meet designer specified tolerances?

10. Identify four consumer products in which meaningful design improvements could be made to accommodate both right- and left-handed users. Describe the improvements you have in mind.

11. Determine the 2nd, 50th, and 80th percentiles of the distribution of men's standing height.

12. Use the human engineering procedure in conjunction with the data in Figures 6-5 and 6-6, to design a telephone booth. In particular,

decide on the booth's height, width, and depth and the heights of the seat and phone which are to be included.

13. Use the data in Figures 6-5 and 6-6 to determine how high to design a doorway which will accommodate 90 percent of the population without stooping.

14. How high could you mount a notice on a bulletin board and still allow it to be read easily by 99 percent of those men who passed the board?

chapter

MACROPROCESSING—BASIC DESIGN

seven

In this chapter, we discuss processing design—what it is and how it can best be accomplished. In order to better understand what processing design involves, the general nature of processing is discussed first. An introduction is provided to service processing and information processing as well as the five basic types of manufacturing processing. Answered next are the questions: what is processing design, when is it done, who does it, and how much processing design effort is justified?

Before processing design can begin in earnest, the processing designers must understand the nature of and demand for the output. For this reason, a brief treatment of output analysis precedes the section on the approach to processing design. In discussing the development of processing design for any stated output, a good deal of attention is given to evaluating processing alternatives; evaluative criteria are often applied successively to settle important aspects of the processing design.

One processing alternative warrants a special section; it is the make-or-buy decision. These decisions not only involve parts but also services like plating, machining, consulting, legal and computer services. Of course, no discussion of processing could be considered complete without an examination of automation. Therefore, the chapter concludes with a discussion of automated processing.

WHAT IS PROCESSING?

Before we can talk about processing design, we must know what the concept of processing implies. In brief, the term "processing" is used to describe *the techniques by which outputs of any system are produced, whether these outputs be products, information, or services.* Because these outputs are so diverse in nature, we would expect that the processing types employed for each would vary quite substantially—as indeed they do. Some idea of the degree of this variation can be gained from examining the characteristics of the main types of processing.

MANUFACTURING PROCESSING

Manufacturing processing is designed to produce material products as opposed to services and information. While many manufactured goods are end products or consumer goods, others are used by producers of consumer goods as either raw materials, parts, tools, or equipment. Firms use bulk plastic for everything from toy ducks to radio cases. Flour may be the end product of huge grain mills, but it is also the input to many food-producing firms. Thus, flour is both a consumer and a producer good.

Let's look at five basic categories of manufacturing processing: extraction, chemical change, preparation, fabrication, and assembly. Figure 7-1 shows which of these main types of manufacturing processing are found in each major industry in the United States. The order in which the five basic types are listed is generally in keeping with the processing sequence flow from natural raw materials to finished goods. Not all finished goods, however, go through the complete sequence. The oil industry extracts oil from the ground following this with chemical change processing to provide us with gasoline, motor oils, asphalt, naphtha, and other petroleum products. Extraction followed by chemical change and fabrication is the typical sequence in the metal industries to produce sheet, bar, and coil stock. These basic outputs are then taken by other industries and fabricated into parts which are assembled, with other elements, into a finished product or consumer good. Packaging, a form of assembly processing, is the final processing stage in many consumer goods industries.

Basic Manufacturing Industries	Extraction	Chemical change	Preparation	Fabrication	Assembly
Aerospace				X	X
Automobiles and transport equipment				X	X
Chemicals and plastics	X	X			
Construction				X	X
Food and beverages			X		
Iron and steel	X	X		X	
Machines and tools				X	X
Mining	X				
Nonferrous metals	X	X		X	
Petroleum	X	X			
Pharmaceuticals and cosmetics	X	X	X		
Rubber	X			X	
Stone, clay, and glass	X	X		X	
Textiles and apparel		X		X	X
Wood products and paper	X			X	

(Column header group: Basic Types of Manufacturing Processes)

Figure 7-1 *A comparison of the basic manufacturing processes involved in different industries*

EXTRACTION PROCESSING

Extraction processing is the task of separating out or decomposing a natural or synthetic material into its desired components. Taking as input a natural or man-made raw material (such as gold ore or crude oil), the extraction process removes by either physical or chemical means the valuable portions (gold, silver, platinum, and lead; or gasoline, heating oil, asphalt, and naphtha). In some cases, like diamond mining or hormone extraction, vast amounts of input have to be reduced through processing steps to produce minute amounts of the desired product. In other instances, the raw materials have such high yields, as in the case of anthracite coal, bauxite, or salt extraction, that little if any purification or concentration is necessary before they can be used.

CHEMICAL CHANGE

Another major type of input-to-output conversion involves chemical reactions, which combine two or more compounds or elements under suitable physical conditions. Such a process would be the combination of water and sulfur trioxide at 470°F to obtain sulfuric acid. These processes are usually described in terms of the chemical reactions taking place. The backbone of the chemical industry, chemical processing, is also widely used in the pharmaceutical industries, where sulfa drugs, antibiotics, and aspirin are produced, and in the metal industries, where metals are alloyed to improve their performance.

PREPARATION

Somewhat related to chemical processing but differing in scope is preparation processing. This process involves such food and beverage industry activities as cooking, baking, blending, mixing, canning, and freezing. Blending and mixing are also used in the preparation of some pharmaceuticals and cosmetics.

FABRICATION   (making the parts, putting them together

Fabrication involves the changing of the physical form and appearance of a raw material without changing its chemical composition. Thus it occurs in the rolling of molten steel and aluminum into sheets, molding rubber into tires, sawing logs into lumber, and, of course, machining of parts to be later assembled into finished goods. Fabrication often occurs in stages, i.e., fibers are spun into thread, thread is woven into cloth, cloth is cut into dress parts, and these are assembled into garments.

ASSEMBLY   *BRINGS PARTS TOGETHER*

The fifth basic type of manufacturing processing is assembly, which brings or combines together two or more distinguishable parts. It is usually the final stages of the manufacture of goods. Assembly can be as simple as bolting together a pair of pliers or as complex as assembling a jet airplane. Packaging may also be considered an assembly process because the product is combined with the packing carton and materials to form a single unit ready for shipment.

SERVICE PROCESSING

Not all processing is manufacturing oriented. In fact, today more than one out of every $2 is spent to purchase services, and more than one out of every two workers is employed by the service sector of our economy. In some ways, service processing is more diverse than its manufacturing counterpart because each service sector has developed designs customized for its particular problems. Then, too, the service professions are often dealing with individual people or goods rather than in mass production or assembly. Each patient in a hospital represents a unique case, as does each legal contract or each television set to be repaired. No matter how thorough the design of service processing, it must always leave room for individual variation. Thus it is an area with challenging problems for the process designer.

The principal types of services are listed in Figure 7-2. Each type

Governmental
Educational
Financial
Medical
Legal
Other professional
    (architects, consultants, etc.)
Utilities
Communications
Transportation
Wholesale—retail sales
Repair
Food and lodging
Entertainment

Figure 7-2 *Principal types
of services*

of service embodies its own particular basic types of processing. Legal processing consists of such activities as drawing up contracts, serving as public advisors concerning the nature of the law, and representing parties in the courtroom. To cure, to heal and repair, and to maintain health are the primary functions of the medical professions. The purpose of transportation services is to move passengers and freight; the purpose of repair processing is to return broken items to a usable state. Indeed, these definitions seem almost self-evident for we have encountered most of these services at some time or another in our lives.

INFORMATION PROCESSING

The most widely used type of processing today may well be information processing. The paperwork found in every organization, from the single proprietary corner grocery to the federal government, is the manifestation of information processing. In sophistication, it ranges from the simplest clerical function to an integrated management information system. No matter what the organization, be it service or manufacturing oriented, it cannot function without records, collected data, written proposals, and procedures. Information processing and ensuing clerical activities involve the reports which must be prepared for the government, management, and stockholders. Firms must also record and store product designs, distribute operating communication between various members of the organization, and gather and tabulate figures in order to price a product. Computer-aided information processing has made great strides in recent years to overcome some of the inherent weaknesses found in existing information systems. Nevertheless, information processing remains one of the most problematic areas in processing design.

SOME BASICS OF PROCESSING DESIGN

Processing design consists of the planning of the methods and means by which outputs will be produced, whether they are manufactured products, services, or information. Thus, it is the selection and design of a series of operations which will be used to transform inputs into the desired outputs. Processing design can be as involved as the design of a chemical processing plant or as simple as a teacher's lesson plan. Whatever the type of processing being considered, however, our purpose in this chapter is to describe an approach generally applicable to all. We shall see that there are several stages in the development of the processing design for a particular output.

TIMING PROCESSING DESIGN ACTIVITIES

Processing design is undertaken everytime a new output is designed or an existing one is redesigned. Designs currently in operation are often reviewed when technological advancement becomes available or when general conditions in the sectors of labor, demand, or design expertise have significantly changed. Many firms carry out such reexaminations of their processes on a periodic basis to be sure that no better approach exists. In redesign situations, the existing processing design is revised or modified wherever possible to reduce the processing time or cost. While we shall focus our attention on processing design for newly designed outputs, the principles and approach described would also be applicable to modifying existing systems for redesigned outputs or to improving existing processing designs even when product design has not changed.

BENEFIT COST CONSIDERATIONS

The amount of effort which should be expended on processing design and improvement depends on the potential returns from such an investment. Sufficient effort should be made so that the marginal benefits from the design effort at least equal the marginal cost of the additional effort on the design. Identifying where that point lies with currently available costing techniques, however, is extremely difficult. Spending too little on processing design may later cause excessive operating costs which might have been avoided. Obviously, a much greater total effort is justified when one is dealing with a million dollar volume than with a thousand dollar one.

PROCESSING DESIGN RESPONSIBILITY   *WHEN DO YOU DO IT?*

The work of processing design is done by many types of people. In large organizations, there are often special groups who handle the major processing design efforts. In consumer goods industries, the group is generally manufacturing planning or industrial engineering. In the chemical, petroleum, and pharmaceutical industries, the group is typically called the "processing planning group" and is staffed largely by chemists and chemical engineers. Mechanical, industrial, and electrical engineers are often included to help design the processing equipment. Throughout business and industry, special groups, often called "systems and procedures groups," are also employed to plan and install major information processing systems.

While much of the processing design work is done by formal POM groups, a great deal is handled by individuals and ad hoc groups. In small firms, a single individual may be responsible for the majority of the manufacturing processing design. Information processing design in very small organizations is often done by persons in addition to their regular duties.

Finally, many firms reach outside their POM organizations to acquire the skills and manpower necessary to develop and put into effect some of their processing designs. Even the largest oil companies contract with a firm specializing in oil refinery design to help work up major installations. The same is true of the paper and textile industries when a new plant is to be built. Consultants may also be a great help in designing service-oriented or information processing systems. A retail chain might contract, for example, with a consultant to develop an appropriate credit policy and associated operating procedures. A hospital might well hire a consultant to design an integrated information system which will handle the necessary information regarding admittance, discharge, billing, and medical records.

use marginal basis - last dollar's worth of effort costs you

OUTPUT ANALYSIS

Efficient processing design begins with a thorough understanding of output design and with knowledge of the marketing plan. If the processing designers are not the output designers, they will have to review the output designer's work and the marketing plan. The processing designers must determine how the parts assemble into a unit of output; then they must identify all the parts of the output and the number of parts needed before beginning to develop a processing plan for any particular part. The more complex the product, the more involved the output analysis will be. The work involved in an output analysis for a toy truck will be similar to, but nowhere near, the magnitude of the study required for a large computer defined by thousands of pages of drawings and specifications.

GRAPHIC AIDS

To understand a specific output, designers use charts to show how the inputs come together to form the output. In the case of an assembled output, a Gozinto (goes-into) chart is helpful in visualizing relationships. A Gozinto chart for a mechanical pencil is given in Figure 7-3. Normally, sketches of parts and assemblies will not be given, but they have been included here so that we can more easily understand the relationships between the parts and their combination into assemblies. The pencil in Figure 7-3 is composed of a cap assembly and a barrel assembly. The cap assembly is composed of two parts—the cap and pocket clip and the barrel assembly is made up of the eraser assembly, barrel, tip, and lead assembly. Thus, even as simple a product as a pencil has levels of assembly. In some very complex products, like computers and aircraft carriers, there may be hundreds of levels of subassembly.

A Gozinto chart is not always the most appropriate graphic means of understanding the relationships between and among all output components. No chart is needed for such simple outputs as a baseball bat, a hammer, a monthly statement for a checking account, or a library overdue notice. In the case of the statement or overdue notice, a sample of each would be sufficient. Some complicated outputs are better examined by specialized schematics which perform a similar function to that of a Gozinto chart. A good example is the production of a chemical compound. How it relates to the components from which it is formed is best described by a diagram which specifies the chemical reactions by which it is produced.

THE MATHEMATICS OF OUTPUT ANALYSIS

Along with the Gozinto chart, most processing designers develop a listing of all the output components and the number of each required. The number of parts needed is determined by the demand for the output multiplied by the number of each part in a unit of output. For a bank's check ledger, the number of each of its components is determined by the number of checking account customers the bank has times the number of transactions each makes during the statement period. In the case of the library overdue notices, it is the number of overdue books. The remainder of this section examines in detail the problem of listing and counting parts for a physical product.

Although product demand forecasts will have been made during the market evaluation phase, these are not sufficient to determine how many parts must be produced in order to meet that demand. Many products utilize the same part in several different subassemblies. A television set, for example, might use a specific type transistor 13 times, a specific type resistor 27 times, the same size screw in 22 places, and so on. Thus, it becomes necessary to compile a list of all the types of parts and the number of each per product unit before processing planning can realistically begin. From this list and count, the total parts requirements for each unit can be determined by simply multiplying the number of parts per product unit by the product's demand forecast.

The product's drawings, specifications, and Gozinto or assembly chart define all the part types and the number of each required per product unit. For a simple product like the pencil of Figure 7-3, compiling a list of all its different parts (9) and counting the number of each needed (1 of each) is an easy job. For complex products like an automobile or a computer, this compilation becomes extremely tedious, and thus a procedure which systematizes the counting process can be helpful.

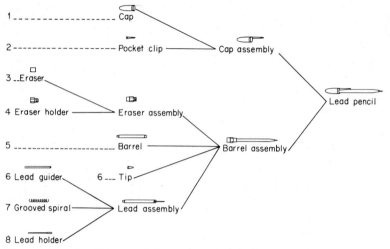

Figure 7-3 *An illustrated Gozinto chart for a mechanical pencil*

ASSEMBLY RELATIONSHIPS *(must Know how thing gross together)*

To develop a parts list and a parts count systematically, we begin by listing
the different types of assemblies and the number of each in the product.
It is convenient to summarize this information in a matrix similar to the
first one of Figure 7-4. Next we determine the different types of subassemblies and the number of each comprising each type of assembly. This information can be summarized in a matrix similar to the second one of Figure
7-4. We next determine the different composition of each level of assembly
until we reach the product's elemental parts; at each stage we summarize
the information in a matrix as in Figure 7-4. Purchased components are
usually excluded from this procedure.

is Sa (?
S_{11} c/ (parts #3321/
multiply 4x2

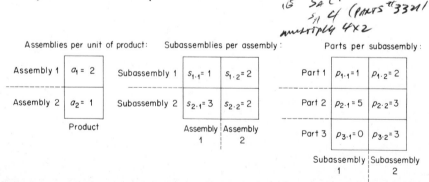

Assemblies per unit of product:		Subassemblies per assembly :			Parts per subassembly :		
Assembly 1	$a_1 = 2$	Subassembly 1	$s_{1.1} = 1$	$s_{1.2} = 2$	Part 1	$p_{1.1} = 1$	$p_{1.2} = 2$
Assembly 2	$a_2 = 1$	Subassembly 2	$s_{2.1} = 3$	$s_{2.2} = 2$	Part 2	$p_{2.1} = 5$	$p_{2.2} = 3$
	Product		Assembly 1	Assembly 2	Part 3	$p_{3.1} = 0$	$p_{3.2} = 3$
						Subassembly 1	Subassembly 2

Figure 7-4 *An example of product assembly relationships*

ASSEMBLY NOTATION

Consider the case of a product with three levels of assembly—parts into subassemblies, subassemblies into assemblies, and assemblies into a product.

Let

a_k be the number of type k ($k = 1, 2, \ldots, K$) assemblies in the product

s_{jk} be the number of type j ($j = 1, 2, \ldots, J$) subassemblies in a type k assembly

p_{ij} be the number of type i ($i = 1, 2, \ldots, L$) parts in a type j subassembly.

When determining the number of type $i = 1, 2, \ldots, L$ parts in the product, it is first convenient to find the number of type $j = 1, 2, \ldots, J$ subassemblies in the product. The latter is the number of type j subassemblies in assembly 1 times the number of type 1 assemblies in the product, plus the number of type j subassemblies in assembly 2 times the number of type 2 assemblies in the product, and so for the other types of assemblies $j = 3, 4, \ldots, J$. Or in mathematical terms the number of type j subassemblies per product is

$$S_j = \sum_{k=1}^{K} s_{jk} a_k \quad j = 1, 2, \ldots, J \qquad \text{7-1}$$

It is easy to determine the number of type $i = 1, 2, \ldots, L$ parts in the product. The answer is the number of type i parts in subassembly 1 times the number of type 1 subassemblies in the product S_1, plus the corresponding multiplications for subassemblies 2, 3, $\ldots$, J. In mathematical terms, the number of type i parts in a unit of product is

$$P_i = \sum_{j=1}^{J} p_{ij} S_j \quad i = 1, 2, \ldots, L \qquad \text{7-2}$$

where the S_j are defined by (7-1).[1]

As an example, let us consider the product described in Figure 7-4. As this figure shows, the product is composed of two types of assemblies ($K = 2$). Each unit of product is composed of two type 1 assemblies ($a_1 = 2$),

[1] Those of you familiar with multiple summations will recognize that 7-1 can be substituted into 7-2 with the result that

$$P_i = \sum_{j=1}^{J} \sum_{k=1}^{K} p_{ij} s_{jk} a_k \quad i = 1, 2, \ldots, L$$

and one type 2 assembly ($a_2 = 1$). Each assembly is composed of two types of subassemblies ($J = 2$), where the type 1 assembly is composed of one type 1 subassembly ($s_{11} = 1$,) and three type 2 subassemblies ($s_{21} = 3$), and so on. Each subassembly is composed of up to three different parts ($L = 3$), where subassembly 1 is built from one type 1 part ($p_{11} = 1$), five type 2 parts ($p_{21} = 5$), and no type 3 parts ($p_{31} = 0$), and so on. The number of type 1 subassemblies in the product

$$S_1 = \sum_{k=1}^{2} s_{1k}a_k = (1 \times 2) + (2 \times 1) = 4$$

and similarly the number of type 2 subassemblies in the product can be shown to be $(3 \times 2) + (2 \times 1) = 8$. The number of type 1 parts in the product are

$$P_1 = \sum_{j=1}^{2} p_{1j} S_j = (1 \times 4) + (2 \times 8) = 20$$

Similarly, you can show that $P_2 = 44$ and $P_3 = 24$.

Mathematical notation provides a systematic approach for counting the components of a product. The approach is readily extended to counting when there are more than three levels of assembly. Knowing what has to be processed, let's look now at how to provide it.

THE PROCESSING DESIGN APPROACH

MAJOR STEPS IN THE OUTPUT

Once the POM processing designer familiarizes himself with the characteristics of the output—its drawings and specifications, its components, and the demand requirements both with respect to time and volume—he is in a position to identify the major steps necessary to provide the output. For a part requiring machining, the major steps are defined by the characteristics of the surfaces needing machining. For each surface to be machined, the appropriate machining operations must be identified. In an extraction process like mining, the steps would include removing the ore from the ground and separating out the desired minerals. In chemical processing, it would be the series of reactions needed to produce the desired outputs. In an executive's annual medical checkup, it would include a delineation of the various tests to run in order to determine the state of his health. In information processing, it is the identification of the information flows and the processes necessary to provide the needed data.

IDENTIFYING ALTERNATIVE METHODS

Next, the alternative methods for accomplishing each major step must be identified. As many alternatives as are warranted by the potential savings should be isolated. Many firms market their processing developments through salesmen and agents. It is hard to imagine designing a large data processing system without calling in a number of companies supplying data processing equipment. These firms have special representatives who will help you design your systems in hopes of selling their company's equipment.

The value of having different groups of processing designers doing their own innovative brainstorming should not be underrated. Occasionally, one group will provide a totally new processing idea which accomplishes something which had not been possible before. The Western Electric Company found that traditionally hardened steel dies were inadequate for drawing some extremely fine wire which was needed in great volume. Seeking an alternative, they began experimenting with diamond dies but found that drilling holes of the necessary minute diameter was beyond the capabilities of conventional techniques. Then someone thought of using a laser as a drill. Since then, Western Electric has found that lasers can also be useful in welding, cutting, measuring, and even inspecting microscopic material.

VIABILITY SCREENING

After the alternatives have been identified, each should be quickly screened for viability to determine if it warrants more detailed evaluation and development. Can the alternative meet the design specifications? Can it produce the firm's demand requirements concerning both volume and time? These are only two of the germane questions to be asked here. Whenever the answer is no, the alternative should be dropped from further consideration or be improved upon so that it remains viable. Occasionally, none of the alternatives considered by the firm may appear viable, and none of them can be improved to a sufficient degree to yield a viable possibility. When this is the case, either the output idea has to be dropped or its design specifications changed.

DETAILED ANALYSIS

Screening is followed by a more detailed analysis of the viable alternatives. In evaluating an alternative, POM considers a number of different factors. The cost and output rate factors are usually of greatest interest. Firms require esitmates of both the cost to set up and operate a processing alternative. Setup costs include not only the cost of any additional equipment and plant investment needed but also the installation cost, and the costs of recruiting and training the personnel to operate and supervise the processing system.

An important category of setup cost is startup costs. While startup effects may be negligible for simple processes, they can be extended and costly in the case of complex processes. A new brewery, a computer-based management information system, or a steel mill don't just begin operating at full capacity. It usually takes weeks and often months for the operating personnel to learn their jobs and to debug the process. It is not uncommon for a hundred million dollar steel mill to experience several million dollars of additional expense during its startup period.

There are such factors as operating flexibility, process expandibility and reliability, and additional managerial burden which are difficult to put in monetary terms even though they ultimately affect the profits of the organization. Typically, their impact is too fragmented and ramifications too indirect to understand their effect in dollars and cents. As a result, such factors are usually evaluated in terms of ordinal ratings such as very good, good, satisfactory, poor, or very poor with respect to each factor considered.

Among the more important of these factors is _operating flexibility,_ first introduced as a POM concept in Chapter 5. Operating flexibility refers to the freedom a processing alternative permits the firm. Does the processing alternative lock the company into an output rate which is expensive to change, or can the output rate be easily changed? Ability to make output rate changes easily and with little expense is important when the output demand is subject to pronounced changes or shifts as with strong seasonal demands. Does the alternative allow some leeway in the time required to get the processing alternative set up and operating? The more leeway an alternative permits, the less impact the installation will have on the organization's other operations. Another dimension of operating flexibility is the possibilities for alternative uses of the equipment. If these are good, then prolonged changes in demand will have less long-run impact upon the firm's profits and employment levels.

Another factor related to operating flexibility is _process expandability._ Especially with a new product, the processing designer must concern himself with how the process can be expanded if demand should increase to the point where additional capacity is required. Some processing designs are expensive to expand. Use of movable equipment and temporary walls are just two of the many ways low-cost expandability can be built into processing designs.

A factor which is strongly related to customer service is _reliability._ If a failure possibility is critical and likely enough, then appropriate standby measures become very important. A firm utilizing a computer-based management information system can be brought to a halt by computer failure.

If the computer is likely to be out of service for more than a few hours, alternative provisions must be made for processing the really critical operating information. You may wonder why the firm couldn't just go back to its precomputer procedures. It could if these were remembered; however, after a few years of computerized operation most of the old procedures are likely to have been forgotten.

An often overlooked, intangible factor in evaluating a processing alternative is the *additional managerial burden* it creates. Even if supervisors are hired to oversee the processing, existing management has to oversee the supervisors. Moreover, additional work might be put on the personnel and accounting departments. As you might expect, it is extremely difficult to assess the magnitude of this additional administrative burden.

Throughout the analysis process, the designers must be concerned with the interrelationships between the various steps. Failure to consider them can lead to an ineffective or worse yet to an unworkable processing design. Finally, a good evaluation considers what happens if the alternative fails. What can be done to salvage the investment? Can the equipment be sold or used elsewhere?

SELECTING AN ALTERNATIVE

Having evaluated each alternative with respect to the previous factors, selection of the *best* processing alternative can begin. Selecting a *best* alternative when there are multiple factors to be considered involves applying the following three steps:

1. See if any of the alternatives can be eliminated because of existing restrictions
2. See if any alternatives are dominated by any of the other alternatives; eliminate the dominated alternatives from further consideration
3. Compare, subjectively if necessary, the remaining alternatives and select the best.

To illustrate the use of these steps consider choosing a *best* alternative from among the four for which evaluation results are given in Figure 7-5. The company choosing between the alternatives has a capital constraint of $235,000; thus alternative 4 is eliminated.

Dominance refers to the situation where one alternative will always be chosen over another. In Figure 7-5, we see that alternative 3 is equal or better in every respect than alternative 2. As a consequence, alternative 3 would always be chosen over alternative 2, and hence, the latter can be eliminated from further consideration.

Thus the choice between alternatives has been narrowed to 1 and 3. Alternative 3's one-time costs are $20,000 more than 1's, yet 3's per

Factors Considered / Alternatives	Investment, set-up, & start-up cost	Per unit operating cost	Operating flexibility	Expandability	Acceptability	Safety
1	$ 200,000	$10.00	G	S	G	G
2	230,000	9.50	G	P	G	S
3	220,000	9.00	VG	P	G	G
4	260,000	8.75	A	P	S	G

Code
VG : very good
 G : good
 S : satisfactory
 P : poor
VP : very poor

Figure 7-5   *A multifactor comparison of four processing alternatives*

unit costs are a dollar less. With the product's projected life of 4 years and yearly volume of 20,000 units, the extra investment appears quite worthwhile since there would be a (4)($1.00)(20,000) — $20,000 = $60,000 savings over the 4-year period. Also in 3's favor is its additional operating flexibility. Since demand is highly dependent on the weather, the increased operating flexibility would be helpful in developing production schedules which will keep the sum of labor, operating, and inventory costs at a minimum. Alternative 1 however is a more expandable design than 3. While in many processing designs, expandability is very important, it is of only minor importance here. If demand exceeds capacity, it would be better to build other plants closer to the demand than to expand this design because of the high transportation costs. These observations when coupled with the equal ratings with respect to the other factors lead one to the conclusion that alternative 3 is the *best* choice.

Although this approach is used in making most processing design decisions, many processing designs are too complex to select all at once. Hence, it is common to find this approach being applied sequentially in several levels. In these situations, management first decides upon the major aspects of the processing design. Next, within the framework of those decisions, the same approach is applied to settle on those aspects of secondary processing importance. Its level by level application is continued until a completed processing design is developed. The appropriate number of levels depends on the particular situation. Consider two examples. First assume we are designing the processing for a part requiring machining in a job shop. Here three analysis levels would be appropriate. At the first level, the machining operations and types of equipment to be used would be selected. At the second level, questions regarding where and what types of inspections to use should be settled. At the final level, the material handling and storage decisions are made. The second example concerns a large national mail-order firm which is designing a material handling system for a new warehouse. At the initial design level, the order demand and merchandise receipts are examined to decide on capacity and other operating requirements for the system. At the second level, the type of system (roller conveyor, overhead monorail, men with carts, etc.) is decided upon. If the overhead monorail type system were chosen, the third level would choose the general layout of the system. Should one large monorail loop be used or should three separate loops be utilized in the receiving, shipping, and storage areas? If the latter were chosen, then the fourth level of analysis would involve deciding on the operating speeds for each of the three loops and the capacity and location of the transfer devices which connect the loops. Selection of the actual equipment to use would be done at the fifth design level, while the sixth level would develop system installation details.

The design level concept can be used effectively to break the development of complex processing designs into a series of more manageable POM problems. At each design level, the same basic steps are applicable in developing that level's portion of the processing design.

EXTERNAL VERSUS INTERNAL PROCESSING

Knowing what and how many components are needed, we are faced with the question of which ones to process internally and which to purchase. Certainly we would not want to go to the trouble of making a product, part, or service if another firm could regularly supply it to us at a cost substantially below our own. On the other hand, if our shop or office has excess capacity, if no new tooling or equipment were required, and if suppliers' cost estimates were high, our firm might well decide to make the piece itself.   *what does it cost to make a part.*

CASES WITH ONE ALTERNATIVE

Sometimes the choice is so obviously internal or external that no formal evaluation of the other alternative is even considered. Generally, when a component falls outside the firm's processing interests or capacities and is needed only in a limited quantity, it is far more economical to purchase it from another firm already engaged in its manufacture. By specializing, such suppliers are able to achieve expertise and economies that the purchasing firm can not hope to duplicate. Thus, clothing manufacturers purchase buttons and zippers; home building contractors buy nails, shingles, and plumbing fixtures; automobile manufacturers buy clocks, radios, and interior textiles; stockbrokerage houses use Standard and Poor's reports

make sure you have source of supply.

for evaluating the financial stability and potential of various companies; and computer owners and leasees depend on the computer manufacturer for maintenance and repair services.

When the firm has the capacity and the component is clearly within the firm's area of processing expertise, internal processing is usually a foregone conclusion. It is hard to imagine General Motors not making any of the engines for its cars, General Electric not making appliance light bulbs for its stoves and refrigerators, or IBM not servicing its own computers. Even without this capacity or expertise, management may decide to provide for internal processing if there is a sufficiently high demand within the firm for the component. Color television tubes, although first supplied to most manufacturers throughout the industry by RCA, increasingly became produced in each company's own facilities as consumer demand for color sets rose.

CASES INVOLVING CHOICE

Not all internal versus external processing decisions, however, are clear cut. In such cases, a careful study of relative advantages and disadvantages to the firm for each alternative must be conducted. To illustrate one approach, we will present first an example of a decision facing the manufacturers of a fictitious product, Smile Toothpaste, and then discuss some of the characteristics of these types of decisions in the context of this example.

SMILE TOOTHPASTE CO.

For many years, the makers of Smile Toothpaste had been using blue plastic caps supplied by Apex Plastics, Inc., a small firm within a few miles of the Smile plant. A few weeks ago, the founder and president of Apex died unexpectedly leaving the business with no one capable of managing the plant. In addition, Mr. Johnson, president of Smile, learned that there was much internal strife at Apex among the heirs, and that they were preparing for a long court fight over who would control the company. Since production had stopped at Apex and there appeared to be no indication of its being normalized in the foreseeable future, Mr. Johnson judiciously decided not to renew Smile's contract with Apex. He was then faced with the decision to make the caps within the Smile plant or to buy them from some other supplier.

Smile's purchasing manager, Mr. Rudolph, was able to locate only one firm, Crestview Container Corp., which was willing to supply the 75 million caps needed each year. Buying from Crestview, however, would cost Smile $4 per thousand to buy caps as compared with the $3 per thousand which they had been paying. The Crestview plant was 350 miles away.

The increased buying cost of $1 per thousand caps set Mr. Johnson to thinking about the possibility of making the caps within his own recently expanded plant. He gave his assistant, Mr. Grimm, the task of evaluating the possibility. Grimm suggested that the best course of action would be to buy a $450,000 plastic-molding machine which, with the right dies, could mold up to 60,000 small parts per hour. The tool and die shop which supplied all of Smile's dies estimated that the cost of the necessary dies would be $15,000. From past conversations with the Apex management, Grimm knew that such dies would last about a year. Further, the manufacturer of the molder would guarantee the machine to have a productive life of 20 years if the owner would purchase the maker's $5,000 a year maintenance contract. This contract was attractive not only because it provided the expert maintenance needed for such a complex machine but also because it included the services of a technician who would train the operator. Operators of equipment like this were earning about $10,000 a year in the area. Grimm also called several bulk plastic suppliers and found that the best delivered price on plastic raw material would be $1.50 per thousand caps. Grimm computed that the inventory costs incurred handling and storing the bulk plastic would be about $.10 per thousand caps.

Grimm figured the cost per thousand caps exclusive of the machine purchase cost to be $2. The latter was made up of $1.50 for plastic, $.10 for inventory and handling the bulk plastic, and $.40 for the operator, maintenance contract, and die costs. This latter cost of $.40 per thousand was figured on the total annual cost of $30,000 ($10,000 operator + $5,000 maintenance contract + $15,000 dies), allocated over 75 million caps. Grimm next calculated that with the $2 cost, excluding the $450,000 machine cost, it would take 3 years, $450,000/(2 × 75,000), to return the price of the machine from the $2 per thousand savings alone.

At first, Mr. Johnson leaned toward the buy alternative, since it was company policy not to make any investment which could not be expected to return its investment within 2½ years. Further reinforcing his initial opinion was the fact that the startup problems and delays associated with new equipment meant headaches for everyone involved.

But Mr. Rudolph indicated that from what he had been able to find out, Crestview was occasionally subject to work stoppages which might interfere with the flow of caps to Smile. In addition, Rudolph noted that there could be trouble with the trucking company because Smile's typical monthly cap shipments would be less than half a truckload. Such partial loads were especially subject to delivery delays until a full truckload for the area was accumulated.

Grimm observed that if Smile made its own caps, the supplier problems could be avoided because the manufacturer of the molding machine had an excellent reputation for customer service. Further he pointed out that the molding machine capacity would not be fully utilized in making caps. In fact, it need only be used 62.5 percent of the time since it could produce up to 480,000 (8 × 60,000) units in an 8-hour day, and only 300,000 (75,000,000/250) caps would be needed each of the 250 working days in the year. Mr. Grimm went on to mention the possibility that the unused capacity could be employed making other molded plastic products. The purchasing manager, Rudolph, thought they could pick up customers who would also be dropping Apex as a supplier. He also stated that competing products to those being marketed by Smile were making increasing use of plastic containers. Perhaps the trouble at Apex was a blessing in disguise, for it was forcing Smile to examine an innovative packaging area which should have been examined several years ago.

After this discussion, Mr. Johnson's thinking changed. Although he would prefer that all investments pay back in at least 2½ years, he realized that payback was not the sole criterion in this case. Further, he was apprehensive about Crestview's potential supply problems, due both to their current labor difficulties and to the prospect of trucking small amounts 350 miles each month. It made sense to him for Smile to have control over the supply. He liked the idea of solving a current problem and at the same time evaluating first hand a processing technology with which Smile was not familiar. As a result of these considerations, Mr. Johnson authorized Mr. Grimm to contract for the molding machine.

GENERAL CONSIDERATIONS

The Smile Corporation example illustrates the variety of factors which must be evaluated in order to reach a good internal versus external processing decision. As it was with Smile, cost is always an important consideration. For external processing alternatives, the total additional cost to the firm must be determined. In the case of Smile, this was the delivered cost plus the additional inventory and handling costs. If Smile produced the caps, the additional costs of internal processing must be evaluated, including extra labor, material, and equipment costs. Usually most important among the noneconomic factors associated with these decisions are future operating flexibility, quality considerations, and supplier service. Maintaining and establishing good supplier relations is also important. Certainly, we would not expect to routinely take work away from a supplier during his slack periods and expect him to take a rush order as a favor to us when his facility is fully loaded.

It is important to remember that each internal-external processing decision situation, whether for parts or service, is unique. As a consequence, care must be taken in each situation to identify and evaluate all the factors relevant to the decision and only those. The relevant factors are those which will change if one of the alternatives is chosen, like the $450,000 which would be spent by Smile for the molding machine if they made caps. Any factor which remains constant regardless of which alternative is chosen has no relevance to the comparison. Mr. Johnson wisely recognized that the cost of the extra space provided in the recent expansion would have to be paid regardless of whether the new machine were installed or not. Hence, it was a constant factor and not relevant to the comparison. If such a constant factor is connected with one alternative and not to the other, a faulty decision may result. Including the cost of the extra space at Smile might have been enough to tip the balance incorrectly towards the external processing alternative.

While the primary example of this section, Smile Toothpaste, has been discussed in terms of whether or not to make or buy a product part, the same general evaluation can be used for related decisions in clerical and service areas as well. Universities must decide whether to continue operating their own food service or to contract with a catering firm. Physicians must choose between sending their diagnostic tests out for analysis or setting up their own small laboratory capable of handling the routine tests. Corporations must decide whether to do internal analysis of their POM problems or to hire special consultants. In each case, the situations may be different, but the same basic principles apply for considering all the relevant factors before choosing the best alternative.

AUTOMATED PROCESSING

Automation is a relatively new term, having been coined in the early 1950s to describe machine control of processes and automatic material handling. It has often been expanded, however, to connote the replacement of human endeavor with that of either machines or computers. In this enlarged sense, automation has been with us a long time. The windmill, cotton gin, and sewing machine are but a few of the classic, early examples of the machine partially replacing man's labor. Yet, it was not such devices which gave rise to the term; it was the development of equipment which eliminated the need to move work manually between processes and of machines which inspected their own output and automatically made the necessary adjustments. To many laymen, however, it is in the computer area where automation seems to have its highest impact. Certainly this is the area which receives the most publicity.

SOME EXAMPLES

Within the experience of a vast majority of people is the automation-related concept of *direct dialing* for placing both local and long distance telephone calls. Most calls today are completed by automatic switching equipment. In the case of long distance calling, the system is designed so that when the normal channels are fully loaded, alternative routings over less direct, but currently available, lines are automatically selected. If a New York to Chicago telephone call is unable to be completed because all the direct circuits are filled, an automatic switching mechanism can place the call through circuits in Washington, D.C. or Cleveland. It is even technically possible for such a call to be relayed through Los Angeles circuits!

Another familiar example is the *computer-controlled reservation systems* in use by most major airlines. To determine if the requested flight is available, the agent keys the inquiry into a small console which is connected to a centrally located master computer that stores up-to-date information on all flights in the near future. The computer immediately responds either by indicating that no seats for that flight are available or by confirming the requested reservation and adding the traveler's name to the passenger list. In some large airports, print-outs of that list may be supplied to the reservation desk at the point and date of departure.

Automated processing in the chemical and oil industries has taken the form of *automatic temperature and pressure control devices* (which act much like the thermostat in private home heating and cooling systems). Today it is not unusual for a single man to control tens of millions of dollars of equipment while seated in a comfort-conditioned control room where instruments keep him informed on how the process is proceeding and where switches and dials enable him to regulate the operation remotely. Further, many aspects of these installations are self-regulating in that the process maintains itself within certain limits set by the operator. In the case of many oil refineries, the degree of sophistication is increasing to the point that in a few years the total operation, except for an unanticipated occurrence, will be computer-controlled. Flow rates, flow routings, temperatures, and pressures will be automatically regulated so that the desired output quantities of regular and premium gasoline, heating oil, motor oil, jet fuel, tars, asphalts, waxes, naphtha, and other by-products are achieved in an optimal manner. Computer programs have already been developed for determining operating schedules for processes within a refinery.

Automated processing has a significant impact on manufacturing industries. There are automatic machines which produce, assemble, and test electric light bulbs at phenomenal rates of speed. Others are capable of filling, cutting, and packaging cigarettes at rates in the thousands per minute while incorporating inspection devices so sensitive that they can detect and reject a package containing a single broken or crushed cigarette.

Another automated application to processing is called *the transfer machine.* These machines are really an integrated system of special purpose machines and conveyors which function as a complete unit to machine a particular part, such as an automobile engine block. The engine blocks to be machined are placed in fixtures permanently attached to the conveyor which properly position and carry them on a stop-and-go basis from one work station to the next. At each station, one or more productive operations are carried out. Also integrated into these machines are stations which inspect the work done by previous stations by using air gages and electronic devices to measure dimensions. If any of these inspections indicate a discrepancy due to tool wear, the transfer machine automatically repositions the worn tool to compensate for that wear. When other problems are indicated, the machine will turn itself off and signal the probable problem source. Transfer machines are really automated production lines.

In the early 1960s, *numerically controlled machine tools* came into use. Operating from instructions punched into paper tape, they are able to machine many different types of parts simply by the operator inserting the appropriate tape. Figure 7-6 shows the main components of one of these machines. Its control unit translates tape instructions into electrical and mechanical signals which cause three-dimensional movement of the tool and work table. Other numerically controlled machines are designed to do all the machining on small intricate parts. These latter machines sometimes have mechanical hands which automatically change tools on tape command.

One final automated processing example is that of an integrated production system built around an *automated warehouse.* One such facility developed by an aircraft parts subcontractor routinely handles 90,000 different parts and tools. The actual warehouse is the size of a football field. Two conveyors take the tools and partially or completed parts to the warehouse. There each load is automatically checked for weight and height and then

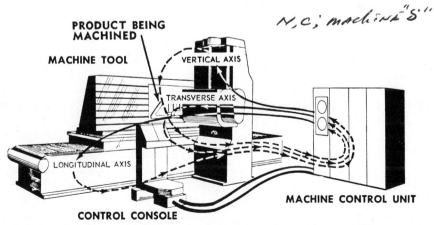

Figure 7-6 *Example of a numerically controlled machine tool* [*From F. G. Moore,* Manufacturing Management, *5th ed. (Homewood: Irwin, 1969), Fig. 7-7, p. 132.*]

transferred to an appropriate storage location by one of the 15 computer controlled, operatorless cranes. The location of this load is then stored in the computer's memory. No attempt is made to move items directly from one department to another. When one section finishes with a part, it so informs the computer (through the use of a remote data collection system), that it is on the way to the warehouse. As a consequence, anyone in the POM system can query the computer as to the status of any part or piece of tooling. Thus the system gives each department up-to-date information for scheduling its work. Plans call for the current system to be only a part of the total, computer-operated, work-scheduling system to be put into effect in the future. In the proposed plan, the computer and its programmed scheduling rules will develop and revise efficient routings of work and tooling from one operation to another (via the warehouse), in such a manner that the firm's work commitments are met effectively.

DETERMINING OPPORTUNITIES FOR AUTOMATED PROCESSING

Whether to automate a particular process, be it clerical or mechanical, is a difficult question facing many executives. Not only does it involve an unusually large capital investment, but it also tends to have significant impact on the firm's modes of operation and the attitudes of its employees.

Let us begin our examination of automation as an attractive alternative for improving processing with the comparison of man to a machine provided in Figure 7-7. From this it may be seen that man can best perform those tasks which cannot be anticipated or which require quick or intuitive judgments based on incomplete information. Recall, for example, the computer-controlled landing system of Apollo XI. If astronaut Neil Armstrong had not taken over manual control, the ship's computer would have landed the vehicle on an area of the moon where it most probably would have been damaged. Machines, on the other hand, perform best where an appropriate and definite response which is technically possible can be developed.

Man's current development of automated machines to perform tasks swiftly follows his own ability to identify, evaluate, and determine optimal reactions to tasks which previously were considered spontaneous processes. While the qualitative assessment should remain in the future essentially as presented in Figure 7-7, there will no doubt be a continual and gradual shifting of tasks from man to machine, with machines increasingly being able to function like a man except faster, more precisely, without fatigue, and with less variation in output.

Nevertheless, being able to accomplish certain tasks better and more rapidly than man is not sufficient reason to automate a process. In a few cases, automation *is* the only viable alternative. In the 1920s, A.T.&T. came to such a realization when forecasts indicated that in 50 years every young woman in the United States would be needed to staff the manual telephone

Production manager - is ultimately responsible. (handwritten)

✓   ✓ (handwritten checkmarks)

Man Excels In	Machines Excel In
Sensitivity to an extremely wide variety of stimuli	Monitoring (both men and machines)
Perceiving patterns and making generalizations about them	Performing routine, repetitive, or very precise operations
Ability to exercise judgment where events cannot be completely defined	Responding very quickly to control signals
Improvising and adopting flexible procedures	Exerting great force, smoothly and with precision
Ability to react to unexpected low-probability events	Storing and recalling large amounts of information
Applying originality in solving problems, i.e., generating alternate solutions	Performing complex and rapid computation with high accuracy
Ability to profit from experience and alter course of action	Sensitivity to stimuli beyond the range of human sensitivity (infrared, radio waves, etc.)
Ability to perform fine manipulation, especially where misalignment appears unexpectedly	Doing many different things at one time
Ability to continue to perform even when overloaded	Deductive processes
Ability to reason inductively	Insensitivity to extraneous factors
	Ability to repeat operations very rapidly, continuously, and precisely the same way over a long period
	Operating in environments which are hostile to man or beyond human tolerance

MACHINES DO LEARN (COMPUTERS THINK) (handwritten)

Figure 7-7 *Man versus machine [From W. E. Woodson and D. W. Conover, Human Engineering Guide for Equipment Designers, 2d ed. (Berkeley: University of California Press, 1966), p. 1-23.]*

exchanges which were then in use. As a result, research efforts were concentrated on signal transmission and switching developments; these ultimately made possible the automatic telephone exchange and direct dialing.

More typical are the situations where automation appears to be the *most profitable* of the available alternatives. Several factors have made it increasingly so. The more important among them are the increases in labor costs, capital availability, and consumer demand. Rather than concentrating on the evolution of each of these factors, let us examine what impact they have had on automation.

Because increasing degrees of automation require greater capital inputs, capital availability is a necessary prerequisite. Without sufficient capital resources to make the initial investment, automated processing is out of the question no matter how attractive the potential cost savings. The impact of labor cost and demand can be seen from Figure 7-8. This diagram illustrates that a society with a higher labor cost can justify the higher fixed cost

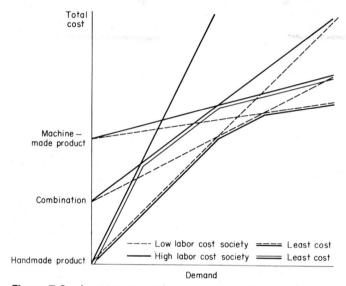

Figure 7-8   *Least-cost modes of manufacture for a product in two societies with differing labor costs*

(i.e., equipment and tooling) associated with increasing degrees of automation at a lower anticipated demand. In Figure 7-8, the higher labor cost society can profitably change from a hand operation to a combination hand and machine at a lower volume than the lower labor cost society. This is one of the reasons why Ford used pre-1940 equipment in an automobile assembly plant it recently built in Mexico.

In cases where current demand may not be entirely sufficient to justify an increased degree of automation, the cost savings passed on to the consumer as a result of the process being automated may raise the future demand above the critical level of cost-changeover point. Indeed, increased demand usually leads to a higher total profit level for the firm in addition to lower unit cost of production. Hence, both the consumer and the producer can mutually benefit from automation.

An ancillary benefit resulting from automation but one difficult to evaluate in monetary terms is that of greater output uniformity. This occurs because the role of the man and, therefore, the product variability are reduced. Increased uniformity leads to all the benefits previously described in discussing part standardization, interchangeability, and tolerances.

To some extent, as we have seen in Figure 7-7, automation can free man from routine and monotonous work. On the managerial level, this means that he is able to concentrate on more important, creative, and rewarding work. Certainly one may legitimately question whether people displaced by automation do find suitable work. Yet, numerous studies have shown that few people are fired as a result of the introduction of automated processes.

Many are shifted to other areas within the organization while some reassignments can be completed only after substantial retraining of the employee. The end result is often a more highly skilled worker.

SOME PROBLEMS OF AUTOMATED PROCESSING

Automation is not completely a positive picture; there are many concomitant problems. The procedure of setting up an automated process can be the cause of much distress for an organization. The transition period involves time, effort, and cost. It takes time to get the aggravating and expensive "bugs" out of the system. Further, the time of transition is often an extremely trying one for operating personnel. The firm must also try to minimize the inconvenience caused by the transition to those outside the company. Customers expect uninterrupted service regardless of what is occurring internally. To avoid production delays, some firms operate the new and old systems together until the new one is operating satisfactorily.

Another consideration in choosing an automated system is its potential reliability. To develop an automated system as reliable as its nonautomated counterpart, the components of the former must be much more dependable than those of the latter. In the automated system, the failure of any one critical part may cause the whole line to stop. For want of a one dollar bearing, a 50 million dollar cat-cracker in an oil refinery can be brought to a standstill, but a nonautomated process may continue to run on built-up inventories while one of its components is fixed. Also, the nonautomated system allows room for improvisation and circumventions of the problem while the automated system is completely rigid. Finally, of no small importance is the fact that the automated system has many more critical parts than the nonautomated one. Not only does it have to have all the machine parts found in its predecessor, but it also has to have material handling and positioning parts as well. If the system is designed to be self-adjusting, it must have parts to do this. For each part added to the system, the reliability of the whole system goes down. Figure 7-9 emphasizes the necessity for high component reliability in huge, automated systems.

A final drawback of automation is inflexibility. Often a relatively simple change in product design or processing improvement can only be incorporated into the system at great cost. In addition, it is difficult and extremely costly to increase the capacity of an automated system once it has been built. As a consequence, the cost of changing such a system tends to discourage product design, processing, and capacity modifications once the system is put into operation. An organization should be careful, however, not to forget that once it has been made, the investment in an automated system is a sunk cost and should not be considered subsequently in evaluating the attractiveness of other alternatives. Only the incremental and opportunity costs associated with the latter are relevant in this analysis.

THE RELIABILITY OF A SYSTEM IS THE   OF IT'S PARTS.

Individual Component Reliability (%)	System Reliability (%)				
	No. of Components				
	10	60	100	250	500
99.99	99.9	99.45	99.1	97.5	95.2
99.9	99.0	94.23	90.5	77.5	60.6
99.0	90.4	54.75	36.6	8.1	1.0*
98.0	81.7	29.77	13.3	0*	0*
				*Approximate	

Figure 7-9 *System reliability as influenced by component reliability* [*Adapted from C. T. Corney, "Reliability and Maintenance," in* The Design Method, *S. A. Gregory, ed. (New York: Plenum Press, 1966) Fig. 24.3, p. 221.*]

The decision to automate a process or system is a difficult one. Because of its potential impact on the company and its workers, it is one which must be made with every deliberate care. Generally, the volume and the duration of work to be done determine the extent to which a firm can profitably automate its operations. The greater the volume and the longer the duration of the demand, the more attractive automation becomes. Yet, the decision cannot be based solely on work volume and duration. Also considered must be the cost of the changeover, the impact upon workers and the POM system, and the future operating flexibility of the system.

QUESTIONS

1. As head of a processing design group, it is your responsibility to take product drawings and to develop an efficient way of manufacturing the products in question. This morning you received the drawing below of a redesigned component for a machine your company markets. The drawing includes dimensions and specifications which have not been reproduced here.

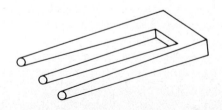

What is the first thing you should do upon examining the drawing?

2. Evaluate this statement: "Breakeven analysis and incremental profit analysis concepts are not pertinent to processing design in nonprofit institutions such as schools and hospitals."

3. What can you say about the firm which made the following statement: "It is just not worth spending $10,000 to cut the production cost by $.10 per unit."

4. Characterize those situations where the following statement would and would not be appropriate:
   "As POM manager of this company, my responsibility is to keep production cost to a minimum."

5. Characterize the situation where each of the following are best used: general purpose machines, special purpose machines, and numerically controlled machines.

6. Identify and characterize four situations where noneconomic factors warrant more consideration than economic ones in deciding among processing alternatives.

7. Evaluate the following statement:
   "The transition from a manual to an automated system, in the long run, will create more productivity and an even greater demand for employees; therefore, I cannot understand why employees are so concerned."

8. You are considering replacing a 2-year-old machine with a new machine. Which of the following factors would you consider (and why) in making your decision? If you think a factor may be used in certain situations but not in others, give an example of each.

   (a) Purchase price of the old machine
   (b) Purchase price of the new machine
   (c) Salvage value of old machine
   (d) Salvage value of new machine
   (e) Financing costs of old machine
   (f) Tax concession on old machine
   (g) Capacity differences
   (h) Differences in amount of operator attention needed

9. Wesley Widget Company has in inventory a certain raw material which cost $11 per unit. Because of a market downturn, the price of this raw material has dropped to $8 per unit and is expected to remain there for some time. The company manufactures left-handed widgets, each of which requires 2 units of this raw material and $5 of labor. If an outside supplier is willing to supply Wesley with all the widgets it needs at $24 each, should Wesley accept? Defend your position.

10. At some colleges preregistration and registration for next semester's courses can be a traumatic experience for many students. What charac-

teristics should a good course registration have? What design steps would you use in developing a system with these characteristics?

11. Characterize the situations where a college should and should not (a) build and operate its own dormitories, (b) operate its own janitorial service.

12. The Dependable Machine Company is considering the purchase of special equipment to be utilized exclusively in the production of a new product they are going to market. There are five alternative methods under consideration for manufacturing the product. Costs for these methods are given in tabular form below. Since the machinery can only be used for a special purpose, it would have no value beyond the life of this project other than for salvage. All of the machines have a useful life of about 15,000 units production; the sales forecast (over the life of the product) is in the process of being made. Give some very explicit quantitative rules which could be applied to determine which process to use.

Process	Hand Labor/Unit	Machine Cost	Salvage Value
A	$1.20	(0)	(0)
B	.80	$ 20,000	2,000
C	.60	40,000	5,000
D	.20	90,000	10,000
E	(0) Automatic	120,000	15,000

13. The More Than One Brewing Company workers have developed the following equations to help them evaluate their existing operating plan for 1972:

$$R = 100V$$
$$TC = 50,000,000 + 50V$$

where

R = Sales revenue
V = Volume in barrels
TC = Total cost

(a) What is the firm's projected breakeven volume?

(b) If the existing operating plans call for a volume of 1,100,000 barrels, what profit is forecasted?

(c) Two additional alternative operating plans have been developed and submitted for evaluation. Propose a course of action.

    (1) The sales manager proposes a 10 percent reduction in selling price and predicts a volume increase to 1,200,000 barrels in 1972.

    (2) The firm's chief industrial engineer suggests an investment in

new automation equipment. He predicts fixed operating expenses including depreciation of the new equipment would increase by 1.5 million dollars but that the decrease in labor required would reduce variable costs by $6 a barrel. Further, he anticipates that sales price and volume would remain the same as they are forecasted in the existing 1972 plan.

14. The Smith Manufacturing Company can produce chairs by using two different processes. They have available the following data:

	Process A	Process B
Fixed Cost	$50,000/yr	$10,000/yr
Variable Cost	$2/chair	$5/chair
Capacity	20,000 chairs/yr	10,000 chairs/yr

(a) For what levels of demand (in chairs per year) would process *A* be preferred to *B*, and for what levels would process *B* be preferred to *A*?

(b) The sales manager thought that the number of chairs that could be sold depended upon the price. The sales forecasts for possible prices are:

   5,000 chairs at $12 per chair
  12,000 chairs at $10 per chair
  20,000 chairs at $ 7 per chair

What process should Smith use and how should they price their chairs?

15. The Auto-Right Co. traditionally has been a components supplier to the auto industry. Because of this relationship, all of its shop workers belong to the U.A.W. Through the U.A.W., the shop workers have achieved a guaranteed annual income from Auto-Right Co. equal to a full year of work at their normal wages. Recently, the company's primary customer withdrew its contract, leaving Auto-Right with only 30 percent of its former volume. In searching for ways of making up its lost volume, the first and, so far, the only possibility located is the chance to make 5,000 units a week of a part at a price of $4 per unit. These parts can be produced and sold to a supplier of auto replacement parts for any part of or all of the next 10 weeks for $4 per unit.

A quick survey has shown that this part can be made in any of the following ways:

(a) Using minimal tooling, the part could be made on existing labor schedules with 1.0 direct labor hour for each part produced.

(b) Using a special die which could be built at Auto-Right in 1 week with 80 direct labor hours, the part could be made with 0.8 direct labor hours per part.

(c) Using a special machine (cost $3,000 and immediately available) the part could be made with 0.3 direct labor hours per part.

Material is expected to cost $1 per unit. The company has a uniform labor rate of $3 per hour, a factory burden rate of 150 percent of direct labor, and a general and administrative expense of 50 percent of direct labor. Auto-Right employs 250 shop employees.

It has been estimated that 25 percent of the factory burden and general and administrative expense varies proportionally with factory activity.

Should Auto-Right take on the job, and if so, what alternative should it use? Justify your answer.

chapter

MACROPROCESSING—PROCESSING MODE AND DESIGN

eight

Here we shall develop the different processing modes available to POM system designers and discuss the conditions of use for each of them. Our approach to facility layout includes a discussion of CRAFT (Computerized Relative Allocation of Facilities Technique) as one approach to process-oriented layout. Under product-oriented processing, we shall introduce both paced and unpaced assembly lines as well as methods for balancing such facilities.

PROCESSING MODE AND PROCESS DESIGN

To this point, our discussion of macroprocessing design has been oriented toward a single product or service. In order to broaden that perspective, we now examine processing design in relationship to the basic processing modes.

FIXED LOCATION PROCESSING

Often it is necessary or desirable to perform a processing operation in a fixed location by bringing

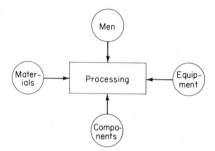

Figure 8-1   *Illustrating fixed location processing*

men, equipment and components, and materials to the work. (See Figure 8-1.) Construction, maintenance, repair of dams, roads, and buildings, and work on telephone, power, water, or sewage lines all require on-site processing. Similarly home and office remodeling, landscaping, and fire fighting must be done on-site. Heavy and bulky materials which are not easily moved are typically processed in a fixed location. Hydroelectric turbines undergo final assembly in a single given location as do diesel engines like those used in locomotives and ships.

Sometimes the decision to do on-site processing is based on marketing considerations. Such decisions often occur in the service sector and affect a firm's competitive strategy. For example, should a television repair service offer in-the-home repair, or should an organization offering nursing home care also provide for home visits by a nurse or therapist?

The nature of fixed location processing design centers primarily on developing and implementing a schedule for coordinating men, equipment materials, and components so that the job is efficiently accomplished. Without this coordination, certain of the resources involved may be idle for long periods of time. Effective construction of large office buildings in crowded metropolitan areas where on-site storage space is sufficient only for a few day's supply of materials requires the most acute attention to scheduling of job resources. The techniques described in Chapter 16 prove invaluable in developing such a schedule. Most notable among these is PERT—a technique for efficiently scheduling complex projects.

PROCESS-ORIENTED PROCESSING   *JoB SHoP*

The most frequently encountered form of processing is one designed around a process or activity-oriented layout. Here similar operations, equipment, personnel, or material are located in a common area; this system can process simultaneously a wide variety of products, information, or services. These may include information retrieval, customer, product, or patient servicing, warehouse order filling, as well as job shop fabrication. Figure 8-2 illustrates how each order is routed individually through the different processing areas according to its own specifications. In order to handle the diverse demands placed upon them, the equipment and personnel used tend to be highly versatile and considerably less specialized than those involved in other forms of processing.

A process-oriented layout is most efficient for handling products or services which cannot justify a specialized, individual layout. A classical illustration is a machine shop which processes a continually changing array of products and customer orders, none of which justifies setting up a special-ized layout. Another familiar example of this type layout is a hospital servic-ing a continual input of patients, each with his own special problems. For each patient, both information describing his condition and materials and personnel used in treating and testing him are routed through operating rooms, recovery rooms, intensive care areas, nursing stations, medical records department, laboratories, laundry, pharmacy, and kitchen.

Initial considerations in process-oriented layout. Rather than being ran-domly located over the processing site, similar operations, personnel, equip-ment, and materials are grouped together in the process-oriented layout to facilitate moving the work, to provide increased utilization of men and equipment, and to provide for increased flexibility and control. Consider a machine shop processing a part requiring grinding which can be done on any of the seven grinders in the shop. If the grinders were scattered throughout the shop, the part would have to be sent to a specific grinder. Without excellent knowledge of current shop conditions, the part might be sent to a grinder with a large backlog of work. On the other hand, if all

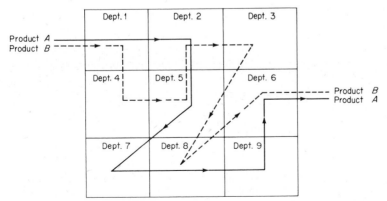

Figure 8-2 *Process-oriented layout showing two of the many different product's and customer orders' routing through nine functionally oriented departments*

the grinders were located in a common area, the part could be sent to this area with instructions that any one of the suitable machines be used. The selection of a specific machine would be made in the grinding area itself in light of first hand knowledge of work loads and worker and grinder availability. Further, this machine grouping allows the grinding foreman to balance work loads for both men and equipment as well as reduce the time the typical order has to wait for processing. In spite of the efficiencies gained by locating similar processes together, the utilization of men and equipment falls somewhere between 60 percent and 90 percent. Although this utilization may seem low, the excess capacity is usually needed to cope successfully with changing product mix and demand variations. It is not atypical for the machine shop to require a month or more to finish an order which involves less than a week's actual machine time. This differential arises because of material handling time and time spent waiting for equipment to become available for processing the order.

Developing a process-oriented layout. In many ways, the most critical dimension of process-oriented processing design is that of locating the departments and work areas. A poor facility layout (see Figure 8-3), results in excessive time and cost lost through unnecessary material, personnel, and information movement. Since layouts are very expensive to alter once they have been installed, an ineffective layout may have to be endured for years. Consequently, a great deal of effort can profitably be put into designing a new layout.

In designing a process-oriented layout, the primary consideration in arranging facilities is to minimize interchange costs between departments. Thus the layout design seeks to minimize:

$$\sum_{i=1}^{N} \sum_{j=1}^{N} C_{ij} D_{ij}$$

where

D_{ij} is the distance in feet associated with moving between departments i and j

C_{ij} is the total interchange cost per foot of moving between departments i and j

N is the number of departments

For a machine shop, C_{ij} would be the average cost for making one foot of the trip between departments i and j times the number of trips to be made. For an oil refinery, C_{ij} would be the cost per foot of the piping between process or storage area i and process or storage area j. For an office building, the relative benefit of offices or departments i and j being a foot closer together could be used as a surrogate for the interchange cost C_{ij}.

Finding the departmental layout which minimizes the interchange costs

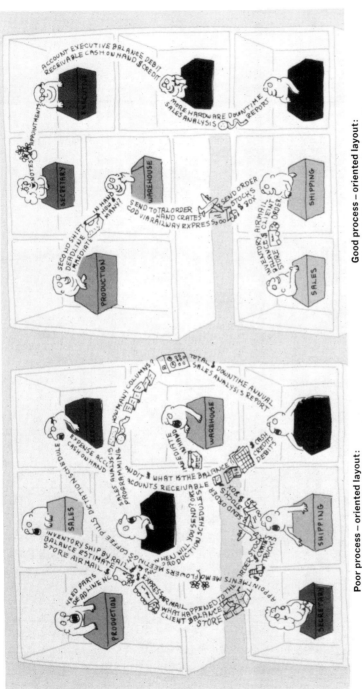

Poor process – oriented layout:
Communications distances are long, and volume and costs are high.

Good process – oriented layout:
Communications distances are shorter and costs are reduced.

Figure 8-3 *Poor versus good process-oriented layout. [From A. S. Volgyesi, "Space-age Approach to Space Allocation," Computer Decisions (New York: Hayden Book Company, Inc., May 1970).]*

179

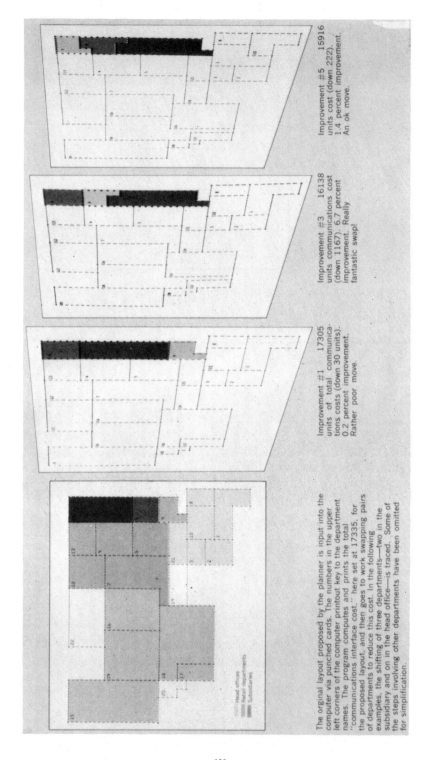

The orginal layout proposed by the planner is input into the computer via punched cards. The numbers in the upper left corners of the computer printout key to the department names. The program computes and prints the total "communications interface cost," here set at 17335, for the proposed layout, and then goes to work swapping pairs of departments to reduce this cost. In the following examples, the shifting of three departments—two in the subsidiary and on in the head office—is traced. Some of the steps involving other departments have been omitted for simplification.

Head offices
Retail departments
Subsidiaries

Improvement #1   17305 units of total communications costs (down 30 units). 0.2 percent improvement. Rather poor move.

Improvement #3   16138 units communications cost (down 1167). 6.7 percent improvement. Really fantastic swap!

Improvement #5   15916 units cost (down 222). 1.4 percent improvement. An ok move.

180

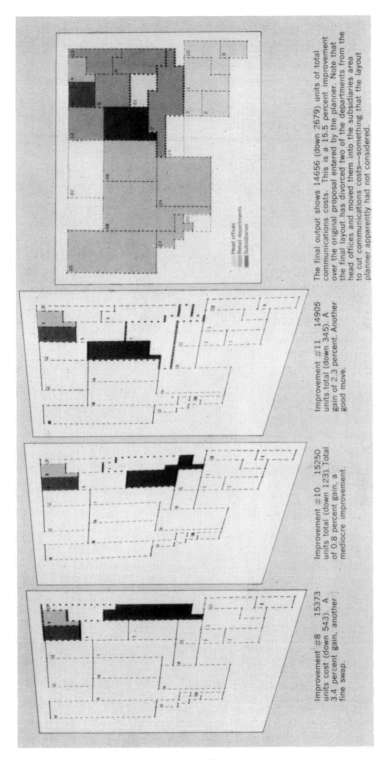

Improvement #8   15373 units cost (down 543). A 3.4 percent gain, another fine swap.

Improvement #10   15250 units total (down 123). Total of 0.8 percent gain, a mediocre improvement.

Improvement #11   14905 units total (down 345). A gain of 2.3 percent. Another good move.

The final output shows 14656 (down 2679) units of total communications costs. This is a 15.5 percent improvement over the original proposal entered by the planner. Note that the final layout has divorced two of the departments from the head offices and moved them into the subsidiaries area to cut communications costs—something that the layout planner apparently had not considered.

Figure 8-4 *Improved office building layout prepared with CRAFT computer program. [From A. S. Volgyesi, "Space-age Approach to Space Allocation," Computer Decisions (New York: Hayden Book Company, Inc., May 1970).]*

is complicated because of the unusually large number of different possible relative positions of the departments. With 10 departments, there are potentially well over one million different relative arrangements. The number climbs to more than 10^{60} when there are 50 departments. As staggering as these numbers are, however, they do not include the possible shape variation of the different departments. For example, a department requiring 10,000 square feet might be assigned to an area 100 by 100 feet, 133.3 by 75 feet, 200 by 50 feet, or any number of other shape possibilities. These two factors, relative positioning and shape, combine to give rise to an almost infinite number of possible layouts.

Utilization of the CRAFT technique. There is an approach which is likely to find a near optimal layout configuration with a reasonable amount of effort. It utilizes a generally available, computerized search technique known as CRAFT (an acronym for *C*omputerized *R*elative *A*llocation of *F*acilities *T*echnique). CRAFT is a heuristic search technique which systematically searches out alternative departmental rearrangements to reduce the total interchange cost. The CRAFT computer program is available free of charge to all users of large IBM computers under program #SDA 3391 from the IBM Share Library of computer programs.

To use CRAFT certain data must be developed. The number and size of the departments to be located and shaped must be determined. Usually only the major departments are considered for two reasons: (1) the required computer time expands rapidly with the number of departments studied, (2) once a basic layout has been chosen, CRAFT can be easily used to help layout the internal arrangement of the major departments already considered. Estimates of how much space is needed can be developed by estimating the number and type of equipment and work areas needed and the space required for aisles and storage. Also needed are estimates of all the C_{ij}'s (the costs per foot of all the interchanges).

Using this information, the layout planners then intuitively develop the best layout they can by trying to minimize interchange costs. Figure 8-4 shows such a plan developed by an architect for rearranging an office building. Figure 8-5 shows a matrix giving the interchange costs associated with the 22 departments to be located in the building. The numbers in the matrix give the priority of the interchanges between the various departments; the higher the priority number the more important is the interchange and the closer the two departments should be.

This preliminary layout is then fed into the computer via punched cards as is the interchange cost matrix. The CRAFT computer program then searches for adjacent pairs of departments which can be swapped and which will reduce the total interchange cost. Any cost reducing swap is made and the search continues until no further cost reducing swaps can be found. Figure 8-4 partially traces some of the department cost reducing swaps made by the computer from the architect's plan. The final layout generated

Communications interface grid

The numbers on both axes represent departments within the company. The numbers from one to six assigned to each interaction between departments represents the priority given to the cost or volume of communications between the two departments involved.

	1	2	3	4	5	6	7	8	9	10	11	12	13	14	15	16	17	18	19	20	21	22
1	-																					
2	3	-																				
3	4	2	-																			
4	5	4	4	-																		
5	4	5	3	1	-																	
6	4	2	2	2	3	-																
7	3	3	4	3	2	3	-															
8	5	6	5	6	6	6	5	-														
9	4	6	6	6	4	6	5	6	-													
10	3	4	5	4	4	5	4	5	6	-												
11	2	4	4	4	2	4	3	4	4	2	-											
12	4	4	6	4	2	3	3	6	4	5	3	-										
13	3	5	6	4	3	4	4	6	6	4	4	2	-									
14	6	5	4	5	6	5	5	5	4	6	2	5	6	-								
15	4	6	4	5	6	5	4	6	4	6	3	4	6	4	-							
16	5	6	4	5	5	5	5	6	4	6	3	4	4	4	4	-						
17	6	6	6	6	5	6	5	6	6	6	5	4	5	1	1	1	-					
18	5	6	4	4	1	5	5	6	6	6	3	3	3	1	1	1	2	-				
19	3	5	5	2	6	6	2	6	6	4	2	5	4	2	2	2	5	1	-			
20	6	6	6	6	6	6	6	6	6	6	6	6	6	6	6	6	6	1	1	6	-	
21	3	3	3	3	2	3	1	5	5	4	2	3	3	4	4	4	4	4	6	6	-	
22	6	6	6	6	6	4	4	4	4	4	4	4	4	4	4	4	4	4	4	4	4	-

Figure 8-5 *Matrix of priority of department interchanges. [From A. S. Volgyesi, "Space-age Approach to Space Allocation,"* Computer Decisions *(New York: Hayden Book Company, Inc., May 1970).]*

by CRAFT shows a 15.5 percent reduction in interchange cost over the preliminary layout.

After finding an effective interdepartmental layout, the CRAFT technique can be continued on the intradepartmental level. In designing a hospital kitchen which has already been located by CRAFT, it would be natural to use CRAFT again to locate stoves, ovens, refrigerators, salad making, baking, other food preparation areas, patient tray assembly, dish washing and storage areas.

Considerations in the use of layout techniques. In view of the expense involved, the use of CRAFT can only be justified in situations too complex to permit the development of an effective layout by more traditional, trial and error methods.) Generally, the larger the number of areas to be arranged, the more complex and costly the interchanges become and the more advantageous the use of CRAFT becomes.

CRAFT is a much more sophisticated technique than described here. It allows a clever planner wide latitude in placing constraints on the types of rearrangements made by the program. It is possible to specify fixed locations for certain areas in advance. This provision is useful, for example, where the plant manager specifies that his office must be in the northeast corner of the plant or where an existing building is being remodeled and there are structural features like elevators or load bearing walls which are too expensive to move from their existing location. When it is desirable to locate two areas adjacent to each other, a very high interchange cost between the two will insure the necessary placement. An even more effective way of proceeding would be to consider the two areas as one unit. Once the CRAFT technique has positioned and shaped the combined area, the layout designers can then worry about the relative positioning of the two areas comprising it.

CRAFT's most serious drawback, besides that of cost, is that it does not alter the exterior shape of the initial layout which is fed into the computer. While this may be a desirable feature when rearranging existing facilities, it can be a major limitation when a new one is being planned. For example, is a new 250,000 square foot plant better built 500 by 500, or 200 by 1,250, or in some irregular shape? At present, all one can do is to try CRAFT with a variety of different, initially proposed building shapes in the hope of locating one which minimizes total interchange cost. Fortunately, it often does not take long or cost much to work with a number of tentative designs especially when fewer than 25 departments are being arranged.

CRAFT's other drawbacks are less serious in nature. Even for a given building shape, CRAFT does not *guarantee* that the least cost layout has been developed because since it is a heuristic, it does not consider all of the possible interchanges and area shapes. Fortunately, it is a characteristic of a facility layout problem that there are many near optimal configurations, and CRAFT almost always finds a near minimum interchange cost layout for a given initial building shape. Since it begins by improving upon a proposed layout, CRAFT's design must be at least as good as the initial layout and hopefully will involve substantial improvement.

PRODUCT-ORIENTED PROCESSING

Flow shop Again

Product-oriented processing, or line processing as it is also commonly known, is an arrangement of work stations which has been set up specifically to process a particular product or group of highly similar products. In the

product always follows same routing.

Know u Diff.

You HAVE INVENTORY FOR EACH POSITION

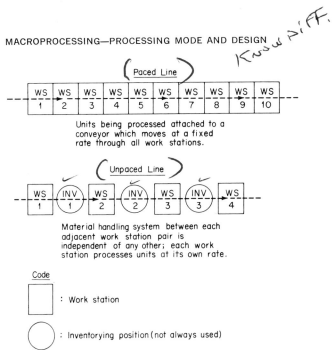

Figure 8-6 *Two types of line processing*

bottling of soft drinks, the making of cigarettes, or the assembly of Chevrolet automobiles, one sees examples of this specialized, high-volume type of processing. The work stations are arranged along a fixed route so that all products are processed through an identical sequence of operations in the same order (see Figure 8-6).

Product-oriented processing typically utilizes more automated and specially designed equipment than is found in the processing of the fixed position and process-oriented types. By far, the best known example of line processing is the Detroit-style automobile assembly line. Frames are attached at the beginning of a moving conveyor which then passes thousands of work stations on its $\frac{1}{4}$-mile route where almost the same set of operations are performed on each passing car. At the end of the line, completed cars are driven off. Telephone receivers, appliances, and most other mass-produced products with many components are line assembled. Bottling and canning operations are still further examples. In fabrication, product-oriented processing is sometimes carried to such an extreme that a completely automatic piece of equipment is developed to do all the necessary operations. Recall the cigarette-making machines and the transfer machine for machining automobile engine blocks described in Chapter 7 in the section on automation.

Although less conspicuous, nonmanufacturing examples of line processing do exist; a cafeteria line is an example. Some of you may well be personally familiar with the selective service physical which processes inductees sequentially through various types of medical exams. Many banks use line processing when handling the personal checks of their depositors; checks are received and verified, and corresponding data cards are punched and fed into a computer which makes appropriate adjustments to customer accounts.

Characteristics. Situations where product-oriented processing is used tend to have certain characteristics in common. Both in rate and duration, the output volume is large enough to justify the time and cost of designing, setting up, and operating a special processing arrangement; the actual volume needed depends on the particular product being produced. Several thousand cigarettes an hour produced around the clock for several years are needed to absorb the cost of a single cigarette-making machine of the type used today. A standard automobile assembly line can be economically justified on the basis of about 25 cars an hour being produced steadily for 4 months. On the other hand, it will take approximately 100 units an hour for over a year to return the cost of General Motor's highly automated line for fabricating and assemblying the bodies for its subcompact, the Vega.

To use line processing, the material being transferred through the line must be movable, although not necessarily light or compact. There are, for example, a few shipyards which fabricate bulky shiphulls, weighing hundreds of tons, on a line basis when there are orders for at least twenty nearly identical vessels.

To institute line processing, there must be complete prior knowledge of what is to be produced. A line can only work with those outputs which it is designed to handle. Even if General Motors would permit it, a Ford could not be put together on a Chevrolet assembly line. Yet some of these lines are designed with sufficient built-in flexibility to assemble several models within the same make of car. For example, on a Chevrolet assembly line you might see a white striped Chevy II, followed by a matador red Camaro dragster, followed by a blue Chevrolet Caprice sedan. The two factors which permit such flexibility in line processing are standardization of work and interchangeability and standardization of components.

Paced and unpaced lines. In designing a product-oriented processing system, a choice must be made between the paced or the unpaced line. (See Figure 8-6.) The former utilizes an automatic material-handling system which moves the material or product through each work station at the same rate. Soft drink bottling, automobile assembly, and cigarette making are all examples of paced lines; the units being produced are spaced at fixed intervals along a conveyor moving at a set speed. When more precise work is required (as in assemblying a telephone), the conveyor often operates on a start-stop basis; that is, each time the line starts up, all the units being processed are advanced to the next station. Regardless of which type conveyor movement is used, there is only a limited amount of time to perform the tasks assigned to each station. The line output rate and the time spent at each station are determined by the speed of the conveyor and the distance covered between each unit.

With an unpaced line (for example, a cafeteria line), or the selective service physical, each work station takes as long as needed to complete the assigned tasks. Inventories between work stations can be used to adjust for differing task time. Instead of an integrated, automatic material-handling system moving through all work stations, separate material-handling facilities (cranes, fork lift trucks, manual methods), move the units between the adjacent work stations.

Conditions for use—paced lines. Because of its automated, continuous material handling, the paced line is well suited for moving large volumes of heavy, bulky materials and products, e.g., cars, refrigerators, and washers. By minimizing worker handling, it may also be desirable for processing fragile items. Since the paced line processes units in a fixed order and moves units at a precise rate, it is possible to schedule a variety of different, though interchangeable inputs into each work station on the line. For example, on an automobile assembly line, it really doesn't matter to the workers responsible for attaching hubcaps which styles they attach to a set of wheels; the task remains essentially the same as long as the particular hubcap will fit whatever wheel is passing on the line. Another advantage of a paced line can be that it does not require inventories between work stations. In the case of large, bulky products, allowing for these inventories can be quite space-consuming; imagine how much space would be needed to allow for even one car between each of the more than 1,000 work stations found on an automobile assembly line.

Paced lines are not without problems. Each worker has only a specified time to complete his assigned tasks before the product has moved to the next station. Consequently, in designing a paced line, the task times are typically those in which at least 95 percent of the workers can complete the tasks. This means slightly reduced labor utilization. Finally any breakdown of the material handling system or one operation along the line or shortage of input components can shut down an entire paced line because of its high degree of integration among work stations.

Conditions for use—unpaced lines. The unpaced line can be justified with a lower output volume because it avoids the high, material-handling investment characteristic of a paced line. While it is possible to schedule a variety of different, interchangeable inputs on unpaced lines, either the order of the units being processed must be preserved (this can be difficult with small units), or each unit must carry instructions as to which type of input to install at each work station. Inventories are typically used between stations on an unpaced line as a means of improving worker utilization; that is, as long as there is a unit available for work and a place to put completed units, workers can remain productive regardless of what is happening at other work stations. Consequently, breakdowns and material shortages are less likely to affect an unpaced line, and individual labor utilization is higher than in paced lines.

Deciding on the output rate of a line. Actual design of a line is accomplished in three phases: (1) deciding how many units an hour the line should be able to produce, (2) determining the work station output rates, and (3) grouping the tasks which must be finished into work assignments so that not only the desired work station output rate will be achieved but also the investment and operating costs of the lines will be minimized. This third phase is commonly referred to as "balancing the line."

Prerequisite to selection of an output rate is a careful analysis of the demand for the product. This demand forecast is then used in calculating how many lines should be used, how many shifts each should be operated, and what capacity each line should have.

Because of the high cost of overtime, employee terminations, and the cost and difficulty of shifting workers, lines are designed to be operated on a full shift basis, i.e., one, two, or three full shifts a day. When labor cost is high compared to the cost of setting up the line (the case in which an assembly line utilizes little equipment and space), single shift line operation would be the obvious choice even if more than one line must be used. On the other hand, lines with high setup costs are commonly operated on a multiple shift basis, as long as the costs of 2nd and 3rd shift wage premiums, extra supervision, and lower 2nd and 3rd shift efficiencies are not prohibitive.

An unpaced line of any capacity can be designed simply by duplicating worker assignments and the pieces of equipment to be used. Figure 8-7 shows an unpaced line for performing four machine-controlled operations, each requiring a separate machine with its own operator. Different line output rates are achieved merely by changing the number of machines and workers utilized. Notice that the equipment and labor efficiency (output rate per machine/operator combination), increases as the line output rate is increased. This observation implies that in a given plant, only one, rather than more than one, unpaced line should be set up to meet demand.

A paced line usually has only a limited range of output rates which are technologically and economically feasible. The longest task which cannot be further subdivided determines the maximum output rate for a paced line. Since that task must be performed on each unit passing down the line, moving the units through each work station at a faster rate would not allow enough time to finish this longest task. If, for example, the longest task requires 0.5 minutes, the paced line cannot produce more than 60/0.5 or 120 units an hour. It is important to recognize that this maximum production rate is only temporarily absolute, i.e., a function of current technology

Machine-controlled Operation	Machine Output Rate in Units per Hour	Number of Machines and Operators Needed to Achieve Output Rate of X Units an Hour				
		$X = 50$	$X = 100$	$X = 150$	$X = 200$	$X = 300$
A	20	3	5	8	10	15
B	25	2	4	6	8	12
C	40	2	3	4	5	8
D	15	4	7	10	14	20
Total:		11	19	28	37	55
Output rate per machine/operator combination		4.5	5.3	5.4	5.4	5.5

Figure 8-7 *Comparison of number of machines and operators needed on an unpaced line to achieve different output rates when there are four machine-controlled operations each requiring its own operator*

and currently anticipated volume. The availability of new equipment may allow an increased output rate; further, a significant increase in anticipated demand may justify the development of equipment not currently available. This is precisely what happened when General Motors decided to retain the same body style on the Vega for several years. Here the previous maximum line output was revised upward from about 70 cars an hour to over 100 an hour, due to the increased use of newly developed automated machinery.

Determining the output rate of individual work station. Once the output rate per hour of the line has been chosen, the ideal output rate for any work station along the line can then be determined. Due to inventory considerations, this particular calculation is more involved for an unpaced line than for a paced one

Paced line output rates. When considering paced lines, the output rates of all the work stations are the same as that selected for the whole line because all the units are equally spaced on the conveyor and travel at the same speed sequentially through all the work stations. The conveyor speed and the spacing of the units determine the line's output rate. Products are usually spaced to allow minimum working clearance between units; allowing excessive space per unit would require the speed of the line to be increased to maintain the desired output rate. For example, if 20 feet per automobile were allowed, and 60 automobiles were to come off the line an hour, the conveyor would have to move at a speed of 20 feet per minute (one automobile per minute), but if the allowance were 30 feet, it would have to travel 30 feet per minute to maintain the same hourly output rate.

It is also important to recognize that the paced line output largely determines the available work time per unit at each work station. The available minutes T for working on each unit moving through each work station is

$$T = \frac{60}{R} - I$$

where

R is the line or work station output rate in units per hour
I is the time in minutes required to advance the next unit to each work place for a paced line operated on a stop and start basis (the time needed for the worker to reposition himself after completing one unit before starting on the next)

Thus if $R = 28$ units an hour and $I = 0.14$ minutes, T would be $\frac{60}{28} - 0.14$ or 2 minutes available for working on each unit. In this example, no more than 2 minutes of work can be assigned to any work station if the tasks are to be completed. Further, to insure a high probability of finishing all the assigned work, the times used should be those that all the workers can meet or exceed 95 percent of the time.

Unpaced line output rates. Determining output rates for the work stations in an unpaced line is a more difficult problem. Basically, there are two choices; in the first, sufficient inventories can be allocated at the work stations to permit each station to operate independently at a rate equal to the desired line output rate. If this option is not available, the only alternative is to increase the output rate sufficient at each work station to compensate for the lost time caused by the interdependencies of these stations.

Allowing for large inventories between work stations insures (1) that there will always be a place to put each unit as it is finished, and (2) that there is always another unit on which to begin work. In this case, the line output rate will be the same as that work station with the *lowest* average output rate. As a result all work stations can be designed with the same output rate as that desired for the line, and because faster workers do not have to wait for slower workers (as in the case of the paced line), employee and equipment utilization is higher than in the paced line.

In the case where inventory between work stations is not allowed, no units can be passed along to the next work station until all stations have finished the unit on which they are working. Hence, the line output rate at any moment is determined by the work station which takes the longest time on the unit it is currently processing. Since processing times at each station are subject to variation, the slowest station may change with different units processed.

It is important to consider the cost of achieving a desired line output rate both by providing interstation inventory storage and by using high work station output rates. First, when working with large, bulky products, providing storage is very costly, and this solution may only be a viable one over a very narrow range. Second, if a firm attempts to obtain a given line output rate by allowing considerably *less* processing time at each station than they think will actually be required, they run the risk of having to provide additional work stations, since the amount of work that must actually be done to complete a unit remains essentially the same regardless of the firm's attempts to reduce it arbitrarily. The optimum amount of interstation inventory should, as Figure 8-8 indicates, be determined by minimizing the total cost of (1) maintaining high inventory levels, and (2) providing additional work stations. Finding the suitable tradeoff between these two which will minimize total cost is extremely difficult in actual practice. Based on past experience with similar lines, many firms have developed adjustment guidelines for determining suitable work station output rates and inventory levels.

Line balancing. The last phase of designing a line is grouping the tasks which have to be performed into balanced work assignments. The objective is to group the tasks so that the output rate of each work station meets, as closely as possible without exceeding it, the time available for working on each unit. Since there is a constant amount of work to be done on each unit, this procedure minimizes the workers and equipment needed

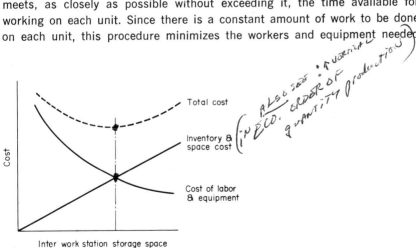

Figure 8-8   *Optimum amount of interstation inventory illustrated*

to operate the line at the desired rate. This process of grouping the tasks is what is meant by "line balancing."

All work must be identified and broken down into elemental tasks. These latter are the minimal units of work which cannot be further divided without the resulting divisions requiring significantly longer to perform than the whole. Drilling a hole, for example, would be considered an elemental task here. If the hole were started on one drill press and completed on another, additional time would be required to withdraw the first drill and remove the part from the press, to position the part on the second press, and to advance this drill to where it makes contact with the part—all unnecessary activities if the task were completed on one machine. Other examples of elemental tasks include soldering a wire to an electrical contact, dishing up a vegetable on a cafeteria line, and putting on and tightening all the nuts on a car wheel with a special power socket wrench which enables the worker to complete the task in one simultaneous operation.

Once all the elemental tasks are identified, the tasks which must immediately precede each of them should be identified and catalogued into a precedence table like the one seen in Figure 8-9. A precedence graph (also shown in Figure 8-9), is a convenient means of visualizing the precedence relationships. There are many examples of immediate precedence relationships. To machine a screw thread in a drilled hole, the hole must first be drilled. Before putting on and tightening the nuts on a car wheel, the wheel has to be attached. Sometimes a task has more than one immediate predecessor; for example, before testing appliances coming down the line to see if they function well, both mechanical *and* electrical parts must be assembled. One task *can* be an immediate predecessor to two or more tasks.

Also catalogued, along with the precedence table and chart, are any other restrictions on the grouping of the tasks; for example, when tasks require differing skills that are not available in a single worker, they must be placed in different work assignments.

An example. When balancing a line, it is usually desirable to use as few workers as possible. To see what is involved in achieving a minimum worker balance, we consider the example in Figure 8-9. Suppose that the maximum time available for processing a unit at any work station is 2 minutes. Further suppose that no restrictions other than the precedence ones exist. Adding up the total time for the 14 tasks, we find that there is $1.0 + 0.6 + 0.4 + 0.8 + 0.7 + 0.5 + 0.5 + 0.4 + 1.7 + 1.0 + 0.5 + 0.4 + 0.7 + 0.5$ or 9.7 minutes of work per unit. Since there are only 2 minutes for working on each unit at each work station, the number of stations needed will be at least 5. From Figure 8-9, we see that task *I* must fill a work station assignment itself since there are no tasks of 0.3 minutes or less which can be combined with it to form an assignment which does

Precedence table

Elemental task	Immediate predecessors	Task time in minutes
A	none	1.0
B	none	.6
C	none	.4
D	none	.8
E	A, B	.7
F	B	.5
G	C, D	.5
H	E	.4
I	F	1.7
J	F, G	1.0
K	H, I	.5
L	J	.4
M	K	.7
N	L	.5

Precedence graph

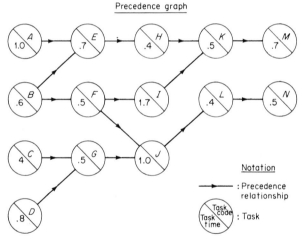

Notation

⟶ : Precedence relationship

(Task code / Task / time) : Task

Figure 8-9 *Precedence table and graph showing elemental tasks and times necessary to produce a simple product*

not exceed 2 minutes. Further, we see that there must be at least one work station assignment following the task *I* assignment in order to complete the product, because both tasks *K* and *M* must follow the task *I* assignment. A work assignment following *I* coming closest to the allowed 2 minutes without violating the precedence relationships would be composed of tasks *J*, *L*, and *N*. The working time of this latter assignment would be 1.9 minutes per unit with 0.1 minute idle time per unit processed. Based on results thus far, we see that we will require at least 9.7 minutes of working time plus 0.3 minutes of idle time per unit at station *I* plus 0.1 minutes of idle time

WORK ELEMENT - SMALLEST SINGLE JOB YOU CAN IDENTIFY.

per unit at the work station performing tasks *J*, *L*, and *N*, or a total of 10.1 minutes of time. Since we are limited to a work assignment time of 2 minutes per unit, we see that a minimum of 6 work stations, not 5, are needed to produce the product at the desired rate.

The station assignments depicted in Figure 8-10 represent the best balance; their duration ranges from 1.5 to 1.7 minutes per unit. Notice that there are only two orders in which the assignments can be arranged along the route without violating any of the precedence relationships.

When there are restrictions other than the precedence ones, they usually reduce the quality of the best line balance. Suppose that in the example of Figure 8-9, the unit being processed cannot be turned over; thus tasks *C*, *D*, *G*, *J*, *L*, and *N* are limited to the line's left side and *A*, *B*, *E*, *F*, *H*, *I*, *K*, and *M* to the line's right side. Since we already know that at least 6 work stations will be needed, we will have to look for 6 work assignments which do not violate this left-right side restriction or any of the precedence restrictions and which total to 2 minutes of work or less per unit. The line design depicted in Figure 8-11 is the best balance which

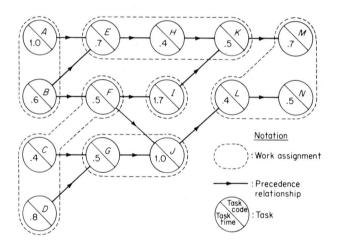

Tasks composing work assignment	Work assignment's order from start of line		Total working minutes per unit processed
A, B	1	1	1.6
C, D, F	2	2	1.7
I	3	4	1.7
E, H, K	4	5	1.6
G, J	5	3	1.5
L, M, N	6	6	1.6

Figure 8-10 *A line design for producing the product in Figure 8-9 when the maximum work assignment working time is 2 minutes per unit*

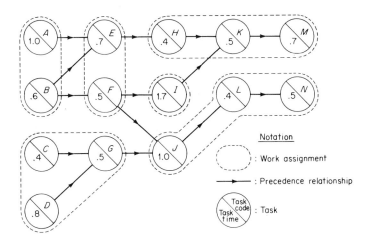

Tasks composing work assignment	Work assignment's order from start of line	Total working minutes per unit processed
A, B	1 on line's right side	1.6
C, D, G	1 on line's left side	1.7
E, F	2 on line's right side	1.2
I	3 on line's right side	1.7
H, K, M	4 on line's right side	1.6
J, L, N	2 on line's left side	1.9

Figure 8-11   *A line design for producing the product in Figure 8-9 when the maximum work assignment duration is 2 minutes per unit and tasks A, B, E, F, H, I, K, and M must be performed on the same side of the line and tasks* C, D, G, J, L, *and* N *on the other side of line*

can be found. Note that the assignments are not as well equalized in duration as when the left-right constraint was not present (the amount of work in the assignments ranges from 1.2 to 1.9 minutes per unit instead of 1.5 to 1.7). When there is such a wide spread, some firms use the low work content assignments (1.2 minutes for instance), as training experiences to get new workers accustomed to the tempo of the line.

More complicated balancing. Although the previous example was a simple one involving only 14 tasks, most real lines needing balancing have hundreds and even thousands of tasks. An automobile assembly may involve 5,000 tasks. Further, the time and effort involved in finding a good balance grows exponentially relative to the number of tasks. Obviously, to find a good balance in a reasonable amount of time, highly efficient computerized line balancing procedures are needed. A number of such procedures have been developed. Articles by Ignall and Mastor review and compare many of these procedures.[1]

Refinements. Whether developed with a computerized balancing technique or by intuition, any balance obtained should be examined for opportunities to reduce the number of workers required to staff the line. Sometimes splitting a task enables a better overall line balance to be obtained, even though the split task is much less efficiently performed. Assume, for example, that in Figure 8-10 task K which presently requires 0.5 minutes per unit can be split into 2 tasks, K_a which takes 0.3 minutes and K_b which takes 0.4 minutes and which must immediately follow K_a. Observe that even though splitting task K increases its time by 40 percent, a 5-man balance can be found (see Figure 8-12), which will maintain the same output rate as the 6-man line.

There are several other techniques which can often be employed to reduce the number of workers and amount of equipment needed on a line.

[1] See E. J. Ignall, "A Review of Assembly Line Balancing," *Journal of Industrial Engineering,* July-August 1965, pp. 244–254 and A. A. Mastor, "An Experimental Investigation and Comparative Evaluation of Production Line Balancing Techniques," *Management Science,* July 1970, pp. 728–746.

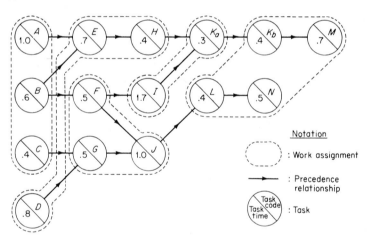

Tasks composing work assignment	Work assignment's order from start of line	Total working minutes per unit processed
A, B, C	1	2.0
D, E, H	2	1.9
F, G, J	3	2.0
I, K_a	4	2.0
K_b, L, M, N	5	2.0

Figure 8-12   *An improved line design over that of Figure 8-9 achieved by splitting task K into tasks K_a and K_b*

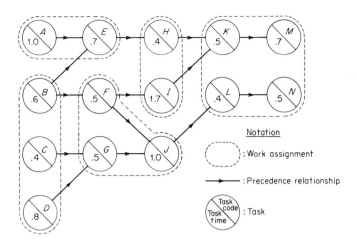

Notation

$\begin{pmatrix}\text{----}\\ \text{   }\\ \text{----}\end{pmatrix}$: Work assignment

⟶ : Precedence relationship

(Task/Task code/Task time) : Task

Tasks composing work assignment	Work assignment's order from start of line		Total working minutes per unit processed
B, C, D	1	1	1.8
A, E	2	3	1.7
F, G, J	3	2	2.0
H, I	4	4	2.1
K, L, M, N	5	5	2.1

Figure 8-13   *Another improved line design over that of Figure 8-9 achieved by increasing the maximum work assignment duration from 2 to 2.1 minute per unit*

Sometimes faster equipment can be used to reduce task time to a point where a better balance is achieved. Sometimes 2 workers can be assigned to the same work assignment to speed up its performance. On a continuously moving paced line, a longer work station can be utilized when extra work assignment time is needed and certain workers can work only on every other unit.

When there appears to be excessive idleness in the balancing design and it cannot be eliminated by utilizing one of the above approaches, the firm might elect to reduce the line output rate a few percentage points to achieve a much less costly balance. For example, in the example of Figure 8-9 when there was no left-right restriction, a 5-man balance can be achieved, by allowing 2.1 minutes per work station instead of 2.0 (see Figure 8-13). Thus, a 5 percent increase in allowed time results in a reduction in the number of line workers from 6 to 5 or a 16.7 percent labor cost reduction. The worthwhileness of this alternative solution would depend on economic analysis of the tradeoffs among labor cost, value of the increased output, and the fixed costs of operating the line.

QUESTIONS

1. How can you recognize a poor process-oriented layout if you see one? A poor product-oriented design?
2. Explain why a restaurant kitchen is like a job shop while a cafeteria line is like a flow shop.
3. Explain how market and demand considerations influence layout design of a:
   (a) Cafeteria
   (b) Hospital
   (c) Automobile assembly line
   (d) Highway
4. Use of a paced assembly line rather than an unpaced one would be more appropriate in which of the following situations:
   (a) Units are bulky
   (b) High worker utilization is desired
   (c) Minimum product handling is desired
   (d) Highly precise and exacting work is required
   (e) The products being assembled have individualized components to be put on particular product units
5. How does the choice of the processing type to be utilized affect the selection of materials-handling equipment?
6. How effective is automation in process-oriented processing? Product-oriented processing? Fixed-location processing? Explain your answers.
7. What are the basic types of data needed to design an efficient process-oriented layout? A production line? A fixed-location layout? Explain your answers.
8. Why is a production-line balancing necessary?
9. Explain what effect a change in output capacity requirements can have on the balance of a production line.
10. Why is labor often more efficiently utilized on an unpaced line than on a paced line?
11. Below is a schematic view of an assembly line with four work stations where each station is staffed by a single worker.

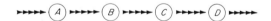

Work enters the line at station A where worker A completes operation A. The work proceeds sequentially through the remaining three stations at each of which a worker completes a different operation on the same unit started by worker A. Finished units leave the line after station D. Partially completed units can be inventoried between operations and need not be processed on a first-come, first-serve basis at each operation. The working time required per unit at each station is shown below:

Operation	Time (in minutes)
A	12.0
B	10.0
C	12.0
D	11.0

The company's industrial engineer has carefully studied this assembly line and found that technologically it is not feasible to divide the work up differently between the four work stations. However, he has come up with an improved method which would decrease the time needed at work station *A* from 12 to 10 minutes.

Justify why the improved method should or should not be installed.

Additional information:

(a) All workers are paid $3 per hour.
(b) The cost to install improved method is $600.
(c) The firm requires all improvements pay for themselves within 4 years.
(d) Any number of units between 10,000 and 12,000 per year can be sold for $10 per unit (assume there are no other possibilities).
(e) All workers work 40 hours per week and 50 weeks a year.
12. Wanderlust, Inc. has badly outgrown their existing facilities and has engaged you to layout a new building for them.

So far, you have determined that the firm has six processing departments each of which can't be subdivided and each of which requires a square shape. Each department's area requirements are given below.

Department	Square footage needs
A	40,000
B	40,000
C	10,000
D	10,000
E	10,000
F	10,000

Building cost considerations restrict Wanderlust to a building design with, at most, six exterior walls. As for travel between departments, the following table summarizes the number of trips made between the six departments in an average week. All trips cost approximately the same per foot traveled.

Average Number of Interdepartmental Trips per Week

	A	B	C	D	E	F
A		100	0	200	300	0
B			100	400	100	200
C				100	300	200
D					100	300
E						300
F						

Design a layout for Wanderlust which minimizes the interdepartmental travel while meeting their stated restrictions. All travel occurs in aisles which are parallel or perpendicular to the outer walls of the building. The one-trip travel distance between two departments can be approximated by computing the distance between the centers of the department. For example, as departments A and C are laid out below, the approximating distance is 200 feet. Note that the approximating distance is independent of which aisles are taken in traveling between A and C as long as movement is always towards the destination.

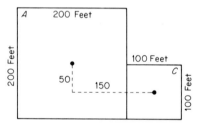

13. Joy Toy Products has decided the best way to assemble a preschool toy is by paced assembly line or lines. The precedence table below summarizes the data they have collected in order to design an appropriate assembly line or lines.

Elemental Task	Immediate Predecessors	Task Time in Minutes
A	none	0.7
B	none	0.2
C	A	0.4
D	A,B	0.2
E	A	0.5
F	C,D	0.5
G	E	0.6
H	F	0.4
I	E,F	0.1
J	G	0.3
K	I,J	0.4

Questions:

(a) Design Joy Toy a line or lines which minimizes the total number of work stations yet can assemble at least 60 units per hour.

(b) Design Joy Toy a line or lines which minimizes the total number of work stations yet can assemble at least 90 units per hour.

(c) To what levels do assembly rates have to be reduced before Joy Toy could get by with one less work station per line?

(d) Tasks *C, D,* and *G* can be split in half with the penalty that after splitting, each half requires 50 percent more time to complete separately than together. How much can you improve your line designs in (a) and (b) by splitting these tasks?

(e) If tasks *A, C, F,* and *H* must be performed on the left side of the line, tasks *B, E, G, J,* and *K* on the right side, and tasks *D* and *I* on either, what line designs will minimize the total number of work stations in (a) and (b)?

CASE

Mr. McCallum, manufacturing manager for the Apex Products, was reviewing an investment proposal prepared by Mr. Cook. Mr. Cook had spent the previous 2 weeks studying the possibility of automating the transfer of material between work stations in the Press Department.

Currently, there were three lines (*A,B,C*) of three work stations each consisting of (1) a blanking operation, (2) a shaping operation, and (3) a punching operation. Work moved down the line from (1) to (2) to (3). Each work station consisted of a press and an operator. In addition, there were two utility men who removed and delivered parts. Thus, a total of 11 men were used. The Press Department is producing 9,000 finished pieces a day with no increase in volume likely.

Mr. Cook's proposal was for automated material-handling equipment to

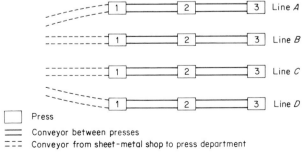

□ Press
═ Conveyor between presses
≡ Conveyor from sheet-metal shop to press department

Figure 8-14 *Proposed layout.*

be installed between the three machines. (See Figure 8-14.) With the proposed equipment, each line would automatically move the work to each press in the line, remove the work from each press, and transport work to the next station. To facilitate the initial loading of each line, Mr. Cook's proposal included a conveyor system from Apex's sheet metal shop. This latter conveyor system (see Figure 8-14) would move sheet metal blanks from the sheet metal shop to automatic feeders for the first press in line. Besides one operator to look after each line, Mr. Cook proposed only one utility man would be needed.

Mr. Cook's proposal included adding a fourth line of presses with automated material handling like he proposed for lines *A, B,* and *C* as well as hiring a roving repairman. The latter would be needed to handle the increasing sophisticated repairs demanded by the automated material-handling system. Whenever repairs of more than a few minutes were encountered, Mr. Cook reasoned that the operator of the downed line could run the fourth line in order to achieve the needed production. The fourth line, *D,* however, would only be run whenever line *A, B,* or *C* was down.

Figure 8-15 summarizes the cost and savings estimates submitted by Mr. Cook.

Explain and justify what Mr. McCallum should do about Mr. Cook's proposal if Apex requires all investments to pay for themselves in under 5 years.

Costs

Automated Material-handling System for Press Department (lines *A, B,* *C,* and *D*)	$ 48,000
Automated Material-handling System from Sheet Metal Shop to Press Department	12,000
Installation Charges $2,000 for Conveyors from Sheet Metal Shop + $4,000 for Conveyors between Presses	6,000
Fourth Line of 3 Presses	$240,000
Roving Repairman for Press Department (yearly salary plus fringes)	9,000
	$315,000

Savings

Direct Labor for the Press Department (from 1 man on each of 9 machines to 1 on each of 3 sets of 3 machines or a savings of 6 men × $7,000)	42,000
Utility Man Labor (from 2 men to 1 man to move work or 1 × $6,000)	6,000
Direct Factory Overhead (25% of direct labor or 25% of $48,000)	12,000
	$ 60,000

Figure 8-15   *Estimated costs and savings*

chapter

MICROPROCESSING DESIGN

nine

A necessary adjunct to equipment and flow processing design of the last two chapters is the design of effective work methods for humans. Man's contribution may be only supervisory, or it may represent the majority of the effort required to complete a particular processing operation. In either case, the worker often expects to be instructed in how to perform his assigned tasks. He also appreciates a carefully planned workplace where he can perform at peak effectiveness and maximum comfort. Suggestions which can improve the effectiveness of the labor required to produce each product should be welcome both to POM personnel and to the employee. Another crucial aspect of microprocessing design is determining the proper division of labor. While examples of totally repetitive short-cycle work assignments, on the one hand, and of jobs following the product or service throughout the entire processing operation, on the other, do in fact exist, the vast majority of jobs in business and industry represent some compromise between these two extremes. It is the task of the microprocess designer to determine the most appropriate mix for his particular processing consideration.

WHAT IS MICROPROCESSING DESIGN?

Despite the advances in automation and mechanization, men continue to play a dominant role in the processing of materials, services, and information. They run drill presses, assemble furniture, drive trucks, sort mail, cash checks, sell merchandise, build skyscrapers, prepare meals, fit eyeglasses—in short, perform an almost endless variety of tasks which we take for granted. Yet, most of these jobs require skill and training. Even highly automated processing requires workers to monitor those functions which the equipment is not designed to regulate and to maintain and repair the equipment whenever necessary. A microprocessing designer, then, is concerned with the development of the work designs which men use in the production process.

The term "microprocessing" is an apt one when discussing the design of human labor and work space, because man's function is usually not an end in itself but is rather only one part, however important, of the whole processing activity. Thousands of people play a multitude of roles in the production of a single jet airliner. In delivering your mail, at least five and often many more postal employees are involved. Thus, microprocessing design can be considered a phase of the total processing design discussed in the preceding chapter. It must be carried out in such a way that the human work assignments are both compatible with the other elements of the overall process design and augmentive to the total effectiveness of the entire processing design.

While microprocessing design is undertaken whenever there is an introduction of a new processing system, its principles and techniques are often used to improve existing jobs. In these latter cases, improvement must be judged in terms of its impact on the total processing system for not all situations merit job improvement effort.[1] This is especially true in assembly and production line situations where the critical work station (the one which uses the most time), regulates the speed of the whole line and tends to nullify any improvements which may be made on other stations.

Organic to our understanding of microprocessing design is the distinction between the following concepts of jobs and work assignments:

"A work assignment" is a set of processing activities which a worker will perform as a single, functional unit.

---

[1] Consider, for example, the case of a paced production line which has four work stations each of which is manned by a single operator. The part being processed moves consecutively from work station A to B to C to D. It takes 4.1, 4.2, 4.3, and 3.9 minutes respectively to process the part at work stations A, B, C, and D. The plant industrial engineer has come up with an idea for reducing the time involved at station B from 4.2 to 4.0 minutes. Upon closer examination, however, he realized that the output rate of the line would not be increased since it was limited by the work station with the longest per unit processing time—station C. Further, the time saved at work station B would be so small that the worker would not have sufficient extra time to take on other duties. Thus, there was no benefit to be gained in improving one man's work methods because no improvement in the overall processing could be effected.

"A job" is the aggregate of the potential work assignments which the worker performing that job may take on.

A work assignment may be a short-cycle repetitive set of tasks, such as bolting one wheel to each car axle coming down the assembly line, key punching IBM cards, or sorting apples. It might also be cyclic or randomly reoccurring, including such diverse examples as performing an appendectomy, giving a traffic ticket, responding to a customer complaint, or handling a labor grievance. Some work assignments are even one shot propositions such as teaching an experimental course, designing a state capitol building, or installing an automated production line.

THIN AND THICK JOBS

For the short-cycle repetitive job, the work assignment and the job are one and the same. When this happens, we call it a "thin job." Most jobs, however, do involve more than one work assignment and many encompass a large variety of tasks every day. These latter would be called "thick jobs." Consequently, the jobs of typist, elevator operator, and inspection line worker would be considered "thin," while tool and die maker, carpenter, university professor, and administrator would be classified as "thick."

When designing both the job and the work assignment, it is most important to define their expected content carefully. For work assignments, the set of activities to be performed must be identified so that the worker will do what is required. For jobs, the set of potential work assignments must be isolated in order to determine what skills are needed to train workers as well as to set the appropriate wage rate for the man's labor.

Every work assignment involves some degree of planning of the work methods to be used. Often this planning is done by the worker as he carries out the assignment. This may occur in any case where the worker is forced to improvise or is himself best qualified to do both the planning and the labor. It may also be the best solution when the benefits of more formal planning do not offset the costs. Whenever a work assignment is done with a high frequency, it is justifiable to preplan the work methods in the assignment and the workplace layout. Substantial design effort is also warranted for thin jobs composed of a few, short-cycle work assignments. The very nature of some work assignments is so critical that their efficient and error-free execution is imperative. However infrequent their occurrence, missile launchings, television spectaculars, and radioactive waste disposals demand carefully planned work assignments for all involved. Occasionally, there are work assignments with sufficient characteristics in common to make it worthwhile to develop generally applicable work methods and work area layouts which are more efficient than ad hoc approaches. It is for this reason that operating rooms and general operating procedures, line-balancing procedures, and labor grievance-handling procedures have been developed.

WORK DESIGN RESPONSIBILITY

The assignment of the responsibility for planning jobs and work assignments and for designing work methods and workplace layout will vary. In small companies, this responsibility usually rests with the same POM men who design the overall processing plan or even the ones who supervise the workers. In larger firms, the need for work design is great enough to justify employing full-time, work design specialists. Those concerned with the design of lower echelon manufacturing jobs often are found in industrial engineering departments, while those concerned with the design of similar, low level jobs associated with information processing activities are centered in systems and procedures groups. These specialists are often aided by the personnel department because of its familiarity with relevant collective bargaining agreement provisions and with the availability of labor skills both within and outside of the firm.

WORK CONTENT

The basic content of many jobs and work assignments has been defined by tradition and long-standing acceptance. Indeed, the majority of skilled and semiskilled labor jobs are so defined. Plumbers, welders, teachers, store clerks, and beauticians basically know what functions they are to perform even before they have been hired for a particular job. The public, too, understands or, at least, is familiar with the general work assignment of television repairmen, general practitioners, and secretaries. Although variation exists, the basic skills required for the job remain constant in each of these situations.

Union contracts also define jobs and work assignments and their content. One has only to look to the railroad industry with its union contract-defined jobs for engineers, conductors, porters, yardmen, brakemen, and firemen.

In our expanding economy, the need for new jobs involving work assignments with unfamiliar content is always present. Much of the content of these new jobs does not fit into the traditional patterns or definitions which have evolved within a company over the years. New, increasingly automated processes which outmode existing ones become available. More sophisticated equipment, products, and whole new areas of technology demand the creation of new skills. Changing volume justifies the higher capital investment in assembly and production line processing procedures. In each of these situations, the company must create new or extend old job definitions to cope with a changing environment. The growing use of rare metals and specialized alloys in the electronic, aircraft, and space industries has called for the development of highly technical welding specialists. These men often have come from the ranks of regular welders through extensive training and experience. Thus their job content has been expanded from existing skills to new ones. So, too, are the cases of the radio repairman who has moved to television and then to color television because of shifting demands for his services and the pilot who began his career flying Constellations and DC-6s but is now captaining super jets. Numerically controlled machines and computers need experts to program them and technicians to operate, maintain, and repair them. Most of these skills did not exist 25 years ago. With increasing production volumes comes the opportunity to develop more specialized job and work assignments.

SKILL REQUIREMENTS

In creating new jobs and work assignments, the designer is concerned with the skills required. There is a genuine effort made to restrict the skills required to as homogeneous a set as possible. In some cases, the volume and type of work are such that these can be restricted to one skill. There are many benefits to be derived from such a practice. Important among them is the fact that it is easier to hire and train employees to perform the work. Further specialization generally provides a greater opportunity for a worker to develop performance proficiency because practice coming from frequent performance enables workers to develop higher degrees of speed and accuracy. Another consideration in specializing work content is the concomitant labor cost. When a job demands a diversity of skills, its wage rate often must be at least as high as that of the highest paying skill in the job. By limiting the skills required on a job, a firm comes closer to achieving the situation where it pays for just the skill being utilized at any particular time. It would be foolish to hire a tool and die maker, at the current rate for such a skilled worker, and use him to operate a drill press full time.

DEMAND REQUIREMENTS

Besides the skill-related considerations, the content of work assignments is also restricted by the demand for the output. If the work which is to be divided into assignments has to be performed so that one unit is completed every minute and if only one worker is to perform each stage of the work, the maximum duration of each repetitive work assignment is one minute. The content of the work assignments formed has to satisfy this condition unless more than one worker is given the same assignment.

COMPLETION REQUIREMENTS

The work completion deadline can also limit the content of an assignment. Under nonrushed conditions, one person might prepare an entire computer program. However, if the programming time using just one programmer is expected to exceed the time available for the program development, the writing of the program would have to be decomposed into two or more simultaneous work assignments.

OTHER REQUIREMENTS

While the above skill and output related considerations push the designer toward defining jobs and work assignments with more and more specialized content, several other factors often tend to limit the movement in that direction. Important among these is the volume of the work to be done. A thin or limited content job or work assignment is typically warranted only when there is sufficient work volume to justify assigning one worker to it full time, as in the case of production or assembly lines. Often the work volume indicates that a thicker job must be utilized in order to keep its holder busy. Sometimes the work to be done entails such high specialization, short duration, or low frequency that it doesn't fit in any job developed by the firm. When this is true, the job will be contracted out to a firm specializing in this work. The maintenance and repair of computers, copying machines, and other delicate equipment requiring highly specialized skill is often handled in this manner. In addition, the more limited the scope of the job, the less flexibility a firm has in shifting workers between work assignments. Finally, very short duration, nonrepetitive work assignments often present problems in scheduling a work load adequate to keep an employee busy.

In recent years, there has been an increased awareness among management that worker satisfaction must also be considered in selecting job content. Extremely thin jobs composed of similar work assignments or a few highly repetitive ones can lead to worker dissatisfaction. This dissatisfaction often results in lower worker morale and increased problems in many areas. Even the attraction of high wages cannot completely overcome the effects of boredom and dissatisfaction over the extreme simplicity and repetitiveness of certain thin jobs. Low morale leads to labor grievances which are trivial and/or imagined as well as honest ones which *should* emerge. If specialization can lead to increased efficiency, it can also cause the sloppy and careless work habits. Overspecialization can reduce the workers' sense of pride or accomplishment to the point where they feel little or no responsibility for the quality of the final product and where they seek other, less productive outlets for their pent up energy and spirit.

To minimize worker dissatisfaction, a number of firms have begun job enlargement and enrichment programs where thicker jobs are designed and where workers are rotated between jobs for which they are qualified. These practices also have the added advantage of providing an extremely flexible labor force which can respond quickly to the firm's changing needs.

The process of selecting job and work assignments is largely a subjective, exceedingly difficult one. It involves weighing the advantages and disadvantages of the various contents in light of a number of factors. These include the type and volume of work to be done, skill requirements and availability, labor costs, union restrictions, and worker satisfaction.

WORK DESIGN

While work content defines what must be accomplished, work design specifies how the worker should perform the labor and what methods, procedures, and work area layout are to be used. Its purpose is to see that the work is accomplished efficiently and that it does not create unreasonable fatigue or mental strain on the worker.

Although work design naturally follows after work content selection, this does not mean that it may not begin much earlier in the design process as it often does. Before settling on the design of a jet aircraft cockpit, a great deal of study goes into examining the efficiency of various cockpit operating procedures in terms of how they are influenced by the many possible instrument-control configurations. Thus, by the time the plane is designed, only the finer details of the recommended operating procedures have to be worked out. Balancing production and assembly lines provides another example. Here, time estimates of the duration of the basic tasks are needed in order to group them into work assignments. Reliable estimates of these task times can only be developed if the designer has a good idea of the methods and layout to be used. The sequence of work design and work content found in these two examples, however, is not typical of most situations. Usually work design is carried out after the work content has been settled. In any case, sufficient preliminary work design should be done to establish the best work content. Any additional work design might be wasted on rejected work content alternatives.

Man is the dominant factor to be considered in work design. The methods, equipment, and work area layout used to perform the work should be designed in light of his capabilities. Since work design is partially a problem of human engineering, the work designer should be familiar with this science's findings and approaches. Since some of these factors have been discussed in detail in a previous section concerning human engineering of products, we shall limit our discussion here to a few additional considerations. Among these are the findings of Figures 9-1 and 9-2. These figures give a great deal of information useful in designing work assignments for male and female employees working in seated and standing positions.

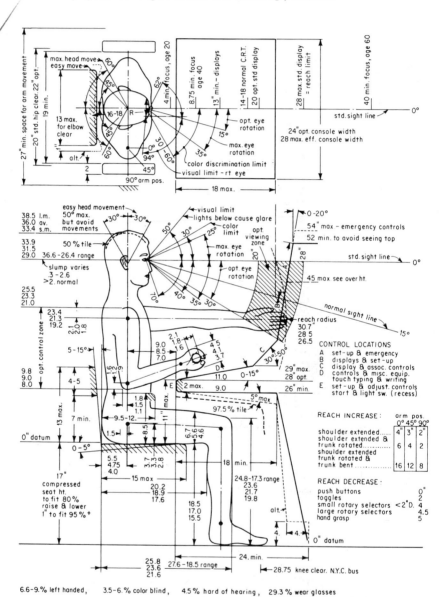

6.6–9.% left handed,   3.5–6.% color blind,   4.5 % hard of hearing,   29.3 % wear glasses

Figure 9-1 *Anthropometric data—adult male seated at console.* [From H. Dreyfuss, The Measure of Man: Human Factors in Design *(New York: Whitney Library of Design, 1967).]*

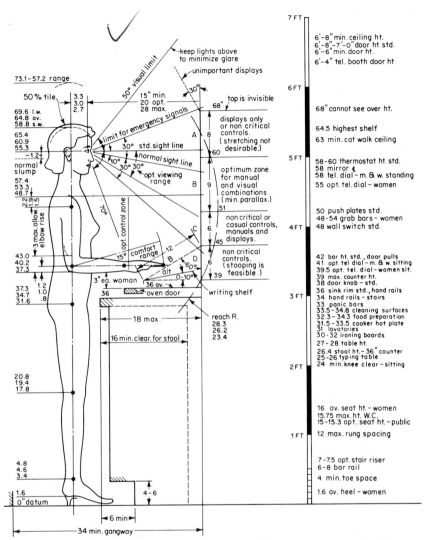

Figure 9-2 *Anthropometric data—adult female standing at control board.* [*From H. Dreyfuss,* The Measure of Man: Human Factors in Design *(New York: Whitney Library of Design, 1967).*]

GRAPHIC AIDS

Over the years, a number of human engineering guidelines have proven to be so useful to the design of jobs that they have become known as the "principles of motion economy." These twenty-two principles listed in Figure 9-3 are arranged according to whether they deal with human body use, workplace arrangement, or tool and equipment design.

These twenty-two rules or principles of motion economy may be profitably applied to shop and office work alike. Although not all are applicable to every operation, they do form a basis or a code for improving the efficiency and reducing fatigue in manual work.

Use of the Human Body

1. The two hands should begin as well as complete their motions at the same time.
2. The two hands should not be idle at the same time except during rest periods.
3. Motions of the arms should be made in opposite and symmetrical directions and should be made simultaneously.
4. Hand motions should be confined to the lowest classification with which it is possible to perform the work satisfactorily.
5. Momentum should be employed to assist the worker wherever possible, and it should be reduced to a minimum if it must be overcome by muscular effort.
6. Smooth continuous motions of the hands are preferable to zigzag motions or straight-line motions involving sudden and sharp changes in direction.
7. Ballistic movements are faster, easier, and more accurate than restricted (fixation) or "controlled" movements.
8. Rhythm is essential to the smooth and automatic performance of an operation, and the work should be arranged to permit easy and natural rhythm wherever possible.

Arrangement of the Workplace

9. There should be a definite and fixed place for all tools and materials.
10. Tools, materials, and controls should be located close in and directly in front of the operator.
11. Gravity feedbins and containers should be used to deliver materials close to the point of use.
12. Drop deliveries should be used wherever possible.
13. Materials and tools should be located to permit the best sequence of motions.
14. Provisions should be made for adequate conditions for seeing. Good illumination is the first requirement for satisfactory visual perception.
15. The height of the workplace and the chair should preferably be arranged so that alternate sitting and standing at work are easily possible.
16. A chair of the type and height to permit good posture should be provided for every worker.

Design of Tools and Equipment

17. The hands should be relieved of all work that can be done more advantageously by a jig, a fixture, or a foot-operated device.
18. Two or more tools should be combined whenever possible.
19. Tools and materials should be pre-positioned whenever possible.
20. Where each finger performs some specific movement, such as in typewriting, the load should be distributed in accordance with the inherent capacities of the fingers.
21. Handles, such as those used on cranks and large screwdrivers, should be designed to permit as much of the surface of the hand to come in contact with the handle as possible. This is particularly true when considerable force is exerted in using the handle. For light assembly work the screwdriver handle should be so shaped that it is smaller at the bottom than at the top.
22. Levers, crossbars, and handwheels should be located in such positions that the operator can manipulate them with the least change in body position and with the greatest mechanical advantage.

Figure 9-3 *Principles of motion economy.* [From R. M. Barnes, Motion and Time Study, Design and Measurement of Work, 6th ed. (New York: John Wiley & Sons, Inc., 1968).]

In applying the principles of motion economy and the other findings and approaches of human engineering, the designer often uses schematic diagrams to help him visualize and evaluate the alternative work designs he is formulating. Among the most useful diagrams are those of the workplace layout being considered. With layout diagrams, he can better simulate the movements and the distances involved.

Schematic diagrams are also employed to depict the actual methods under consideration. While there are specific charts existing (*each* with

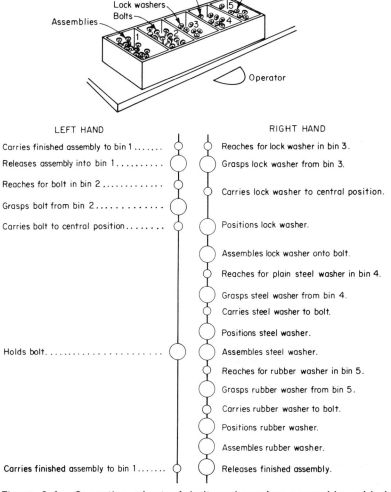

Figure 9-4 *Operation chart of bolt and washer assembly—old design.* [*From R. M. Barnes,* Motion and Time Study, Design and Measurement of Work, *6th ed. (New York: John Wiley & Sons, Inc., 1968).*]

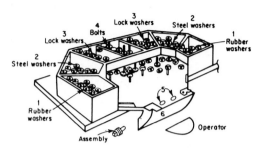

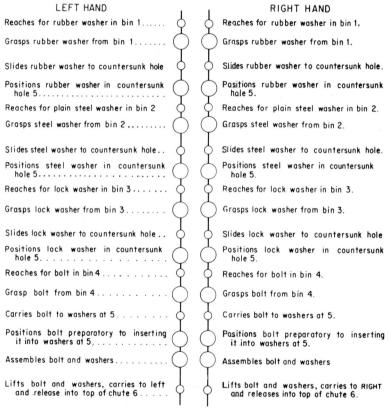

LEFT HAND			RIGHT HAND
Reaches for rubber washer in bin 1......	○	○	Reaches for rubber washer in bin 1.
Grasps rubber washer from bin 1.......	○	○	Grasps rubber washer from bin 1.
Slides rubber washer to countersunk hole	○	○	Slides rubber washer to countersunk hole.
Positions rubber washer in countersunk hole 5........................	○	○	Positions rubber washer in countersunk hole 5.
Reaches for plain steel washer in bin 2	○	○	Reaches for plain steel washer in bin 2.
Grasps steel washer from bin 2.........	○	○	Grasps steel washer from bin 2.
Slides steel washer to countersunk hole..	○	○	Slides steel washer to countersunk hole.
Positions steel washer in countersunk hole 5..........................	○	○	Positions steel washer in countersunk hole 5.
Reaches for lock washer in bin 3.......	○	○	Reaches for lock washer in bin 3.
Grasps lock washer from bin 3........	○	○	Grasps lock washer from bin 3.
Slides lock washer to countersunk hole..	○	○	Slides lock washer to countersunk hole
Positions lock washer in countersunk hole 5.	○	○	Positions lock washer in countersunk hole 5.
Reaches for bolt in bin 4...........	○	○	Reaches for bolt in bin 4.
Grasp bolt from bin 4...........	○	○	Grasps bolt from bin 4.
Carries bolt to washers at 5........	○	○	Carries bolt to washers at 5.
Positions bolt preparatory to inserting it into washers at 5.............	○	○	Positions bolt preparatory to inserting it into washers at 5.
Assembles bolt and washers..........	○	○	Assembles bolt and washers
Lifts bolt and washers, carries to left and release into top of chute 6.....	○	○	Lifts bolt and washers, carries to RIGHT and releases into top of chute 6.

Figure 9-5 *Operation chart of bolt and washer assembly—improved.*
[*From R. M. Barnes,* Motion and Time Study, Design and Measurement of
Work, *6th ed. (New York: John Wiley & Sons, Inc., 1968).*]

its own name), for just about any situation, almost all these charts are
constructed along similar lines. They have a column for each element whose
activities the designer wishes to follow over a certain time period. In Figures
9-4, 9-5, and 9-6 there are two columns, one for each of the worker's
hands, while in Figure 9-7 there is a column for the worker and one for
each machine that he services.

MICROMOTION STUDY

SIMO CHART

PART Bolt and Washer Assembly–Improved Method DEPARTMENT AY16 FILM NO. X75

OPERATION Assemble 3 washers on bolt   OP. NO. A32

OPERATOR M.S. Bowen   1C4327   DATE   MADE BY S.R.M. SHEET NO. 1 OF 1

DESCRIPTION LEFT HAND	THERBLIG SYMBOL	TIME	TIME IN 2000THS OF A MIN.	TIME	THERBLIG SYMBOL	DESCRIPTION RIGHT HAND
Reaches for rubber washer	TE	10			10 TE	Reaches for rubber washer
Selects and grasps washer	St G	1			1 St G	Selects and grasps washer
Slides washer to fixture	TL	13	20		13 TL	Slides washer to fixture
Positions washer in fixture and releases	P RL	14			14 P RL	Positions washer in fixture and releases
			40			
Reaches for steel washer	TE	12			12 TE	Reaches for steel washer
Selects and grasps washer	St G	1			1 St G	Selects and grasps washer
			60			
Slides washer to fixture	TL	17			17 TL	Slides washer to fixture
Positions washer in fixture and releases	P RL	13	80		13 P RL	Positions washer in fixture and releases
Reaches for lock washer	TE	12			12 TE	Reaches for lock washer
Selects and grasps washer	St G	1	100		1 St G	Selects and grasps washer
Slides washer to fixture	TL	14			14 TL	Slides washer to fixture
Positions washer in fixture and releases	P RL	8	120		8 P RL	Positions washer in fixture and releases
Reaches for bolt	TE	10			10 TE	Reaches for bolt
Selects and grasps bolt	St G	10			10 St G	Selects and grasps bolt
			140			
Carries bolt to fixture	TL	12			12 TL	Carries bolt to fixture
Positions bolt	P	8	160		8 P	Positions bolt
Inserts bolt through washer	A	48	180		48 A	Inserts bolt through washer
			200			
Withdraws assembly	DA	3			3 DA	Withdraws assembly
Carries assembly to top of chute	TL	10			10 TL	Carries assembly to top of chute
Releases assembly	RL	1	220		1 RL	Releases assembly

Figure 9-6 *Simo chart for bolt and washer assembly—improved design.* [*From R. M. Barnes,* Motion and Time Study, Design and Measurement of Work, *6th ed. (New York: John Wiley & Sons, Inc., 1968).*]

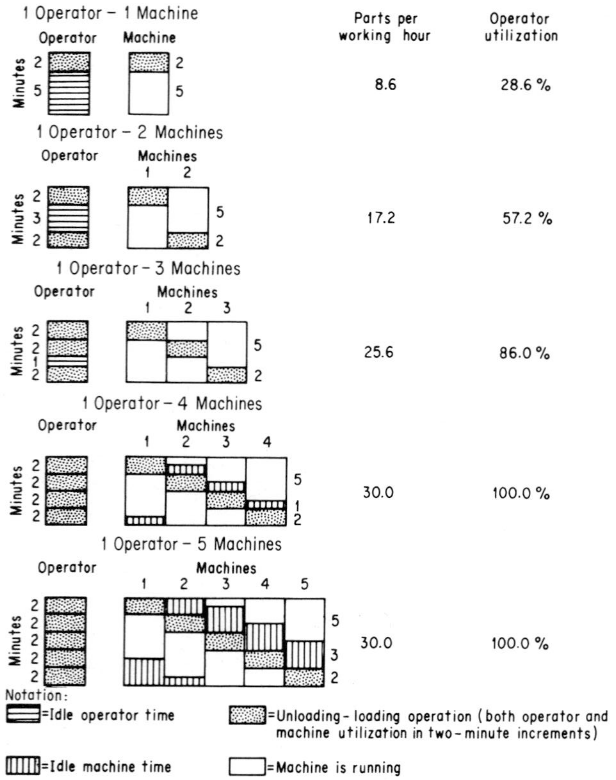

Figure 9-7 A comparison of man-machine combinations

	Parts per working hour	Operator utilization	Machine utilization	Operators needed to produce 100 parts per hour	Machines needed to produce 100 parts per hour
1 Operator – 1 Machine	8.6	28.6 %	100.0 %	11.7	11.7
1 Operator – 2 Machines	17.2	57.2 %	100.0 %	5.85	11.7
1 Operator – 3 Machines	25.6	86.0 %	100.0 %	3.9	11.7
1 Operator – 4 Machines	30.0	100.0 %	87.5 %	3.3	13.2
1 Operator – 5 Machines	30.0	100.0 %	70.0 %	3.3	16.5

Notation:

= Idle operator time

= Unloading–loading operation (both operator and machine utilization in two-minute increments)

= Idle machine time

= Machine is running

The type of chart which can be of greatest value depends on the particular situation—whether the work is primarily manual or semi-automatic, whether the worker is seated or standing, and the nature of jobs which he is required to do. Repetitive, short-cycle work of long duration involving many workers justifies elaborate and detailed work design effort. These situations are often encountered in the electronics and automotive industries where examinations are carried out in minute detail in the hopes of saving a few additional thousandths of a minute per cycle. For such detailed jobs, a chart like the simo chart of Figure 9-6 is often appropriate. A similar work assignment, but one held by only one worker, would typically justify a less detailed examination, but it would probably still be worth examining the activities of both hands with an operations chart like Figure 9-4. Longer-cycle, less repetitive jobs typically warrant even less detailed consideration in their design, and there are appropriate charts available for this level of effort too.

You may wonder how the time entries listed in several of these charts can be estimated during the work-design phase. This is done in various ways. When better data aren't available or worth gathering, these times are often simply the best guesses made by people experienced in estimating work times. Some firms have banks of standard time data which they have built up from past experience. The latter have been translated into a form which can readily be used to project time estimates for many types of work. Some firms also use time estimates built up from predetermined times for such elemental tasks as reach, grasp, and position. A number of organizations sell entire systems of predetermined time data. The idea here is simply to find a system compatible with the firm's needs.

APPLYING THE PRINCIPLES OF MOTION ECONOMY

The principles of motion economy (Figure 9-3) can often be very helpful in spotting ways to improve a method being considered. Consider the method and layout in Figure 9-4 for putting together a bolt-lock washer-flat washer-rubber washer assembly.[2] Going through the principles of motion economy, we see that the work design of Figure 9-4 doesn't satisfy principles 1, 2, and 3. To incorporate those principles, it is necessary to put together an assembly with each hand simultaneously. Doing this requires the use of two special fixtures to hold the bolts in proper position. Also the old design does not make use of gravity feed or drop delivery (principles 11 and 12). The latter, however, also appear to be good ideas for making the parts

---

[2] The rubber washer holds on the other two washers on the bolt. The assembly is used in bolting together various appliances. Their preassembly has been found to be necessary to the operations of several appliance assembly lines.

available to the worker and for disposing of the completed assemblies. Many of the changes we have discussed are shown in Figure 9-5.

The detailed analysis of the new design in Figure 9-6 reveals what a notable improvement the new design is. With this new design, 2 assemblies require 0.11 minutes or 0.055 minutes per assembly; the old design needed 0.075 minutes per assembly.

Thus, we have seen with a simple example how the work methods and workplace layout can be designed using the principles of human engineering, schematic diagrams, and a good deal of human judgment. Solutions for more complex situations, however, are not as easy to design, and the services of a skilled work-design specialist or consultant are often warranted.

MULTIPLE WORK ASSIGNMENTS

Several times in our discussion, we have alluded to work assignments involving more than one machine, worker, or type of output. In view of the widespread use of such compound work assignments, this special type of microprocessing design deserves more than passing notice.

Once they are functioning properly, most semi-automatic machines only need to be loaded and unloaded. Because of their typically long machining time and comparatively short loading and unloading time per part, it is often possible for a worker to service more than one machine. Spinning machines in the textile industry (commonly called frames), only require attention when a feed spool is empty, a take-up spool is full, the fiber or yarn breaks, or a frame malfunctions. Thus it is not uncommon for a few men to look after 20 or more spinning frames which are simultaneously processing many yarn types. Another example of multiple machine assignments occurs in the case of the familiar vending machine route man (whether he be servicing soft drink or food machines, slot machines, or parking meters), who usually replenishes and maintains many machines in various locations during the course of each day. You should be able to identify numerous other multiple assignment situations. How many nurses should be assigned to a hospital ward? Which stores in a large retail chain should draw their stock from which warehouse? How many bank tellers are needed to service customers?

The purpose of such multiple assignments is obvious: to make most efficient use of men and machines. However, their use is not justified in every situation. One notable situation where such assignments might not be justified is where the jobs would be of short duration. In a job shop, it is not uncommon to find most semi-automatic and numerically controlled machines with their own individual operator. There, most of the jobs being processed are of short duration—a few hours or less. Thus, any particular multiple assignment involving such jobs would at best be efficient for only a few hours; at worst such assignments would be confusing for all involved. As a consequence, few multiple assignments are found where the jobs being processed are of short duration. Another situation where they would not be used is when multiple work assignments are prohibited by collective bargaining agreements.

To illustrate the development of efficient multiple assignments, let us examine the simple situation where repetitive tasks with constant task times are involved. While such a case may at first seem highly unrealistic, it is actually a good approximation of reality in many situations. Consider semi-automatic and numerically controlled machines where the duration of machining time per part is highly predictable and the variation in the manual handling time per part is typically negligible when compared to the total man-machine cycle time. To appreciate what is involved in designing an efficient multiple assignment in such cases, let's consider the following example. Each working day, 600 units of a particular part need to be machined. The workers assigned to the machines are expected to be involved in machine tending only 6 hours out of the 8 they spend in the plant (the remaining 2 hours are for lunch, rest, personal needs, clean-up, material shortages, and breakdowns). As a result, for each actual working hour, 600/6 or 100 parts should be produced. Each part requires 5 minutes to machine and 2 minutes to load and unload from the machine.

Figure 9-7 commonly known as an activity or man-machine chart, shows some of the alternative man-machine assignments possible in this particular situation as well as their more important statistics. Let us now examine how these statistics were derived. First, consider the parts produced per actual working hour. In the case of one worker tending three machines, this worker and his three machines will turn out three parts every 7 actual working minutes. In other words, one part is produced on an average of every 7/3 or 2.34 actual working minutes which means his hourly production is 60/2.34 or 25.6 pieces.

Worker and machine utilization are easy to calculate for each alternative. If a worker tends two machines, we see from Figure 9-7 that the shortest period in which a part can be produced with a single machine is 7 actual working minutes (5 for machining and 2 for loading and unloading it). With two machines, the worker spends only 4 minutes out of every 7 working minutes in the nonidle activities of loading and unloading. As a consequence, his worker utilization is $(4/7) \times 100$ or 57.2 percent. For a look at machine utilization, consider the example in Figure 9-7 of one operator for five machines. Here the critical resource is the man; it takes him 10 minutes to service each of the five machines once. In those 10 minutes, each machine in his care is actually running or unavoidably tied up by the worker loading and unloading it 7 out of every 10 minutes. As a consequence, its utilization is $(7/10) \times 100$ or 70 percent.

When deciding on the most economic alternative, another factor of interest is the number of operators needed to produce the 100 parts per actual working hour under various man-machine alternatives assignments. Since we have calculated that a ratio of one man to three machines can produce 25.6 parts per hour, we conclude that 100/25.6 or 3.9 of these one man-three machine configurations would be needed to obtain the 100 parts per hour. Forget for the moment the problem of what to do about the fractional part of a man-machine assignment. Consider now the number of machines needed with a one worker-four machine configuration. Here the equivalent of 3.3 such configurations are necessary (100/30.0). Since each configuration consists of four machines, 3.3 × 4 or 13.2 machines are necessary.

The statistics in Figure 9-7 serve as useful guidelines in deciding on the final man-machine configuration. They lead us to two very important conclusions. First, a one man-three machine assignment is more efficient in this example than an assignment with fewer machines. Assignments involving one and two machines require the same number of total machines to produce the 100 units an hour as a three machine assignment, but the one and two machine assignments require more workers than the three machine assignments. The second conclusion we should make here is that a one man-four machine configuration is more efficient than a configuration of five machines per operator. Although the number of operators remains the same in moving from a four to five machine assignment the total number of machines needed to achieve the 100 units an hour increases from 13.2 to 16.5. Both these conclusions could have also been reached by examining the man and machine utilizations in the assignments from Figure 9-7. As a consequence of these two observations, it is clear that the most efficient man-machine assignment would be either one to three or one to four.

Now, let's return to the fractional part of each assignment which remains and see how it might be handled. In the case of one man tending three machines, it could probably be resolved by using four such one man-three machine assignments and living with a 100 × (4 − 3.9)/4 or 2.5 percent underutilization of each configuration. It is highly unlikely we would find other work which would be flexible enough for scheduling into the little excess time available. Only if the job duration were short would three such assignments and the use of overtime be a viable alternative to the use of four such assignments. When we examine the amount of overtime needed to produce output equivalent to 0.9 of a configuration, we see that three one man-three machine configurations would require 8 × (.9/3) or 2.4 hours of daily overtime per man to produce the 600 units needed daily. Besides being expensive for the firm, such an amount of overtime is usually quite fatiguing on the workers if continued for more than a few weeks.

Now let us explore the implications of the one worker-four machine assignment. Having four such configurations rather than three means that there is $100 \times (0.7/4)$ or 17.5 percent excess capacity per assignment. If other, equally profitable work can be scheduled to take up this slack, there is no opportunity lost. If, however, there is no other scheduled work available, using three one man to four machine configurations and overtime would probably be the selected alternative. In this case, the required overtime would be $8 \times 0.3/3$ or 0.8 hours a day, an amount which is usually acceptable to the worker and management even over a period of a few months.

MAKING THE DECISION

In making the actual decision between the one man-three machine or one man-four machine configurations, the choice will depend on the various economic and noneconomic factors relevant to the situation. To illustrate the use of the appropriate type of analysis, consider the case of Mr. Lewis, of Casemate Corp., who is faced with the multiple assignment problem we have already partially analyzed. The processing operation in question is the machining of the metal base of a hand planer. Demand is such that Casemate anticipates machining 600 planer bases a day for the next 3 years. Having just decided to add planes to their line of hand wood tools, Casemate has neither men nor machines available to do the work.

Lewis has found that while skilled workers are in short supply, the type required can be hired at an average wage of $3 an hour and double time for overtime. Further, the personnel department has estimated that the extra costs Casemate will incur in hiring and training the needed workers will average $400 a worker. Using figures both from the machinery manufacturer and Casemate's industrial engineering department, Mr. Lewis computed the installed cost of each machine as $15,000. Each is guaranteed to run at least 15,000 hours if it is properly maintained. Maintenance costs are expected to average $.50 for each hour the machine is run.

Following the reasoning discussed previously, Mr. Lewis concluded that it would be best to utilize either four one man-three machine assignments or three one man-four machine assignments. Since Casemate only operates a single shift and plans to do so for the foreseeable future, Lewis didn't evaluate any alternatives using more than one shift a day. He reasoned that the hiring, training, and wage costs associated with each alternative would be relevant because they would be expenses not presently covered by the firm and would vary with the alternative chosen. If the four one man-three machine configurations were used, there would be a total of $1,600 or $400 × 4 in hiring and training costs and $96 a day in wages (this latter figure is simply $3 a man hour times 8 hours a day times 4 men). On the other hand, if the three one man-four machine configurations were used, Lewis figured there would be a total of $1,200 in hiring and training costs and $86.40 in daily wages. The latter was made of $72 in regular wages and $14.40 in overtime earnings (the overtime was figured at $6 a man hour times 0.8 hours a day overtime per man times 3 men).

Mr. Lewis also considered many other factors in the evaluation but ruled most of them out as irrelevant. He reasoned that the cost of machines would be irrelevant to the comparison because each alternative utilized twelve machines. He also found it unnecessary to include maintenance costs in the comparison since all the machines would run the same number of total hours. The excess capacity of 2.5 percent for each one man-three machine configuration was too small to be of value and did not enter the decision.

Thus Mr. Lewis based his choice on the hiring, training, and wage expense of one alternative versus the other. Since the three one man-four machine configuration with respect to each of these costs involved less expense than the other, it clearly was the better choice—$1,200 hiring and training expense and $86.40 daily cost as compared respectively to $1,600 and $96. Additional indirect savings could be realized because this decision meant fewer workers to supervise, to carry on the payroll, or to lay off if the work should take a sudden and prolonged down turn.

WORK ENVIRONMENT

An associated but sometimes neglected dimension of work design is the conscious planning of the work environment. The physiological and psychological impact of the environment can significantly affect the workers' productivity. A well designed environment is not only conducive to ongoing activities but also encourages a generally relaxed and pleasant atmosphere. As a consequence, organizations are increasingly becoming concerned with the design and control of such environmental factors as noise, dirt, illumination, temperature, humidity, and pollution, and they are equally interested in the development of a healthy, positive attitude among employees toward their work and toward the company. Proper attention to both these factors is important not only in the shop but also in the office, in retail stores, banks, hospitals, and schools—wherever a man finds employment.

THE PHYSICAL ENVIRONMENT

Let us begin by considering some of the more common physical aspects of environmental design. Proper levels of glareless illumination should be provided so that the workers may perform their work without developing eyestrain. As the human engineering findings in Figure 9-8 illustrate, more detailed work generally requires more light. To avoid eye fatigue, it is important to position lights so that glare is minimized. In the service fields, lighting affects both the employee, clerk or professional, and the customer.

Harsh illumination can lead to a psychologically uncomfortable atmosphere which makes everyone irritable while judiciously placed light fixtures may create any number of diverse, favorable moods. Here the guidelines provided in Figures 9-8 and 9-9 are helpful.

GENERAL ILLUMINATION LEVELS

Task Condition	Level (foot candles)	Type of Illumination
Small detail, low contrast, prolonged periods, high speed, extreme accuracy	100	Supplementary type of lighting. Special fixture such as desk lamp.
Small detail, fair contrast, close work, speed not essential	50–100	Supplementary type of lighting.
Normal desk and office-type work	20–50	Local lighting. Ceiling fixture directly overhead.
Recreational tasks that are not prolonged	10–20	General lighting. Random room light, either natural or artificial.
Seeing not confined, contrast good, object fairly large	5–10	General lighting.
Visibility for moving about, handling large objects	2–5	General or supplementary lighting.

RECOMMENDED ILLUMINATION LEVELS, INDUSTRIAL AND MANUFACTURING

Type of Work	Level (foot candles)	Type of Work	Level (foot candles)
Drilling, riveting	30	Drafting	100
Layout and template	50	Lofting	150
Welding	30	Machining:	
At work point	1,000	Rough	20
Assembly	30	Extra fine	200
Extra-fine assembly	300	Sheet metal:	
Finishing, inspection	200	Punch, stamp	30
Paint booth	30	Scribing	100
Glass—grind, polish	50	Receiving, shipping	10

Figure 9-8 *Illumination data. [From W. E. Woodson and D. W. Conover, Human Engineering Guide for Equipment Designers, 2d ed. (Berkeley: University of California Press, 1966).]*

SPECIFIC RECOMMENDATIONS, ILLUMINATION LEVELS

Location	Level (foot candles)	Location	Level (foot candles)
Home:		*School:*	
Reading	40	On chalkboards	50
Writing	40	Desks	30
Sewing	75–100	Drawing (art)	50
Kitchen	50	Gyms	20
Mirror (shaving)	50	Auditorium	10
Laundry	40		
Games	40	*Theatre:*	
Workbench	50	Lobby	20
General	10 or more	During intermission	5
		During movie	0.1
Office:			
Bookkeeping	50	*Passenger Train:*	
Typing	50	Reading, writing	20–40
Transcribing	40	Dining	15
General correspondence	30	Steps, vestibules	10
Filing	30		
Reception	20	*Doctor's Office:*	
		Examination room	100
		Dental-surgical	200
		Operating table	1,800

Figure 9-8 *(Continued)*

Extremes in temperature, humidity, dust, and dirt have a noticeable impact on work efficiency. Although for many years it has been common to centrally heat buildings, cooling them is a more recent innovation. The effects of warm temperatures on human efficiency are illustrated in Figure 9-10. Here we see that the average number of errors made during an information transmission process goes up at an increasing rate with the degree of temperature and the duration of exposure to it. With good reason, the practice of central air conditioning is spreading throughout many manufacturing and service fields. Where, in the past, companies were only air conditioning their offices, now shops, warehouses, and material handling areas are enjoying the benefits of cool air. Most store, restaurant, and professional building owners feel that air conditioning is a necessity.

In some cases, temperature and humidity are kept constant because of the special requirements of expensive machinery or valuable products. The only way highly precisioned machines can be made to reproduce parts to extreme tolerances is under constant temperature, humidity, and dust free conditions. The same is true in the assembly of missile guidance systems

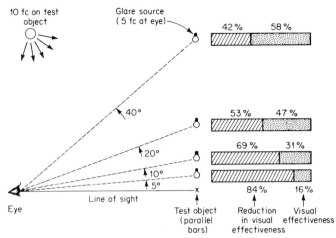

Figure 9-9 *Effects of direct glare on visual effectivenss. The effects of glare become worse as the glare source gets closer to the line of sight. [From E. J. McCormick,* Human Factors Engineering *(New York: McGraw-Hill Book Company, 1964).]*

where every piece of dust or dirt represents a potential disaster. Perhaps the best known example of climate control is found in the large art museums where the priceless collections must be completely protected against deterioration or damage.

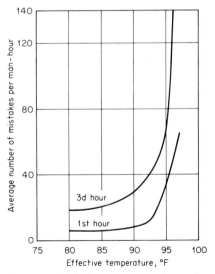

Figure 9-10 *Average number of mistakes in Morse code receiving in relation to effective temperature. [From E. J. McCormick,* Human Factors Engineering *(New York: McGraw-Hill Book Company, 1964).]*

In the past, noisy workplaces were considered to be a fact of factory and office life. However, as more and more studies have shown, prolonged exposure to excessive noise results in decreased work efficiency and the possibility of permanent hearing impairment. Consequently, organizations have begun multifaceted programs to reduce overall noise levels. Equipment can often be sound conditioned. Even an ordinary piece of office machinery like a typewriter can be extensively improved. Cases have been lined with sound absorbent materials, linkages and rollers redesigned to soften the old clickety-clack, and rubberized legs added to help reduce the vibration transmission to typing tables and desks. Even more extensive efforts have been made in designing buildings with their acoustical ceilings, carpeted and vinyl cushioned floors, and structural wall and ceiling sound baffles. Certain operating procedures are also being modified to help control noise. Jet takeoffs at reduced power provide a well known and dramatic example. Yet sound conditioning is not all noise control. Music is often used to drown out moderate noise with its own more pleasant sound which is conducive to many activities which do not require total concentration; these activities include assembly work and most secretarial work. It also provides a pleasant background in service areas as shops, restaurants, and hospitals.

Color is another dimension of environmental design in the areas of visual discrimination, identification, and mood creation. It can be used to differentiate between similarly appearing objects. In hospitals or other buildings where directions are necessary, the simple device of painting all of the names of the sections in one particular area one color can be a great help to the person wandering through the endless corridors. "Follow the yellow arrows" is an easily understood directive which can be quickly followed because the eye can identify the color yellow long before it can read a similar-sized printed direction. Through constant usage certain colors have become standard cues. Red used in traffic signals denotes "stop," while in industry it indicates danger areas. An extension of these meanings is found in the use of red for anything associated with fire trucks, fire exit signs, and fire alarm boxes. Yellow is generally used as a signal for caution, and green often means "safe" or "go."

As Figure 9-11 implies, the psychological implications of color are also very useful. Years ago, hospital rooms tended to be painted a dove gray. Contrast the overcast mood created by gray and its effects on patient recovery with that of the cheerful, warm, and restful pastels in use today. This latter use of color is in keeping with the current trend to make color play a positive, constructive role in environmental design. Everyone is familiar with light green and its restful, nondisturbing qualities. Designers are now turning to bright, bold, and strong colors and using them as stimulating accents to avoid the negative effects usually encountered when they are used in great quantity. One wall of an entrance may be painted cranberry,

Color Psychology

Color	Mood Created	Sample Associations*
Red	Stimulating to the nervous system; positive	Fire, danger, blood, stop, hot, 4th of July
Yellow	Cheerful, warm	Sun, caution
Orange	Like red	Pumpkin, oranges, heat, Halloween
Yellow-green	Neutral	Sunlit grass, mustard
Green	Restful, cool, tranquil	Nature, vegetation, go, St. Patrick's Day
Blue	Opposite to red; cool, contemplative, subduing	Sky, water
Purple	Solemnity	Mourning, royalty, Easter
White	Neutral to positive effects	Snow, marriage (death in China)
Gray	Neutral, contemplation	Overcast day, navy
Black	Neutral, sorrow	Death, darkness, black is beautiful

* Many variations exist in cultures past and present.

Figure 9-11 *The psychology of color. [From H. Dreyfuss,* The Measure of Man: Human Factors in Design *(New York: Whitney Library of Design, 1967).]*

a color of richness and welcome. Deep blue carpets and chairs mixed with rosewood desks can actually help banks create the new, progressive image they are seeking to convey. Brightly colored desks, filing cabinets, and typewriters are being used to produce a more stimulating work environment but not an overpowering one.

THE ENVIRONMENT AND EMPLOYEE ATTITUDES

Undoubtedly the most important single, psychological factor associated with work design is employee attitude. Poor worker attitudes have caused more than one company to close its doors. Being aware of this, firms put a diverse array of beneficial programs into effect to encourage good employee relations.

Perhaps the most classic studies in industrial relations were conducted at the Hawthorne plant of the Western Electric Company in Chicago, Illinois. These studies were designed to measure how output is affected by illumination level and other physical factors of the environment, but their results were more far reaching in their relevance than the researchers anticipated.

A group of workers were chosen and relocated in a special section of the plant where the work environment could be carefully controlled. As the level of illumination was increased, the group's output also continually increased as predicted. Then one of the researchers thought to cross-check the results by reducing the illumination levels. As this was done down to the point where the workers could hardly see, the group's output rose to even higher levels. This startling and, at first, conflicting result was finally found to be due to the worker's desire to please the experimenters. The workers liked the attention they were receiving and were unconsciously straining to meet what they thought were the expectations of the researchers. Thus it was found that positive worker attitude can overcome, to some extent, physical limitations.

Positive attitudes toward work and the employing organization can benefit everyone. They can help increase productivity and profits and can cause pleasant working conditions. Worker loyalty is directly related to fewer job turnovers, absenteeism, grievances, work stoppages, court litigations, and costly strikes.

Many of the most common approaches used to foster positive employee attitudes are monetarily related. Besides a job's regular wage rate, many companies use incentive systems to motivate extra effort by workers. Profit sharing and stock purchase plans, commonly used incentives for motivating and rewarding management itself, are being increasingly used at all organizational levels. Fringe benefits abound. Some firms operate company stores and purchase plans where the firm's product can be bought at substantial discounts. Some retailers offer employee discounts on everything that they sell and some have special shops for slightly damaged merchandise at drastically reduced prices. Partially or even wholly paid health and life insurance plans can help relieve employee apprehension of the uncertain future. Paid vacations are gaining increased popularity as are earlier retirement programs.

Nevertheless, organizations should not overlook the benefits to be gained from nonmonetary approaches. Company papers, athletic and social events, and worker-of-the-week contests are but a few which have been used successfully for many years. Employee suggestion boxes and programs which involve the workers in environmental design are just two more examples. An increasing number of organizations, from manufacturing concerns to hospitals and banks, have successfully conducted "in-house" campaigns to foster an attitude of genuine concern for the quality of the employees' work. Hospitals' "Tender Loving Care" campaigns and factories' "Zero Defects" or "Do it Right the First Time" programs are useful in attitude development. Another interesting approach is the use of inspection tickets for products of all types which actually give the inspector's full name. Needless to say, such an inspector feels more personally responsible for the quality of the goods which pass his station than one who simply stamps "inspected" on the case as it goes by. Such practices encourage the worker's pride in a job well done. Enlightened POM personnel realize only too well the effect of positive employee attitudes on all aspects of POM microprocessing.

QUESTIONS

1. How does *microprocessing* differ from *macroprocessing?* Which is more important to the whole processing activity? Why?
2. Characterize the role of microprocessing design in:

   (a) Performing surgery
   (b) Delivering mail
   (c) Working on a fast moving assembly line
   (d) Putting together a do-it-yourself Health-kit amplifier

3. When considering product-oriented processing, process-oriented processing, and fixed-location processing, for which one would microprocessing design be the most important and for which one the least? Explain you answer.
4. Which of the following would be more likely to be automated and why: a work assignment which justifies a great deal of microprocessing design or one which justifies little such design?
5. How can you do microprocessing design for jobs which have not yet been done? Why would you want to do that?
6. What are the implications of the Hawthorne study to the POM manager?
7. Since jobs on an automobile assembly line are quite frustrating to many of the employees working on them, why do American automobile assembly lines utilize such thin-job assignments?
8. Discuss the role of both physical and psychological environment designs for consumers in

   (a) Retail stores
   (b) Education
   (c) Public transportation

9. Betty, a college coed, being short on money but liking her morning toast and coffee, purchased an old, nonautomatic, two-slice model electric toaster. Each side is operated independently, and the bread must be turned, since only one side of a slice is toasted at a time. When the door is opened, metal fingers inside push the bread so that it partially hangs over the door edge and, hence, can be grasped without burning one's fingers. Springs on each side of the toaster hold the door shut while stops hold each door in a horizontal position when a door is open all the way.

The following are the times it takes Betty, on the average, to perform various tasks associated with operating this toaster.

Task	Time in Minutes
Preheat toaster (only required once when toaster is in continuous use).	0.5
Place slice of bread in toaster using either hand by itself.	0.1
Toast either side of a piece of bread.	0.5
Turn over slice using either hand by itself.	0.1
Remove toast from toaster using either hand by itself.	0.1
Move piece of toast from one side of toaster to the other using either hand by itself.	0.1

Not being exactly a "bounce-out-of-the-bed" type and being faced with an 8 o'clock class, Betty is trying to salvage every second of sleep she can. Design for Betty the fastest method of toasting the three slices of toast she eats with coffee every morning. Chart your proposed method and give the length of time your proposed method requires.

10. Explain and justify how you would instruct your school's janitorial staff to wash, wax, and polish floors in classrooms with movable furniture.

CASE

Carolina Products manufactures a line of water pumps. Because of demand changes, the firm is faced with the problem of how to readjust production of several pump components. Over the past year, the firm's requirements for cover plate A-31 has increased from 100,000 to 140,000 units a year. Projections indicate the firm's need for this cover plate will increase to approximately 170,000 units a year in about 3 years.

Each cover plate A-31 must be ground and drilled. Below is given the work content of the two operations required on cover plate A-31.

Load grinder	0.60 min/cover	Load drill press	0.50 min/cover
Machine-controlled grinding	2.00 min/cover	Machine-controlled drilling	0.60 min/cover
Unload grinder	0.30 min/cover	Unload drill press	0.30 min/cover

Currently Carolina Products has only four grinders and two drill presses available for machining cover plate A-31. Additional drill presses and grinders can be purchased for $3,000 and $7,000 each.

Most of the Carolina Products shop works only a single shift with the average machine operator earning $4 an hour including fringe benefits. Overtime carries a 50 percent premium and is allowed up to a half day per week.

Second shift operation is currently used for a few critical operations and carries with it a 10 percent wage premium. If a second shift is employed utilizing more than one operator, one worker will have to be made a supervisor who earns a 10 percent wage premium for each worker he supervises.

In the past, Carolina Products has had no difficulty installing multiple task work assignments as long as 20 percent of total time of each shift is allowed for personal time, tool changes, and contingencies. The firm does not pay bonuses for multiple assignment work and has standard 8-hour shifts.

Discuss and justify how you think Carolina Products should go about grinding and drilling the needed plates.

chapter

MEASUREMENT

ten

Any successful organization must have the ability to make and use time estimates. Without these there is little basis for evaluating its past performance or planning its future activities.

Development of effective work methods and work area layouts, whether in a machine shop or in a hospital surgical suite, calls for estimates of the times required by alternative motion patterns. Developing realistic cost estimates and delivery dates is still another area of application.

Since the type of time estimates required depends on their intended use, a review of the more important uses and the time estimates appropriate to each of them is made. We will first consider subjective methods of estimation and then the more formal approaches. In covering the formal approaches, the general strategy of formal work measurement is discussed followed by a description of the three major work measurement approaches— time study, work sampling, and predetermined data.

Since these three approaches depend, either directly or indirectly, on observation of work activities, they are suitable for studying physical labor

but not for observing general mental activities like planning or making decisions. Here performance has to be subjectively gauged according to the
finished product or output. Nevertheless, many of the concepts underlying
time study, work sampling, and predetermined data prove helpful in making
these subjective estimates.

The estimation of machine-controlled times, although just as important
as those for either mental or physical activities, is basically an engineering
problem and will not be discussed here. For commonly used simple machines,
like drill presses, grinders, or punches, there are readily available tables,
graphs, and formulas for calculating their associated processing times.[1]

EVALUATION OF ACTUAL PERFORMANCE

 Evaluating worker performance is a necessary function of management. Such
evaluation becomes essential when an organization uses wage incentives.
In these cases, a worker is paid a base wage plus a premium for performance
above a certain level.

To evaluate worker performance and to operate a successful wage
incentive system, fair and equitable standards of comparison have to be
used; the evaluation should also be easy to perform. Since it is easy to
determine how long activities take, it is often convenient to evaluate worker
performance by comparing the actual time taken against a standard time.
This form is especially useful when there are a variety of outputs with
different time standards for each. Worker performance in this case can
be defined as:

$$\frac{\text{Standard time}}{\text{Actual time}} \times 100$$

Thus, if a worker uses an entire 8-hour shift to do work that was supposed
to take 6.0 hours, his performance would be 75 percent, or $(6.0/8) \times 100$,
indicating considerably below standard performance on his part. His performance would have been above standard had he produced 9.6 standard
hours of work during the same shift, i.e., a performance rating of 120
percent, or $(9.6/8) \times 100$. For the standard and actual time to be comparable,
this standard time must reflect not only normal productive time but also
a fair and equitable allowance for nonworking time, i.e., rest breaks, delays
in receipt of work, and the like.

For repetitive jobs producing only one type of readily countable output,
it is faster to compute performance in terms of unit output:

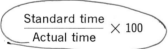
$$\frac{\text{Units produced per shift}}{\text{Standard units per shift}} \times 100$$

[1] W. A. Nordhoff, *Machine-shop Estimating,* New York, McGraw-Hill, 1947.

There are many workable bases for defining what is standard performance. The only necessary criteria are that the basis selected leads to consistent evaluation and that all who are involved understand and accept its meaning.

Through tradition and experience, certain comparative bases of performance have gained wide acceptance. One such definition of standard time is the expected amount of time needed by a typical, qualified worker using the proper work method and layout and performing at a pace which can

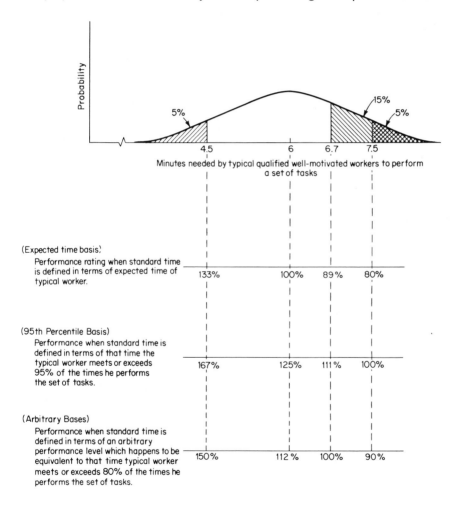

Performance $= \dfrac{\text{standard time}}{\text{actual time}} \times 100\%$

Figure 10-1 *Comparison of different bases used in defining standard time*

be maintained throughout the day without undue fatigue. Figure 10-1 shows how performance can vary using this expected time basis in one particular situation. Here the standard time which would correspond to a performance of 100 percent would be 6 minutes.

Over the long run, any organization has every right to expect the performance of its employees to average about 100 percent with the expected time basis, providing it trains the workers in the proper method, provides a steady supply of work and appropriate workplaces, and sufficiently motivates them. Management prefers to use this expected time basis for establishing work standards because it reflects realistically how long work can be expected to take, and time standards based on it can be utilized without any conversion factor in scheduling and costing out work and in making delivery promises.

Workers, for psychological reasons, tend to prefer time standards which they can usually expect to exceed. Understandably a 110 percent performance sounds better, is more ego building, than one of 88.5 percent, even though both may represent identical output. For this reason, management sometimes defines standard time in terms of that amount of time that the typical worker can meet or exceed 95 percent of the time. With this basis and the situation in Figure 10-1, the standard time would be 7.5 minutes. In this case, management expects worker performance to average out to about 125 percent. Because performance can normally be expected to exceed this standard, this 95 percent basis is often used in designing wage incentive systems.

Just as students and teachers often support grading on a curve but often cannot agree on where to define the various grade ranges, worker and management may similarly agree that using one of the above bases is a good idea but may be unable to agree on what that basis stands for. Confusion and misunderstanding can be avoided by choosing an absolute basis which can be readily visualized and consistently applied. For example, it is not unusual to define standard walking performance as 3 miles per hour. Once selected, the standard hours for the walking involved in any job become simply the distance to be traveled in feet divided by 5,280 and multiplied by 3 miles per hour. Another commonly accepted definition of standard performance for hand movements has been in terms of dealing a deck of cards into four piles, one at a time, in 40 seconds. Finally, some organizations define their standards using a predetermined data system; details of these systems are discussed later in this chapter.

TIME PREDICTION

Without reliable and appropriate time estimates, it would be impossible to improve existing operations or effectively plan new ones. It would be difficult to compare "make or buy" alternatives; select processing and material handling equipment; decide on layout and routing considerations; or design work methods. In addition, without appropriate time data, the efficiency of work scheduling and labor and equipment load assignments would be in doubt, along with the reliability of any delivery date or cost quotation. Thus, an inability to estimate the times of future alternatives and activities could place an organization, whether it be a factory, airline, or consulting firm, at a severe competitive disadvantage.

In estimating the times of human activities, organizations often make the estimates in terms of the typical worker. There are good reasons why it may not be advisable to tailor time estimates to an individual's performance. Sheer cost of developing estimates for every worker would be prohibitive. Further, every time an employee was replaced, considerable reestimation and redesign of work methods and assignments would be needed to compensate for the new employee's specific characteristics. When data are developed in terms of the typical worker, however, it is necessary to revise the time estimates only when the work method is changed.

When estimating times for activities, it is important to develop them in the form which is most relevant for their intended use. Forms commonly employed are expected working time, working time that 95 percent of the qualified workers can meet, and expected working time plus nonworking time allowances. Let us examine each of these three time forms to see how each is developed and where and why it is used.

Expected working time estimates are needed to develop efficient work methods and work area layouts and to ensure that equipment conforms to good human engineering design. Without knowing the expected times of various alternative movement sequences, it would be hard to compare their respective efficiencies.

Balancing a paced production or assembly line requires yet another type of time estimate. Due to the fixed speed of the line, each worker has only a limited amount of time to complete the tasks assigned to him. If he cannot complete his assignment, either the whole line will have to slow down or his task will simply not be completed. Either situation defeats the objective of the paced line. Hence in assigning tasks to work stations, there must be a very high probability that all tasks can be accomplished in the time available. The estimates most typically used are those in which each task can be completed 95 percent of the times it is attempted. These time estimates should not include allowances for nonworking time because a paced line is operated so that material shortages and equipment failure have a very low probability of occurring and because replacement workers are used to relieve regular line employees.

Developing labor cost estimates and delivery time quotations and scheduling and routing work call for time estimates which include both productive and nonproductive times. Employees cannot be expected to work straight through the day; they need time for personal needs, fatigue, and coffee breaks. Further, employees may be interrupted by material shortages, equipment malfunctions, and conferences with the supervisor. Yet these nonproductive periods affect how long it takes and how much it costs to accomplish work. Therefore nonworking time needs to be included in calculations for this type of estimate.

INFORMAL VERSUS FORMAL METHODS

While the primary purpose of this chapter is to introduce methods of formal work measurement, some emphasis must be given to the less formal, but no less valid, approaches to time estimation. Formal work measurement methods can only be employed effectively where the activity can be observed repeatedly during estimate development. There are many situations which do not satisfy this condition. Hence, there is the necessity for the use of less formal approaches. Even when the formal approaches can be used, the additional time and cost required to apply them may not be offset by their higher reliability in developing accurate estimates.

An informal approach is often employed to determine whether or not the additional time, cost, and accuracy of the formal approaches are worthwhile. Choosing between alternatives where slight differences can be significant often suggests that a formal procedure follow an informal evaluation. After all, who would make a really strong case for alternative A being 5 percent better than B when the comparison is based on an informal evaluation with an estimating error of 100 percent? On the other hand, if an informal evaluation shows alternative A to be 50 times as efficient as B, no more accurate estimation is needed to make a rational choice.

When a formal work measurement approach is not appropriate, the needed estimate can usually be generated subjectively. While subjective estimates are quick and inexpensive to make, their accuracy is often in question. Errors arise because of estimator bias and the unavailability of complete information about the activities whose times are being estimated.

Several procedures have been developed to reduce error potential. Assigning the estimate to the person most familiar with the activity is one way. The more time he spends thinking through the nature of the activity and the conditions that may affect it, the more confidence one can place in his estimate compared with an "off the top of the head" estimate. Having several knowledgeable people make estimates and averaging them is yet another way of proceeding. In this situation, the old saying "two heads are better than one" has an even more appropriate corollary of three, four, or more heads. Each estimator often takes into account factors which didn't occur to the others. Hence the average estimate typically reflects the true nature of the real situation more adequately than the individual one.

To compensate for individual bias, we can use an adjustment factor. If the estimator tends to be overly optimistic and has in the past underestimated times by 10 percent, a more nearly unbiased estimate can be obtained if we multiply his estimates by 100/90. Usually it takes a good while to develop the ability to correctly interpret and modify the opinions of one's subordinates.

When previous time data exist, they can often be used in estimating. In some cases, a sufficiently accurate estimate can be reached by averaging existing past times. Such a procedure however is not without pitfalls. The work methods, equipment, material, or product design may have been changed, or the performance of the workers on these earlier jobs may have been different.

Existing records must be used with care when developing time estimates. The estimator must ask himself in what ways the data differ and how they will have to be modified to produce the desired estimate. Such modification involves eliminating times for activities not relevant to the ones you are attempting to derive, applying adjustment factors to those which are not quite like those for which you have data, and even estimating from scratch the times for those activities for which no related times exist. Our introduction to the procedures of formal work measurement will produce ways in which such modifications can be made.

FORMAL WORK MEASUREMENT—STRATEGY

OVERVIEW

Any organization must be able to obtain the various time estimates needed by its management in a way that overcomes the errors in historical records or educated guesses. A method that experience has proven effective involves first developing normal times by adjusting observed time for work-pace differences and then adding necessary nonworking time allowances.

Normal time is the productive time needed to perform a task when utilizing appropriate work methods and work area layout and when performing at a pace the firm defines as normal. Normal pace *could* be defined as the working effort that can be expected of a typical qualified worker or as that pace which can be met or exceeded by 95 percent of the qualified workers, or as any other arbitrary level of effort accepted by labor and management. Any individual's pace is rated as a percent of the work pace which the firm defines as normal. A faster pace than normal would result in a rating over 100 percent and conversely for a slower pace.

If a firm knows the normal time associated with a set of work activities, other types of required time estimates can quickly be generated. Suppose, for example, that a firm defines its normal time in terms of the pace that 95 percent of the qualified workers could be expected to meet or exceed. If this firm then requires times useful in grouping activities into work assignments for the purpose of designing a paced production line, no adjustment would be necessary, because with 95 percent of the employees completing their assembly line activity in the time allowed, one could be reasonably assured that, once balanced, the line would continue to operate effectively. If, however, one were designing an unpaced assembly line, expected working times estimates would be needed to reflect that output expected from the entire work group. These are obtained by multiplying the 95 percent time by the average pace the group was expected to achieve.

If, however, job time estimates are needed for routing and scheduling work or for developing delivery time and labor cost estimates (all longer-term activities), we would have to add allowances for nonworking time to the working time. When nonworking allowances are added directly to normal time, the resultant time is known as standard time. Today, most organizations evaluate performance in terms of the pace they define as normal and in terms of the standard time or output rate associated with that pace. The terms "normal time" and "standard time" tend to be used to connote time estimates applicable to two different situations; normal time is generally used when a "working time only" type of estimate is required, and standard time is typically used when an "actual time required to do the job" type of estimate is required.

NORMAL TIME AND PACE RATING

The normal time associated with a set of tasks is determined by a process of actual measurement and pace adjustment. In stopwatch time study, for example, a worker is observed performing the work for which the normal time is sought. While measuring his productive time, the worker's pace is simultaneously rated with respect to the pace the firm has defined as normal. The relationship among observed time, normal time, and pace rating is given by this equation:

Normal time = [observed time $\times$ pace rating (in percent)]/100

Thus, theoretically, three time study analysts could each perform a time study on three different employees all performing the same operation but at dissimilar pace levels and still arrive at the same normal time for that operation. Assuming that the three analysts could estimate pace quite accurately, here is how their findings might appear:

	Observed Time	Pace Rating	Normal Time
1st employee	10 min/unit	120%	12 min/unit
2nd employee	12 min/unit	100%	12 min/unit
3rd employee	15 min/unit	80%	12 min/unit

Thus, the application of a pace rating to an observed time compensates for individual pace differences of employees and produces a normal time achievable by any qualified employee. In the example above, the first employee worked at a pace 20 percent *faster* than normal; therefore his time had to be *increased* to make it representative of performance expected from a typical employee. In the case of the third employee, he worked at a pace 20 percent *slower* than normal; therefore the time he required had to be *reduced* to make it a representative time.

How does the analyst learn to rate work pace with respect to an abstract concept like normal pace? The answer lies in proper training and experience. Most analysts start the learning process using rating training films. Many companies have produced films showing various types of commonly encountered work being done at a variety of different work paces, in terms of the firm's own concept of normal pace. Others use films distributed by the Society for the Advancement of Management which show different shop and office tasks being performed at a variety of work paces. The apprentice analyst rates each performance in the film and compares his rating with those previously established. In this way, he calibrates his mental image of various work paces in different situations to correspond to that of the film.

ALLOWANCES

In order to evolve an on-the-job time estimate, it is necessary to add allowances to the normal time for justifiable nonworking time. Allowances are added for personal time, for rest to overcome fatigue, and for delays beyond the worker's control, such as lack of work, equipment failure, conferences with supervisors, and work area cleanup for which the worker is responsible.

Today labor and management often negotiate the values for allowances, especially personal and fatigue time. Figure 10-2 illustrates the fatigue allowances employed by one company for different types of activities. A 5 percent personal allowance (roughly equivalent to 10 to 15 minutes, twice a day) is typical for most firms.

Because they tend to occur irregularly and to be of uncertain duration, allowances for unavoidable delays due to lack of work, equipment failure, and conferences with supervisors can often be developed using work sampling, a technique discussed later in this chapter.

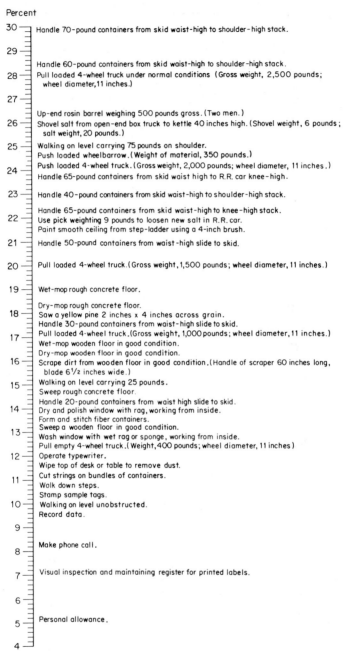

Percent

30 — Handle 70-pound containers from skid waist-high to shoulder-high stack.

29 —

Handle 60-pound containers from skid waist-high to shoulder-high stack.
28 — Pull loaded 4-wheel truck under normal conditions (Gross weight, 2,500 pounds; wheel diameter,11 inches.)

27 —

Up-end rosin barrel weighing 500 pounds gross. (Two men.)
26 — Shovel salt from open-end box truck to kettle 40 inches high. (Shovel weight, 6 pounds; salt weight, 20 pounds.)

25 — Walking on level carrying 75 pounds on shoulder.
Push loaded wheelbarrow. (Weight of material, 350 pounds.)
Push loaded 4-wheel truck. (Gross weight, 2,000 pounds; wheel diameter, 11 inches.)
24 — Handle 65-pound containers from skid waist high to R.R. car knee-high.

23 — Handle 40-pound containers from skid waist-high to shoulder-high stack.

Handle 65-pound containers from skid waist-high to knee-high stack.
22 — Use pick weighting 9 pounds to loosen new salt in R.R. car.
Paint smooth ceiling from step-ladder using a 4-inch brush.

21 — Handle 50-pound containers from waist-high slide to skid.

20 — Pull loaded 4-wheel truck. (Gross weight, 1,500 pounds; wheel diameter, 11 inches.)

19 — Wet-mop rough concrete floor.

Dry-mop rough concrete floor.
18 — Saw a yellow pine 2 inches x 4 inches across grain.
Handle 30-pound containers from waist-high slide to skid.
17 — Pull loaded 4-wheel truck. (Gross weight, 1,000 pounds; wheel diameter, 11 inches.)
Wet-mop wooden floor in good condition.
Dry-mop wooden floor in good condition.
16 — Scrape dirt from wooden floor in good condition. (Handle of scraper 60 inches long, blade 6½ inches wide.)
15 — Walking on level carrying 25 pounds.
Sweep rough concrete floor.
Handle 20-pound containers from waist high slide to skid.
14 — Dry and polish window with rag, working from inside.
Form and stitch fiber containers.
Sweep a wooden floor in good condition.
13 — Wash window with wet rag or sponge, working from inside.
Pull empty 4-wheel truck. (Weight, 400 pounds; wheel diameter, 11 inches)
12 — Operate typewriter.
Wipe top of desk or table to remove dust.
Cut strings on bundles of containers.
11 — Walk down steps.
Stamp sample tags.
10 — Walking on level unobstructed.
Record data.

9 —

Make phone call.
8 —

Visual inspection and maintaining register for printed labels.
7 —

6 —

Personal allowance.
5 —

4 —

Figure 10-2 *Personal and fatigue allowances used by one company having mainly handling and hand-truck operations. The allowances given included personal time.* [*From R. M. Barnes,* Motion and Time Study, Design and Measurement of Work, *6th ed. (New York: John Wiley & Sons, Inc., 1968).*]

Allowances are applied in either of two ways—as a percent of normal time or as a percent of the work day. Fatigue allowances are often given in the former form, while personal and delay allowances are more commonly stated in the latter manner. Whether the allowances are expressed as a percent of on-the-job time or of working time, it is irrelevant as long as everyone concerned understands which terminology is being used. For example, if the worker is allowed an hour out of each 8-hour shift as nonworking time, allowances may be expressed as $\frac{1}{8}$, or 12.5 percent, of his on-the-job time or as $1/(8-1)$, or 14.3 percent, of his working time. If we assume a normal time of 10 minutes per unit, we would calculate the standard work expected using the first alternative as follows:

$$\frac{7 \text{ hours}}{10 \text{ min/unit}} = \frac{420 \text{ min}}{10 \text{ min/unit}} = 42 \text{ units expected per day}$$

If, on the other hand, we use the second approach, we get the same result:

$$10 \text{ min/unit} \times 14.3\% = 1.43 \text{ min/unit (allowance time)}$$
$$10 \text{ min/unit} + 1.43 = 11.43 \text{ min/unit (standard time)}$$
$$\frac{8 \text{ hours}}{11.43 \text{ min/unit}} = \frac{480 \text{ min}}{11.43 \text{ min/unit}} = 42 \text{ units expected per day}$$

TIME STUDY

To many, formal work measurement and time study are synonymous. While this is not actually the case, time study was the first and is still the most fundamental and frequently used of the formal work measurement techniques. Time study utilizes direct observation of activities to develop normal times for those activities.

A wise preliminary step is to examine first the work methods, work place layout, and other such work-affecting factors as input and output scheduling and the condition of the processing equipment. Here the object is to increase efficiency before spending time and money on developing time estimates for an inefficient design.

JOB BREAKDOWN

Once the final work design has been established, the job to be timed should be broken down into timeable *elements,* each with a clearly identifiable beginning and end. An experienced time study analyst can accurately time elements as short as 0.05 minutes. Machine-controlled job elements should be separated from operator-controlled ones. Job elements occurring in every work cycle (unit produced) should be separated from elements occurring with lesser frequencies.

These deviations are made with good reason. While the operator-controlled elements must be pace rated, normal times for machine-controlled elements can often be determined by separate engineering calculations. Often each operator-controlled element must be individually rated, for it is not unusual for a worker's work pace to vary between job elements. For example, although their physical strength may enable them to move heavy weights efficiently, some workers are poor at job elements involving precision hand motions; this results in a higher rating for the former than for the latter. Job elements with different frequencies of occurrence should be listed separately in order to prorate their times on a per unit basis. For example, a 10-minute tool sharpening activity which is required after every 100 parts, appears in the work standard as 0.1 minute per part produced. Timing individual job elements also facilitates building up predetermined data, a concept introduced later in this chapter.

WORKER SELECTION

The worker studied should be thoroughly experienced in the use of the work method and work area layout, thus making him less likely to deviate from the prescribed work design. It is much more difficult to pace rate an inexperienced worker, and the resulting pace ratings are less accurate than those based on the work of an experienced man.

MAKING THE STUDY

Figure 10-3 shows a time study work sheet used in developing a time standard for a grinding job. The level of recorded detail is typical of that needed to respond knowledgeably should any question about the validity of the standard arise. Further, such a detailed record makes it possible to derive other types of time estimates without completely restudying the job.

In Figure 10-3, notice how the unusual times (i.e., conferring with supervisor and dropping a part) were deleted from the calculation of the normal time. Nonproductive allowances added to the normal time compensate for these particular situations. The fatigue allowance is applied only to the operator-controlled normal time. Since personal and delay allowances are stated in minutes a day, they are therefore applied to both machine- and operator-controlled times. Standard time job element 6, which occurs only once every 200 ground parts, is prorated over the per part standard.

<u>Date of study:</u>   August 7, 1971

<u>Analyst:</u>   John Bowlin

<u>Worker studied:</u> Glen Parker -- 3 1/2 years of experience in use of a
wide variety of grinding equipment and operations;
classified as experienced in grinding of Part #1003-A

<u>Work area layout and equipment:</u> (determined by John Bowlin)

<u>Work method:</u> (developed by John Bowlin)

Job element no.	Job element description	Frequency
1	Get unground part, place in fixture, start machine	Every part
2	Wait for grinder to finish top of part (machine controlled)	Every part
3	Cut off machine, turn over part, start machine	Every part
4	Wait for grinder to machine bottom of part (machine controlled)	Every part
5	Cut off machine and put in finish parts bin	Every part
6	Replace grinding wheel with new or redressed (overhauled) wheel and readjust grinder	Every 200 parts

Allowances and other relevant data:

1. Element 6 is common to many grinding operations and has previously
been established to have a time standard of 10 minutes; this includes
typical allowances plus an allowance for the possibility of improper
adjustment of the grinding wheel which occasionally occurs.

2. For routine grinding jobs such as this one the appropriate
allowances are:

Personnel — 30 minutes (or 6.25) of the 8-hour shift

Fatigue — 15% of the normal time or actual working time for
elements 1, 3, and 5

Unavoidable delay — 30 minutes (or 6.25) of the 8-hour shift

3. The operator on this job is not responsible for work area cleanup
or for moving parts between workplaces.

Figure 10-3   *Time study work sheet for developing time standard for
grinding of part #1003-A*

Time Study Data and Analysis

Job element	Rating	Observed time in minutes per part										Average observed minutes per part excluding unusual times	Normal minutes per part = average observed minutes x (rating / 100)
		Part 1	Part 2	Part 3	Part 4	Part 5	Part 6	Part 7	Part 8	Part 9	Part 10		
1	80%	.23	.24	.25	.47*	.26	.27	.24	.25	.45**	.26	$.25 = \left(\dfrac{\begin{array}{c}.23 + .24 + .25 + .26 \\ + .27 + .24 + .25 + .26\end{array}}{8} \right)$	$.20 = .25 \times 80/100$
2	100%	.30	.30	.30	.30	.30	.30	.30	.30	.30	.30	.30	$.30 = .30 \times 100/100$
3	110%	.22	.23	.20	.18	.19	.18	.20	.20	.21	.19	$.20 = \left(\dfrac{\begin{array}{c}.22 + .23 + .20 + .18 + .19 + \\ .18 + .20 + .20 + .21 + .19\end{array}}{10} \right)$	$.22 = .20 \times 110/100$
4	100%	.30	.30	.30	.30	.30	.30	.30	.30	.30	.30	.30	$.30 = .30 \times 100/100$
5	120%	.15	.14	.39*	.15	.16	.16	.14	.15	.15	.15	$.15 = \left(\dfrac{\begin{array}{c}.15 + .14 + .15 + .16 + .16 \\ + .14 + .15 + .15 + .15\end{array}}{9} \right)$	$.18 = .15 \times 120/100$

* Conferred with foreman

** Dropped part

Analysis

Normal machine-controlled minutes per part	$.6 = .3 + .3$
Standard machine-controlled minutes per part	$.684 = .6 \times \dfrac{100}{100} \times \dfrac{100}{100 - (6.25 + 6.25)}$
Normal worker-controlled minutes per part (excluding job element 6)	$.6 = .20 + .22 + .18$
Standard worker-controlled minutes per part (excluding job element 6)	$.786 = .6 \times \dfrac{100 + 15}{100} \times \dfrac{100}{100 - (6.25 + 6.25)}$
Standard worker-controlled minutes per part (including job element 6)	$.836 = .786 + \dfrac{10}{200}$
Standard minutes per part	$1.520 = (.684 + .836)$
Standard output per worker per shift	$316 = \left(\dfrac{480}{1.520} \right)$
Standard labor cost per unit applying average grinding dept wage of $ 2.70 / hr	$\$ .0685 = \$ 2.70 \times \dfrac{1.520}{60}$

Figure 10-3   *(Continued)*

NUMBER OF CYCLES TIMED

Are the 10 timed cycles for the job in Figure 10-3 enough? Certainly the more job cycles timed and observed, the more information the time study analyst has on which to base the times and pace ratings of the observed job elements. This will result in more accurate normal time estimates.

Figure 10-4 lists the minimum number of cycles that one company recommends. This number depends on both the cycle duration and the number of cycles occurring per year. For jobs with longer cycle times, Figure 10-4 shows that additional observations are needed to achieve the equivalent accuracy associated with the shorter cycle times. If some of the job elemental

Time/cycle (hours)	Minimum Number of Cycles to Study		
	Activity: Over 10,000/yr.	Activity: 1,000 to 10,000/yr.	Activity: Under 1,000/yr.
8.000	2	1	1
3.000	3	2	1
2.000	4	2	1
1.000	5	3	2
0.800	6	3	2
0.500	8	4	3
0.300	10	5	4
0.200	12	6	5
0.120	15	8	6
0.080	20	10	8
0.050	25	12	10
0.035	30	15	12
0.020	40	20	15
0.012	50	25	20
0.008	60	30	25
0.005	80	40	30
0.003	100	50	40
0.002	120	60	50
Under 0.002	140	80	60

Figure 10-4 *Recommended minimum number of cycles to be observed. [From G. B. Carson (ed.),* Production Handbook, *2d ed. (New York: The Ronald Press Company, 1958).]*

times eventually become part of a predetermined data system, additional cycles should be included to ensure a highly accurate estimate. Finally, more than the minimum recommended number should be observed whenever the chances of error are abnormally high, i.e., when studying a learning worker or a job whose cycles were subject to an unusually high degree of time and pace variations.

The determination of the number of cycles to be observed can be treated in a precise statistical manner once the reliability sought has been specified. The object of such statistical approaches is to ensure that a specified minimum level of confidence can be placed in the fact that the average observed time is within a specified percentage of the worker's average time.

WORK SAMPLING

The expense of using time study to develop time estimates for long-cycle or infrequently or irregularly occurring activities is often prohibitive. Studies to analyze delay time from machine breakdown or material shortages can require that an analyst continuously observe and time the activities of a worker for a week or longer to obtain a representative picture of the occurrence of these activities. In this case, the cost of the analyst's time could exceed the value of the time estimates.

There is a formal, direct observation approach to work measurement that avoids the need for continuously observing and timing the activities of one worker by utilizing sampling techniques. This approach, most commonly known as work sampling, involves randomly taking a series of instantaneous observations over a prolonged period from which activity times are then inferred. By randomly making a large number of observations over an extended period, we would expect to observe nearly the same percentage of occurrence of an activity as would truly occur if a continuous time study were carried out. For example, if we observed whether or not your roommate was studying at 1,000 randomly chosen times and we found him studying 250 of these times, we could infer correctly that, on the average, he studies 6 hours a day ($24 \times 250/1000$).

TWO TENETS OF WORK SAMPLING

There are two basic tenets of work sampling. One holds that the percentage of the total number of random observations falling on a particular activity indicates approximately the proportion of time that activity actually occurs. The other tenet holds that the greater the number of observations taken, the greater the accuracy of the findings.

Let us continue the example of your roommate's study habits. If we had been lazy and observed his activities only 5 times instead of 1,000, we would have obtained a much less reliable estimate. In fact, we might never have seen him studying any of the 5 times we looked in on him, or he may always have been studying. If either of these situations occurred, we would have incorrectly inferred either that he never studies or that he never moves, eats, sleeps, plays tennis, or kills time. (From Figure 10-5,

X	
0	.236
1	.396
2	.264
3	.088
4	.015
5	.001

Figure 10-5 *Chances of seeing roommate studying X times out of five if he actually studies 25 percent of the time*

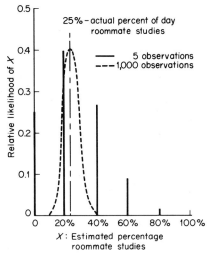

Figure 10-6   *Comparison of relative likelihoods of estimating different percentages of day spent studying using 5 as opposed to 1,000 observations*

we see that the probability of not seeing him studying any of the 5 times we observed him is .236 while the probability of always seeing him studying is .001.) Further, if we should repeat such a 5-observation study, we would probably see him studying a different number of times, thus leading to a different estimate of his actual study time. By increasing the number of observations, we substantially increase our chances of accurately estimating his actual study time of 6 hours. This fact is demonstrated in Figure 10-6, which compares the probability of estimating different studying times using 5 observations as opposed to 1,000.

THE USES OF WORK SAMPLING

But, of course, work sampling has more important applications than finding out about your roommate's study habits. Like time study, it is suited for estimating times of types of activities which reoccur over a given time period and which can be clearly identified. On the other hand, it is not as well suited as time study for estimating times for activities of extremely short duration. Although it is best suited for estimating times of activities whose percent of total working time is significant, it does not matter whether these activities occur regularly or irregularly, frequently, or infrequently. As a consequence, work sampling is a useful tool in developing standards needed to plan cost and evaluate the long-cycle or irregularly occurring activities commonly found both in manufacturing and in such indirect labor operations as repair, maintenance, janitorial, warehousing, retailing, office, and health care operations.

Perhaps the most common use of work sampling is in estimating unavoidable delay allowances which are needed to develop time standards (i.e., standard time = normal time + allowances). Since unavoidable delays happen because of such random occurrences as machine breakdowns and material shortages, work sampling provides an excellent method of estimating the percentage of each work day consumed by these delays.

Another important use of work sampling is determining resource utilization patterns. Consider the case of the research manager interested in increasing the efficiency of his highly skilled professionals by adding more technicians and support personnel. He could conduct a work sampling study to determine the time spent by his researchers in performing work which could more profitably be delegated to less skilled aides. If the total time spent on unskilled tasks did not justify the addition of more personnel, the manager would reject this possibility for improving efficiency. On the other hand, if the amount of time spent on such tasks was high, his work sampling study would indicate just how many support personnel could be efficiently utilized. Further, if his laboratory received a large new contract, these work sampling results would be useful in planning the type and number of support personnel that should be added as additional researchers are recruited.

RANDOM OBSERVATIONS

In order not to bias the results of a work sampling study, the observations must be made in a random manner. Using the example of your roommate, if you observed him every hour on the hour during his rest breaks, you might mistakenly infer that he never studies. Or if you consciously avoided observing him during the times you knew he would be in class or studying, you might mistakenly underestimate his actual study time.

Therefore, there is a real need for selecting observation times randomly; setting up a lottery, where observation times are chosen by picking numbers out of a hat, is one possible method. A more sophisticated approach involves the use of a random number table. These tables are generated by computers in such a manner that every number being considered has an equal chance of occurring at each table position.

Figure 10-7 is a portion of a random number table. Let's see how it can be used to generate random times for making 10 daily observations of activities in a plant which operates from 8 a.m. to 5 p.m. For each number in Figure 10-7, let its first three digits denote the number of hours after the start of the shift to make an observation. The first number, 037183, indicates we should make an observation at 0.37 hours into the shift, or

037183	742942
750066	485453
978142	610163
268787	211559
347104	356141
989408	220985
674192	362686
096124	785915
825300	163214
595132	069133
907093	950622
687432	133869
437817	899093
326355	269577
866478	947189
783807	
194660	
414101	
168942	
679380	

Source: A table of 14,000 random units, *Handbook of Tables for Mathematics*, 3rd ed., Cleveland: The Chemical Rubber Co., 1967, pp. 928–932.

Figure 10-7   *Portion of a random number table*

at 8:22 a.m., $8 + (0.37 \times 60)$. The second number, 750066, indicates we should make an observation 7.50 hours into the shift at 3:30 p.m. The third number, 978142, indicated we should make an observation 9.78 hours after the start of the shift, but since the shift is only 9 hours long, this number has no relevance and would be discarded. Figure 10-8 shows how this procedure was employed to produce the 10 required observation times. A new set of observation times, however, should be generated for each day to avoid observations made at the same time each day. To generate a new observation set, we need only start at a different place in the random number table.

NUMBER OF OBSERVATIONS

The second tenet of work sampling states that the more observations taken, the greater the accuracy of the findings; we know then that to select the

Random Number	Hours After Shift Start	Observation Time	Observations to Be in This Sequence
037183	0.37	8:22 a.m.	8:22 a.m.
750066	7.50	3:30 p.m.	8:58 a.m.
978142	9.78	not relevant	10:41 a.m.
268787	2.68	10:41 a.m.	11:28 a.m.
347104	3.47	11:28 a.m.	12:22 p.m.
989408	9.89	not relevant	1:57 p.m.
674192	6.74	2:44 p.m.	2:44 p.m.
096124	0.96	8:58 a.m.	2:52 p.m.
825300	8.25	4:15 p.m.	3:30 p.m.
595132	5.95	1:57 p.m.	4:15 p.m.
907093	9.07	not relevant	
687432	6.87	2:52 p.m.	
437817	4.37	12:22 p.m.	

Figure 10-8   *Generation of ten observation times from table*

proper number of observations we first need to decide how accurate we want to be.

Figure 10-9 shows how the desired accuracy affects the number of observations needed to ensure that accuracy. Note that this number depends not only on the stated accuracy but also on the percent of the total working time occupied by the activity being observed. Thus, for an activity which occurs 10 percent of the time, we would have to make 900 observations to be 95 percent certain that the observed frequency of its occurrence was with ± 2 percentage points of 10 percent, i.e., between 8 and 12 percent. If we desired to be 95 percent sure that the observed percentage was within ± 1 percentage point, 3,600 observations should be made. It is interesting to note that doubling the desired accuracy quadruples the number of observations needed.

Thus, while closer accuracy greatly increases the total observation cost, it reduces costs due to sampling inaccuracies (see Figure 10-10). What we would really like to find is the accuracy level where the sum of the two costs is minimum, the minimum point on the total cost curve of Figure 10-10. Sampling inaccuracy costs are only vaguely predictable; choosing an accuracy level is generally done by intuition. In determining the appropriate unavoidable delay allowance for a time standard underlying a wage incentive system affecting many workers, it would be reasonable to specify a 95 percent certainty that the observed unavoidable delay percentage was within ± 1 percentage point of its actual value. Here if the actual value happened to be 10 percent, 3,600 observations would have to be taken to ensure this level of accuracy.

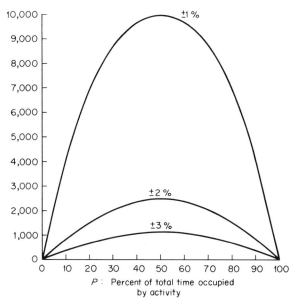

Figure 10-9 *Number of observations required to be 95 percent sure that the observed percentage of occurrence of an activity is within 1, 2, or 3 percentage points of its actual value. [From R. M. Barnes, Motion and Time Study, Design and Measurement of Work, 6th ed. (New York: John Wiley & Sons, Inc., 1968).]*

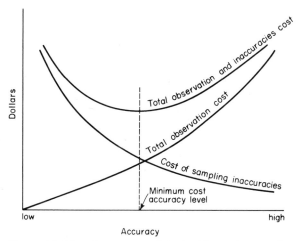

Figure 10-10 *Costs associated with work sampling*

On the other hand, consider the position of a research laboratory manager interested in increasing the number of unskilled support personnel as a means of making the researchers' time more productive. If it generally requires about 10 percent time occurrence of unskilled work to justify one additional support person, the manager needs to determine the percentage occurrence of unskilled tasks only to the nearest 10 percent (i.e., 0 percent, 10 percent, 20 percent, . . . , 100 percent). Here only enough accuracy is needed to determine *which* 10 percent is nearest to the actual one. Should a preliminary sample of 400 observations demonstrate a 12 percent occurrence of such tasks, we would be 95 percent certain that it is the true percentage ±3 percent (i.e., between 9 and 15 percent). Consequently, it is very likely that two additional support personnel could be profitably utilized.

PROCEDURE

Performing a work sampling study is not difficult if certain steps are carefully followed. Consider the case of Steer-Rite, Inc., a chain of auto repair shops specializing in front end alignment. The founder, Al Wonden, has been telling his son, Al junior, how the firm needed a good estimate of the time necessary

Information	Source Data	Data
No. of man-hours the realigners worked	Time cards	2,000 hours
No. of cars realigned during study	Sales records	2,000 cars
Realignment time as percent of total time	Work sampling	64%
Nonworking time due to unavoidable delays (other than no customers) as percent of total time	``	5%
Nonworking time due to no customers as percent of total time	``	18%
Other nonworking time as a percent of total time	``	13%
Average rating	Work sampling (see below)	94.8%
Personal time allowance	Union contract	7%

Figure 10-11 *Steer-Rite data and calculation for developing a time standard for realigning a car*

Rating Data and Calculation of Average Rating

Each time a realigner was observed working, he was rated to the nearest 5%, e.g., 95, 100, or 105. The findings are given below.

Rating as %	No. of times made
120	0
115	50
110	150
105	400
100	1,500
95	2,000
90	1,600
85	400
80	300
75	0
	6,400 Total

$$\text{Average rating} = \frac{\begin{array}{c}115(50) + 110(150) + 105(400) + 100(1,500) \\ + \ 95(2,000) + 90(1,600) + 85(400) + 80(300)\end{array}}{6,400}$$

$$= 94.8\%$$

$$\text{Normal hours per car} = \frac{\left(\begin{array}{c}\text{total hours} \\ \text{put in}\end{array}\right)\left(\begin{array}{c}\text{fraction of} \\ \text{total time} \\ \text{spent rea-} \\ \text{ligning cars}\end{array}\right)\left(\begin{array}{c}\text{average} \\ \text{rating as} \\ \text{a fraction}\end{array}\right)}{\text{total number of cars realigned}}$$

$$= \frac{2,000 \times 0.64 \times 0.948}{2,000} = 0.606 \text{ hours per car}$$

$$\text{Standard hours per car} = \begin{array}{c}\text{normal hours} \\ \text{per car}\end{array} \times \left(\frac{100}{100 - \left(\begin{array}{c}\text{personal time allow-} \\ \text{ance plus allowance} \\ \text{for unavoidable de-} \\ \text{lays other than due} \\ \text{to no customers} \\ \text{both as a percent}\end{array}\right)}\right)$$

$$= 0.606 \times \left(\frac{100}{100 - (5 + 7)}\right) = 0.688 \text{ hours per car}$$

Figure 10-12   *Calculation of time standard*

to realign a car. Such a standard, he explained, would be invaluable in promising delivery times, setting prices, evaluating worker performance, and planning staffing and equipment needs for the shops. Young Wonden suggested that they conduct a work sampling study to develop the needed time standard. Figure 10-11 shows the type of information Al junior decided to collect for this study.

He knew to begin a study he had to decide first on the accuracy required and the number of observations needed to produce it. Realizing that this standard would be quite widely used and that his own labor was free, he decided it should be quite accurate, i.e., he wanted there to be at least a 95 percent chance that all observed percentages be within ± 1 percentage point of the actual occurrence of any activity.

In order to determine how large a sample should be taken, he observed from Figure 10-9 that 10,000 observations would guarantee that any observed percentage of occurrence of an activity would be within ± 1 percentage point of its actual value.

It took young Wonden 20 days to make the 10,000 observations of the workers realigning cars. Each day he made 50 observation rounds, each accomplished at random times. During each round he obtained 10 observations, 1 on each of the 10 realigners.

His findings along with the other data collected for establishing the realignment standard are shown in Figure 10-11. The final step was to analyze the work sampling results. Young Wonden's development of the standard hours to realign a car is shown in Figure 10-12. In explaining his findings to his father, he pointed out that the workers in the shop where he conducted the study were only about 95 percent efficient and were taking too much personal time (13 percent instead of the allowed 7 percent). In addition, he explained that 18 percent nonworking time due to no customers had initially disturbed him. He now felt it was reasonable to have a 15 percent level of idleness in order to handle business when it peaks unpredictably. The excess 3 percent idleness plus the present efficiency and 5 percent excess nonworking time meant that currently only 9 realigners were really justified.

PREDETERMINED DATA

When a large number of accurate time estimates is needed for reoccurring work involving many similar elements, developing them by individual time studies or work sampling studies is expensive and time consuming. In such cases, it is often wise to consider analyzing the similar elements initially and recording the results for future use in synthesizing times for work that contains these types of elements. Although the initial cost for synthesizing needed times is higher, it is incurred only once. Figure 10-13 indicates

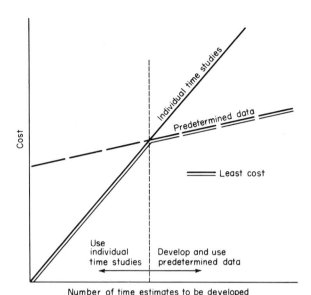

Number of time estimates to be developed

Figure 10-13   *Economics of predetermined data*

that if the number of estimates to be made is large, it is better to develop and use predetermined data (also often referred to as standard data). Another valuable application of predetermined data is in estimating times for work still in the planning or design stages, when observation of actual operations is not possible.

There are two basic types of predetermined data. One is "macro-data," which is applied to much more aggregated work activities like packing a box, washing a floor, or loading a machine. The other is "micro-data," which is expressed in terms of elemental body movements like reaching, grasping, turning, and releasing.

MACRO-DATA

When there is a large number of different short-cycle jobs involving many similar activities, macro-data often provide a useful method of organizing time estimation data. Consider the case of Span & Spic, Inc., an office cleaning firm. Since most of Span & Spic's work is obtained through competitive bid, they need an accurate and fast procedure for estimating how long it takes to wash and polish variously sized rooms. Because the time required to wash and wax a floor is highly dependent on area, management determines how long it takes to clean and polish 13 different-sized floors from among those that they are currently serving. These 13 were picked to represent as nearly as possible the range of floor sizes usually encountered. In each case, Span & Spic rated the workers' performance to obtain normal time

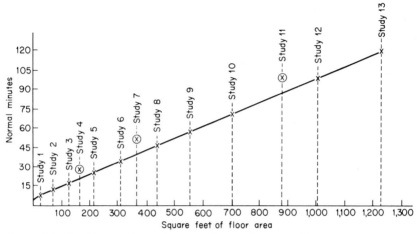

Figure 10-14   *Normal times for washing and waxing floors*

estimates. Their findings are given in Figure 10-14. The results indicate that there is a strong linear relationship between normal time and the area to be serviced.

Span & Spic began using their new scheme for time estimating. Whenever a bid was requested, they determined the square feet in each room and found the appropriate normal time from the graph in Figure 10-14. If the room had 600 square feet, for example, the time allowed would be 65 minutes; to this time was added estimates for the setup and travel time. Total or standard time estimates were then obtained by adding allowances for fatigue, personal time, and delays. This last figure, when multiplied by relevant wage rate, was an estimate of Span & Spic's cost to do the job.

As a result of their success in floor estimates, they started to develop predetermined data for the other job components such as cleaning windows, vacuuming carpets, dusting, and washing walls. In each case, they looked for the independent variables which enabled them to predict the time as accurately as possible. For example, the time to clean windows was found to depend upon the size of the window, the number of panes, the location (interior or exterior), and the travel time between windows. They used the results of their studies to produce tables which would give the normal time for a wide range of office situations which might be encountered.

Predetermined macro-data are commonly used in synthesizing times for many types of work besides janitorial and maintenance. By far their widest use is in machine shop estimating, where collecting data on operations such as drilling, grinding, and milling has been a long-standing tradition. Other areas of application include office and secretarial work, especially in estimating typing and filing times, warehousing work, and data processing.

MICRO-DATA

When using micro-data, manual work is viewed as a series of elementary motions such as reaching, grasping, positioning, and disengaging. Charts are available which list the time it takes for an average worker to complete various elementary motions. Since almost any physical task can be broken down into an appropriate listing for micromotions, these charts of micro-data allow organizations to compute time estimates for tasks before they are actually performed.

TABLE I—REACH—R

Distance Moved, Inches	Time TMU TMU = .0006 min				Hand in Motion		Case and Description
	A	B	C or D	E	A	B	
¾ or less	2.0	2.0	2.0	2.0	1.6	1.6	A Reach to object in fixed location, or to object in other hand or on which other hand rests.
1	2.5	2.5	3.6	2.4	2.3	2.3	
2	4.0	4.0	5.9	3.8	3.5	2.7	
3	5.3	5.3	7.3	5.3	4.5	3.6	B Reach to single object in location which may vary slightly from cycle to cycle.
4	6.1	6.4	8.4	6.8	4.9	4.3	
5	6.5	7.8	9.4	7.4	5.3	5.0	
6	7.0	8.6	10.1	8.0	5.7	5.7	
7	7.4	9.3	10.8	8.7	6.1	6.5	C Reach to object jumbled with other objects in a group so that search and select occur.
8	7.9	10.1	11.5	9.3	6.5	7.2	
9	8.3	10.8	12.2	9.9	6.9	7.9	
10	8.7	11.5	12.9	10.5	7.3	8.6	
12	9.6	12.9	14.2	11.8	8.1	10.1	
14	10.5	14.4	15.6	13.0	8.9	11.5	D Reach to a very small object or where accurate grasp is required.
16	11.4	15.8	17.0	14.2	9.7	12.9	
18	12.3	17.2	18.4	15.5	10.5	14.4	
20	13.1	18.6	19.8	16.7	11.3	15.8	
22	14.0	20.1	21.2	18.0	12.1	17.3	E Reach to indefinite location to get hand in position for body balance or next motion or out of way.
24	14.9	21.5	22.5	19.2	12.9	18.8	
26	15.8	22.9	23.9	20.4	13.7	20.2	
28	16.7	24.4	25.3	21.7	14.5	21.7	
30	17.5	25.8	26.7	22.9	15.3	23.2	

Figure 10-15 *Time values for various classifications of motions. Times are recorded in a special time unit called a time measurement unit (TMU), 1 TMU = 0.0006 minute (MTM Association for Standards and Research)*

TABLE II—MOVE—M

Distance Moved, Inches	Time TMU TMU = .0006 min				Wt. Allowance			Case and Description
	A	B	C	Hand in Motion B	Wt. (lb.) Up to	Factor	Constant TMU	
¾ or less	2.0	2.0	2.0	1.7	2.5	1.00	0	
1	2.5	2.9	3.4	2.3				
2	3.6	4.6	5.2	2.9	7.5	1.06	2.2	A Move object to other hand or against stop.
3	4.9	5.7	6.7	3.6				
4	6.1	6.9	8.0	4.3				
5	7.3	8.0	9.2	5.0	12.5	1.11	3.9	
6	8.1	8.9	10.3	5.7				
7	8.9	9.7	11.1	6.5	17.5	1.17	5.6	
8	9.7	10.6	11.8	7.2				
9	10.5	11.5	12.7	7.9	22.5	1.22	7.4	B Move object to approximate or indefinite location.
10	11.3	12.2	13.5	8.6				
12	12.9	13.4	15.2	10.0	27.5	1.28	9.1	
14	14.4	14.6	16.9	11.4				
16	16.0	15.8	18.7	12.8				
18	17.6	17.0	20.4	14.2	32.5	1.33	10.8	
20	19.2	18.2	22.1	15.6				
22	20.8	19.4	23.8	17.0	37.5	1.39	12.5	
24	22.4	20.6	25.5	18.4				C Move object to exact location.
26	24.0	21.8	27.3	19.8	42.5	1.44	14.3	
28	25.5	23.1	29.0	21.2				
30	27.1	24.3	30.7	22.7	47.5	1.50	16.0	

Figure 10-15 *(Continued)*

Such small motions as grasping, disengaging, and reaching are of too short duration to time accurately with a stopwatch. To build up a catalog of these times, you would typically take fixed-speed movies (1,000 film frames per minute, for example) of an operation. The film frames applicable to each movement could then be counted and converted into time. You would also rate the overall performance of the participating worker in order to translate observed time into normal time. In order to build a sufficiently

TABLE III—TURN AND APPLY PRESSURE—T AND AP

| Weight | Time TMU for Degrees Turned TMU = .0006 min | | | | | | | | | | |
	30°	45°	60°	75°	90°	105°	120°	135°	150°	165°	180°
Small—0 to 2 Pounds	2.8	3.5	4.1	4.8	5.4	6.1	6.8	7.4	8.1	8.7	9.4
Medium—2.1 to 10 Pounds	4.4	5.5	6.5	7.5	8.5	9.6	10.6	11.6	12.7	13.7	14.8
Large—10.1 to 35 Pounds	8.4	10.5	12.3	14.4	16.2	18.3	20.4	22.2	24.3	26.1	28.2

APPLY PRESSURE CASE 1—16.2 TMU. APPLY PRESSURE CASE 2—10.6 TMU.

TABLE IV—GRASP—G

Case	Time TMU	Description
1A	2.0	Pick Up Grasp—Small, medium or large object by itself, easily grasped.
1B	3.5	Very small object or object lying close against a flat surface.
1C1	7.3	Interference with grasp on bottom and one side of nearly cylindrical object. Diameter larger than $\frac{1}{2}''$.
1C2	8.7	Interference with grasp on bottom and one side of nearly cylindrical object. Diameter $\frac{1}{4}''$ to $\frac{1}{2}''$.
1C3	10.8	Interference with grasp on bottom and one side of nearly cylindrical object. Diameter less than $\frac{1}{4}''$.
2	5.6	Regrasp.
3	5.6	Transfer Grasp.
4A	7.3	Object jumbled with other objects so search and select occur. Larger than $1'' \times 1'' \times 1''$.
4B	9.1	Object jumbled with other objects so search and select occur. $\frac{1}{4}'' \times \frac{1}{4}'' \times \frac{1}{8}''$ to $1'' \times 1'' \times 1''$.
4C	12.9	Object jumbled with other objects so search and select occur. Smaller than $\frac{1}{4}'' \times \frac{1}{4}'' \times \frac{1}{8}''$.
5	0	Contact, sliding or hook grasp.

Figure 10-15 *(Continued)*

TABLE V—POSITION*—P

Class of Fit		Symmetry	Easy to Handle	Difficult to Handle
1—Loose	No pressure required.	S	5.6	11.2
		SS	9.1	14.7
		NS	10.4	16.0
2—Close	Light pressure required.	S	16.2	21.8
		SS	19.7	25.3
		NS	21.0	26.6
3—Exact	Heavy pressure required.	S	43.0	48.6
		SS	46.5	52.1
		NS	47.8	53.4

*Distance moved to engage—1″ or less.

TABLE VI—RELEASE—RL

Case	Time TMU	Description
1	2.0	Normal release performed by opening fingers as independent motion.
2	0	Contact release.

TABLE VII—DISENGAGE—D

Class of Fit	Easy to Handle	Difficult to Handle
1—Loose—Very slight effort, blends with subsequent move.	4.0	5.7
2—Close—Normal effort, slight recoil.	7.5	11.8
3—Tight—Considerable effort, hand recoils markedly.	22.9	34.7

TABLE VIII—EYE TRAVEL TIME AND EYE FOCUS—ET AND EF

Eye travel time $= 15.2 \times \dfrac{T}{D}$ TMU, with a maximum value of 20 TMU.

where T = the distance between points from and to which the eye travels.
D = the perpendicular distance from the eye to the line of travel T.

Eye focus time = 7.3 TMU.

Figure 10-15   *(Continued)*

TABLE IX—BODY, LEG, AND FOOT MOTIONS

Description	Symbol	Distance	Time TMU
Foot Motion—Hinged at Ankle.	FM	Up to 4″	8.5
With heavy pressure.	FMP		19.1
Leg or Foreleg Motion.	LM	Up to 6″	7.1
		Each add'l. inch	1.2
Sidestep—Case 1—Complete when leading leg contacts floor.	SS-C1	Less than 12″	Use REACH or MOVE Time
		12″	17.0
		Each add'l. inch	.6
Case 2—Lagging leg must contact floor before next motion can be made.	SS-C2	12″	34.1
		Each add'l. inch	1.1
Bend, Stoop, or Kneel on One Knee.	B,S,KOK		29.0
Arise.	AB,AS,AKOK		31.9
Kneel on Floor—Both Knees.	KBK		69.4
Arise.	AKBK		76.7
Sit.	SIT		34.7
Stand from Sitting Position.	STD		43.4
Turn Body 45 to 90 degrees—			
Case 1—Complete when leading leg contacts floor.	TBC1		18.6
Case 2—Lagging leg must contact floor before next motion can be made.	TBC2		37.2
Walk.	W-FT	Per Foot	5.3
Walk.	W-P	Per Pace	15.0

Figure 10-15 *(Continued)*

extensive catalog which would enable you to synthesize time for a wide variety of manual work, you would have to film and rate a tremendous number of micromotion sequences not only to cover the different types but also to identify how each was affected by such factors as distance moved, weight handled, and preciseness of movement.

It is no wonder, then, that a few consulting firms have independently produced generalized, predetermined micro-data which they offer for sale to industry. The package includes use of the data and training of technicians. Part of the micromotion data of the Methods—Time Measurement System (MTM), one of the better known systems, are given in Figure 10-15. The

Formal Measurement Techniques

Type	Application	Examples	Requirements
1. Direct Time Study	a. Establish standards for repetitive, short-cycle work performed at essentially one work station.	Typing Filing Packaging Assembly Machining	Time recording with stopwatch or camera (micromotion). Establishing statistical reliability. Definition of concept of normal pace. Detailed methods description. Determining and applying allowances. Rating pace. Highly standardized method.
	b. Establish standards for irregular, medium- to long-cycle work, frequently performed by moving about several work stations.	Repair Janitorial Warehousing Clerical	Time recording with stopwatch or camera. Determining and applying allowances. Fairly standardized method. Establishing statistical reliability (optional). Definition of concept of standard. Rating pace. Gross methods description.
	c. Develop predetermined data.	See Types 3 & 4	
2. Work Sampling	a. For management information: i.e., determination of delays, utilization of people and equipment, work distribution, feasibility studies, performance checks, et al.	Any work	Make instantaneous observations and tally. Define elements and end points. Set up random schedule. Determine percent of total time spent on various categories of work and nonwork.
	b. To establish standards for irregular work where a work unit may be determined which is highly correlated to input.	Rebuild Indirect labor Repair Warehousing	Establish number of observations required. Set up random schedule. Make instantaneous observations and tally. Gross description of method. Define elements and end points. Choose level of accuracy desired.

		Applications	Method/Procedure
		Clerical	Obtain production count during study. Apply allowances. Rate pace (random sampling). Establish number of observations required for statistical reliability.
3. Predetermined Macro-Data	a. Establish standards for repetitive short- and medium-cycle work where volume is high.	Assembly Filing Packaging Machining Typing	Average the variables into small categories. Determine and define motion patterns (elements). Determine time values from predetermined time standard tables. (In some instances, from direct time studies.)
	b. Establish standards for repetitive work where volume is low, or for long, irregular-cycle work where volume is high.	Repair Warehousing Assembly Clerical Packaging Maintenance Machining	Determine time values from direct time studies or predetermined time standard tables. Determine and define motion patterns. Average the variables into gross categories.
4. Predetermined Micro-Data	a. Establish standards for repetitive short-cycle work where volume is high.	Machining Assembly	Application of allowances. Precise measurement of all variables, such as distance. Determination of time values from tables. Highly standardized method. (Break down into basic motions.)
	b. Check consistency of direct time study standards.	Machining Assembly	Same as above.
	c. Develop predetermined macro-data.	See Type 3	See Type 3.

Figure 10-16 *Measurement summary.* [*From B. L. Hansen, Work Sampling for Modern Management (Englewood Cliffs, N.J.: Prentice-Hall, Inc., 1960).*]

265

Informal Measurement Techniques

Type	Application	Examples	Requirements
1. Technical Estimate	a. Establish standards for irregular work.	Repair Maintenance	Evaluate and record to improve ability to estimate. Break down into small elements. Apply allowances. Make estimate of time it *should* take to perform work (estimate made by supervisor, inspector, analyst, etc.). Use historical reports, standard data, time study, experience, etc., for each element.
	b. Scheduling and controlling projects for priority, status, evaluation, and costing.	Technical projects	Same as above, except estimates to be made by supervisor, project chief, etc.
2. Historical Standards	Establish standards for irregular work where a work unit may be determined.	Indirect labor Warehousing Administrative	Select realistic work unit and correlate input to output. Measure central tendency (mean, median, mode, quartile, regression, etc.). Apply allowances. Develop and/or analyze historical records of man-hours expended and related output in units produced.
3. Staffing Patterns	Establish staffing ratios for highly irregular work for which no work unit may be determined.	Support activities Administrative	Determine ratios of number of support personnel to supported personnel. Analyze historical records of similar activities.

Figure 10-16 *(Continued)*

MTM time values listed are in 0.00001 hours (equivalent to 0.0006 of a minute). The degree of precision with which the different micromotions are characterized in the MTM system is illustrated by the fact that MTM lists 11 different times for grasping an object, each dependent upon a particular set of conditions affecting that movement.

The many predetermined micro-data systems available on the market differ in several ways. Each system may define and encompass a different set of micromotion classifications. The rating basis used to convert observed time to standard time may vary. One system may base its times on an expert worker and another on an average qualified worker. Some systems even include allowances for such special considerations as fatigue or learning time. As a result, any firm entertaining the idea of using one of these predetermined micro-data systems must search for the appropriate system.

Another caution when exploring the possibility is the considerable time involved in setting up and operating a system. As much as 6 months may be needed to train a man in the system before he becomes proficient in its use. It also takes a good deal of time for even an experienced micro-data analyst to break down jobs into appropriate micromotions and then to total up the micromotion times.

However, micro-data offers many advantages. No other time estimating system can be used to build up such a wide variety of time estimates of tasks which are yet to be accomplished. By forcing minute review of motion patterns, it also increases the chance of developing a better method of performing the task under study.

CONCLUSION

The chapter has presented a variety of measurement techniques, each of which produces data useful to one or more POM needs. The choice among measurement methods involves tradeoffs between cost and required accuracy; the final application of the time values is itself the major determinant of which method is most effective in the long run. Figure 10-16 presents a brief summary of the major formal measurement techniques.

QUESTIONS

1. Why do you agree or disagree with the following statements:
   (a) "We can't perform reliable time studies because our workers always try to bluff our time-study men."
   (b) "Pace rating is a highly subjective process, and, therefore, it should be eliminated from formal work measurement methodology."

(c) "When using predetermined times, there is little need to worry about the appropriate concept of normal performance."

(d) "We don't use wage incentives because our employees would strive for quantity rather than quality."

(e) "What we want are the actual times tasks are going to take and not some adjusted performance or pace-rated time."

(f) "We can't use work measurement because our workers are poorly motivated."

2. Explain the significance of the law of large numbers in work measurement.

3. Does the growth of automation increase or decrease the need for work measurement? Support your answer.

4. If you were a local union steward, what particular factors might you use as a basis for challenging the accuracy of a company's time-study results and why?

5. Why bother timing jobs element by element?

6. Rather than use random sampling theory to determine the sample size (number of cycles observed) in time-study methodology, some companies resort to rule of thumb methods of determining the sample size as 30 minutes' worth of observation or an hour's worth. What risks and what possible advantages are associated with this home vintage answer to the problem?

7. Describe the difficulties you might encounter in trying to establish labor standards with predetermined data.

8. For each work measurement technique, indicate those types of tasks where it might be utilized.

1. Time study	A. Repetitive tasks
2. Work sampling	B. Nonrepetitive tasks
3. Micro predetermined time data	C. Short-cycle task
4. Macro predetermined time data	D. Long-cycle task
5. Historically and subjectively based estimates	E. Low-production volume
	F. High-production volume
	G. Single-man task
	H. Multi-man task
	I. Man-machine task

9. Consider the case of a certain projected job assignment which has not yet been performed. It is extremely repetitive and short cycle in nature and will be performed by 50 workers for the next 2 years. Which work measurement approaches would be most appropriate for estimating a standard time for this job prior to actually performing the job and why?

10. At the Hoy Corporation, an assembly operation has recently been time studied. Three observations were taken on a complete cycle of the operation. The cycle times recorded for the three observations were 2.10 minutes, 2.40 minutes, and 2.25 minutes respectively. The observations had respective performance ratings of 1.20, 1.00, and 1.04. If plant practice is to have a 25 percent allowance for this type of operation, what should the standard time for this operation be?

11. Bohlin Publishing has just discovered that the pace rating used in developing a print-setting standard was in error. The man who performed the original study rated the operator's pace at 130 percent when the rating should have been 110 percent. If the current standard of 5 minutes includes a 20 percent of the normal time allowance, what should the corrected time standard be?

12. How many working minutes do you expect it would take a worker to produce a part for which the time standard is 10 minutes if the allowances for this work are 25 percent of the normal time and the worker is rated at 80 percent where normal pace is defined on an expected pace base?

13. After the application of appropriate work simplification techniques, Jay Oliver took a direct time study of a simplified job and obtained the following elemental times in minutes:

| Job Element | Cycles | | | | |
	1	2	3	4	5
#1	.16	.12	.13	.15	.24
#2	.60	.60	.60	.60	.60
#3	.33	.50	.35	.37	.35
#4	.50	.50	.50	.50	.50
#5	.24	.24	.25	.27	.25

In addition, he determined the following information about this job:

(a) Job elements 2 and 4 are machine controlled and cannot be speeded up by the operator.

(b) Jay Oliver observed two irregular occurrences while timing the job. These were elemental times which vary from the average of each element's average by more than 25 percent.

(c) He rated the operator at 110 percent when he was working.

(d) Management and the worker's union have negotiated the following allowances for this job:

Personnel—30 minutes a day
Unavoidable delay—20 minutes a day
Fatigue—10 percent of the operator's actual, physical working time

(e) A worker holding this job earns $4 per hour.

(f) Material cost is $.50 per unit

(g) Total overhead cost is added in at a rate of 100 percent of the sum of direct labor and material cost.

(h) A shift is 8 hours long.

What should the standard minutes per unit be for this job?

What should the shift output standard be?

What should the standard cost per piece be?

14. Below are the results of a work sampling study which took place over a 300-hour period during which the worker was observed while processing 27,000 parts.

	No. of observations
Working	1,600
Nonworking (personal & idle)	400

The worker, when working, was rated at 80 percent normal performance. For this type work, the allowances (personal, fatigue, unavoidable delay, etc.) should be 10 percent of the total work day (8 hours). Find the standard number of units the worker should process an hour.

15. In the preceding problem, would the standard have better been set by a time study rather than a work-sampling study? Explain.

16. As a maintenance officer in the Air Force, you are charged with the responsibility of setting a time standard (in minutes) for uploading bomb loads. The following study was conducted over a period of 300 hours with 600 uploadings performed.

Composite Performance Rating	Activity	No. of Observations
80	Manually check and lift bombs into trailer.	200
200	Correct above defects (this time will be reduced by 50% by an additional inspection during manufacture).	300
100	Tow-loaded tractor to aircraft.	250
80	Check electrical contacts holding pins and safety wires (called "wiring out").	200
100	Correct any malfunctioning observed during wiring out.	200
100	Load bombs into bomb bay with automatic lift.	200
100	Return tractor and trailer to bomb storage area.	250
	Personal or idle time.	400

Official United States Air Force personal time allowance is 15 percent of total 8-hour work day *unless otherwise stated,* and it is not otherwise stated here.

What would be an appropriate time standard for uploading the bombs?

17. At the Motivated Pickle Pickers Corporation wage incentives are utilized to motivate the pickle pickers. All pickle pickers are guaranteed an hourly wage of $2 regardless of how many pecks are picked. If, however, they exceed Motivated Pickle Pickers shift standard base on 3 minutes per peck, the pickle pickers pick up a pickle-picking bonus per peck picked.

The bonus is a one-to-one bonus in that for every peck of pickles picked over the 8-hour shift standard, the standard pickle-picking labor cost per peck is earned. How much would a pickle picker earn a day at Motivated Pickle Pickers if he picked 140 pecks of pickles? 190 pecks of pickles?

chapter

FACILITY LOCATION

eleven

In this chapter, we examine the process of locating an operating facility, whether it be a manufacturing plant, retail store, warehouse, bank, or office. Up to this point, our discussion has assumed implicitly that the geographical location of the facility being designed was already known. Actual decision making under such an assumption can lead to an operating system design which is optimal for *one given site* but may also result in a site and operating system design combination that may not be optimal for the organization. Often, the design of the new facility imposes restrictions on the selection of a site. A power utility's decision to build a nuclear generating plant, for example, requires a site having access to substantial quantities of water for reactor cooling. Alternatively, in those cases where the facility location is selected before the details of its operating system design are settled, the impact of location on design is equally significant. In the retailing and service industries, certain locations have a greater potential to attract customers than others. Hence, the selection of a particular site influences the design capacity of the facility. Labor and land costs vary widely geographically. Locating in high-labor cost areas can sometimes only be justified by using a higher degree of processing automation, and the choice between single or multistoried facilities often depends on the price of the land. Such interactions must be considered in developing a site-operating system design combination which best meets the needs of the organization.

In our consideration of such location-design interrelationships, we will consider first the reasons for performing locational analysis as an ongoing process rather than as an ad hoc one. Following this is a discussion of the nature of the alternatives which should be included in a locational analysis study. Finally, a comprehensive example of a location decision is presented to illustrate just how the decision is actually structured.

MOTIVATING FACTORS

The circumstances motivating organizations to seek the most advantageous location for their facilities can be many. In the case of a new venture, decisions have to be made immediately about where to build, buy, or rent facilities. Mergers often create the problem of duplicate or overlapping facilities—which should be kept and which phased out. Even firms who have optimally located their facilities at some past time can often profit from periodic locational reassessment.

Probably the most frequently occurring condition which forces management to examine its facility locations and designs is significant changes in the demand for the goods and services it offers. Increasing demand requires a decision on where to add the additional capacity; decreasing demand forces the organization to decide which facilities to phase out or change over to production of more profitable goods or services. Geographical shifts in demand can also precipitate location analysis studies. The phenomenal growth of Southern California, for example, has caused many national retail and manufacturing concerns to add manufacturing, warehousing, and selling facilities in that area to capitalize on the increasing importance of western markets. In urban areas, the growth of outlying suburban communities has forced many downtown stores and banks to open suburban branches. This same growth and shift pattern in demand has resulted in locational problems in the education, utility, and health service areas as well.

Other factors precipitating relocation include changes in the cost of raw materials, services, and labor. Mining and lumbering industries are constantly moving their basic operations to new sources of supply as existing sources become depleted. Many organizations relocate because of rising labor costs, a classic example here being the movement of textile companies from New England to the southeastern United States during the last 50 years. Increasing labor costs in the electronics and camera industries have motivated a number of American manufacturers to locate factories in foreign countries and then export their products to the United States.

While demand changes and rising operational costs are the primary factors motivating locational reassessment, there may be other reasons. A fire or other catastrophe opens the question of whether now is the time to relocate or to rebuild at the same location. Often the land on which older facilities are located has so increased in value that it is financially wise to sell and relocate. Firms even relocate to maintain offices commensurate with their growing prestige in the business or professional community. Today some companies are finding that upgrading old facilities to meet the costs of new pollution control regulations is prohibitively costly. When conditions within the inner cities have sufficiently worsened to make the business no longer profitable or facilities and employees no longer safe, firms are faced with the difficult decision of whether or not to relocate in a more hospitable environment. Some firms choose relocation, but often others elect to stay and become an active catalyst in improving the quality of life around their current locations.

Certainly every existing organization should periodically reassess its environment to determine if long-term changes have occurred which may make it advantageous for it to alter or possibly relocate some portion of its facilities. With such periodic studies, a firm is much more likely to perceive the desirability of these changes before the need for them actually makes itself felt. A diminished competitive position, severe labor recruitment problems, and abrupt power or water shortages often reveal the failure of an organization to perform such periodic, formal reexaminations.

The frequency of location analysis studies depends on the firm's particular situation. Often different types of alternatives need to be examined at different time intervals. As a general rule, the high rate of return needed to justify significant locational adjustments is only likely to be realized when there have been significant shifts in the market or in operating costs. Because these decisions represent major capital expenditures, they need to be examined less frequently than minor ones but in considerably greater detail. Often pilot studies or surveys are conducted as indicators of when to perform more complete analysis.

Most well-managed organizations have found it best to reassess the locational analysis possibilities on a 1- to 3-year schedule. The longer period is used for reassessing such costly alternatives as locating a new manufacturing plant or building a major addition to an existing one. The shorter period naturally tends to be employed when examining such less expensive changes as reassessing the firm's rental warehouse configuration or leasing additional space adjacent to offices already occupied.

THE ALTERNATIVES

In this section, we examine first those environments in which an organization may prefer to modify an existing facility in lieu of locating a new one; next we will review those criteria which usually suggest a new location as the better alternative. From these discussions, it becomes apparent that the potentially attractive alternatives may well be so great in number as to require an efficient screening technique to identify the best alternative.

ALTERNATIVES TO NEW LOCATIONS

Although this chapter is primarily directed toward the problems of locating new facilities, locational analysis studies often determine that it is most advantageous to expand or modify existing facilities. There are many ways to adapt to a changing environment solely by utilizing existing processing locations. Temporary and minor demand changes can usually be handled without permanently upgrading the firm's physical capacity. Overtime, longer work weeks, and temporary help are commonly used devices to increase output. When demand shifts can be anticipated, suppliers of physical goods often elect to meet at least a portion of the projected need with inventory built up during slack selling periods. Another method for coping with demand increases is to contract out work to other organizations; printers and construction firms, as well as garment manufacturers, have used this option advantageously. Temporary drops in demand can also be handled without changing physical capacity. Workers can be assigned to other jobs, put on short work weeks, given extended vacations, and if other options fail, laid off.

When demand changes appear to be more permanent, many organizations still find it desirable to stay in the same location but to make more permanent changes in their capacity. Given a long-term demand increase, most firms find it beneficial to add equipment and employees. Sometimes replacement of outdated equipment with that of higher capacity provides a practical alternative to relocation. If there is room at the existing site, physically expanding the overcrowded plant or office can reduce the inefficiencies inherent in overcrowded facilities. Use of second and even third shifts is another popular method. The latter option is particularly attractive in heavy manufacturing and computer processing operations where additional facilities require significant capital investments. Long-term demand decreases, if not more difficult to deal with, are definitely more trying. Other jobs for the workers must be found, or they must be laid off. Occasionally, it may even be best to phase out a facility location—a decision never made lightly.

Geographical shifts in demand can also be handled effectively in some cases without adding additional manufacturing locations by altering a distribution system. Additional warehouses often make it possible for an organization to service these new demand areas competitively. By installing efficient ordering, order filling, and shipping procedures, some firms have even been able to compete successfully without warehouses in new areas. The J.C. Penney Company, for example, by teletyping orders to its Milwaukee fashion center and shipping out by air, is able to get dresses to its stores and customers, on the average, 2 days after the orders are placed without local or regional warehouse support.

NEW LOCATIONS

Since they represent a greater and more costly break with existing conditions, alternatives involving the introduction of new sites generally are considered only when the operating environment has significantly been altered, i.e., major long-term changes in the level of demand, availability and delivery costs of raw materials, or distribution and operating costs.

Obviously there are situations where only new site alternatives would be considered. The most obvious of these would be the case of the new firm which, of necessity, must build, buy, or rent the facilities needed. Another situation where a new location is the only available alternative occurs where the process is dependent on locally available resources which have been depleted. Thus, the lumber and mining industries must seek out new forests and mineral deposits if they are to maintain economic viability.

If the needed increase in capacity is more than double the minimum economic operating size for a new facility, there is the additional alternative of adding more than one new facility. For example, most towns of any substantial size need several grade school and fire station locations. Many states, including California, Virginia, Pennsylvania, and North Carolina, permit branch banking. Manufacturing firms often employ regional warehousing as well as several plants to meet most efficiently the demands for their products. Although multifacility location problems are much more difficult to handle, they can be resolved with currently available tools of analysis. A firm should also not overlook the possibility of increasing the capacity of some of its existing facilities instead of acquiring all the needed capacity increase with new facilities.

COUNTING ALTERNATIVES

Some idea of the number of location options involved when demand justifies the use of multifacilities can be gained by examining Figure 11-1. Figure 11-1 shows the different options available if the firm can utilize 1, 2, 3, or 4 facilities of various sizes in any of 4 locations. As can be seen there are 15 different alternative facility location configurations.

Suppose your firm's need for additional capacity can be met by 1 large plant or 2, 3, or 4 smaller plants. Further suppose there are only 4 possible plant sites, A, B, C, and D.

If only 1 plant is built, it can be located at A, B, C, or D.

If 2 plants are used instead, they can be located at A&B, A&C, A&D, B&C, B&D, or C&D.

If 3 plants are used, they can be located at A&B&C, A&B&D, A&C&D, B&C&D.

If 4 are used, there is only one possibility, A&B&C&D.

Thus the total number different geographical configurations that are involved are $15 = 4 + 6 + 4 + 1$.

Figure 11-1   *Example illustrates the counting of the alternative geographical configurations that can result as the number of facilities increases*

Figure 11-2 also shows that the number of different facility-location configurations increases rapidly with the number of potential location areas when anywhere from one single facility up to one at each area can be utilized. In fact, the number exceeds a million with only 20 areas and a trillion with only 40 areas. While the total number of potential areas almost always exceeds the maximum feasible number of facilities, Figure 11-2 does give some idea of the number of alternatives when more than one facility can be expanded, phased out, or added. Figure 11-2 values probably do not understate the actual number of alternatives associated with the number of candidate areas when the capacity options are also included. The options concerning the time at which various capacity and location

Number of Potential Location Areas (N)	Number of Different Geographical Configurations $(2^N - 1)$
1	1
2	3
3	7
4	15
5	31
10	1,023
20	1,048,575
50	over 10^{15}
100	over 10^{30}

Figure 11-2   *The number of different geographical plant configurations that can result when the use of more than one plant in each potential location area is feasible*

decisions can be undertaken still further increase the number of alternatives which can be considered.

The vast number of both the options and the influencing factors affecting them makes it impossible to evaluate all alternatives individually. As a consequence, a location analysis study must be conducted in a highly systematic and efficient manner if the optimal course of action is to be disclosed. Later in this chapter, we shall examine one method by which this can be done.

PRELIMINARY SURVEY

In most cases, a location analysis study should begin with a preliminary survey to determine whether or not a full-scale study is warranted. If this initial survey reveals that critical environmental factors have not changed significantly, there is little likelihood that further analysis is necessary. On the other hand, if important changes in the critical aspects of markets or operating costs are disclosed, the study should obviously be expanded.

The preliminary survey should also indicate whether or not the use of *new* facility sites might be justified. When it is not, consideration need not be given to determining the requirements of or collecting supportive data for the new site. If the survey indicates, however, that new sites may be desirable, detailed analysis which carefully evaluates all possible alternatives should follow. The remainder of this chapter examines analysis appropriate for this latter situation.

FACILITY LOCATION ANALYSIS

Procedures for the analysis of facility location are often organized in terms of three sequential phases. The first identifies the relevant background factors needed to begin the screening for the optimal location of the firm's proposed facilities. These include potential markets, competition, processing costs, and labor requirements. The second phase narrows down areas to be searched for site possibilities. Evaluating and comparing specific site alternatives is done in phase three. Using this approach enables the usually large number of potential sites and many significant locational factors to be managed successfully.

Although each particular situation requiring the location of a new facility varies, the differences in approaching the analysis are often minor. At this point, then, a comprehensive example will help illustrate the general methodology in location analysis.

BACKGROUND FACTORS

Have-Another, Inc., a leading, nationally known producer of beer, has breweries in Milwaukee, Dallas, Baltimore, and Los Angeles. Due to a steadily increasing demand for its beer, brought on by a successful advertising campaign, the firm's sales and market share have increased significantly over the past few years. Even with an expansion of its Milwaukee brewery 2 years ago, the Have-Another market research department still projects that the demand for the product will exceed its current total production capacity within a year. Further, they project that demand for Have-Another will increase by at least 10 percent a year over the next 5 years and at a somewhat faster rate in areas such as the Northwest and the Southeast.

As a consequence, Have-Another management recognizes that if it is to maintain its growth rate in sales and profits, total brewing capacity must be expanded. Financially, Have-Another can commit a total of $60 million to expansion over the next 2 years; this translates into being able to add about 4.5 million barrels of annual brewing capacity during this period.

Management asks the market research department to project demand for Have-Another beer by major geographic regions of the United States for 2 years and 5 years hence. The results of their study are given in Figure 11-3. Note that demand estimates for each region are stated in

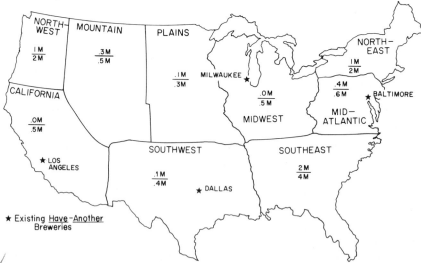

Figure 11-3 *Additional sales potential by regions for 2 years and 5 years (2 yrs/5 yrs); numbers are additional millions of barrels per year of brewing capability needed to satisfy sales potential*

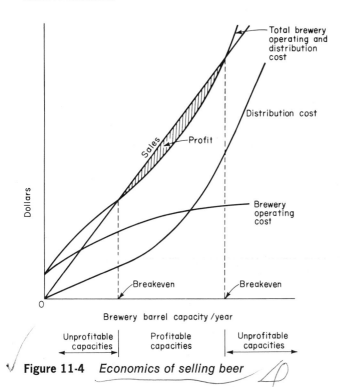

Figure 11-4   *Economics of selling beer*

terms of the *additional capacity* needed to take advantage of the demand both 2 and 5 years in the future. These figures *do not* indicate that expansions of present facilities or new breweries should be added in each region. As a matter of fact, the economics of brewing and distributing beer preclude any but major expansions.

To understand how Have-Another utilized the findings compiled in Figure 11-3, it is first necessary to review briefly the economics of producing beer illustrated in Figure 11-4. Here we see the typical relationship among revenues, costs, and capacity in a modern brewery. Costs fall into two main categories—facilities operation and distribution of finished product. When the brewery is operating at capacity, the costs show significant economies of scale with increased capacity. On the other hand, distribution costs behave in just the opposite fashion. In order to generate the demand necessary to operate larger and larger capacities, distribution areas must be expanded. Moving the beer over longer distances causes higher distribution costs with additional sales. While the exact nature of the costs, revenues, profits, and breakeven points varies from one location to another, generally a highly clustered demand like that associated with the New York metropolitan area is required to breakeven on a million barrel brewery. The less clustered the demand, the larger the brewery must be to operate profitably if the economies of scale realized in production are to offset the higher distribution costs. Consequently, in a dispersed market like the Mountain States, it would probably require at least a 2 million barrel brewery to operate profitably.

From Figure 11-3, the company management quickly sees that sales potential and need for additional brewery capacity to supply it will be the greatest in the three regions without breweries—the Southeast, the Northeast, and the Northwest. Of these, the Southeast offers the greatest additional sales potential. Further, it is the only region whose need for brewing capacity comes anywhere near making an expansion economically justifiable.

Management also recognizes that a brewery in the Southeast has nationwide advantages. If sufficiently large, it could supply the southern part of the Mid-Atlantic region; this would enable Have-Another to supply all the demand in that region and also free part of the Baltimore brewery output to be distributed more extensively in the Northeast region. Similarly, if the new Southeastern brewery supplied the southern part of the Midwest region, the Milwaukee division could relieve Baltimore of some of the demand found in the western parts of the Mid-Atlantic and Northeast. Finally, if released from some of its eastern coverage by the new facility, Dallas could supply more to the Plains, Mountains, and California regions. This released capacity at the Los Angeles brewery could then be used in meeting demand in the Northwestern and Mountain regions. Thus locating a brewery in the Southeast potentially has far-reaching operating ramifications for the firm.

After an analysis of the short and long-run advantages of locating in the Southeast and after conducting studies to determine the optimal size of the facility, Have-Another concludes that it should build a 4.5 million barrel per year brewery in the Southeastern region.

CHOOSING A SPECIFIC AREA

Having selected the Southeast for a brewery site, Have-Another is in position to begin the search for a specific area within that region. Since there would be an excessive amount of work involved in identifying and comparing all of the areas within that region which meet its requirements for water, transportation, and labor sites, the company must reduce the alternatives to a workable number. It becomes clear from reviewing the location-influencing factors that the factor which tends to dominate the location choice is profit which, in turn, is most heavily dependent on distribution costs; i.e., the brewery cannot be too far from the minimum cost distribution location without diminishing profits. Figure 11-5 illustrates that the farther the brewery is from the location which minimizes its distribution costs, the more rapidly the distribution costs increase. Generally, this undesirable effect starts to be significant about 200 miles from the minimum distribution cost point. Thus,

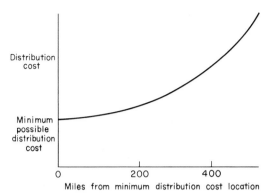

Figure 11-5   *How distribution costs vary with a brewery's distance from the minimum distribution cost location*

the search for feasible brewery locations can be limited to a circle of 200-mile radius centered at the minimum distribution cost point.

In locating this minimum distribution cost area, management cannot know with certainty which customers from other regions will be served by the new brewery until after the facility is operational. However, in a practical sense, Have-Another can assume that the market served will be much the same as the one planned when they were first deciding whether or not to add a brewery in the Southeast. The outline of that market is shown in Figure 11-6.

To find the minimum distribution cost location for the market depicted in Figure 11-6, they proceed as follows. First, the market is gridded off into a number of demand areas for which forecast demand data are available, 35 in this case. They then estimate the number of deliveries per year necessary to service demand area 1 to be t_1, for demand area 2, t_2, and so on. Letting the delivery cost per mile be c and letting d_i be the distance

Figure 11-6   *Area served by Have-Another's Southeastern Brewery*

in miles from the brewery to the center of a demand area, the cost per year to distribute beer to demand area 1 is ct_1d_1, and for area 2, ct_2d_2, and so forth. The total cost to distribute beer from the Southeastern brewery to all the 35 demand areas is $\sum_{i=1}^{35} ct_i d_i$. By minimizing this expression, the demand area which minimizes the total distribution cost can be identified as the best brewery site.

Even though a reasonably efficient mathematical solution to this problem was not developed until the early 1960s, a practical solution had been available for many years; it used a physical analog technique known as "drop the string." Have-Another's management choses to employ this technique. They first lay out the 35 demand areas on a sheet of plywood and drill a hole in the center of each as shown in Figure 11-6. Through the hole for demand area 1, they thread a piece of string with a weight corresponding to ct_1 hanging below the plywood sheet. Similarly through demand area 2 hole, they thread a string with a weight corresponding to ct_2 and so on for all 35 holes. The free ends of the strings will then be tied together and dropped. This knot will then be pulled by the weights to a point which minimizes the total distribution costs.[1]

When Have-Another "drops the string," the knot settles in northeastern Georgia. As a consequence, they will search the area shown in Figure 11-7

---

[1] This knot is pulled to the center of gravity of the mass distribution. It is also interesting to observe that the distance between the knot and every hole corresponds to the straight line or as-the-crow-flies distance. Since one rarely travels directly between two points on the ground. Have-Another's use of the "drop the string" approach is only an approximation. It is, however, a sufficient one for their purposes.

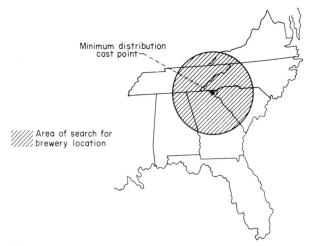

Minimum distribution cost point

Area of search for brewery location

Figure 11-7   *Have-Another's narrowed area of search for location of its new brewery*

for locations satisfying the brewery's labor, water, and transportation services requirements. Checking with the state development agencies of North and South Carolina, Georgia, Alabama, and Tennessee and the appropriate sources listed in the *Directory of Federal Statistics for Local Areas,* Have-Another is able to identify 12 feasible sites in the 200-mile area shown in Figure 11-7.

Have-Another now attempts to reduce the set of candidates even further. Because location desirability is highly dependent on how much the firm's profits can be increased by locating in an area, they estimate the increased total corporation profitability associated with each of the 12 locations. The five most profitable locations produce estimates which are within $300,000 a year of each other. However, the break between the 5th and 6th ranked locations in profitability turns out to be slightly over $1.5 million a year—a figure that Have-Another's management considers too large to overcome, regardless of how otherwise desirable the 6th, 7th, . . . , or 12th profit-ranked areas are with respect to other factors. As a consequence, they will make their choice between the five most profitable areas.

CHOOSING A SPECIFIC SITE

Have-Another must now choose one specific facility location from among the five final candidates. This phase of the location analysis first identifies all the factors which may influence the choice of a specific brewery site. These are listed in Figure 11-8. Notice that these factors are broken down into three categories: requirements, objective factors, and subjective factors. Management has decided that it is sufficient for their purposes to evaluate all these factors on the basis of the first 5 years of the new brewery's operations. The main exception is the water supply requirement, which is so important to the total operation that the quantity and quality has to be judged over a 25-year period.

The first three requirements concerning labor, water, and transportation are by far the most limiting. Because the required 100 acres of land would more than likely be available in most areas in which the firm wants to locate, it need only be considered in the final stage of the actual site selection.

Of the objective factors, the ones most affecting the choice of locational areas are sales and distribution costs. They play a dominant role in determining profits and are highly variable with changes in location. Of secondary importance are water and tax rates, with all other profit influencing factors having even less impact on the choice of location areas. Due to a national labor contract requiring the same wage scales for all Have-Another breweries,

Requirements

Labor
 Must be able to hire locally
  150 mechanics
  100 electricians
  200 semiskilled workers

Water
 Must have assured supply of 10 million gallons of water a year of needed quality
 (not specified here).

Transportation Services
 Must have required minimum rail and truck services (not specified here).

100 acre site

Objective (for Southeast and entire U.S. except where noted otherwise)

$ Sales

Costs
 Distribution
 Delivered cost of raw materials
 Operating cost
 Labor (same regardless of location hence not relevant to choice)
 Water
 Electric
 Taxes (state, local)
 Other (fuel, etc.)

Profit not including investment costs

Construction costs (only for new brewery)

Land cost

Subjective

 Laws affecting brewery operation and costs
 Water supply quantity & quality (must be identified, effect assessed, and possibility
 of change assessed)
 Labor supply
  Quantity
  Quality
  Labor unrest
 Transportation service (quantity & quality)
  Rail
  Truck
  Air
 Other utilities (electricity, etc.)
 Community
  Attitude toward brewery
  Finances & services
  Quality of life

Figure 11-8   *Factors influencing choice of brewery site*

labor cost is constant regardless of location. Hence, in this case, labor cost has little role to play in the choice of a brewery location.

The subjective factors in Figure 11-8 are quite relevant to choosing a brewery location even though they cannot be evaluated on a precise dollars-and-cents basis. Local and/or state laws may affect the production and distribution of beer. Such laws relevant to any seriously considered site must be identified and assessed in terms of their potential impact on the operations of the firm.

The labor supply of any seriously considered area should be analyzed as to quantity and quality. Have-Another prefers areas having a plentiful rather than a minimal labor supply, so that its hiring of 450 workers will be less likely to disrupt and antagonize another area employer. From past experience, Have-Another management assumes that it should have little trouble attracting employees if they are available since it will be offering very competitive wages because of its national labor contract. Although Have-Another has never had any major labor problems itself it prefers to avoid communities with histories of labor unrest.

Of the remaining subjective factors, two related to the community warrant further explanation. Community finances and services should be examined in order to determine if tax rates are likely to increase significantly. A community with a high bonded indebtedness or an obvious need for a major increase in community services is likely to raise taxes. Quality of life, a factor summarizing the desirability of the area as a place for families to live, can be important in attracting and keeping employees.

Each area under serious consideration is then visited to determine available sites. Management then carefully evaluates each area with respect to all factors influencing the final choice. Figure 11-9 gives their evaluation in a somewhat abbreviated form. As a result of this phase of the location analysis study, Have-Another decides to build their Southeastern brewery in area 4.

Capsulizing their deliberations, we see that they have been reluctant to elect area 1 or area 2 because of the desired extra margin of safety associated with the rail service and water supply quantity offered by the other alternatives. Area 3 has been passed over principally because of its substantially higher investment cost in relationship to its profit; further, area 3's labor supply appears to be more limited than Have-Another would like. Moving into the area would undoubtedly cut heavily into the other employer's work forces. Except for the problem of laws prohibiting Sunday work and taxing product inventories, area 4 is preferred over area 5 mainly because of its higher quality water supply. Thus, if the unfavorable laws can be reworked, Have-Another plans to build on a selected site in area 4. In the event of failure, Have-Another would locate in area 5 and would plan to add at a cost of $300,000 extra filtration and aeration equipment to ensure there would never be any problem with the quality of the water.

Factors:	Area 1	Area 2	Area 3	Area 4	Area 5
Increased yearly profit (millions)	17.51	17.46	17.31	17.27	17.22
Construction & land costs (millions)	32.5	33.0	33.6	32.1	31.9
Water supply					
Quantity	G	A	G	V	V
Quality	V	O	G	O	A
Transportation services					
Rail	A	V	G	V	G
Truck	G	V	V	V	G
Air	A	G	V	G	V
Labor					
Quantity	V	G	A	G	O
Quality	V	G	G	G	G
Community	A	V	O	G	G
Laws	V	A	A	Unacceptable But Willing To Modify	V

Code A—acceptable G—good V—very good O—outstanding

Figure 11-9   *Site evaluation information for Have-Another Breweries*

CONCLUSION

Certain specialized techniques have been developed to aid management in facility location decisions. The "drop the string" technique utilized by Have-Another, Inc., is one of these. Others are described in the references at the end of this book. For aiding the location of plants, service facilities or stores, there also are available a variety of computer-aided mathematical techniques for locating the points which minimize total distribution costs, minimize average service time, and maximize the customer drawing power. Most of these are directed at finding the number, size, and location of facilities which will minimize the sum of the operating and distribution expenses. As Figure 11-10 indicates, total operating costs usually increase with the number of facilities used. Greater fixed expenses are incurred, and there are fewer opportunities to achieve operating economies of scale due to the lower average volume being processed at each facility. Total distribution costs, however, usually decrease because the average plant-to-customer expense is lower.

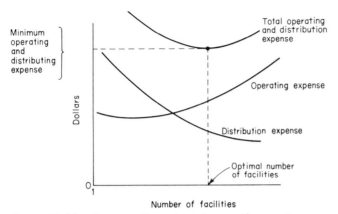

Figure 11-10   *Composition of total operating cost*

Some facility location techniques are especially well suited for designing warehouse and multiple plant systems. Various types of related techniques can be successfully applied to such problems as decomposing school, fire, and police districts, and market areas into service or sales regions and locating regional sales offices, long distance telephone switching centers, branch banks, and stores. One of the most interesting applications is to nonpartisan political redistricting of legislative bodies.

With all these techniques, however, the responsibility rests with the analyst for determining if and at what stage of his locational analysis study they are appropriate. He must be careful not to let their apparent sophistication fool him into believing they automatically produce optimal answers. Rarely do real life situations conform exactly to the abstracted environments in which these techniques are designed to optimize. Thus, it cannot be overemphasized that the final responsibility rests with the analyst in deciding if and how these techniques can aid him in solving his particular location problem.

QUESTIONS

1. Why are plant-location decisions important in relation to production-system design? What production factors are involved?
2. Why do you agree or disagree with the following statement? "We should recognize that increasing production or productivity is an everyday concern of the firm so that a plant-location problem is not basically a new type of problem but rather one of a different order of magnitude."
3. List ways you can increase output without increasing a plant's physical capacity. Discuss the cost and operating implications of each.

4. Why is there a movement by industry to leave the big cities? What are the gains? What are the losses?

5. Why is the multifacility location problem more complicated than the single-facility location problem?

6. What characteristics are associated with firms which locate near their sources of raw materials? Near their markets?

7. What factors are most important in locating the following types of facilities and why?
   (a) Warehouses
   (b) Gas stations
   (c) Garbage dumps
   (d) Hospitals
   (e) Interstate highways

8. Why is facility location done in stages? Explain and justify what stages you would use in locating the following types of facilities.
   (a) Automobile assembly plant
   (b) Professional sports stadium
   (c) Airport
   (d) Oil refinery
   (e) Junior college

9. Hill Associates are planning Aquarius, a new satellite city from scratch. Among the many facilities to be located are one or more fire stations. Aquarius is to be composed of four areas, A, B, C, and D. To protect these areas three potential fire-station locations looked promising—w, x, and y. Determine which of the locations to use and how large of a station to build on each in order to minimize the expected annual fire-loss cost plus annual fire-station cost.

The following data collected by Hill Associates will be needed.

Area	A	B	C	D
Expected Number of Fires/yr.	20	40	10	20
Average Building Value	$20,000	$30,000	$40,000	$80,000

Average minutes from each potential fire station location to each area

	A	B	C	D
w	2	4	5	6
x	5	3	3	7
y	6	7	3	2

Minutes to Respond to Fire	On the Average the % of Building Value Lost
2	5%
3	10%
4	20%
5	30%
6	45%
7	65%

Equivalent annual cost of building and operating different-sized stations at each different location

Potential Station Location	Number of Areas Served		
	1	2	3
w	$12,000	$19,000	$26,000
x	10,000	16,000	21,000
y	15,000	24,000	30,000

10. Ace Trucking has recently decided to relocate its distribution centers. After much study, Ace Trucking grouped its customers into five geographical regions, A, B, C, D, and E. Ace further decided to restrict its consideration of locations for distribution centers to four—w, x, y, and z. Ace then went on to calculate both the yearly variable cost of serving each region out of each potential center location and the yearly fixed cost of operating each center. A summary of Ace's calculations are given below.

Potential Distribution Center Location	Distribution Center Yearly Fixed Cost	Yearly Variable Costs of Serving Each Region from Each Distribution Location				
		A	B	C	D	E
w	$45,000	$ 30,000	$100,000	$ 80,000	$180,000	$140,000
x	60,000	90,000	40,000	60,000	50,000	50,000
y	60,000	120,000	60,000	100,000	40,000	80,000
z	80,000	80,000	60,000	50,000	120,000	90,000

Where should Ace Trucking have distribution centers in order to minimize its costs?

part

**OPERATING AND CONTROLLING THE PRODUCTION/
OPERATIONS MANAGEMENT SYSTEM**

four

chapter

DYNAMICS AND CONTROL

twelve

In earlier chapters you encountered the notion of capacity in several places. The simplest statement of capacity is *the number of units of output per time unit that the system is designed to produce.* An airplane is said to have the capacity to carry 180 passengers between New York and Los Angeles in 6 hours. A steel mill produces 1,500 tons per day. A barber shop with 5 men and 5 chairs can give 18 haircuts per hour. A highway can handle 10,000 cars per hour and a tunnel with its toll gates 4,000. All of these examples provide good static definitions of the capacity of a system. But what if there are strong headwinds on the flight or landing delays? What if that steel mill has orders for only semifinished goods? What if only 15 customers an hour arrive at the barber shop? What if the highway leads into the tunnel?

This chapter introduces the sequence of chapters relating to this question of how capacity is managed dynamically. Chapters 13 through 17 go into much greater detail concerning the methods and approaches used to get the most out of an existing system, as well as a proposed one, under variable conditions of use. Drawing on the analogy from the traditional engineering curriculum, we might say that the chapters which follow relate to the prior ones as dynamics relates to statics. This chapter discusses the interrelationships between these methods and also explains how historical information concerning capacity has to be evaluated.

FACTORS AFFECTING CAPACITY

The discussion of a strategy for POM in Chapter 4 already has indicated that there is a great deal more to the idea of capacity than just a single output rate for a given product mix. There are many aspects to be evaluated and then adjusted (controlled) so that the system can meet the fluctuating rates that the marketplace requires. A system, once designed, must be operated over time to gain the best continuous results. Figure 4-4 describes a complex feedback system with flows of material and information that perform the eight basic elements of the POM system discussed in Chapter 4. What is still to be explained is exactly how one interprets the information in this feedback loop and then adjusts that process by the correct amount. The designed capacity levels are attainable only if the control system is operated effectively. In many cases, the design capacity can be exceeded when the control system is operating unusually well. Chapters 13 through 17 outline the approaches developed to improve operations.

The effective capacity of the process over time, as well as the cost of operation, is likely to depend on the following factors:

1. Forecasting accuracy
2. Levels of resource input
3. Levels of operation and degree of operations balance
4. Control of the work moving through the process
5. Utilization of facilities
6. Utilization of manpower
7. Quality of work performed and accepted
8. Uses made of inventories
9. Improvement of methods and process
10. Quality of the POM information system which integrates the other factors to provide an efficient operation

The description of how these factors affect capacity follows.

FORECASTING ACCURACY

Forecasting is the subject of Chapter 13. Without reasonably good forecasts of both the marketplace and the developing technology, the POM group is flying blind. Mathematical approaches to many management problems are based theoretically on perfect information, the technical equivalent of 20–20 hindsight. This seldom, if ever, occurs in a business or service organization, so the manager must bet on his best guess about what is going to happen, using his knowledge of the concept of expected values of key variables, as described in Chapter 3. His forecasts, therefore, need not be limited to point values but may be estimates of the frequency distributions likely to be encountered. These distributions may be very numerous. A paint company which sells and stocks 6,000 types, sizes, and colors must develop 6,000 individual forecasts. Shaky as they may be, forecasts are essential for control of the POM system.

INPUTS

Nothing comes out of a POM system unless resources—men, capital equipment, raw materials, and information—are put into it. One of the more critical decisions in this area and one faced at regular intervals is how many men are to be employed to operate the available equipment. This decision is discussed in Chapter 14. How much equipment to use for a known demand was covered in Chapters 7 and 8. The question remains of how many shifts of how many hours each should be manned. The two factors—manpower levels and equipment levels—have been separated somewhat arbitrarily. As you know from elementary economics, labor and capital are substitutable for each other within relatively wide limits. One rationale behind these separate treatments of labor and of capital is the permanence of capital equipment investments and the long periods of planning and delivery governing their purchases. You do not hire and lay off machines, except at a considerable loss. As you will see in Chapter 14, one does not hire or lay off workers without costs either, but the penalties, the risks, and the length of time required to carry out changes can be much less. Raw materials purchases usually are planned over a relatively long period to assure sources of supply, but since they can be stored as inventory, the input rate can vary considerably in the short run without incurring such major costs. Even where contractual relationships exist, the vendor's desire to please the purchaser usually permits changes in shipping schedules. The information input is a function of the information and control system, a part of the internal environment which is covered in detail in Chapter 16.

Manpower is a quite different resource from the others. It is purchased by the hour and is a complete loss if it is not consumed as it becomes available. Chapter 15 explains that labor is storable in the form of inventory, while a surplus of labor leads to either enforced or voluntary idleness. Even where workers operate on an incentive system as described in Chapter 10, it is the responsibility of management to see that there is enough work in front of each man to enable him to produce at the limit of his capacity. Otherwise, management must find a way to compensate him for his time at a level reflecting his past performance and skills. In fact, one of the real drawbacks of a wage incentive system is the fact that it motivates against a number of tasks that contribute to overall company productivity but do not increase incentive earnings. How does the worker react to orders to train others, to inspect and correct the work of others, to try out proposed new methods, to experiment with new products, or to rush through a piece that pays a low wage rate but is needed to keep other workers busy? In such situations, management may have to offer special premiums for these tasks. The incentive system is a very consistent control device for increasing direct output, but it is often one which leads toward suboptimization. Management has to maintain its freedom to allocate men, equipment, and materials to both the principal and the supporting operations of the organization if it is to achieve its desired profit level.

OPERATING LEVELS AND COSTS

Related to, but not necessarily the same as, the manpower scheduling problem is the question of the operating level and balance of facilities. You know from basic courses in economics that the cost per unit of production in a facility is not linear, especially when it operates at or near capacity. Profits do not decline when the plant operates above 100 percent, at least not until the operating rate is well above capacity. What happens is illustrated in Figure 12-1. The incremental contribution per unit increases as the demand increases from very low levels and then falls as demand exceeds the design optimum. The causes of this loss of efficiency at high levels are multiple. As the plant starts out at a low level of operation, men and equipment are not fully utilized. Management can afford to be more lax in scheduling and use of men. Then as demand rises, it becomes necessary to run a tighter ship.

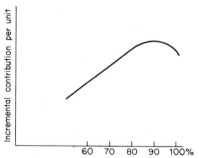

Figure 12-1   *Incremental contribution per unit with increasing demand*

Everyone works just a bit harder to meet the challenge. As the system is stretched even further, however, the weaknesses show up. Bottlenecks begin to appear as departments that are not balanced get out of phase and as other workers are held up for lack of inventory, parts deliveries, or paperwork. As the demand rises even more, men are put on overtime at a 50 percent premium; some parts produced more cheaply internally are farmed out to suppliers, and orders are expedited, upsetting schedules, tempers, and efficiency. The equipment used to meet the low or average levels of demand is the newest and most efficient. Equipment pressed into service to meet peak demand is likely to be the oldest, least efficient, and most difficult to maintain. The pressure of meeting full schedules may also lead to increased wear and to deferred maintenance, both of which may lead to higher costs later.

Because of peak loads in demand and anticipated growth, most companies maintain capacity which is somewhat greater than the average demand. Since this peak load occurs only a small proportion of the time, the plant is designed to operate at maximum efficiency at the more frequently encountered lower levels. In general, companies build their plants to operate best between 80 and 90 percent of capacity. Yet, output rates must match the needs placed on the system by the external environment and the organization both, even if it means a somewhat less satisfactory cost level at certain production volumes.

Each firm has to find its own strategy for coping with this need for extra capacity. Automobile assembly lines run only two shifts instead of the usual three, saving the third shift for overtime operation when needed and for maintenance. Oil refineries which must operate 24 hours per day, 7 days per week use price cuts and storage to adjust demand to relatively inflexible output rates. Electric power companies trade power rather than build extra generating capacity for peak loads. Steel mills have the same inflexible work schedule, but the presence of multiple units allows flexibility in output rates. By starting and shutting down blast furnaces, oxygen inverters, and open hearths, the rolling mills can be supplied with varying amounts of material for their intermittent operation. The fundamental problem of the steel company often is to balance coke facilities, ore supply, blast furnaces, oxygen inverters, rolling mills, and finishing mills against the changing mix of product requirements from the marketplace. In some novelty and toy businesses, the only way to maintain employment stability is to build a supply for the peak Christmas selling season throughout the calendar year, selling out during good years and dumping excess inventory in bad ones. In Chapter 15 on inventory control, we will discuss the several uses of inventory that can alleviate capacity constraints on the POM system and provide much flexibility.

CONTROL

Putting resources and workers into a system of sufficient designed capacity is not enough. Somehow the production must be guided, prodded, pushed, and routed through the process. At the beginning of this book, the process was treated as a single, relatively homogeneous activity, a black box with inputs issuing into one end and outputs from the other. Then, in Chapter 4, you saw many different sets of operations yielding multiple products. There are alternative ways of organizing these operations into a flow shop, a job shop, or a project. Each such configuration presents a distinct challenge to the POM group who must control and schedule the movement of products and services. The value of the output is determined by its utility. This relates to the timing and location of its availability as well as its functional purpose. Therefore, the output must be controlled to arrive at the proper place in the proper amounts at the proper time. This is the subject of chapters yet to come on inventory control and scheduling.

UTILIZATION

Management is trying to obtain the best possible utilization of the men and the equipment at the same time. This again will require efficiency in scheduling and use of inventory. But there remains the fundamental choice between one or the other. This is especially true in the job shop where the number of men and machines are not necessarily the same. Which one is the objective of the scheduling activity will vary from time to time. When the product mix and the demand produce constraints on output due to a lack of manpower, then manpower obviously will be the resource to be conserved in the scheduling process. If specific pieces of equipment form a bottleneck, then the utilization of those machines should be the aim of the scheduling activity, even at the expense of some idle manpower. These logical choices will be based on the concept of opportunity costs discussed in Chapter 3.

QUALITY

A company profits little if the process is very efficient but the output is of poor quality. It cannot maintain its position in a market unless the output delivered at the right place at the right time is also of the right quality. Quality affects resource uses and output rates, making it a legitimate factor in the evaluation of the capacity of the firm. The control system plays an important motivational role in the area of quality. If the company does not emphasize quality in all its operations and pushes hard for output and labor efficiency, then workers can easily fall into the attitude that the company doesn't give a hoot about the product. Morale and craftsmanship or both will be lost. The company must make conscious choices about where it stands in the marketplace with respect to quality. That is a strategic position which will in turn determine the selection of labor skills, equipment, standards, and output rates, as well as volume and price.

Chapter 17 will discuss techniques for designing quality control systems. This is one part of POM systems that traditionally has been set apart as a specialty, the private domain of statistical experts. There are reasons why quality control and inspection personnel are kept somewhat separated from the other production employees, but their efforts are an important and integral part of the total information and control system and help determine overall capacity and efficiency.

INVENTORY

The functions of inventory are numerous and varied. They are listed and described in Chapter 15. Inventory stores capacity available at one point in time for use at another time. In this manner, it provides a powerful tool for flexibility in the manager's arsenal. Inventories also serve as cushions and shock absorbers in the internal environment. They allow the separate subsystems to achieve enough short-run independence to schedule work efficiently, produce goods in the economical lot sizes, and adjust to the uncertainties in the external environment. Without these cushions, the POM group would have to be much larger and do a great deal more running around to avoid crippling delays and idle men and machines. The costs of an inventory system, however, are substantial. There is capital tied up in these materials and costs of moving, controlling, protecting, and administering them. Chapter 15 will outline the methods used to balance off these costs and benefits to bring about the most economical total system.

IMPROVEMENT OF METHODS AND PROCESS

In Chapters 6, 7, 8, 9, and 11, emphasis was placed on the role of engineering, operations reasearch, and methods groups in designing the best process. These POM support groups devise improvements that are steadily being incorporated into the physical and management processes to increase capacity and effectiveness. It is not unusual to hear, for example, that the steel industry is operating at 108 percent of capacity. That is possible in many plants with overtime and subcontracting. But it is often the case that the capacity figures refer to a specific date in the past. Meanwhile, there has been a steady series of modifications of equipment and procedures. POM groups are motivated to accomplish continuing improvement through the

Table 12-1 *Standard costs per pound of rayon, corrected for input-price changes, 1940–1950 (in cents)*

DuPont Plant	Old Hickory		Spruance I		Spruance III	
	Total Direct Factory Costs	Percentage Capacity Operated	Total Direct Factory Costs	Percentage Capacity Operated	Total Direct Factory Costs	Percentage Capacity Operated
1940	16.15	93.2	20.17	99.5	13.75	97.7
1941	15.46	93.2	19.25	100.0	13.28	100.0
1942	15.90	98.0	20.16	99.7	12.65	99.3
1943	15.36	99.7	20.40	100.0	12.50	99.2
1944	15.41	98.8	20.01	99.6	11.91	98.8
1945	15.71	98.8	19.32	99.0	11.68	99.5
1946	15.38	99.3	19.47	97.0	11.51	94.2
1947	14.92	98.0	18.80	99.7	11.01	96.7
1948	14.65	99.3	18.10	97.7	11.02	97.7
1949	14.61	98.0	17.48	77.2	10.91	99.1
1950	14.29	98.0	17.09	99.9	10.72	100.0

Taken from Table 4.1, 4.7, 4.19, C.1, C.2, and C.4 in S. Hollander, *The Sources of Increased Efficiency: A Study of DuPont Rayon Plants*, (Cambridge: The MIT Press, 1965).

budgetary process. If a manager achieves a good operating efficiency and output rate one year, he will undoubtedly end up with a budget for the next that calls for him to do even better. This is how he earns his salary year after year. No manager is allowed to get a process operating and then assume a passive, caretaker role until he draws his pension. He has to show continued achievement year after year. Table 12-1 is a series of annual costs from DuPont rayon plants over the years 1940 to 1950. These cost reductions were made without really major or radical changes in the process or the technology. Yet, over the 10-year period, constant dollar costs fell 11.5 to 22.0 percent.

People learn and so do organizations. What is evident in Table 12-1 is the ability of various corporate contributors to improve on the physical and management processes. This improvement can be plotted in the same manner as the learning curve. This new curve is called a "manufacturing progress function" and can be a useful control tool for management. Mathematically, it is treated the same as the learning curve. Figure 12-2 contains manufacturing progress functions from selected industries. These improvements are a contractual requirement in the aerospace industry. The government and the contractor agree that the costs of producing an aircraft will decrease

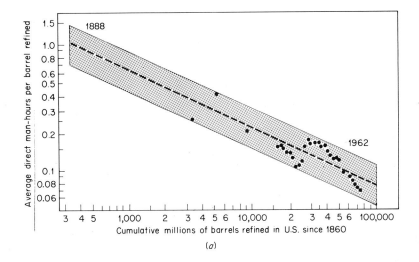

(a)

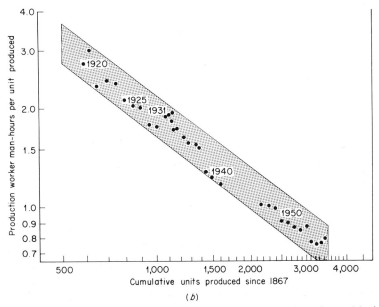

(b)

Figure 12-2 *(a) Manufacturing progress functions in selected industries.*
[Source: W. B. Hirschmann, "Profit from the Learning Curve," Harvard
Business Review, *vol. 42, January-February 1954, pp. 125–139.] (b)*
Man-hours per unit of output in United States basic steel industry—
suggested learning curve decline 1935–1955. [Source: U.S. Department of
Labor Statistics, Bulletin 1200, September 1956, and other sources.]

according to a function called a "learning curve." In the aerospace industry, this function is summarized as a percentage figure. An "80 percent learning curve" would mean that the cost of planes drops 20 percent from the nth to the $2n$th unit. The second plane would cost 80 percent of the first, the fourth 80 percent of the second, etc.

These decreases in costs per unit mean that the company gets more output with the same inputs, that capacity effectively has been increased without major capital investments over a period of time. This is accomplished in many ways. Workers are learning. Production engineers are finding new methods and standards to apply to the manufacturing of existing designs. Designers are modifying products to use more economical materials and processes. Purchasing agents are locating new suppliers and negotiating better prices. Managers and staff specialists have been improving work flows and schedules. Maintenance and tool and die men have been designing new equipment and modifying old equipment. Each member of POM has been contributing his skills to the improvement process which shows up mathematically in the manufacturing progress function.

The steel capacity figures, for example, are set up as of a certain date; then as time passes by, the basic units are rebuilt or replaced and the process control improved so that actual capacity exceeds the standard base figure. Units must be shut down regularly for relining with new firebrick and for maintenance, and it is common practice to make modifications and improvements at that time. Sharon Steel Corporation used its "Mary" blast furnace in Ohio for almost a hundred years, but this claim was a lot like the old New England farmer and his axe. He used to tell summer visitors, "Don't make things today liken they used ter. Why, I bin usin' ther same axe ter chop wood fer sixty year." What he doesn't tell is that he has replaced nine heads and five handles.

INTEGRATING SYSTEMS

Integrating these factors is the communication and control system discussed in Chapter 4, this chapter, and Chapter 16. Chapter 4 argued that such a system is necessary to provide the conditions under which intersystem conflicts can be resolved. To perform this function it must (1) state decision rules explicitly, (2) state exception conditions and responses, (3) provide a mechanism for performing the best tradeoffs, and (4) assure a fair evaluation of the results in terms of overall rather than subsystem results. At the same time, it must put flesh on the skeleton of the information system discussed in Chapter 4. POM management is responsible for the quantity and quality (including timeliness) of information input, its routing and processing, and for using the output for actuating and evaluating the other subsystems.

ORGANIZATIONAL COMPONENTS OF THE
CONTROL AND PLANNING PROCESS

It is not surprising that many of the factors affecting capacity appear as labels on the POM organization charts, as subsystems of the total system, or as topics for several chapters in this text. This book attempts to emphasize the overall systems viewpoint of POM, but it frequently becomes more convenient to treat each area separately and to assign it to individuals who can become specialists.

Each area has its own information system, either separately for its own use, or as a segment of the total information system. Chapter 4 listed information-system applications. Many of these applications can be grouped to indicate the genesis of the departments and titles in the traditional POM organization. Figure 12-3 is an organization chart showing these groupings. There obviously are many interactions among these groups in both the static design of capacity and the dynamic tasks of adapting to changing conditions and demands of the environment.

TOP MANAGEMENT

Top POM men carry titles like vice president—manufacturing, vice president—operations, plant manager, and superintendent. These men participate in the definition of the customer, the market, and the strategy of the firm. Most of the subsystems under them are creating adaptive responses within the constraints of company policies they help set. These policies may vary from the very broad to the trivial, but they set ground rules common to each group. The term aggregate schedule, for example, refers to the decision as to how many men will be employed over the next several months and what shall be their hours of work. This is a primary response to adjust capacity to meet anticipated future demands. To do this the top management must make reasonable forecasts of demand and process performance over the relevant time period. Then they must continually perform the balancing act outlined in Chapter 4, making sure that the evaluation and reward system leads to the best overall operating results. Cyert and March have suggested that firms often fail to resolve many of these problems, using instead slack in the system to avoid the difficult value questions that would have to be faced, the numerous potential conflicts to be resolved, and the considerable, associated psychic cost and interpersonal conflict.[1] These authors argue that, therefore, organizations frequently fail to set specific operational goals for all departments and establish instead only generalized, nebulous aims which can be interpreted by each department according to its own point of

[1] Cyert and March, *The Behavioral Theory of the Firm* (Englewood Cliffs, N.J.: Prentice-Hall, Inc.), 1960.

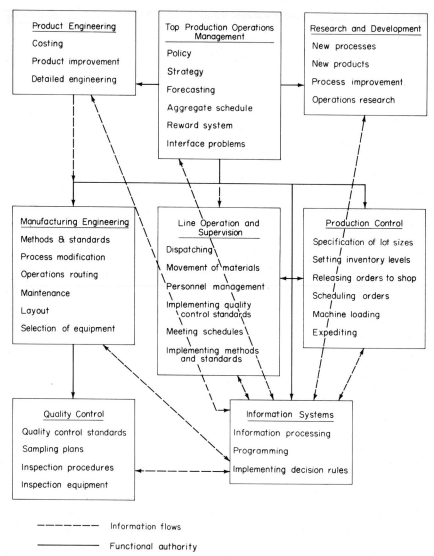

Figure 12-3 *Typical groupings of functions for control and administration in POM*

view. The result is that excess inventories may be carried to avoid conflicts over delivery schedules, that orders are run in nonoptimal lots to meet unrealistic delivery promises, etc. An alternative is to face these issues directly through problem-solving activities and indirectly through the information system and the reward system of the firm.

CHANGE AGENTS

Reporting to top POM are two groups responsible for basic and occasionally radical improvements. These are research and development, and product development or applied engineering groups. In one of these groups, or in a separate department at the same level, sits the operations research group. All are resident innovators motivated to bring about changes in products, processes, or procedures. Without them, the organization is hampered in its efforts to adapt promptly to a changing environment.

R & D and engineering do not necessarily invent new ideas. The company benefits when they do, but the likelihood of the big breakthroughs coming in one's own laboratories is small. Table 12-2 shows the sources of DuPont's major money-making products over the period 1920 through 1950. Relatively few of these came from the inside. Innovative groups must be willing to serve as the eyes and ears of the company and to adapt whatever they find to the strategy and capabilities of the company. They must develop, evaluate, and then recommend new and improved products and processes. The operations research group has the added function of presenting new ways of going about the ancient task of controlling, modeling, and evaluating the process. It is their work over recent years that has led to the array of models, techniques, and approaches for dealing with dynamic control problems that are the topics of the next five chapters. Seeing problems and searching out the approaches to similar problems in mathematics, the physical sciences, and the social sciences, they have drawn together the best techniques from all of these disciplines and added on to them to provide the improved management methods. These approaches have been made even more powerful by the advent of the computer which has let analysis and information processing, unthinkable 20 years ago, become relatively simple and routine procedures.

These innovative departments will continue to contribute to the firm for some years to come. They can and do, however, present a series of problems for top management. Change is necessary to the adaptive process, but there always is the question about bias in new recommendations, especially those from groups whose basic justification is the introduction of changes. This problem is heightened by the fact that these people are professionally trained specialists. Earlier chapters have commented on some inherently conflicting interests within the organization. The staff professional is the locus of several such conflicting motivations. He joins the organization to practice his professional skill, but his lack of knowledge of the business as a whole, and the narrowness of his training often limits his outlook to his professional role. His stock-in-trade is dependent as much or more on his reputation than on his service to the firm. This recognition will be based on the brilliance he shows in developing new systems of even greater com-

Table 12-2   *DuPont's 24 most important product and process innovations between 1920 and 1950, rated from 1 to 5 on the basis of their relative commercial and technological importance**

Year Introduced	Product and Press Innovations	Relative Importance (5 Denotes Greatest Importance)
1920	Viscose rayon	4†
1923	Duco lacquers	3
1923	Tetraethyl lead (bromide process)	3†
1924	Tetraethyl lead (chloride process)	2†
1924	Cellophane	4†
1926	Synthetic ammonia	1
1927	Moistureproof cellophane	3
1927	Methanol and higher alcohols	1
1928	Dulux finishes	2
1929	Acetate rayon	3†
1931	Freon	2
1931	Neoprene	2
1931	Titanium pigments	2†
1934	Cordure high-tenacity rayon	2
1936	Lucite acrylic resin	1
1939	Nylon	5
1940	Polyvinyl acetate and alcohols	1
1941	Rutile titanium dioxide	1
1942	Fermate fungicides	1
1943	Teflon	1
1944	Alathon polyethyliece plastic	1
1948	Orlon acrylic fiber	3
1948	Titanium metal	3†
1949	Polymeric color film	1
1949	Fiber V (Dacron)	3†

* Based on *Fortune*, October 1950, p. 114, except for viscose rayon, tetraethyl lead (chloride process), plain cellophane, acetate rayon, and titanium pigments. These were added by the author.

† This is the author's estimate of the relative importance of these products and processes. In all other cases, the relative importance is that given each product in *Fortune*.

Taken from W. F. Mueller, "The Origins of the Basic Inventions Underlying DuPont's Major Product and Process Innovations," in *The Rate and Direction of Inventive Activity*, National Bureau of Economic Research, Princeton University Press, 1962, pp. 323–346.

plexity and scope. The POM managers, on the other hand, are not interested in becoming the owners of a grand edifice architected by its staff. They are interested in a tradeoff between efficiency and flexibility, trying to hold investments in systems and in changes to the level appropriate for the firm's strategy and markets. Furthermore, the individual manager may have only a shadowy comprehension of the speciality from which a recommendation arises. He may have to say yes or no based primarily on biased information, his general understanding of the crucial aspects of the business, his experiences in judging people and ideas, and his knowledge of the underlying problems.

MANAGING CHANGE AGENTS

The chances are less than one in five that you personally will ever be working in one of the POM groups in Figure 12-3 (excluding of course top management). Yet, all managers have these problems in responding to numerous requests and proposals for new systems, to modifications for the old ones, and to glowing promises and forecasts. That is why it is worthwhile to master the somewhat technical material in these chapters. You certainly cannot expect to avoid a complete "snow job" by specialists and other managers unless you acquire a basic knowledge of what is going on in their areas and what is or is not important to them. Time and time again you will want to get something done that is of value to you and to the company, and as often as not, you will be told, "It can't be done." How do you expect to know whether or not to accept that reply at face value? Only by knowing enough about what is behind the man's reply will you know whether he means that it is a physical impossibility, or just something he doesn't want to do, or a case where you have to show that the benefits will outweigh the perceived costs. You can't hope to win working off a base of complete ignorance. Every bit of knowledge that you gain about how other groups operate is really a weapon in your own arsenal.

DEFINING THE WORK

Between the highly innovative staff groups and the operating groups sit the processing design groups. They translate general specifications for products and process into the routing and manufacturing methods used to transform the input most efficiently, given current process capabilities. These groups also work to update these instructions with new ideas and techniques. Most of the activities of these groups were described in earlier chapters. They usually have responsibility for all methods and standards, for machine and materials handling layouts, for developing final specifications of equipment and materials to be purchased, and for procedures for maintenance and quality control.

DEFINING AND CONTROLLING QUALITY

The function of quality control may be entrusted entirely to a separate specialized group. In many cases, the several quality control functions are split between the engineering staff and the group supervising line operations. This ambiguity in the organizational structure is explained in Chapter 16. Quality control standards are quite technical, but line management has the ultimate responsibility for seeing to it that both quality *and* quantity meet market demands. There are tradeoffs between quality and quantity that must be made, and there are close interrelationships between worker supervision and quality of output that must be administered carefully in the context of overall training and efficiency objectives.

CONTROL IN SYSTEMS

The remaining three major groups in Figure 12-3 are responsible for capacity and efficiency on a day-to-day basis. These three functions are difficult to separate in some systems. The integrated nature of these POM activities can be illustrated by the final six information-system applications in the Chapter 4 list. All are from the service industries. They are air traffic control, traffic flow control in cities, scheduling hospital activities, improving stock exchange and brokerage information flows, hotel reservation and registration systems, and bank clerical operations. Each processes a large volume of information as well as physical units of output. Several have already been described in simple systems terms in Figure 4-1; here is a more comprehensive look at three such POM systems, all from service industries.

    Traffic control. Take the air traffic controller example. The system manager of an air traffic control center receives forecasts in terms of the airline schedules and messages from pilots and other control centers. From this, he can estimate the number of men needed at certain hours of the day and may, on occasion, issue prohibitions against the addition of flights at certain hours because the capacity of the men, machines, and runways will be overtaxed. These decisions would correspond to the aggregate scheduling decision of the factory. As aircraft enter the control area, they present themselves as orders for landing or takeoff guidance. For each type of aircraft, there are ordering conditions related to weight, available fuel, landing speeds, priority, costs of delay, and instrumentation. These specifications usually are known by the controllers, although the communication system can be used to notify the ground of fuel shortages or other emergency situations. The controllers then handle the several units of capacity— storage space in the three-dimensional holding pattern, the progression of aircraft down through the pattern to the runways, the number of runways in use, and the landing rates allowable by regulation or organizational policy.

The controllers, intent on their radar scopes and plotting boards, move planes about in the waiting lines (queues) according to their priorities and the aircrafts' technical requirements. During peak periods, the bottleneck resource usually is runway capacity expressed in terms of takeoffs and landings per minute. The schedule of planes on the taxiways and in the holding pattern is continually revamped to get the planes on and off, despite their differing speeds, at the closest allowable intervals. In cases of peak demand, the controllers use their own judgment and experience in reducing this interval between planes (which is really a safety or quality factor) to achieve the necessary rate of landings and improve passenger service (quality of another sort). The effective performance of this process depends on a combination of men, machines, and information to utilize the currently critical capacity. It involves both long-run and short-run scheduling, management of a supply or inventory of items, and the immediate and close control of the flow of items and information.

Hospitals. The task of operating a hospital to service the needs of arriving patients is complex also. Patient arrivals are relatively difficult to predict, although the aggregate demand for frequently required services like the delivery of babies is relatively easy to forecast. Once these demands are known through the admitting procedure, then a number of tasks can be scheduled. One can think of the hospital as a job shop system. Some patients need only beds, doctor visits, and nursing care, while others will go through X-ray units, operating rooms, recovery rooms, and intensive care units. There is a limited capacity for each type of unit, and they do not necessarily balance out evenly. The most commonly cited measure is the bed capacity, but that is becoming less and less indicative of the real level of activity. More and more patients are walking in, being taken care of in outpatient clinics, and going home immediately. Beds also may be limited in their usefulness by certain regulations and procedures. For example, concern over infant infections has led some states to pass laws that maternity beds may not be used when idle to house other types of patients. Internal policy may also assign specific beds to other medical specialties. This will lessen flexibility and reduce effective capacity, but it does allow the specialists to be assured of room for their own patients and to schedule them more easily. Even the availability of a bed does not assure smooth flow of the patient through the care system. In some hospitals, whole floors of beds are shut down because of a shortage of nurses. To utilize scarce and frightfully expensive resources, hospitals have begun to place more and more emphasis on management techniques.

At Childrens Hospital Medical Center in Boston, Mass., a computer information system is used to keep track of the location of each child on the hospital floors and identify each empty bed available for new assignments. This system is a response to problems generated by the practice of moving patients from room to room based on their needs for nursing care. Those requiring special care are located nearest to the nursing stations. As the patient improves, he is progressively moved to the more distant locations. This saves on nursing labor, but it requires a rapid updating of each patient's position. Hospitals are traumatic enough for parents without them discovering that the hospital has temporarily lost their little darling. Here the speed of the information system has allowed the hospital to keep their records at the visitors' entrance up-to-date and thus allowed the hospital to use more efficient methods without serious loss of quality of service. Other information systems are rapidly being developed to improve the speed and accuracy of laboratory test results and to schedule patients for clinic visits.

Any hospital has a series of inventory systems to be managed. Some, like drugs and laundry supplies, are handled the same as these items elsewhere. But the hospital also has several inventories of patients. There are patients in clinic waiting rooms, allowing the physician to utilize his time fully. There are patients due for surgery for which there is no urgency; these can be used to fill to capacity beds and operating rooms as the real emergencies fluctuate. There is the pool of patients in the hospital for observation, therapy, and teaching purposes readily available for diagnosis, treatment, and therapy at the convenience of the hospital staff. Having them there increases the efficiency of the staff but all too often at the expense of the patient. Somewhere in the management of this process there has to be a more equitable tradeoff of patient idleness versus hospital utilization. Inventory and scheduling theory play a useful role in these decisions.

Financial institutions. The bank and the brokerage house both are large systems that transfer information to facilitate the utilization of capital. In each, time and fast information at high volumes are paramount. Each has gone more and more to a POM approach in its operations with heavy investments in equipment and specialized manpower. Far into the night, batches of paperwork are processed according to predetermined schedules by second and third shift employees. Inventories of cash, securities, and loans are very carefully managed to obtain improved rates of return and still meet variations in their demand. In the case of the stock brokerage houses, this new technology with its dependence on high capital investments has contributed to the major shift in the structure of the firms from partnerships to public corporations able to seek substantial equity financing.

SPECIALIZATION OF FUNCTIONS

In the more traditionally organized manufacturing firm, POM activities are assigned to separate groups. There will be a man or men responsible for overall production operations. Under him are department heads and foremen each responsible for a physical area or a group of men in the shop. It is their job to take the tasks routed to them, assign them to individual men and machines, and see that they are done on time and with the proper quality. It also is their task to evaluate the individual worker's performance and handle labor relations and personnel matters at the first level. In the course of their activities, foremen also perform the most detailed step in the scheduling function called dispatching. This is the hour-by-hour or minute-by-minute act of choosing the lot that will go on each machine next. Where there are 7 turret lathes, the schedulers are likely to treat them all alike, whereas the foreman will know that numbers 3 and 6 are the only ones capable of meeting the tolerance requirements of a special job for an important customer. It is the foreman who has those last degrees of flexibility to make the various bits and pieces fall into place and try to keep everyone reasonably happy.

The production planning and control group supports the line managers with information and schedules. This group usually has three principal functions: order processing and scheduling, production control, and inventory control. Each may be assigned to a separate group of specialists. The order processing and scheduling group takes the order and checks its availability against inventory (stock status) if finished goods or parts stocks are maintained. If that product is out-of-stock, they estimate the time required for production and notify the customer of the anticipated delivery date. After this, the scheduling activity begins in earnest. The order is "exploded" into the much longer lists of parts to be manufactured or assembled from a parts inventory. These are then translated into stock withdrawals, purchase orders, and manufacturing orders to be delivered by a certain date. The production control organization translates these promises into production lots assigned to specific operations for production by specific dates and follows up on their progress. An inventory control group determines the levels of inventory needed to meet fluctuations in demand, to provide cushions between the production subsystems, and to equate demand to capacity. As inventory levels drop below those considered satisfactory, the inventory control group releases replenishment orders to the shop in the most economical lot sizes.

APPROACHING SPECIALIZED AREAS

In the chapters which follow, we will be discussing some of the more technical aspects of the POM control functions. Each topic could be and is the subject of several books. We cannot and should not attempt to cover all available material in depth here. Yet, you need to study the problem enough to know which proposals are sensible and plausible. Each chapter, therefore, starts with a statement of the problem followed by an analysis of the economics involved, a series of simple models linking decision rules with the economic facts of the problem, an outline of the routes to more complex models, and a look at the practical information and control systems that lead to the effective implementation of this knowledge. Our objective is to let you first understand the problem and then develop a method of problem-solving and analysis that can be carried over to other areas, a method of thinking about business problems that is rigorous but does not mislead you into thinking that this is just another mathematics course. Some topics like the economic lot size calculation, forecasting demand, and statistical quality control are covered more extensively than others. These topics are stressed because they involve relationships that behave contrary to the typical man's intuition or first approximation. Where simple linear (straight-line) models suffice, it does not seem as important to use a quantitative approach. You would tend to arrive intuitively at the right solution anyway. Where the notions are foreign to your way of thinking, it takes many more pages of explanation to drive the point home and leave you with sufficient understanding to deal effectively with the situation when you encounter it again.

QUESTIONS

1. What are the factors determining effective capacity? Define each in terms of your school.
2. Identify three primary bottlenecks in the educational process of your university, and classify each of them as to the factors determining its capacity and the measures necessary to expand capacity.
3. Why does the incremental contribution per unit decline as demand exceeds the design optimum? How does one improve the contribution as demand continues to increase?
4. What does the *New York Times* mean when it reports that the United States steel industry is operating at 108 percent of capacity?
5. Can maximum efficiency and quality be achieved simultaneously in a production process? How?
6. Evaluate this statement: "Demand does not determine quality and output rate, since firms use predetermined policies, schedules, and objectives."
7. How should Tony's Pizza Parlor deal with the tasks of controlling quality, quantity, and efficiency?
8. How can Tony's cope with the changing demand for pizza? It operates both table and take-out service.

9. How might the concept of organizational slack be used to explain the organizational problems of a teaching hospital?
10. How does one evaluate the performance of the major change agent groups in a firm?

CASE: NONFERROUS METALS CORP.

Between May and August of 1968, the Brass Wire Mill of Nonferrous Metals Corp. had fallen considerably behind its scheduled delivery commitments. The problems appeared to center around a wire-cleaning unit which was a bottleneck in the manufacturing process. A number of corrective measures had been taken including adding equipment, changing manufacturing methods, increasing manpower, and providing new work standards. By the end of August, however, output was, if anything, lower than ever.

Mr. Harry Brown, the mill manager, and most of the senior executives were reasonably certain that the low rate of output now was due to resistance by the workers to the new methods and standards which would have required considerably greater output in order to allow the cleaning-unit workers the same take-home pay. Like most other workers in the plant, they were paid on the basis of the number of pounds of wire cleaned under a complex system of separate rates for each type and size of wire.

The new output levels required of the workers, who had been supplied some new automatic materials-handling equipment, were almost double their old performance. Mr. Brown's boss had recommended disciplinary action against the workers. The personnel director had advised against such a policy since the local union contract soon was to be renegotiated and the disciplining of the workers would give the union a cause to rally the workers for a strike. Mr. Brown also suspected that the workers might soon file a grievance under the union contract against the new standards. He felt that the new standards were soundly constructed, but it would be difficult for any arbitrator to accept such a large reduction in standard times. He could foresee the company losing ground in the final settlement.

The chief industrial engineer argued strongly against any concessions on the new standards since they were based on the procedures and techniques used to justify all standards and wages in the company. They had been checked and rechecked. He did suggest a couple of minor points that the company might compromise on without endangering the plant-wide system.

Mr. Brown would have to make the final decision himself. His company had a firm policy of delegating such decisions to the individual mill manager. Mr. Brown's job description stated that his performance would be judged on the following factors:

1. Meeting scheduled, monthly output targets in pounds of wire.
2. Meeting cost per pound targets.
3. Achieving a high percentage of on-time deliveries.
4. Achieving a favorable inventory-to-sales ratio.
5. Achieving a low percentage of quality complaints and returns.
6. Achieving a favorable percentage product yield.
7. Staying within his budgets.
8. Having a high percentage of workers at or above standard output and compensation.

In the current seller's market, when customers were clammering for material, Mr. Brown believed that his output volume was the variable being watched most carefully by top management.

chapter

FORECASTING FOR PLANNING

thirteen

Forecasting is something many a manager says he could not do, even if his job depended on it. And since it does, he forecasts all the time. This apparent contradiction rests with the acceptable degree of accuracy intended. No one forecasts sales of an item to the accuracy desired by the users of the information. Yet decisions must be made with the best information available. Therefore, the topic of this chapter is not whether or not forecasts are necessary or good but how to develop and use the existing art with its admixture of science. Improving your forecasting will be a critical aspect of your managerial performance; it is one major difference between the $20,000 and the $40,000 executive.

This chapter focuses on the prediction of market demand for the output of an operating system. Effective management also depends on an ability to anticipate changes in technology, price structure, labor demands, social changes, etc. In each case, however, the same methods can be applied. Information inputs and outputs may differ, but the process remains the same.

In this process, the manager must:

1. Set the objectives of the planning process for which forecasts are an input.
2. Select the period over which the projection will be made.
3. Select the methodology or approach needed.
4. Gather the pertinent information.
5. Prepare a forecast.
6. Evaluate it.

Forecasting is not something done in a vacuum. Demand forecasts, for example, enable the organization to meet the needs of its customers, needs which may not yet be fully determined. The better these forecasts, the better the company will be able to seek out and meet customer demands, either in the short run through revised inventory and production schedules or in the long run through the acquisition of products, personnel, and facilities. Serious failure in either area can threaten the growth of the organization.

PURPOSES OF FORECASTS AND THEIR TIMING

Forecasts can serve a wide variety of purposes, but to be effective each must be tailored to fit its primary purpose. A decision made on Wednesday whether or not to schedule overtime next Saturday is unlikely to depend heavily on a 3-year forecast of demand. On the other hand, selection of the size of a new factory building will. Forecasts will vary in more than just the time period being considered. The 3-year demand forecast may include markets, products, and processes not presently used. It may be in terms of total machine-hours, man-hours, or even sales dollars. Forecasts of short-run shop loads have to be laid out in terms of specific times, activities, and machines. They also may differ in the way that they are developed. The shop foreman may merely look at the orders on the books and then compare the ability of his men and machines to produce those orders, or he may also estimate what new work will come in. The long-range forecaster will be looking systematically at the environmental system (e.g., past sales trends, population trends, technological trends, and competitor behavior) and at the firm's strategy.

Using the example of a grocery products manufacturer, Magee has developed a series of forecasting requirements each with its own individual time span, characteristics, and techniques of analysis. These are shown in modified form in Table 13-1 and Figure 13-1.

Within the uses of forecasts outlined in Table 13-1, the level of detail increases as the time span decreases. While the same statistical methods may be applied to each purpose, the units of measurement will differ. Employ-

Table 13-1 *Forecasting requirements*

Use	Time Span	Characteristics	Techniques
Business Planning: Product planning Research programing Capital planning Plant location and expansion	Generally 5 years or more; sometimes less	Broad outline forecast, often qualitative only	Technical-economic studies; economic and population studies; marketing studies
Intermediate Operation Planning: Capital and cash budgets Sales planning Production planning, especially in seasonal business Setting production and inventory budgets	Generally 6 months to 2 years at least through one cycle in seasonal business	Used for analysis of alternative operating plans; numerical; not necessarily detailed by item; estimate of reliability needed	Collective opinion; trend analysis; seasonal index analysis; correlation with economic indices; combination techniques
Short-run Production Control: Adjusting production and employment levels to account for departures of total inventory from plan	One to 6 weeks; span equals lag between decision to adjust operating rates and time output is actually affected	Forecasts of operating activity, not item forecast	Statistical trend extrapolation; explosion of short-term product or product-class forecasts
Forecast of Item Requirements: Placing purchase orders Scheduling items into production Replenishing warehouse stocks: controlling decisions when and how much to replenish	Span equals lead time between placing order or scheduling run and receipt or completion; estimate of error, or maximum demand needed to protect service	Designed for routine use in manual, punched-card, or electronic systems	Explosion of end-product demands; graphical, statistical, or numerical techniques

From: Magee, J. F., *Production Planning and Inventory Control* (New York: McGraw-Hill Book Company, 1958), p. 119.

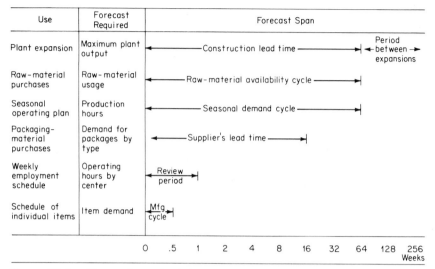

Figure 13-1   *Illustrative schedule of required forecasts*

ment schedules must be based on a prediction of man-hours needed by skill or labor classification. Packaging requirements must be broken down by product and by size within product. Where special promotions are used, such as "7¢ off" on a box, the planners must include this in the schedule. To plan raw material purchases, it may be necessary to know only pounds of product to be packaged, and not whether it is shipped in 5 or 10 pound packages. Yet the man designing the box-filling lines may be interested only in the total demand by size without regard to package printing or even ingredients. Within a large manufacturer, like General Foods or Pillsbury Corporation, these decisions may be the responsibility of different individuals. To avoid needless duplication of effort, such firms often have forecasting specialists who attempt to maintain consistency among the plans and who possess technical skills helpful to better forecasts. In each case, however, it is fully understood that the decision-maker is the one who will look good or bad on the basis of the forecast.

It also is important to recognize that a situation which is stable in the long run may be highly variable in the short run. The marketing department of an air conditioner manufacturer may be right on the button in predicting the total annual demand for air conditioners, but, if it misses a pronounced April warm spell, that potential may never be realized. Similarly, the forecasts of total product demand may be accurate, but the forecast of individual items and markets may be in error. A plentiful supply of 8-ounce cans in Omaha will not do a brewer much good when his customers are out of quart bottles.

Thus, the most important step is the careful definition of the specific forecast that is required, its time span, its appropriate unit or units of measure, and its accuracy requirements.

TECHNIQUES OF FORECASTING

Organizations commonly use five approaches to the forecasting of demand: (1) expert opinion, (2) "can do" commitments, (3) extension of past history, (4) association with other events, and (5) identification of leading events. The first two approaches involve subjective estimates of what is likely to transpire in the future. The latter three require the application of statistical methods to the available current and historical data. In many cases, the manager's actions are based on a combination of several, if not all, of these approaches.

EXPERT OPINION

Each manager makes his decisions based on what he anticipates will happen and what he hears from others. Outside experts may be consulted; other executives will be asked to submit estimates based on their information and experience. Salesmen regularly are asked to forward their knowledge of customer plans and preferences and competitors' activities. All of these estimates are subjective, biased, and based on incomplete information. They do, however, have the advantages of requiring little mathematical sophistication and taking little management time.

Even the use of world renowned outside experts in the most critical decisions is subject to bias. When the first great hydroelectric plant at Niagara Falls, New York, was being planned, two groups submitted proposals. The Edison interests offered to supply direct-current equipment such as they had provided throughout the United States. A second group led by two mavericks named Nicola Tesla and George Westinghouse argued for the use of a new technology called "alternating current." Thomas Edison was a recognized expert and obviously not a disinterested one. The promoters of the power project consulted Lord Kelvin in England and he replied tersely, "Do not commit the monstrous folly of using alternating current." The decision-makers, as you know, made their own investigation and chose alternating current, a decision that has held up well over 50 years. Experts and experienced managers will be useful as guides and sources of information, but you will have to make your own decisions.

CAN DO FORECASTS

In many situations, forecasts serve as goals as well as predictions. Salesmen and production managers are regularly asked what they "can do." If the salesman tells the general manager that he will sell a million widgets, it will matter little, for many purposes, whether the salesman achieves it through a general upsurge in demand or by hundred-hour work weeks. The forecast in many firms becomes a self-fulfilling prophesy. As such, it is useful to the top manager and to the production planner. Both must be cautious, however, in recognizing that this introduction of commitment into the forecasting process brings with it a likelihood of bias. Different men will react in different ways to the challenge. Some will be incurable optimists, while others will be risk avoiders and submit the lowest believable estimates. Then, you as an effective manager will have to apply your own correction factors for each individual. You may even go so far as to develop a numerical weighting factor, such as the following:

$$\text{Actual to forecast ratio for Joe} = \frac{\Sigma \text{ Joe's last 5 yearly actual sales}}{\Sigma \text{ Joe's last 5 yearly forecasts}}$$

Then when Joe gives you his estimate for next year, you would actually plan on the basis of that figure times his "actual to forecast ratio."

EXTENSION OF PAST HISTORY

When we take past history as our starting point for predicting the future, it does not necessarily mean that we expect that March will be identical to February and to January. We need to respond to seasonal factors, to trends, and to changes in the process generating our information. Figure 13-2 represents the retail demand for a small home appliance. It is apparent that the peak selling period is the Christmas market. What happens in December pretty much determines the year's success. At the same time, there appears to be an upward trend which, *if continued,* would affect future sales. Finally, of course, there are the random monthly fluctuations. The forecaster of total sales will have to work with raw data containing elements of all three—cyclicality (or seasonality), trend, and random variation.

Seasonality or cyclicality adjustments. The usual procedure is to deal with the seasonality first. Let us start with the 3-year historical demand for this appliance. The first step is to determine which portion of the annual sales falls in each month of the year. Table 13-2 illustrates one process used to generate the seasonal indices for the small appliance. January 1967, January 1968, and January 1969 had sales of 39.0, 33.9, and 36.4. These average to 36.43. For the last 3 years as a whole, sales averaged 50.83 per month. The percentage ratio of January's sales to the all months' average

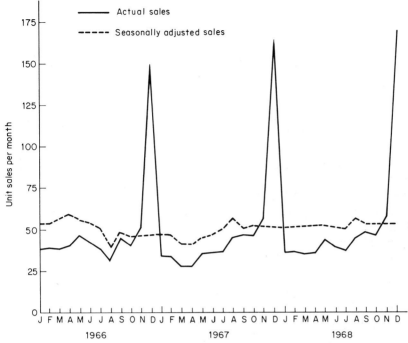

Figure 13-2 *Sales of household appliance*

Table 13-2 *Determination of the season index for small appliance*
(based on 3 years' sales experience)

	1966	1967	1968	Three Year Mean	Index: Month's Mean as % of Overall Average
January	39.0	33.9	36.4	36.43	71.7
February	39.2	33.8	37.2	36.73	72.3
March	38.4	27.7	34.8	33.63	66.2
April	40.8	27.6	36.1	34.63	68.1
May	46.9	36.9	43.8	42.53	83.7
June	42.7	36.8	39.7	39.73	78.2
July	38.4	37.2	37.2	37.60	74.0
August	31.2	45.1	45.0	40.43	79.5
September	44.6	46.5	48.9	46.67	91.8
October	40.8	46.8	47.2	44.93	88.4
November	50.3	57.6	58.6	55.50	109.2
December	149.2	164.3	169.8	161.10	317.0
Total	601.5	594.2	634.7	609.91	
Average/month overall				50.83	100

was 71.7. This is called the *seasonal index* for January. This index can be used as follows to predict 1970 sales:

Actual January 1970 sales = 40.2 thousand units.
Does the annual sales rate equal 12 × 40.2 or 482.4?

No! January's sales usually are 71.7 percent of the monthly average. Therefore, a better estimator would be the "seasonally adjusted" sales volume or (40.2/.717) × 12 = 672.8. Going on through Table 13-2, we arrive at comparable values month by month. These have been placed on Figure 13-2. Now the evidence of a trend in the data becomes clearer, and statistical analysis or moving average techniques can be applied. Figure 13-3 presents a series of data in which the trend is even more pronounced. The fact that there is a trend line can be determined by using the simplest statistical approach, least squares regression.

Least squares regression. Our objective is a trend line, preferably one of maximum statistical significance. Therefore, the line through our data will be a simple linear equation

$$Y = a + bX$$

where

Y = the value for which the estimates are being made, the dependent variable (next period's sales)
a = the point at which the trend line intercepts the Y axis
b = the rate of change (slope) of the trend line (sales growth per period)
X = the independent variable

The criterion for fitting a line (or any other curve) to a set of data is the least squared error. With this as our target, we try to minimize the

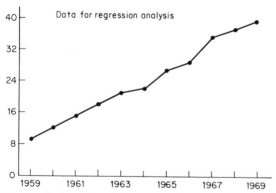

Figure 13-3   *Plot of Y versus years as per data in Table 13-3*

sum of the squares of the vertical (or Y) differences (deviations) between the observed data points and the points with the corresponding X values on the trend line. This is an arbitrary choice basic to much of statistics. For a discussion of its merits, look at any basic statistics text.

Once we accept this criterion, we know that for any observed point X, Y and the corresponding point on a potential regression line X, Y', the value of the deviation will be

$$y = Y - Y'$$ 13-1

Since $Y' = a + bX$ is the formula for the line, we can substitute for Y':

$$y = Y - Y' = Y - (a + bX)$$ 13-2

and for n points our criterion will be to minimize:

$$Z = \sum_{i=1}^{n} y_i^2 = \sum_{i=1}^{n} [Y_i - a - bX_i]^2$$ 13-3

This minimum value occurs when

$$\Sigma Y_i = na + b\Sigma X_i$$ 13-4

and

$$\Sigma(X_i Y_i) = a\Sigma X_i + b\Sigma X_i^2$$ 13-5

Equations 13-4 and 13-5 can be taken on faith or on the basis of calculus as demonstrated in footnote 1.[1] Since we started with observed values for every point $X_i Y_i$, we can substitute these values in the terms of Equations 13-4 and 13-5. This will give us two equations with the two unknowns a and b, and we can quickly solve them to find out the appropriate equation for the trend line.

In the special case where the data are based on a time series with an odd number of years, say 1959 through 1969 (11 years), we can number the years from −5 to +5 consecutively and simplify the calculations considerably. Then $\Sigma X_i = 0$ and Equations 13-4 and 13-5 reduce to:

$$a = \frac{\Sigma Y_i}{n}$$ 13-6

$$b = \frac{\Sigma(X_i Y_i)}{\Sigma(X_i^2)}$$ 13-7

[1] At the minimum value of Equation 13-3, the partial derivatives of Z with respect to a and b will be:

$$\frac{dZ}{da} = 0 = -2[\Sigma Y_i - a - bX_i]$$ 13-8

$$\frac{dZ}{db} = 0 = -2\Sigma X_i[Y_i - a - bX_i]$$ 13-9

These can be transformed readily into the relationships in Equations 13-4 and 13-5.

Table 13-3

Year	X	Y	XY	X²
1959	−5	9	−45	25
1960	−4	12	−48	16
1961	−3	15	−45	9
1962	−2	18	−36	4
1963	−1	21	−21	1
1964	0	22	0	0
1965	+1	27	27	1
1966	2	29	58	4
1967	3	35	105	9
1968	4	37	148	16
1969	5	39	195	25
Totals	0	264	338	110

Table 13-3 shows the process for fitting the best trend line to the points plotted in Figure 13-3. The resulting values of a and b are $a = 264/11 = 24.0$, and $b = 338/110 = 3.08$. The equation for the trend line would be $Y' = 24 + 3.08X$. The estimate of 1970 demand, therefore would be $Y' = 24 + 3.08 (1970 - 1964) = 24 + 3.08(6) = 42.5$. Now that you have the answer, we would suggest that you try to do the same data but treat the time series so that $1959 = 1$ and $1969 = 11$ in Equations 13-4 and 13-5.

ASSOCIATION WITH OTHER EVENTS

Once that line has been fitted to the data, the question remains as to the goodness of fit of the regression line to the data. Statisticians accept the least squared error criterion as their basis of comparison, and, therefore, they logically accept the idea that the line which reduces that squared error the most has the best fit. Rather than compare contending lines (or curves) directly, the statistician compares each with a straight line representing the mean value of the dependent variable, $\bar{Y} = \Sigma Y_i / N$. For this mean value, the squared error is $\Sigma(Y_i - \bar{Y})^2$. For the fitted lines, the squared error is $\Sigma(Y_i - \bar{Y})^2 - \Sigma(Y_i - Y_i')^2$. This is most commonly expressed in terms of a ratio change where complete explanation, a perfect fit, would be 1.0 and no improvement would be 0.0. This ratio called the "coefficient of determination," or r^2, is computed by the formula:

$$r^2 = \left[1 - \frac{\Sigma(Y_i - Y_i')^2}{\Sigma(Y_i - \bar{Y})^2} \right]$$

13-10

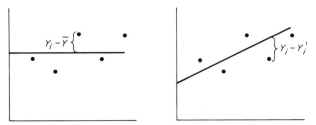

Figure 13-4 *Comparison of error in the mean with error in the regression line*

The sign of r^2 is determined by the sign of the slope of the regression line. The square root of this term, r, is called the coefficient of correlation.[2] Exact interpretation of values of r^2 or r for their significance with either linear or curvilinear fits is a tricky business. The difference in errors between the mean and the regression line is illustrated in Figure 13-4.

FORECASTING FROM LEADING EVENTS

If we assume that there are events that are associated with or even cause the events that we are forecasting, then we can use statistical analysis to see which events are most closely associated, i.e., give the largest r^2. For example, we may have an inkling that sales of brick in the United States are closely related to building activity and might even be able to prove it statistically. Yet we may get the data on building activity too late to help us schedule the production and shipment of bricks. Well, we could try the reported figures for construction contracts let, for building permits issued, or for planned capital expenditures. One or some combination of more than one might better meet our needs. We could also try out several different time lags. For example, brick consumption in a given month might not be related to housing starts in that month but rather to those 3 months earlier. The variables and the lags which give us the highest r^2 would be the ones that we would most likely use as the basis of our forecasts. The lags in the response are useful to us because they give us time to get the information before decisions must be reached.

[2] If one wishes to calculate the coefficient of correlation directly from the observed values of X and Y, he can use Equation 13-11.

$$r = \frac{N\Sigma XY - \Sigma X\Sigma Y}{\sqrt{[N\Sigma X^2 - (\Sigma X)^2][N\Sigma Y^2 - (\Sigma Y)^2]}}$$

13-11

where
N = the number of observations
ΣX = sum of the observed values of X_i
ΣY = sum of the observed values of Y_i
ΣXY = sum of the products X_iY_i

In the preceding section, we illustrated how regression lines might be used to develop a projection of future sales. One assumption of this approach is that the underlying process generating our sales is consistent over time. This may not always be our best assumption. If market changes are suspected, then the more recent sales information may be our best indicator. Here, however, we are faced with the knowledge that there will be substantial random fluctuation in the reported period-to-period sales. If last month was a poor one, it does not necessarily follow that this next one will be poor too. In fact, it may be excellent due to purchases delayed from last month. Similarly, once we have decided that building permits 3 months ago are best predictors of this month's brick shipments, we still may not choose to double shipment schedules when one month shows a 100 percent increase in the volume of permits issued. As in all control systems, one key decision that we must make is the rapidity and magnitude with which we respond to new information. Too rapid a response leads to lots of hopping around in our production and inventory levels. Too slow a response means not being able to meet changing conditions. One way of adjusting our response to changes is the use of averaged, rather than individual, figures as our inputs.

Moving averages. Averages that are updated as new data are received are called "moving averages." We control our speed of response by the number of periods included in the moving average and the weighting assigned to each. In its simplest form, the periods are weighted equally. Thus a 3-month moving average used to forecast July sales would contain sales figures for April, May, and June. Once the July figures are in, April is dropped, and July is added to forecast August.

One can argue that this equal weighting for each month is not the best approach because the newer information is more representative of current events. He might declare that he would weight the latest month as heavily as the preceding 2 months and the next-to-last month twice the one 3 months ago. In this case, the forecast for next month, F_4, would be based on the actual sales, A_i, for the preceding 3 months as follows:

$$F_4 = \frac{(3A_3 + 2A_2 + A_1)}{6} \qquad\qquad \text{13-12}$$

As new data come in, they displace the oldest piece of information. But suppose that a company has 8,000 items (often called "stockkeeping units," or SKU's) for which it must regularly forecast demand. If it uses a 6-month moving average, uniformly weighted or otherwise, then someone has to take the new figures, add to them the figures for the preceding 5 months, and compute the new moving average. This is a lot of work, even for a computer. For 8,000 SKU's you would have to store and retrieve 48,000 monthly sales figures, although a trick or two might enable you to get this figure down to retrieval of only 16,000 figures at a time. If nonuniform weightings are used, then the amount of work increases sharply. To many decision-makers, it has seemed logical to think that the more current information should be weighted most heavily, but the computational burden has discouraged them from using anything other than the implied uniform weighting.

Exponential smoothing. A technique called "exponential smoothing" overcomes some of these disadvantages of nonuniform weighting schemes. The only piece of information manipulated is the most recent forecast for the item in question and a single weighting factor called "alpha." The latter can be selected to minimize the anticipated forecast error for each item. In use, this single weighting factor, alpha, has proved as effective as other more complex weighting schemes.

Most forecasting schemes use past experience as a mirror of the future. Exponential smoothing certainly is no exception. The underlying assumption is that the basic processes generating future demand will remain constant or at least nearly so. If this assumption is true, then, *in the absence of a trend,* the forecast for last month should be the forecast for this month and next month as well, and we can dismiss variations as being merely random error. Obviously, however, we would like to be able to adjust to changes as they occur. One way is to look at the differences between our forecasts and the actual results for the forecast period. This difference will consist of two components, randomness and trend. To the extent that it is trend, we would like to adjust our forecast by that amount. If we say that 50 percent of that error is trend, then we will add 50 percent of the observed error to our last forecast to get the next. If we were wrong, the error will widen next time, and the new correction will increase too. So long as the errors persist, we will continue to make corrections. Presumably, the random errors around the true value will cancel each other out, and over time we will reach the new correct value. The fraction of the error that one chooses to add will be the alpha α factor that was mentioned above.

The size of the alpha will depend on the speed with which one wishes to respond to real changes in demand. This has to be weighted against the risks of overresponding to random fluctuations. As we will see later, it is possible to experiment with various alternative values of alpha ranging from zero to one to see which value would have best served our interests in the past. Table 13-4 gives three sets of forecasts of the same series of events using α values of 0.3, 0.5, and 0.7 and Equation 13-13. The results are plotted in Figure 13-5. Larger alphas do not necessarily result in better forecasts. Two major factors come into the evaluation of alternative α values: (1) the distribution of random errors around the true value, and (2) the costs attributable to errors in the forecast. Think about the problem of a factory manager who must revise production upwards or downwards

Table 13-4 *Calculations of exponentially smoothed moving averages*

			$\alpha = 0.3$	$\alpha = 0.5$	$\alpha = 0.7$
Month	Actual	Forecast for Month	100	100	100
A	100	B	100	100	100
B	110	C	103	105	107
C	120	D	108.1	112.5	116.1
D	130	E	114.7	121.5	125.8
E	140	F	122.3	130.7	135.7
F	150	G	130.6	140.4	145.7
G	150	H	136.2	145.2	148.7
H	140	I	137.3	142.6	142.6
I	130	J	135.1	136.3	133.8
J	120	K	130.6	128.1	124.1
K	110	L	124.4	117.0	114.2
L	100	M	117.1	108.5	104.3

depending on changes in demand, but each time he makes changes there are costs proportional to the amount of overtime authorized or the number of people hired or laid off. If he believes that much of the variation from week to week is random, then he may prefer a very low value of alpha. If he sees demand as being well-behaved, as in Figure 13-5, and faces relatively low costs due to changeover and relatively high costs when sales and production are not at the same rate, then he will want a high alpha.

$$\text{New Forecast} = \text{Old Forecast} + \alpha\,(\text{Actual} - \text{Old Forecast})$$
$$= (1 - \alpha)\,\text{Old Forecast} + \alpha\,\text{Actual} \qquad \textbf{13-13}$$

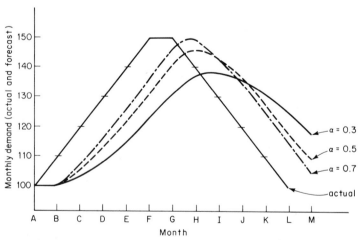

Figure 13-5 *Plot of actual and forecast monthly demands*

Trend adjusted exponential smoothing. During a period when there is an upward trend, an exponentially smoothed forecast will be low, but it will be high during a downtrend. There is, however, a trend adjustment factor that can be added to the new forecast to minimize this effect. Here again we start with an "old trend" which contains the residual errors from prior forecasts. Then there is a new correction factor, called "current trend," which is "new forecast minus old forecast." Again using the alpha weights, we arrive at new trend = α (new forecast − old forecast) + (1 − α) old trend. Once we are equipped with both a new forecast and a new trend, we compute the trend adjusted demand.

"Trend adjusted expected demand" = "new forecast" + (1 − α)/α "new trend." If we take the data for α = .5 from Table 13-4 [and remember that this makes the term (1 − α)/α equal to 1.0], we get the following estimates:

Month	Actual	New Forecast with α = .5	New-Old Forecasts	Old Trend	New Trend	Expected Demand
		100	0	0	0	100
A	100	100	0	0	0	100
B	110	105	5	0	2.5	107.5
C	120	112.5	7.5	2.5	5.0	117.5
D	130	121.5	9.0	5.0	7.0	128.5
E	140	130.7	9.2	7.0	8.1	138.8
F	150	140.4	9.7	8.1	8.9	149.3
G	150	145.2	4.8	8.9	6.8	152.0
H	140	142.6	−2.6	6.8	2.1	144.7
I	130	136.3	−6.3	2.1	−2.1	134.2
J	120	128.1	−8.2	−2.1	−5.2	122.9
K	110	117.0	−11.1	−5.2	−8.2	108.8
L	100	108.5	−8.5	−8.2	−8.3	100.2

Note that during the periods of steady increase in demand and later during steady decrease, the trend adjusted forecast at α = .5 tracked sales better than the unadjusted forecast with α = .7, but it also overshot the mark when the trend reversed itself. Again one has to make choices between speed of response and costs of overresponse.

Exponential smoothing has several advantages over the moving averages. It is not necessary to keep track of every period's sales in order to drop an old figure and add the new one to get the next forecast. Secondly, the weighting can be tested and adjusted more easily to represent new opportunities and new risks. Finally, where a computer system is used to update the forecasts for thousands of items, it is required to do fewer calculations with less storage and retrieval. The only stored data would be alpha, which may be uniform for all products or vary with each, the latest forecast, and, at the time of calculation, the newly entered latest actual period sales. If a trend adjustment is used, the new trend also will be stored.

The techniques of statistical and model-building forecasts outlined here are only the most elementary ones. Special texts on forecasting methods are available for further study. The important things to remember are (1) that there are such methods and places to find them, and (2) that they can be useful, provided the future is likely to reflect closely the activities of the recent past.

TECHNOLOGICAL FORECASTING

The higher one goes in management, the more he must concern himself with the external environment as well as the internal. We have been concentrating on market demands in this chapter. But there are many broader questions like "When will someone come up with a new idea to make computerization of our information system feasible?" or "When I locate our new plant, how much attention should I give to proximity to a major airport?" or "How likely is it that a new process will come along to make our present one uneconomical?" These questions are much harder to answer than those about next year's demand, but they are very important to the future profitability and security of an organization.

At the start of this chapter, we indicated that the same approaches would apply at all levels of forecasting and they do. Expert opinion is widely used to predict major social and technological changes. The objective here is to concentrate, over the long range, less on the means and more on the results. This may be the reason why science fiction writers like Jules Verne were better predictors of the future than the foremost scientists of their day. They recognized the social, economic, and psychological forces leading man to new accomplishments like faster and more individualized methods of land travel, conquest of dreaded diseases, flight, etc. The technical specialist could not yet see the means and, therefore, couldn't predict the results. Those who saw broad forces at work felt that these would motivate many men to search for means and some would succeed. For some cases, especially those closely related to your product line, it may be necessary to guess the correct means, but for many long-range decisions, only the ends need to be known.

One example of a frequently needed forecast is the future of computer costs. One may not know much about computers or who is planning to bring out what new piece of equipment next, but the data in Figure 13-6 show what has happened and forecast machine speeds and costs per calculation. This is a combined output of historical analysis and of expert

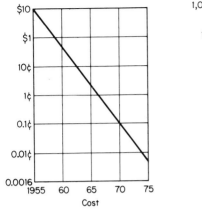
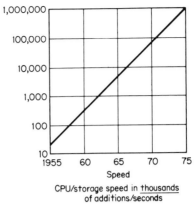

Figure 13-6 *Trends in computer processing.* [*Source: W. H. Ware, "Future Computer Technology and Its Impact," Report P-3279, The RAND Corp., Santa Monica, Calif., March 1966).*]

opinion. A similar judgment was responsible for America's success with the Polaris nuclear-missile submarine program. Existing American nuclear warheads were far too heavy for the Polaris missile at the time that the program was started, but the Navy recognized that research and development underway by the Atomic Energy Commission had steadily reduced the size and weight of nuclear warheads. The Navy gambled that by the time their rocket was perfected, the required payload would have been reduced down to its carrying capacity. That gamble, or you may call it a forecast if you wish, was correct. This meant that a smaller rocket was sufficient to do the job, even though the Navy personnel were not knowledgeable about the day-to-day progress in atomic weaponry.

S. W. Herwald of Westinghouse Electric Corporation has suggested a five-step procedure for keeping up with and exploiting the very rapid rates of technological change experience today:

> First, choose those areas of the technology that bear on a particular functional performance.
>
> Second, time the program of development so that the new product reaches the market soon enough to reap the premium profits that are possible only in the early phase of a new product's life.
>
> Third, pay particular attention to those technologies that are likely to change the *mode* of business we're in.

Fourth, think in terms of the new technology related to the lines which we really don't know about.

Fifth, determine the pace that must be set and do it by making an unemotional, objective assessment of the facts.

By using such an approach to the problem, we can perhaps make a more intelligent appraisal of the effects of the technology on the corporate future and increase our batting average on profitable successes.[3]

The manager has to start by looking at his business and its technologies and then developing a list of areas to be followed directly. He has to develop in himself, or in others assigned to specific areas, the will to follow regularly the trade journals and news releases. He must comprehend the basic significance of what is observed to the future of the company in general and the POM department in particular. The third point is a warning that the biggest changes are likely to come from the outside and from unexpected places. The buggy-whip industry died, not because of changes in buggy-whip technology, but because of the application of the internal combustion engine to small, low-cost vehicles. Management must stay loose in its thinking and forecasting.

CONTINUAL FORECASTING AND STRATEGIC PLANNING

Just learning about a new technology is not enough. It must be followed and evaluated continually. Numerically controlled machine tools are new technologies which have affected strongly the design and operation of metal cutting processes and electronics wiring. Great things were expected of this development from the start, but the economic impact ended up being almost the opposite of that initially predicted. With this technology, small computer-like units attached to a machine operated it in accordance with a program punched into a paper tape or stored in a small memory unit. The original evaluation of its impact was that it would lead to a new era of mass production, replacing equipment operators and performing simple operations over and over flawlessly. This assumption seemed logical on the basis of the history of automation. Yet, for very long production runs, it proved cheaper to build special-purpose mechanical systems to do the highly repetitive tasks and not invest in the general-purpose electronic systems. On the other hand, the new machines that were developed to capitalize on the control system have paid their way handsomely in making small runs of high-complexity, high-accuracy pieces. Here the very flexible control system can move the equipment flawlessly through intricate patterns that a human operator could

---

[3] S. W. Herwald, "Appraising the Effects of the Technological State of the Art on the Corporate Future," in J. R. Bright, ed., *Technological Planning on the Corporate Level* (Boston: Harvard Graduate School of Business Administration, 1962), pp. 65–66.

not accomplish because of the timing and hand-eye coordination. Also, where very high-cost materials like titanium are used, it is possible to pretest the control tapes and equipment using a lower-cost material until all the bugs are removed from the control tape. Then the expensive material can be machined right the first time, saving the cost of the rejects. Very expensive materials and high-volume production seldom go together, so effective uses tend to be at low volumes. Those who bet on numerically controlled machine tools for mass production were disappointed. But, furthermore, if they gave up at this point, they failed to learn by the experiences of others and lost out again when its potentials were fully understood and exploited in a new generation of equipment.

The use of atomic energy for commercial power generation is another example of the need to follow a technology over an extended period of time. In his paper, Herwald included the diagram in Figure 13-7 to show the typical responses of evaluators to technological accomplishment over time. Presumably, there is some threshold level at which the problems will be mastered and the development will pay off. At time A, an early optimism that the problems are on their way toward solution will lead many companies to jump on the bandwagon as they did with atomic energy in the 1950s and oceanography in the 1960s. Then as the technical and economic problems become clearer in the ongoing work, the enthusiasm wanes and finally reaches a low at time B. With time, additional work and progress in the supporting technologies lead to new improvements and ultimately to economical use for those who could afford to persevere or who followed the rate of progress carefully and rejoined the chase at time C. Usually at least three ingredients must be present before a new technology can be exploited: (1) the invention or new approach, (2) the supporting technology, and (3) the social or economic need. By supporting technology, we mean the technology needed to allow its exploitation, like the metallurgy for the high temperatures and corrosive environments and the control and measurement devices needed for commercially adequate atomic energy sys-

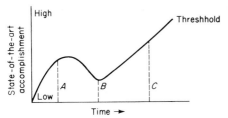

Figure 13-7 *Appraising new developments. [Source: S. W. Herwald, "Appraising the Effects of the Technological State of the Art on the Corporate Future," in J. R. Bright, ed.,* Technological Planning on the Corporate Level *(Boston: Harvard Graduate School of Business Administration, 1962), p. 64.]*

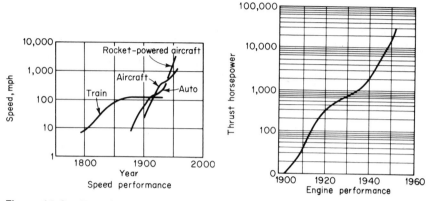

Figure 13-8   *Trends in aircraft design. [Source: Battelle Memorial Institute, "A Feasibility Study of Techniques for Measuring and Predicting the State of the Art," Columbus, Ohio, 1959, pp. A-21, A-27.]*

tems. Where all three have come together progress is rapid and profitable. Many items like penicillin were invented or discovered long ago but forgotten, because they could not be manufactured. When the technology was ready, new industries were formed. The successful forecaster must be ready to look at all three factors.

It often pays to keep a plot of the fundamental environmental and economic variables affecting a business over time. Figure 13-6 shows one set for the user or maker of computers. Figure 13-8 shows a similar set pertaining to the commercial and military aircraft industry. Here the weight, complexity, and speed of commercial aircraft have continued to rise steadily over the years and plans on the drawing boards indicate a continuation of these trends. That a forecast of these factors would have been helpful for aircraft users and for airport designers and operators is painfully evident to any of us who use airports regularly. Similar plots also can be made of capacity trends in any industry and of price levels. The extension of a line on a graph is not a real prediction of the future, but it is a piece of evidence that cannot be overlooked without good reason and it keeps away a lot of wishful thinking about the future.

SOCIAL FORECASTING

As people have become convinced that forecasts of the social and economic environment are needed for effective planning, expert opinion has been marshaled more and more systematically to keep decision-makers informed of what is likely to occur to people and society as technology progresses. A number of books have appeared that display forecasts of the life of available physical resources and the state of technology and of society by the

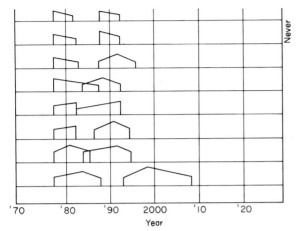

The left-hand figure represents 50% probability estimates, the figure on the right the 90% probability estimates. The highest point represents the mean estimate.

13. In all of the larger hospitals, pharmacists (or some type of personnel trained in pharmacy) will make ward rounds with doctors and act as drug consultants*

16. Serious diseases will be treated at special centers which may be located quite a distance from a patient's home*

5. There will be few, if any, MD's in solo private practice

1. Over half of the visits by patients outside of the hospital will be specifically to non-MD medical personnel; i.e., the MD will not see these patients

28. Today, insurance covers about 20% of the USA's health bill; eventually, it will cover 75% of all costs

21. There will be widespread use of computers for monitoring devices attached directly to the patient in his home

27. There will be compulsory, comprehensive medical insurance (including hospital, medical, and surgical coverage) for all

7. The typical MD will spend less than one-quarter of his time on direct patient care†

* Consensus at both the 50% and 90% probability levels
† Consensus at the 90% probability level

Figure 13-9 *Forecasts of future events in technology*

year 2,000. One technique used to gain agreement of the expert opinions is the Delphi technique which requires experts to predict the dates at which stated events are likely to happen. Then the results of each set of estimates are analyzed and reported back to each expert separately, along with any comments that the other experts may have presented to buttress their views. After receiving this new information, the experts have an opportunity to revise their estimates on the basis of the new information and to predict the technical and social consequences of that event at that time. Figure 13-9 shows some of the predictions of one Delphi study. This type of forecasting is far afield from short-range market estimates, but one of the same techniques, expert judgment, is used. Even though the technological and social forecasts are so far afield, they also are necessary for predicting customer desires and needs for long-range planning.

QUESTIONS

1. Edmund Burke once said, "You can never plan the future by the past." What is the significance of that statement to the POM manager?
2. In an operation with wide fluctuations in weekly demand, what are the advantages of exponential smoothing or moving averages for forecasting?
3. The longer the time period covered by a demand forecast, the more aggregate these forecasts tend to be. Why?
4. In what detail and for what units does the POM of a cafeteria need daily forecasts? What about the POM of an airline? A ski lodge? A men's jewelry factory?
5. What are the effects of seasonal fluctuations in demand on production? How can they be handled in forecasting procedures?
6. Are dollar or unit forecasts better for production and inventory control? Why?
7. How is the need for short-range (i.e., less than a week into the future) forecasting changed when a process design improvement decreases the time needed to produce a product from 3 to 2 weeks?
8. A statistician from your corporate staff delightedly reports that he has discovered a very high coefficient of determination in the relationship between your monthly sales of baby strollers and traffic deaths on the Los Angeles Freeway. How do you respond?
9. Your company has developed a new home garbage compactor. Marketing forecasts annual sales of 10 thousand, 40 thousand, and 100 thousand units respectively for the next 3 years. As POM manager, what course of action are you going to take if there is a lead time of 8 months in acquiring and starting up production facilities? Why?
10. Company R has operated successfully for a number of years. They have recently been purchased by company T which wants to prepare various short- and long-range forecasts. Company R executives have complained about the waste of time involved, pointing to their successes in the past without forecasting procedures. Do you see any need for additional forecasts? Why?
11. Why is technological forecasting so difficult?

PROBLEMS

1. Use exponential smoothing and the data in the table to determine the uncomputed monthly forecasts. (The slots marked by X's.)

Year	Month	Actual Monthly Demand	Monthly Demand Forecast Using a Smoothing Factor of		
			= .2	= .5	= .8
'71	April	120	120	120	120
	May	140	X	X	X
	June	160	X	X	X
	July	110	X	X	X
	Aug.	120	X	X	X
	Sept.	110	X	X	X
	Oct.		X	X	X

(a) Plot the actual demand and each of the forecasts against time.

(b) Which of the smoothing factors works best in this problem
   (1) If the criterion is to minimize the sum of the absolute forecast deviations from actual demand?
   (2) If the criterion is to minimize the sum of the squared forecast deviations from the actual demand?

2. The Aqua Water Ski Company has asked you to forecast the demand for their Speed Pro Model skis for the second, third, and fourth quarters of 1971 and the first quarter of 1972. The data they supplied on past quarters unit demand of this model (a unit is one pair) is given in the following table.

Year	1	Quarter 2	3	4
1967–68	700	1400	1500	1100
1968–69	1100	1800	1900	1500
1969–70	1400	2200	2400	1800
1970–71	1900	—	—	—
1971–72	—			

Use the least squares regression line (quarter demand versus time) seasonally adjusted to help you in your forecast.

3. You are production control manager for the XYZ Machine Shop which has just received a large order for widgets from a major customer. Since most parts made in the shop can be used in several different products, your new policy is to produce parts in lot sizes based on

annual demand. Prepare a forecast of 1972 demand for parts *A, B, C*, and *D* based on the following data:

Year	Widget Industry Sales	Index of Goods Manu- factured	Part A	Demand at XYZ Part B	Part C	Part D
1967	100	1.05	6600	5350	2500	7100
1968	103	1.21	6450	5600	2200	8200
1969	112	1.26	6800	5700	1800	9100
1970	104	1.35	7025	6200	1750	9800
1971	116	1.47	6940	6500	1400	10400
1972	120*	1.56*	?	?	?	?

* Estimated

4. What is the coefficient of determination or r^2 between XYZ Machine Shop's data on widget industry sales and the index of goods manufactured?

CASE: EVANDER MARINE AND SPORTS CENTER

On January 1, 1969, Mr. Harold Burkhart of Evander, S.C., opened his new Evander Marine and Sports Center. The Center sold boats, motors, go-carts, minibikes, tape players, sporting goods, guns, ammunition, and marine accessories. The business had grown rapidly. 1969 net sales were $193,000, growing to $279,000 in 1970.

Mr. Burkhart felt that the Center could continue to grow rapidly for a number of years. Evander was a county seat with a population of only 15,000, but it was located only 12 miles from a large navigable lake and less than 50 miles from the Atlantic Ocean. The Center held the exclusive franchise in the four county area, including the lake, for one of the county's most famous lines of motors and boats. Sales in 1969 had been held down by supplier strikes and by diversions of boats and motors to Vietnam, but deliveries were satisfactory during 1970. Boats and motors accounted for 72 percent of these sales but were highly seasonal. Table 13-5 shows 1970 sales by month.

Mr. Burkhart felt that he could increase his sales at least 50 percent with added display space for boats, and he could add sailboats and campers to his lines. But these would not solve the basic problem of seasonal business. "What we need," said Mr. Burkhart, "is a fill-in line of merchandise which would help us get through the months when we aren't selling many boats and motors." Sixty-six percent of the marine sales occurred in March through July. The Center had carried a prime line of motorcycles for 6

Table 13-5 *Total sales by the month*

January	$ 15,678
February	19,109
March	35,319
April	36,594
May	50,036
June	36,021
July	24,679
August	14,707
September	19,753
October	4,983
November	9,744
December	12,307
	$278,930

months, but they had not proved profitable and did not fit well with the other lines.

Mr. Burkhart did feel that if he rented an empty building next door, he might be able to use the extra space and his displayroom during the off-season to store up to 50 boats. If he could get $10 to $15 per month per boat, he felt that he could breakeven on the rental and handling costs. But sales were not the only forecasting problem.

"A repair shop is a necessary evil. Most businesses lose money on them, but it's necessary to have one in order to keep the customers happy," Mr. Burkhart admitted. Table 13-6 shows the monthly billings of the repair department in 1970.

Table 13-6 *Repair shop volume*

	Labor	Parts	Total
January	$ 517.37	$ 298.69	$ 816.06
February	517.00	647.77	1,164.77
March	817.35	1,106.44	1,923.79
April	1,150.85	901.21	2,052.06
May	422.97	281.80	703.77
June	934.48	889.25	1,823.73
July	498.18	317.81	815.99
August	1,121.18	956.17	2,077.35
September	891.75	793.42	1,685.17
October	341.50	547.10	888.60
November	351.87	528.67	880.54
December	358.25	212.23	570.48
	$7,922.75	$7,480.56	$15,403.31

chapter
AGGREGATE SCHEDULING
fourteen

Armed with a set of forecasts, POM groups can get down to the business of planning future operations. Exactly how long the forecasts and the resulting plans are to remain in force is a strategic decision. These plans could hold until the company's capital spending activities change its capacity, but they certainly shouldn't outrun management's ability to forecast with adequate reliability. For the most part, these plans, also called "aggregate schedules," commit the company to a level of activity for 2 to 12 months, depending on processing times and the frequency with which revised forecasts and plans are drawn up.

COST FACTORS

There are major costs associated with a given planned level of production and with changes in that level. This is why the planning decision is such an important one. It forms the POM framework within which all other activities go forward and sets the limits within which the company can react to

343

changes. At the same time, it allows the other groups to anticipate a relatively stable set of conditions toward which to plan their activities. Vacation schedules can be set up and maintenance shutdowns arranged in advance so that craftsmen and equipment can be available and ready to go. Much can be done to reduce the unfavorable effects of layoffs on the workers and the community, if adequate warning is given. Also the personnel department can do a much better job of finding and training new workers when it has time to do its job. The accounting and financial departments will prepare budgets and cash flow projections on the basis of this plan. These budgets are top management's way of holding POM and marketing to that plan.

RESPONSES

In developing a production plan, there are a number of methods of adjusting the aggregate schedule so that it provides the amount *and* balance of capacity needed to meet the anticipated demands. They are listed below:

1. Making versus buying
2. Cross-training of personnel and use of multipurpose equipment
3. Changes in workforce levels or composition
4. Overtime or short hours
5. Deferred preventive maintenance
6. Refusing business and contribution pricing
7. Adjustments in backlog levels
8. Adjustments in inventory levels
9. Modifying the length of production runs
10. Product modification
11. Process modification
12. Dispatching and short-run scheduling

MAKE OR BUY

You have probably encountered this approach previously. A company often can find another firm willing to take some of the overflow of work. This usually involves a higher cost per unit of output to compensate the subcontractor for his overhead, profits, and greater variability of demand, but it meets the customer's needs without introducing him to a current competitor. This method, however, is least reliable when it is needed most. A need for greater capacity often is associated with a general improvement in economic conditions or at least in total industry demand. At this time, the potential subcontractors will also tend to have their hands full and may even be looking for supplementary capacity too. So subcontracting becomes most expensive and least flexible when it is needed most.

CROSS-TRAINING

All products and services that a company provides are not necessarily in peak demand at the same time. If workers are trained to shift from one product line to another and the equipment also is multipurpose, they can be moved from product to product in response to demand. Here again, however, this approach is least helpful in periods of general economic strength when overall need is greatest. This is precisely when all product lines are likely to boom at once. The costs incurred in using this response are the time and effort invested in training workers for multiple jobs which they perform only occasionally and the substantially lower labor efficiencies from changing jobs.

WORKFORCE AND HOURS CHANGES

When management science specialists study the aggregate scheduling problem, they often emphasize the cost related to the changes in labor force, in working hours, and in inventory and backlog levels. These are the usual means for adjusting production levels in industries with seasonal fluctuations, business cycles, or marked changes in competitive position. All these are of interest to the economist as well as the manager, because the method of response can either dampen or accentuate the economic swings involved. Inventory levels, employment rates, and hours of work are all topics of government and social interest.

Costs of hours changes. The most frequently used method of increasing capacity is overtime operation. American companies tend to operate 8 to 9 hours on a shift but with time off for lunch, coffee breaks, and shift changes. If more output is needed, the process can be operated on Saturdays or on extended hours on weekdays when third shifts are not scheduled. Federal law requires that workers be paid time-and-a-half for all hours per week over 40, and union contracts and company policy sometimes have extended this premium to all hours above a scheduled work week of 35 or 37½ hours too. This 50 percent premium does not, however, represent the full added cost of overtime. Productivity generally is not high during overtime hours due to the fatigue of long days and a lack of motivation on Saturdays. On the other hand, the 50 percent premium paid the worker is not accompanied by a corresponding increase in fringe benefits, which usually are equal to about 25 percent of the direct hourly wage. Social security premiums are not assessed against the employer once total annual income passes a given level; and medical, welfare, and pension insurance benefits are based on man-months worked or straight time earnings. When the alternative to overtime is the hiring and training of new workers and providing new machines for them, that 50 percent premium is not a particularly large penalty. In industries where a union contract guarantees the workers full employment or at least most of their annual income, the overtime alternative looks far preferable to adding workers who might have to be laid off again in the near future. Companies, however, avoid offering steady overtime over any lengthy period. Workers get accustomed to the higher standard of living quickly and find it hard to adjust to the loss when they return to regular hours. This leads to unrest and strong pressures for wage increases. Long hours also tend to build up cumulative fatigue and a backlog of personal errands and seem to lead to more accidents, illness, and absenteeism.

Costs of employment changes. Adding workers to the payroll also leads to new costs. New men must be recruited and trained to take over the lower classified jobs. Then the older employees must be retrained to fill the more skilled positions opening up. In many plants, the workers are able to request the new jobs on the basis of seniority. This is the "bidding" procedure found in many labor-management contracts. If the company opens up an added position for a welder B in labor grade 5, any man who thinks he has the welding skills to meet the minimum job requirement can sign up on the announcement sheet on the official bulletin board. This is his formal request for the job. The man meeting the minimum skills and having the highest seniority gets the job. In practice, this often amounts to giving it to the highest seniority man in labor grade 4 and showing him what to do, rather than arguing about his qualifications. If the man who gets the welder's job is a punch press operator, then that press job is available for someone else to bid on, and so it continues until a new man comes on the payroll as a sweeper or laborer. Obviously, the sequence of job changes upsets the efficiency of the whole operation and makes management think twice about frequent additions of a worker or two. It seems better to plan a little farther ahead and get all of the changes in personnel made at once, so things will run along smoothly for a while. Where seniority governs layoff, the situation can be even more chaotic. If the welder B post is eliminated, that man looks around for someone with less seniority to "bump." If he can meet the minimum requirements, he can claim any job in the shop held by a man with less seniority. Then the next man looks around for someone else with the next best job and bumps him out of it. Several changes may take place even before anyone is moved out of labor grade 5. The changes finally get down to the man with least seniority who is actually the one who becomes unemployed. The net result is a large number of switches in jobs and the continual buffeting about of the new entrants into the labor force, generally the young and the recently trained minority group workers.

Employment stability and morale. Bumping and guaranteed annual wages are not the only reasons that employers wish to avoid layoffs if possible. Each trained worker represents an investment in training and skills that will be lost if he finds work elsewhere. To the worker, the unemployment benefits are part of the Social Security package, but they are administered differently from the company's point of view. Employer payments are more like insurance premiums for casualty losses. Those who represent the highest risks pay the highest premiums. Once an employer has a number of layoffs, his premium rate rises markedly and stays that way for several years. Employers also value the loyalty and high morale of employees. One of the best ways to build these is to offer the security of steady employment. In fact, many companies have policies that call for steady employment despite the cost of that policy. Partly, they believe that it will pay off in the long run; and partly, they wish to have their good name associated with that kind of organization. When the chips are down and losses are incurred, that well-intended policy must fall. But employment often can be reduced without formal layoffs. There is the normal turnover or attrition among employees, and as people leave, they may not be replaced. It also is possible to suggest to some people that everyone would be happier if they sought employment elsewhere. As the backlog gets smaller and smaller and inventory higher, the smarter employees will often see the handwriting on the wall and find someplace else to work, often someplace better. The unfortunate aspect of this from the company's viewpoint is that often the more perceptive employees are the ones to leave first.

The cumulative effects of employment ups and downs also determine over time the quality of labor available to the company and the prestige of its managers in the community. Word gets around about a firm as a place to work. If it offers security as well as good wages and challenging work, it will have its pick of the people in the area. If it earns a poor reputation, it will be the last stop on everyone's search for work.

A short-run alternative to layoffs on any large scale are shorter work weeks or idle time. The latter means that the company absorbs the cost of paying a man to do nothing. This is the only alternative to layoff unless the lack of work is widespread. Then, it may be possible to put a whole department and facility on a shortened work week, usually 4 days. This will work well if it can be applied impartially to all employees and where group solidarity is high. Before long, however, the skilled workers will leave for a firm that can offer a better income, and they may not return when demand improves.

DEFERRED MAINTENANCE

In periods of high demand, it is possible to keep the machinery running longer by not shutting it down as scheduled. Underloads also will allow the company to consider shutdowns earlier than originally scheduled. The flexibility gained from this device generally is neither repeatable nor long lasting.

REFUSING BUSINESS OR REDUCING SERVICE

Certainly there is no law of business that says that the company cannot decline an order when its capacity has been filled. The airlines do this and so does the dentist. Yet, this act usually sticks in the businessman's craw. He works hard to gain customers and service them, and he hates to see them turned over to a competitor. If capacity is short throughout his industry, he will be able to lengthen his delivery promises, and the customer, knowing the situation, will have to wait or pay the extra costs of overtime or subcontracting. The supplier then adds the order to the "backlog" of work and performs it in turn. Working off a substantial backlog is a desirable situation for the producer, if he can remain competitive on delivery. He is minimizing his finished goods inventory and has greater flexibility in selecting orders to fill in the gaps in his schedule. This gives better utilization of men and equipment, but it means poor delivery service, something which is acceptable only if no major competitor offers much better delivery at comparable price and quality levels.

ADJUSTMENTS IN BACKLOG LEVELS

Some industries operate only off a backlog, maintaining no finished goods inventories. In fact, one can think of an inventory as a negative backlog or a backlog as a negative inventory. Manufacturers of heavy capital equipment especially tend to operate that way. Their business is subject to great swings of demand based on business expectations and the firms cannot afford to carry enough capacity to meet peak demands. Secondly, the specifications for the equipment tend to vary from order to order on the basis of advances in technology and of changing applications and product designs. There is little payoff in stocking an assembled machine only to find that the customer wants ten or fifteen things done slightly differently to take advantage of what he has learned from using an earlier machine.

ADJUSTMENTS IN INVENTORY LEVELS

This does not mean, however, that the manufacturer cannot stock the more commonly used parts and have them ready for assembly at any time. The effect of the stock of parts is to allow the manufacturer to store up hours of labor and machine time during low periods and relieve the congestion in the shop during peak loads. The special parts that are needed to complete the machine will still have to go all the way through the production cycle, but they will not have to compete with all the standard parts for machine time. Delivery would be shorter. Even that reduction in delivery time could be short-lived. It will bring in an increased share of the demand and greater workloads until the delivery of the company is more nearly like that of its competitors. The net effort, however, would be a substantially increased share of the market over the total business cycle.

Where the POM group can see an increase in demand coming, a seasonal peak for example, then it often is feasible to go to a higher level of operations immediately and store up the capacity in the form of inventory. Here the effect is to increase capacity, but it comes at the costs and risks of building the inventory. The costs are related primarily to the opportunity costs of the capital invested and the risks to the obsolescence and shrinkage that accompany the holding of inventory for any length of time. Much of the discussion which follows is really predicated on the problems of a business with seasonal ups and downs. There are several alternative ways of meeting these swings that are almost sure to come, even though their amplitude is relatively uncertain.

CHANGING PRICE LEVELS

To keep his men busy or avoid the embarrassment of turning down orders, the supplier also can manipulate prices, especially on heavy capital goods where individual price quotations are offered subject to negotiation. If you have mastered the appendix on linear programming, you are familiar with the method for calculating "shadow prices" or opportunity costs for each unit of capacity and for a specific unit of product. The businessman who deals in units whose prices vary from order to order can move his prices up and down to reflect conditions in his shop. When demand is high, he can raise prices to increase his total contribution, and in the low periods, he can lower his prices toward variable costs to hold his workforce together and keep work coming in to cover portions of his overhead. The increased price levels also represent a more graceful way of turning away customers who are not the firm's supporters during lean times and still keep the door open for negotiations leading to an eventual longer-term buyer-seller relationship.

MODIFYING PRODUCTION LOT SIZES

In the chapter on inventory control, you will learn the importance of the selection of the correct quantities for production lots. These choices are important because they determine in large part the average level of inventory investments and the amount of the firm's capacity and manpower that is devoted to the nonproductive activity of setting up or changing over equipment from one production run to another. Normally, the POM group would prefer to have the longest possible runs because increased length tends to increase the ratio of production running time to nonproductive setup time. However, if men sit idle anyway for lack of work, there is no incremental cost to these setups. One could then afford to reduce lot sizes. Reducing the lot sizes reduces inventory investment and the costs related thereto. During boom periods, the manufacturer would like to increase his runs to utilize scarce men and machines most effectively. This is doable up to a point, but then the large runs begin to clog an already overloaded shop and contribute to the lengthening backlog. More often than not, the response to a capacity limitation accompanied by missed delivery promises is a reduction in the length of the manufacturing runs and a net loss of capacity due to more setups.

REVISIONS TO PRODUCT OR PROCESS

Where the problem of capacity is related to the imbalance of facilities, it is possible for manufacturing engineering personnel to make revisions in the product design or the process routing, so that a number of orders can be steered around the bottlenecked equipment, reducing the potential backlog and improving deliveries. This approach sounds nice in theory but is seldom practiced. The manufacturing engineering group is a processing center with its own concepts of efficiency and capacity constraints. The redesign or redevelopment of an alternative production routing is something that is seldom done. People who study the problems of scheduling talk about alternative routings as if they were commonly used, but POM procedures call for selection of one "best" routing at the time the order is first processed. Developing more than one would be a waste of time until there is evidence of a need for a specific alternative routing based on current shop load. A typical order is out on the shop floor for several weeks before someone discovers it hasn't been coming through the process. It finally is discovered in a queue of orders behind the overtaxed machine. This is the first time that anyone has data to justify the investment in a new routing. By that time, it is really too late to do anything about that order and who knows where the bottleneck will be if and when the reorder comes through next time? As more and more companies become willing and able to use the computer to simulate the movement of orders through the shop and this technique proves effective in forecasting bottlenecks before the order is entered, then the preparation of alternate routings will become a more reasonable response.

DISPATCHING AND SHORT-RUN SCHEDULING

In a later chapter, you will look at the alternatives for scheduling and dispatching work through the process. The selection of the relevant objective and the corresponding decision rules can contribute considerably to the ability of the production/operations management system to meet shifting capacity requirements. Even though the planning horizon for individual scheduling decisions may be a week to only a few hours, a change in decision rules can have considerable cumulative effect on capacity over the longer planning periods associated with aggregate scheduling.

ONE ANALYTIC APPROACH TO AGGREGATE SCHEDULING

The section above has identified the aggregate scheduling or planning problem, the alternatives open to POM, and the costs and benefits associated with each one. Next comes the task of putting together an objective function, a single cost picture that relates these costs to one another. Once this has been done, the analyst can study the tradeoffs involved and recommend modes of operation that are at or near the lowest cost point. Management can take it from there, adding the nonquantitative factors and validating, i.e., double checking the suggestions against their experiences with similar situations in the past.

The objective function for evaluating aggregate scheduling is not well behaved like the ones in the exercises on linear programming exercises in Appendix 1. The costs involved are not direct outputs of the accounting system; the relationships are only tentatively understood; and the tradeoffs are multiple and complex. There is a virtually infinite number of alternatives available from a steady level output rate to a rate which varies with every order that comes in. Somewhere between these two there exists a good policy for the firm to follow. Table 14-1 lists the costs involved in changing

Table 14-1 *Cost items involved in changing production levels (workforce and rate)*

Costs of Increased Levels	Costs of Decreased Levels

1. Employment and Training:
  (a) Interviews and selection.
  (b) New personnel records, physical examinations, payroll setup.
  (c) Training new workers.
2. Service and Staff Functions:
  (a) Production and inventory control.
  (b) Purchasing, receiving, inspection, and materials handling.
3. Added Shifts:
  (a) Supervision.
  (b) Shift premium.
4. Overtime costs related to the increase level.
	1. Unemployment compensation insurance.
	2. Contributions to union funds.
	3. Costs of employee transfer and retraining.
	4. Intangible effects on public relations.
	5. Production and inventory costs of revising schedules, order points, etc.
	6. Idle time costs due to lags in decisions and action.

Taken from Buffa, *Production-Inventory Systems*, Figure 5.5, p. 127.

production levels. These all could be included in the objective function, but they are usually regrouped into the simple factors that are included in the following equation; total costs for a production level per period (one period, one product) = straight time costs + overtime costs + costs of decreasing capacity + costs of increasing capacity.

If we define some terms, however, we can examine some simple constraints and develop an objective function.

Let

c_1 = marginal costs of production of a unit on regular time
p = number of units produced on regular time
c_2 = marginal costs of production of a unit on overtime
ϕ = number of units produced on overtime
c_3 = marginal costs of adding one unit of production capacity
u = number of units of production capacity added
c_4 = marginal cost of dropping one unit of production capacity
v = number of units of production capacity dropped
d = demand for the period in units
s = capacity of production system in units at start of the period
r = the ratio of maximum overtime capacity in units to straight time capacity

SIMPLE ASSUMPTIONS

This is the simplest formulation of the problem based on the assumption that output is not carried over from period to period. As we look carefully, we see that certain constraints would logically follow. The number of overtime units would be confined to a range between zero and a specified limiting percentage of the straight time output. If we identify r as that maximum ratio of overtime to straight time, we have an initial linear constraint on the system. The increased cost of overtime will lead the decision-maker to avoid any overtime until the straight time has been used. If one has a policy that overtime will not be used beyond 10 hours per week and straight time hours are 40, then $r = .25$ and the constraint becomes $\phi \leq .25s$. The objective would be to minimize $c_1 p + c_2 \phi + c_3 u + c_4 v$. As you may have surmised, we are heading gradually toward a linear programming formulation for the selection of an aggregate schedule. The pedagogical purpose of taking up the LP, linear programming, method at this point is to further illustrate the problem and its structure.

AN LP FORMULATION

The linear programming formulation should provide as much production as possible on regular time before any of the other more costly changes are made. The formulation also should recognize some overall capacity constraints in effect at the beginning of the period. This takes the form:

$$p \leq s \quad \text{and} \quad p + \phi \leq (1 + r)s$$

Now one can add the effects of the changes in capacity to the formulation of the problem. When would the manager choose to add to his capacity? Well, he would add overtime when overtime costs less than adding capacity (when $c_2 < c_3$) and capacity when $c_2 > c_3$ or when $p + \phi = (1 + r)s$ (when output has reached overtime capacity). If $p < s$ (i.e., output equal to demand is below capacity), then he would make no change when $c_1 < c_4$ (idle labor costs are below the costs of dropping capacity) and he would drop capacity when $c_1 > c_4$ (vice versa). No linear programming analysis is required, and the decision rules are clear-cut. The one-period problem is trivial and too simple to be realistic.

If a manager looks ahead to next year and sees that he must add capacity in the third quarter to meet his needs, just after he has cut back in the second quarter, he hopes that there are better alternatives. Why not make some inventory in the second quarter and then ship it out during the third? The holding costs would be incurred for only a quarter of a year. That makes sense, but as so often happens, it will expand the complexity of the model immensely. Look at the example of a company with the forecast demand shown in Table 14-2.

AN EXAMPLE

Table 14-2 reflects several problems of fitting any plan to the real world. Most companies manufacture several products. They also have month-to-month fluctuations in both demand and output. The two must be compared, and this requires use of a common denominator for capacity. Direct labor hours, usually standard hours developed by the industrial engineers, are the common choice. No one knows for sure how long a job will take, but in an organization with accurate standards, standard labor hours should provide an adequate estimate. If they do not, then the whole exercise is rather futile. Demands for each product are forecast and monthly demands translated into standard labor hours. These are indicators of the output rates needed to meet the monthly demands. They are not really the true rates required because a production lead time requirement dictates that the buildup precede the increased output. In a business with a 13-week production cycle, the plant must start responding to April demand in January, not in April.

USE CUMULATIVE FIGURES

In order to avoid this month-by-month compartmentalization of planning and to dampen out the psychological effects of large monthly variations,

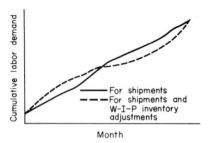

Figure 14-1   *Cumulative graph of labor demand forecast in Table 14-2*

the standard procedure is to express aggregate production requirements graphically as a cumulative figure. Figure 14-1 is a cumulative graph of the demand shown in Table 14-2.

This is not enough, for Table 14-2 includes three other gentle reminders of the problems of real life. As output increases, work-in-process inventories will have to rise correspondingly. This W-I-P inventory will contain productive hours that won't be shipped immediately. This W-I-P inventory change, therefore, means even greater production variations are needed to meet demand changes because it takes up more capacity in periods of rising demand and releases more during economic slowdown. The dotted line in Figure 14-1 reflects adjustments for work-in-process or "buffer" inventory requirements. Then there is the fact that each month does not contain the same number of working hours. The natural variation is due to the length

Table 14-2   *Production requirements in thousands of man-hours*

Month	Expected Demand	Cumulative Demand	Required Buffer Stocks (W-I-P)	Production Days	Cumulative Days
Jan.	700	700	300	22	22
Feb.	900	1,600	340	18	40
Mar.	1,100	2,700	375	22	62
Apr.	900	3,600	340	21	83
May	650	4,250	290	22	105
June	600	4,850	275	21	126
July	550	5,400	265	21	147
Aug.	400	5,800	230	13	160
Sept.	400	6,200	230	20	180
Oct.	400	6,600	230	23	203
Nov.	500	7,100	255	21	224
Dec.	600	7,700	275	20	244

of the month, the number of weekends, and the placement of holidays. Furthermore, the schedule indicates that an August vacation shutdown has to be allowed for. Any work due out in late August or early September must be virtually complete by the end of July.

Now the manager can begin to see the cumulative daily output rates needed to meet each month's requirements. If, for example, he is to meet the first quarter needs of 2,700 thousand man-hours shown in Table 14-2 without reducing finished goods inventories and increase buffer stocks by 75 thousand, then he must produce at the rate of 45 thousand standard labor hours per day. By October 1, under the same rules, he will have had to produce 6,200 less 70 or 6,130 thousand man-hours in 180 working days, or an average of 34.1 thousand per day. For the year as a whole, he will have to produce 7,675 thousand in 244 working days, or 31.5 thousand per day. These three calculations would be represented by the alternative straight "production" lines in Figure 14-2. The differences between these production plans and the adjusted demand lines can be interpreted as follows: if the cumulative production line is above the cumulative demand line, the difference represents a buildup in inventories or a reduction in the backlog. Where the cumulative production line is below the cumulative demand line, there is either an increase in the backlog or a reduction in inventories. Any useful model will have to allow for major swings in inventories.

If the firm whose estimates are outlined in Figure 14-1 is in a seasonal business, then planning for the fourth quarter cannot go forward in a vacuum. It will depend in large part on the forecast for the quarters which follow. If this firm does not already have a substantial inventory on hand in anticipa-

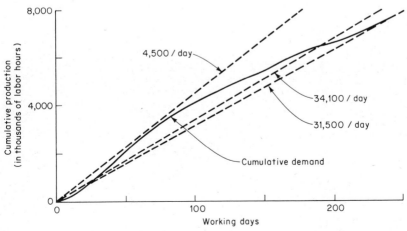

Figure 14-2 *Graphic representation of several production plans*

tion of the first 3 months of the next year, it is headed for a repeat of the serious problems of production smoothing that we saw in the first quarter of the coming year. The most critical forecast of the cycle is the one for a year ahead starting in April or May. Figure 14-2 illustrates that as much as a 50 percent change in required daily production rates may be necessary unless an inventory buildup starts during the summer months from a production plan determined by the late spring.

AN EXPANDED MODEL

To compare these costs and determine the desired level of operation from quarter to quarter, it is necessary to revise the analytical models presented above to allow for these alternatives. In the first quarter, it is possible to produce goods to be shipped in each of the four quarters. In the second period, there would be three alternative times of sale, if one adopts the simplifying assumption that there can be no carryover into the following year. For the third period, there would be two opportunities and for the fourth only one. That restriction is most unreal, but it is offset somewhat by the fact that the fourth quarter for this plan would be the third quarter 3 months hence and the second quarter 6 months from now, assuming quarterly replanning. But in a highly seasonal business, this could be a dangerous assumption, since an inventory buildup period of 9 months might be required for products such as Christmas toys or calendars. Really the only justification for such a cutoff rule is the difficulty imposed by the degrees of complexity that occur as more and more periods are linked together.

Objective function. Remember that the one period case provided the formula

$$c_1 p + c_2 \phi + c_3 u + c_4 v$$

In a four-period model, this four-term objective function expands as follows: $c_1 p$ becomes

$$c_1 p_{11} + c_5 p_{12} + c_6 p_{13} + c_7 p_{14} + c_1 p_{22} + c_5 p_{23} + c_6 p_{24} + c_1 p_{33} \\ + c_5 p_{34} + c_1 p_{44}$$

where

c_1 = marginal costs of production of a unit on regular time

p_{ij} = number of units produced on regular time in the ith period for sale in the jth period

$c_5 = c_1 +$ marginal cost of holding a unit until sold one quarter hence

$c_6 = c_1 +$ marginal cost of holding a unit until sold two quarters hence

$c_7 = c_1 +$ marginal cost of holding a unit until sold three quarters hence

$c_2\phi$ becomes

$$c_2\phi_{11} + c_8\phi_{12} + c_9\phi_{13} + c_{10}\phi_{14} + c_2\phi_{22} + c_8\phi_{23} + c_9\phi_{24} + c_2\phi_{33} + c_8\phi_{34} + c_2\phi_{44}$$

where

$c_2 =$ marginal costs of production of a unit on overtime

$\phi_{ij} =$ number of units produced on overtime in period i for sale in period j

$c_8 = c_5 + c_2$

$c_9 = c_6 + c_2$

$c_{10} = c_7 + c_2$

$c_3 u$ becomes

$$c_3 u_1 + c_3 u_2 + c_3 u_3 + c_3 u_4$$

where

$c_3 =$ marginal cost of adding one unit of product capacity

$u_i =$ number of units of capacity added in the ith period

$c_4 v$ becomes

$$c_4 v_1 + c_4 v_2 + c_4 v_3 + c_4 v_4$$

where

$c_4 =$ marginal cost of reducing one unit of product capacity

$v_i =$ number of units of capacity dropped in the ith period

The objective function has expanded from four terms to twenty-eight, and there is a corresponding increase in the number of constraints and their complexity. To see that demand was met, one would have to replace $d = p + \phi$ by

$$d_1 = p_{11} + \phi_{11}$$
$$d_2 = p_{22} + \phi_{22} + p_{12} + \phi_{12}$$
$$d_3 = p_{33} + \phi_{33} + p_{13} + \phi_{13} + p_{23} + \phi_{23}$$
$$d_4 = p_{44} + \phi_{44} + p_{14} + \phi_{14} + p_{24} + \phi_{24} + p_{34} + \phi_{34}$$

Constraining equations. The changes in capacity could be related by a new set of constraint equations:

$$p_{11} + p_{12} + p_{13} + p_{14} \leq u_1 - v_1 + s$$
$$p_{22} + p_{23} + p_{24} \leq u_1 + u_2 - v_1 - v_2 + s$$
$$p_{33} + p_{34} \leq u_1 + u_2 + u_3 - v_1 - v_2 - v_3 + s$$
$$p_{44} \leq u_1 + u_2 + u_3 + u_4 - v_1 - v_2 - v_3 - v_4 + s$$

where

s = capacity of the production system in units at start of first period. The constraints on overtime would be expressed as:

$$\phi_{11} + \phi_{12} + \phi_{13} + \phi_{14} \leq r(p_{11} + p_{12} + p_{13} + p_{14})$$
$$\phi_{22} + \phi_{23} + \phi_{24} \leq r(p_{22} + p_{23} + p_{24})$$
$$\phi_{33} + \phi_{34} \leq r(p_{33} + p_{34})$$
$$\phi_{44} \leq r(p_{44})$$

What was a set of three constraints has grown to twelve, and it still is only a quarterly model that ends abruptly, treats the whole product line as one, treats the firm as one facility, and assumes linearity. Why bother with it? There are two major reasons. It is a formulation that allows you to reach an analytic solution through the use of linear programming. Within the accuracy of the assumptions, you can arrive at an answer using the skills that have been acquired in Appendix 1. The matrix would look huge, with its twenty-eight variables, but it is solvable with currently available computer codes. If you have such a program available to you, you can use these equations to answer question 3 at the back of this chapter. Thus, you can see a situation where LP was occasionally applied, but beyond illustrating use, there is a second pedagogical point. This has been a relatively simple problem which illustrates the rapid rate at which an analytical solution expands in complexity in any combinatorial situation, especially when you really try to give the manager the answer he wants. If he makes ten or twelve different products, each with a different capacity requirement in several manufacturing departments and if total, as well as departmental, constraints on workforce and machine capacities are taken into account, you can realize the difficulties of approaching an "optimal" solution. This is why most companies have not adopted this technique; but with increasing computer capabilities, management sophistication, and familiarity with the strengths and weaknesses of the available approaches, acceptance will increase. In addition to linear programming, there are approaches based on dynamic programming and on heuristic rules, i.e., effective rules-of-thumb for production planning.

SIMPLE APPROACHES FOR SMOOTHING EMPLOYMENT

There are powerful reasons, economic and humanitarian, for wishing to maintain a level rate of production. How does one evaluate ways of smoothing production without a major analytical investment in models? There are several simple steps that can give first approximations of the effects of production smoothing policies, although much spadework must be done.

The first step might be a graphical one similar to that illustrated in Table 14-2 and Figure 14-1. A forecast would have to be made of demand month-by-month and a cumulative tabulation prepared. Cumulative output lines representing policies being seriously considered would be drawn and compared against the sales figures which have been altered to reflect inventory adjustments. This will tell the story of the monthly shortages or excesses. Table 14-3 illustrates three programs aimed at leveling the rate of production and reducing the number of changes in employment levels. Plan A calls for level production through the year at the average requirement level of 31,455 units per day. This program eliminates all but the initial employment level change for at least a year. It may tend to reduce workforce change costs substantially, but by April, it leads to an inventory deficit of over a million units and total monthly inventory shortages of over 6 million units unless there was a large starting inventory. Plan B calls for two levels of production, a high rate of 43,855 units during the busy first 4 months and a lower 25,065 units during the final 8 months. This markedly reduces the inventory shortages, but it leads to a 43 percent production rate drop. Plan C calls for a somewhat smaller peak output rate of 40,380 units per days over the first 5 months and 24,714 during the last 7 months. Plan B follows demand quite closely, but it might completely outstrip the constraints on capacity forcing one to adopt something more like plan C and to accept the inevitable loss due to some shortages.

Numerous other plans might be tried as well. Which one is selected will depend on the actual cost structure of the firm including those assigned for this purpose to inventory shortages, inventory storage costs, and costs of workforce changes in either direction. One of the assumptions of the linear programming formulation presented earlier in this chapter was that the costs of actions such as labor force changes are uniform regardless of the magnitude of the change. This may not be the case. As one approaches capacity, costs may rise rapidly; changes of more than a certain percentage of the workforce may lead to catastrophic reductions in productivity, and a company can drown in a flood of inventory. This is why a number of other approaches have been proposed using nonlinear cost functions or special cost structures which simulate more closely those of a specific firm.

Table 14-3 Examples of three comparative workforce leveling strategies (1,000 units)

Month	Expected Demand	W-I-P* Invent. Adjust.	Cum. Need	Cum. Prod. Level (31.445/day)	Net Gain or Loss	Cum. Prod. Level (43.855/day) / (25.065/day)	Net Gain or Loss	Cum. Prod. Level (40.38/day) / (24.714/day)	Net Gain or Loss
Prev. Dec.	700	None	700						
Jan.	700	None	700	692	− 8	798	+ 89	726	+ 26
Feb.	900	+40	1,640	1,258	− 292	1,745	+ 105	1,615	− 25
Mar.	1,100	+35	2,775	1,950	− 825	2,719	− 56	2,504	− 271
Apr.	900	−35	3,640	2,611	− 1,029	3,640	None	3,351	− 289
May	650	−50	4,240	3,303	− 937	4,191	− 49	4,240	None
June	600	−15	4,825	3,963	− 862	4,718	− 107	4,759	− 66
July	550	−10	5,365	4,624	− 741	5,244	− 121	5,279	− 86
Aug.	400	−35	5,730	5,033	− 697	5,570	− 160	5,599	− 131
Sept.	400	None	6,130	5,662	− 468	6,071	− 59	6,104	− 26
Oct.	400	None	6,530	6,385	− 145	6,648	+ 118	6,662	+ 132
Nov.	500	+25	7,055	7,046	− 9	7,174	+ 119	7,181	+ 126
Dec.	600	+20	7,675	7,675	None	7,675	None	7,675	None
Cum. Invent.									
Shortages					−6,013		−551		−932
Overages					+None		+431		+284
Size of Capacity Shifts Needed After the Initial One					None		18.8/day		15.7/day

*Based on estimates from Production Control Department.

360

SENSITIVITY TO SEASONALITY

One word of caution! The choice of plan can be quite sensitive to the selection of the beginning and ending dates of the planning period if the business is highly seasonal. Table 14-4 shows a new version of plan A from Table 14-3. The same production level (31.445 thousand units per day) is maintained but evaluated over a year starting in May instead of January. This version shows a very large inventory buildup instead of the tremendous inventory shortages predicted in Table 14-3. Of course, the trick would be how to get from January to May without a tremendous swing in employment in order to meet that seasonal peak.

OTHER ANALYTICAL AND NOT-SO-ANALYTICAL APPROACHES

Trial and error approaches with actual costs naturally lead the analyst into a search for a systematic way of looking for better policies. A historically important approach was developed by Holt, Modigliani, Muth, and Simon of Carnegie-Mellon University. This is the "linear decision rule" in which

Table 14-4 *Program of level employment starting in May (thousands of units)*

Month	Requirements			Revised Plan A	
	Expected Demand	W-I-P Invent. Adjust.	Cum. Need	Cum. Prod. Level	Net Gain or Loss
May	650	−50	600	692	+ 92
June	600	−15	1,185	1,352	+ 167
July	550	−10	1,725	2,013	+ 288
Aug.	400	−35	2,090	2,422	+ 332
Sept.	400	None	2,490	3,051	+ 561
Oct.	400	None	2,890	3,774	+ 884
Nov.	500	+25	3,415	4,435	+1,020
Dec.	600	+20	4,035	5,064	+1,039
Jan.	700	+15	4,750	5,756	+1,006
Feb.	900	+25	5,675	6,322	+ 647
Mar.	1,100	+35	6,810	7,914	+ 204
Apr.	900	−35	7,675	7,675	None
Total Monthly Invent.					+6,240
Prod. Rate (31.455 units/day)					

the costs of changing workforce levels is approximated by a quadratic (U-shaped) function. Quadratic functions also are used to represent the overtime and undertime costs and inventory and shortage costs. These cost functions have two major advantages over the linear representation of the linear programming approach. They emphasize the idea that the farther one departs from normal operating and service levels, the greater the incremental cost per unit of deviation. These costs also can be differentiated easily to yield simple linear rules for determining workforce and production rates. They also do not depend on deterministic demand rates estimates. The linear decision rule approach, however, has the drawback of requiring a large number of estimated cost parameters.

E. H. Bowman of MIT has suggested that on the average the judgment of experienced managers in planning aggregate production levels is relatively good and reflects their knowledge of basic costs such as those of inventory shortages which are not available from accounting records. He believed that excess costs reflected the tendency of these same managers to respond too frequently to stimuli from their environment and to change production levels too often. Therefore, he suggested that the statistical study of past choices would lead to a simple formula for production planning reflecting true costs, which could be used to set a more measured response to the pressures to change production levels frequently. Bowman's method has been verified in practice and seems to yield improved results, but it is quite sensitive to the quality of the past judgments by management and to the assumption that the best fit of the historical data is to be achieved by a simple linear regression.

Yet another approach is the simulation of the operations of the firm on a computer followed by use of that simulation model to search out a good aggregate scheduling policy. Jones of Harvard has suggested a heuristic method for evaluating the simulation to come up with a simple pair of decision rules based on the setting of four parameters. While this does not promise an optimal result, it does allow the investigator to work with any cost structure that can be incorporated into the simulation. Taubert and Buffa of UCLA have suggested building into the simulation a routine to search the structure of the simulation, variable by variable, until an apparent best result Is reached.

Well beyond the scope of this book are methods of search for the optimal result using dynamic programming and control theory techniques. All these approaches hold considerable promise in the long run because of their adaptability to individual cost structures, uncertain demand, and their ability to deal with longer planning horizons. At present, however, they are more the province of the scholar than the individual manager or even his operations research staff. But the trend of the future, especially in aggregate scheduling, is reflected in this statement:

> At this point no single optimization technique can solve all mathematical models. This means that optimization is still, in reality, an art involving a careful match between technique and model. This match must be made skillfully, with constant concern for the fundamental fact that a solution to a model can be no better than the model itself. Consequently, the model builder faces the dilemma that the more complicated and realistic he makes the model, the lower his probability of finding the global optimum. In the past, this problem was so serious that the model builder had to restrict his attention to simple models that could be solved by analytic techniques. Today the computer has made possible many quasi-analytical and heuristic search techniques. These techniques have increased significantly the probability of finding the global optimum of a complex model and have placed before the model builder a very powerful set of mathematical tools.[1]

Buffa and Taubert have concentrated on heuristic search routines for an approximate answer to the aggregate scheduling problem. The trends they cite apply as well to the newer analytical approaches. Important improvements in this critical decision-making area are on the horizon.

QUESTIONS

1. Why are budgeting and production planning considered complementary activities?
2. Evaluate the following statement: "Long-range plans are just window-dressing. It is easier to be on your toes and ready for a change than to be wrong."
3. What are the forecasting requirements for planning production over a 2-year period at a Pascagoula, Miss., cat-food cannery? At a Le Sueur, Minn., pea packery? At Boy Scout headquarters in Washington, D.C.?
4. What impact would an aggregate schedule have upon an inventory control system?
5. Explain the pure economic arguments for avoiding layoffs of employees, using as examples Army lieutenant colonels during peacetime, nurses at a city hospital, and black welder-apprentices by a bridge building contractor.

[1] E. S. Buffa and W. H. Taubert, "Aggregate Production Planning," *Industrial Management Review* (Fall 1967), p. 21.

6. In an automobile plant, what are the factors to be considered by POM when deciding between extensive use of overtime and hiring more employees?

7. How does a manager decide whether or not to maintain a level rate of production with a seasonal demand for his product? How does he select the best starting point for his aggregate schedule?

8. As POM manager, you have to build up the finished goods inventory to 30 percent above normal in anticipation of a long strike. How do you go about reducing that inventory when the strike is avoided?

9. What are the strengths and weaknesses of a linear programming formulation for determining the desired aggregate plan?

10. In a firm with 50 employees, would it be better to hire 2 new production employees per month or 12 at once to meet increased demand?

11. If you face wide fluctuations in employment which seem unavoidable, what can you do to maintain your firm's reputation in the community?

PROBLEMS

1. The graph below shows how the cumulative demand for a given product for the coming year changes.

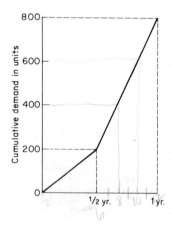

(a) If you want to maintain stable employment throughout the year and meet all demand, you should produce at what rate? What would be your maximum inventory?

(b) If you want to minimize inventory costs yet meet all demand, you should produce at what rate?

2. Prepare an annual production plan for the Halyard Rope Company which as of December 31 will have a workforce of 65 direct employees and an inventory of 4,000 units. Output per direct employee is esti-

mated at 1,000 units per direct employee per month. It is estimated that overtime manufacture costs $.30 additional per unit but is limited to 40 percent of the then current capacity. Inventory carrying cost is $.10 per unit per month. Management estimates that it costs the company $200 to hire and train a new direct employee and $600 when an employee is laid off. Marginal revenue per unit is $.12 per unit and management wishes to have the same inventory at the end of next year. Forecast monthly demands for next year are:

January	60,000	July	95,000
February	80,000	August	86,000
March	75,000	September	80,000
April	75,000	October	75,000
May	80,000	November	72,000
June	87,000	December	74,000

3. Set up a linear programming set of equations on a quarterly basis for Halyard Rope assuming that production is constrained by employees only.

CASE: EVANDER MARINE AND SPORTS CENTER

In addition to the forecasting problems outlined at the end of the preceding chapter, Mr. Burkhart realizes that he has corresponding problems in planning for the flow of goods and repair work through his operation. Looking back over what he considered to be a successful year in 1970, Mr. Burkhart commented, "We have too much money tied up in inventory. Here it is January 1, and we should have almost nothing in inventory. But I would venture to say that an accounting would show as much as $100,000 in inventory. One of the reasons for this excess is the fact that we order early and at odd times to get special discounts. Some companies offer as much as 8 percent, but with money up over 9 percent, much of this is lost in carrying the merchandise. There is no way to avoid a certain amount of this kind of buying, but I would like to cut down the size of our inventory." Table 14-5 lists the purchases month-by-month during 1970.

On the other hand, many items also could be received on a 2-day order cycle including most boats and motors. Of course, these rush shipments or trips to pick up boats increased operating costs and lost seasonal discounts. But they generally enabled the Center to get the customer what he wanted, and sales were seldom lost due to a customer unwilling to wait a day or two for delivery of a major item.

The repair department performed a lot of warranty work for the motor manufacturer, for which the Center was paid $8.50 per mechanic hour.

Table 14-5

	Boats and Motors	Parts	Other
January	$ 22,175.98	$ 1,042.01	$ 3,596.26
February	6,303.00	1,572.86	6,048.19
March	22,576.03	661.56	153.82
April	13,545.32	1,289.43	12,147.71
May	51,030.33	2,252.72	5,150.59
June	24,730.31	650.28	2,564.45
July	18,740.84	608.52	853.31
August	21,083.87	1,442.36	1,369.58
September	7,509.74	1,920.18	264.34
October	3,532.58	203.69	1,608.45
November	10,109.06	727.88	1,454.01
December	18,609.47	363.26	1,234.89
Totals	$219,946.53	$12,934.77	$36,445.60

TOTAL $269,326.90

But the payment was made on the basis of the time that the factory standards showed it should take for the repair. If the Center's mechanics were slower or inefficient, then the Center was not reimbursed for the excess time. There were three men in the repair department full time. Frank McGuire, the chief mechanic, received $175 per week, while the other repairmen, Tom Ribock and Hank Riker, each earned $125 per week.

Mr. Burkhart noted, "We have more work than we can take care of during our busy season, but there is slack at other times. It is necessary for us to keep three employees, so we will have them during the busy months. At least one man is on 24-hour call. The repair department is half our weekly payroll."

There had been three different chief mechanics since the business opened. Each head mechanic had to be factory trained with the Center paying travel and support expenses. All repairmen also were sent to a yearly refresher course in boat and motor repair.

chapter

INVENTORY CONTROL

fifteen

In Chapter 4, several ways of looking at the POM system were presented. These included identities called inventories, or stocks, or stored goods. In this chapter, these identities are discussed in more detail together with the means of planning and controlling them to the overall benefit of the organization. This includes dealing with them as the money account shown in Figure 4-7, at the interface between marketing and POM as in Figure 4-4, as a response to forces in the environment with respect to incoming labor and materials and outgoing products as in Figure 4-1, and as a cushion between components of the POM system as in Figures 4-2 and 4-3. Even though inventory occurs at different interfaces in the system, it frequently serves similar functions at each. This chapter will first deal with the inventory as a familiar balance sheet asset, then with the functions of inventory, with the ways of analyzing inventory policies, and finally, it will treat the methods of using these policies to make the system work smoothly and economically.

INVENTORY AS A MONEY STOCK

The balance sheets of most firms show three major working capital asset accounts: cash (and securities), accounts receivable, and inventories. Cash usually is the smallest of these. It can be put to work profitably elsewhere. Which of the remaining two is greatest depends on the nature of the marketing environment and the POM process. In some cases, the inventory account is the largest single asset account. Certainly then, management of this asset should be a major activity in the organization and one understood by all responsible managers. Yet it is one area where a great deal of misunderstanding and friction arises. Even the simple question of "How big should inventories be?" becomes complex because each functional manager has a very different point of view.[1] The production manager wants large work-in-process inventories to ease his scheduling task, while the sales manager wants large finished goods stocks to avoid disappointed customers. The problem is compounded further by the fact that inventory decisions often involve indirect or imputed costs not available directly from the cost accounting system and because specific stocks of material may at any instant be serving multiple purposes.

The first step to a rational set of inventory policies based on company-wide net benefits is to recognize that the inventory is not a single money stock but the summation of many separate investments—each with its own returns and purposes. The second step is acceptance of a working definition of the relevant costs and savings associated with each inventory activity. Accepting this as a way of evaluating inventory often means that the traditional stock turnover ratio of sales to inventory cannot be used as a measure of inventory management efficiency. Indeed, it will be shown that in some situations reduced turnover can actually increase overall efficiency. This is not to say that the turnover figure should not be computed. The discovery that competitors have a different ratio could indicate that they have developed different ways of going about their business which should be investigated. But the treasurer or controller who says that stock turnover is too low must take on the burden of proving exactly how a lower *total cost system* can be set up that will also produce a higher turnover.

The controller legitimately can challenge each incremental inventory investment on the grounds that it is an allocation of capital. The funds invested in a unit of raw materials must compete on a rate-of-return basis with new equipment, research and development projects, advertising campaigns, stockholder dividends, or a new carpet for the executive dining room. The objective then of most inventory investigations will be to show that

---

[1] John F. Magee, *Production Planning and Inventory Control* (New York: McGraw-Hill-Book Company, 1958), p. 5.

investments are being made only so long as they achieve a specified rate or that the rate actually achieved is the maximum for that investment. Generally, that rate can be improved either by reducing the amount of inventory used to perform a specific function or by achieving lower total costs by reallocating a fixed investment.

FUNCTIONS OF INVENTORY

To avoid the pitfalls of thinking of inventory as a single money stock, one has to develop a habit of looking at the functional contribution made by each inventory item. The inventory investments are relatively easy to identify. They are the piles of raw materials and finished goods in the warehouse. They are truckloads of breakfast cereal *en route* to grocery stores. They are patients waiting outside the doctor's office, seats on an airplane, spaces in the dormitory parking lot, and gasoline in the tank between pit stops at Indianapolis. The benefits are less obvious. To spot them one must look at the reasons why the inventory is of value or costs someone time and money when it isn't there. One has to look carefully at the functions that an inventory serves and how the quantity available and the administration of that quantity affects organizational performance. Function will relate to the position of a good or service in a given amount in time and space and its usefulness at that location at that time.

One way to establish the reasons for having inventories is to try to visualize a world in which there are no inventories. Without them the shoe store shelves would be bare when your loafers wear out. You would have to wait for the man to make what you want and need. Going back even further, he would have to wait until the tanner kills a cow, skins it, and tans the hide. Beyond that, the tanner would have to wait for the cow to grow, for that cow's mother to have a calf, for the . . . , etc. Obviously people don't wish to remain dependent on all these other processes and are willing to compensate merchants, processors, and farmers for supporting inventories of shoes, hides, cattle, calves, etc. These inventories give us freedom to time our activities more freely and plan them more efficiently. When they are not present in the right location in the right quantities, then those who rely on them become inconvenienced and often irked.

Yet what may be one man's convenience may be another man's inconvenience. The doctor's office is an example of this. To the physician, the full waiting room means that he wastes no time waiting for patients to arrive. For the patient, the time waiting is often time wasted. The real decision is that of assessing the value of these resources and the impact of gaining one at the loss of the other. If the doctor never loses any time and the patients are made to wait for hours, then the assumption must be that doctor's time is infinitely valuable and the patient's valueless. Perhaps there is a happier exchange.

The empty seat on the airplane means that you can go somewhere at the last minute. To the airline, it means lost revenue. Here again there can be a minimum-cost number of seats idle on the airplane given the travelers' fluctuating needs and high fixed costs of buying and operating available aircraft. Note though that the minimum total cost will be arrived at only if we have a common denominator for evaluating costs to both the airline and the customer. This can be agreed to by both parties or it can be arrived at through the market mechanism. In the airline industry, for example, the companies watch the load factors (percent seats occupied) and experiment not only with charges for passengers who do not show up to take their reserved seats but also with inducements to potential passengers to take the seats that have not been filled by flight time at a reduced rate. Implementation of these arrangements is difficult. Witness the ups and downs of no-show penalties and youth-fare rates.

Within the organization, inventories are used to give subsystems freedom to operate independently. Work-in-process inventories are a necessity unless one is willing to walk each item from machine to machine, set up the machine for that one piece, carry it to the next machine which must be waiting idle, set that machine up, run the piece, go to the next machine, etc. The costs would be astronomical because of handling, idle machinery, repeated setups, and the manpower to worry over costs and coordination enough to get work into the shop and out of it. To some extent, the patients in the hospital are work-in-process inventory for the physician. The patients are there all day, presumably because they are too sick to be at home, but they also enable the doctor to see all of his patients during rounds which he schedules for his convenience or for his teaching schedule.

The situations described above and others can be generalized into a list of the functions of inventory like the one in Table 15-1.

Table 15-1 *Functions of inventory*

Maintaining a rate of flow through a process
Covering gaps in a discontinuous process
Providing multiple access to supply
Allowing purchase or production in more economical lots
Allowing portions of a system or process to operate at different rates, at least
  temporarily
Meeting fluctuations in supply, process, or consumption
Modifying and then storing otherwise perishable commodities, especially labor
Speculating against anticipated charges in costs or availabilities
Displaying motivational information

COVERING GAPS IN SUPPLY

Companies that shut down to allow all their employees to take vacation at once let customers know several weeks in advance so they can build inventories in anticipation of this break in their supply process. Similarly, the airliner leavng Honolulu for Los Angeles must carry enough fuel for 5 thousand miles, despite the fact that the more fuel a plane carries the more fuel it must burn to support the added weight.

MULTIPLE SOURCES OF SUPPLY

Most people recognize that institutions continue to exist only if they provide the goods and services we desire at a convenient time and place. It would be much more economical from an investment point of view to have each little-used book in only one library for all the schools and other organizations in New York City, but the Nobel prize physicist at Columbia might be very dissatisfied if he had to go to New York University for his copy of a late nineteenth-century book on celestial mechanics. The obvious ways around this are to minimize anticipated inconvenience by having the one copy closest to the greatest concentration of potential users or having multiple copies (a large inventory) in several locations. One alternative has lower investment and greater inconvenience, while the other reverses these two costs. In some cases, the customer has a choice of going directly to the factory and buying at low prices or paying his local merchant much higher prices to compensate him for his time and his capital. Here again one trades one set of costs for another. The frustrating thing to consumer and supplier both is the fact that accounting systems spell out neither set of costs well but do much better with inventory carrying costs than with costs of customer inconvenience or the compensations for serving a customer well.

PURCHASE OR PRODUCTION IN LOTS

The more commonly studied inventory decisions are those which involve production or procurement of materials in lots and those which allow the firm to respond to most fluctuations in supply, process, or demand. Here is the point at which the sales manager, the POM manager, and the controller are likely to collide. The salesman's life would be much easier if he could rest assured that whenever the customer requested any item in any amount, immediate shipment of the full order would be made. The factory manager would abet this tendency for huge inventories. He could avoid listening to telephone pleas for rush production to cover stock shortages or to help out an important customer who miscalculated. Moreover, he could maintain a very steady rate of production in large lots and show a sharply reduced per unit manufacturing cost. If more customers were gained by this improved service, both men could point to the added revenue and increased utilization of productive capacity. The controller, however, could cite the very major investments involved, the other investment opportunities lost, and the response of customers who, sensing this willingness to take the risks and investments, would shift even more burdens back on the supplier.

ALLOWING TEMPORARY VARIATIONS IN OPERATING RATES

The same urges for independence between supplier and user exist even within one company. Even though assembly might be a continuous process, it might prove more economical to operate parts manufacture by making larger, more infrequent lots. Some departments might operate three shifts, others one. Buffers of inventory between departments and between machines serve to allow a less rigid control of flow rates and negate the need to respond to every minor fluctuation in production rates or efficiencies. Coordination and control are virtues about which we talk as if the more we have the better. Yet, there is a point of diminishing returns beyond which the added effort is not worth the costs of the inventories that could substitute for them.

MEETING FLUCTUATIONS IN SUPPLY OR DEMAND OR STORING PERISHABLES

Many companies operate in environments with major seasonal fluctuations. They do not necessarily operate at a rate which fluctuates immediately with the demand or supply levels. Their supplies such as labor or raw materials may be available only at a different rate. An inventory system is used to balance the two rates. The salmon packer in Washington must process fish as they are caught during the salmon run and hold his output until it is ordered throughout the year. The assembler of air conditioners may be able to get parts delivered at any rate he desires, but he may not be able to maintain a reliable workforce unless he provides stable employment. To store up the excess labor during the winter, he has the men produce as much as they can all year round. He holds the extra output until the peak selling season when demand exceeds production rate and his inventory declines.

ALTERNATIVES TO INVENTORY

Crowded hospitals often have more people awaiting surgery than they have operating rooms or beds for recuperating patients. To avoid overflows, certain delayable operations like removal of tonsils and repair of hernias are put off for days or weeks until space is available. This backlog of operations to be performed, like backlogs in manufacturing, is really a negative inventory. Many organizations providing products only to individual specifications have no finished goods inventory. They operate entirely off a backlog. In some situations, such as airline transportation to Europe during the tourist season, when both the inventory and the backlog are quite limited, business is actually turned away because the added capacity (plane seats) for just the peak load would be too expensive. Power companies who must have enough capacity for peak loads adjust to the situation by charging large users extra high rates if they draw over a certain amount during the peak load period. These companies also invest heavily in transmission lines to allow them to get more capacity from nearby companies which may have a slightly different peak demand pattern.

SPECULATING

There are organizations that hold inventories primarily because they anticipate that price levels will change in the future. Investment bankers have "inventories" and so do the speculators on the commodity exchanges. Agricultural markets are a natural arena for this type of dealing. Most POM organizations consider this type of gambling to be outside of their normal operating policies, yet they do not hesitate to increase raw material purchases in the face of a warning that prices will rise or to speed up capital investments in an obviously inflationary period.

INVENTORIES AS MOTIVATORS

At times, the presence of inventory has a motivational effect on the people around it. It is a common belief that large piles of goods displayed in a supermarket will lead the customer to buy more. Yet, too much piled up in everyone's way leaves a negative impression on buyer and employee alike. Similarly, it is understood that workers should be able to see work ahead of them in an appropriate amount. If there is not enough work in sight, they may slow down to protect themselves from short hours or layoffs. If the pile is so imposing as to appear impossible, they may get discouraged or even quit.

FACTORS AFFECTING AN INVENTORY SYSTEM

In later sections of this chapter, specific uses of inventory will be examined one at a time. When one looks at the total inventory system of the company, he sees a number of separate inventories; but he also has to be aware that these derive from the total system and its interactions. Table 15-2 lists a number of factors that are likely to affect the design and operation

Table 15-2 *Factors affecting an inventory system*

Demand Related Factors

  Size and frequency of orders
  Uniformity or predictability of sales
  Service requirements or allowable delay in filling orders
  Physical and economic structure of the distribution
  Accuracy, frequency, and detail of sales forecasts
  Costs associated with failure to meet demand

Process Related Factors

  Form of production organization: product line, job shop, project
  Number of process stages
  Degree of specialization and differentiation of product at specific stages
  Physically required processing times and batch sizes at specific stages
  Time required to respond (lead time) to changes in production plans
  Production process capabilities and flexibility
  Capacity of production and warehousing stages
  Type of processing—batch vs. continuous
  Quality requirements, shelf-life, obsolescence risks

Organization Related Factors

  Organizational structure
  Information system available
  Data processing capabilities—speed, volume, cost
  Rate of return on capital available elsewhere
  Amount of capital available
  Labor relations policies

Other

  Exogenous events like inflation, rail strikes, wars

of the inventory system. When one is faced with a relatively novel or unstructured description of an organization's inventory problems, this list can serve as a checklist to start the analysis at a sufficiently broad level. Most of the factors are not new after the examples discussed thus far. Those which might still be new to you relate to the successive differentiation of product and to the speed and efficiency of a paperwork and information processing system.

A TOTAL INVENTORY SYSTEM—AN EXAMPLE OF ADAPTATIONS TO SUCCESSIVE PROCESS STEPS

Let us take the example of a manufacturer of upholstered furniture. It illustrates the inventory uses between process steps, the successive differentiation of the product inventories, the information needs generated, and the times required to produce and modify inventories. The process starts out with a supply of raw lumber. This consists of two or three grades in a few standard thicknesses and widths. As needed, these boards are dried in the kilns for about one week and stored for further use.

The lumber is then machined in a rough mill into fifty or so standard shapes. It usually takes 1 or 2 weeks to get a lot through the rough mill although it could be done in a day or two, if necessary. According to production schedules, these rough parts are withdrawn from inventory and finished into one of five hundred or more finished wood parts used in the assembly of furniture frames. These parts are withdrawn from inventory as the assemblers need them. Within a day or two after the frames are assembled, they are covered with any one of a hundred available fabrics to produce the item on order. The finishing of parts, the assembly of frames, and the upholstering take anywhere from 2 days to a week depending on sequencing and urgency.

As the lumber moves through the process, it becomes more highly differentiated. As dried board, it could be made into almost any piece in the product line. The risk of obsolescence is nil. Each time it is processed it becomes more specialized, usable in fewer products. At the same time, however, it gains a greater labor content the more it is processed and hence greater capacity to store labor. Also the closer the product is to completion the sooner it can be used in response to a rush order. Thus, each stage in the process has its own set of attributes as a place for carrying inventory, a set that becomes evident only with a thorough study of the process and the environment.

In this same furniture company, the system for processing orders also plays a major role in the timing of information and material flows and hence in the implementation of any inventory policies. Figure 15-1 shows both the flow of materials and the flow of information in the control process. Orders may arrive weeks before the scheduled shipment period, but they are held in the office until 3 weeks before the shipment date to allow maximum flexibility in the scheduling of freight shipments. The orders scheduled for shipment are released to the production control department once a week only. Then it takes several days for the clerks to translate the order (explode it) from the list of finished units needed into the much longer list of quantities and specifications for parts. Then these parts-requirements lists are passed on as shop orders to the parts finishing foreman. He must get parts to assembly and upholstering soon enough for them to do their operations before the shipping date. What looks like a 3-week lead time for manufacturing is almost half eaten up by the processing of paperwork and by the fact that some actions must be taken at least 10 days prior to shipment. The paperwork delays are occasioned in part by the desire

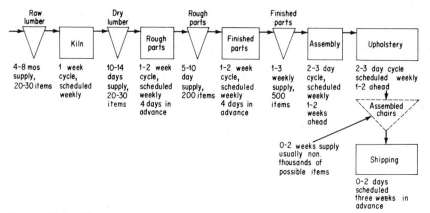

Figure 15-1 *Flow of goods and information in a furniture plant*

to batch clerical tasks for flexibility and efficiency. Some decisions, such as the choice of the wood to be dried, must actually occur before the orders and shipment schedules are known, so no adjustment is possible. All scheduling of the kilns has to be done on the basis of forecasted, not actual, demand. This important question of the design of the information and control (paperwork) system is a major area for consideration to be covered in the latter parts of this chapter.

Figure 15-1 provides a summary of the process steps, an identification of the inventories, the number of SKU's, the average size inventory, and the scheduling and production cycles. These are the majority of the process related factors affecting an inventory system listed in Table 15-2. You should have at least as good an overall command of any operating system before you presume to deal with specific inventory and production control problems within it.

USING MODELS

This chapter started with a discussion of the relationships between the inventory policies of the firm and the POM environment. This led to an analysis of the functions of inventory and the relevant characteristics of the firm. Such analysis is broad and sets the stage for an equally necessary analysis of the specifics of each proposed inventory investment. Like the newspaper reporter, the analyst should determine who, what, where, when, and how, as well as how much. Inventory has a usefulness only when it is in the right place in the right amount at the right time. The word "right" implies a one true answer or what is called an "optimal solution." It implies that numerical models are to be used with considerable precision. In the inventory field, there are many models of extreme arithmetic precision. The unfortunate fact is that there are a limited number of situations to which they can be applied precisely. Relevant costs are only approximations at best. Customer and supplier behavior is uncertain, if not capricious. Relationships are not constant over a full range of values. Yet, these models can be modified to suit many, many situations. This text covers only a few of the models available. Even more importantly, a highly abstract model can be used to give the student and later the businessman a much improved basis for highly imprecise decisions that he already makes implicitly or by default.

The models presented here are only the most elementary ones. They deal with the basic tasks of defining relevant costs, the amount of inventory needed to maintain a continuous flow of goods through a transportation or materials-handling system, the quantity to use in placing an order, and the point in time to place the order.

INVENTORY RELATED TO FLOW RATES

If a gasoline distributor has a fleet of 50,000 barrel tankers moving between the refineries in Texas and his terminal in New Jersey, he has a set of inventory decisions to make about two inventories in transit: tankers and barrels of gasoline. Assume that his stations sell on the average 25,000 barrels per day, and he has enough inventory tankage at his terminal to cover fluctuations in demand. If his tankers take 5 days to make the trip one way and he has to have a tanker arriving every 2 days to meet the demand rate, there must be five ships in movement, on the average, all of the time. Table 15-3 shows the status of his fleet on 10 successive days. Every other day a ship arrives with 50,000 barrels of gasoline in movement, on the average $2\frac{1}{2}$ ships are at sea with a load, so that his inventory of gasoline in movement averages 125,000 barrels, or a 5-day supply. This is no accident. The formula for the computation of simple transit inventories is *the throughput (demand) per unit period times the number of periods in transit.*

This same formula applies to the amount of inventory on a conveyorized system like an automobile assembly line. If there is a line $\frac{3}{4}$ of a mile long and there are cars spaced every 15 feet, then there are 264 cars in that inventory. The inventory is expressed in terms of a number of feet, but the belt has a known speed in feet per minute or miles per hour and the formula of throughput per unit period times the number of periods to traverse the line would still apply.

In the job shop, transit inventories are much more variable. Once an operation is completed the move men must be notified, have their work scheduled, and then perform the transfer between operations. Actually goods

Table 15-3 *Tanker schedule to meet 25,000 BPD demand*

Day	1	2	3	4	5	6	7	8	9	10
Ship										
Flying Z										
Status	L	U	U	U	U	U	L	L	L	L
Destination	N.J.	Tex.	Tex.	Tex.	Tex.	Tex.	N.J.	N.J.	N.J.	N.J.
Tiger Power										
Status	L	L	L	U	U	U	U	U	L	L
Destination	N.J.	N.J.	N.J.	Tex.	Tex.	Tex.	Tex.	Tex.	N.J.	N.J.
Sgt. Stripes										
Status	L	L	L	L	L	U	U	U	U	U
Destination	N.J.	N.J.	N.J	N.J.	N.J.	Tex.	Tex.	Tex.	Tex.	Tex.
Quick Clam										
Status	U	U	L	L	L	L	L	U	U	U
Destination	Tex.	Tex.	N.J.	N.J.	N.J.	N.J.	N.J.	Tex.	Tex.	Tex.
Labor West										
Status	U	U	U	U	L	L	L	L	L	U
Destination	Tex.	Tex.	Tex.	Tex.	N.J.	N.J.	N.J.	N.J.	N.J.	Tex

often can be transported much more promptly but are held up waiting for the machine to become available for the next operation. Under these conditions, it becomes difficult and somewhat academic to say what is transit inventory and what is a backlog for men and machines to work off. The installation of automatic materials-handling equipment such as paced conveyers may or may not reduce transit inventories depending on the situation at the time. If the distance between work stations is great, then there may be many units between the stations. This may or may not offset the old buffer stocks formerly kept between these operations.

HOW MUCH TO MAKE OR BUY AT ONE TIME

One of the most commonly recognized functions of inventory is that of reducing the frequency with which an order is placed. When the refrigerator and the home freezer came into common use, well-organized housewives stopped shopping every day. They bought and stored larger quantities for use over long periods and to take advantage of lower prices. The hospital, the factory, and the laboratory all have similar opportunities to save by ordering more at a given time. The manufacturer also has additional opportunities to reduce the frequency with which machinery must be adjusted, retooled, and restarted, since larger lots mean fewer changes from product to product.

This selection of the quantity to make or buy in one lot is one for which there are a number of standardized analyses that will give you the number to be ordered. One can find book after book discussing and elaborating on equations and models to be used under various possible circumstances. This section will follow much the same route. A very simple version is presented first and then elaborated slightly to cover a more comprehensive set of problems. One major reason for covering this model in such detail is the fact that its recommendations are quite contrary to the intuitive rules that even experienced businessmen follow until they come to understand the underlying economic analysis.

THE SIMPLEST CASE

The task of working with the economic order quantity model also can serve to drive home the importance of urgings, elsewhere in this book, that you give very careful attention to the question of what costs are relevant to a particular decision. As always, you will be interested only in those cash flows or opportunities for income foregone that pertain to the particular decision at hand. The question can be reduced to whether to select a lot of size n or of $n + 1$, so that the analysis will be based on incremental analysis.

The choice of a size of lot to be manufactured is the simplest form of the economical order quantity problem. The direct costs of the lot to be manufactured will be the sum of the variable costs per unit and those costs which are fixed for each lot going through. The fixed costs could include the setup labor and the equipment idle time during setup, the pieces spoiled during startup, and the paperwork and other administrative costs associated with putting a lot into production and getting it completed and stored. The relevant costs of producing a lot can be expressed symbolically as:

Direct variable cost per lot $= S + QV$

where

S = the fixed costs associated with a lot

Q = the quantity in the lot

V = variable manufacturing cost per unit

Reducing cost per lot certainly is not the firm's objective. That could be accomplished by reducing Q to zero, but the firm wouldn't last long under those conditions. Demand must be met over the longer run at a minimum of total cost. The period used most commonly is a calendar year, although some other period such as a month or a week can be used in appropriate cases.

$$\text{Total direct manufacturing costs per year} = (R/Q)(S + QV) = \frac{RS}{Q} + RV$$

where

R = the total required production for the year, usually assumed to be total annual demand

The term R/Q merely represents the number of lots ordered per year of lot size Q. The term RV is independent of the value of Q that is being sought and is generally omitted from further analysis in the simple case.

If the manager stops his analysis here, he will reach the conclusion that the larger the lot the lower the cost, so why not make each product only once a year. After all, the numerator is constant, so increasing the denominator continuously reduces the cost. The application of this finding will leave the company knee-deep in inventory or at least headed in that direction until the controller begins to ask his legitimate questions.

Inventory cannot be had for nothing. Every dollar of material and labor put into the units sitting on the warehouse shelf represents an outlay of cash which might be used somewhere else. There also are other costs attributable directly to the amount of inventory carried. Many states treat manufacturing inventories as taxable property; so the more you have the higher your tax bill. If the warehouse burns down, the amount to be replaced will be dependent on the amount that was there. Therefore, insurance coverage requirements and their accompanying premiums will vary with inventory investment.

The savings that increased lot sizes can provide to offset insurance and tax costs and justify the use of the capital invested in the inventory and the storage space should be high enough to compensate the company for the risks which result from leaving goods around. In the newspaper business, a day-old product is worth little or nothing. For each business, there will be an appropriate return for the risks of obsolescence or deterioration or shrinkage. Obsolescence is the risk that an item will lose value because of a shift in styles or consumer preference. Deterioration is bound to occur to any item as it gets older. Some things like pies and cakes get worse by the hour. For granite tombstones, it takes a bit longer. Shrinkage represents the fact that inventory quantities tend to decrease over time. Things get lost, strayed, or stolen, mostly stolen. The problem is so bad with small hand tools that many companies do not provide them to their workers at all. Each employee is expected to provide and protect his own.

Handling and storage costs are other factors that must be considered. These costs may or may not be relevant to the lot size decision. If a company has a very large storage space for which it has no alternative uses, there would be no need to include those storage costs relating to space in the calculation of the optimum lot size. The problem here is that a company may start out with excess storage space, not charge for space, produce everything in very large lots, and then run out of space. The procedure here would be to recognize that space was beginning to acquire an opportunity cost and add that to the costs of carrying inventory, thus depressing the future optimum lot sizes.

The whole set of indirect costs listed above frequently are grouped under the single title of "carrying costs." Since most of them are related to the dollar value of the goods, you will frequently see them stated as either a cost per unit per year or a percentage rate to be multiplied times the actual variable manufacturing cost V for the specific unit being ordered. The latter is more suitable if decisions must be made about parts and assemblies of differing value.

When a purchased or manufactured lot size Q arrives at the storage area, the inventory there jumps by the amount Q. This inventory then declines again in response to demand until the next lot arrives. In a best-of-all-possible-worlds market, orders would be shipped out at a known steady rate, and the time that it would take for a lot to arrive would be known with certainty. Under these conditions, the smart man would plan his orders to arrive as the material runs out and just before the next user demands some more. Thus, the inventory would be zero each time a lot of Q units arrives. The average inventory would then be $(Q + O)/2 = Q/2$. Figure 15.2 shows this situation graphically.

THE INITIAL ASSUMPTIONS

The conditions illustrated in Figure 15-2 are very simple, but they also require the following very rigid and unreal set of assumptions:

1. The demand rate is assumed constant, continuous, and known.
2. The lot is assumed to arrive all together at one time.
3. All cost and savings are assumed to remain constant over the planning period.
4. The lot is assumed to arrive exactly at the time planned.

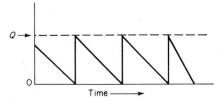

Figure 15-2 *Inventory fluctuations with constant demand*

5. The lot size decision is assumed to be independent of other decisions; e.g., there is no consideration of the fact that the choice could also depend on the plant capacity available.

The POM group operates in an environment much more complex and dynamic than the assumptions behind this model. Fortunately, there are many related models available for application to these more complicated situations.

COMPUTING ORDER QUANTITY

If we wrap all the carrying costs into a single rate per dollar of manufacturing cost i, we are then in a position to arrive at the total cost function which is associated with the actual selection of an economic order quantity for manufacture. Total cost associated with manufacturing lot size = setup cost + average inventory carrying cost = $SR/Q + Q/2 \times Vi$. These costs have been plotted in Figure 15-3.

There is a minimum cost lot size associated with the total-cost curve in Figure 15-3. The footnote below shows the derivation of that minimum value using the differential calculus.[2] Another way of looking at the minimum cost situation is to think of the costs associated with the addition of a small increment Δ to the lot size. Assume that you start with a lot of size Q. The total relevant cost of that lot is $SR/Q + QVi/2$. By adding an increment, the value of Q becomes $Q + \Delta$. The rational decision-maker will add that

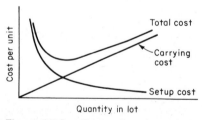

Quantity in lot

Figure 15-3 *Cost related to selection of economic order quantity*

---

[2] The total cost equation will be at a minimum when its first derivative is zero and its second derivative is positive.

$$TC = \frac{RS}{Q} + \frac{Q}{2} Vi$$

$$\frac{dTC}{dQ} = \frac{-RS}{Q^2} + \frac{Vi}{2} = 0 \quad \text{or } Q = \sqrt{\frac{2RS}{Vi}}$$

$$\frac{d^2TC}{dQ^2} = +2 \frac{RS}{Q^3} > 0$$

which holds for all situations where R, S, and Q are positive.

unit only so long at it reduces total cost, when

$$\frac{SR}{Q+\Delta} + \frac{(Q+\Delta)}{2} Vi < \frac{SR}{Q} + \frac{Q}{2} Vi$$

The opposite relationship would lead to a reduction in the lot size. One would quit only when the two total costs were identical. At that point,

$$\frac{SR}{Q+\Delta} + \frac{(Q+\Delta)}{2} Vi = \frac{SR}{Q} + \frac{Q}{2} Vi$$

By multiplying both sides by Q and $Q + \Delta$ this equation simplifies to

$$-SR + Q(Q+\Delta)\frac{Vi}{2} = 0$$

The limit of $Q(Q + \Delta)$ as Δ approaches zero is Q^2 and this reduces the equation further for the continuous case to

$$-SR + Q^2\frac{Vi}{2} = 0$$

and we arrive at the same solution as the calculus that $Q = \sqrt{2RS/Vi}$. Table 15-4 shows the results for a specific item

where

$R = 30$ units used per year

$S = \$15$ fixed charges per order for paperwork and setup

$V = \$100$ variable cost per unit

$i = 0.25$, i.e., 25 percent return required per year to cover all carrying charges and opportunity costs

According to the formula:

$$Q = \sqrt{\frac{2RS}{Vi}} = \sqrt{\frac{2 \times 30 \times 15}{100 \times 0.25}} = \sqrt{\frac{900}{25}} = \frac{30}{5} = 6$$

Notice that the losses due to small errors in the region of the optimum lot size are relatively small. If the lot actually scheduled were 5, 6, or 7, the additional costs would be slight. This happens because the formula is a square root function. This is fortunate. The factors used in the computation of the lot size are not precise. R, the annual demand, is only a forecast, and the carrying costs are not readily obtainable from standard cost accounting systems. For example, if the true rate of return needed was 0.25 and the manager used 0.20, that would have been a 20 percent error in the

Table 15-4 *Calculations to determine an economical order quantity (annual demand = 30)*

Lot Size	Carrying Cost	Procurement Cost	Total Cost
Q	$Q/2 \times Vi$	RS/Q	
1	$ 12.50	$450.00	$462.50
2	25.00	225.00	250.00
3	37.50	150.00	187.50
4	50.00	112.50	162.50
5	62.50	90.00	152.00
6	75.00	75.00	150.00
7	87.50	64.29	151.79
8	100.00	56.25	156.25
9	112.50	50.00	162.50
10	125.00	45.00	170.00
30	375.00	15.00	390.00

input, yet, the error in the lot size would have been in the ratio of

$$(\sqrt{0.25}/\sqrt{0.20}) - 1 = 11 \text{ percent}$$

If the total cost function is so insensitive to changes in *R*, *S*, *V*, and *i*, one might ask why the formula is considered so important. The reason is that the manager who is not familiar with the formula is likely to pick a simple, but arbitrary, rule for his orders like 3 months' supply for fast-moving items and once a year for the slow ones. If the unit in Table 15-4 was considered to be a fast mover, his lot size would be 6 or 7 (3 months' supply); but if it were a slow-moving item, it would be 30 (a year's supply), and costs would be more than double what they should be. Understanding the meaning of the formula drives home the two facts that each item should be considered separately in the light of its own relevant costs and demand rate and that the relationships between the costs are not simple linear ones.

ECONOMICAL ORDERING QUANTITY FOR PURCHASES

The simple model has been described thus far in terms of the lot to be ordered into manufacture. The mathematics is the same for purchased materials unless there are quantity discounts available. Under the fixed price system there is a variable unit cost (the purchase price) and a fixed ordering cost (comparable to *S* for setup costs). Unfortunately, *S* is not a cost collected by the accounting system but one estimated by management and sufficient to cover the incremental costs of securing quotations, typing the order, keeping track of it, receiving the merchandise, delivering it, processing the account payable, etc. Most of these operations are done by overhead, "fixed cost" departments, in which the labor input is not going to vary with each order. Yet, the assumption that placement of an order has only a negligible marginal cost ultimately leads to a flood of orders and, hence, to the addition of personnel throughout the system. To avoid these additional costs which would be incremental and would actually result from the logical assumption of zero incremental costs associated with any *one* order over a succession of decisions, many organizations assume relatively arbitrarily that there is an incremental cost, say \$25 or \$50, and use it as the value of S. From there on, the usual formula $Q = \sqrt{2RS/Vi}$ applies.

QUANTITY DISCOUNTS

In many situations, a vendor offers his product at prices that vary with the amount ordered. The more you order the larger the lot he processes in shipping and in manufacture. In most price lists, identical prices are applied to any quantity ordered within a certain range. The result is that the average cost per unit and total cost curves as discontinuous as shown in Table 15-5 and Figure 15-4 which are taken from an actual industrial price list. It is obvious from the total price column that if the usual lot size calculation had showed a lot size of 24, the purchasing agent should buy 25, the smallest quantity which will qualify him for the 25–49 price break. To take this into account, it is obvious that the simple lot size model will have to be expanded to include these breaks in price.

In the section on the determination of the proper lot size, a function was presented showing manufacturing and purchasing costs. It was $RS/Q + RV$. The RV term was dropped because it did not vary with Q.

Table 15-5 *Evaluation of a quantity discount scheme*

List Prices per Unit		Selected Total Order Costs	
Quantity	Unit	Quantity	Total Price
1 to 11	\$4.20	11	\$46.20
12 to 24	3.60	12	43.20
25 to 49	3.20	13	46.80
		—	
		24	86.40
		25	80.00
		26	83.20
		27	86.40

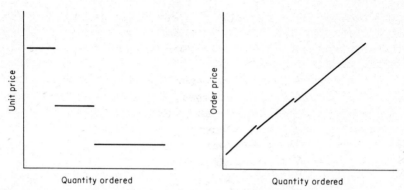

Figure 15-4   *Effect of price discounts on unit and order prices*

In this case of quantity discounts, *V* does vary with the quantity ordered, and the *RV* term has to be added back into the calculation. The new total cost associated with the lot size is then:

$$TC = \frac{RS}{Q} + RV + \frac{Q}{2} Vi$$

The graph of this curve where quantity discounts are offered is shown in Figure 15-5. The choice of *Q* may or may not be affected by the introduction of the quantity discounts. The usual approach is to experiment with the lot size and total cost equations, emphasizing areas around the price breaks in the search for a minimum. Specific formuli covering the lot size decision with quantity discounts are available in most specialized books on inventory control.

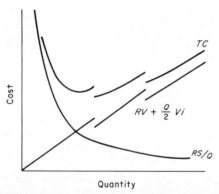

Figure 15-5   *Total costs of lot size decision with quantity discounts*

SETTING A REORDER POINT

This chapter has been concerned with the amount of material to be ordered at a given time. The next question is how to tell when that time has arrived. Again the primary approach will be to look first at a situation which outlines both the problem and a model commonly used to deal with it. The definition is again based on relevant costs and then manipulation of the cost function to reduce total costs as much as possible. The perfect knowledge assumptions used to develop the simple lot size model are modified here to fit the more realistic case where one cannot predict perfectly either the arrivals of customer's orders or the delivery date of your replenishment orders once they have been placed.

When it was assumed that the manager had perfect knowledge of the future, there was little or no problem in telling him when to order. To keep the inventory carrying costs at a minimum, he would like to have the goods arrive after he has run out but just before the next customer walks in. In this way, he would carry only the $Q/2$ average unit inventory. The reorder point (ROP), the point in time, and inventory level at which the next order is to be placed would be exactly equal to the amount that would be shipped during the period that it would take to obtain delivery of the new lot. The amount to be ordered would be Q, the economic lot size.

The amount to be shipped during the interval while the firm awaits the receipt of goods is a function of both the length of time in days in the waiting period L and the demand rate or daily usage U during that period. Therefore, the reorder point under conditions of perfect information can be defined as:

$$ROP = U \times L$$

As long as the manager has perfect information, he need not go lower without reordering because he is sure to lose sales or have a dissatisfied customer, and he will not reorder at a higher level because of the costs of carrying unneeded inventory. Figure 15-6 shows this situation graphically.

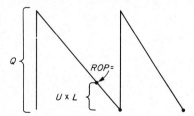

Figure 15-6   *Reorder point under perfect information*

SAFETY STOCKS TO MEET UNCERTAINTY

When the real world shows its usual variability, however, either in daily demand or the delivery time or both, then it becomes necessary to consider departures from this very simple model. Take the case of a radio repairman who has to decide when to reorder the amplifier tubes commonly failing in portable television sets. If he has been in business for a while, he can go over his records and determine how many amplifier tubes he sold during each of the periods that he was awaiting an order. Let us assume that his experience could be summarized in Table 15-6. His first notion, particularly if he was familiar with the ROP formula presented above, would be to determine the expected value of the usage by adding up all the demands and dividing by 20. This mean demand during lead time is 150 units. The fact is that placing an order when there were 150 units in stock would have avoided a stockout in only 11 of the 20 reorder periods, i.e., demand exceeded 150 in 9 cases. If he is not willing to run out 9 out of 20 (almost half) times, then he had better consider carrying a cushion to reduce the probability of running out to a level acceptable to him.

His decision problem is a typical one, and this frequently needed cushion is called a "safety stock." If he decides that the best situation is one in which the customer is serviced 19 out of 20 times from stock, then he must place his order when the stock is at a level of 164 units. Of this total reorder level quantity, 150 would be attributable to the mean demand during the reorder cycle, and the remaining 14 would be the safety stock cushion SS. $ROP = U \times L + SS$ where U is the mean daily usage and L is the mean waiting period in days. Figure 15-7 shows the new model with variable demand and a safety stock.

Table 15-6 *Demand experienced for amplifier tubes during reorder cycle*

Demand during Reorder Period	Number of Periods with This Demand	Cumulative No. of Periods of Demand $\leq$ This Amount
132 units	2 periods	2 periods
146	4	6
148	3	9
150	2	11
152	3	14
154	4	18
164	1	19
172	1	20

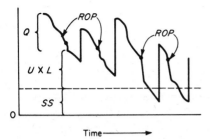

Figure 15-7   *Inventory system behavior with uncertainty about demand and delivery*

DESIRED SAFETY STOCK LEVELS

The next question is that of determining the safety stock level that will give the repairman the least total cost. Here, as in so many other cases, he will be balancing two sets of costs against each other. As the safety stock and the reorder point are increased to give greater and greater protection, the likelihood of a stockout, and the annual costs associated with stockouts are decreased. On the other hand, his firm incurs added costs by carrying this inventory cushion. The problem then becomes one of finding a safety stock level which minimizes the system cost. The annual carrying cost will be a function of the size of the safety stock in units times the annual carrying charges per unit. The average added inventory will be approximately the whole safety stock. As Figure 15-7 indicates, the safety stock will not be eaten into most of the time, only during some of the reorder cycles. As a reasonable approximation, one can say that the annual carrying cost for safety stock will be *SS* times *Vi*. The related costs of stockout will be a function of the number of stockouts per year and the cost of a stockout. The number of stockouts per year will be determined by the number of periods during which the material is on order and the risk of a stockout during each such period. Thus, the manager will wish to minimize the following quantity:

$$\text{Total cost of safety stock decision} = SS\,(Vi) + A\left(\frac{R}{Q}\right)P(S)$$

where

  SS = safety stock in units

  Vi = cost of carrying a unit of inventory for a year

  A = cost of incurring one or more stockouts during a reorder period

R/Q = annual demand divided by the number in lot, or the number of orders placed

$P(S)$ = probability of one or more stockouts each time that an order is placed

You have encountered Q, the lot size variable, before. The appearance of this term in the costs to be minimized by the selection of the safety stock indicates that the lot size decision was not really independent of the safety stock decision after all. This can be seen in the following comparison. Consider an item C which is ordered once a year and an item D ordered 50 times a year. Each has a safety stock such that on the average there is a stockout every 25 orders. This means that $P(S)$ is $\frac{1}{25}$ or 0.04. Item D will be out-of-stock on the average twice every year. Obviously then, the selection of the same low $P(S)$ and the maintenance of the safety stock to achieve it would seem out of proportion unless the cost of a stockout for item C is 50 times the corresponding cost for item D. This sort of analysis quickly brings into question the practices of many companies who merely set a safety stock equal to a certain fixed proportion of the normal demand and apply it to all items.

ESTIMATING STOCKOUT COSTS

The variable A is extremely difficult to define. It represents the cost of a stockout of one or more units during a reorder period. The firm seldom gets a notice that the customer went elsewhere for an item or that a major client may be considering giving his business to a competitor due to slow deliveries or split shipments. Other costs also could be included in this value such as that of maintaining a staff to expedite orders and handle customer inquiries and the production inefficiencies suffered when orders are rushed or setups broken. The value of A also may vary from stockout to stockout, since several customers might be inconvenienced during one shortage and a different one the next. This value A always is a highly subjective thing estimated roughly by managers from scanty evidence. Yet, it is necessary to have some estimate to start building a rational inventory policy.

If a *unit* cost A' of A can be estimated, it is then possible to compute the appropriate value of $P(S)$ from the equation below. All the other constants are those used in the computation of the economic lot size.

$$P(S) = \frac{Vi}{(A'R/Q) + Vi}$$

This formula can be derived from *marginal* analysis of the expected costs and expected savings from adding a *marginal* unit to the safety stock. With a given safety stock, there will be a probability of stockout $P(S)$.

If one more unit added to the safety stock will avoid the unit cost of stock-out (A'), then each time a reorder takes place, the expected saving will be $P(S) \times (A)$. The number of reorders per year is R/Q. Therefore, the expected annual savings due to this extra unit is

$$\frac{P(S) \cdot A' \cdot R}{Q}$$

On the other hand, the added unit will sit in inventory when there is no stockout. The expected cost, therefore, will be

$$[1 - P(S)] \cdot Vi$$

The rational businessman will continue to add to his safety stock so long as expected savings exceed expected costs. Thus the desired safety stock occurs when expected costs and savings are equal. Symbolically, this is expressed as:

$$\frac{P(S) \cdot A' \cdot R}{Q} = [1 - P(S)]\, Vi$$

Multiplying the two terms on the right side of the equation, we get

$$\frac{P(S) \cdot A' \cdot R}{Q} = Vi - P(S) \cdot Vi$$

Collecting terms containing $P(S)$, we get

$$\frac{P(S) \cdot A' \cdot R}{Q} + P(S) \cdot Vi = Vi$$

and this can be regrouped to give the result

$$P(S) = \frac{Vi}{(A'R/Q) + Vi}$$

IMPLICIT EVALUATION OF STOCKOUT COSTS AND PROBABILITIES

It may be possible to establish that elusive value of A' by an implicit or backward induction type of analysis. Organizations frequently have adopted a policy rule-of-thumb that sets the level of service to be provided $P(S)$ by their inventory systems; e.g., they say that the customer's order should be filled from stock 98 percent of the time. This is equivalent to saying that the desired $P(S) = 0.02$. Knowing the annual carrying cost for an item Vi, the number of times it is ordered per year R/Q, as well as $P(S)$, one can compute the corresponding A'. For example, if Vi is $1, R/Q

is 12, and $P(S)$ is 0.02, then

$$P(S) = \frac{Vi}{(A'R/Q) + Vi} \quad \text{becomes} \quad 0.02 = \frac{\$1}{12A' + \$1}$$

and A' is $4. It is then up to the businessman to decide whether this value for A' is a reasonable one.

IMPLICATIONS OF A UNIFORM $P(S)$

One immediate implication of the formula for evaluating $P(S)$ is that a uniform policy for all items may not be the best solution. Suppose that a firm makes many similar items, each with the same holding cost but different sales rates. Consequently, it orders goods with varying frequency ranging from weekly for some fast-moving items to once a year for some slow-moving ones. Table 15-7 illustrates the stockout costs implied by a constant stockout frequency policy and carrying cost per unit. Note that the highest stockout costs are attributed to the slowest moving items and the lowest to the fast moving, high-volume items. Perhaps it would be better for management to set a uniform cost of stockout A', or one which recognizes higher costs for stockouts in the faster moving items. This will be a further managerial analysis that takes into account the need for an economically administerable system as well as for a logically consistent one. Each POM management has to work out its own values of $P(S)$ and A' in response to analysis such as this as well as the demands of customers and the responses of competitors.

USING CUMULATIVE DISTRIBUTIONS TO SET SAFETY STOCKS

Once a value of $P(S)$ has been accepted, it is possible to use a frequency distribution of demand during reorder cycles like that shown in Table

Table 15-7 *Variation in implied stockout costs with constant P(S), Vi, and varying order frequency*

Frequency of Order R/Q	$P(S)$	Carrying Cost/Unit Vi	Implied Stockout Cost A'
1	.02	$1	$49.00
3	.02	1	16.33
6	.02	1	8.16
12	.02	1	4.08
26	.02	1	1.88
52	.02	1	0.94

15-6 and determine the choice of *SS* and *ROP* that would provide the calculated protection against stockout. If the television repairman determined that his costs in lost customers or in time wasted and extra costs incurred getting tubes from other local sources warranted a 5 percent chance of stockout, he would reorder at 164, because demand was greater than 164 in only 1 out of 20 (5 percent) of the prior periods. If 10 percent was better, he would wait until his inventory had dropped to 154 before reordering.

In most situations, there are many items for which a reorder point must be established and a fairly small amount of data available concerning actual demand during the reorder periods. The latter problem is usually overcome by estimating a typical or mean reorder period and using a frequency distribution based upon historical demand during periods of similar length. If the bulk of the demand during these reorder periods is well enough behaved to fit a known mathematical distribution like the normal distribution with a mean of $U \times L$ and standard deviation $\sigma(U \times L)$, the readily available tables of the cumulative probabilities of that distribution can be used to determine the safety stock directly, given the mean, standard deviation, and target $P(S)$. Two commonly used distributions are the normal and the Poisson. The former has the advantages of being understood by many decision-makers and having the cumulative probability tables readily available. The Poisson distribution has the advantages of seeming to be more representative of the true order arrival situation and having a standard deviation that is the square root of its mean. Its cumulative probability tables are less readily available and more difficult to use, but if the demand is large, the normal tables can be used with relatively little error. This sequence has led some organizations to adopt a decision rule of the form $ROP = U \times L + z \sqrt{U \times L}$, where z represents the number of standard deviations needed to provide the $P(S)$ specified by company policy. In cases where they remember to change z with each item and the real distribution of demand during lead time approximates the Poisson, this is all right. The television repairman could be used as a case in point. His historical figures showed a mean of 150 units. A Poisson distribution of this magnitude can be approximated safely by the normal distribution, so one gets from the normal tables in Appendix 2 the fact that for $P(S) = 0.05$, z should be 1.64. This would yield $ROP = 150 + 1.64 \sqrt{150} = 150 + 20.1$, or about 170. That is quite different from the value of 164 arrived at using the empirical distribution. Firms with "better behaved" demand will, of course, achieve better results. To some extent, the choice between the empirical demand and the formuli will rest on the cost and effort involved in getting, maintaining, and evaluating the empirical distributions for each product. Figure 15-8 gives a comparison between the television repairman's empirical and normal distribution of demand with a mean of 150 and a standard deviation of 12.25, which is the square root of 150.

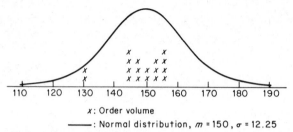

x: Order volume

———: Normal distribution, $m = 150$, $\sigma = 12.25$

Figure 15-8 *Comparison of empirical and theoretical distribution of demand during reorder period with mean = 150*

This section has relaxed another of the constraints on the simple inventory models first introduced. The single total cost equation has been adjusted by Q and SS to fit the needs of real situations. No formula has been offered, however, that minimizes total cost by adjusting both Q and SS to get the best overall result and remove the independence assumption. More specialized texts deal with this and with situations where customer orders are for multiple units and items, where backordering is permitted only under certain conditions, etc. These are grist for the inventory specialists' mill.

RELAXING MORE ASSUMPTIONS

The simple model with its simple assumptions was examined first. Then the discussion removed the assumption that all prices were constant with the quantity ordered. This was a partial relaxation of the assumption that "all costs and savings are assumed to remain constant over the period." One usual component of normal inventory systems was next described— reorder points including safety stocks. These exist to allow the system to overcome discontinuous, uncertain demand rates and the uncertain interval between reordering and receipt of the goods. Two other assumptions have not yet been dealt with, namely, the instantaneous arrival of the lot and the independence of the lot size from other factors such as available capacity.

ARRIVAL OF LOTS OVER AN EXTENDED PERIOD

When a product is produced in large volume and the production run is stretched out over a number of days, it is obvious that one need not carry enough inventory to get by until the whole lot is delivered. Once the first portion of the lot becomes available, the demand can be met day by day from the newly completed stock. Figure 15-9 shows the inventory level under these circumstances when the other conditions of the simple lot size formula are in effect. One can proceed to develop a total cost equation just as

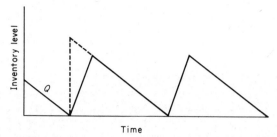

Figure 15-9 *Inventory behavior with extended production and delivery of lot*

before. The fixed costs related to the processing of the lot will remain the same, but the average inventory will be modified. If we define the usage rate per day as D and the production or delivery rate per period as P, we can recognize that the average inventory is $Q/2$ less the material shipped out daily and not stored at all. This amount shipped is D units per day over the length of the production run. The length of the production run is the lot Q divided by the production rate of P or (Q/P) days, and the storage cost avoided would be

$$\frac{Vi}{2} \cdot \frac{DQ}{P}$$

Then the total cost would be

$$TC = \frac{RS}{Q} + \frac{Q}{2} Vi - \frac{Q}{2} \frac{D}{P} Vi$$

$$TC = \frac{RS}{Q} + \frac{Q}{2} Vi \left[\frac{P - D}{P} \right]$$

Using the same procedure for deriving the minimum that was used to define the simple lot size formula,[3] one arrives at the formula

$$Q = \sqrt{\frac{2RS}{Vi} \left[\frac{P}{P - D} \right]}$$

[3] The total cost equation will be at a minimum when its first derivative is zero and its second derivative is positive.

Given that

$$TC = \frac{RS}{Q} + \frac{Q}{2} Vi \left[\frac{P - D}{P} \right]$$

$$\frac{dTC}{dQ} = -\frac{RS}{Q^2} + \frac{Vi}{2} \left[\frac{P - D}{P} \right] = 0 \quad \text{or} \quad Q = \sqrt{\frac{2RS}{Vi} \left[\frac{P}{P - D} \right]}$$

$$\frac{d^2TC}{dQ^2} = +\frac{2RS}{Q^3} > 0$$

holds for all situations where R, S, and Q are positive.

WHAT HAPPENS WHEN THE ORDERS RELEASED
DO NOT EQUAL PRODUCTION

Once an inventory system has been set up, the inventories will be filled for each stockkeeping unit (SKU), and these levels will move up and down in response to demand and to production. Each SKU will respond independently of the others. There will be times when the orders released to the POM system as the inventories pass through reorder points will not be equal to the planned production rate. There is no assurance that the orders released in each period will be constant, even with a constant demand. When lots released do not equal capacity, something has to give.

Capacity can be varied over the short run by adding overtime or by letting people stand idle at company expense or their own through short work weeks. Over a slightly longer period, there are the alternatives of transferring, hiring, and firing personnel or equipment. These alternatives are considered in detail in the chapters on POM system capacity and on production planning.

When it is impossible to increase capacity, the alternatives are to extend delivery times (increase backlog) or to reduce the lot sizes processed. Lengthened lead time without a corresponding change in the reorder points amounts to a reduction in safety stock coverage and increases the probable frequency of stockouts. Reducing the lot size frees equipment time temporarily. It will, however, mean more frequent orders and more charges for paperwork and setups. More setups mean that less time is actually available to produce parts, so neither alternative is particularly attractive. Several researchers have analyzed this unhappy situation. The results are not wholly conclusive, but they do indicate that the better response in many cases is to let the lot size remain at its calculated optimal value at all times and adjust the available capacity by raising or lowering the reorder points in response to available capacity and fluctuating demand.

INVENTORY SYSTEM RESPONSE TO BUSINESS CYCLES

Failure to recognize the cumulative effects of a mismatch between capacity and demand results in serious trouble. Let us assume that a manufacturer uses the economic order quantity and reorder point rules described in detail in this chapter to set his finished goods inventory policies. He sets a Q and an ROP for each item. The system works well during a period of relatively steady demand. Then demand increases rapidly. Recognizing the increase in demand, he recomputes new values of Q with larger demand R and for ROP with the larger usage during reorder period U. This immediately increases the size of the lots released to the factory. Since both average demand during the reorder cycle and the safety stock requirements have increased, *ROP* is increased and reorders are placed at inventory levels higher than before. As the demand approaches and then exceeds the capacity of the factory, the backlog situation is worsened by the inventory system. Larger lots are released sooner. Not only is the company straining its capacity to meet the increases in demand, but it also is behaving as if it wished to build up the safety stock portion of its inventory at the same time. This will cause increased backlogs, and lengthened delivery times will be observed. Responding to the new, longer lead times (L), the inventory system will again raise the reorder points due to the increased value of L. This triggers lots into production sooner, and the spiral continues with the company trying to produce even more for both shipment and inventory.

A serious problem can also occur in a corresponding fashion as demand falls in a recession. The knowledgeable manager, seeing orders off and backlogs decreasing, will estimate lower values of R and U for the next period or so. New lower values of R, U, and L will be substituted into the lot size and reorder point formuli. This may be exactly the wrong thing to do. Each lot released to the shop will be smaller, which absorbs labor with more setups, but as the inventory on each item falls in response to the new demands, the time that it takes to reach the new *ROP*'s will lengthen due to slowed demand and new lower *ROP*'s. This reduction in the workload will again be reflected in faster deliveries and yet another reduction in the lead time used to plan the inventory requirements; lower *ROP*'s, even smaller backlogs, and personnel reductions greater than necessary will likely result.

The economist has this sort of phenomenon in mind when he talks about the role of business expectations and inventory fluctuations as an accelerator of cyclical economic swings. Changing business expectations make the manager more willing to invest in assets but, even on a more rational basis, lead him to modify his estimates of the demand and lead times for his products and indicate that he should carry more inventories per unit sales volume in times of rising outlook and smaller ones during a downswing. It is up to the inventory manager to understand these dangers and respond to them appropriately by recognizing that inventory levels can be controlled to dampen production level changes if capacity and demand do not correspond.

AN ALTERNATIVE SYSTEM: FIXED ORDER CYCLE

Unlike the situations just described (fixed reorder point), there are a number of situations where the frequency with which orders are placed is predetermined by the technology or by the order processing system. Orders can

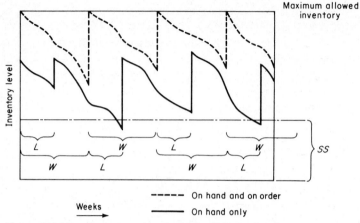

Figure 15-10　*Inventory levels in fixed order cycle*

be placed on a fixed interval cycle. Think of the supermarket which receives a delivery from the warehouse or wholesaler every Tuesday and Friday morning. The models we have looked at were based on a fixed order quantity and fixed reorder point. The supermarket manager is dealing with a fixed ordering time, but the amount in stock at that time and the amount that he orders will vary according to the demand since the last order was placed and the expected demand until the following order arrives. He wishes to meet the demand over the period until he can next make an adjustment in his orders and receive the merchandise. That period will consist of the time between orders or the review period W plus the delivery time required for the next order to arrive, the lead time L. Figure 15-10 shows how such an inventory system would function.

On Saturday, the store manager reviews his stock and writes up his order for delivery the following Tuesday. He knows that any error cannot be corrected until he writes his next order on Wednesday and receives those goods on Friday. Therefore, the stock that he has on hand plus what he orders must be sufficient to carry him over until then. Where there is uncertainty about the demand, he would add a safety stock. This decision rule can be expressed as

$$I + Q = SS + \bar{U}(W + L)$$

$$Q = SS + \bar{U}(W + L) - I$$

where

　　I = the inventory in units on hand

　　Q = the quantity in units to be ordered

SS = the safety stock calculated the same way as for the fixed reorder point rule, except that the period is $W + L$

$\bar{U}$ = expected usage per period during the decision period

W = the number of periods until the next order is placed

L = the number of periods for delivery of the next order

OTHER INVENTORY SYSTEMS

This chapter has concentrated primarily on the one system in which the quantity to order Q is fixed and the reorder point R is fixed in time or inventory level. The reorder point model dealt with the fixed reorder point in units and the replenishment cycle model dealt with the fixed reorder time period. There are many variations of this system in terms of mathematics, control, and administration. Usually stock records are kept and reviewed every time a withdrawal is recorded to determine whether or not the reorder point has been reached. In some companies, the records are adjusted as each order is shipped. In others, the paper work is held until a number of orders are collected, and the stock records are processed in a larger batch. This is more efficient from the point of view of the clerical staff, but the efficiency comes at the expense of some delays in the shipment of goods and the placement of reorders.

TWO-BIN SYSTEM

One variant of the fixed reorder point system is the two-bin system. The physical inventory is placed in two separate lots. One lot is equal to the reorder point quantity. Employees are instructed to fill all orders first from the other lot or bin. When the stock clerks use up the one lot and must begin to use the lot representing the amount equal to the reorder point, they know that it is time to reorder. Presumably, they then notify the purchasing or inventory control departments that it is time to place a new order. This system has the advantage that no inventory records need be kept day by day. As you might guess, it is used most commonly for items of low unit value like nuts, screws, and clerical supplies. The cost of keeping track of such items could easily exceed their value. The major drawback of such a system is the reliance which it places on the employees to use the right bin and to notify supervision or purchasing that it is time to reorder. If they are not reliable enough, then a continuous inventory record may have to be kept in order to avoid the costs of stockouts. The problem, however, is that employees who are not reliable enough to use this system generally are not reporting the amount of the withdrawal accurately either. There is little use in having people keeping neat and up-to-date records that don't represent the actual amounts available. The usual response to this situation is to keep all but a few reliable employees out of the inventory storage area. Even if there are no highly reliable personnel available or willing to do that sort of work, it is wise to limit the number of employees with access. They at least can be supervised and held accountable for the inventory placement and records.

FIXED DOLLAR CONTROLS

In some businesses, especially retailing, it is standard practice to hold a department to a fixed dollar amount of inventory. This amounts to an incentive to consider inventory decisions on the basis of turnover, a practice which was frowned on at the start of this chapter. Yet it may make good sense in style merchandizing, because it essentially motivates the departmental buyer to get rid of old inventory by taking markdowns in order to make room for the new, more stylish merchandise that carries a higher profit margin. Before one judges a fixed-dollar system in retailing, he must determine whether or not the allocation of inventory capital among the departments reflects their expected return on their investments. If that is the case, the system may be a good one, because it eliminates the recording and the calculation of reorder points for many items that have seasonal, fluctuating demand or are likely to become obsolete at an early date. The system uses the logic of inventory investment analysis to set the amount that can be committed by the department, but within that limit, the buyer has great flexibility in pricing and inventory decisions.

CYCLICAL ORDERING

In some businesses, the production process appears to require that orders be placed and processed in a specified sequence. This may occur when a number of similar orders must be grouped to use an expensive special setup which will be available only at predetermined intervals. Extreme examples are space vehicle launches which must take place when the moon or planets are closest to Earth. In some processes with colored dyes and chemicals, the order in which the products are processed markedly affects the time required to clean the equipment. This leads to a production lot quantity which varies with the demand during the period between runs.

Many companies use a mixed system. Each individual subsystem of the process could have its own inventory policy. In one factory, it would not be surprising to have raw materials purchased partly on lot size and partly on speculation, while parts fabrication is entirely on a fixed lot size and fixed reorder point basis. Yet, final assembly is performed only upon receipt of a firm order. These choices depend on a variety of characteristics of the company and its component organizations. This observed variation in policies will extend beyond the models and decision rules discussed here to the organization of the groups responsible for inventory control and the administrative tasks they perform in the context of the total production control system.

QUESTIONS

1. Thinking in terms of the total manufacturing firm, in what ways can you see inventories reducing costs? Increasing costs?
2. Indicate the various functions performed by the inventory of a service station, a quick-service hamburger stand, a beauty parlor, and an oil refinery.
3. What motivational effect on the worker does a large raw materials inventory have? A large finished goods inventory?
4. What is meant by carrying costs of inventory? How will lower carrying costs of inventory affect the economic order quantity? Give a numerical example.
5. If you were a men's clothing retail store manager, would you prefer ordering goods periodically or when inventories reached certain levels?
6. For a given item, why will an optimal fixed order cycle system result in a higher average inventory than an optimal fixed reorder point system?
7. The higher the safety stock, the fewer stockouts occur. Why should a firm allow stockouts?
8. Under what circumstances would a firm be unable to maintain its desired safety stock levels?
9. A common index used in inventory control is inventory turnover, i.e., the total value of the units moved out of inventory during the period divided by the average inventory during the period. Describe two dangers of trying to raise this index higher and higher.
10. Evaluate the following statement: "I can't use a reorder point because my turnover is so rapid that inventory runs out before an order arrives."
11. As the manager of an inventory control department, you receive a report based on your perpetual inventory records indicating that the quantities on hand of five fast-moving parts are 14, −3, 8, −9, and 64,000, respectively. What should you do and why?
12. In developing reorder points for your wholesale inventory of refrigerators, would you state them in units or in total dollar value?

PROBLEMS

1. The Micron Company purchases a key raw material in the amount of $30,000 a year and wishes to make its purchases on an optimum

basis. If the carrying cost on average inventory is 12 percent, the company believes it costs $40 to place an order, and the supplier offers a 2 percent discount for orders of $10,000 or more, how should Micron order?

2. Micron orders another item in optimal order quantities 12 times a year. Average usage is 6 units per day and the average reorder period is 24 days. The cost to carry and store a unit for one year is $5 and the cost of a stockout is $25. What should be the reorder point when demand during the reorder period is distributed as follows?

Usage during Reorder Period	Probability of This Usage
108	0.15
120	0.10
132	0.15
144	0.20
156	0.10
168	0.20
180	0.10

3. What is the optimum number of units for Micron to run when the production rate is 30 units per day and the daily usage is 20 units? Setup cost is $30 per unit and factory cost is $900 per unit?

4. Widget, Inc. buys components A and B from Acme Supply. Widget's management believes they can reduce costs by ordering A and B at the same time instead of independently. So far, the following has been determined: A and B are used in the same assembly (one unit of each) and in that assembly only. Demand for that assembly is expected to remain stable at 100,000 per year. It costs $10 to carry a unit of A or B for one year, and the cost of placing an order with Acme is $75 per order. How should Widget order A's and B's?

5. At Hollowdale Plastics, a manufacturing run of golf tees is being planned. The customer order is for 6,000 tees. This one customer has placed orders averaging 5,000 units per month for several years. The molding machine produces 600 units per hour and costs $180 to set up. Management believes that the tees can be inventoried at an annual cost of $10 per thousand tees. How large a production run should be scheduled?

CASE: THE TECHO COMPANY

The Techo Company designs and distributes technical service manuals for many of the major electronic equipment manufacturers. The format and content of each new manual is first determined by Techo's staff. Once these specifications are decided, the actual printing and binding operations are performed by the Slick Press Printing Company.

Because of the diversification program, Techo has found itself short of working capital. Casting around for possible sources of funds, Techo's president has questioned the heavy investment in finished manuals. He has figured that if this inventory would be cut in half, the firm's cash budget for the next year could be made much more respectable. He realizes, however, that if the capital presently invested in finished stocks was being effectively utilized, then other sources of funds would have to be investigated.

The President has asked his assistant, Fred Ivy, a recent MBA graduate, to analyze the situation and to report his findings.

Fred found that the finished goods inventory was determined by the ordering practices of the sales manager. As each one of the several hundred different manuals reaches its reorder level, the sales manager would forecast next year's requirements and then order a year's supply. Upon receipt of a purchase order, the Slick Press Company would run off each order complete and deliver it to Techo's rented warehouse. Orders from dealers and repair shops all over the United States were filled immediately upon receipt from these warehouse stocks.

Since all stocked manuals were quite similar, Fred Ivy elected to center his analysis on a typical manual, No. B50. He reasoned that if he could justify the proposed 6 months ordering rule for this manual, his logic would apply to all others as well. His preliminary findings were as follows:

1. The cost of processing a routine purchase order had never been studied. However, the Purchasing Agent thought that it couldn't be much more than $2.
2. Accounting records showed that the annual rental cost of the warehouse space had been about 5 percent of the average inventory value for the last few years.
3. Opinions as to the cost of capital varied from 5 to 15 percent. There appeared to be little hope of tying this figure down.
4. The Slick Press printing and binding price for an order of manuals depended upon the quantity ordered as was shown in their pricing formulas: $100 + .40N$ where N is the number of manuals in the order.
5. Demand for all manuals was quite stable during the year and obsolescence was not a major problem. Currently, about 6,000 B50 manuals were being ordered a year.

Fred Ivy feels he must prepare a report which justifies either the present one year's supply ordering rule or the proposed 6 month's rule.

chapter

PROCESSING CONTROL AND SCHEDULING

sixteen

Within the capacity of an operating system, many decisions must be made about who does what activities and when, in order to meet the firm's criteria for efficiency. Employees must be told to report at definite hours on specific days, purchasing must seek delivery of materials to meet service schedules, and preventive maintenance must be planned for those periods when production will be least affected. Each input and output and each processing step must be controlled day by day to achieve the planned capacity and to do an acceptable job of meeting customer demands. This function of controlling the sequence and timing of events goes on under a number of labels. You saw several, including planning, scheduling, and dispatching in Chapter 13. While discussing the subject of aggregate scheduling, we mentioned the interrelationship between the capacity available and the way in which it is to be scheduled from day to day. If the capacity available is not scheduled efficiently, men and equipment can be idle, reducing effective capacity. If the work taken on is too much for the available resources, then the scramble to meet customer complaints and expedite deliveries will make operations less efficient, making the situation even worse. Although scheduling decisions and their implementation are highly detailed and are tactical rather than strategic, they are important to the long-run success of the organization.

As we look at the task of selecting a desired timing and sequencing for operations and activities in the organization, we will assume that the sequence in which the operations are to be performed on a single customer, customer order, or project has been predetermined by the designers of the product and process, and that the precedence (required order) of operations has been established. What remains to be faced is sequencing concurrently all these demands and their related operations within a single facility. The generalizations that can be made about sequencing and timing procedures center around two sets of attributes: (1) the process type, i.e., flow shop, job shop, or fixed location (project), and (2) the nature of the uncertainties encountered, e.g., the arrival of tasks, the length of tasks, the flow of tasks, and the completion dates of tasks. In each case, careful attention has to be given also to the specific criteria by which the choice of a sequence is to be judged.

There are a number of managerial and organizational considerations to be taken into account in understanding the context of scheduling and dispatching decisions. To illustrate these, the section which follows this introduction outlines the information processing and decision-making tasks which help determine the sequences of activities for orders in a job shop manufacturing organization. It corresponds to a listing of the precedence relationships between many of the control tasks shown in Figure 12-3. From it, one can derive an understanding of the sequencing problems faced in organizations.

In succeeding sections, specific approaches to short-run scheduling questions in flow shops, job shops, and project-organized operating systems are discussed. Each opens the way to methodological approaches for dealing with the complexities of scheduling. Figure 16-1 shows the heirarchy of sequencing decisions in an organization. Long-range planning involves the sequencing of events at a high level of aggregation far into the future.

Figure 16-1 *Simple heirarchy of sequencing decisions*

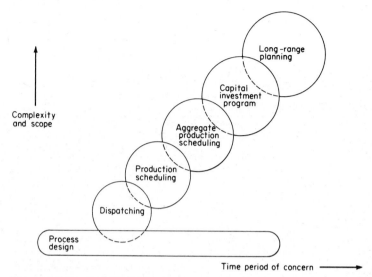

Figure 16-2   *Relationships among areas making sequencing decisions*

The dispatch of the next job to Lathe 722 when the current job is completed is the most immediate and minute sequencing decision involving multiple orders. But experience has shown that none of these sequencing decisions is really independent of the others. Figure 16-2 illustrates the much more complex but realistic relationships between sequencing decisions.

THE PRODUCTION PLANNING AND CONTROL PROCESS

In any large operation, there are many persons involved in controlling various aspects of the production process. Control is an information and decision-making process which must be operated parallel to the physical or information conversion processes to be controlled. In order to meet the needs of the organization, all these activities, both direct production and indirect control, must be managed smoothly. Some indirect processes, such as production engineering and data processing, must be scheduled carefully in order to keep things moving—scheduled as carefully as metal working machines or airline equipment. Development of this parallel information system has been the subject of many recent studies in operations management. As techniques for process and product design have gradually enabled management to reduce direct labor and material requirements, managers have begun to look for other ways to compete. Consequently, greater importance has been attached to labor and equipment utilization, to reduced volumes of work-in-process and finished goods inventory, and to the ability of the system to respond to proliferating product lines and to demands for improved delivery and product quality.

INFORMATION PROCESSING IN PRODUCTION PROCESSES

This information process has its own series of operations which are outlined in Table 16-1. A metal-working job shop is used for this example because its associations with grease and metal chips contrast so sharply with the information system which must function effectively in order for the machines to be used efficiently. Paperwork is for white collar workers and grease and metal chips for blue collar workers, but both run production processes which must be managed carefully. Production engineering activities were outlined in Chapters 6 through 11. This group must schedule their operations to meet estimates of delivery times, which may be prepared by production engineering, marketing services, or inventory control. It specifies the operations to be performed, which in turn determine the sequence of operations, the equipment to be used, and the purchases that are to be made. The purchasing department secures vendor delivery estimates. Production control predicts how the order is likely to progress through the manufacturing process, while marketing has to adjust these predictions to the competitive demands of marketplace. For this reason, the quoted delivery time may be shorter than the latest experiences with similar orders. In addition, the delivery experience can change markedly during the period between the quotation and the receipt of the order. Most companies, therefore, review the order received to see that it conforms to the original quotation and acknowledge the delivery performance that is expected given the current state of inventories and the system's backlog.

TURNING ORDERS INTO PRODUCTION ORDERS

When the ordered material is not in stock, it must be "exploded" into its individual components and materials, all of which must be controlled if the desired output is to come out of the system. Manufacture of a large piece of specialized equipment may require keeping track of and marshalling hundreds or even thousands of different components. The volume of items to be controlled can be very large compared to the number of products produced. Each component, subassembly and assembly, has to be checked to see if it is in inventory, purchased if it is out of stock and normally is procured outside, and ordered into production if it is normally manufactured and stock is low or nonexistent. Since an output does not occur until every single component and assembly is completed, this output is dependent upon timely inputs of materials, shop orders from production control, and product specifications and operation sheets from production engineering.

Table 16-1 *Sequences of activities in the production control system*

Department	Step
Production Engineering	A. Receive specifications and request for costing
	B. Plan manufacturing methods, standards
	C. Make cost and delivery estimates
Production Control	D. Accept and acknowledge receipt and delivery date of order
	E. Explode order into component parts and materials
Inventory Control	F. Check parts and materials against inventory
	G. Adjust inventory available figures for stock items
Production Control	H-1. Requisition purchase of materials and components not stocked
	I-1. Write shop orders for manufactured items not stocked
Inventory Control	H-2. Requisition purchase of stock items below reorder point
	I-2. Write shop orders for manufactured items below reorder point
Purchasing	I-3. Negotiate purchase orders for requisitioned items
Production Engineering	J. Order tools, jigs, and fixtures for new jobs
Production Control	K. Issue operations lists, routing sheets for shop orders
	L-1. Schedule operations against equipment capacity
	M. Estimate probable delivery dates and notify marketing
	N. Release jobs to the shop floor on schedule
Purchasing	L-2. Advise production control of acknowledged delivery dates on purchased items, expedite where necessary
Shop Supervision	O. Dispatch orders to machines and men as needed
	P. Notify production control of quantity completed and date after each scheduled operation
Production Control	Q. Arrange movements of materials as required
	R. Evaluate revised order schedules and set priorities
	S. Handle change orders
	T. Handle rush or expedited orders
	U. Advise shipping and inventory control when job is completed
	V. Advise production engineering and marketing of general delivery performances

Just the materials is not enough; all these must arrive to meet the start of the production schedule. In firms with long delivery periods or large backlogs, the shop orders are held by the production control department until the point at which the materials are available and the shop is due to start on the order.

RELEASING SHOP ORDERS

This decision as to when the work is to start into the process in order to meet the promised delivery date is one of the more critical ones in production control. It relates to the amount of work on hand and to the availability of materials and tooling. A POM model which could predict the progress of each shop order through the system from operation to operation would be of considerable value. This would have to produce many individual predictions. Figure 16-3 shows the progress of one order through a job shop. The prediction must include the estimate of the time required to obtain materials, the time required to move them to the area where operation 1 will be performed, the time waiting in queue for operation 1, the time in operation 1, the time to be moved to operation 2, etc. In a job shop with a hundred machines and hundreds of different orders, this is a staggering task, but one which computer methods will assist with in the future.

FOLLOWING THE PROGRESS OF ORDERS

An order is not turned over to the men on the shop floor with full trust that it will appear on the shipping dock by the anticipated date. A record, visual or computerized, is kept of the time at which each operation should be completed according to the routing assigned to the order. When a man completes an assigned operation, the number of pieces completed and the actual labor or machine time expended on the completed operation are reported to production control. On the basis of this information, orders which are behind can be expedited. In a process where scrap losses are

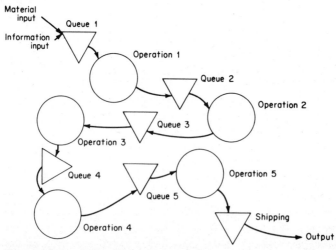

Figure 16-3 *Order flow in a job shop*

high, it is important to know the number of items surviving each operation. Once it is obvious that the attrition is going to exceed the scrap allowance, someone has to take action either to order another lot into production or to advise the customer that the quantity supplied will be less than that ordered. The information on actual hours taken to complete the job can be used to improve future estimates of costs and processing times.

MOVEMENT ORDERS

In many shops, the notification that an operation has been completed triggers an order to the group responsible for moving the material on to the next operation. Move men and lift truck operators may or may not be under the control of departmental foremen. If not, a system has to be set up to get the moves scheduled in response to varying work loads, relative efficiency of alternative routings, and the backlogs ahead of the various departments. In some cases, no move orders are written, but lift trucks circulate systematically throughout the work areas seeking out loads visually marked for movement to other areas. This may lead to much travel without a load, but it reduces the costs of the clerical system and can reduce the delays which occur while the move orders are written up and distributed. It takes a somewhat more disciplined and responsible type of driver, but this is a typical tradeoff in operations management. People who can get the job done with less supervision and control will operate well with less costly information systems, but they usually command higher wages, if they are available at all. The choice between better men and better systems is an economic choice.

DISPATCHING

Once a job is in the area where an operation is to be performed, someone must determine who does the job and when, and the sequence in which waiting orders are processed. The barber shop where every customer takes a number upon entering or the aircraft in single file on the airport runways are simple cases where the sequence is determined by simple rules rigidly adhered to. But in these cases, the system and the criteria for service are simple. Having each job taken in turn based on its arrival sequence is acceptable to the customer and economically satisfactory to the server. But in a more complex situation, this first-come-first-served (FCFS) rule may not be acceptable at all. Think of the hospital, typically organized as a job shop. Here patients with acute problems are assigned high priorities for services in X-ray or the operating rooms. Patients who are visiting the clinic have to be serviced fairly rapidly in X-ray or the laboratory, if they are to get out the same morning or by evening, whereas patients who are hospitalized for long periods can be used to fill in the gaps in the X-ray schedule at the convenience of the operators. But what about the patient who was hospitalized on Saturday in order to be operated on Monday morning? Laboratory and X-ray procedures must be completed ahead to meet the critical schedule of the surgeon and the availability of operating rooms. This question of "looking ahead" beyond the next task to the needs of other departments is another facet of the real scheduling problem.

ORGANIZATIONAL RESPONSIBILITY

The hospital example also illustrates another aspect of the scheduling and control system, namely, where does the final authority for the sequencing of jobs rest in each part of the organization? Who sets the priorities and to whose benefit? One area of possible conflict and overlap of authority is between the physician who is responsible for the general progress of the patient and the functional supervisors of the nurses, pharmacists, X-ray technicians, and orderlies. The physician may wish to see lab results on his evening rounds and then perform surgery at 8 a.m. the next morning. The lab supervisors may have conflicting demands which exceed laboratory capacity or lead to inefficiencies that they have to resolve, not always to the satisfaction of an individual doctor.

FLEXIBILITY FOR THE FOREMAN

A corresponding point of potential overlap and conflict exists in the job shop between production control and the supervisors (foremen) responsible for the efficiency of each production area. A foreman sees a group of orders awaiting processing as a way to accomplish a number of ends. He can, by careful selection of the man, job, and machine, seek to gain the highest long-run productivity in his area. He can sequence orders to reduce setup times, for example, or get John Doe who did a really tricky task well to do it again, rather than have someone else make the same mistakes, etc. He can use the assignment of orders as one of the few direct rewards under his control to discipline and motivate his men. This selection of which job goes on the open machine next is called "dispatching" and is one of the limited areas where the foreman still exercises discretion within the context of a well-developed production control system. The scheduler usually sets general priorities on jobs and the dates by which each order should leave an area, but the foreman makes the final dispatching decisions, hopefully within the constraints set by the schedule. Yet a foreman often may tend to make suboptimal (not best for the total system) decisions because he does not know what work will be available in the near future and its priority and often is not aware of the work situation in other areas with operations following his. Here again operations management is faced with a choice between centralized, complex information systems exercising tight control to sequence all work from hour to hour as opposed to reliance on a group of individuals who will make individually motivated, occasionally suboptimal decisions about sequencing as and when required.

EXPEDITING

Finally, each job emerges from the process and is shipped, mostly on or about the date promised in the acknowledgement of the order. Those orders which do not emerge as planned or come from an important customer who wants and demands earlier delivery are expedited; i.e., special steps are taken to see that they are processed earlier than normally at each work station in order to get them out more quickly. The net result for the expedited order can be surprisingly fast delivery, but this comes at the cost of slowing the by-passed orders. This potential speedup can be illustrated by comparing the delivery of two items, one made on a paced conveyor line and the other in a job shop. Assuming that each was out-of-stock and required ten operations of about equal processing times of $\frac{1}{2}$-hour each, the item on the conveyor might be completed in 5 to 24 hours depending on the spacing between stations. But in the job shop where the queues ahead of each machine average 2 days and it takes on the average a day to complete a move of a batch from one area to the next, one could spend at least 30 calendar days to complete the 5 hours of work. Obviously, the management of the job shop has to concern itself with the management of the queues in order to keep this from becoming 50 days.

EVALUATING SCHEDULES

Finding the best sequence of activities is a difficult task, but it can be simplified by having a set of criteria for evaluating the results. In most scheduling situations the decision-maker would like to:

1. Meet the required delivery dates as often as possible.
2. Have the minimum average lateness, when there has to be some.
3. Avoid really serious latenesses.
4. Reduce quoted (usually average) lead times, subject to 1, 2, and 3.
5. Maximize efficiency of manpower and machine utilization.
6. Reduce costs of setups and changeovers.
7. Minimize work-in-process inventory investments.
8. End up with the maximum possible net income.

These have some inherent conflicts, but they can be represented by an array of indices for ranking scheduling strategies.

To obtain a comparable set of experimental results on which to rank these strategies, POM researchers simulate the flow of a predetermined set of orders through a production system under each of the alternative strategies. After the shop has been run with this set of orders for a given period, it is possible to collect the following indices of system performance:

1. The number of jobs and standard hours of work completed.
2. The percentage of the jobs completed on time.
3. The average time required to complete an order.
4. The variation in the order completion times.
5. The mean lateness of the late orders.
6. The average work-in-process inventory.
7. Expediting costs (e.g., overtime costs) where allowed by the rules and the simulation program.

With these results, it is possible to obtain a reasonably good comparison of the strategies under controlled conditions. To some extent, the results are sensitive to the structure of the set of orders and the shop simulated, but enough situations have been compared to give a relatively representative picture of how the strategies operate. Equipment and manpower inefficiencies, like extra setups, show up in the failure of the system under one rule to complete as many jobs or as many standard hours of work during the period allowed as another rule does. Average completion times in a system where the jobs compared have identical due dates usually is a good indicator of the jobs late but is not necessarily good enough. It is possible that some scheduling rules would get jobs completed in less time on the average but still lead to a larger percentage of late jobs because they failed to expedite those jobs with the more demanding delivery requirements. Or consider the situation where a scheduler is offered a substantial bonus to reduce the percentage of jobs late. If he was being compensated solely on that basis, he might choose to gain his bonus by suspending work on any job once it appeared obvious that it was going to be late. The other jobs could then move ahead and run less risk of being late, but those orders already late could become very, very late. Some dispatching and scheduling rules, as you will see, may prove quite effective on many criteria but do not guarantee that all orders will get completed. This is why some rules have to be coupled with other special rules to take care of the situations which show up as marked irregularities in the variance of the order completion times and the mean lateness figures.

A SIMPLE COMPARISON

Where these criteria are not of equal importance because of competitive pressures or cost structures, a single evaluation figure may be developed using a weighted ranking of the outcomes. Table 16-2 shows two comparisons

Table 16-2

Criteria*	1	2	3	4	5	6	7	8	9	10	Total
Relative Weight	1	1	1	1	1	1	1	1	1	1	Relative Rank
Rule											
MINPRT	1.00	.83	1.00	.20	1.00	1.00	.76	.91	1.00	1.00	8.70
MINSOP	.87	1.00	.63	1.00	.73	.52	.96	.99	.92	.92	8.54
FCFS	.86	.54	.54	.20	.73	.38	.84	.98	.93	.93	6.93
MINSD	.84	.48	.46	.22	.68	.36	.91	1.00	.91	.91	6.77
MINDD	.94	.62	.64	.24	.84	.51	1.00	.99	.87	.87	7.52
RANDOM	.84	.68	.79	.20	.67	.66	.80	.93	.92	.91	7.40

Criteria*	1	2	3	4	5	6	7	8	9	10	Total
Relative Weight	2	5	5	5	1	1	4	2	3	2	Relative Rank
Rule											
MINPRT	2.00	4.15	5.00	1.00	1.00	1.00	3.04	1.82	3.00	2.00	24.01
MINSOP	1.74	5.00	3.15	5.00	.73	.52	3.84	1.98	2.76	1.84	26.56
FCFS	1.72	2.70	2.70	1.00	.73	.38	3.36	1.96	2.79	1.86	19.20
MINSD	1.68	2.40	2.30	1.10	.68	.36	3.64	2.00	2.73	1.82	18.71
MINDD	1.88	3.10	3.20	1.20	.84	.51	4.00	1.98	2.61	1.74	21.06
RANDOM	1.68	3.40	3.95	1.00	.67	.66	3.20	1.86	2.76	1.82	21.00

* KEY TO CRITERIA:

1. Number of orders completed
2. Percent of orders completed late
3. Mean of the distribution of completions
4. Standard deviation of the distribution of completions
5. Average number of orders waiting in the shop
6. Average wait time of orders
7. Yearly cost of carrying orders in queue
8. Ratio of inventory carrying cost while waiting to inventory cost while on machine
9. Percent of labor utilized
10. Percent of machine capacity utilized

KEY TO THE DISPATCH RULES:

MINPRT   Minimum processing time next operation
MINSOP   Minimum slack per operation—time until due date less total processing time remaining, divided by number of operations left
FCFS   First-come-first-served
MINSD   Order with earliest (minimum) planned start date in schedule of this work center
MINDD   Order with earliest (minimum) planned due date in overall schedule
RANDOM   Orders randomly selected

Taken from E. LeGrande, "The Development of a Factory Simulation Using Actual Operating Data," *Management Technology,* vol. 3, no. 1, May 1963.

of a set of results from a series of simulations. A series of simulation runs was made in which a rule was programmed into the computer and used to dispatch the orders at each work station. The data indicates that the MINPRT (minimum processing time next operation) rule produced the largest number of orders completed and received a relative rank of 1.00. It achieved 83 percent as good a performance on percent of orders completed late as the MINSOP (minimum slack per operation) rule and received a relative rank of 0.83 for this second criterion. In the first set, the relative weights were simply summed to give an implicitly equal weighting to each criterion. The second shows the results with a revised weighting. Obviously, even more sophisticated weighing schemes could be devised, but let us proceed to the question of how strategies are formulated and implemented, starting with the simplest flow shop case.

THE FLOW SHOP

The assembly line is the most rationalized flow shop, and the procedures used to balance lines in earlier chapters show how a flow shop can be managed to obtain better sequences of operations. The assembly line requires that the operations be grouped to give essentially the same operating times to all stations, nicely sequenced due dates, and orders placed into production at predetermined intervals. But all flow shops do not necessarily make only one item at a time on a fixed schedule. As one looks at a very simple flow shop where tasks are of varied lengths, some of the alternative strategies for scheduling procedures become evident.

What if you had only one machine and a series of orders to be processed? What would determine the best sequence, if the costs were (1) sequence independent, or (2) sequence dependent? If costs are sequence independent and there is time to do all the work before the first order is due, then one can sequence the jobs with the highest invested dollar value first to minimize work-in-process carrying costs or take the jobs with the shortest processing times first to minimize the average time to complete an order. If all jobs cannot be done before the first order is due and lateness is of concern, then one is more likely to process the orders in terms of their due dates; i.e., jobs due out first are processed first. This procedure works when for every delivery date the sum of the processing times of all the orders due up to and including that date are less than the equipment and manpower time available; i.e., the system is operating below capacity. Once this condition breaks down, then it is necessary to compare alternative schedules and evaluate them by the most relevant criteria.

If costs are sequence dependent—for example, where the setup costs vary depending on what order precedes the current one—the problem becomes even more complicated. Where there are N jobs to be processed, there are $N!$ or $N \times (N-1) \times (N-2) \times \ldots \times 1$ possible sequences. Take the trivial case shown in Table 16-3. There are only three jobs, so there are $3 \times 2 \times 1$ sequences to choose from on the basis of total cost. Table 16-4 contains a complete enumeration of these six sets of costs, assuming that the initial cost of going to A, B, or C is the same. The least-cost sequence need not be unique, and, in this case, A-B-C and B-A-C are equivalent. Some investigators have suggested that one use a rule-of-thumb called the "next best rule." One starts with a given job and then looks for the next job with the least ("best") setup cost. In the trivial example above, the scheduler would start with B and go to A because that is the lowest cost requirement. Then the only possible next step is to go from A to C. This gives the lowest cost equal to $4. Starting at C, however, one would pick A over B and then go to B for a total cost of $5. But note that we have had to investigate only three alternatives instead of six. With four jobs, complete enumeration would require $4 \times 3 \times 2 \times 1$, or 24 evaluations, while the "next best rule" would require only four. In general, the comparison is $N!$ versus N evaluations, a very marked simplification and one which gives pretty good results almost every time. A rule of this type, which is good but not proven optimal, is called a "heuristic."

With multiple machines (more than one stage or operation in the process), the problem becomes much more complicated. Now it becomes necessary to look ahead beyond the machine currently being scheduled and see how each choice will affect machines serving later operations as well. Each machine with its own queue can be thought of as a server in a queuing theory model. From queuing analysis, one can determine how long a queue should be maintained to secure the desired rate of equipment utilization. A production control system should be able to look ahead to report if that queue exists.

Table 16-3 *Setup costs for sequencing jobs*

Going to	A	B	C
From A	$0	$2	$3
B	1	0	2
C	3	4	0

Table 16-4 *Total costs of possible sequences*

Sequence	Cost
A-B-C	$2 + 2 = $4
B-C-A	2 + 3 = 5
C-A-B	3 + 2 = 5
A-C-B	3 + 4 = 7
B-A-C	1 + 3 = 4
C-B-A	4 + 1 = 5

THE GANTT CHART

The device frequently used to keep track of multiple machine schedules is the Gantt chart. It is named after Henry Gantt, a pioneer in scientific management, who developed it over 50 years ago. We might call it a bar chart, but one modified to identify specific orders. It can take several forms. The simplest form is a loading chart like the one shown in Figure 16-4. This reports the work loads on the typesetting, printing, and bindery operations of a publishing organization. It does not indicate that any one job will come out of the typesetting department 35 days after the start of the chart. It merely shows that there are 35 days of work ahead of the department. No allowance has been made for delays due to maintenance, vacations, or idleness waiting for orders tied up in other departments. For example, look at the case of the bindery. The publishing process allows most of the photographic composition work and the typesetting to go forward in parallel, but these must precede the printing, which in turn must precede binding. If all of the typesetting work cannot come out before 35 days are up, certainly all of the bindery work cannot be started, let alone completed, until some time after that period.

It is evident that the load chart does not tell the scheduler what he needs to know about the date at which an order should be completed. Assuming that order F is started into the typesetting department only after orders A through E are completed, it cannot be completed before day 35. Since printing must follow both photography and typesetting, order F cannot be completed before day 39 (35 + 4 in printing), and the bindery cannot finish up until day 42 (39 + 3 days in bindery).

Actual scheduling of orders A through F requires that the jobs be put on a time scale in the sequence that they can go through the steps of the process. If job A goes into photography and typesetting at the same

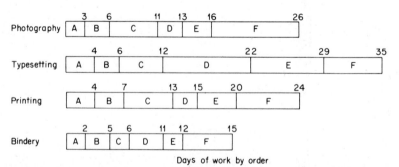

Figure 16-4 *Load chart for publishing operations new load booked in cumulative days of work in order of arrival*

time, then its actual schedule would look as follows:

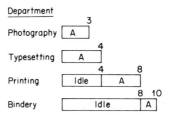

Most schedulers would be dissatisfied to have the printing department idle for 4 days and the bindery for 8. Unless they are constrained to take orders first-come-first-served (FCFS rule), they would like to push through jobs with shorter processing times up to that point (using the MINPRT rule) in order to reduce idleness. On this basis, order *B* would go first, then *A*, followed by *C*. The revised Gantt chart for orders *A* and *B* appears in Figure 16-5. Idleness has been reduced.

A further question arises with orders *D* and *E*. After *A*, *B*, and *C* are through the first two parallel operations on day 12, a first-come-first-served rule would select order *D*. But this would mean that the printing department would sit idle from day 19 until day 23. If job *E* is taken first, then the printing presses can roll again on day 20. Here again it has been useful to "look ahead" at other work groups and to change rules depending on the situations encountered. It is important to recognize that one cannot recommend any one scheduling or dispatch rule such as FCFS over another unless he knows the specific problem encountered and the criteria currently being emphasized.

The criteria and especially the nature of the problem become more variable as the uncertainties increase, especially those concerning the arrivals of orders and their delivery priorities as well as the processing and waiting times applying to specific orders. In Figure 16-5, we assumed that the printing department and the bindery would have remained idle. Yet in an on-going shop, they might have been busy processing the final operations of orders received prior to order *A*. Likewise, orders *A* through *F* might

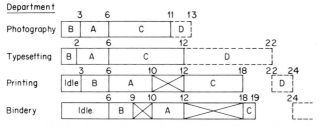

Figure 16-5 *Gantt chart schedule for orders* A, B, *and* C *with possible schedule for* D

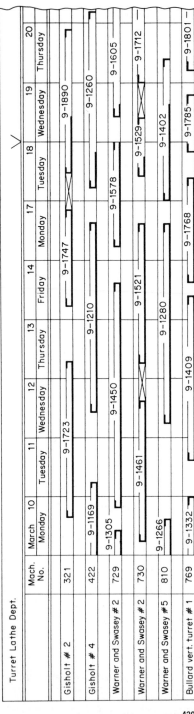

Turret Lathe Dept.

Figure 16-6 *Gantt layout, or reserved time planning chart,* [*From E. S. Buffa, Models for Production and Operations Management, John Wiley & Sons, Inc., New York, 1963, p. 64.*]

have had different due dates and priorities, and there might suddenly come an order G that is needed in a real rush. Thus, one of the prime objectives of the scheduler is flexibility in his schedule.

Once a schedule is made, it is subject to change and to obsolescence as actual job completion times vary from the expected times of completion. Because of this, many schedules use a form of the Gantt chart that can be updated regularly to show the current date, the jobs scheduled, whether the work completed is on schedule, and where time has been reserved for maintenance, rush orders, training, and just catching up. Figure 16-6 shows one such chart and the notation used to let the decision-maker spot problems quickly.

THE JOB SHOP WITH ITS UNCERTAIN FLOWS

The techniques for controlling the larger, more complex flow shops can be extended to the job shop, where the routings are highly variable. These routings also tend to be coupled with higher variability in waiting times, processing times, and delivery requirements. Here Gantt charts are used as control devices to follow orders and schedule equipment, but one has to rely more and more on arbitrary scheduling rules as uncertainty and complexity increase. The capacity of the individual to spot developing problems and "look ahead" and then develop alternate schedules is limited and any large job shop usually overtaxes this capacity.

TACTICS

The current schedule of a shop usually has been arrived at by starting with the old schedule and adding to it the operations required by the newly arrived jobs. The first new operation is scheduled into the earliest opening for the proper equipment of sufficient length in the old schedule. Then each operation is scheduled into the first opening in the appropriate department which is of adequate length *and* starts after the preceding operation has been completed. A reasonable time also has to be allowed for the material to move from department to department. The succeeding operations are scheduled in the same manner to increase equipment utilization without violating precedence relationships. This is called a "left-shifted" or "left-justified" schedule. Often it leads to an acceptable utilization of the facility and meeting of delivery requirements, whereupon it may be accepted as is.

If the results are not satisfactory on completion of this initial left-shifted schedule, then one has to start all over again using a new set of scheduling rules or else use a trial-and-error procedure to shift jobs around until an adequate schedule is reached. One heuristic way to start is to treat the due date of the last operation of an order as the right-hand margin for the schedule of that order and shift that final operation as far to the right as possible. Then the next to last operation is shifted as far to the right as the new start of the last operation allows. Each additional operation is similarly scheduled working toward the first. This, when done to each job, moves everything to the right and gives flexibility in scheduling the start of jobs with early delivery requirements and/or short processing times, depending on the criteria being applied. Once these adjustments are made, the schedule is again left-shifted to close gaps in the schedule and get the work out as soon as possible.

DISPATCHING

Much the same process takes place on the factory floor as the foreman selects (dispatches) the orders to be done next. He may ignore everything and pick them randomly, be "fair" and treat them first-come-first-served, get the most jobs out by using a shortest processing time rule, or speed deliveries by selecting the one with the earliest due date, or just juggle orders in response to expediters' requests.

But these simple rules do not necessarily function adequately. Just because the first and second operations of a job have very short processing times does not mean that the fifth one might not. Pity the job with the single longest operation in the whole shop backlog. So long as it is always one of two orders ahead of the equipment performing that fifth operation, it will wait under a strict MINPRT (minimum processing time) rule and never be completed. Likewise, an earliest due date (MINDD) rule will select on Thursday the job due next Monday with only 15 minutes of work remaining and bypass an order due next Tuesday with 7 operations and 86 hours of work remaining. Rules are needed to compare orders on the basis of their work remaining as well as their due dates and to guarantee that they get out of the shop within a reasonable period.

COMPOUND RULES

These problems have led to the development of new sets of compound scheduling and dispatching rules for use in complex job shops that control on the basis of remaining work and the time available to do it. They are most useful when there is a computer system following the progress of the order and supplying the people on the floor with current information on the status of orders and on the latest priorities. One of the more interesting rules is based on the slack time remaining divided by the number of operations remaining (MINSOP). Since the computer has to have instructions about what to do in case of ties, a shortest processing time rule is used as a tie breaker. Slack time represents the difference between the time it would take to complete all remaining operations if there were no waiting in queue and the time available between now and the due date. In effect, this MINSOP rule computes the time available to wait in queue before each operation on the average. It hustles through these orders which have the least waiting time available. This dynamic rule increases the priority of the order as it waits in the queue.

An increasing number of firms with large job shops are beginning to build computer models of their own operations. An array of orders with their routings and processing times, including those booked and those likely to arrive, is fed into the system at the anticipated intervals. An appropriate Monte Carlo simulation is made of the arrival intervals and the variations in processing times of these orders. Scheduling rules are used to move the orders in the queues in front of each set of machines. Experiments are then made with the model to test the impact of changes in the decision rules and of alternative aggregate scheduling and equipment purchases. Several reports of these efforts are quite encouraging, explaining how management has come to understand much better what really is going on. These reports claim cuts in production lead time and work-in-process inventory.

THE PROJECT AND ITS UNCERTAIN SCHEDULE

Many of the systems that you will manage will be unique or at least novel. One has to develop a control system for most new research projects, advertising campaigns, building contracts, and surgical emergencies. All these nonrepetitive undertakings are frequently called "projects" in order to distinguish them from similar, but more repetitive, production processes. Proper sequencing of its activities and their timing is critical to a project's objectives. To accomplish this, the project manager has to invest time in arriving at a proper schedule. To do so, he must add to his bag of tricks techniques that are responsive to a higher degree of uncertainty and still are inexpensive because they will not produce schedules whose costs can be amortized against thousands of units of production.

Each project manager usually starts off with a background of experiences which tells him a great deal about the activities necessary and how long they will take. If he lacks this information, the men who will manage the individual tasks usually can supply it. On the other hand, he knows that this project will not be exactly like the others and that many of the specialized people who contribute to the project will face uncertainties and also may be servicing multiple projects. Just how these specialists will perform on the project and when they will be available is something that he must attempt to anticipate and, in the latter case, control. Thus, he must approach his job with a special concern for the interrelationships among tasks and for the impact that variations in the performance of these tasks are likely to have upon his project. Most of all, he needs to be able to identify the flexibilities that he has in adjusting to these uncertainties.

NEW TOOLS

For many years, the project manager has had a simple tool to help him, the use of bar or Gantt charts for scheduling. Then in the 1950s, managers faced with very large projects such as the annual maintenance shutdown of multi-million dollar chemical plants and the development of a submarine-missile system found new techniques to help plan and control large, complicated, and rapidly changing projects. Names were coined with great abandon for these systems and their computerized versions, but two acronyms have achieved the greatest fame. They are CPM (Critical Path Method) and PERT (Program Evaluation and Review Technique). We will emphasize the latter.

AN EXAMPLE

Let us take the case of Harvey Crimson and Eli Swinger, two young men about town who wish to start their own business. After a reasonably careful study, they believe that they have the proper specifications for a product: sells for a dollar, costs a dime to make, is patentable, is habit-forming and, temporarily at least, is legal and not taxable. A friend has indicated that he can develop such a product if guaranteed a reasonable income for the period that it takes to get the product on the market, as well as a share of the profits of the firm. Before making this commitment, Harvey and Eli wanted to estimate the actual length of that commitment. They put together in Table 16-5 the list of activities to be performed. Then they studied the order in which to do them and the length of time for each. They were both amazed at the total of 36 man-months required to perform all of the tasks. Eli noted that it would take a year and a half (36 ÷ 2 = 18 months) if both Harvey and he worked full-time on the project. Harvey, however, observed that some periods would require only part-time effort and some activities could be delegated to specialists and agents. But there were some probable delays that would have to be included in the schedule. The engineer who had agreed to do the development of the process stated that he needed at least 2-months warning to free himself to do the required work. Some of the plants that could undertake the manufacture of equipment for this type of product had a 6-month backlog. Therefore, a tentative order would have to be placed at least 3 months before activity *m* could be started.

BAR CHARTING

The first step that Harvey and Eli undertook was to develop the "must follow" sequence shown in Table 16-5. They then drew their results out on a simple bar chart shown in Figure 16-7. On each bar, the activity is designated by a letter and its length by a number. The bars on the chart are proportional to the length of each activity and have been positioned so that each activity starts immediately on completion of all the activities which it must follow. It does not, however, show explicitly which activities must control which other ones nor, consequently, which activities might be delayed without lengthening the project. They quickly ran into a number of questions. Their resources were scarce, and it made sense to put off most of their investments until the last possible moment. How could they represent the full set of alternative choices in starting times for each activity? What would be the resulting schedule if the process engineer was not

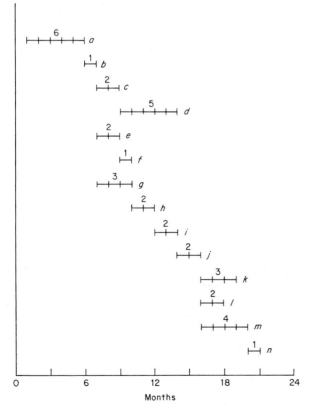

Figure 16-7 *Bar chart of schedule for developing the new product and the firm*

Table 16-5 *Activities in developing a product and a firm*

Activity	Length	Must Follow
(a) Develop idea for product	6 months	—
(b) Evaluate the idea for product	1	a
(c) Prepare prospectus for investors	2	b
(d) Raise money	5	c
(e) Prepare marketing strategy and methods	2	b
(f) Design market test of new product	1	e
(g) Develop product from initial idea	3	b
(h) Develop process for marking product	2	g
(i) Make initial (pilot) manufactured lot to test process and supply market test	2	h
(j) Test market product	2	d,f,i
(k) Raise more money	3	j
(l) Develop distribution system	2	j
(m) Get full-scale production started	4	j
(n) Fill distribution channels	1	k,l,m

available for 4 months or if equipment lead times were shortened to 4 months? It was to answer questions like these that the PERT technique was developed.

PERT FUNDAMENTALS

Two fundamental definitions underlie PERT (Program Evaluation and Review Technique):

1. *Events:* An event is a milestone, a specific accomplishment that can be identified with a recognizable point in time.
2. *Activities:* An activity is the package of time and work required to accomplish a specific task, i.e., reach a specific event.

Each activity can be associated graphically with two events, its start and its finish. The start of one activity is frequently an event identical to the finish of another. With these two distinctions in mind, it is possible to make the transition from the simple bar chart to a PERT network. The bar chart tells us that the particular activity d follows activity c but not its interrelation with activities a, g, or m. We can overcome this limitation by building a network or arrow diagram to replace the bar chart. In this PERT network, the activities are represented by arrows and the event by

numbered circles called nodes. Thus, we can represent the search for a
new product idea by a pair of arrows.

The next step is to develop the entire network so that all interrelationships
are indicated by the resulting network. Thus, the introduction of a new
product can be represented by the network in Figure 16-8. Eli and Harvey
still have to deal with the question of the waiting times for the engineer and
the equipment, but let us look at the advantages of this simple network as a
tool for analysis and control.

1. Indicates explicitly all the relationships among all activities on the
   project.
2. Makes redundant the listing of tasks and their "must follow" relationships.
3. Allows application of networking techniques such as PERT, using computers if the project is very large.
4. Allows the use of probability theory for the estimation of completion
   dates when there is uncertainty about the length of the activities.
5. Allows us to ask a number of "what if" questions without a complete
   redrawing of the lines.

THE NETWORK

In the network in Figure 16-8, the project starts at a point in time, an
event preceding one or more activities. The start is itself instantaneous. The
activities represented by the arrows are the sole consumers of time and
other resources. By numbering the events, it is possible to designate the
activities and also identify those events that are shared. The activity of
finding a product, designated activity 1-2, can be identified readily as the
one which comes immediately ahead of activity 2-3. We also can see that
activity 8-9 must follow activities 4-8, 5-8, and 7-8, even when the drawing

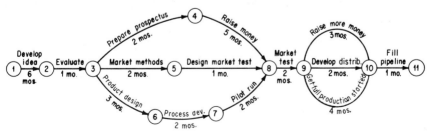

Figure 16-8 *Preliminary network for developing the product and firm*

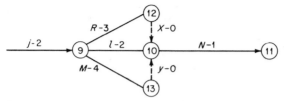

Figure 16-9   *Modified network section*

of the network is not in front of us. The "all-roads-lead-to-activity" 8-9 is a common phenomenon. Here it means that there is no use going ahead with any of the other activities until the market test proves successful. After event 9, the completion of the market test, several things can go forward at once.

DUMMY VARIABLES

At least one modification must be made to the network in Figure 16-8 before a standard computer program could be used. For most programs, each activity must be identified by a unique pair of event numbers. It would confuse the computer to have activities k, l, and m all identified as 9-10 but with three different lengths. To get around this problem, it is possible to put in "dummy activities" represented by a dotted line. Two dummy activities x and y of zero time durations can be used to uniquely identify activities k, l, and m as in Figure 16-9. This complicates the drawing of the network, but it removes any ambiguity.

     A second condition under which the dummy variable is useful is the following. An activity r must be preceded by activities q and p. Activity q also must precede activity s, but the latter is not dependent upon completion of activity p. Figure 16-10 shows the use of a dummy activity z to avoid a misleading network.

A PROCEDURE

The procedure that our would-be entrepreneurs followed is a generally applicable one. The initial step is to break down the project into a complete list of activities, their times and their interrelationships. The more detailed

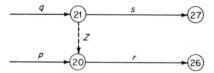

Figure 16-10   *Use of dummy for complex precedence condition*

the list at the start the better. At first, the list is likely to be nothing more than all the things that you can think of that someone must do and be responsible for. Such a list can be useful by itself, because gaps in planning may come to light and the list will be available for continued reference as the project progresses. This list should be the joint undertaking of the manager and the technical specialists responsible for the project activities. In this way, a number of things are accomplished:

1. A mutual understanding of the necessary steps is established.
2. A mutual understanding of the interrelationships is established.
3. Project goals and objectives are made explicit.
4. Commitments are made as to time and resource requirements which later can serve to guide and motivate performance.

With this commonly accepted agreement as to the activities needed, the time required, and the interrelationships, it is possible to develop the initial PERT network. For example, Table 16-6 contains a detailed description of a new product program for Swinger and Crimson, which includes the modification in Figure 16-9 and the delays that were left out above.

Figure 16-11 shows the final network presentation of these events.

Table 16-6 *Description of activities and events of final network*

Activity No.	Length	Activity Description	T_E	T_L	S^*
1-2	6	Develop product idea	0	0	0
2-3	1	Evaluate new product idea	6	6	0
3-4	2	Prepare financial prospectus	7	9	2
3-5	2	Prepare marketing strategy	7	13	6
3-14	2	Wait for engineer to get free	7	7	0
4-8	5	Raise funds	9	11	2
5-8	1	Design market test	9	15	6
14-6	3	Develop product	9	9	0
6-7	2	Develop process	12	12	0
7-8	2	Make pilot production run	14	14	0
8-9	2	Market test	16	16	0
9-12	3	Raise more money	18	25	7
9-10	2	Develop distribution system	18	26	8
12-10	0	Dummy activity	21	28	7
9-13	6	Wait for equipment	18	18	0
13-10	4	Get production started	24	24	0
10-11	1	Fill distribution pipeline	28	28	0
Finish			29	29	0

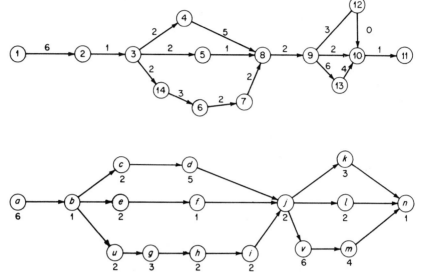

Figure 16-11 *The final network schedule.* T_E = *earliest start date for each activity;* T_L = *latest start date for each activity; S = slack in each activity and defined at* $T_L - T_E$. *The computation of these values is explained on the following text pages. An alternative and acceptable diagramming convention puts activities on circles and events on arrows. This type of network often is easier to draw initially, but it does not lead directly to the data needed for computer analysis and is somewhat more difficult to analyze.*

The addition of the delays as activities 3-14 and 9-13 has complicated the network, but several questions have now become evident. The delays occasioned by the wait for the engineer and the equipment delivery leave much leeway in timing the starts of the fund raising and the marketing program. When can we start these much shorter tasks? The definition of the delay for equipment availability becomes important. Is it a delay that can be worked around and to what gain? What will be the length of the project now? We know the sum of the original activities was 36 months and the delays may be 10 months, but that does not necessarily mean a 46-month project.

Analysis of any network is concerned primarily with the length and cost of the project, the earliest date at which an activity can start, and the latest such time. Once a network has been drawn up, it is possible to follow all paths (required sequences) through the network. The longest of these will be the planned length of the project. For example, there are three paths between events 3 and 8 in Figure 16-11: 3-4-8 of length 7,

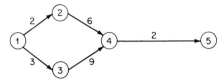

Figure 16-12 *Sample network for analysis*

3-5-8 of length 3, and 3-14-6-7-8 of length 9. Since event 8 cannot occur until activities 4-8, 5-8, and 7-8 all are completed, event 8 cannot occur until 9 months after 3.

To explain the procedure for network analysis systematically, let us look at the sample network in Figure 16-12. It is obvious that activity 4-5 can be started only after all activities on both paths 1-2-4 and 1-3-4 have been completed. The length of path 1-2-4 is 8 and of 1-3-4 is 12, and thus, the earliest allowable starting time T_E for activity 4-5 will be 12. We shall call this longest path(s) the "critical path(s)," because it controls directly the length of the project. In Figure 16-12, the critical path is 1-3-4-5, and the project length is 14.

We can proceed to set up the earliest allowable start time T_E for each activity by working from the start of the project through toward the project's finish. For each activity, T_E will be the length of the longest path leading to that activity's starting event. It also is evident that some activities need not start at their earliest allowable start time if the project is allowed a 14-period duration. Activity 2-4 can start as late as period 6 and still not delay the project, while activity 1-2 could start as late as period 4. To provide the manager with this useful information, we will calculate the latest allowable start time T_L for each activity and the amount of slack S available in the schedule for each activity equal to $T_L - T_E$. Slack represents to the manager the amount of time that he can delay completion of an activity without lengthening the critical path. If an activity is on the critical path, its slack will be zero unless the project is late in starting, in which case slack could be represented by a negative number. By inspection of Figure 16-12, we can arrive at Table 16-7.

The same approach is used to find the corresponding figures for much more complicated networks. One goes through the network front to back

Table 16-7

Activity	1-2	1-3	2-4	3-4	4-5	Finish
T_E	0	0	2	3	12	14
T_L	4	0	6	3	12	14
$S = T_L - T_E$	4	0	4	0	0	0

to calculate T_E for each activity. The value of T_E for the last activity plus the length of that activity is the length of the project and the length of the critical path. Armed with the length of the project, one uses the same approach from back to front to find T_L for each activity. Here, as shown in Table 16-7, one computes the lengths of paths from the finish of the project to the start of the activity, including the activity's own length. By subtracting the maximum of these from the total length of the project, we get T_L for that activity. If $T_L = T_E$, there is no slack and the activity is on one or more of the critical paths. Multiple critical paths are possible since path lengths are not unique. This same mechanical procedure can be applied to any project regardless of its complexity and is sufficiently straight forward that it can be assigned to a computer.

Once a network has been laid out and analyzed to determine the earliest and latest allowable start times and slack for each activity, the length of the project, and the location of the critical path, this information can be put to good use. First of all, the developer of the network has secured commitments from all parties that they can do their own activities within a given time period. He also has an estimate of the project length and has identified for each activity how much, if any, a given delay on a given activity will affect the length of the project. Now the manager can think about the opportunities available to him to shift resources from slack tasks to critical tasks and reduce project length. The new product development project shown in Figure 16-11 offers some examples. Activity 9-13 is a 6-month delay for delivery of equipment. Could we place a tentative order with the manufacturer 6 months ahead of event 9 and then cancel if the market test was unsuccessful? Well, you might jump the gun—if cancellation charges are not too high—but probably not by 6 months. Activities 6-7 and 7-8 involve development of the process and initial pilot plant production. It would be doubtful that one could specify to the manufacturer the production capacity and process requirements until these two activities were completed. Could these two activities be started earlier then? No, the calculation of slack indicates that these two activities are on the critical path, so there is no flexibility in starting date without adding more resources.

Returning to Table 16-6 and Figure 16-11, let us assume that our engineer was able to join the project immediately—eliminating activity 3-14. Now paths 3-4-8 and 3-14-6-7-8 are both of length 7. Both paths will require intensive attention, and, if the money raising goes at all slowly, the whole effort will now be delayed.

The usefulness of PERT is not limited to the initial planning phase of a project. As activities are performed, it becomes evident that the original estimates were not perfect forecasts. But as soon as these discrepancies arise, favorable or unfavorable, it is relatively easy to reevaluate the network to determine the impact of unexpected developments and see what adjustments, if any, are necessary.

UNCERTAINTY

It also is possible to set up a PERT network which takes into account the uncertainty surrounding activity lengths. To do this, one typically secures three time estimates for each activity. They are:

1. *The most likely time*—represents the most frequently occurring time that the activity would require if the work were done again and again under identical conditions, the time that the manager would give when only one point estimate is called for.
2. *Most optimistic time*—estimates the time that it would take if everything went along perfectly with no problems, no delays, etc. Needless to say, this would have a very low probability of occurring, maybe once per hundred projects.
3. *Most pessimistic time*—represents the time it might take to complete the activity if everything went wrong. This too would be unusual, but it should be given some weight in any distribution of outcomes.

These three estimates are then used as the basis for fitting a probability distribution to the time for the activity so that we can arrive at an expected value for the time of each activity and a standard deviation for that time. Historically, a probability distribution called the beta distribution has been used to represent the distribution of completion times for PERT activities.

where

a = most optimistic time

b = most pessimistic time

m = most likely time

the applicable beta distribution will have:

$$\text{a mean activity time} = \frac{a + 4m + b}{6}$$

and

$$\text{standard deviation} = \frac{b - a}{6}$$

The beta distribution was selected because it could be fit easily to the three time estimates and could represent both symmetric and asymmetric distributions. Armed with these two parameters for each activity time, it is possible to prepare a frequency distribution of the total length of the project and estimates of the likelihood of completing the project before specific dates.

CRITICAL PATH METHOD

Once the project manager has the network in front of him and knows the anticipated length of the project, he usually wants to improve the cost of the project and its completion date. Unfortunately, these two objectives usually are at crossed purposes. In most cases, it is possible to shorten the project only by increasing the input of resources and the cost. Thus, the manager often must expand his project analysis to consider both time and cost by using a cousin of PERT called "Critical Path Method" (CPM). In CPM, one also gathers specific estimates of the cost of each activity, which may or may not be directly variable with the time schedule. For the PERT analysis, we have already dealt with the naturally allowed length of an activity—or the *normal* time.

CPM uses the same network construction principles as PERT and the normal time. In addition, one secures the normal direct cost associated with the crash time. The "crash time" is the time that would be required if no costs were spared in trying to reduce the project time. "Crash cost" is then the cost of the activity when the manager does everything possible to speed it up. He could be willing to incur this cost for a number of reasons, e.g., securing progress payments or avoiding lateness penalties.

For example, let us look at a road construction project. Suppose that one activity is the grading of the roadbed, and the normal time and cost estimate are 4 months and $1 million for 12 miles of roadbed. The contractor recognizes that it is possible to work 4 hours overtime each day at time-and-a-half and to work a seventh day at double pay. It also might be possible to do some of the work on a night shift, knowing that there would be added costs of supervision, inefficiencies despite an investment in lighting equipment, and high premiums to attract second-shift labor. In fact, all three approaches could be taken to achieve round-the-clock speed—if the cost of a delay to the contractor were high enough to warrant the added costs.

CALCULATING CRASH COSTS

We can represent this situation graphically, as in Figure 16-13. The vertical axis represents the cost of completing the project, and the horizontal axis represents the time required for completion. We have the original estimates of 4 months and $1 million. Now suppose that with a crash effort the same manager estimates completion could be made in 2 months at a crash cost of $2 million. These two points are connected with a straight line in Figure 16-13. This line is referred to as the "approximate time-cost curve." We use the term "approximate" because there is no proof that this cost line will be straight. In many cases, we should expect it to curve like the dotted line in Figure 16-13. Such a curved line would indicate a

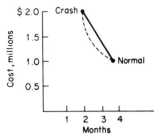

Figure 16-13 *Crash time and cost compared with normal time and cost*

diminishing return from each incremental input of resources to improve the activity's actual duration. Which lines, straight or curved, would be the more useful approximation of the true situation again is a matter of judgment on the part of managers familiar with the project. Many times, however, it will be adequate to proceed on the basis of the straight-line relationship. You can easily imagine the accounting problems involved in determining the true time-cost curve, particularly if there are thousands of activities on a project each with its own curve. For this reason, the linear approximation often is used instead. If, as a manager, you think that a more accurate fit is significant to some major activity, then by all means construct your best nonlinear estimate of the true curve and use it.

SHORTENING THE CRITICAL PATH

To look at the procedure for shortening a network, let us start with the job at the left of Figure 16-14. Here it is presented with its normal times which result in a project length of 16 weeks. In Table 16-14, we have listed the normal and crash times and cost for all activities. We can see that the normal cost of the project is $35,000. If all activities were crashed, the project would cost $47,000. By looking at the network with all of its crash times at the right of Figure 16-14, we can see that a minimum crash project length would be 10 weeks, i.e., the total crash time for path 1-2-4-5. But

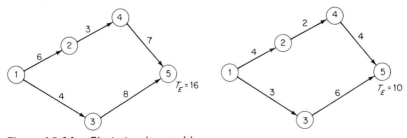

Figure 16-14 *First step in crashing*

Table 16-8

Activity	Times		Cost		Average Cost to Reduce per Week
	Normal	Crash	Normal	Crash	
1-2	6	4	$10,000	$14,000	$2,000
1-3	4	3	5,000	8,000	3,000
2-4	3	2	4,000	5,000	1,000
3-5	8	6	9,000	12,000	1,500
4-5	7	4	7,000	8,000	333

there is an obvious waste of resources here, since we have reduced the shorter secondary path (1-3-5) to 9 weeks; that is, we seem to have ended up paying for unnecessary slack on that path. A policy of complete crashing that buys this slack could prove extremely costly on a larger project with hundreds of activities. Therefore, we have to follow a procedure which selects only those activities on the critical path (or paths) for crashing. Furthermore, it would be desirable if the procedure allowed the manager to see the cost for each possible additional reduction of the project length. With that information, he could then choose the project length which incurs the minimum total project costs including both crashing costs and comparable penalties or lost revenue.

This procedure starts out by establishing the cost of reducing each activity per period. Referring back to Table 16-8, we notice that the least expensive activity to crash on the critical path is activity 4-5; here, time can be reduced for a cost of $333 per week. The minimum crash time to which we can reduce this activity is 4 weeks at an additional total cost of $1,000. When we have done this, we will have the network as shown in Figure 16-15 which will be 13 weeks long and have a total cost of $36,000. Then we must proceed to the next least expensive activity on the critical path, reducing activity 2-4 from 3 to 2 weeks. Then we have a project lasting 12 weeks and costing $37,000. This is shown in Figure 16-16.

It is apparent from Figure 16-16 that paths 1-2-3-5 and 1-3-5 are both critical: each path requires 12 weeks for performance of the work

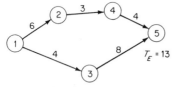

Figure 16-15 *Network for a 13-week, $36,000 project*

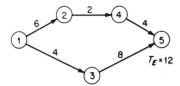

Figure 16-16 *Network for a 12-week, $37,000 project*

required. Any reduction of the time on one path by further crashing without a corresponding reduction of time on the other path will not reduce the T_E of the network-ending event any further. Therefore, we would choose to crash activity 3-5 from 8 to 6 weeks at a total cost of $3,000 ($1,500 per week) and then crash the only remaining uncrashed activity on the upper path (activity 1-2) from 6 to 4 weeks at a total cost of $4,000 ($2,000 per week) to achieve the network shown in Figure 16-17. In that network, the project can be completed in 10 weeks at a total crashed cost of $44,000. This is $3,000 less than the cost of crashing all activities, yet it achieves the same results.

The recapitulation of what we have done appears in Table 16-9.

Remember that in crashing this project to its lowest possible time at the minimum possible cost, we have taken into account only the *direct* costs associated with the project. Nothing has been said about (1) indirect costs (the overhead costs that go on almost irrespective of the time required to complete the work, e.g., bonding and insurance), or (2) costs sometimes referred to as *utility* costs (e.g., penalties for being late and bonuses for finishing the project early). The behavior of these two types of cost can certainly influence the decision about the desirability of crashing a project. Assume that a contractor in his original contract promised delivery in 12 weeks and further agreed to pay a penalty of $10,000 per week if he delivers later than 12 weeks. Thus, when the contractor sees that he would not normally finish before 16 weeks, he faces a possible total penalty of $40,000. No doubt then, he would be glad to incur crashing costs that would reduce T_E to 12 weeks as long as these costs are less than $40,000. On the other hand, there is no reason why he would want to spend additional money to reduce the project time to under 12 weeks unless the reduction in indirect costs is greater than the crashing costs. There are many possible ways in

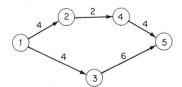

Figure 16-17 *Network for a 10-week, $44,000 project*

Table 16-9   *The network in Figures 16-14, 15, 16, 17*

Steps	Length of Network (weeks)	Total Network Cost
1. Original network	16	$35,000
2. Crash activity 4-5	13	36,000
3. Crash activity 2-4	12	37,000
4. Crash activity 3-5	12	40,000
5. Crash activity 1-2	10	44,000

which these three types of costs, direct, indirect, and utility, can be combined
in project planning and control.

PERT AS A CONTROL SYSTEM

Once the project has been planned, it is possible to use the network as
a motivational and control device. The times scheduled are there for everyone
to see, and the impact of delays on any specific activity upon the other
activities and their managers is painfully evident. The project manager, in
attempting to assign scarce personnel to alternative tasks, can use the slack
for each activity as a priority ranking device. When different activities
could be started next by a carpenter, his foreman knows immediately that
he should assign the man to the next task on the critical path and after
that to the next task with the least slack. It also is important to recognize
the possibility that, as the actual activities are completed, they may run longer
or shorter than the planned schedules with the result that the available slacks
and actual makeup of the critical path may change. Therefore, it is useful
to update the network and the calculations of T_E, T_L, and S as the project
proceeds and actual lengths are observed. With this update comes new
insights into the anticipated project completion date and revised priorities
to be used in assigning scarce resources and incurring added costs.

CONCLUSION

PERT and CPM exemplify the opportunities that lie ahead in POM systems.
We saw in the earlier chapters the importance of precedence relationships to
the development of an effective operating system. In PERT and CPM, we
have developed a somewhat more sophisticated tool for management built
around the analysis of the resulting network. A step-by-step analysis is made
of each activity, and, in CPM, alternatives are developed for time and cost
tradeoffs. Once a manager has established his criteria for cost and overall

time schedule, it is possible to analyze and evaluate a series of alternative systems designs to systematically enhance the results. Once the manager has set his schedule, it is possible to take the actual results as they are reported and substitute them into the initial network, especially when the computer is used for calculations. The analysis of this revised network returns feedback to the manager based on a revised forecast of the anticipated outcomes. The manager can then respond intelligently to this new information.

Computerized PERT and CPM systems even give the manager a printout which first lists those items with no slack, then those with one unit of slack, then two, etc. This makes it easier for him to operate with a true management-by-exception approach, focusing his skill and efforts on those activities most critical to the timely completion of the project. A series of these responses will take place over the life of the project, provided there is sufficient emphasis on responsiveness and control. In the future, these techniques, especially their computerized versions, will be developed well beyond the scope of this book. Where the stakes are very high, even more elaborate procedures can be utilized to help the manager allocate resources for multiple projects and between activities to provide a much improved system performance.

QUESTIONS

1. Compare the production scheduling and control problems of a flow shop, a job shop, and a project.
2. What types of graphic control methods are available for use in production control? What are their strengths and weaknesses? When and where would you use each one?
3. What are the relationships and conflicts between production control and inventory control?
4. What are the differences between Gantt charts and PERT charts? Could you combine the two into one?
5. Who should handle the scheduling of a flow shop? The foreman or the scheduling department? What about a job shop?
6. How does the aggregate schedule (production plan) affect the activities of the production scheduler and the foreman?
7. If a manager becomes aware that his firm is seriously short of working capital, which dispatch rule might he adopt to obtain temporary relief?
8. Evaluate the following statement: "The usefulness of PERT is limited to the initial planning phase of a project."
9. List the PERT steps involved in starting your car (the one with a stick shift), getting it out of the driveway, and achieving a speed of 30 miles per hour.

10. Under what conditions must dummy variables be used in PERT diagrams? In what other situations are they customarily used?

11. PERT is viewed as an administrative as well as a planning tool. How can a project manager use PERT to improve the effectiveness of his operation?

PROBLEMS

1. Kellown Manufacturing Company has the fixed weekly cyclic demand shown below:

Monday	9	Friday	19
Tuesday	17	Saturday	9
Wednesday	2	Sunday	14
Thursday	0		

Company policy is to maintain a constant daily production rate. The production and shipping departments work 7 days a week, and each day's production is available for shipment on the following day. If it costs $4 a day for every unit short and $1 a day for every unit over, how much stock should be on hand at the start of business on Monday when all the unfilled demand is backordered? When no unfilled demand is backordered?

2. You are the production control man for the XYZ Machine Shop. You have just received an order for 180 widgets from a large customer. Since most of the parts that are made in the shop can be used in several finished products, your new policy is to produce parts only in economic lot sizes. The normal operating conditions for the shop are: 8 hour days, and 5 day weeks. You never work overtime because of excessively high labor costs. Present volume of work makes it economically impractical to schedule a second shift. At the present time, the inventory of parts A, B, C, and D is zero. What is the earliest date that the customer above can pick up his order for 180 widgets?

Estimated annual requirements are:

Part	Annual Usage	Carrying Cost per Item
A	7,100	$1.52
B	6,800	1.67
C	1,300	3.79
D	12,000	0.75

The routing sequence for all four parts is machine 11, 21, 13, 14, 25. The company has one of each type machine. Table 1 indicates the assembly requirements for the widgets on the new order.

Table 1 *Gozinto chart for a widget*

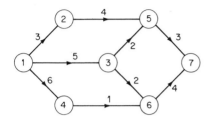

Assembly of a widget (see above) takes place only after all parts have been machined. Each widget requires 0.080 hours to assemble completely.

Table 2 *XYZ Machine Shop—setup costs per machine per lot*

Machine Number	Parts			
	A	B	C	D
11	$ 8.75	$1.75	$ 9.85	$ 5.95
13	3.05	3.85	4.35	14.65
14	4.70	9.15	25.25	2.85
21	21.50	5.35	5.55	5.65
25	14.45	5.08	25.00	3.51

Table 3 *Setup times per machine per lot of parts*

Machine Number	Parts			
	A	B	C	D
11	3 hr	½ hr	4 hr	2 hr
13	1 hr	1½ hr	2 hr	4 hr
14	2 hr	3 hr	8 hr	½ hr
21	7 hr	1½ hr	2 hr	2 hr
25	4 hr	1½ hr	8 hr	1 hr

Table 4 *Operation times per machine per part*

Machine Number	Parts			
	A	B	C	D
11	0.025 hr	0.015 hr	0.085 hr	0.025 hr
13	0.009 hr	0.030 hr	0.061 hr	0.016 hr
14	0.017 hr	0.080 hr	0.090 hr	0.009 hr
21	0.058 hr	0.043 hr	0.036 hr	0.017 hr
25	0.031 hr	0.041 hr	0.176 hr	0.010 hr

Conditions to be observed in scheduling:

1. No alternate job routings are permitted.
2. Productive facilities are available as shown.
3. No split operations; once a lot is started, it is completed.
4. No delay between machines (ignore travel time).

3. Bodyclean, Inc., makers of a complete line of men's toiletries, have been disturbed by the popularity of a competitor's new deodorant. Top management, worried about eroding profits, has decided to fight fire with fire by introducing their own new deodorant, called "B-O-B Gone." This will be accomplished by slightly altering their present production process and completely redesigning the package.

The production manager has been asked to develop a plan for getting the new product to the market as soon as possible. Accordingly, he has set down the following PERT schedule:

Activity	Duration in Weeks	Initial Event	Terminal Event
(a) design product	6	1	2
(b) design package	2	1	3
(c) test market package	4	3	5
(d) distribute to dealers	2	5	6
(e) order package materials	3	3	4
(f) fabricate package	4	4	5
(g) order materials for product	3	2	4
(h) test market product	4	2	7
(i) fabricate product	4	4	7
(j) package product	3	7	5

(a) Construct the PERT diagram.

(b) Find T_E and T_L for each activity.

(c) Determine the critical path and the expected completion time for the project.

4. The project director at Bitey Computer has suddenly received word that a new memory must be designed within 8 months. The only way to do this would be to add engineers and allow 2-man teams to work on individual activities. When 2 men work on a task, it can be completed in half the time, but the quality of the design suffers somewhat. Therefore, he wishes to meet the 8-month schedule by doubling up on the fewest tasks.

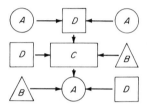

Using the above diagram, indicate the new times for each task that would give an 8-month schedule but double up the men on the fewest activities.

5. Listed is the set of activities, sequence, requirements, and estimated activity times required for completing a new project.

Activity	Immediate Predecessors	Normal Time (days)
a	start	2
b	start	4
c	a	2
d	a,b	4
e	b	3
finish	c,d,e	

(a) Draw a network illustrating this project. (Indicate any dummy activities by dotted lines.)

(b) Compute the slack associated with activity "a."

(c) You now discover that activity "d" can start when activity "b" is half finished. However, second half of "b" must be completed by the completion of activity "d," and "b" still must be totally complete before "e" can be started. Revise your network in part (a) to include this discovery.

CASE

Thad Procrastinator, graduate student, faces the prospect of five term papers due on the same day in the very near future. He estimates that each paper will take the following number of days to complete:

Course	Working Time in Days
A	$6\frac{1}{2}$
B	11
C	7
D	4
E	$7\frac{1}{2}$

Planning further, he attempts to develop schedules that will minimize the time required to complete the five papers and minimize the average days late.

A fellow student suggests that he really try to attempt to minimize the lateness penalty that might be applied by the various professors. Between them, their best estimate is that the professors deduct the following number of percentage points for each day of lateness:

Course	Lateness Percentage Penalty/Day
A	3
B	7
C	4
D	6
E	2

Faced with bleak prospects of passing, Thad convinces his wife to edit and type each of his papers once he has drafted them. On this basis, he lists the following estimated times to complete each phase of each paper.

Course	Research and Writing Time	Editing and Typing Time
A	$3\frac{1}{2}$	3
B	6	5
C	$4\frac{1}{2}$	$2\frac{1}{2}$
D	2	2
E	3	$4\frac{1}{2}$

He develops a schedule which looks marginally acceptable with his wife's assistance. But he hears of a film festival lasting 3 days that he and his wife would like to attend. A friend offers to work for him editing the papers at $20 per day. They estimate that the editing and typing can be split as follows:

Course	Editing Time	Typing Time
A	1½	1½
B	2	3
C	1	1½
D	1	1
E	2	2½

Develop the best schedule for friend Thad.

chapter

QUALITY CONTROL SYSTEMS

seventeen

The subject of quality has been introduced in several chapters. It is obvious that the capacity of an operation can be altered markedly by changing standards and procedures with respect to quality. People and machines can be asked to go only so fast and for so long before they start to make many more mistakes. Therefore, the choice of the level of quality to be provided is a major strategy decision, one which reaches beyond the boundaries of the POM system. The image of the company and even the status of its employees in the community are affected by the performance and appearance of its products. The profit margins it can demand and the share it can hold of different segments of the market are functions of its quality standards. Its quality level reflects the design of the product, the choice of equipment, the labor skill levels maintained, the wages paid, the amount of testing and inspection done, and the proportion of the output rejected for one reason or another.

In the area of quality, just as with the inventory policy, it is unlikely that any firm would choose perfection as its policy. In fact, as much as you as a consumer may dislike the idea, the objective of quality control is to find that level of disservice that leads to the best set of total system costs and revenues. Thus, the approaches outlined in this chapter will be quite similar in philosophy to those in the chapters on inventory control and production planning and control. Cost and revenue outcomes will be compared to find the best net outcome.

THE MARKET'S DEMANDS

The primary determinant of product quality is the needs of the customer. There is little doubt that the rational customer will buy a product or service only if it meets his minimum needs for performance. After that, he may be willing to pay for more quality to the extent that its increased utility exceeds the increased cost. Marketing groups in the firm assess consumer wants, providing the initial informational input to the quality decision. They express and interpret for the engineering and production staff their impressions of the market, using terms that are relevant to POM activities, like tolerances, color, and reliability.

POM REINTERPRETS THE MARKET

The engineering department interprets these marketing requests in the design and specification of the product. The design process is a continuous series of choices between cost and ability of the product to function as you saw in Chapter 6. For example, it is the process engineer who specifies the tolerances on each dimension of each part. The tolerance is the range of a dimension that the engineer is willing to accept. He calculates what each addition to this range is likely to do to the product's performance and to its cost. If he is specifying the inside diameter of an oil seal that goes around a shaft, he will have to keep in mind that too small an inside diameter will cause the shaft to bind and that too great a diameter will cause leakage of lubricant, overheating, and then damage. Such constraints set the limits of the allowed range. Then, as it was explained in Chapters 6 and 7 he must select the material and the machining process to be used. These two together are expected to produce a specified variation in the inside diameter. Some parts may be expected to be outside the tolerance limits. If the cost of such errors is significant, there is the choice of selecting either a process which reduces that range or an inspection system which removes a sufficient number of the unsatisfactory pieces. The design of these inspection and testing procedures is the major focus of this chapter; but it is important to remember that a process change should be one alternative considered when more inspection or testing is proposed.

POM ADMINISTERS THE QUALITY CONTROL SYSTEM

Once the product and processes, including the inspection process, have been designed, the POM group takes on responsibility for administering the process and the inspection and testing. There are two stages to this task. The first is to achieve the specified results efficiently with the designed process. The second is to learn when that process is not behaving as intended and take corrective action. Each process has its own "normal" or random variation. Once a product is placed into production, there is no assurance that further variations will not be introduced by differences in the behavior of the men, machines, raw materials, or operating conditions. To some extent, this possibility was taken into account in figuring the normal variation. But, any systematic error introduced by an operator using the wrong method, a worn cutting tool, or a machine out of adjustment would produce a distribution different in either mean or variance or both. The amount of money and effort devoted to the avoidance or correction of these errors will be determined again by costs and benefits, and it will be useful to think about the functions of quality control in a general sense before taking a closer look at the models appropriate to specific tasks.

FUNCTIONS OF QUALITY CONTROL

Table 17-1 lists functions of quality control or quality related activities. These functions can be simplified into two basic activities: (1) designing a product or service so that the associated standards give the customer the most for his money, and (2) seeing that the product or service meets the standards to which it is to conform. In addition to meeting customer specifications, quality control is involved in the following activities.

Table 17-1 *Functions of quality control*

Meeting customer specifications
Providing interchangeability and fit of parts for manufacture
Meeting legal conditions of contract, warranty, or liability
Maintaining organizational morale and discipline
Reducing the costs of rework and scrap and reducing unnecessary addition of value
  to rejects
Monitoring the production process for changes
Linking responsibility for errors to specific employees, machines, etc.
Providing checks on quantity produced in order to reveal location of waste and
  spoilage

PROVIDING INTERCHANGEABILITY

This function is not to be taken lightly. Today people expect a replacement part to fit as well as the original, but less than 200 years ago in America, this was not true. At the time of the War of 1812, Eli Whitney was manufacturing the first American product that had truly interchangeable parts, rifles. This was a difficult but significant feat made possible by the development of waterpower machine tools and careful manufacturing standards. Our whole industrial efficiency is dependent upon this capability.

MEETING LEGAL RESPONSIBILITIES

The primary objective of the quality control system is one of supplying the quality level that the customer wants and leaving the reputation of the company in good standing. Today, a company is increasingly likely to be held publicly accountable and liable for any damage done through failure of the product to perform safely under reasonable conditions of use. Legal action can be based on something as concrete as a warranty or as nebulous as the fact that the manufacturer failed to warn the user of the safe limits of operation.

MAINTAINING EMPLOYEE MORALE

At the same time the management is worried about the external image of the company, it also must be concerned about internal conditions. There is a strong economic argument that the company need not make everything letter perfect, but there are dangers on the other side. Too much haste and shoddiness may destroy the pride and skill of the workforce and lead to absenteeism and employee turnover. Many companies operate with internal standards that are somewhat higher than their customers require, simply to be consistent with their own sense of values and to let all employees know that there is a clear minimum acceptable standard of performance.

REDUCING SCRAP LOSSES

There are other primarily internal reasons for inspection and quality control. It is important to reduce the labor that goes into pieces destined for the scrap heap. The initial defense against this is to have no defective work at all. In fact, some companies, especially those in the aerospace program, have "zero defects" programs. These are essentially gimmicks and contests to get the workers interested in avoiding all errors. Where the stakes are smaller and the customer is not willing to pay the exorbitant costs of perfection, then some error rate has to be accepted.

Where errors are anticipated, then steps may be taken to catch them before they cause other errors or jeopardize the work done at succeeding stations. Thus, it is common to inspect incoming parts and materials before they are incorporated into a product and to inspect before costly components are added or irreversible processes started. In some cases, the rejected assemblies or materials may be corrected, and in others, they have to be scrapped completely. One of the more interesting questions in this area is what one does when a defect is discovered in an auto on a fast-paced assembly line. A worker has just so many minutes to do his specific elements. If he tries to correct a defect that he sees, he will fall behind and probably create more defects through haste or missed operations. If the line is stopped for the correction for one minute, the loss is one minute times the number of men on the line. If the defect is not corrected then and there, it may go all the way through to the end, but hopefully will be observed and corrected during final inspection and repair. The usual response is to let the item go through and try to correct the defect later.

A QUALITY INFORMATION SYSTEM

The process in a POM system will be under control in most cases, but the management can control it only to the extent that it continues to have current information on the latest condition of that process. A quality control system has to be designed to indicate to management when the process is tending to stray from its intended state. This usually requires a regular sampling procedure that shows the condition of the system over time. The presentation of this information usually is graphical so that variations and trends can be noted promptly.

GRADING OUTPUT

Many processes yield distributions of quality outcomes which are not just good or bad. Some products may be rejects, but others fall into one or several categories or grades having different values. A testing and inspection function is used to assign each unit to an appropriate grade. You see this in "choice" beef, "C" students, and "factory seconds" in shirts and dresses. The grading procedure determines the method of distribution and the price to be commanded. For example, transistors coming off a single production line are graded according to a number of performance characteristics. Those meeting stringent military specifications might be sold to military contractors at a dollar a unit. The lesser quality ones meeting minimum standards could go to radio and toy manufacturers at a quarter a piece or less, even though both products have identical production costs and come from the same manufacturing lot. The grading process is quite flexible in some cases and can respond to market conditions. If the demand for high priced products is low, it is easy to call a high quality piece a second and increase shipments. Going the other way is not as easy, since the product still must meet the higher market or customer quality standards.

DETERMINING RESPONSIBILITY FOR ERROR

A certain amount of inspection must be done merely to keep workers aware that quality still counts. To make an inspection system effective and to facilitate improvement, it must show which individual worker or machine is responsible for the errors that are uncovered. This means that there must be a system for identifying errors, reporting them to management in exception and summary reports, and keeping the employee informed of his batting average. In many cases, the errors may not be the worker's fault, but he cannot take corrective action nor seek help unless he is made aware of how well or how poorly he is doing. In companies that pay workers an incentive wage, the motivation and communication are provided quite simply. Parts or goods that fail to pass inspection are returned to the worker claiming credit for the work to redo or repair on his own time. In more elaborate systems where only a small percentage of the worker's output is inspected, the amount of inspection remains low so long as what is examined indicates good work. Then if errors appear to become more numerous, the percentage of his work inspected is increased until he again shows an adequate run of good work.

DETERMINING SPOILAGE RATES

Management also needs a check on the spoilage rates within the process in order to identify the places where losses are occurring. In one industrial firm known to the authors, a product was redesigned to eliminate casting defects occurring in a thick portion of the casting. If the employees were conscientious, they would reject the parts which showed these defects during machining, but this problem would not have been identified merely by the fact that 70 castings entered the process and only 45 finished parts emerged. Someone had to keep track of the errors and losses at each stage, find out the causes, and seek out corrective action when the losses were high.

INSPECTION

A worker generally is held responsible for the quality of his own work. Yet, it is unrealistic to expect him to serve as his own judge and jury.

The firm, therefore, typically employs a separate group of employees known as inspectors. These men usually have different immediate supervisors than the production workers. Quality is so important and so threatened by the pressures to achieve high rates of production and lower costs that it is necessary to have a system of checks and balances. To have a product shipped from a plant it must in effect be passed by two groups—inspection and production. At a higher level, both groups report to the same man who must resolve basic conflicts, but the inspectors usually do have the right to hold up shipment unless their orders are countermanded from above.

LOCATION OF INSPECTION

Inspection may take place right in the processing area or at a separate inspection station. The choice of location depends on the process flows and on the problems of scheduling the inspection function which must be treated as yet another operation in the total process. The first line of defense is the worker who can avoid making defects and see them in the work in front of him. *Then* come the inspectors who are usually trained separately from the workers to obtain the benefits of specialization. They are taught to use gauges, test instruments, micrometers, and procedures at which they become increasingly proficient. At inspection stations on the floor and in special inspection and quality control departments, there may be thousands of dollars of test equipment. As this equipment becomes larger, more complex, and more expensive, as with heavy machine tools, it pays to have only one each of such machines located in a special area and have work brought to it job shop fashion. Some machines like X-ray equipment also require special quarters with a heavy investment in shielding and wiring that make it uneconomical to place them in the production line. Thus, the work may have to leave the normal flow to go to an inspection station.

Roving inspectors also may be used to spotcheck the quality of work or the conditions of operation. They know the requirements of the process and circulate among the work stations to see what quality of work is being done. This, of course, leads to some game playing and to personal frictions between workers and inspectors that are more intense than the usual ones involving employees faced with fixed inspection stations and procedures. It is both easy and human for the worker to interpret frequent selection of his work as being motivated by a personal bias.

Government agencies responsible for the quality and safety of regulated services make considerable use of roving inspectors. Airline pilots never know until just before takeoff whether or not a Federal Aviation Agency inspector is going along in the cockpit to "observe." All food preparing and serving institutions are subject to local health inspection and grading to force maintenance of sanitary conditions. Similar inspections are made of nursing homes and hospitals in many states. Bank examiners and company auditors perform a similar function in protecting against embezzlement and fraud. In professional environments such as teaching and medicine, roving inspectors are not acceptable to most individuals, but the possibility that a colleague will see the results of one's work still serves to keep a man on his toes. One of the strong arguments in favor of a group medical practice as opposed to an individual or "solo" practice is this element of continuous review by others.

Where roving inspectors make spot checks, the scheduling problem is essentially a sampling task like that encountered in market research but with a behavioral element and the POM element of reducing the travel and time costs. You have encountered work sampling techniques before in Chapter 10. If a man knows that you are on your way to inspect his nursing home, he will have sufficient nurses on duty, the patients all nicely cared for, and the kitchen scrubbed clean. If the inspector visits a town and looks at only two nursing homes but twelve get spruced up, you can count that as getting extra value from the inspector. On the other hand, you'll never find out how bad things can get between inspections. The inspection scheme has to be designed to introduce an overall impression of randomness. But a truly random system might place the inspector in the northwest corner of his territory for one inspection and in the southwest for the next. Travel costs and time could get out of hand very easily. The usual solution is to select a series of relatively low-cost travel routes through the territory, and then select one of these at random for the next swing through. This introduces some uncertainty into the system and still keeps inspection costs at a reasonable level.

ADDING INFORMATION

This section has not made clear whether one inspects every item of output or just samples from a set of outputs. This is an economic question. Sometimes the answer is 100 percent inspection and testing and other times none at all. The latter choice is equivalent to making the customer your quality control department. In most cases, the answer is somewhere between these two choices. The general rule is to inspect as long as the expected value from the inspection keeps increasing. This can be expressed as:

$$E \text{ (inspection)} = -\text{ Cost} + \Sigma E \text{ (gains)} + \Sigma E \text{ (losses avoided)}$$

The costs are the labor time and administrative effort going into the inspection system. The gains include the returns for higher grades, the improved worker productivity and ease of assembly due to good matching of parts. The losses avoided include the value added that is not wasted on parts destined for the scrap heap, the savings in the manpower to handle customer complaints and the losses of goodwill avoided. The expectation is calculated just as it was in Chapter 3. All the events included in the economic evaluation are probabilistic except the planned costs. These events are probabilistic because no one knows the quality distribution of the future output.

AN EXAMPLE

Let us look at an example. Suppose that the quartermaster of a Latin American Republic's army is approached by an international trader who offers him 1,000,000 rounds of ammunition for the army's standard automatic rifle. Ammunition stocks are somewhat depleted but not yet in critical supply. Delivery will be made promptly from three separate countries, and, for obvious reasons, the deal will be cash-and-carry. The trader has a reasonably good, but not a totally unblemished, record in international arms shipments. How should the quartermaster go about reaching his decision?

Undoubtedly, he will want to test some of the ammunition, and the trader has offered to let his representatives fly to two of the countries and test out some of the ammunition. The third country is closed for understandable diplomatic and political reasons. Before the representatives leave, however, the quartermaster must give them specific instructions on how to test and evaluate the ammunition. This will include instructions on two types of characteristics, *variables* and *attributes*.

ATTRIBUTES AND VARIABLES

Attributes are binary (yes or no) conditions which lead one to accept or reject, e.g., pass-fail grades in courses and fire—no fire tests for bullets.

Variables are characteristics of a system that are measurable and can take on multiple, usually continuous values, e.g., the diameter of a ball bearing, the temperature of a patient, and weight of powder in each cartridge.

As a general rule, variables may be treated as attributes, but attributes cannot always be treated as variables. For example, elementary school rules may say that students may not attend classes if they have a temperature. Temperature is recorded as a variable, but the decision is based on whether or not the individual is in a state above or below 98.6°F. Then in practice that rule is subject to interpretation. The school nurse might let someone stay if a routine physical uncovered a reading of 98.8 but send her home when she complained of a headache and stiff neck at that temperature.

The quartermaster can designate a number of attributes and variables for his men to examine, including:

1. What percentage of the bullets fired jam in the weapon?
2. What percentage fail to achieve a reasonable accuracy at 1,000 feet?
3. What is the impact velocity distribution at 500 feet, 1,000 feet, and 500 yards?
4. Is there a bias in the bullet trajectory, and how bad is it?
5. Do the bullets appear corroded or tampered with?
6. Don't accept any made by the XYZ Company.

For many characteristics, he also must set levels at which he will or will not accept the ammunition. These may or may not be independent of each other. If 15 percent of the bullets jammed in the weapons, he wouldn't be interested at any price. His whole complement of automatic weapons would be out of action in no time at all. If ¾ of 1 percent misfired but did not jam the weapons and the ammunition had high range and accuracy, he might be willing to accept the high proportion of misfires in return for these other qualities and the use of the ammunition.

TO SAMPLE OR NOT TO SAMPLE

The size of the sample to be inspected and tested also is a major decision that he must make before he sends his men on the trip. Obviously, a 100 percent test of range and accuracy is out of the question. The testing process destroys the utility of the product. Each bullet fired reduces the number available, and, certainly, the trader will put a limit on the number fired or charge full price for those consumed. Visual inspection of the condition of the bullets and measurement of their outside diameter would be feasible in two of the countries. Even where it is feasible to test these qualities, however, it would be prohibitively expensive in time and money to process every piece. A sampling procedure must be developed first and then followed exactly.

ALWAYS UNCERTAINTY REMAINING

The bullets located in the inaccessible country present a much more difficult problem. The tests conducted in the other two countries will assess the results of one or more bullet-making processes. Are the bullets in the third country the output of the same processes? If the quartermaster believes that they are, then he will be governed by the data from the other two countries. If not, then he has altogether a different problem. His plight is somewhat like that of a manager of a major league baseball team who must decide the fate of a promising minor league outfielder just before the player draft. Last year, this young man was up with the team at the start of the season. He had looked good in spring training, but he batted .212

once the season started, striking out 40 percent of the time. He was sent down to the team's top minor league club and hit .340 with 20 percent strikeouts and 30 homers. Now the manager faces a tough decision. He has two sets of data. He recognizes that each is the outcome of a different process involving the same individual but at different levels of experience and against different classes of pitchers, fielders, and ball parks. Neither will be exactly the same this coming year. The player will be another year older and maybe another year smarter. The manager will have to rely almost entirely on his subjective judgment as to the correspondence between the processes tested and the one in question. So will the quartermaster.

OBSERVER AND TEST RELIABILITY

Another factor that should concern the quartermaster will be the quality of the testers. Errors can be introduced by the testing process as well as the product. What if the men sent to fire the bullets can't or won't count carefully, are careless in maintaining their weapons, are very poor shots, or are in the pay of the opposition. Any one of these characteristics can lead to acceptance of bad ammunition or rejection of good lots. Classical statistics texts refer to acceptance of bad lots as Type I errors and rejection of good lots as Type II errors. This is a problem of special concern in medicine where patients vary considerably in their responses to diagnostic tests and where the tests may be relatively inconclusive anyway. The choices can be illustrated by the figures in Table 17-2. It indicates that for every 100 patients who were tested by this method after they saw a physician about some symptoms that indicated this disease as a possibility, 80 showed a positive reaction. When these 80 patients were further studied by surgery, X-ray, or autopsy, a final diagnosis was reached. Of the 80 patients showing a positive test, 56 patients did have the illness and 24 did not. Of the 20 patients with negative test results, 4 were later found to have had this disease. This means that the test diagnosed 72 percent (56 + 16 out of 100) correctly and 28 percent in error. The attractiveness of the test for

Table 17-2 *Probabilities associated with a diagnostic test for illness*

		Results of Test		
		Positive	*Negative*	*Percent*
Condition of	*Ill*	56	4	60
Patients Tested	*Well*	24	16	40
	Percent	80	20	

use would depend on these data, alternative tests available, *and* the relative costs of the errors. If a patient who receives a false negative test result were to die for lack of treatment, then the search for better tests would continue. Actually, there are a number of tests that could be given economically on a wide scale for kidney disease and other ills, but the probability of false alarms is sufficiently great to make physicians hesitant to use them. There could be a widespread negative public reaction if many people had to undergo further tests and evaluation for treatment only to find that they were all right after all. This has to be weighed against the lives that might be saved by such testing. Too often, we assume that having an inexpensive test solves the inspection problem.

Now that the general problem has been discussed, this chapter, like its predecessors, moves on to consider specific models and approaches to be applied to the individual problem. Three types of models are considered: least-cost inspection, sampling attributes, and sampling variables. The chapter then concludes with a discussion of the quality control organization and its administration.

LEAST-COST INSPECTION

Assume that a production assembly line is being designed to make an item, and there are four logical sites for the location of inspection stations. Which ones should be selected? Table 17-3 lists the locations in order of their occurrence in the process, the work value that has gone into the item up to that point, the percent defectives added between possible stations and

Table 17-3 *Data concerning candidate inspection stations*

Station	Mfg. Value at Station	New % Defectives Added Since Preceding Inspection Station	Variable Costs of Inspection per Piece
A	$2.38	10	$0.10
B	2.79	4	0.08
C	3.35	7	0.10
D	3.62	6	0.07

K → L → M → (A) → N → O → (B) → P → Q → R → (C) → S → T → U → (D)

O   Inspection operation

Figure 17-1   *Process flow with all possible inspection stations*

the variable cost of inspection at each station. Figure 17-1 illustrates the sequence of operations and the possible inspection stations. For each possible location there will be two sets of values to be calculated:

I = inspection cost

S = savings due to inspection

For each configuration of inspection stations, there will be a specific set of costs and savings. If inspection is performed at A, B, C, and D, the inspection cost will be $.10 + .08 + .10 + .07 or $.35 per unit. The savings are a little harder to visualize. Figure 17-1 shows the flow in the assembly process in which A through D are potential inspection stations and K through U are required assembly operations. Inspection at A, in Figure 17-1, cannot reduce the errors at operations K, L, and M even though they amount to 10 percent. They already have occurred. The pieces that have been ruined in these operations can be removed by inspection so that value is not added to the defective 10 percent at operations N through U. Similarly, inspection at station C can avoid the loss of $0.27 = $3.62 − $3.35 in the value added at operations S, T, U. One very sure way of finding out the best combination of stations would be to look at each possible set of stations and calculate the costs and benefits of each combination. There are 15 possible combinations of 1, 2, 3, or 4 stations:

One Station	Two Stations	Three Stations	Four Stations
A	AB	ABC	ABCD
B	AC	ACD	
C	AD	ABD	
D	BC	BCD	
	BD		
	CD		

This exhaustive evaluation obviously is time consuming and degenerates rapidly as more alternative stations are added, hence it is seldom used. The usual first step in practice is to look at each station separately and evaluate the costs and benefits there before worrying about the multiple combinations. (Table 17-5 shows the calculations for the 4 stations individually.) From the data in Table 17-4, it is evident that the search for the

Table 17-4 *Evaluation of individual stations*

Station	Inspection Cost per Piece	Savings until Next Station	Savings if Piece Goes to End of Process without Another Inspection
A	$.10	$.41 × .10 = $.041	$1.24 × .10 = $.124
B	.08	.56 × .04 = .022	.83 × .14 = .116
C	.10	.27 × .07 = .019	.27 × .21 = .057
D	.07	0	0

right answer can be simplified considerably.[1] This table also illustrates that a final inspection at D does not eliminate wasted investments at future operations. Thus, the value of that final inspection cannot be justified on the basis of the data presented here. It very well might be justified on other grounds like keeping the 6 percent or more defectives out of the customer's hands. Temporarily at least, one can now eliminate the alternative configurations D, AD, BD, CD, ACD, ABD, BCD, and ABCD from further consideration once D has or has not been selected, and we now need consider A, B, and C. That leaves only seven more possibilities still to be evaluated.

Inspection at station C seems unwarranted under any set of circumstances. Even if no defectives were removed at earlier stations leaving the incoming error rate at 21 percent, the additional labor wasted on these bad pieces at operations S, T, and U would average under $.06 per piece inspected, less than the $.10 cost of inspection. Thus, inspection station C would cost more than it saves and is not to be used. That eliminates alternatives C, AC, BC, and ABC, leaving only AB to be evaluated and compared with A alone, which has a payoff of $.124 − .100 or $.024, and B alone, which yields $.116 − .080 or $.036. Stations at A and B would involve an inspection cost of $.180 per unit. The 10 percent error would be removed at station A for an expected value of $.124 and the 4 percent at B for an expected value of $.033 for an expected total benefit of $.157 which is less than the inspection cost. Inspection at B, plus D if that is selected, appears to be the best decision. A similar procedure can be followed with the design of most inspection systems using relevant costs, expenses, and arrays of alternatives.

---

[1] Table 17-4 is simplified too. It assumes that the tests are completely accurate at each station and that the number of defectives found at one level is independent of the number removed at another. The calculations also assume that only one error occurs on any one piece which is unlikely, but avoids considerable complication in the analysis at the cost of some accuracy.

SAMPLING

The quartermaster evaluating ammunition, whose situation was described earlier in this chapter, has a number of problems approachable with statistical techniques. These relate not only to the total number of bullets tested but also to how those tested should be chosen to provide a representative sample of the population of bullets about which a decision must be made. To decide, he must first understand some simple terms and concepts.

There is a universe or population of bullets (a defined set of events or objects that are all those in question). If he took a 100 percent sample with complete accuracy, he would know the population or at least those characteristics of the population that he measured. The decision-maker usually is interested in a well-defined population, such as families who have automobiles, students who major in chemistry, women who have three or more living children, or parts in Lot #53116 coming off the #7 boring mill. If he does not have the unambiguous definition of the population, he can't expect real help from statistical analysis.

RANDOM SELECTION

In working with statistical quality control methods, one seeks a *random* method of sample selection. For example, if a market research firm wishes to ask questions of a random 20 percent sample of airline passengers on selected flights, it probably would pick a long series of random numbers from 1 to 10 and then check the next random number every time a passenger came off, questioning only those who went by when the numbers 1 and 2 appeared in the list. A sample based on every fifth passenger would not be a random sample and could be biased by any property of the spacing of passengers. This method of sampling, however, might be chosen anyway to keep the interviewers' workload smooth.

The measures of characteristics gathered in a sample can be grouped into a *frequency distribution* (a table or plot of the number of times that a particular value has occurred in the sample). Frequency distributions were illustrated in Chapter 3. If the values are introduced at random from a well-behaved and symmetrically shaped frequency distribution of the population, they often can be approximated very well by a *normal distribution,* also called a Gaussian distribution. Most statistical tests and most plans for quality control are based on the assumption that the values in the population are normally distributed. Any time that the decision-maker has good reason to believe that the desired characteristic of the population is not normally distributed and will not yield a normally distributed set of samples, he should seek expert advice and not attempt to use the standard quality control approaches in the basic texts.

THE NORMAL DISTRIBUTION

The normal distribution has a set of properties which you should recall from Chapter 3. An estimate of its mean is:

$$\bar{x} = \Sigma x/n$$

where $\bar{x}$ is the mean of the set of values of x in the sample of size n

A second measure is needed to indicate the degree of the dispersion of the values around the mean. As we saw in Chapter 3, statistical analysis relies on one measure of dispersion called the standard deviation, the square root of the sum of the mean squared deviation. An estimate of the standard deviation is determined by the equation:

$$\sigma = \sqrt{\Sigma(x_i - \bar{x})^2/n}$$

where

σ = the standard deviation, the measure of dispersion

x_i = the value of x for the ith observation in the sample, $i = 1, 2, \ldots, n$

$\bar{x}$ = the mean value of x for the sample = $\Sigma x_i/n$

n = the number of observations in the sample

Note that the standard deviation σ is expressed in the same dimensional units as x. If x is the distance of the hemline above the knee, then σ is in inches and can be expressed on a graph or number line with a value in inches equal to $\bar{x}$ plus or minus a number of σ's. If the mean of the distribution of skirt heights above the knee is 3 inches and has a standard deviation of 0.5 inches, then the observations at 4 inches can be expressed as $3.0 + 2\sigma$ inches. A normal curve is frequently expressed this way because many users are familiar with the proportion of the observations in a normally distributed sample that are less than or equal to a specific value of the constant k in $\bar{x} \pm k\sigma$, where k is the number of standard deviations either way from the mean. These values are frequently listed in tables like the one in Appendix 2 of this book. The three most widely used values are illustrated in Figure 17-2. These drawings indicate the percentage of normally distributed observations in a large sample falling between and outside the limits of $\bar{x} \pm 1\sigma$, $\bar{x} \pm 2\sigma$, and $\bar{x} \pm 3\sigma$. These percentages are proportional to the integral of the function above the lower and below the upper limit and, therefore, to the area enclosed by them. Appendix 2 also shows the percentages that apply to fractional standard deviations. Table 17-5 shows the observations of the foul shooting averages made by State U and the calculations necessary to provide a value of the standard deviation of the sample. If these were randomly

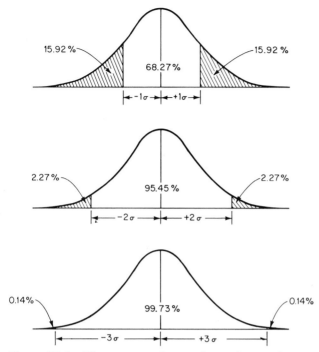

Figure 17-2   *The areas under portions of normal curves*

selected from a normally distributed population, then we would anticipate that for any one game 68.27 percent of the time the foul shooting percentage should fall between 62.6 and 81.4 ($\bar{x} \pm 1\sigma$), 95.45 percent between 53.2 and 90.8 ($\bar{x} \pm 2\sigma$), and 99.73 percent between 43.8 and 100 ($\bar{x} \pm 3\sigma$).

CONTROL CHARTS

These 2σ and 3σ values are important information. When the man responsible for controlling process quality sees that the observed results are outside of a set of values, he can then quickly judge how likely it is that these values were the *random* output of the process being controlled. If that likelihood is very small and these values occur more than once, it is a good indicator that the underlying process may be changing. To allow for a quick response to changes in the process, many quality control systems employ charts which plot the observed results over time against the prior mean value and the limits which would indicate that the process is not the one anticipated originally. Figure 17-3 shows the data from Table 17-5 plotted this way in what is called a "control chart." The supervisor looking

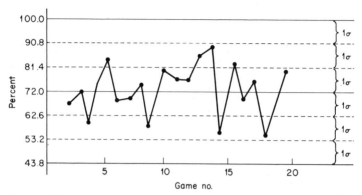

Figure 17-3   *Chart plotting the percentages in Table 17-5*

Table 17-5   *Observations of State U's foul shooting percentage*

Date of Game	Percentage Made	Mean Percentage	Deviations	Dev. Squared (D²)
Nov. 6	68	72	−4	16
Nov. 9	72	72	0	0
Nov. 13	60	72	−12	144
Nov. 18	74	72	+2	4
Nov. 21	82	72	+10	100
Nov. 30	67	72	−5	25
Dec. 4	68	72	−4	16
Dec. 8	74	72	+2	4
Dec. 13	58	72	−14	196
Dec. 18	78	72	+6	36
Dec. 28	75	72	+3	9
Dec. 29	75	72	+3	9
Jan. 7	86	72	+14	196
Jan. 9	88	72	+16	256
Jan. 13	56	72	−16	256
Jan. 16	82	72	+10	100
Feb. 2	69	72	−3	9
Feb. 9	74	72	+2	4
Feb. 13	54	72	−18	324
Feb. 16	80	72	+8	64
N = 20	1,440		0	1,768

= number
of samples $\sigma = \sqrt{\Sigma D^2/N} = \sqrt{1,768/20} = \sqrt{88.4} = 9.4$

at this chart can readily see whether or not the process is stable. Moreover, he does not even have to be present. He can instruct the quality control staff to inform him when a stated number of results occur outside the $\pm 2\sigma$ or $\pm 3\sigma$ limits on the chart.

SAMPLING PLANS

A similar logic governs the rules for one important quality control procedure called "acceptance sampling." This consists of taking a sample or set of samples of a stated size, which will lead to acceptance of the population (often called the "lot") as the one from which the sample was drawn, if the number of defects in the sample is equal to or less than a stated number c. Assumedly, there is an underlying proportion of defectives in a population that is under control. If that is true, the sample properly drawn seldom will produce more than c defectives. When it does, the sampling plan, therefore, will reject the lot as bad on the basis that the proportion defective in the population must be much higher than that proportion planned if it generates such a high defective proportion in even an occasional lot.

Sampling plans can be classified into four general categories:

1. Control charts using variables
2. Control charts using attributes
3. Acceptance sampling using attributes
4. Acceptance sampling using variables

The first and third classes of quality control plans are those most frequently encountered in the literature and in practice. Therefore, they will be the primary focus for the sections that follow.

CONTROL CHARTS USING VARIABLES

The manager starts out with a process designed to produce a planned population frequency distribution of values for each variable being controlled. Presumably, any sample from the process would have a mean, a standard deviation, and a range representative of that population. Each of these three characteristics can be followed on control charts for each variable. Figure 17-4 shows the frequency distribution of the population superimposed on a control chart.

Note that the actual population, unlike that in Figure 17-3, may not necessarily be normally distributed, but the distribution of the means of a large number of samples will be normal and lead to a distribution like that in Figure 17-4. The sample's mean should be the same as the popula-

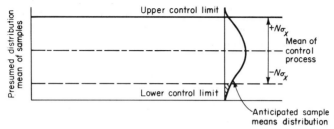

Figure 17-4 *x̄ or mean control chart with sample distribution*

tion's mean, but the variability is much less. Within a set of samples

$$\sigma_{\bar{x}} = \frac{\sigma}{\sqrt{N}}$$

where

$\sigma_{\bar{x}}$ = standard deviation of the sample means

σ = standard deviation of the population

N = the number of samples taken.

Figure 17-4 is a completed $\bar{x}$ chart with the addition of the upper and lower control limit (UCL and LCL) lines. They are established at a selected k standard deviations away from the mean planned for the controlled process. The usual values of k are 2 or 3, although a careful economic analysis is unlikely to generate such an integer value. The relevant costs are those of investigating the process when the control limits are exceeded (indicating out-of-control conditions) and the risks associated with not investigating at that level.

A series of $\bar{x}$ charts are shown in Figure 17-5 together with a set of interpretations that a manager might apply to what he observes. There will be some variability in the means recorded, but once a pattern of variability has been observed, the manager frequently can tell at a glance whether or not there is trouble brewing.

Beyond the mean. When the mean of the process is well behaved, this is no assurance that the process is under control. It is possible that the distribution of the output has many more than the acceptable number of errors, but that those above the limits offset those below the limits, producing a mean well within the established limits. Therefore, the careful quality control manager tends to supplement his $\bar{x}$ charts with control charts for variability. The same sample observations which provide the mean also can be used to compute a standard deviation and new UCL and LCL values. Then a sequence of sets of samples can be plotted against the mean $\sigma_{\bar{x}}$. Not only does this require many calculations involving means, deviations, total squared errors, and square roots thereof, but the resulting values are difficult for the decision-maker to interpret physically. Most quality control systems, therefore, retreat to a much less accurate but easier to obtain and understand measure, the range. A range or *R* chart is a plot of the difference between the highest and lowest values in each sample against time. Again the UCL and LCL limits are computed from standard deviations likely to occur in the desired population and serve as warnings that the process variability is in control or is tending out of it. Figure 17-6 is an *R* chart.

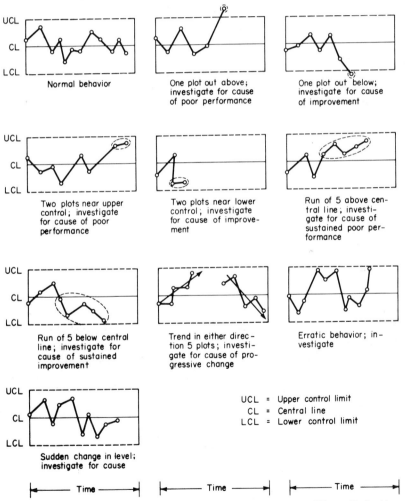

Figure 17-5 *Control chart evidence for investigation. [From B. L. Hansen, Quality Control (Englewood Cliffs, N.J.: Prentice-Hall, Inc., 1963), p. 65.]*

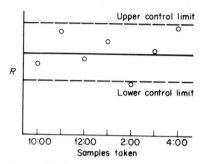

Figure 17-6   *A range or* R *control chart*

The procedure for preparing an *R* chart is virtually the same as for an *x* chart. Assume that a sample has been taken of the five judges' scorings at diving competitions. Their values for back twisting dives performed by one man were:

Back Twisting Dive	Values Scored by the Five Judges	Mean	Range
A	6,7,7,8,8	7.2	2
B	4,5,5,6,7	5.4	3
C	5,6,6,6,6	5.8	1
D	8,8,8,9,9	8.6	1
E	5,6,6,7,7	6.2	2
F	6,6,6,6,6	6.0	0
G	5,5,7,7,7	6.2	2
H	7,7,7,7,8	7.2	2
I	5,5,6,6,7	5.8	2
J	6,6,7,7,8	6.8	2

The diver might chose to keep an *x* chart of his dives to see whether his performance on back twisting dives was improving or lessening. This would be important to him in the selection of dives to be performed in the free-style portion of his exhibition. If he were suspicious of the agreement of the judges on these dives, he might also wish to keep track of the range. The mean range is 1.6, and the standard deviation of the range is 0.8. Figure 17-7 is a range chart for the diving scores. Note that one can get into difficulties with range charts because there are no negative values of the range. This is not serious, however, because the concern usually centers on increases in variation rather than on decreases, although in some cases the latter could represent the results of too great an investment in attempting to control the process.

Equipped with both a mean chart and a range chart, the manager

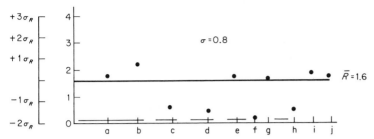

Figure 17-7 *Range chart of judges' agreement on back twisting dives*

can be reasonably certain that his process is under control, although there is some slight possibility that variability is not. He still must face the question of how frequently and how intensively to sample. This, like other decisions concerning the purchase of information, is a function of a number of costs and benefits.

Data for process design. Control charts give signals if processes are changing. They also serve, in many cases, as a record of process behavior useful for future reference. The process may be designed to yield one frequency distribution of a variable, but the samples taken for quality control purposes serve to establish what the real results have turned out to be. This information then is available for the design of similar processes or in the modification of current operating procedures to reduce costs or increase output rates or output quality. The sample has to be big enough to catch shifts in the true process that are potentially costly to the company. Duncan[2] in a basic and useful book has suggested a rule of thumb. If the control system needs to catch only relatively large shifts in the mean, say 2σ or greater, than samples of 4 or 5 are adequate. If the chart is to detect shifts as small as 1σ, then samples of 15 or 20 are better. He also suggests that in a continuous process where the shift can cause a large loss, it is better to take small samples (4 or 5) more frequently rather than 8 to 10 at once.

CONTROL CHARTS USING ATTRIBUTES

The attributes of a sampling system can be expressed as a continuous distribution by plotting the proportion of the times that the material is accepted or rejected. The mean proportion defective, usually designated $\bar{p}$ and called the "percent defective," can be plotted on a control chart, called for obvious reasons a p-chart. The probability distribution for this type of vari-

[2] A. J. Duncan, *Quality Control and Industrial Statistics,* 3d ed. (Homewood, Ill.: Richard D. Irwin, Incorporated, 1965), p. 398.

able is the binomial, which has a mean of *p* and a standard deviation
of

$$\sigma = \frac{p(1-p)}{n}$$

where

p = the mean proportion defective in the lot (or population)

n = the number of units in the sample

As with other distributions, the behavior of a substantial number of binomial
samples can be assumed to follow the normal distribution and the normal
tables can be used to set the upper and lower control limits of the p-chart.
Figure 17-8 contains a p-chart for a product sampled on a once-per-shift
basis. A similar chart can be prepared based on the number of units defective
rather than the proportion. The data would, of course, be dependent on
a constant sample size. This variable, the *number of defectives* per sample
of size *n*, characteristically is identified by the letter *c*. The plot of *c* is
designated by a c-chart. The choice between a p-chart or a c-chart is relatively arbitrary. It is primarily a question of which the manager feels most
comfortable with. If there is a possibility of variation in sample sizes from
time to time, that would tend to tip the decision in favor of the p-chart.
Unless the sample size stays constant, the plot of *c* is relatively meaningless,
although the standard deviation of the p-chart and the control limits derived
for it also are sensitive to *n*, the sample size. If the proportion or the
number defective increases, the manager knows that a correction should
be made. If the proportion stays below the designated level, he also should
investigate a new set of process conditions that will lead to equal or better
quality at consistently lower costs.

Chemical engineers have developed a statistical technique called EVOP
(for evolutionary operation) to analyze quality and yield data accompanying
very small variations in process settings. These variations may be either

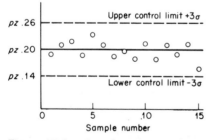

Figure 17-8   *A p-chart for product sampled once per shift*

planned or the results of minor adjustment errors. As the variations are made and the results analyzed, those associated with statistically significant improvements in the results are incorporated into the process. Then a new experiment is started based on minor deviations from the new setting. The objective of this procedure is to have a sequence of minor shifts which in time will amount to the equivalent of major process changes without the costs of large experiments and the risks of major changes in key variables. The manager may not adopt a sophisticated plan such as EVOP, but he certainly should be willing and able to use the data that are provided both by choice and by accidental variations to improve his operations over time.

ACCEPTANCE SAMPLING BY ATTRIBUTES

Knowing that the mean proportion defective is within the tolerance limits set by the designer of a process is important, but it fails to answer to the important question: "When should a lot of material, ingoing or outgoing, be accepted as meeting quality standards or rejected as unsatisfactory?" The purchaser, for example, cares little about the process percent defective of his supplier. He cares about the percent defectives entering his own process and about holding the vendor to their agreement on specifications for acceptance or rejection. These specifications usually take the form of a sample of size n from a lot of size U and a maximum allowable number of defective pieces. These agreements also generally spell out the frequency of the sampling, the procedure to assure randomness, and the exact nature of a defect or set of conditions defining a defective. In a plan, all sorts of combinations are possible to allow for the presence of multiple defects, the presence of both major and minor defects, multiple sampling, and sequential sampling. The latter involves the acceptance of a lot if the observed errors are at or below one value, rejection of the lot if they are at or above another, and the taking of one or more additional samples if the value is between the first two. The first two sets of conditions are clearly indicative of good or bad lots; but the intermediate values could be due to sampling error, and a new larger sample is required to give adequate information for a decision.

Selecting a sampling plan. The first step in the sampling procedure is the selection of the proportion defective that would separate acceptance from rejection, if the true value of that proportion were known with certainty. If the knowledge was certain or at least came from a relatively reliable 100 percent inspection, the acceptance-rejection decision would be relatively simple. When the proportion defective was less than the target Acceptable Quality Level (AQL), the lot would go out. If it were greater than that, it would be rejected. Figure 17-9 shows this relationship in an Operating Characteristic (OC) curve (which plots the probability of accepting a lot against its true lot percent defective under a given sampling plan).

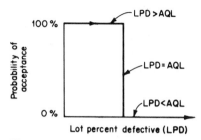

Figure 17-9 *Operating characteristic curve with 100% inspection*

The number of defectives can be expressed as a percentage or as *c*, the number of units defective in a sample of *n* taken from a lot of size *U*. One hundred percent inspection means that $n = U$. Where one has 100 percent inspection but breaks the lot into separate samples that are accepted or rejected independently, some lots may be rejected even when the average percent defective is the one targeted, simply because the errors will be distributed randomly among the individual samples. Figure 17-10 contains the results of 48 tosses of an unbiased coin which produced the anticipated equal distribution of heads and tails. The proportion of acceptable units (heads or *H*) is 50 percent, and the sampling plan when each 6 tosses is treated as a separate sample is $c = 3$, $n = 6$. This means that any lot with 3 or more heads would be accepted. In this case, then, the 2 circled lots would be rejected. Had heads rather than tails represented rejects, then 3 of the 8 lots, those in a broken circle, would have been rejected. In either case, the rejections would have been due entirely to the randomness of the samples rather than the underlying proportion of defectives. But that is the price one pays for using samples and controlling work in the more convenient small lots.

More realistic problems. In the real situation, where the underlying process percent defective changes from hour to hour and the sample contains only a small fraction of the total production, it is easy to see how the task becomes much more complicated. We would like to reject all lots with $p > $ AQL and accept those with $p \leq$ AQL, but once the sampling procedure is introduced, one incurs a risk of rejecting a good lot or accepting a bad lot because the sample did not represent the true population. Therefore,

Figure 17-10 *The results of breaking observations into small independent samples*

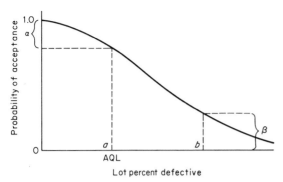

Figure 17-11 *Typical OC curve with sampling errors*

the ideal operating characteristic curve shown in Figure 17-9 begins to flatten out and look like the one in Figure 17-11. At the prescribed AQL, there will still be a real probability that the lot will be rejected. This error will exist even when the process percent defective is really well below the AQL. This probability of rejection is referred to as the "producer's risk" or α. Producer's risk exists primarily below the AQL level of p. On the other hand, once the underlying $p > $ AQL, there remains some probability of acceptance which reduces rapidly as the process worsens. This probability of accepting a bad lot is called the "consumer's risk" or β. Figure 17-11 also illustrates that at any given point, the producer's risk of rejection, α, can be determined directly as one less the probability of acceptance; this is expressed notation-ally as $\alpha = 1 - \beta$. If the process worsens and the value of p shifts up to b, then the consumer's risk of accepting these lots is β.

    Choosing a final plan. Selecting a sampling plan is not an easy task. A sample size n and an acceptance number c must be chosen from a virtually infinite array of possible plans. The final choice will be the one which leads to the lowest total cost. Normally one would like to keep the sample size n as small as possible so as to hold down the cost of selecting, handling, and sampling. On the other hand, the larger that sample, the closer the curve is to the ideal in Figure 17-9. This relationship of sample size to error risks is shown in Figure 17-12, where samples of n equal to 100, 200, and 300 are compared. The actual target AQL is 1.5 percent, and the sample $c/n = p$ in each case is 1 percent. Note that as the sample increases, there is an increased probability of rejecting a lot when the lot percent defective approaches AQL $= 1.5$ percent.[3] There also is a reduced probability of rejecting the lot when the true p approaches zero, but this

---

    [3] Figure 17-12 has the same ratio of c to n for each alternative sampling plan. If AQL $= 1.5$ per-cent was the target, then $c = 1$ was the obvious choice for $n = 100$. The choice of $c = 2$ would have led to the acceptance of many lots with too high a p value. For the case where $n = 200$, it would be logical to evaluate $c = 3$ also, and for $n = 300$, $c = 4, 5$, and 6.

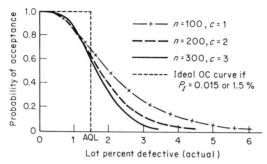

Figure 17-12   *Examples of OC curves*

has been accomplished at the expense of a high probability of rejecting good lots in the area just below the AQL line. Error always can be reduced but only at the cost of larger samples or a greater likelihood of error some-place else. Therefore, two other variables must enter into the analysis: the costs associated with each type of error and the frequency distributions of the true process percent defective that is likely to be observed over time.

The two types of errors are likely to produce different costs and to have separate decision-makers involved, one for the supplier and one for the user. But, let us assume that they are one in the same for the purposes of this example. Let us further assume that the manager believes that the mean error rate p will be 1.5 percent and will be randomly distributed with a standard deviation of 0.2 percent. Each sampling plan will have its own OC curves from which one can read off the probabilities of each kind of error for any given value of the unknown quantity p. If we add to this the cost of the sampling plan being considered, we have all of the ingredients for a total cost calculation. Table 17-6 illustrates a method of approximating the expected value of the sampling errors. A more rigorous approach would involve integration as outlined in the footnote to this page.[4]

[4] Total cost of a sampling plan $= C_1 \int_0^{AQL} \left[(\alpha|c, n, p_i) P(p_i) \right] dpi$

$$+ C_2 \int_{AQL}^{1.00} \left[(\beta|c,n,p_i) \cdot P(p_i)dp_i \right] + C_3$$

where

p_i = value of p at any point i, $0 \leq i \leq 1$

α = probability of rejecting a good lot given c, n, and p_i

C_1 = the cost of rejecting a good lot

$P(p_i)$ = probability that p will take on the value p_i

β = probability of accepting a bad lot given c, n, and p_i

C_2 = the cost of accepting a bad lot

C_3 = the cost of sampling given c, n

Table 17-6 *Procedure for computing expected error costs*

Lot Percent Defective	Prob. of P Being in This Range	Prob. of Rejecting	Cost of Rejecting	Prob. of Accept.	Cost of Accept.	Total Error Costs
1.05 or less	.0122	Determined*	$10	Determined*	$ 0	Determined*
1.05–1.15	.0279		10		0	by
1.15–1.25	.0655	by	10	by	0	sampling
1.25–1.35	.1210		10		0	plan
1.35–1.45	.1747	sampling	10		0	c,n
1.45–1.50	.0987		10	sampling	0	OC
1.50–1.55	.0987	plan	0	plan	30	Determined*
1.55–1.65	.1747		0		30	by
1.65–1.75	.1210	c,n	0	c,n	30	sampling
1.75–1.85	.0655		0		30	plan
1.85–1.95	.0279	OC	0	OC	30	c,n
1.95 or more	.0122		0		30	OC

*These values of α would be read from OC curves for the alternative plan c,n being evaluated.

To arrive at the expected values, evaluation of the frequency distribution of P has been broken down into several ranges which are assumed to average out to the midpoint of the range. Using the tables for the normal distribution and the midpoint of the ranges, it is possible to estimate the probability that the process will be in that range. For example, the process generating the $p = 0.015$ will have a 0.1747 probability of being in the range 0.0125 to 0.0135. Going to the candidate OC curve for the plan $n = 100$, $c = 1$, the analyst will find that about 45 percent of the lots in this range will be rejected. The cost of rejecting a good lot is $10, so the average rejection error cost per lot would be $4.50 for this range, and the total expected cost of rejection in this range will be $4.50 × 0.1745 or $0.785. In the corresponding area from 1.55 to 1.64, it appears that the probability of accepting a bad lot with the plan $n = 100$, $c = 1$ is 50 percent, so the total expected cost of that sector is 0.50 × $30 × 0.1745 or $2.618. For the plan $n = 300$, $c = 3$, the probability of acceptance of a bad lot looks to be 25 percent, so that the expected costs would be $1.31 (0.25 × $30 × 0.1745) for that section. These figures would have to be added to similar data from the other ranges of the manager's frequency distribution to arrive at the total cost function.

An alternative approach would be to simulate the process in question drawing successive values of p from a table or computer program providing normally distributed random numbers. These would represent successive lots. Then, the selection of another uniformly distributed random number would determine whether the lot was accepted or rejected in accordance with the probabilities on the OC curve being tested and the given value of p. Where either of the two types of error occurred, the appropriate costs would be added to a total cost function. After a suitable number of simulated lots had been processed, the average costs per lot for the plan being tested could be compared with those of other plans being considered and with the final choice made.

Shortcuts needed. The procedures for evaluating each plan are cumbersome, especially when one considers all the alternative plans that could be used. Figure 17-13 shows the alternative when c over n is held constant at 0.01 and the sample size is varied. Figure 17-14 shows the OC curves that result when n is held at 50 and c is allowed to vary. Obviously, a simple procedure for evaluating the alternative would be preferred by many managers, even at the cost of some accuracy or of some experiments to reduce total system costs.

In a frequently used short-cut procedure, the manager starts out by specifying a pair of percent defective levels. One, which he designates AQL, represents a low rate of defectives considered to be good quality performance. He would like to accept most lots when $p = $ AQL or is close to it. He also sets a value for α, the producer's risk, equal to the small per-

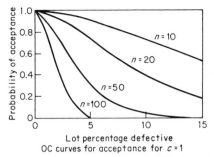

Figure 17-13   *OC curves with constant c and variable n*

centage of good lots that he is willing to have rejected at this low *p* value. Then, he selects a second level of *p* which would be considered poor quality or something bordering on it where he would want a very small β or consumer's risk. This level of *p* he would call his "lot tolerance percent defective" (LTPD). He now has two points on a desired operating characteristic curve (AQL, α) and (LTPD, β). His next job is to look in one of the many books displaying potential OC curves and pick the ones that go through or close to these two points at a reasonable sampling cost. Then, it is possible to evaluate the better ones with a more thorough evaluation of sampling costs versus closeness to the curve which minimizes error costs. Figure 17-15 shows a plot of the two points used to evaluate curves and the several candidate sampling plans.

Average outgoing quality level. The purchaser really may not care at all about AQL, LTPD, or α. He wants a specific level or fewer defects in the incoming materials, or he will reject it. That level is determined partly by costs and partly by the quality that competitive suppliers are willing to offer. He wants assurances that the average incoming defect levels will not exceed a stated proportion. He couldn't care less how the producer meets it, but he demands an "average outgoing quality level" (AOQL) that

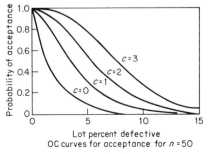

Figure 17-14   *OC curves with constant n and variable c*

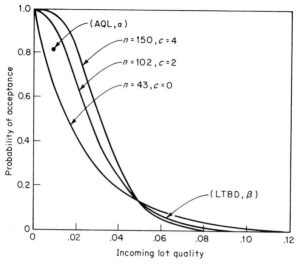

Figure 17-15 *Comparing OC curves using two base points*

must be met. The supplier can meet this limit in the following manner. If there are zero percent defectives, then none is rejected. As the value of p in the true process increases, some defects will be shipped out. For any given sampling plan c,n, this quality level will be approximated over time by the process percent defective p, times the probability of acceptance [Prob. (A)] of any lot with that value of p as shown in the plan's OC curve times the number of units in the lot or $[(p \cdot \text{Prob.} (A) \cdot N)]$. At the same time, another group of defects will not be shipped out because the lot was rejected, and, over time, this would contain $[p \cdot (1\text{-Prob.} (A)) \cdot N]$ defects. If these rejected lots are 100 percent inspected and are replaced by good pieces, then we will obtain, on the average, from accepted and

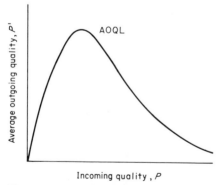

Figure 17-16 *Average outgoing quality curve*

rejected, then reworked lots a reduced p, or p'. In the case where the entire rejected lots are 100 percent inspected and all rejects replaced with good pieces, the new p' would be equal to $p' \cdot$ Prob. (A). As p increases, the value of p' increases for a while and then decreases as a greater and greater percentage of the lots are rejected and then reworked. This means that there will be a maximum p' value for any given sampling plan as illustrated in Figure 17-16. This maximum can be set at the AOQL that the customer is demanding and his requirements will be met, at least on the average. There are other variations of the AOQL system in which only the samples are reworked rather than the whole lot, but if the samples are a goodly portion of each lot, the same limiting effect can be realized.

ACCEPTANCE SAMPLING BY VARIABLES

Each of the units in a sample can be evaluated for its specific values of a variable as well as its attributes. These values can be averaged to provide a mean value for the sample, which hopefully is representative of the lot from which the sample was drawn. Presumably, this sample mean can have two limits just like the situation with the control charts for variables. The same data are commonly used in both a control chart system for trend analysis and a sampling plan for deciding whether or not to accept specific lots. Again, it is assumed that the population, the lot of size N, has an underlying distribution of unit measures which may or may not be the one for which the process was designed originally. On the basis of the design and the several costs of rejection and acceptance errors, upper and often lower limits of acceptance are again established knowing that the set of samples will have its own normal distribution of means.

In many cases, either an attributes sampling plan or a variables sampling plan can be used. The variable measure contains more information, since one actually measures the value rather than merely classifying it good or bad. Actual measurement obviously leads to higher inspection, recording, and computation costs per unit than attribute classification, and the control limits calculations are more complicated as well. On the other hand, the fact that the variable sampling plan supplies more information means that it requires a much smaller sample size to give the same level of protection. Table 17-7 provides a comparison of the sample sizes needed for similar levels of protection. The manager will have to be the final judge as to which plan will have the best net effect.

In many sampling plans, a single sample often must be fairly large if it is to provide the desired amount of assurance to the manager that the output quality is acceptable. An alternative that often is attractive, especially where there is no great hurry to ship the lot, is to take one smaller sample, and if that gives a slightly ambiguous result, then take a second

Table 17-7 *Sample sizes needed to achieve a given level of protection*

With Attributes Plan	With Comparable Variables Plan	Percent Reduction in Sample Size with Variables Plan
10 units	7 units	30%
20	13	35
40	20	50
75	35	53
150	60	60
300	85	72
750	125	83
1,500	200	87

Source: Bowker, A. H., and H. P. Goode, *Sampling Inspection by Variables* (New York, McGraw-Hill, 1952).

larger one. This is called a "double-sampling plan." Figure 17-17 shows the operating characteristic curve of a double-sampling plan with an initial *n* of 50. This is a much smaller sample than that needed for a comparable single-sampling plan. The first sample of 50 is drawn, and the lot is accepted if the number of observed defects is 2 or fewer. It will be rejected if the number of defects is equal to or greater than 7. If the observed number of defects is 3, 4, 5, or 6, then a second sample of 100 units is selected. That sample is inspected until the total number of defects uncovered in both lots reaches 7. At that point, the lot is rejected, and no further inspection is required. In Figure 17-17, there are three curves. The left-most one, lettered A, is the curve for the initial sample of 50. The second curve, lettered B, is the principal OC curve which governs the overall probability of acceptance of the lot on the basis of a full n of 150. c, the third curve, shows the probability, increasing with increasing p, that a lot will be rejected ($c \geq 7$) on the first sample. If the lot percent defective was 4 percent, then there was a .68 chance of acceptance on the first sample and a virtually zero percent chance of rejection. After the second sample, an added 10 percent of the lots would be accepted and the remaining 22 percent rejected. That means that about 5 out of 11 of the lots with $p = 0.04$ reaching the second sampling stage would be accepted.

If two samples are better than one, why not try three or four or 100? There are numerous sequential sampling plans available. Each relies on a plan of sampling and rejecting if a given number of defects are uncovered, accepting if a much lower number are found, and continuing sampling when intermediate numbers are found. The sequence of samples does tend to delay the movement of the goods, and, more importantly, the administrative com-

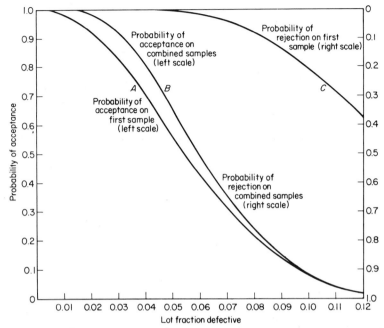

Figure 17-17 *Operating characteristic curves for a double sampling plan.* [*From A. J. Duncan,* Quality Control and Industrial Statistics *(Homewood, III.: Richard D. Irwin, Inc., 1965), p. 165.*]

plexities and the costs of sequential sampling quickly begin to outweigh the advantages of the smaller initial samples.

THE QUALITY CONTROL FEEDBACK SYSTEM

The quality control subsystem of the firm is a particularly clear illustration of the concepts of a general system involving feedback and control as outlined in Chapter 2. You will recall that the feedback system had five elements:

Processor: the activity that is being controlled, generally the converter of inputs into outputs.

Sensor: a device or procedure which measures characteristics of the process or the output.

Comparer: a device which compares the information gained by the sensor with a standard or a predetermined value.

Memory: a device for holding the standard or value to be compared with the signals from the sensor, and, in a closed-loop system, it may contain instructions for the effector.

Effector: a device which can modify the production process in response to signals from the comparer and memory.

The quality of a process output is measured in the sampling plan which, when executed, is the sensor. Although these several definitions use the word "device," it is painfully evident that a man can and often does perform the same functions, and that the existence of a man at any one function is not necessarily the difference between an open and a closed loop. If a clerk is explicitly ordered to shut down the process whenever the line on the process chart crosses the upper control limit, it matters little whether that action is taken by man or machine; the procedure is determined by the design of the system, and no discretion is intended. The inspector looking for bruised peaches at the cannery and the automatic machine weighing packed cans are both sensors; and they can be programmed to serve as comparers and effectors as well, since each compares the items with a standard and discards the rejects. Both could also record the number of rejects, if that information is considered useful. In an open-loop system, where the manager has a great deal of flexibility in using his information to select adjustments in the process, the control chart is a memory unit for the short-run comparer (the QC clerk) and for the long-run comparer (the manager who looks at trends and tries to anticipate where the process is headed). Then, the short-run or long-run comparer can effect any one of a number of potential modifications to the process.

AUTOMATED CONTROL

Many automated systems already have quality control loops built into them. Diameters of automotive pistons coming off a line are examined automatically, and any significant deviation sends off a signal alarm. Several companies already are working on systems to achieve an adaptive control capability in a process. This would involve using a computer to analyze successive measurements of variables of the output of the process. If there are no major process errors, the values recorded will appear to be randomly distributed; but trend analysis, especially multiple correlation, can be performed almost instantaneously by a computer to spot minor trends due to gradual tool wear or changes between batches of raw materials. Once the trend is spotted, it is possible to make gradual and continuous process adjustments to compensate for these changes and reduce the number of defects substantially. Both adaptive control and its cousin, EVOP, can be used as responses to the fact that the means of process outputs shift with use of the equipment. They lead to regular adjustments in order to maintain a relatively constant output frequency distribution despite process variation. One major reason for variation is the wear and tear on the equipment. In the machine shop, cutting tools and bearings wear out while in the chemical plant, heat exchangers take on new heat transfer characteristics with use. Output predictable from the process design is known reliably only over a short period of time. The advantage of small, frequent adjustments is that they entail less risk of upsetting the process due to excessive reaction.

Like so many others, the quality control loop will gradually continue to close as the technology improves. Think about the automobile as an open loop with the driver closing it. He now looks at the traffic and road signs and adjusts acceleration and direction to meet traffic conditions. In some cars, he also adjusts gear ratios with the shift and clutch. On a few cars, mostly antique or sports, he adjusts carburation further with a choke; and, on even fewer, he adjusts the ignition spark. Ignition spark, throttle, choke, and shifting once were open loops in the standard car. One by one they have been closed. Even today engineers are recommending potential new systems with computers to guide automobiles along tracks between major traffic points to improve speeds (flow rates) and quality (safety).

SIMULATION OF QC SYSTEMS

Because of the probabilistic nature of the process results and the candidate sampling plans, Monte Carlo simulation of each plan seems to be one reasonable way to evaluate sampling plans. The use of simulation to check individual sampling plans has been mentioned earlier in this chapter. The added advantages of a simulation model of a quality control system lie in the ability one gains to simulate the results using multiple frequency distributions representing multiple variables and attributes, alternative sampling plans, and special error distributions associated with the more common or more severe process malfunctions. By running a sequence of simulation experiments, it is possible to check for interactions among the various frequency distributions and select better control limits than the usual arbitrary and often uneconomical 3σ limits.

Figure 17-18 is a generalized flow chart for a simulation model proposed by Barish et al. for computer simulation of a QC scheme. Once the program is set up, it checks to see whether the next event is to be a sample. If so, the sample is generated by the computer on the basis of the given process frequency distribution and random draws from it. The sample is then compared with the standard. If it is an acceptable sample, the results are recorded, and then the simulated time (the event clock) is moved forward to the next event. If it is not accepted, the process adjustment is recorded and the next event occurs. If the next event is to be a malfunction of the process, that is noted, and the process frequency distribution is modified for the next scheduled sample. A record is made of the time of the malfunction, so that the cumulative errors until the next adjustment and the resulting total number of defectives are known for the

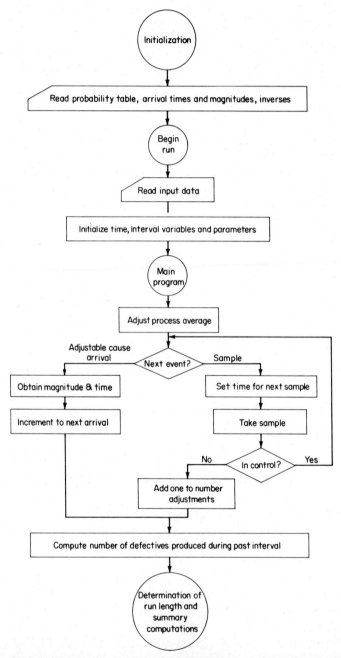

Figure 17-18 *Flow chart for simulation of QC system. [From N. Hauser, N. N. Barish, and S. Ehrenfeld, J.* Ind. Eng., *vol. 17, no. 2, February 1956, p. 80.]*

final cost calculations. The next sample may or may not catch the new error rate, depending on the sampling plan and the luck of the draw. When the error is caught, an adjustment is made to correct it, and the new samples can again be generated from the prescribed frequency distribution until a new disturbance occurs. The analyst can experiment by changing the input data several ways to provide for different sample plans, different types and frequencies of disturbances, and their specific costs. The system costs can be calculated by the computer at the end of the simulation run. The phrase "determination of run length" refers to the parts of the computer program that determine whether or not the experiment has run long enough to give stable relationships and provide a realistic comparison. Given the arbitrary choices in the usual process of selecting sampling schemes, computer simulations appear to hold considerable promise for developing more rational and more accurate sampling plans.

QUESTIONS

1. Who determines product quality? Why?
2. What is the relationship between quality and cost? Quality and profits?
3. List at least five places in a production process where inspections should be considered.
4. A plant superintendent proposes elimination of all inspections except at the end of the work in each department. He argues that, even in machining work, losses will be small because machine operators who work on tasks late in the job sequence can lay aside bad pieces that reach them. How does this recommendation sound to you?
5. Evaluate the following statement: "A common industrial practice is to use ± 3 standard deviation control limits to minimize the risks of saying the process is out of control when it is in control and of saying it is in control when it is out of control."
6. As it is used in defining operating characteristic curves, what is the meaning of "producer's risk"?
7. In quality control, compare the procedures for controlling attributes with those for controlling variables.
8. If the cost of accepting a defective item is very low compared with the cost of rejecting a good item, would you use wider or narrower limits compared to situations where the two costs are the same?
9. Discuss a procedure for setting up an r-chart.
10. What statistical sampling method should you use to inspect transistors for use in the navigational computers of a manned spacecraft headed for the moon? Why?

11. What are the advantages and disadvantages of having roving inspectors in production?

12. In inspecting products, what factors would influence the amount of inspection performed? Why?

PROBLEMS

1. If the cost of inspecting an item is $.50 and the cost if it is not inspected and is later found defective is $5, at what process percent defective should a manufacturer be indifferent as to whether he does or does not inspect that item?

2. Where would it be most advantageous to place a second inspector, given that every unit is inspected after operation 5? Inspectors receive $2 per hour. Starting with operation 1, parts are processed sequentially in ascending number of operation.

Operation	1	2	3	4	5
Percent rejects traceable to operation	8	2	1	4	3
Inspection time per piece in minutes	4	1	3	5	2
Cumulative incremental material, labor, and overhead value per piece	1.50	1.80	2.00	2.50	3.00

3. Samples of 4 items each are taken from Hardy Motors' manufacturing process at regular intervals. A certain quality characteristic (i.e., diameter, width, etc.) is measured and $\bar{X}$ (mean) and R (range) values are computed for each sample. After 25 samples, $\bar{X} = 15,350$ and $R = 411.4$

(a) Compute limits (3 sigma) for $\bar{X}$ (mean) and R (range) charts.

(b) Suppose that all the points (i.e., $\bar{X}$'s) on the $\bar{X}$ and R charts fell within control limits. Tolerance requirements for this particular quality characteristic are $16,610 \pm 15$. If the quality characteristic is normally distributed with the distribution centered at $\bar{X}$ (i.e., mean of the sample means), what percentage of the product, if any, would you expect to find outside the specified tolerances?

(c) Any item that falls below the lower tolerance limit of 15,595 must be scrapped, whereas any above the upper tolerance limit of 16,625 may be brought within specifications by rework operations. It is suggested that the process ought to be centered at a level so that not more than 0.1 percent of the product will be scrapped. If the quality characteristic is normally distributed with the dispersion indicated by the control chart data, and if it is believed that satistical control can be maintained, what should be the aimed-at value $\bar{X}'$ (i.e., the centering of the process) to make this scrap exactly 0.1

percent? What percentage of rework should be expected with this centering?

4. A p-chart is to be used to analyze the September record for 100 percent inspection of toy radio tubes. The total number inspected during the month was 2,196, and the total number of defectives was 158.

 (a) Compute the average fraction defective P.

 (b) Compute individual 3-sigma control limits for the following 3 days, and state whether the fraction defective fell within control limits each day.

Date	Number Inspected	No. of Defectives
Sept. 14	54	8
15	162	24
16	213	3

5. A package filling machine at Crummy Cake has associated with it acceptable tolerance limits of 2.50 ± 0.04 pounds. Samples of weights have revealed that $\sigma = 0.01$ (i.e., sample standard deviation), and the process is normally distributed. With $\bar{X} = 2.51$, what percentage of individual boxes do you expect to fall outside the tolerance limits?

CASE: STATIC ELEVATOR CORPORATION

Robert Zipf has recently been assigned a special project as part of his product engineering job at Static Elevator. His task is to interpret and track down a number of complaints about high service costs and low reliability.

One of the first quality procedures he has studied concerns the production of the critically important elevator support hooks. The process has been operated to achieve hooks with an average strength of 30,000 pounds per square inch (psi) to break. The occasional tests run on hooks with a mean breaking strength of 30,000 psi have indicated a standard deviation in breaking strengths reported of 500 psi.

The test equipment at Static Elevator could handle up to 16 tests per day on top of the current workload. Harry Void, the Chief Inspector, has suggested that Zipf worry only about downward shifts in the breaking strengths and set up a process control chart accordingly. Because of the safety aspects involved, the company usually costs its processes to assume the process to be out of control when 15 percent of the sample means appear to be outside of the control limits.

Mr. Zipf has also discussed the breaking strength requirements with Joe Dulcet, the engineer who designs the hooks and similar parts of the elevator system. Joe indicated that the 30,000 psi figure was an industry and government standard set in 1954. Spot checks on current designs indicate that the force on the hooks seldom exceeds 28,500 psi.

Mr. Zipf feels that he ought to prepare a test procedure for elevator hooks and then talk it over with senior management to get their opinions on strategies and cost alternatives involved.

bibliography

1. Ackoff, R. L., and M. W. Sasieni. *Fundamentals of Operations Research.* New York: Wiley, 1968.
2. Ackoff, R. L., and Patrick Rivett. *Manager's Guide to Operations Research.* New York: Wiley, 1963.
3. Ackoff, R. L. *Scientific Method: Optimizing Applied Research Decisions.* New York: Wiley, 1962.
4. Alderson, Wroe, and Stanley J. Shapiro, eds. *Marketing and the Computer.* Englewood Cliffs, N.J.: Prentice-Hall, 1963.
5. Anthony, Robert N. *Planning and Control Systems; a Framework for Analysis.* Boston: Harvard, 1965.
6. Archibald, Russell D., and Richard L. Villoria. *Network Based Management Systems (PERT/CPM).* New York: Wiley, 1966.
7. Baker, Bruce N. *An Introduction to PERT-CPM.* Homewood, Ill.: Irwin, 1964.
8. Barlow, C. Wayne. *Corporate Packaging Management.* New York: American Management Association, 1969.
9. Barrett, D. A. *Automatic Inventory Control Techniques.* New York: International Publishers, 1969.
10. Battersby, Albert. *Network Analysis for Planning and Scheduling.* New York: St. Martin's, 1964.
11. Baumol, William J. *Economic Theory and Operations Analysis.* 2d ed. Englewood Cliffs, N.J.: Prentice-Hall, 1965.
12. Beer, Stafford. *Cybernetics and Management.* New York: Wiley, 1959.

13. Beer, Stafford. *Decision and Control; the Meaning of Operational Research and Management Cybernetics.* New York: Wiley, 1966.
14. Beer, Stafford. *Management Sciences: The Business Use of Operations Research.* Garden City, N.Y.: Doubleday, 1968.
15. Belsey, David A. *Industrial Production Behavior: The Order-stock Destinations.* Amsterdam: North-Holland Publishing Co., 1970.
16. Bernes-Lee, C. M., ed. *Models for Decision Making.* New York: Gordon and Breach, 1969.
17. Biegel, John E. *Production Control: A Quantitative Approach.* Englewood Cliffs, N.J.: Prentice-Hall, 1963.
18. Blanchard, B. B., Jr., and Edward E. Lowery. *Maintainability: Principles and Practice.* New York: McGraw-Hill, 1969.
19. Boot, Johannes Cornelius Gerardus, and Edwin B. Cox. *Statistical Analysis for Managerial Decisions.* New York: McGraw-Hill, 1970.
20. Bosc, George E. P., and Norman R. Draper. *Evolutionary Operation: A Statistical Method for Process Improvement.* New York: Wiley, 1968.
21. Bowman, D. L. et al. *Organization for Manufacturing.* New York: Society of Manufacturing Engineers, 1970.
22. Bowman, Edward H., and Robert B. Fetter. *Analysis for Production Management.* Rev. ed. Homewood, Ill.: Irwin, 1961.
23. Brabb, George Jacob. *Introduction to Quantitative Management.* New York: Holt, 1968.
24. Branch, Melville Campbell. *The Corporate Planning Process.* New York: American Management Association, 1962.
25. Brichta, A. M., and Peter E. M. Shark. *From Project to Production.* New York: Pergamon, 1970.
26. Brinkloe, W. D. *Managerial Operations Research.* New York: McGraw-Hill, 1969.
27. Broadwell, Martin M. *The Supervisor and On-the-job Training.* Reading, Mass.: Addison-Wesley, 1969.
28. Buffa, Elwood S. *Models for Production and Operations Management.* New York: Wiley, 1963.
29. Buffa, Elwood S. *Modern Production Management.* 3d ed. New York: Wiley, 1969.
30. Buffa, Elwood S. *Operations Management: Problems and Models.* 2d ed. New York: Wiley, 1968.
31. Buffa, Elwood S. *Production-Inventory Systems; Planning and Control.* Homewood, Ill.: Irwin, 1968.
32. Cabell, Randolph W., and A. Phillips. *Problems in Basic Operations Research for Management.* New York: Wiley, 1961.
33. Candlin, D. B. *O and M, A Management Service.* New York: Pergamon, 1969.

34. Cantor, J. *Profit Orientated Manufacturing Systems.* New York: American Management Association, 1969.
35. Caplen, R. H. *A Practical Approach to Quality Control.* New York: International Publishers, 1969.
36. Chorafas, D. N. *How to Manage Computers for Results.* London: Gee and Co., 1969.
37. Chorafas, D. N. *Systems and Simulation.* New York: Academic, 1965.
38. Chu, Kong. *Quantitative Methods for Business and Economic Analysis.* Scranton: International Textbook, 1969.
39. Churchman, Charles West, et al. *Introduction to Operations Research.* New York: Wiley, 1957.
40. Churchman, Charles West. *Prediction and Optimal Decision.* Englewood Cliffs, N.J.: Prentice-Hall, 1961.
41. Churchman, C. West. *Systems Approach.* New York: Dell, 1969.
42. Cleland, David I. *Systems, Organizations, Analysis, Management, A Book of Readings.* New York: McGraw-Hill, 1969.
43. Dean, Burton V. *Operations Research in Research and Development.* New York: Wiley, 1963.
44. DiRoccaferrera, Guiseppe M. Ferrero. *Introduction to Linear Programming Processes.* Cincinnati: South-Western Publishing Co. Inc., 1967.
45. Dooley, Arch R. et al. *Operations Planning and Control.* New York: Wiley, 1964.
46. Driebeck, Norman J. *Applied Linear Programming.* Reading, Mass.: Addison-Wesley, 1969.
47. Drucker, Peter F. *Managing for Results; Economic Tasks and Risk-taking Decisions.* New York: Harper & Row, 1964.
48. Drucker, Peter F. *Technology, Management and Society.* New York: Harper & Row, 1970.
49. Duncan, Acheson Johnston. *Quality Control and Industrial Statistics.* Homewood, Ill.: Irwin, 1965.
50. Dyckman, T. R. et al. *Management Decision Making Under Uncertainty.* New York: Macmillan, 1969.
51. Eddison, R. T., et al. *Operational Research in Management.* New York: Wiley, 1962.
52. Eilon, Samuel. *Elements of Production Planning and Control.* New York: Macmillan, 1962.
53. Emery, J. C. *Organizational Planning and Control Systems.* New York: Macmillan, 1969.
54. English, J. Morley, ed., *Cost Effectiveness: Economic Evaluation of Engineering Systems.* New York: Wiley, 1968.
55. Enrick, Norbert Lloyd. *Management Operations Research.* New York: Holt, 1965.

56. Enrick, Norbert Lloyd. *Quality Control.* New York: The Industrial Press, 1960.
57. Enrick, Norbert Lloyd. *Quality Control and Reliability.* Metuchen, N.J.: Textile Book Service, 1969.
58. Ertell, Glenn G. *Numerical Control.* New York: Wiley, 1969.
59. Evarts, Harry F. *Introduction to PERT.* Boston: Allyn and Bacon, 1964.
60. Fabricant, Solomon. *A Primer in Productivity.* New York: Random House, 1969.
61. Fabrycky, Wolter J., and P. E. Torgersen. *Operations Economy: Industrial Applications of Operations Research.* New York: Prentice-Hall, 1966.
62. Fetter, Robert Barclay. *The Quality Control System.* Homewood, Ill.: Irwin, 1967.
63. Flagle, Charles D. et al., eds. *Operations Research and Systems Engineering.* Baltimore: John Hopkins, 1960.
64. Fuhro, Wilbur J. *Work Measurement and Production Control with the F-A-S-T System.* Englewood Cliffs, N.J.: Prentice-Hall, 1963.
65. Gavett, J. William. *Production and Operations Management.* New York: Harcourt, Brace & World, 1968.
66. Gavett, J. William, and John M. Addlerige. *Operations Analysis in Small Manufacturing Companies.* Ithaca, N.Y.: Cornell, 1962.
67. Gillis, F. E., Jr. *Managerial Economics: Decision Making under Certainty for Business and Engineering.* New York: Addison-Wesley, 1969.
68. Goddard, Laurence S. *Mathematical Techniques of Operational Research.* Reading Mass.: Addison-Wesley, 1963.
69. Goldfarb, Nathan, and William K. Kaiser, eds. *Gantt Charts and Statistical Quality Control.* Hempstead, N.Y.: Hofstra, 1964.
70. Gordon, G. *System Simulation.* Englewood Cliffs, N.J.: Prentice-Hall, 1969.
71. Grabbe, Eugene M. et al., eds. *Handbook of Automation, Computation and Control.* 3 vols. New York: Wiley, 1958, 1959, 1961.
72. Grant, Eugene Lodewick. *Statistical Quality Control.* 3d ed. New York: McGraw-Hill, 1964.
73. Greene, James H. *Production Control: Systems and Decisions.* Homewood, Ill.: Irwin, 1965.
74. Greene, James H. *Production and Inventory Control Handbook.* New York: McGraw-Hill, 1970.
75. Groff, G. K. and John F. Muth. *Operations Management: Selected Readings.* Homewood, Ill.: Irwin, 1969.
76. Gue, R., and M. Thomas. *Mathematical Methods in Operations Research.* New York: Macmillan, 1968.

77. Hagan, J. T. *A Management Role for Quality Control.* New York: American Management Association, 1968.
78. Haley, Keith Brian. *Mathematical Programming for Business and Industry.* New York: Macmillan, 1967.
79. Hamilton, William F. et al. *Linear Programming for Management.* Newburyport, Mass.: Entelak, 1969.
80. Hammer, P. L., and S. Rudeanu. *Boolean Methods in Operations Research and Related Areas.* New York: Springer-Verlag, 1968.
81. Hansen, Bertraud L. *Quality Control; Theory and Applications.* Englewood Cliffs, N.J.: Prentice-Hall, 1963.
82. Hanssmann, Fred. *Operations Research in Production and Inventory Control.* New York: Wiley, 1962.
83. Hanssmann, Fred. *Operations Research Techniques for Capital Investment.* New York: Wiley, 1968.
84. Harris, Douglas H., and F. B. Chaney. *Human Factors in Quality Assurance.* New York: Wiley, 1969.
85. Hillier, F., and G. J. Lieberman. *Introduction to Operations Research.* San Francisco: Holden-Day, Inc., 1967.
86. Holdren, Bob R. et al. *Operations Research in Small Business.* Ames, Iowa: Iowa State University Press, 1963.
87. Holt, Charles C. et al. *Planning Production Inventories and Work Force.* Englewood Cliffs, N.J.: Prentice Hall, 1960.
88. Hopeman, Richard J. *Production; Concepts, Analysis, Control.* 2d ed. Columbus, Ohio: Charles E. Merrill Books, Inc., 1970.
89. Hopeman, Richard J. *Systems Analysis and Operations Management.* Columbus, Ohio: Charles E. Merrill Books, Inc., 1969.
90. Horowitz, I. *Modern Theory of the Firm and Operations Analysis.* New York: Holt, 1970.
91. Hu, T. C. *Integer Programming and Network Flows.* Reading, Mass.: Addison-Wesley, 1969.
92. Iannone, Anthony L. *Management Program Planning and Control with PERT, MOST and LOB.* Englewood Cliffs, N.J.: Prentice-Hall, 1967.
93. Jaiswal, N. K. *Priority Queues.* New York: Academic, 1968.
94. Jedamus, Paul, and Robert Frame. *Business Decision Theory.* New York: McGraw-Hill, 1969.
95. Johnson, Richard A. et al. *Operations Management.* Boston: Houghton Mifflin, 1970.
96. Johnson, Richard A. et al. *Theory and Management of Systems.* 2d ed. New York: McGraw-Hill, 1967.
97. Juran, Joseph M. *Quality Control Handbook.* 2d ed. New York: McGraw-Hill, 1967.
98. Kaufmann, Arnold. *Methods and Models of Operations Research.* Englewood Cliffs, N.J.: Prentice-Hall, 1963.

99. Kaufmann, Arnold, and R. Faure, *Introduction to Operations Research.* New York: Academic, 1968.

100. Kaufmann, Arnold, and G. Desbazelle. *The Critical Path Method: An Application of the PERT Method and Its Variants to Production and Study Programs.* New York: Gordon and Breach, 1969.

101. Killeen, Louis M. *Techniques of Inventory Management.* New York: American Management Association, 1969.

102. Kirkpatrick, Elwood G. *Quality Control for Managers and Engineers.* New York: Wiley, 1970.

103. Koepke, Charles A. *Plant Production Control.* 3d ed. New York: Wiley, 1961.

104. LeBreton, Preston P., and Dale A. Henning. *Planning Theory.* Englewood Cliffs, N.J.: Prentice-Hall, 1961.

105. Levin, Richard I., and Charles A. Kirkpatrick. *Planning and Control with PERT/CPM.* New York: McGraw-Hill, 1966.

106. Levin, Richard I., and Charles A. Kirkpatrick. *Quantitative Approaches to Management.* 2d ed. New York: McGraw-Hill, 1971.

107. Levin, Richard I., and Robert B. DesJardins. *Theory of Games and Strategies.* Scranton: International Textbook, 1970.

108. Levin, R. I., and R. P. Lamone. *Linear Programming for Management Decisions.* Homewood, Ill.: Irwin, 1969.

109. Levin, R. I., and R. P. Lamone. *Quantitative Disciplines in Management Decisions.* Belmont, Calif.: Wadsworth, 1969.

110. Lindsay, Franklin A. *New Techniques for Management Decision Making.* New York: McGraw-Hill, 1963.

111. Lockyer, K. G. *An Introduction to Critical Path Analysis.* New York: Pitman, 1964.

112. Lowe, C. W. *Critical Path Analysis by Bar Chart.* London: Business Books, 1969.

113. McElhiney, Paul J., and Robert J. Cook. *The Logistics of Materials Management: Readings in Modern Purchasing.* Boston: Houghton Mifflin, 1969.

114. McKenney, J. L., and R. S. Rosenbloom. *Cases in Operations Management.* New York: Wiley, 1969.

115. McLaren, K. G., and E. L. Buesnel. *Network Analysis in Project Management.* London: Cassell, 1969.

116. MacNiece, E. H. *Production Forecasting, Planning and Control.* 3d ed. New York: Wiley, 1961.

117. Magee, J. F., and David M. Boodman. *Production Planning and Inventory Control.* 2d ed. New York: McGraw-Hill, 1967.

118. Makower, Michael Stanley, and E. Williamson. *Teach Yourself Operational Research.* London: English Universities Press, Ltd., 1967.

119. Manne, Alan S., and Harry M. Markowitz, eds. *Studies in Process*

Analysis: Economy-Wide Production Capabilities. New York: Wiley, 1963.

120. Mansfield, Edwin, ed. *Managerial Economics and Operations Research.* New York: Norton, 1966.

121. Martin, E. Wainright, Jr. *Mathematics for Decision Making: A Programmed Basic Text.* Homewood, Ill.: Irwin, 1969.

122. Martino, R. L. *Critical Path Networks.* Wayne, Pa.: Industrial Development Institute, 1967.

123. Maynard, Harold Bright. *Handbook of Modern Manufacturing Management.* New York: McGraw-Hill, 1970.

124. Meier, R. C. et al. *Simulation in Business and Economics.* Englewood Cliffs, N.J.: Prentice-Hall, 1969.

125. Miller, David W., and M. K. Starr. *Executive Decisions and Operations Research.* 2d ed. Englewood Cliffs, N.J.: Prentice-Hall, 1960, 1969.

126. Miller, Ernest Charles. *Objectives and Standards of Performance in Production Management.* New York: American Management Association, 1967.

127. Miller, Robert Wallace. *Schedule, Cost, and Profit Control with PERT.* New York: McGraw-Hill, 1963.

128. Moder, Joseph J., and Cecil R. Phillips. *Project Management with CPM and PERT.* New York: Reinhold, 1964.

129. Moore, Franklin G. *Manufacturing Management.* Homewood, Ill.: Irwin, 1969.

130. Morris, L. N. *Critical Path Construction and Analysis.* New York: Pergamon, 1967.

131. Morris, William Thomas. *Engineering Economy: The Analysis of Management Decisions.* Homewood, Ill.: Irwin, 1960.

132. Muth, John F., and G. E. Thompson, eds. *Industrial Scheduling.* Englewood Cliffs, N.J.: Prentice-Hall, 1963.

133. Naylor, Thomas H., and John M. Vernon. *Micro-economics and Decision Models of the Firm.* New York: Harcourt, Brace & World, 1969.

134. Niland, Powell. *Production Planning, Scheduling, and Inventory Control: A Text and Cases.* New York: Macmillan, 1970.

135. O'Brien, J. J., ed. *Scheduling Handbook.* New York: McGraw-Hill, 1969.

136. Optner, Stanford L. *Systems Analysis for Business Management.* 2d ed. Englewood Cliffs, N.J.: Prentice-Hall, 1963.

137. Panico, J. A. *Queuing Theory: A Study of Waiting Lines for Business, Economics and Science.* Englewood Cliffs, N.J.: Prentice-Hall, 1969.

138. Pierce, John F., ed. *Operations Research and the Design of Management Information Systems.* New York: Technical Association of Pulp and Paper Industry, 1966.

139. Pierce, John F., Jr. *Some Large-scale Production Scheduling Problems in the Paper Industry.* Englewood Cliffs, N.J.: Prentice-Hall, 1964.
140. Plossl, G. W., and O. W. Wright. *Production and Inventory Control; Principles and Techniques.* Englewood Cliffs, N.J.: Prentice-Hall, 1967.
141. Prentice-Hall Editorial Staff. *Encyclopedic Dictionary of Production and Production Control.* Englewood Cliffs, N.J.: Prentice-Hall, 1964.
142. Pritzker, Robert A., and Robert A. Gring, eds. *Modern Approaches to Production, Planning and Control.* New York: American Management Association, 1960.
143. Putnam, Arnold O. et al. *Unified Operations Management; A Practical Approach to the Total Systems Concept.* New York: McGraw-Hill, 1963.
144. Radcliffe, Byron Mason et al. *Critical Path Method.* Chicago: Cahners Publishing Co., 1967.
145. Rago, Louis J. *Production Analysis and Control.* Scranton: International Textbook, 1963.
146. Ramlow, D., and E. Wall. *Production Planning and Control.* Englewood Cliffs, N.J.: Prentice-Hall, 1967.
147. Rappaport, Alfred. *Information for Decision Making.* Englewood Cliffs, N.J.: Prentice-Hall, 1970.
148. Reinfeld, Nyles V. *Production Control.* Englewood Cliffs, N.J.: Prentice-Hall, 1959.
149. Reynolds, Anthony, and Jeffrey Coates. *Cost Control for Production Management.* New York: Machinery Technical Books, 1962.
150. Richmond, Samuel B. *Operations Research for Management Decision.* New York: Ronald, 1968.
151. Riggs, James L., and Charles O. Heath. *Guide to Cost Reduction through Critical Path Scheduling.* Englewood Cliffs, N.J.: Prentice-Hall, 1966.
152. Robertson, Donald Campbell. *Project Planning and Control; Simplified Critical Path Analysis.* Cleveland: CRC Press, 1967.
153. Rudwick, Bernard H. *Systems Analysis for Effective Planning; Principles and Cases.* New York: Wiley, 1969.
154. Saaty, Thomas L. *Mathematical Methods of Operations Research.* New York: McGraw-Hill, 1959.
155. Sadowski, Wieslaw. *Theory of Decision-Making.* New York: Pergamon Press, 1965.
156. Sasieni, Maurice W. et al. *Operations Research.* New York: Wiley, 1959.
157. Scheele, Evan D. et al. *Principles and Design of Production Control Systems.* Englewood Cliffs, N.J.: Prentice-Hall, 1960.

158. Schellenberger, Robert E. *Managerial Analysis.* Homewood, Ill.: Irwin, 1969.
159. Schlager, Kenneth J. *Production Research through Industrial Systems Simulation.* Madison, Wisconsin: U. of Wisconsin Press, 1963.
160. Schlaifer, Robert. *Probability and Statistics for Business Decisions.* New York: McGraw-Hill, 1959.
161. Schmidt, J. W., and R. E. Taylor. *Simulation and Analysis of Industrial Systems.* Homewood, Ill.: Irwin, 1970.
162. Schwartz, H. C., and H. L. Gilmore. *Integrated Product Testing and Evaluation: A Systems Approach to Improve Reliability and Quality.* New York: Wiley, 1969.
163. Sengupta, S. Sankar. *Operations Research in Sellers' Competition.* New York: Wiley, 1967.
164. Shaffer, Louis Richard et al. *Critical Path Method.* New York: McGraw-Hill, 1965.
165. Shuchman, Abraham. *Scientific Decision Making in Business.* New York: Holt, 1963.
166. Silvester, Eugene T. *Computer Process Control: A Guide Book for Management.* Stamford, Conn.: Technical Publishers, 1970.
167. Simms, Britten. *Project Network Analysis and Critical Path.* London: Machinery, 1969.
168. Singh, Jagjit. *Great Ideas of Operations Research.* New York: Denver Publications, 1968.
169. Smith, A. C. *Numerical Control for Tomorrow.* Ann Arbor, Mich.: U. of Michigan.
170. Smith, C. S. *Quality and Reliability: An Integrated Approach.* New York: Pitman, 1969.
171. Solomons, David. *Divisional Performance: Measurement and Control.* New York: Financial Executives Research Foundation, 1965.
172. Spencer, Milton H., and Louis Siegelman, *Managerial Economics, Decision Making and Forward Planning.* Homewood, Ill.: Irwin, 1964.
173. Sporn, Philip. *Technology, Engineering and Economics.* Cambridge, Mass.: M.I.T. Press, 1969.
174. Starr, Martin K. *Production Management: Systems and Synthesis.* Englewood Cliffs, N.J.: Prentice-Hall, 1964.
175. Stires, David M., and Maurice M. Murphy. *Modern Management Methods PERT and CPM.* Boston: Materials Management Institute, 1963.
176. Stok, Theodous Leonardus. *The Worker and Quality Control.* Ann Arbor, Michigan: U. of Michigan Press, 1965.
177. Stoller, David S. *Operations Research: Process and Strategy.* Berkeley: U. of California Press, 1964.
178. Theil, Henri et al. *Operations Research and Quantitative Economics.* New York: McGraw-Hill, 1965.

179. Thierauf, Robert J. *Decision Making through Operations Research.* New York: Wiley, 1970.
180. Thomas, A. B. *Inventory Control in Production and Manufacturing.* Boston: Cahners, 1969.
181. Thompson, W. W. *Operations Research Techniques.* Columbus, Ohio: Charles E. Merrill Books, Inc., 1967.
182. Timms, Howard L. *The Production Function in Business: Fundamentals and Analysis for Management.* Homewood, Ill.: Irwin, 1962, 1970.
183. Tonge, Fred M. *A Heuristic Program for Assembly Line Balancing.* Englewood Cliffs, N.J.: Prentice-Hall, 1961.
184. Ullman, J. E., and S. E. Glynck. *Manufacturing Management, An Overview.* New York: Holt, 1969.
185. Ulman, David B. *New Products Program: Their Planning and Control.* New York: American Management Association, 1969.
186. van der Veen, B. *Introduction to the Theory of Operational Research.* New York: Springer-Verlag, 1967.
187. Vernon, Ivan R., ed. *Introduction to Manufacturing Management.* Dearborn, Mich.: American Society of Tool and Manufacturing Engineers, 1969.
188. Villers, Raymond. *Research and Development: Planning and Control.* New York: Financial Executives Institute, 1964.
189. Voris, William. *The Management of Production.* New York: Ronald, 1964.
190. Wagner, Harvey M. *Principles of Management Science, with Applications To Executive Decisions.* Englewood Cliffs, N.J.: Prentice-Hall, 1970.
191. Wagner, Harvey M. *Statistical Management of Inventory Systems.* New York: Wiley, 1962.
192. Wethermill, G. B. *Sampling, Inspection, and Quality Control.* London: Methuen, 1969.
193. White, D. J. *Decision Theory.* London: G. Allen, 1969.
194. White, Douglas et al. *Operations Research Techniques: An Introduction.* International Publishing Service: 1969.
195. Wiest, J. D., and F. K. Levy. *A Management Guide to PERT/CPM.* Englewood Cliffs, N.J.: Prentice-Hall, 1969.
196. Williams, N. *Linear and Non-linear Programming in Industry.* London: Pitman, 1967.
197. Yang, Wen-Jei, and Masami Masubuchi. *Dynamics for Process and System Control.* New York: Gordon and Breach, 1970.
198. Zeyner, Lewis R. *Production Manager's Desk Book.* Englewood Cliffs, N.J.: Prentice-Hall, 1969.

appendix
THE SIMPLEX METHOD OF LINEAR PROGRAMMING
one

SETTING UP THE INITIAL BASIC SOLUTION

To solve a problem by the simplex method requires (1) arranging the problem equations and inequalities in a special way and (2) following systematic procedures and rules in calculating a solution. These steps will be demonstrated using a simple product-mix problem; consider a company which can produce two products P_1 (chairs) and P_2 (tables) in its two machine centers. Both products must pass through both centers. Its profit objective would be:

maximize: Profit = $\$8P_1 + \$6P_2$ Although we shall use the word *profit*, we shall actually be referring to the accounting term *contribution*, i.e., price/unit — variable cost/unit.

subject to

$$4P_1 + 2P_2 \leq 60 \text{ hr} \qquad \text{machine center 1 processing hours}$$
$$2P_1 + 4P_2 \leq 48 \text{ hr} \qquad \text{machine center 2 processing hours}$$

The first step is to convert the inequalities into equations by adding slack variables:

$$4P_1 + 2P_2 + S_1 = 60 \text{ hr}$$
$$2P_1 + 4P_2 + S_2 = 48 \text{ hr}$$

In the simplex method, any unknown that occurs in one equation must appear in all equations. The unknowns that do not affect an equation are written with a zero coefficient. For example, since S_1 and S_2 represent unused time which yields no profit, these variables are added to the objective function with zero coefficients. Furthermore, since S_1 represents unused time in machine center 1 only, it is added to the equation representing machine center 2 with a zero coefficient. For the same reason $0S_2$ is added to the equation representing the time constraint in machine center 1. Thus the equations are:

$$\text{Maximize: Profit} = \$8P_1 + \$6P_2 + \$0S_1 + \$0S_2$$

subject to

$$4P_1 + 2P_2 + S_1 + 0S_2 = 60 \text{ hr}$$
$$2P_1 + 4P_2 + 0S_1 + S_2 = 48 \text{ hr}$$

To simplify handling the equations in the problem, they can be put into tabular form.

It will be helpful to describe the simplex tableau and to identify the parts and function of each.

1. See Table 1. The two *constraint equations* are shown in the simplex tableau as

	P_1	P_2	S_1	S_2
60	4	2	1	0
48	2	4	0	1

Note first that row 1(4, 2, 1, 0) represents the coefficients of our first equation and row 2(2, 4, 0, 1) the coefficients of our second equation.

2. Each *variable column* contains all the coefficients of one unknown. For example, under P_1 is written $\begin{pmatrix} 4 \\ 2 \end{pmatrix}$, under P_2 is written $\begin{pmatrix} 2 \\ 4 \end{pmatrix}$, under S_1 is written $\begin{pmatrix} 1 \\ 0 \end{pmatrix}$, and under S_2 is written $\begin{pmatrix} 0 \\ 1 \end{pmatrix}$.

3. The constants (60 and 48) have been placed to the left of the equations. We have simply rearranged the terms in the constraint equations to form the simplex tableau.

We must establish an initial solution. The starting solution will be the zero-profit solution. This solution would be to make no tables or chairs, have all unused time, and hence realize no profit. If no tables and chairs were produced, if $P_1 = 0$ and $P_2 = 0$, then the first solution would be

$$P_1 = 0 \qquad P_2 = 0 \qquad S_1 = 60 \qquad S_2 = 48$$

Table 1 *Parts of the simplex tableau*

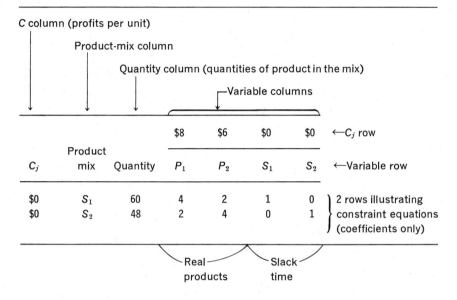

C column (profits per unit)

Product-mix column

Quantity column (quantities of product in the mix)

Variable columns

	Product		$8	$6	$0	$0	←C_j row
C_j	mix	Quantity	P_1	P_2	S_1	S_2	←Variable row
$0	S_1	60	4	2	1	0	} 2 rows illustrating
$0	S_2	48	2	4	0	1	constraint equations (coefficients only)

Real products   Slack time

This first feasible solution is shown in the initial simplex tableau as

Product mix	Quantity	P_1	P_2	S_1	S_2
S_1	60	4	2	1	0
S_2	48	2	4	0	1

Note that the *product-mix column* contains the variables in the solutions. The variables in the first solution are S_1 and S_2 (the slack variables). In the *quantity column* we find the quantities of the variables that are in the solution.

$S_1 = 60$ hr available in machine center 1
$S_2 = 48$ hr available in machine center 2

Since the variables P_1 and P_2 do not appear in the mix, they are equal to zero.

The C_j *column* in Table 1 contains the profit per unit for the variables S_1 and S_2. For example, the zero appearing to the left of the S_1 row in Table 1 means that profit per unit of S_1 is zero.

The last two columns in the initial simplex tableau consist of the coefficients of the slack variables that are added to the constraint inequalities to make them equations.

The third and fourth columns consist of the coefficients of the real product variables, P_1 and P_2. For example, the element 4 in the P_1 column of the table means that if we wanted to make 1 unit of P_1 (to bring 1 table into the solution), we would have to give up 4 hours of S_1 in machine center 1.

Similarly, the element 2 in the P_2 column indicates that the manufacturing of 1 unit of P_2 (bringing 1 chair into the solution) would force us to give up 2 hours of S_1 in machine center 1.

The elements in the third and fourth columns thus represent rates of substitution.

The element 1 in the S_1 column tells us that to bring in 1 hour of S_1 (to make 1 hour of S_1 available) we would have to give up 1 of the 60 hours of S_1 now in the solution. As there are only 60 hours in center 1 available, we must give up 1 of the 60 if we want an hour for some other purpose.

The zero in the S_2 column immediately under the S_2 means that making 1 hour in machine center 2 available for other purposes has no effect on S_1, the amount of slack time in center 1.

In our examination of substitution rates, we have treated two types of action.

1. The *addition* of real products, P_1 and P_2, into the production schedule or solution.

2. The *withdrawal* of time, S_1 and S_2, from the total amounts of time available in each of the two machine centers—withdrawal so as to make time available for other purposes.

Up to this point, setting up the initial simplex tableau has not involved any computations. We have simply rearranged the problem equations to form the first simplex tableau.

To find the profit for each solution and to determine whether the solution can be improved upon, we need to add two more rows to the initial simplex tableau: a Z_j row and a $C_j - Z_j$ row. This has been done in Table 2. The value in the Z_j row under the quantity column represents

Table 2 *Initial simplex tableau completed (two rows added)*

			$8	$6	$0	$0
C_j	Product mix	Quantity	P_1	P_2	S_1	S_2
$0	S_1	60	4	2	1	0
$0	S_2	48	2	4	0	1
2 rows	Z_j	$ 0	$0	$0	$0	$0
added	$C_j - Z_j$		$8	$6	$0	$0

the total profit from this particular solution: zero, in this case. In this first solution, we have 60 hours of unused time in machine center 1 ($S_1 = 60$) and 48 hours of unused time in machine center 2 ($S_2 = 48$). The total profit from this solution is found by multiplying the profit per unit of S_1($0) by the quantity of S_1 in the solution (60 hours) plus the profit per unit of S_2($0) times the quantity of S_2 in the solution (48 hours).

Total profit for the first solution is

Number of unused hours of $S_1 =$	60
Times profit per unit of S_1	$\times$ $0 = $0
Number of unused hours of $S_2 =$	48
Times profit per unit of S_2	$\times$ $0 = $0
Total profit	$0

The four values for Z_j under the variable columns (all $0) are the amounts by which profit would be reduced if 1 unit of any of the variables (P_1, P_2, S_1, S_2) were added to the mix. For example, if we want to make 1 unit of P_1, the elements $\begin{pmatrix} 4 \\ 2 \end{pmatrix}$ under P_1 tell us we must give up 4 hours of S_1 and 2 hours of S_2. But unused time in each machine center is worth $0 per hour; consequently, there is *no* reduction in profit.

How much profit is lost by adding 1 unit of P_1 to the production schedule or solution?

Number of hours of S_1 given up $=$	4
Times profit per unit of S_1	$\times$ $0 = $0
Number of hours of S_2 given up $=$	2
Times profit per unit of S_2	$\times$ $0 = $0
Total profit given up	$0

C_j has been defined as profit per unit; for tables (P_1), C_j is $8 per unit. $C_j - Z_j$ is the *net* profit which will result from introducing, i.e., adding, 1 unit of a variable to the production schedule or solution. For example, if 1 unit of P_1 adds $8 of profit to the solution *and* if its introduction causes no loss, then $C_j - Z_j$ for $P_1 = $8.

The calculation of Z_j's for Table 2 follows:

Z_j (total profit) $= $0(60) + $0(48) = $0
Z_j for column $P_1 = $0(4) + $0(2) = $0
Z_j for column $P_2 = $0(2) + $0(4) = $0
Z_j for column $S_1 = $0(1) + $0(0) = $0
Z_j for column $S_2 = $0(0) + $0(1) = $0

Calculations of *net* profit per unit of each variable follow:

Variable	Profit/unit $-$ C_j	Profit lost/unit $=$ Z_j	Net profit/unit $C_j - Z_j$
P_1	\$8	\$0	\$8
P_2	6	0	6
S_1	0	0	0
S_2	0	0	0

By examining the numbers in the $C_j - Z_j$ row of Table 2, we can see, for instance, that total profit can be increased by \$8 for each unit of P_1 (tables) added to the mix of by \$6 for each unit of P_2 (chairs) added to the mix. Thus a positive number in the $C_j - Z_j$ row (\$8 in the case of the P_1 column) indicates that profits can be improved by that amount for each unit of P_1 added. On the other hand, a negative number in the $C_j - Z_j$ row would indicate the amount by which profits would *decrease* if 1 unit of the variable heading that column were added to the solution. Hence the optimum solution is reached when no positive numbers remain in the $C_j - Z_j$ row; i.e., no more profit can be made.

DEVELOPING THE IMPROVED SOLUTIONS

Now that the initial simplex tableau is established, the next step is to determine how improvement is to be made.

We now introduce a computation procedure which will generate the correct second and subsequent tableaus of the problem. In this section we shall not attempt to explain the logic of this method, but the next section, Justification and Significance of All Elements in the Simplex Tableau, will demonstrate that the procedures are in fact completely logical and, if properly followed, will generate the appropriate values in each step of the problem. The computational procedure for the second solution follows.

Step 1. Determine which variable will add the most per unit to profit. The numbers in the $C_j - Z_j$ row tell exactly which product will increase profits most. As stated previously, the presence of positive numbers in the $C_j - Z_j$ row indicates that profit can be improved; the larger the positive number, the greater the improvement possible.

We select as the variable to be added to the first solution that variable which contributes the *most* profit per unit. In Table 3, bringing in P_1 (tables) will add \$8 per unit to profit. The P_1 column is the optimum column.

Table 3 *Optimum column in initial tableau*

			$8	$6	$0	$0
C_j	Product mix	Quantity	P_1	P_2	S_1	S_2
$0	S_1	60	4	2	1	0
$0	S_2	48	2	4	0	1
	Z_j	$ 0	$0	$0	$0	$0
	$C_j - Z_j$		$8	$6	$0	$0

↑ └—Optimum column

By definition, the *optimum column* (Table 3) is that column which has the largest positive value in the $C_j - Z_j$ row or, stated in another way, that column whose product will contribute the most profit per unit. Inspection of the optimum column tells us that the variable P_1 (tables) should be added to the mix, replacing one of the variables presently in the mix.

Step 2. The next step is to determine which variable will be replaced. This is done in the following manner: divide 60 and 48 in the quantity column by their corresponding numbers in the optimum column and select the row with the smaller or smallest nonnegative ratio as the row to be replaced. In this case, the ratios would be:

$$S_1 \text{ row: } \frac{60 \text{ hr available}}{4 \text{ hr required/unit}} = 15 \text{ units of } P_1$$

$$S_2 \text{ row: } \frac{48 \text{ hr available}}{2 \text{ hr required/unit}} = 24 \text{ units of } P_1$$

Since the S_1 row has the smaller positive ratio (15:1 rather than 24:1), it is called the *replaced row* because it will be replaced in the next solution by 15 units of P_1. The elements common to both the S_1 and S_2 rows *and* the optimum column are called *intersectional elements*. Thus the intersectional element of the row to be replaced (S_1 row) is 4, and the intersectional element of the S_2 row is 2 (see Table 4). Row replacement means that in the next solution, the variable S_1 (unused time) will be replaced by 15 units of P_1 (15 tables).

Step 3. Having selected the optimum column and the replaced row, we can develop the second simplex solution, an *improved* solution.

The first part of the new tableau to be developed is the P_1 row. The P_1 row appears in place of the replaced row (S_1) of Table 4. The P_1 row of the new tableau is computed as follows: divide each number in the replaced

Table 4 *Replaced row and intersectional elements in initial simplex tableau*

			$8	$6	$0	$0	
C_j	Product mix	Quantity	P_1	P_2	S_1	S_2	
$0	S_1	60	④	2	1	0	←Replaced row
$0	S_2	48	②	4	0	1	Intersectional
	Z_j	$ 0	$0	$0	$0	$0	elements
	$C_j - Z_j$		$8	$6	$0	$0	

↑——Optimum column

row (the S_1 row) by the intersectional element (4) of the replaced row:

$$^{60}\!\!/_4 = 15 \qquad ^4\!\!/_4 = 1 \qquad ^2\!\!/_4 = \tfrac{1}{2} \qquad ^1\!\!/_4 = \tfrac{1}{4} \qquad ^0\!\!/_4 = 0$$

Thus the new P_1 row should be (15, 1, $\frac{1}{2}$, $\frac{1}{4}$, 0).

Note in Table 5 that for the first time there is a dollar figure in the C_j column ($8 per unit). Also note that S_2 and its profit per unit ($0) remain in the new tableau.

Step 4. To complete the second tableau, we compute new values for the remaining rows. *All* remaining rows of the variables in the tableau are calculated using the formula

$$\begin{pmatrix} \text{Elements in} \\ \text{old row} \end{pmatrix} - \left[\begin{pmatrix} \text{intersectional} \\ \text{element of old row} \end{pmatrix} \times \begin{pmatrix} \text{corresponding} \\ \text{elements in} \\ \text{replacing row} \end{pmatrix} \right] = \begin{pmatrix} \text{new} \\ \text{row} \end{pmatrix}$$

Table 5 *Replacing row in second simplex tableau*

			$8	$6	$0	$0	
C_j	Product mix	Quantity	P_1	P_2	S_1	S_2	
$8	P_1	15	1	$\frac{1}{2}$	$\frac{1}{4}$	0	←Replacing row
$0	S_2						
	Z_j						
	$C_j - Z_j$						

Using the formula, the new S_2 row is

Element in old S_2 row	$-$	Intersectional element of S_2 row	$\times$	Corresponding element in replacing row	$=$	New S_2 row
48	$-$	(2	$\times$	15)	$=$	18
2	$-$	(2	$\times$	1)	$=$	0
4	$-$	(2	$\times$	$\frac{1}{2}$)	$=$	3
0	$-$	(2	$\times$	$\frac{1}{4}$)	$=$	$-\frac{1}{2}$
1	$-$	(2	$\times$	0)	$=$	1

The new S_2 row as it appears in the second tableau is shown in Table 6. The method for computing the Z_j and $C_j - Z_j$ rows (the profit opportunities) has already been demonstrated in developing the initial simplex tableau.

The computation of the Z_j row of the second tableau is as follows:

Z_j (total profit) $= \$8(15) + \$0(18) = \$120 =$ total profit of second solution

Z_j for P_1: $\$8(1) + \$0(0) = \$8$
Z_j for P_2: $\$8(\frac{1}{2}) + \$0(3) = \$4$ Profits given up by introducing
Z_j for S_1: $\$8(\frac{1}{4}) + \$0(-\frac{1}{2}) = \$2$ 1 unit of these variables
Z_j for S_2: $\$8(0) + \$0(1) = \$0$

Thus the computations above indicate that introducing a unit of P_1 would lose \$8 for us. How can this be?

1. We currently make 15 units of P_1.
2. Production of 15 tables uses up all the time originally available in machine center 1.
3. To introduce another P_1, we would have to give up 1 of the current 15 P_1's.
4. Giving up a table would cost us \$8.

Table 6 *Replacing row and new S_2 row in second tableau*

			\$8	\$6	\$0	\$0
C_j	Product mix	Quantity	P_1	P_2	S_1	S_2
\$8	P_1	15	1	$\frac{1}{2}$	$\frac{1}{4}$	0
\$0	S_2	18	0	3	$-\frac{1}{2}$	1
	Z_j					
	$C_j - Z_j$					

The new $C_j - Z_j$ row (net profit per unit) is

Variables	Profit/unit $-$ C_j	Profit lost/unit $=$ Z_j	Net profit/unit $C_j - Z_j$
P_1	$8	$8	$0
P_2	6	4	2
S_1	0	2	-2
S_2	0	0	0

The completed second tableau is shown in Table 7. Certainly the total profit from this second solution ($120) is an improvement over the zero profit in the first solution.

The presence of a positive number ($2) in the P_2 column of the $C_j - Z_j$ row of the second solution (Table 7) indicates that further improvement is possible. Therefore the same process used to develop the second solution must be repeated to develop a third solution.

Step 1. A look at the $C_j - Z_j$ row of the second tableau (Table 7) shows that P_2, chairs contributes a *net* profit of $2 per unit.

$$
\begin{aligned}
&C_j: \quad \text{Profit per unit of } P_2 \qquad \qquad \$6\\
&Z_j: \quad \text{Profit lost per unit of } P_2\,(-)\ \underline{\ 4\ }\\
&C_j - Z_j: \text{Net profit per unit of } P_2 \quad \$2
\end{aligned}
$$

The optimum column, therefore, in Table 7 is the P_2 column. Chairs will now be added, replacing one of the variables P_1 or S_2 in the second solution.

Step 2. The replaced row is found as before by dividing 15 and 18 in the quantity column by their corresponding numbers in the optimum column and selecting the row with the smaller ratio as the replaced row.

Table 7 *Second simplex tableau completed*

			$8	$6	$0	$0
C_j	Product mix	Quantity	P_1	P_2	S_1	S_2
$8	P_1	15	1	½	¼	0
$0	S_2	18	0	3	$-$½	1
	Z_j	$120	$8	$4	$2	$0
	$C_j - Z_j$		$0	$2	$-$2	$0

$$P_1 \text{ row: } \frac{15}{\frac{1}{2}} = 30$$

$$S_2 \text{ row: } \frac{18}{3} = 6$$

The S_2 row, the one with the smaller positive ratio, is designated as the replaced row. The optimum column, replaced row, and intersectional elements of the second tableau are shown in Table 8.

Step 3. The replacing row of the third tableau is computed by dividing each number in the replaced row by the intersectional element of the replaced row.

$$\frac{18}{3} = 6 \qquad \frac{0}{3} = 0 \qquad \frac{3}{3} = 1 \qquad \frac{-\frac{1}{2}}{3} = -\frac{1}{6} \qquad \frac{1}{3} = \frac{1}{3}$$

Thus the replacing row of the third tableau is $(6, 0, 1, -\frac{1}{6}, \frac{1}{3})$. It assumes the same row position as the replaced row of the second tableau (see Table 9).

Table 8 *Optimum column, replaced row, and intersectional elements of second tableau*

			$8	$6	$0	$0	
C_i	Product mix	Quantity	P_1	P_2	S_1	S_2	Intersectional element of P_1 row
$8	P_1	15	1	⟨½⟩	¼	0	
$0	S_2	18	0	③	$-\frac{1}{2}$	1	←Replaced row (S_2)
	Z_j	$120	$8	$4	$2	$0	Intersectional
	$C_i - Z_i$		$0	$2	$-2	$0	element of S_2 row (replaced row)

Optimum column

Table 9 *Replacing row of third tableau*

			$8	$6	$0	$0	
C_j	Product mix	Quantity	P_1	P_2	S_1	S_2	
$8	P_1						
$6	P_2	6	0	1	$-\frac{1}{6}$	$\frac{1}{3}$	←Replacing row
	Z_j						
	$C_i - Z_i$						

Step 4. The new values of the P_1 row are

Element in old P_1 row	—	Intersectional element of P_1 row	×	Corresponding element of replacing row	=	New P_1 row
15	—	$(\frac{1}{2}$	×	$6)$	=	12
1	—	$(\frac{1}{2}$	×	$0)$	=	1
$\frac{1}{2}$	—	$(\frac{1}{2}$	×	$1)$	=	0
$\frac{1}{4}$	—	$(\frac{1}{2}$	×	$-\frac{1}{6})$	=	$\frac{1}{3}$
0	—	$(\frac{1}{2}$	×	$\frac{1}{3})$	=	$-\frac{1}{6}$

The new P_1 row is $(12, 1, 0, \frac{1}{3}, -\frac{1}{6})$. In Table 10 it has been added to the third tableau.

The Z_j's of the third tableau are computed as follows:

Z_{total}: $\$8(12) + \$6(6) = \$132 =$ total profit from third solution

Z_{P_1}: $\$8(1) + \$6(0) = \$8$
Z_{P_2}: $\$8(0) + \$6(1) = \$6$
Z_{S_1}: $\$8(\frac{1}{3}) + \$6(-\frac{1}{6}) = \$5/3$
Z_{S_2}: $\$8(-\frac{1}{6}) + \$6(\frac{1}{3}) = \$2/3$

The new $C_j - Z_j$ row (net profit per unit) is computed as follows:

Variable	Profit/unit C_j	—	Profit lost/unit Z_j	=	Net profit/unit $C_j - Z_j$
P_1	$\$8$	—	$\$8$	=	$\$0$
P_2	$\$6$	—	$\$6$	=	$\$0$
S_1	$\$0$	—	$\dfrac{\$5}{3}$	=	$-\dfrac{\$5}{3}$
S_2	$\$0$	—	$\dfrac{\$2}{3}$	=	$-\dfrac{\$2}{3}$

Table 10 *Replacing row and new P_1 row in third tableau*

			$\$8$	$\$6$	$\$0$	$\$0$
C_j	Product mix	Quantity	P_1	P_2	S_1	S_2
$\$8$	P_1	12	1	0	$\frac{1}{3}$	$-\frac{1}{6}$
$\$6$	P_2	6	0	1	$-\frac{1}{6}$	$\frac{1}{3}$
	Z_j					
	$C_j - Z_j$					

Table 11 *Third simplex tableau completed*

			$8	$6	$0	$0
C_j	Product mix	Quantity	P_1	P_2	S_1	S_2
$8	P_1	12	1	0	$\frac{1}{3}$	$-\frac{1}{6}$
$6	P_2	6	0	1	$-\frac{1}{6}$	$\frac{1}{3}$
	Z_j	$132	$8	$6	$5\frac{2}{3}$	$2\frac{2}{3}$
	$C_j - Z_j$				$-$5\frac{2}{3}$	$-$2\frac{2}{3}$

The completed third tableau is shown in Table 11. As there is no positive $C_j - Z_j$ value, as no further profit improvement is possible, the optimum solution has been obtained. It is

$$P_1 = 12 \quad P_2 = 6 \quad S_1 = 0 \quad S_2 = 0$$

Profits will be maximized by making 12 tables and 6 chairs and having no unused time in either machine center. The variables P_1 and P_2 appear in the product-mix column with their values represented by the corresponding numbers in the quantity column. The variables S_1 and S_2 do not appear in the product-mix column and therefore are equal to zero.

The Z_j total, $132, represents the profit obtained under the optimum solution. The above solution also can be verified by substitution in the initial problem equations:

Objective function:

$$Z = \$8P_1 + \$6P_2 + \$0(S_1 + S_2)$$
$$= \$8(12) + \$6(6) + \$0 = \$132$$

Problem constraints:

$$4P_1 + 2P_2 \leq 60 \quad \text{machine center 1}$$
$$4(12) + 2(6) \leq 60$$
$$60 \leq 60$$
$$2P_1 + 4P_2 \leq 48 \quad \text{machine center 2}$$
$$2(12) + 4(6) \leq 48$$
$$48 \leq 48$$

SUMMARY OF STEPS IN THE SIMPLEX PROCEDURE

In summary form, the steps involved in the simplex procedure for maximization problems are as follows:

1. Set up the inequalities describing the problem constraints.
2. Convert the inequalities to equalities by adding slack variables.

3. Enter the equalities in the simplex table.
4. Calculate the C_j and Z_j values for this solution.
5. Determine the entering variable (optimum column) by choosing the one with the highest $C_j - Z_j$ value.
6. Determine the row to be replaced by dividing quantity column values by their corresponding optimum-column values and choosing the smallest nonnegative quotient.
7. Compute the values for the replacing row.
8. Compute the values for the remaining rows.
9. Calculate C_j and Z_j values for this solution.
10. If there is a positive $C_j - Z_j$ value, proceed as indicated in step 5 above.
11. If there is no positive $C_j - Z_j$ value, the final solution has been obtained.

JUSTIFICATION AND SIGNIFICANCE OF ALL ELEMENTS IN THE SIMPLEX TABLEAU

Up to now, the discussion has centered on the mechanics or rules and procedures involved in solving a simplex problem. In addition to the solution, however, the simplex method provides us with important information concerning various alternative solutions and the effect of changes in the basic data upon the solutions. Frequently, this information is as valuable and revealing as the answer itself.

Thus our objective in this section will be to explain the justification and economic significance of all the elements in the simplex tableau, to give meaning to the procedures learned thus far.

Table 12 *Second simplex table*

C_j	Product mix	Quantity	$8 P_1	$6 P_2	$0 S_1	$0 S_2
$8	P_1	15 (1)	1 (12)	½ (16)	¼ (4)	0 (8)
$0	S_2	18 (2)	0 (13)	3 (17)	−½ (5)	1 (9)
	Z_j	$120 (3)	$8 (14)	$4 (18)	$2 (6)	$0 (10)
	$C_j - Z_j$	(15)	$0	$2 (19)	$−2 (7)	$0 (11)

In Table 12 we have reproduced the second simplex tableau from the preceding section (see Table 7) and have numbered each element. Our general interpretation, keyed to each circled number, is as follows.

1. THE QUANTITY COLUMN

①In the initial simplex tableau (Table 2) we noted that P_1 (tables) made the larger contribution per unit to profit and thus should be added to the second solution. To find the quantity to be added, we proceeded as follows:

$$\frac{60 \text{ hr available in center 1}}{4 \text{ hr required/table}} = 15 \text{ tables}$$

We found that 15 was the largest quantity which could be made without violating any of the time restrictions in either center.

Making 15 tables required all the hours available in center 1 (4 hours per unit × 15 units = 60 hours). Thus P_1 replaced S_1 in the solution.

②Each of the 15 tables requires 2 hours in machine center 2. Thus to make 15 tables requires 30 hours (2 hours per unit × 15 units). Since 48 hours are available and only 30 hours are required, we have 18 hours left in center 2.

In the quantity column we see 15 tables, 18 hours, and $120. Including three different types of item in the same column may seem confusing. This quantity column, however, will never be added. The figure 15 is significant as an element of the P_1 row and not as an element of the quantity column. In similar fashion, 18 is an element of the S_2 row, and $120 is an element of the Z_j row.

③The $120 represents the total profit from the variables in the product mix.

Number of units of P_1 (tables)	= 15
Times profit/unit of P_1	× $8 = $120
Number of units of S_2 (unused hours)	= 18
Times profit/unit of S_2	× $0 = 0
Total profit of second mix	$120

2. SUBSTITUTION RATES

④ Since 1 unit of P_1 (1 table) requires 4 hours in center 1, the second solution uses up all the 60 hours in center 1. Therefore, the production of anything else in this machine center would require that some of the tables be given up. For example, if 1 unit of S_1 (1 hour) is made available for other purposes, $\frac{1}{4}$ table would have to be given up; or stated in another way, every hour of S_1 added to the solution reduces the production of P_1 (tables) by $\frac{1}{4}$ unit.

⑤ Reducing the production of P_1 (tables) by $\frac{1}{4}$ unit certainly must have an effect on center 2 because *chairs and tables* must be processed through both machine centers. Because P_1 requires 2 hours per unit in center 2, and because adding 1 unit of S_1 reduces the production of P_1 (tables) by $\frac{1}{4}$ unit, $\frac{1}{4} \times 2 = \frac{1}{2}$ hour is freed in center 2. We can illustrate this another way:

Units of P_1 now in mix	15
If 1 unit of S_1 is added to the mix, P_1 is reduced by	$- \frac{1}{4}$
New quantity of P_1	$14\frac{3}{4}$
2 hr/unit of P_1 required in center 2	$\times 2$
Total hr required to make $14\frac{3}{4}$ units of P_1 (in center 2)	$29\frac{1}{2}$
Total hr required to make $15P_1$ (2×15)	30
Total hr freed by adding 1 unit of S_1	$\frac{1}{2}$

⑧ Adding 1 unit of S_2 has no effect (0) on P_1. Why? Since machine center 1 is the limiting center (all hours have been used), making available 1 hour of S_2 in machine center 2 will have no effect on the production of tables. Since 18 hours are still available in center 2, we can make one of them available without reducing our production of tables.

⑨ Withdrawing 1 unit of S_2 removes 1 unit of S_2. Why? Since there are only 18 hours available in center 2 in the second solution, we can withdraw 1 hour ($1S_2$) only if we remove 1 hour ($1S_2$) from the 18 hours now available. Adding 1 hour ($1S_2$) would increase the time available in center 2 by 1 hour, making the total 49 hours. But this is impossible, because the total time available in center 2 is 48 hours. Thus in the second solution, if we add 1 hour ($1S_2$), we must subtract 1 hour ($1S_2$) in order not to exceed the 48 hours.

⑫ Here again we have a 1-for-1 substitution; i.e., each unit of P_1 added to the production schedule replaces 1 unit of P_1 in the solution. From ① we found that 15 was the largest quantity of tables that could be processed in center 1. Thus in order to add another table ($1P_1$) and at the same time satisfy the time restriction in center 1 (60 hours available), we must subtract or give up 1 table to make the necessary time available.

⑬ Adding 1 unit of P_1 to the production schedule has no effect on S_2. Why? From ⑫ we found that adding 1 table ($1P_1$) required giving up 1 table ($1P_1$), so that the net change in center 2 must be zero ($1 - 1 = 0$). Since there is no real change in center 1, neither is there any change in center 2; no additional hours are required.

⑯ Adding 1 unit of P_2 (chair) to the program replaces $\frac{1}{2}P_1$ (table): a chair ($1P_2$) requires 2 hours per unit in center 1, and a table ($1P_1$) requires 4 hours. Now, because center 1 is the limiting center (time is ex-hausted), processing 1 chair would require giving up $\frac{2}{4}$, or $\frac{1}{2}$, table ($\frac{1}{2}P_1$). Stated in another way, processing a chair in center 1 takes 2 of the 4 hours required to make a table. Thus for every chair processed in center 1, $\frac{1}{2}$ table must be given up to provide the necessary 2 hours.

(17) Adding 1 unit of P_2 (chair) replaces 3 units of S_2 (3 hours). The problem originally stated that $1P_2$ required 4 hours in center 2. How can we justify this apparent inconsistency? First note that adding 1 chair ($1P_2$) replaces $\frac{1}{2}$ table (from (16)). Second, a table requires 2 hours in center 2. Thus giving up $\frac{1}{2}$ table frees 1 hour in center 2 ($\frac{1}{2} \times 2$ hours required per unit of $P_1 = 1$ hour). The 4 hours required to make a chair in center 2 minus the 1 hour freed equals 3 hours net change. Processing a chair still requires 4 hours per unit: 3 hours plus the 1 hour freed equals the 4 hours required. The inconsistency therefore disappears when we consider the effect of a change in not *one* center but *both* centers. Chairs and tables must be processed in both machine centers in order to make a completed unit. Thus any change in center 1 must have an effect in center 2.

In summary, the eight elements we have discussed represent marginal rates of substitution between the variables in the product mix and the variables heading the column. We found that a positive rate of substitution, e.g., (16) indicates the decrease in P_1, that occurs if 1 unit of P_2 is added to the program. On the other hand, a negative rate of substitution, e.g., (5) indicates increase in S_2, that is, $\frac{1}{2}$ hour freed, that occurs if 1 unit of S_1 is added to the program.

3. THE Z_j ROW

We turn now to an explanation of the elements in the Z_j row; these represent the loss of profit that results from the addition of 1 unit of the variable heading the column.

(6) Adding 1 unit of S_1 results in two changes: (1) P_1 is decreased by $\frac{1}{4}$ unit (see (4)); (2) S_2 increased by $\frac{1}{2}$ unit ($\frac{1}{2}$ hour freed; see (5)). How much profit would we lose if these two changes took place? Since profit per unit of P_1 is \$8 and P_1 is decreased by $\frac{1}{4}$ unit, the profit lost from this change would be \$8 $\times \frac{1}{4}P_1 = \$2$. Because profit per unit of S_2 is \$0, the increase in S_2 by $\frac{1}{2}$ unit results in no loss (\$0 $\times \frac{1}{2}S_2 = \$0$). The *total* profit lost, then, is the sum of the losses resulting from the two changes, or \$2 + \$0 = \$2.

The same reasoning process applies to the other elements of the Z_j row. We want to know (1) the changes which occur when 1 unit of the variable heading the column is added, (2) the loss of profit from each change, and (3) the total profit lost, the sum of the loss of each change.

⑩ With the addition of 1 unit of S_2:

Change 1. No change in P_1 (see ⑧)   0
Profit per unit of P_1 $\times$ \$8
     Loss   \$0

Change 2. $1S_2$ given up (see ⑨)   1
Profit per unit of S_2 $\times$ \$0
     Loss   \$0
Total loss   \$0

⑭ With the addition of 1 unit of P_1:

Change 1. $1P_1$ given up (see ⑫)   1
Profit per unit of P_1 $\times$ \$8
     Loss   \$8

Change 2. No change in S_2 (see ⑬)   0
Profit per unit of S_2 $\times$ \$0
     Loss   \$0
Total loss   \$8

⑱ With the addition of 1 unit of P_2:

Change 1. $\frac{1}{2}P_1$ given up (see ⑯) $\frac{1}{2}$
Profit per unit of P_1 $\times$ \$8
     Loss   \$4

Change 2. $3S_2$ given up (see ⑰)   3
Profit per unit of S_2 $\times$ \$0
     Loss   \$0
Total loss   \$4

4. THE $C_j - Z_j$ ROW

Each positive number in the $C_j - Z_j$ row represents the net profit obtainable if 1 unit of the variable heading that column were added to the solution. The following examples help to illustrate this point.

⑲ The positive number 2 represents the net profit if 1 unit of P_2 (1 chair) were added.

Total profit per unit of P_2 \$6
Less total profit per unit lost (see ⑱) $-\ 4$
     Net profit   \$2

So long as there is a positive dollar figure in the $C_j - Z_j$ row, further improvement in profit can and should be made, because for each unit of P_2 added, we can increase the profit of $120 by $2. Element ② (18 hours) and element ⑰ (3 hours per chair) indicate that 18/3, or 6 chairs can be added.

⑮ Total profit per unit of P_1		$8
	Total profit per unit lost (see ⑭)	− 8
	Net profit	$0

For every unit of P_1 added, total profit will not change. The explanation is that we are already producing as many tables as possible under the time restrictions in machine center 1. If we add $1P_1$ to the solution, we must give up $1P_1$. Adding 1 unit of P_1 results in a profit increase of $8, but giving up 1 unit of P_1 results in a profit decrease of $8. Thus nothing is added to total profit.

⑪ Total profit per unit of S_2		$0
	Total profit per unit lost (see ⑩)	− 0
	Net profit	$0

Each unit of S_2 added to the program will not change total profit. Again the explanation is that center 1 limits the production of tables to 15. Therefore adding 1 unit of S_2 has no effect on P_1 (see ⑧). Total profit, then, cannot be increased by adding any units of S_2.

⑦ Total profit per unit of S_1		$0
	Less total profit per unit lost (see ⑥)	− 2
	Net loss	−$2

A negative number (a net loss) in the $C_j − Z_j$ row indicates the decrease in total profit if 1 unit of the variable heading that column were added to the product mix. In this case, each unit of S_1 added to the program will decrease total profit by $2. Why? From ④ we found that for every unit of S_1 added, ¼ table would have to be given up. Profit per unit of S_1 is $0, but profit per unit of P_1 is $8. So each S_1 added would result in a $2 loss ($8 × ¼ = $2).

A negative number in the $C_j − Z_j$ row under one of the columns representing time (S_1 or S_2) has another interpretation. A negative number here represents the amount of increase in total profit if the number of hours available in that center could be increased by 1. For example, in ⑦ if 1 more hour ($1S_1$) were available in machine center 1 (i.e., if $S_1 = 61$ instead of 60 in the initial solution, Table 2), then total profit could be *increased* by $2. This can be proved by using the equation representing the time restriction in center 1 altered to reflect the addition of 1 hour. If

$$4P_1 + 2P_2 + S_1 = 61$$

and we let

$$S_1 = 0 \qquad P_2 = 0$$

(since P_2 and S_1 are not in the second solution, they are equal to 0), then

$$4P_1 + 2(0) + 0 = 61$$
$$4P_1 = 61 - 2(0) - 0 = 61$$
$$P_1 = 61\frac{1}{4}$$

Substituting $P_1 = 61\frac{1}{4}$ for P_1 in the objective function yields the following total profit:

$$\text{Profit} = \$8P_1 + \$6P_2 + \$0S_1 + \$0S_2$$
$$= \$8(61\frac{1}{4}) + \$6(0) + \$0 + \$0 = \$122$$

Note that making available 1 additional hour in center 1 would increase total profit by $2.

With this information, the manager may want to investigate the possibilities of expanding the capacity in center 1.

In summary, a *positive number* in the $C_j - Z_j$ row indicates the amount of increase in total profit possible if 1 unit of the variable heading that column were added to the solution. A *negative number* in the $C_j - Z_j$ row indicates the amount of decrease in total profit if 1 unit of the variable heading that column were added to the solution. A negative number in the $C_j - Z_j$ row *under one of the columns representing machine time* can be thought of as the amount of increase in total profit obtainable if 1 more hour in the center heading that column were available.

A MINIMIZATION PROBLEM

Up to this point the discussion has involved a profit maximization problem. The simplex method can also be used in problems where the objective is to minimize costs.

For example, an animal feed company must produce 200 pounds of a mixture consisting of ingredients X_1 and X_2. X_1 costs $3 per pound, and X_2 $8 per pound. No more than 80 pounds of X_1 can be used, and at least 60 pounds of X_2 must be used. The problem then is to find how much of each ingredient should be used if the company wants to minimize cost.

The cost function can now be written as

$$\text{Cost} = \$3X_1 + \$8X_2$$

One restriction or constraint in the problem is that we must produce 200 pounds of the mixture—no more, no less. Stated mathematically, this statement becomes

$$X_1 + X_2 = 200 \text{ lb}$$

This equation means that the number of pounds of X_1 plus the number of pounds of X_2 must equal 200 pounds.

The second restriction is that no more than 80 pounds of X_1 can be used. We may use less than 80 pounds, but we must not exceed 80 pounds. In mathematical language this is written

$$X_1 \leq 80 \text{ lb}$$

The third restriction is that at least 60 pounds of X_2 must be used. We may use more than 60 pounds but not less than 60 pounds. Mathematically, this is expressed

$$X_2 \geq 60 \text{ lb}$$

In summary, then, the problem stated in mathematical form is:

$$\text{Minimize: Cost} = \$3X_1 + \$8X_2$$

subject to

$$X_1 + X_2 = 200 \text{ lb}$$
$$X_1 \leq 80 \text{ lb}$$
$$X_2 \geq 60 \text{ lb}$$

At this point, it might be helpful to state that irrespective of whether the goal is to maximize profits or minimize costs, the steps in setting up the problem are similar, and once the first solution is formulated, the procedure is much the same.

Now consider the first restriction in this minimization problem represented by an equality:

$$X_1 + X_2 = 200 \text{ lb}$$

Remember from the manufacturing problem that our first need was for a solution—*any* technically feasible solution—so that we could start moving toward the final, the optimum, solution. Our first solution in the manufacturing problem netted us zero profit. This was a ridiculous solution profitwise, *but* it served as a starting point or base for improvement and refinement.

In this cost minimization problem, we once again need a starting solution. It too will be ridiculous costwise. It too will be a point of departure in our search for the lowest cost mixture.

Suppose we decide to let $X_1 = 0$ and $X_2 = 200$. We have observed all restrictions; our solution is

$$X_1 + X_2 = 200$$
$$0 + 200 = 200$$
$$200 = 200 \qquad \text{restriction is satisfied}$$
$$X_1 \leq 80$$
$$0 \leq 80 \qquad \text{restriction is satisfied}$$
$$X_2 \geq 60$$
$$200 \geq 60 \qquad \text{restriction is satisfied}$$

In a more realistic problem, one involving 12 ingredients (and each with its own restrictions), finding a first solution by inspection is almost impossible. Our need, then, is for a simple procedure which will generate a first solution in all problems, no matter how complicated.

Let us start by not putting any X_1 or X_2 into our first solution. Instead, start with 200 pounds of A_1—an artificial variable representing a new ingredient.

$$X_1 + X_2 + A_1 = 200$$
$$0 + 0 + 200 = 200$$
$$200 = 200 \qquad \text{restriction is satisfied}$$

Just what is A_1? It can be thought of as a very expensive substance ($100 a pound) which could substitute satisfactorily for our end product.

Our first solution, then, consists entirely of 200 pounds of A_1 at $100 per pound. Although this is ridiculous costwise, it does represent a technically feasible solution in that the product *would* fill our customers' needs.

Because of its high price ($100 versus $8 and $3), A_1 must not be present in our optimum solution.

In linear programming terminology, this type of variable (A_1) is called an *artificial variable*. It is only of value as a computational device; it allows two types of restrictions to be treated, the equality type and the greater-than-or-equal-to type.

The second restriction in this problem is of a type with which we are familiar

$$X_1 \leq 80 \text{ lb}$$

Because X_1 in the final solution may turn out to be less than 80 pounds, we must add a slack variable in order to form an equation.

$$X_1 + S_1 = 80 \text{ lb}$$

The slack variable S_1 represents the difference between 80 pounds of X_1 and the actual number of pounds of X_1 in the final solution.

Finally, there is a third restriction

$X_2 \geqslant 60$ lb

To convert this inequality into an equation, we must *subtract* a slack variable

$X_2 - S_2 = 60$ lb

The negative slack variable S_2 represents the amount by which X_2 will exceed 60 pounds in the final solution. For example, if X_2 in the final solution equals 130 pounds, then S_2 must equal 70 pounds in order for the equation to hold. Of course, if X_2 equals 60 pounds in the final solution, then the value of S_2 would have to be 0.

We see at once that if $X_2 = 0$ in the first solution, then $0 - S_2 = 60$, or $S_2 = -60$. This equation is not a feasible one in the first solution because -60 pounds of an ingredient is not possible: -60 pounds makes no more sense than -12 tables or -6 chairs. What shall we do?

One approach is to prevent S_2 from appearing in the first solution. But what takes its place to keep the equation in balance? If X_2 is zero and S_2 is zero in the first solution, then we must introduce a new ingredient, one that is an acceptable substitute for X_2, one that will take the place of X_2 in the first solution. As in the case of A_1, this new ingredient (A_2) can be thought of as a very expensive substance ($100 a pound). The high price of A_2 assures us that it will never appear in our final solution. Thus the original restriction of $X_2 \geqslant 60$ was first changed to $X_2 - S_2 = 60$ by the addition of a slack variable; now the present change revises this into $X_2 - S_2 + A_2 = 60$ by the inclusion of an artificial variable. The equation in the first solution still holds because $X_2 = 0$ and $S_2 = 0$.

We stated that the artificial variables A_1 and A_2 would be assigned a very high cost, $100 a pound. To avoid having to work with extremely large numbers, we let the letter M represent 100. This will simplify the calculations to follow.

The cost function and the restriction equations ready for the initial simplex tableau are shown below:

Minimize: Cost $= \$3X_1 + \$8X_2 + \$0S_1 + \$0S_2 + \$MA_1 + \$MA_2$

subject to

$$
\begin{aligned}
X_1 + X_2 + A_1 \quad\quad\quad &= 200 \\
X_1 \quad\quad\quad + S_1 \quad\quad &= 80 \\
X_2 \quad\quad - S_2 + A_2 &= 60
\end{aligned}
$$

We show zero cost for the slack variables S_1 and S_2, and we show $M cost for the artificial variables A_1 and A_2.

Any unknown that occurs in one restraint equation must appear in all equations. Consequently we must now insert the appropriate variables with zero coefficients into the restraint equations.

Here is our problem ready for the simplex solution:

$$\text{Minimize: Cost} = \$3X_1 + \$8X_2 + \$0S_1 + \$0S_2 + \$MA_1 + \$MA_2$$

subject to

$$X_1 + X_2 + A_1 + 0S_1 + 0S_2 + 0A_2 = 200$$
$$X_1 + 0X_2 + 0A_1 + S_1 + 0S_2 + 0A_2 = 80$$
$$0X_1 + X_2 + 0A_1 + 0S_1 - S_2 + A_2 = 60$$

The first simplex tableau is shown in Table 13. Note that the total cost of the first solution, $260M, is extremely high. Since the objective is to minimize costs, the optimum column is found by selecting that column which has the largest *negative* value in the $C_j - Z_j$ row (that column whose value will decrease costs the most). A glance at the $C_j - Z_j$ row shows only two negative values, $3 - \$M$ and $8 - \$2M$. As $8 - \$2M$ is the larger negative number in the $C_j - Z_j$ row ($8 - \$2M$ is $- \$192$, while $3 - \$M$ is only $-\$97$), X_2 is the optimum column.

The computational procedures for finding the replaced row, the replacing row, all other new rows, the Z_j row, and the $C_j - Z_j$ row are exactly the same as those for the maximization problem.

Table 13 *Initial simplex tableau: minimization problem*

			$3	$8	$M	$0	$0	$M
C_j	Product mix	Quantity	X_1	X_2	A_1	S_1	S_2	A_2
$M	A_1	200	1	1	1	0	0	0
$0	S_1	80	1	0	0	1	0	0
$M	A_2	60	0	1	0	0	-1	1 ←
	Z_j	$260M	$M	$2M	$M	$0	-$M	$M
	$C_j - Z_j$		$3 - \$M	$8 - \$2M	$0	$0	$M	$0

↑————Optimum column   Replaced row

Computations for the initial tableau Table 13 are as follows.

Z_j row:
$$Z_{total} = \$M(200) + \$0(80) + \$M(60) = \$260M$$
$$Z_{X_1} = \$M(1) + \$0(1) + \$M(0) = \$M$$
$$Z_{X_2} = \$M(1) + \$0(0) + \$M(1) = \$2M$$
$$Z_{A_1} = \$M(1) + \$0(0) + \$M(0) = \$M$$
$$Z_{S_1} = \$M(0) + \$0(1) + \$M(0) = \$0$$
$$Z_{S_2} = \$M(0) + \$0(0) + \$M(-1) = -\$M$$
$$Z_{A_2} = \$M(0) + \$0(0) + \$M(1) = \$M$$

$C_j - Z_j$ row:
$$C_{X_1} - Z_{X1} = \$3 - \$M = \$3 - \$M$$
$$C_{X_2} - Z_{X2} = \$8 - \$2M = \$8 - \$2M$$
$$C_{A_1} - Z_{A1} = \$M - \$M = \$0$$
$$C_{S_1} - Z_{S1} = \$0 - \$0 = \$0$$
$$C_{S_2} - Z_{S2} = \$0 - (-\$M) = \$M$$
$$C_{A_2} - Z_{A2} = \$M - \$M = \$0$$

Replaced row:

A_1 row: $200\!/\!1 = 200$

S_1 row: $8\!/\!0$ Since $8\!/\!0$ is not a mathematical concept, this row is not considered

A_2 row: $60\!/\!1 = 60$, replaced row (smallest quotient)

Table 14 *Second simplex tableau: minimization problem*

			$3	$8	$M	$0	$0	$M
C_j	Product mix	Quantity	X_1	X_2	A_1	S_1	S_2	A_2
$M	A_1	140	1	0	1	0	1	−1
$0	S_1	80	1	0	0	1	0	0←
$8	X_2	60	0	1	0	0	−1	1
	Z_j	$140M + $480	$M	$8	$M	$0	$M − $8	$8 − $M
	$C_j - Z_j$		$3 − $M	$0	$0	$0	$8 − $M	$2M − $8

Optimum column   Replaced row

The second solution is shown in Table 14. Computations for the second simplex tableau are as follows.

Replacing row (X_2):

$$^{60}\!/_1 = 60$$
$$^0\!/_1 = 0$$
$$^1\!/_1 = 1$$
$$^0\!/_1 = 0$$
$$-^1\!/_1 = -1$$
$$^1\!/_1 = 1$$

A_1 row:

$$200 - 1(60) = 140$$
$$1 - 1(0) = 1$$
$$1 - 1(1) = 0$$
$$1 - 1(0) = 1$$
$$0 - 1(0) = 0$$
$$0 - 1(-1) = 1$$
$$0 - 1(1) = -1$$

S_1 row:

$$80 - 0(60) = 80$$
$$1 - 0(0) = 1$$
$$0 - 0(1) = 0$$
$$0 - 0(0) = 0$$
$$1 - 0(0) = 1$$
$$0 - 0(-1) = 0$$
$$0 - 0(1) = 0$$

Z_j row:

$$Z_{total} = \$M(140) + \$0(80) + \$8(60) = \$140M + \$480$$
$$Z_{X_1} = \$M(1) + \$0(1) + \$8(0) = \$M$$
$$Z_{X_2} = \$M(0) + \$0(0) + \$8(1) = \$8$$
$$Z_{A_1} = \$M(1) + \$0(0) + \$8(0) = \$M$$
$$Z_{S_1} = \$M(0) + \$0(1) + \$8(0) = \$0$$
$$Z_{S_2} = \$M(1) + \$0(0) + \$8(-1) = \$M - \$8$$
$$Z_{A_2} = \$M(-1) + \$0(0) + \$8(1) = \$8 - \$M$$

$C_j - Z_j$ row:

$$C_{X_1} - Z_{X_1} = \$3 - \$M = \$3 - \$M$$
$$C_{X_2} - Z_{X_2} = \$8 - \$8 = \$0$$
$$C_{A_1} - Z_{A_1} = \$M - \$M = \$0$$
$$C_{S_1} - Z_{S_1} = \$0 - \$0 = \$0$$
$$C_{S_2} - Z_{S_2} = \$0 - \$(M - 8) = \$8 - \$M$$
$$C_{A_2} - Z_{A_2} = \$M - \$(8 - M) = \$2M - \$8$$

Replaced row:

A_1 row $^{140}\!/_1 = 140$
S_1 row $^{80}\!/_1 = 80$ replaced row
X_2 row $^{60}\!/_0$ not defined

Table 15 *Third simplex tableau: minimization problem*

			$3	$8	$M	$0	$0	$M
C_j	Product mix	Quantity	X_1	X_2	A_1	S_1	S_2	A_2
$M	A_1	60	0	0	1	−1	1	−1
$3	X_1	80	1	0	0	1	0	0
$8	X_2	60	0	1	0	0	−1	1
	Z_j	$60M + $720	$3	$8	$M	$3 − $M	$M − $8	$8 − $M
	$C_j − Z_j$		$0	$0	$0	$M − $3	$8 − $M	$2M − $8

Optimum column ─────── Replaced row

The third simplex tableau is shown in Table 15. Computations for the third simplex tableau are as follows.

Replacing row (X_1):
$$80/1 = 80$$
$$1/1 = 1$$
$$0/1 = 0$$
$$0/1 = 0$$
$$1/1 = 1$$
$$0/1 = 0$$
$$0/1 = 0$$

A_1 row: X_2 row:
$$140 − 1(80) = 60 \qquad 60 − 0(80) = 60$$
$$1 − 1(1) = 0 \qquad\quad 0 − 0(1) = 0$$
$$0 − 1(0) = 0 \qquad\quad 1 − 0(0) = 1$$
$$1 − 1(0) = 1 \qquad\quad 0 − 0(0) = 0$$
$$0 − 1(1) = −1 \qquad 0 − 0(1) = 0$$
$$1 − 1(0) = 1 \qquad\quad −1 − 0(0) = −1$$
$$−1 − 1(0) = −1 \qquad 1 − 0(0) = 1$$

Z_j row:
$$Z_{\text{total}} = \$M(60) + \$3(80) + \$8(60) = \$720 + \$60M$$
$$Z_{X_1} = \$M(0) + \$3(1) + \$8(0) = \$3$$
$$Z_{X_2} = \$M(0) + \$3(0) + \$8(1) = \$8$$
$$Z_{A_1} = \$M(1) + \$3(0) + \$8(0) = \$M$$
$$Z_{S_1} = \$M(−1) + \$3(1) + \$8(0) = \$3 − \$M$$
$$Z_{S_2} = \$M(1) + \$3(0) + \$8(−1) = \$M − \$8$$
$$Z_{A_2} = \$M(−1) + \$3(0) + \$3(0) + \$8(1) = \$8 − \$M$$

$C_j - Z_j$ row:
$C_{X_1} - Z_{X_1} = \$3 - \$3 = \$0$
$C_{X_2} - Z_{X_2} = \$8 - \$8 = \$0$
$C_{A_1} - Z_{A_1} = \$M - \$M = \$0$
$C_{S_1} - Z_{S_1} = \$0 - \$(3 - M) = \$M - \$3$
$C_{S_2} - Z_{S_2} = \$0 - \$(M - 8) = \$8 - \$M$
$C_{A_2} - Z_{A_2} = \$M - \$(8 - M) = \$2M - \$8$

Replaced row:
A_1 row $^{60}\!/_1 = 60$ replaced row
X_1 row $^{80}\!/_0$ not defined mathematically
X_2 row $60/(-1) = -60$ negative ratio

The fourth simplex tableau is shown in Table 16. Computations for the fourth tableau are as follows.

Replacing row (S_2):
$^{60}\!/_1 = 60$
$^{0}\!/_1 = 0$
$^{0}\!/_1 = 0$
$^{1}\!/_1 = 1$
$-^{1}\!/_1 = -1$
$^{1}\!/_1 = 1$
$-^{1}\!/_1 = -1$

X_1 row:
$80 - 0(60) = 80$
$1 - 0(0) = 1$
$0 - 0(0) = 0$
$0 - 0(1) = 0$
$1 - 0(-1) = 1$
$0 - 0(1) = 0$
$0 - 0(-1) = 0$

X_2 row:
$60 - (-1)(60) = 120$
$0 - (-1)(0) = 0$
$1 - (-1)(0) = 1$
$0 - (-1)(1) = 1$
$0 - (-1)(-1) = -1$
$-1 - (-1)(1) = 0$
$1 - (-1)(-1) = 0$

Table 16 *Fourth simplex tableau (optimum solution): minimization problem*

			$\$3$	$\$8$	$\$M$	$\$0$	$\$0$	$\$M$
C_j	Product mix	Quantity	X_1	X_2	A_1	S_1	S_2	A_2
$\$0$	S_2	60	0	0	1	-1	1	-1
$\$3$	X_1	80	1	0	0	1	0	0
$\$8$	X_2	120	0	1	1	-1	0	0
	Z_j	$\$1,200$	$\$3$	$\$8$	$\$8$	$-\$5$	$\$0$	$\$0$
	$C_j - Z_j$		$\$0$	$\$0$	$\$M - \$8$	$\$5$	$\$0$	$\$M$

Z_j row:

$Z_{total} = \$0(60) + \$3(80) + \$8(120) = \$1,200$

$Z_{X_1} = \$0(0) + \$3(1) + \$8(0) = \$3$

$Z_{X_2} = \$0(0) + \$3(0) + \$8(1) = \$8$

$Z_{A_1} = \$0(1) + \$3(0) + \$8(1) = \$8$

$Z_{S_1} = \$0(-1) + \$3(1) + \$8(-1) = -\$5$

$Z_{S_2} = \$0(1) + \$3(0) + \$8(0) = \$0$

$Z_{A_2} = \$0(-1) + \$3(0) + \$8(0) = \$0$

$C_j - Z_j$ row:

$C_{X_1} - Z_{X_1} = \$3 - \$3 = \$0$

$C_{X_2} - Z_{X_2} = \$8 - \$8 = \$0$

$C_{A_1} - Z_{A_1} = \$M - \$8 = \$M - \$8$

$C_{S_1} - Z_{S_1} = \$0 - (-\$5) = \$5$

$C_{S_2} - Z_{S_2} = \$0 - \$0 = \$0$

$C_{A_2} - Z_{A_2} = \$M - \$0 = \$M$

Since in the fourth tableau (Table 16) no negative values remain in the $C_j - Z_j$ row, we have reached the optimum solution. It is to use 80 pounds of X_1 and 120 pounds of X_2. This results in a cost of $1,200, the minimum cost combination of X_1 and X_2 which satisfies the restrictions in the problem. We have the 200 pounds of our mixture (120 + 80) required. Note that the slack variable S_2 is also in the solution. S_2 represents the amount of X_2 used over the minimum quantity required (60 pounds). Substituting the values for X_2 and S_2 in the constraint equation $X_2 - S_2 + A_2 = 60$, we have

$$120 - 60 + 0 = 60$$
$$60 = 60$$

Since the artificial variable A_2 is not in the solution, it is equal to zero.

Of course this problem could have been solved simply by visual inspection; unfortunately this is just not the case with many problems involving mixtures, etc. For example, instead of the limited raw materials and constraints, imposed upon the animal feed company of our earlier example, consider the following animal feed mixture requirements:

Raw materials: $X_1, X_2, X_3, X_4, X_5, X_6$

Constraints:

1. We need 1,000 pounds of the mixture.
2. X_1 cannot be more than 200 pounds.
3. X_2 must be at least 150 pounds.
4. X_3 must equal 300 pounds.
5. X_4 cannot be more than the sum of X_1 and X_2.
6. X_5 must be more than the sum of X_3 and X_4.
7. X_6 must be between 50 and 100 pounds.

Here is a problem that one would have difficulty solving by inspection; without actually setting up and solving the simplex tableaus for this problem, let us formulate the constraints as follows:

1: $X_1 + X_2 + X_3 + X_4 + X_5 + X_6 = 1,000$
2: $X_1 \leq 200$
3: $X_2 \geq 150$
4: $X_3 = 300$
5: $X_4 \leq X_1 + X_2$
6: $X_5 \geq X_3 + X_4$
7a: $X_6 \geq 50$ We use two constraints to
7b: $X_6 \leq 100$ ensure that X_6 will be between 50 and 100 pounds; the first one ensures that X_6 will be 50 or more; the second that X_6 will be 100 or less.

Getting these constraints ready for the first simplex tableau would involve bringing all the variables to the left side and adding appropriate slack and artificial variables as follows:

1: $X_1 + X_2 + X_3 + X_4 + X_5 + X_6 + A_1$ $= 1,000$
2: X_1 $+ S_1$ $= 200$
3: X_2 $- S_2 + A_2$ $= 150$
4: X_3 $+ A_3$ $= 300$
5: $-X_1 - X_2$ $+ X_4$ $+ S_3$ $= 0$
6: $- X_3 - X_4 - X_5$ $- S_4 + A_4$ $= 0$
7a: X_6 $- S_5 + A_5 = 50$
7b: X_6 $S_6 = 100$

SUMMARY OF STEPS IN THE SIMPLEX PROCEDURE

In summary form, the steps involved in the simplex procedure for minimization problems are as follows:

1. Set up the inequalities and equalities describing the problem constraints.
2. Convert any inequalities to equalities by adding or subtracting slack variables as necessary.
3. Add artificial variables to any equalities involving negative slack variables and to any equalities which were not altered by adding slack variables initially.
4. Enter the resulting equalities in the simplex table.
5. Calculate C_j and Z_j values for this solution.
6. Determine the entering variable by choosing the one with the largest negative $C_j - Z_j$ value.
7. Determine the row to be replaced by dividing quantity column values

by their corresponding optimum-column values and choosing the smallest nonnegative quotient.

8. Compute the values for the replacing row.
9. Calculate the values for the remaining rows.
10. Calculate the C_j and Z_j values for this solution.
11. If there is a negative $C_j - Z_j$ remaining, proceed as indicated in step 6 on page 528.
12. If there is no negative $C_j - Z_j$ value remaining, the final solution has been obtained.

appendix

THE NORMAL DISTRIBUTION

two

Directions: To find the area under the curve between the left-hand tail and any point, determine how many standard deviations that point is to the right of the mean then read the area directly from the body of the table. *Example:* The area under the curve from the left-hand tail and a point 1.81 standard deviations to the right of the mean is .96485 of the total area under the curve.

Areas under the curve

	.00	.01	.02	.03	.04	.05	.06	.07	.08	.09
0.0	.50000	.50399	.50798	.51197	.51595	.51994	.52392	.52790	.53188	.53586
0.1	.53983	.54380	.54776	.55172	.55567	.55962	.56356	.56749	.57142	.57535
0.2	.57926	.58317	.58706	.59095	.59483	.59871	.60257	.60642	.61026	.61409
0.3	.61791	.62172	.62552	.62930	.63307	.63683	.64058	.64431	.64803	.65173
0.4	.65542	.65910	.66276	.66640	.67003	.67364	.67724	.68082	.68439	.68793
0.5	.69146	.69497	.69847	.70194	.70540	.70884	.71226	.71566	.71904	.72240
0.6	.72575	.72907	.73237	.73536	.73891	.74215	.74537	.74857	.75175	.75490
0.7	.75804	.76115	.76424	.76730	.77035	.77337	.77637	.77935	.78230	.78524
0.8	.78814	.79103	.79389	.79673	.79955	.80234	.80511	.80785	.81057	.81327
0.9	.81594	.81859	.82121	.82381	.82639	.82894	.83147	.83398	.83646	.83891
1.0	.84134	.84375	.84614	.84849	.85083	.85314	.85543	.85769	.85993	.86214
1.1	.86433	.86650	.86864	.87076	.87286	.87493	.87698	.87900	.88100	.88298
1.2	.88493	.88686	.88877	.89065	.89251	.89435	.89617	.89796	.89973	.90147
1.3	.90320	.90490	.90658	.90824	.90988	.91149	.91309	.91466	.91621	.91774
1.4	.91924	.92073	.92220	.92364	.92507	.92647	.92785	.92922	.93056	.93189

	.00	.01	.02	.03	.04	.05	.06	.07	.08	.09
1.5	.93319	.93448	.93574	.93699	.93822	.93943	.94062	.94179	.94295	.94408
1.6	.94520	.94630	.94738	.94845	.94950	.95053	.95154	.95254	.95352	.95449
1.7	.95543	.95637	.95728	.95818	.95907	.95994	.96080	.96164	.96246	.96327
1.8	.96407	.96485	.96562	.96638	.96712	.96784	.96856	.96926	.96995	.97062
1.9	.97128	.97193	.97257	.97320	.97381	.97441	.97500	.97558	.97615	.97670
2.0	.97725	.97784	.97831	.97882	.97932	.97982	.98030	.98077	.98124	.98169
2.1	.98214	.98257	.98300	.98341	.98382	.98422	.98461	.98500	.98537	.98574
2.2	.98610	.98645	.98679	.98713	.98745	.98778	.98809	.98840	.98870	.98899
2.3	.98928	.98956	.98983	.99010	.99036	.99061	.99086	.99111	.99134	.99158
2.4	.99180	.99202	.99224	.99245	.99266	.99286	.99305	.99324	.99343	.99361
2.5	.99379	.99396	.99413	.99430	.99446	.99461	.99477	.99492	.99506	.99520
2.6	.99534	.99547	.99560	.99573	.99585	.99598	.99609	.99621	.99632	.99643
2.7	.99653	.99664	.99674	.99683	.99693	.99702	.99711	.99720	.99728	.99736
2.8	.99744	.99752	.99760	.99767	.99774	.99781	.99788	.99795	.99801	.99807
2.9	.99813	.99819	.99825	.99831	.99836	.99841	.99846	.99851	.99856	.99861
3.0	.99865	.99869	.99874	.99878	.99882	.99886	.99889	.99893	.99896	.99900
3.1	.99903	.99906	.99910	.99913	.99916	.99918	.99921	.99924	.99926	.99929
3.2	.99931	.99934	.99936	.99938	.99940	.99942	.99944	.99946	.99948	.99950
3.3	.99952	.99953	.99955	.99957	.99958	.99960	.99961	.99962	.99964	.99965
3.4	.99966	.99968	.99969	.99970	.99971	.99972	.99973	.99974	.99975	.99976
3.5	.99977	.99978	.99978	.99979	.99980	.99981	.99981	.99982	.99983	.99983
3.6	.99984	.99985	.99985	.99986	.99986	.99987	.99987	.99988	.99988	.99989
3.7	.99989	.99990	.99990	.99990	.99991	.99991	.99992	.99992	.99992	.99992
3.8	.99993	.99993	.99993	.99994	.99994	.99994	.99994	.99995	.99995	.99995
3.9	.99995	.99995	.99996	.99996	.99996	.99996	.99996	.99996	.99997	.99997

index

index